Introduction to
World Religions

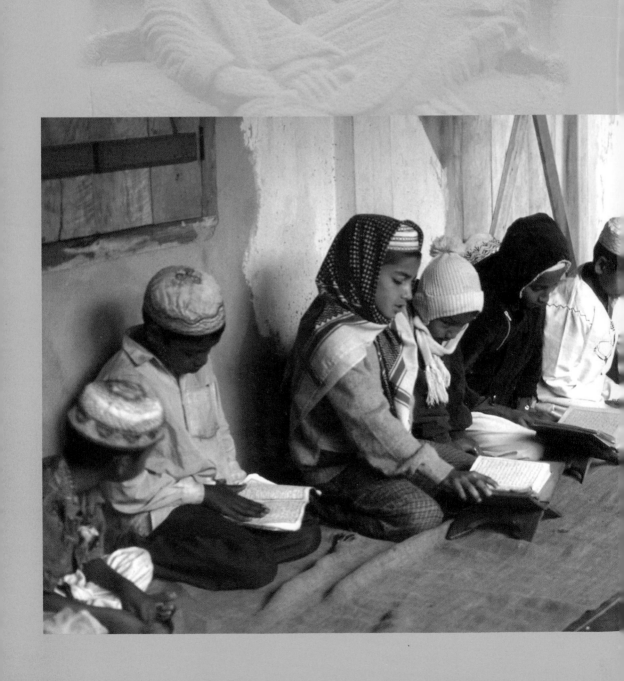

Introduction to
World Religions

Christopher Partridge
General Editor

Fortress Press
Minneapolis

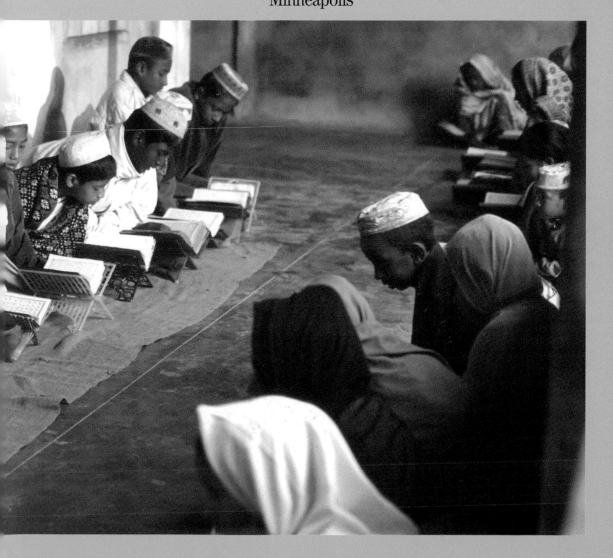

INTRODUCTION TO WORLD RELIGIONS,
WITH CD-ROM

First Fortress Press edition 2005

Published in the United Kingdom as *The New
Lion Handbook*, *The World's Religions*,
3rd edition.

Cover design by Diana Running
Cover images: Hand Holding Prayer Beads
© Royalty-Free/CORBIS; View from Below of
Temple © Jim Zuckerman/CORBIS.

ISBN 0-8006-3714-3

Printed in Singapore.

CONSULTING EDITORS

Professor Veikko Anttonen
Professor of Comparative Religion,
School of Cultural Research,
University of Turku, Finland

Dr Eric S. Christianson
Senior Lecturer, Biblical Studies,
University College Chester, UK

Professor Diana L. Eck
Professor of Comparative Religion
and Indian Studies,
Harvard University, Cambridge, MA, USA

Professor Gavin Flood
Professor of Religious Studies,
University of Stirling, Scotland, UK

Professor Andreas Grünschloß
Professor of Religious Studies
(Religionswissenschaft),
University of Goettingen, Germany

Professor Robert Kisala
Associate Professor,
Nanzan University, Nagoya, Japan

Professor Anthony N.S. Lane
Professor of Historical Theology
and Director of Research,
London School of Theology, UK

Professor Nicholas de Lange
Professor of Hebrew & Jewish Studies,
University of Cambridge, UK

Professor Mikael Rothstein
Associate Professor, Head of Studies,
Department of History of Religions,
University of Copenhagen, Denmark

Professor Lamin Sanneh
Professor of History and
of World Christianity,
Yale University, New Haven, CT, USA

Professor Garry W. Trompf
Professor in the History of Ideas
University of Sydney, Australia

Dr Linda Woodhead
Senior Lecturer in Christian Studies,
Lancaster University, UK

Contents

Preface   9

Understanding Religion

PART ONE

Religions of Antiquity

PART TWO

Indigenous Religions

PART THREE

Hinduism

Jainism

Buddhism

Sikhism

CONTENTS

Zoroastrianism

Judaism

Christianity

Islam

The Religions of East Asia

The Bahá'í Faith

Religion in Today's World

Preface

In the small, complicated world of the twenty-first century there is a widespread and growing awareness of the significance of religions and beliefs. This has been accompanied by an increasing desire for, and arguably a need for, reliable and accessible knowledge. Not only have religions contributed to the foundation of civilizations throughout history, but also they have directly influenced contemporary international relations and significant world events. Whether one thinks of the globalization of 'fundamentalisms', religiously motivated politics, the emergence of numerous new religions, or our increasingly plural societies, the informed twenty-first-century citizen cannot afford to neglect acquiring some understanding of religious belief and practice.

This book is a collection of insightful, stimulating and accessible introductions to the histories, beliefs and practices of religions from pre-historic times to twenty-first century developments. As well as being accessible, the articles are accurate and authoritative, having been written by an international team of acknowledged experts. Moreover, making the religions visible, the book is richly illustrated with numerous photographs, maps and diagrams. Consequently, there are few, if any, volumes to rival it as an attractive, readable and reliable resource for those wanting basic introductions to the world's religious traditions. It is particularly suitable for teachers, students, interested laypeople, and professionals who need clear, accurate, comprehensive overviews of the world's principal religious beliefs and practices.

Those familiar with earlier editions of this book will immediately see that this edition has been completely revised. Not only has much of it been rewritten in order to bring it up to date with current scholarship, but the layout has also significantly changed, with each of the principal religions given its own discrete section. A further particularly stimulating feature of this new edition is the inclusion of short articles written by 'ordinary' believers about what their faith means to them and how their lives are shaped by their beliefs. In other words, the short 'insider' articles in the book seek to take readers 'under the skin' of faith traditions, by allowing individual believers from around the world to speak for themselves. Although, of course, they only allow a single believer's perspective (with which other believers may disagree), they do enable some understanding of what it means to be a believer within a particular faith.

While the sections dealing with particular religions are not absolutely identical, being shaped to a large degree by the emphases within the faith, there has been an effort to ensure that all such sections address the following principal areas: (1) historical overview; (2) sacred writings; (3) key beliefs; (4) worship and festivals; (5) family and society; and (6) developments in the modern world. Therefore, if you read through any section in its entirety you will come away with a good introductory knowledge of these six principal areas of the respective faith.

As well as sections on particular religions, the book begins with an important section on the study of religion, in which readers are introduced to some of the key thinkers in the history of the modern study of religions and to some of the key issues and approaches taken to the study of religion. Again, the Rapid Fact-Finder at the end of the book, which many readers have found particularly useful, has been thoroughly updated. Finally, the last main section includes discussions of some particular developments in the modern world, such as the emergence of new religions and alternative spiritualities, the impact of postmodernism on religious thought, and issues surrounding the decline of once dominant forms of religion (such as Christianity in the Western world). Again, these articles draw on the latest research and thinking in their respective areas and thus provide important introductions to religion in the modern world.

CHRISTOPHER PARTRIDGE

Understanding Religion

PART ONE

What is Religion?

RUSSELL T. McCUTCHEON

'To define is not to finish, but to start. To define is not to confine but to create something... To define, finally, is not to destroy but to construct for the purpose of useful reflection... In fact, we have definitions, hazy and inarticulate as they might be, for every object about which we know something... Let us, then, define our concept of definition as a tentative classification of a phenomenon which allows us to begin an analysis of the phenomenon so defined.'

Brian K. Smith

Although no one is certain of the word's origins, we know that 'religion' derives from Latin and that languages influenced by Latin have equivalents to the English word 'religion'. What in British scholarship was once called 'Comparative Religion' is known in Germany as *Religionswissenschaft*, religion's systematic study (or *Wissenschaft*), and in France it is known as *les sciences religieuses*. Although the ancient words to which we trace 'religion' had nothing to do with today's meanings – for it seems to have come from words that meant: to pay careful attention to some activity (*religere*) or to tie something tightly (*religare*) – it is today commonly used to refer to those beliefs, behaviours, and social institutions that have something to do with speculations on any, and all, of the following: the origin, end and significance of the universe; what happens after death; the existence and wishes of powerful, non-human beings such as spirits, ancestors, angels, demons and gods; and the manner in which all of this shapes human behaviour. Because each of these makes reference to an invisible (i.e. non-empirical) world that somehow lies outside of, or beyond, human history, the things we name as 'religious' are commonly thought to be opposed to those institutions that we label as 'political'. We therefore operate under the assumption that, whereas religion is a matter of personal belief that can never be settled by rational debate, such things as politics are observable, public and thus open to rational debate.

The essence of 'religion'

Although this common-sense distinction between private and public, sentiment and action, is itself a historical development – it is sometime around the seventeenth century that we first see evidence that words that once referred to one's behaviour, public standing and social rank (such as piety and reverence) became sentimentalized as matters of private feeling – today the assumption that we all have an inner core of belief that is somehow expressed publicly in ritual is so widespread that questioning it appears

Pilgrims light candles of yak's butter at Buddhism's most important site in Tibet, the Jokhang Temple, Lhasa.

David Beckham's successes as a soccer player have given him iconic status in the eyes of many.

counter-intuitive. It is just this assumption that inspires a number of people who, collectively, we could term 'essentialists'. They are 'essentialists' because they maintain that 'religion' names the outward behaviours that are inspired by the inner thing they call 'faith'. Hence, one can imagine someone saying, 'I'm not religious, but I'm spiritual.' Implicit here is the assumption that the institutions associated with religions – hierarchies, regulations, rituals and so on – are merely secondary and inessential. The important thing is the inner faith, the inner 'essence' of religion. Although the essence of religion, the thing without which someone is thought to be non-religious, is known by various names (faith, belief, the Sacred, the Holy and so on), essentialists are in general agreement that the *essence* of religion is real and non-empirical (i.e. it cannot itself be seen, heard, touched and so on); it defies study and must be experienced first-hand.

The function of 'religion'

Apart from an approach that assumes an inner experience, which underlies religious behaviour, scholars have used the term 'religion' for what they consider to be curious areas of observable human behaviour, which requires an explanation. Such people form theories to account for why it is that people think, for example, that an invisible part of their body (usually called 'the soul') outlives that body; that powerful beings control the universe; that there is more to existence than what is observable. These theories are largely functionalist; that is, they seek to determine the social, psychological, or political role played by the things we refer to as 'religious'. Classically speaking, we have such functionalists as:

● Karl Marx (1818–83), whose work in political economy understood religion to be a pacifier that both deadened oppressed people's sense of pain and alienation while, simultaneously, preventing them from doing something about their lot in life, since ultimate responsibility was thought to reside with a being who existed outside history;

● Émile Durkheim (1858–1917), whose sociological definition of religion understood sets of beliefs and practices to enable individuals who engaged in them to form a shared, social identity; and

● Sigmund Freud (1856–1939), whose psychological studies prompted him to liken religious behaviour to the role dreams play in helping people to vent antisocial anxieties in a manner that does not threaten their place within the group.

Although all three of these classic approaches are rather different, each can be understood as *functionalist* insomuch as religion names an institution that has a role to play in helping individuals and communities to reproduce themselves.

The family resemblance approach
Quite apart from the *essentialist* way of defining religion (i.e. there is some non-empirical, core feature without which something is not religious) and the *functionalist* (i.e. that religions help to satisfy human needs), there is a third approach: *the family resemblance definition*. Associated with the philosophy of Ludwig Wittgenstein (1889–1951), a family resemblance approach assumes that nothing is defined by merely one essence or function. Rather, just as members of a family *more or less* share a series of traits, and just as all things we call 'games' *more or less* share a series of traits, none of which is distributed evenly across all members of those groups we call 'family' or 'games', so too all things – including religion! – are defined insomuch as

they more or less share a series of delimited traits.

'Religion' as classifier
The moral of the story is that the word 'religion' likely tells us more about the user of the word (i.e. the classifier) than it does about the thing being classified. For instance, a Freudian psychologist will not conclude that religion functions to oppress the masses, since the Freudian theory precludes coming up with this Marxist conclusion. As well, any scholar who adopts Wittgenstein's approach will sooner or later come up with a case in which something seems to share some traits but perhaps not a sufficient number to count as 'a religion'. If, say, soccer matches satisfy many of the criteria of a religion, what might not also be called religion if soccer is? And what does such a wide usage do to the specificity and thus utility of the word 'religion'? As for those who adopt an essentialist approach, it is likely no coincidence that only those institutions with which one agrees are thought to be expressions of some authentic inner experience, sentiment or emotion, whereas the traditions of others are criticized as being shallow and derivative.

So what is religion? As with any other item in our lexicon, 'religion' is a historical artefact that different social actors use for different purposes: to classify certain parts of their social world to celebrate, degrade or theorize them. Whatever else it may or may not be, religion is at least an item of rhetoric that group members use to sort out their group identities.

Phenomenology and the Study of Religion

CHRISTOPHER PARTRIDGE

There is a long history of curiosity and scholarship regarding the religions of other people. However, the study of religions is a relative newcomer to the halls of academia. Greatly indebted to the impressive work and influence of the German scholar Friedrich Max Müller (1823–1900), the first university professorships were established in the final quarter of the nineteenth century. By the second half of the twentieth century the study of religion had emerged as a prominent and important field of academic enquiry. In a period of history in which the rationalism of the earlier part of the century had seen a decline and in which there had been a rise of interest in particularly non-Christian spirituality, since 1945 there has been a growth in academic institutions offering courses and modules in the study of religion. Moreover, work done in other disciplines has increasingly converged with the work done by students of religion (see 'The Anthropology of Religion', 'The Psychology of Religion', 'The Sociology of Religion', and 'Critical Theory and Religion'). These factors, amongst others, have made it possible for the study of religion in Western universities to pull away from its traditional place alongside the study of Christian theology in order to establish itself as an independent field of enquiry. That is to say, whereas earlier in the century the study of non-Christian faiths was usually undertaken in faculties of Christian theology and studied as part of a theology degree, there was a move, particularly in the late 1960s and 1970s, when the term 'religious studies' became common currency, to establish separate departments of religious studies.

Religionsphänomenologie

Phenomenology is distinct from other approaches to the study of religion, in that it does not necessarily seek to understand the social nature of religion, it is not concerned to explore the psychological factors involved in religious belief, and neither is it especially interested in the historical development of religions. Rather its main concern has been descriptive, the classification of religious phenomena: objects, rituals, teachings, behaviours and so on.

The term *Religionsphänomenologie* was first used by the Dutch scholar Pierre Daniel Chantepie de la Saussaye (1848–1920) in his work *Lehrbuch der Religions-geschichte* (1887) which simply documented religious phenomena. This might be described as 'descriptive' phenomenology, the aim being simply to gather information about the various religions and, as botanists might classify plants, identify varieties of particular religious phenomena. This classification of types of religious phenomena, the hallmark of the phenomenological method, can be seen in the works of contemporary scholars such as Ninian Smart (1927–2001) and Mircea Eliade (1907–86). Such typologies (certainly in earlier works) tend to lead to accounts of religious phenomena which, to continue with the analogy, read much the same as a botanical handbook. Various species are identified (higher religion, lower religion, prophetic religion, mystical religion and so on) and particular religious beliefs and practices are then categorized, discussed and compared.

As the study of religion progressed, phenomenology came to refer to a method which was more complex and claimed rather more for itself than did Chantepie's mere cataloguing of facts. This later development in the discipline – which was due in part to the inspiration of the philosophy of Edmund Husserl (1859–1938) – recognized how easy it is for prior beliefs and interpretations to unconsciously influence one's thinking. Hence, scholars such as Gerardus van der Leeuw (1890–1950) stressed the need for phenomenological *epoché* (the 'bracketing' or shelving of the question about the ontological or objective status of the religious appearances to consciousness). Thus the question about the objective or independent truth of Kali, Allah or the Holy Spirit is initially laid aside. The scholar seeks to suspend judgment about the beliefs of those he studies in order to gain greater objectivity and accuracy in understanding. Also central to phenomenology is the need for empathy (*Einfühlung*) which helps towards an understanding of the religion *from within*. Students of a religion seek to feel their way into the beliefs of others by empathizing with them. Along with this suspension of judgment and empathy, phenomenologists spoke of 'eidetic vision', the capacity of the observer to see beyond the particularities of a religion and to grasp its core essence and meaning. Whilst we often see only what we want or expect to see, eidetic vision is the ability to see a phenomenon without such distortions and limitations. Hence, later phenomenologists did not merely catalogue the facts of religious history, but by means of *epoché*, empathy and eidetic vision sought to understand their meaning for the believer. Although phenomenologists are very aware that there will always be some distance between the believer's understandings of religious facts and those of the scholar, the aim of phenomenology is, as far as possible, to testify only to what has been observed.

It aims to strip away all that would stand in the way of a neutral, judgment-free presentation of the facts.

The idea of the holy

Some scholars have gone beyond this simple presentation of the facts and claimed more. A classic example is Rudolf Otto's (1869–1937) *Das Heilige* (*The Idea of the Holy*, 1917). On the basis of his study of religions, he claims that central to *all* religious expression is an a priori sense of 'the numinous' or 'the holy'. This, of course, necessarily goes beyond a simple presentation of the facts of religious history to the development of a particular philosophical interpretation of those facts. The central truth of all religion, claims Otto, was a genuine feeling of awe or reverence in the believer, a sense of the 'uncanny' inspired by an encounter with the divine. Otto does more than simply relate facts about religion. He assumes the existence of the holy – accepting the truth of encounters with the supernatural.

For some scholars, such as Ninian Smart, such an assumption in the study of religion is unacceptable. To compromise objectivity in this way, Smart argues, skews the scholar's research and findings. What the scholar ends up with is not an unbiased account of the facts of religion, but a personal *theology* of religion.

Neutrality?

Whilst Otto's type of phenomenology clearly displays a fundamental lack of objectivity, it is now generally recognized that this is a problem for the study of religions as such. Although many contemporary religious studies scholars would want to defend the notion of *epoché* as an ideal to which one should aspire, there is a question as to whether this ideal entails a certain naivety. For example, the very process of selection and the production of typologies assumes a level of interpretation. To select certain facts rather than others and to present them with other facts as a particular type of religion presupposes some interpretation. What facts we consider important and unimportant, interesting or uninteresting, will be shaped by certain ideas that we hold, whether religious or non-religious. To be an atheist does not automatically make the scholar more objective and neutral. Hence, the belief in detached objectivity and the claim to be purely 'descriptive' are now considered to be naive. The important thing is that, as we engage in study, we recognize and critically evaluate our beliefs, our

presuppositions, our biases and how they might shape the way we understand a religion (see 'Critical Theory and Religion').

Insiders and outsiders

Another important issue in contemporary religious studies is the 'insider/outsider' problem. To what extent can a non-believer ('an outsider') understand a faith in the way the believer ('an insider') does? It is argued that outsiders, simply because they are outsiders, will never fully grasp the insider's experience; even people who experience the same event at the same time will (because of their contexts and

Pilgrims in their millions converge on the Sangam at the *Maha Kumbh Mela* at Allahabad, India.

personal histories) interpret that experience in different ways. However, some scholars have insisted there is a definite advantage to studying religion from the outside (sometimes referred to as the *etic* perspective). Members of a religion may be conditioned by, or pressurized into accepting, a particular and often narrow understanding of their faith, whereas the outsider is in the scholarly position of not being influenced by such pressures and conditioning. Impartiality and disinterest allow greater objectivity.

Although there is undoubtedly a value to scholarly detachment and while the scholar may have a greater

knowledge of the history, texts, philosophy, structure and social implications of a particular faith than the average believer, not to have experienced that faith from the inside is surely to have a rather large hole in the centre of one's understanding. Indeed, many insiders will insist that scholarly 'head-knowledge' is peripheral to the 'meaning' of their faith. Hence, others have noted the value of studying a religion as an 'insider' or at least relying heavily on the views of insiders (sometimes referred to as the *emic* perspective).

Listening and dialogue

In order to take account of the *emic* perspective, along with the emphasis on participant observation (see 'The Anthropology of Religion'), some have spoken of the 'response threshold' in religious studies. The crossing of the response threshold happens when insiders question the scholar's interpretations – *etic* interpretations are challenged by *emic* perspectives. An insider's perspective, which may conflict with scholarly interpretations, is felt to carry equal if not more weight. Wilfred Cantwell Smith (1916–2000) has even argued that no understanding of a faith is valid until it has been acknowledged by an insider. Religious studies is thus carried out in the context of a dialogue which takes seriously the views of the insider, in order to gain a deeper understanding of the insider's world view.

Beyond phenomenology

In a book entitled *Beyond Phenomenology* (1999) Gavin Flood has argued that what is important in studying religions is 'not so much the distinction between the insider and the outsider, but between the critical and the non-critical'. Flood makes use of theories developed within the social sciences and humanities. With reference to the shift in contemporary theoretical discourse, which recognizes that all knowledge is tradition-specific and embodied within particular cultures (see 'Critical Theory and Religion'), Flood argues, firstly, that religions should not be abstracted and studied apart from the historical, political, cultural, linguistic and social contexts. Secondly, he argues that scholars (who are likewise shaped by their own

Catholic Albanians attend Mass.

contexts) always bring conceptual baggage to the study of religion. Hence, whether because of the effect research has on the community being studied or because the scholar's own prejudices, preconceptions, instincts, emotions and personal characteristics significantly influence that research, the academic study of religion can never be neutral and purely objective. Flood thus argues for 'a rigorous metatheoretical discourse' in religious studies. Metatheory is the critical analysis of theory and practice, the aim of which is to 'unravel the underlying assumptions inherent in any research programme and to critically comment on them'.

Metatheory is thus important because it 'questions the contexts of inquiry, the nature of inquiry, and the kinds of interests represented in inquiry'. In so doing, it questions the idea of detached objectivity in the study of religion and the notion that one can be a disinterested observer who is able to produce neutral descriptions of religious phenomena free of evaluative judgments. Hence, scholars need always to engage critically with and take account of their own assumptions, prejudices and presuppositions.

This means that holding a particular faith need not be a hindrance to the study of religion. One can, for example, be a Christian theologian and a good student of religion. But for scholars such as Flood, the important thing is not the faith or lack of it, but the awareness of and the critical engagement with one's assumptions: 'It is critique rather than faith that is all important.'

It is worth noting that recent theological work and philosophy of religion, mainly in France, sees new possibilities for the philosophy of religion through a turn to phenomenology. Much of this work has been done in response to the important French Jewish philosopher Emmanuel Levinas (1905–95). The names particularly associated with this turn are Jean-Luc Marion, Dominique Janicaud, Jean-Luc Chretien, Michel Henry and Alain Badiou. Marion, for example, has written on the phenomenology of the gift in theology, Badiou has responded to Levinas arguing against his emphasis on the importance of 'the other', and Chretien has written on the phenomenology of prayer.

The Anthropology of Religion

FIONA BOWIE

Anthropology approaches religion as an aspect of culture. Religious beliefs and practices are important, because they are central to the ways in which we organize our social lives. They shape our understanding of our place in the world and determine how we relate to one another and to the rest of the natural (and supernatural) order. The truth or falsity of religious beliefs or the authenticity or moral worth of religious practices are seldom an issue for anthropologists, whose main concern is to document what people think and do, rather than determine what they ought to believe or how they should behave.

An early observation in the anthropology of religion was the extent to which religion and social structure mirror one another. Both the French historian Fustel de Coulanges (1830–89), drawing on Classical sources, and the Scottish biblical scholar William Robertson Smith (1846–94), who studied Semitic religions, demonstrated this coincidence in form. For example, nomadic peoples such as the Bedouin conceive of God in terms of a father and use familial and pastoral imagery to describe their relationship with God. A settled, hierarchical society, by contrast, will depict God as a monarch to whom tribute is due, with imagery of servants and subjects honouring a supreme ruler. These early studies influenced the French sociologist Émile Durkheim (1858–1917), whose book *The Elementary Forms of the Religious Life* (1912) was foundational for later anthropological studies of religion. Rather than seeing religion determining social structure, Durkheim argued that religion is a projection of society's highest values and goals. The realm of the sacred is separated from the profane world and made to seem both natural and obligatory. Through collective rituals people both reaffirm their belief in supernatural beings and reinforce their bonds with one another.

The totemism of Australian Aboriginals, which links human groups with particular forms of animal or other natural phenomena in relations of prohibition and prescription, was regarded by many nineteenth-century scholars as the earliest form of religion and as such was of interest to both Durkheim and anthropologist Edward Burnett Tylor (1832–1917), who postulated an evolutionary movement from animism to polytheism and then monotheism. However, as evolutionary arguments are essentially unprovable, later work built not on these foundations but on the more sociological insights of Durkheim and anthropologists such as Alfred Radcliffe-Brown (1881–1955) and Sir Edward Evan Evans-Pritchard (1902–73).

Evans-Pritchard sought to retain the historical perspective of his predecessors while replacing speculation concerning origins with data based on first-hand observations and participation in the life of a people. His classic 1937 ethnography of witchcraft, oracles and magic among the Azande in Central Africa demonstrated that beliefs which from a Western perspective appear irrational and unscientific, such as the existence of witches and magic, are perfectly logical once one understands the ideational system on which a society is based.

While Durkheim was avowedly atheist, some of the most influential anthropologists of the later twentieth century, including Evans-Pritchard, were or became practising Roman

> 'The belief in a supreme God or a single God is no mere philosophical speculation; it is a great practical idea.'
>
> Maurice Hocart

UNDERSTANDING RELIGION

Myths and Symbols

DOUGLAS DAVIES

If we had just heard a moving piece of music, we would find it strange if someone asked us whether the music were true or false. Music, we might reply, is neither true nor false. To ask such a question is inappropriate. Most people know that music can, as it were, speak to them even though no words are used.

As with music so with people. The question of what someone 'means' to you cannot fully be answered by saying that he is your husband or she is your wife, because there are always unspoken levels of intuition, feeling and emotion built into relationships. The question of 'meaning' must always be seen to concern these dimensions as well as the more obviously factual ones.

Myths

Myths take many forms depending on the culture in which they are found. But their function is always that of pinpointing vital issues and values in the life of the society concerned. They often dramatize those profound issues of life and death, of how humanity came into being and of what life means, of how we should conduct ourselves as a citizen or spouse, as a creature of God or as a farmer, and so on.

Myths are not scientific or sociological theories about these issues. They are the outcome of the way a nation or group has pondered the great questions. Their function is not merely to provide a theory of life which can be taken or left at will; they serve to compel a response from humanity. We might speak of myths as bridges between the intellect and emotion, between the mind and heart – and in this, myths are like music. They express an idea and trigger off our response to it.

Sometimes myths form an extensive series, interlinking with each other and encompassing many aspects of life, as has been shown for the Dogon people of the River Niger in West Africa. On the other hand, they may serve merely as partial accounts of problems such as the hatred between people and snakes, or the reason for the particular shape of a mountain.

One problem in our understanding of myths lies in the fact that Western religions – Judaism, Christianity and Islam – are very concerned with history. They have founders, and see their history as God's own doing. This strong emphasis upon actual events differs from the Eastern approach to religion, which emphasizes the consciousness of the individual. Hinduism and Buddhism possess a different approach to history, and hence also to science.

In the West the search for facts in science is like the search for facts in history, but both these endeavours differ from the search for religious experience in the present. In the West, history and science have come to function as a framework within which religious experiences are found and interpreted, and one consequence of this is that myths have been stripped of their power to evoke human responses to religious ideas.

The eminent historian of religion Mircea Eliade has sought to restore this missing sense of the sacred by helping people to understand the true nature of myths. The secularized Westerner has lost the sense of the sacred, and is trying to compensate, as Eliade sees it, by means of science fiction, supernatural literature and films. One may, of course, keep a firm sense of history and science without seeking to destroy the mythical appreciation of ideas and beliefs.

Symbols

Religious symbols help believers to understand their faith in quite profound ways. Like myths, they serve to unite the intellect and the emotions for the task of discipleship. Symbols also integrate the social and personal dimensions of religion, enabling individuals to share certain commonly held beliefs expressed by symbols, while also giving freedom to read private meaning into them.

We live the whole of our life in a world of symbols. The daily smiles and grimaces, handshakes and greetings, as well as the more readily acknowledged status symbols of large cars or houses – all these communicate messages about ourselves to others.

To clarify the meaning of symbols, it will help if we distinguish between the terms 'symbol' and 'sign'. There is a certain arbitrariness about signs, so that the word 'table', which signifies an object of furniture with a flat top supported on legs, could be swapped for another sound without any difficulty. So the Germans call it *tisch* and the Welsh *bwrdd*.

A symbol, by contrast, is more intimately involved in that to which it refers. It participates in what it symbolizes, and cannot easily be swapped for another symbol. Nor can it be explained in words and still carry the same power. For example, a kiss is a symbol of affection and love; it not only signifies these feelings in some abstract way; it actually demonstrates them. In this sense a symbol can be a thought in action.

Religious symbols share these general characteristics, but are often even more intensely powerful, because they enshrine and express the highest values and relationships of life. The cross of Christ, the sacred books of Muslims and Sikhs, the sacred cow of Hindus, or the silent, seated Buddha – all these command the allegiance of millions of religious men and women. If such symbols are attacked or desecrated, an intense reaction is felt by the faithful, which shows us how deeply symbols are embedded in the emotional life of believers.

The power of symbols lies in this ability to unite fellow-believers into a community. It provides a focal point of faith and action, while also making possible a degree of personal understanding which those outside may not share.

In many societies the shared aspect of symbols is important as a unifying principle of life. Blood, for example, may be symbolic of life, strength, parenthood, or of the family and kinship group itself. In Christianity it expresses life poured out in death, the self-sacrificial love of

Christ who died for human sin. It may even be true that the colour red can so easily serve as a symbol of danger because of its deeper biological association with life and death.

Symbols serve as triggers of commitment in religions. They enshrine the teachings and express them in a tangible way. So the sacraments of baptism and the Lord's Supper in Christianity bring the believer into a practical relationship with the otherwise abstract ideas of repentance and forgiveness. People can hardly live without symbols because they always need something to motivate life; it is as though

abstract ideas need to be set within a symbol before individuals can be impelled to act upon them. When any attempt is made to turn symbols into bare statements of truth, this vital trigger of the emotions can easily be lost.

An ornately dressed dancer performs the Hindu epic, the *Ramayana*, in which the gods take centre stage and interact with humankind. Myths and symbols tend to have a stronger place in Eastern religions than in those of the West.

Catholics. This is true of Mary Douglas (b. 1921) and Victor Turner (1920–83), both of whom were particularly interested in the symbolic aspects of religion. They were influenced not only by Durkheim and Evans-Pritchard, but more particularly by Durkheim's gifted pupils Marcel Mauss (1872–1950) and Henri Hubert (1864–1925), who wrote on ceremonial exchange, sacrifice and magic. In her influential collection of essays *Purity and Danger* (1966), Douglas looks at the ways in which the human body is used as a symbol system in which meanings are encoded. The body is seen as a microcosm of the powers and dangers attributed to society at large. Thus, a group that is concerned to maintain its social boundaries, such as members of the Brahman caste in India, pays great attention to notions of purity and pollution as they affect the individual body. In examining purity rules Douglas is primarily concerned with systems of classification. In her study of the Hebrew purity rules in the book of Leviticus, for example, Douglas argues that dietary proscriptions were not the result of medical or hygienic concerns, but followed the logic of a system of classification that divided animals into clean and unclean species according to whether they conformed to certain rules (such as being cloven hooved and chewing cud) or were anomalous, and therefore unclean and prohibited. Like Robertson Smith, Douglas observed that rituals can retain their form over many generations, notwithstanding changes in their interpretation, and that meaning is preserved in the form itself as well as in explanations for a particular ritual action.

In the work of Mary Douglas we see a fruitful combination of the sociological and symbolist tradition of the Durkheimians and the structuralism of Claude Lévi-Strauss (b. 1908). Lévi-Strauss carried out some fieldwork in the Amazonian region of Brazil, but it is as a theoretician that he has been most influential, looking not at the meaning or semantics of social structure, but at its syntax or formal aspects. In his four-volume study of mythology (1970–81), he seeks to demonstrate the universality of certain cultural themes, often expressed as binary oppositions, such as the transformation of food from raw to cooked, or the opposition between culture and nature. The structuralism of Lévi-Strauss both looks back to Russian formalism and the linguistics of the Swiss Ferdinand de Sassure (1857–1913), and forwards to more recent psychoanalytic studies of religion, both of which see themselves as belonging more to a scientific than to a humanist tradition. On the symbolist and interpretive side Victor Turner produced a series of sensitive, detailed studies of ritual and symbols, focusing on the processual nature of ritual and its theatrical, dramatic aspects, based on extensive fieldwork among the Ndembu of Zambia carried out in the 1950s. Clifford Geertz (b. 1923) is equally concerned with meaning and interpretation, and following a German–American tradition he looks more at culture than at social structure. For Geertz, religion is essentially that which gives meaning to human society, and religious symbols codify an ethos or world view. Their power lies in their ability both to reflect and to shape society.

A Kogi man from Colombia playing the flute. The Kogi have retained a theocratic form of social organization led by religious leaders known as *manas*.

'Man is an animal suspended in webs of significance he himself has spun. I take culture to be those webs.'

Clifford Geertz

The Sociology of Religion

MALCOLM HAMILTON

The sociological study of religion has its roots in the seventeenth- and eighteenth-century Enlightenment, which sought not only to question religious belief but also to understand it as a natural phenomenon, a human product rather than the result of divine revelation or revealed truth. While contemporary sociology of religion has largely abandoned the overtly critical stance of early theoretical approaches to the truth claims of religion, the discipline retains the essential principle that an understanding of religion must acknowledge that it is, to some degree at least, socially constructed and that social processes are fundamentally involved in the emergence, development and dissemination of religious beliefs and practices.

Methodological agnosticism

While some sociologists consider that some religious beliefs are false, and that recognition of this is crucial to a sociological understanding of them, the dominant position in the sociology of religion today is that of 'methodological agnosticism'. This method states that it is neither possible nor necessary to decide whether beliefs are true or false in order to study them sociologically. Theology and philosophy of religion, not sociology, discuss questions of religious truth. The conditions which promote the acceptance or rejection of religious beliefs and practices, which govern their dissemination, and the impact they have on behaviour and on society can all be investigated without prior determination of their truth or falsity.

Roots in individual needs

Theoretical approaches in the sociology of religion can usefully, if a little crudely, be divided into those which perceive the roots of religion to lie in individual needs and propensities and those which perceive its roots to lie in social processes and to stem from the characteristics of society and social groups. The former may be further divided into those which emphasize cognitive processes – intellectualism, and those which emphasize various feelings and emotions – emotionalism.

In the nineteenth century intellectualist theorists such as Auguste Comte (1798–1857), Edward Burnett Tylor (1832–1917), James G. Frazer (1854–1941) and Herbert Spencer (1820–1903) analysed religious belief as essentially a pre-scientific attempt to understand the world and human experience, which would increasingly be supplanted by sound scientific knowledge. The future would thus be entirely secular with no place for religion.

Emotionalist theorists, such as Robert Ranulph Marett (1866–1943), Bronislaw Malinowski (1884–1942) and Sigmund Freud (1856–1939) saw religions as stemming from human emotions such as fear, uncertainty, ambivalence and awe. They were not attempts to explain and understand but to cope with intense emotional experience.

Roots in social processes

The most influential sociological approaches which consider that the roots of religion lie in society and social processes, not in the individual, are those of Karl Marx (1818–83) and of Émile Durkheim (1858–1917).

For Marx religion was both a form of ideology supported by ruling classes in order to control the masses and at the same time an expression of protest against such oppression – 'the sigh of the oppressed creature'. As a protest,

The influential sociologist Karl Marx.

> *'Religion is the sigh of the oppressed creature and the opium of the people.'*
>
> Karl Marx

however, it changed nothing, promoting only resignation and promising resolution of problems in the afterlife. Religion is 'the opium of the people' in the sense that it dulls the pain of the oppressed and thereby stops them from revolting. Hence, the oppressed turn to religion to help them get through life; the ruling classes promote it to keep them in check. It will simply disappear when the social conditions that cause it are removed.

Durkheim saw religion as an essential, integrating social force, which fulfilled basic functions in society. It was the expression of human subordination, not to a ruling class as Marx had argued, but rather to the requirements of society itself and to social pressures which overrule individual preferences. In his famous work *The Elementary Forms of the Religious Life* (1912), he argued that 'Religion is society worshipping itself.' God may not exist, but society does. Rather than God exerting pressure on the individual to conform, society itself exerts the pressure. Individuals, who do not understand the nature of society and social groups, use the language of religion to explain the social forces they experience. Although people misinterpret social forces as religious forces, what they experience is real. Moreover, for Durkheim, religion fulfils a positive role in that it binds society together as a moral community.

Max Weber and meaning theory

Later theoretical approaches in the sociology of religion have all drawn extensively on this earlier work, attempting to synthesize its insights into more nuanced approaches in which the various strands of intellectual, emotional and social factors are woven together. A notable example is the work of Max Weber (1864–1920), probably the most significant contributor to the sociology of religion to this day. His work

included one of the best-known treatises in the sub-discipline, *The Protestant Ethic and the Spirit of Capitalism* (1904–1905) and three major studies of world religions.

Weber's approach to religion was the forerunner of what has become known as 'meaning theory', which emphasizes the way in which religion gives meaning to human life and society in the face of apparently arbitrary suffering and injustice. Religion offers explanation and justification of good and of bad fortune by locating them within a broader picture of a reality which may go beyond the world of immediate everyday perception, thereby helping to make sense of what always threatens to appear senseless. So those who suffer undeservedly in this life may have offended in a previous one; or they will receive their just deserts in the next life or in heaven. Those who prosper through wickedness will ultimately be judged and duly punished.

Rational choice theory

The most recent, general theoretical approach in the sociology of religion, which synthesizes many previous insights, is that of 'rational choice theory'. Drawing upon economic theory, this treats religions as rival products offered in a market – by religious organizations (which are compared to commercial firms) and leaders – to consumers who choose by assessing which best meets their needs, which is most reliable and so on. This approach promises to provide many insights. However, it has been subjected to trenchant criticism by those who question whether religion can be treated as something chosen in the manner that products such as cars or soap powders are chosen, rather than something into which people are socialized and which forms an important part of their identity which simply cannot be easily set aside or changed. Furthermore, if religious beliefs are a matter of preference and convenience, why do their followers accept the uncongenial demands and constraints they usually impose and the threat of punishments for failure to comply?

Secularization and new movements
The sociology of religion was for many decades regarded as an insignificant branch of sociology. This situation has changed in recent years, especially in the USA. Substantive empirical inquiry has been dominated by two areas: secularization and religious sects, cults and movements. It had been widely assumed that religion was declining in modern industrial societies and losing its social significance – the secularization thesis. This has been questioned and found by many, especially rational choice theorists, to be wanting. The result has been intense debate. The dominant position now, though not unchallenged, is that the secularization thesis was a myth.

Central to this debate is the claim that, while religion in its traditional forms may be declining in some modern, Western industrial societies, it is not so in all of them, the USA being a notable exception, and that novel forms of religion are continuously emerging to meet inherent spiritual needs. Some new forms are clearly religious in character. Others, it is claimed, are quite unlike religion as commonly understood. They include alternative and complementary forms of healing, psychotherapies, techniques for the development of human potential, deep ecology, holistic spirituality, New Age, the cult of celebrity and nationalist movements and even sport. Whether such things can be considered forms of religion depends upon how religion is defined, a matter much disputed.

A second crucial element in the secularization debate is the rise of a diversity of sects and cults – the New Religious Movements – which have proliferated since the 1960s and 1970s. For the anti-secularization (or sacralization) theorists this flourishing of novel religiosity gives the lie to the thesis, while for pro-secularization theorists such movements fall far short of making up for the decline of mainstream churches and denominations. Whatever their significance for the secularization thesis, the New Religious Movements, and sects and cults in general, have fascinated sociologists whose extensive studies of them form a major part of the subject.

Heavy concentration on New Religious Movements has been balanced more recently by studies of more mainstream religious churches and communities and by studies of the religious life of ethnic minorities and immigrant communities, among whom religion is often particularly significant and an important element of identity. Added to the interest in new forms of religion and quasi-religion, such studies make the contemporary sociology of religion more diverse and varied than ever.

The Psychology of Religion

FRASER WATTS

Three key figures dominate the psychology of religion that we have inherited from the pre-war period, William James, Sigmund Freud and C.G. Jung.

William James (1842–1910)

The undoubted masterpiece of the early days of the psychology of religion is the classic *Varieties of Religious Experience*, written at the end of the nineteenth century by William James. James assembled an interesting compendium of personal reports of religious experience and embedded them in a rich and subtle framework of analysis. He thought that religious experience was essentially an individual matter and was the foundation on which religious doctrine and church life were built. However, from the outset his critics argued that religious experience is in fact interpreted within the framework of inherited religious teaching and shaped by the life of the institution. James hoped to put religion on a scientific basis through the scientific study of religious experience, although he was unable to make a really convincing case for accepting religious experience at face value. Despite these issues, even his critics have never doubted the quality of his work. It is as hotly debated now as when it was first written.

Sigmund Freud (1856–1939)

Another important figure in the development of the psychology of religion was Sigmund Freud, although his approach was very different from that of James. Freud built his general theories on what patients told him during their psychoanalysis, although he reported only one case study in which religion played a central part. That was the so-called 'wolf man', in whom religion and obsessionality were intertwined, which led Freud to suggest that religion was a universal form of obsessional neurosis. In fact, Freud's psychology of religion was hardly based on data at all. It was a blend of general psychoanalytic theory and his own personal hostility to religion. He wrote several books about religion, each taking a different approach. The clearest is *The Future of an Illusion*, which claims that religion is merely 'illusion', which for him is a technical term meaning wish-fulfilment. Freud's successors have argued that what he called illusion, including religion, is in fact much more valuable to people in helping them to adjust to life than he realized.

C.G. Jung (1875–1961)

Freud's approach to religion was continued in modified form by Carl Gustav Jung. Whereas Freud had been a harsh critic of religion, Jung was favourably disposed to it. However, his approach to religion was so idiosyncratic that many have found him an uncomfortable friend. Jung made a distinction between the ego, the centre of conscious life, and the self, the whole personality that people can potentially become. For Jung the self is the image of God in the psyche, and the process of 'individuation' (i.e. from ego-centred life to self-centred life) is in some ways analogous to religious salvation. Jung was evasive about the question of whether there was a god beyond the psyche and usually said it was not a question for him as a psychologist. Jung took more interest in the significance of Christian doctrine than most psychologists and, for example, wrote long essays on the Mass and on the Trinity.

> '*Religious ideas... are illusions, fulfilments of the oldest, strongest and most urgent wishes of mankind.*'
>
> Sigmund Freud

Sigmund Freud, whose influence on psychology and religion is undisputed.

Young worshippers pray during a church service at The Hiding Place at Chittenango, New York, USA.

The psychology of religion today

The psychology of religion went relatively quiet around the middle of the twentieth century, but has been reviving in recent decades. It has become more explicitly scientific, and most psychological research on religion now uses quantitative methods. There are currently no big psychological theories of religion, but important insights have been obtained about various specific aspects of religion. The following examples give the flavour of current work.

● *Individual differences*. One useful distinction has been between 'intrinsic' religious people (those for whom religion is the dominant motivation in their lives) and 'extrinsic' religious people (those for whom religion meets other needs). Intrinsics and extrinsics differ from one another in many ways. For example, intrinsically religious people show less social prejudice than the non-religious people, whereas extrinsically religious people show more.

● *Religious development*. Children's understanding of religion follows a predictable path, moving from the concrete to the abstract. However, acquiring a better intellectual understanding of religion is not necessarily accompanied by a more spiritual experience. In fact, spiritual experience may actually decline as children grow up. There have been attempts to extend a development approach to religion into adulthood. For example James Fowler has developed a general theory of 'faith development'. Although this has identified different approaches to faith in adults, it is not clear that higher levels of faith necessarily follow the earlier ones, nor that they are superior.

● *Mental health*. Despite Freud's view that religion is a form of neurosis, scientific research has shown that there is often a positive correlation between religion and health, especially mental health. It is most likely that religion actually helps to improve people's mental health, although that is hard to prove conclusively. Religion probably helps by providing a framework of meaning and a supportive community, both of which enable people to cope better with stressful experiences.

● *Conservative and charismatic Christianity.* There has been much interest in both fundamentalism and charismatic religion. One key feature of fundamentalism is the 'black and white' mindset that maintains a sharp dichotomy between truth and falsehood, and between insiders and outsiders. The charismatic phenomenon that has attracted most research interest is speaking in tongues. It seems very unlikely that this is an actual language, more a form of ecstatic utterance. One line of research has explored the social context in which people learn to speak in tongues. Another has explored the unusual state of consciousness in which people surrender voluntary control of their speech.

Although psychology has generally taken a detached, scientific view of religion, there are other points of contact. One is the incorporation of psychological methods into the Christian church's pastoral care, something begun by Freud's Lutheran pastor friend, Oskar Pfister (1873–1956). Another is the dialogue between religious and psychological world views, an aspect of the more general dialogue between science and religion. Some psychologists consider that humans are 'nothing but' the product of their evolution or nervous systems, whereas religious faith emphasizes their importance in the purposes of God.

Critical Theory and Religion

JEREMY CARRETTE

Our knowledge of 'religion' is always politically shaped and is never an innocent or a neutral activity. Knowledge about religion can always be questioned and scholars of religion are finding that 'religion' and talk about 'religion' is involved with questions of power. Critical theory questions knowledge about 'religion' and reveals the social and political nature of such ideas.

Defining critical theory

Critical theory arises from a long tradition in Western thought which has questioned the truth and certainty of knowledge. It carries forward the work of the 'three great masters of suspicion', Karl Marx (1818–83), Friedrich Nietzsche (1844–1900) and Sigmund Freud (1856–1939). Following Marx critical theory is aware that all knowledge is linked to economic and political ideology; following Nietzsche it understands that all knowledge is linked to the 'will to power'; and following Freud it understands that all knowledge is linked to things outside our awareness (the unconscious). The ideas of these three great thinkers influence, and are carried forward in, the work of critical theory. They started to question the view that knowledge was neutral and rational.

There are two basic understandings of 'critical theory', a strict definition and a loose definition. The former relates to the Frankfurt School of Critical Theory, an important group of German intellectuals who tried to think about society according to the ideas of Marx and Freud. They included Theodor Adorno (1903–69) and Max Horkheimer (1895–1973) who jointly published *Dialectic of Enlightenment*, a seminal work in which they questioned Western rational thought since the Enlightenment. What did it say about the potential of human knowledge if it could lead to the ideology of Nazi Germany and the horrors of the Holocaust? Culture was understood to be formed by propagandist manipulation.

The loose definition incorporates a wider range of critical theories, which emerged, largely in France, after the student riots of 1968 in Paris. This date is a watershed in modern Western intellectual history because it reflects, among many things, a shift in the thinking about state power and the control of ideas. It is an event that brings the questions of 'power' and 'politics' to the question of knowledge and truth.

Post-structuralism

The critical thinking that emerged in 1968 in France is known as 'post-structuralism' because it comes *after* an intellectual movement known as 'structuralism'. Structuralism believed one could identify a given number of structures in myth, language and the world. Post-structuralists argued that these structures were not 'given' in the fabric of the world but created by different societies at different points of history and in different cultures. Michel Foucault (1926–84) examined the historical nature of ideas, showing that the ways we think about the world were related to political institutions and regimes of power. Jacques Derrida (1930–2004) showed that our ways of representing the world in texts held hidden contradictions and tensions, because language was unstable and built upon assertions of power not truth. The instability of language is

French students throwing stones at police in the riots of 1968, beginning what was to become a nationwide protest.

CRITICAL THEORY AND RELIGION

like the discovery that the meaning of words in a dictionary simply means other words (rather than something indisputable and fixed in the world) and that meanings are simply asserted or agreed (rather than having a strong foundation given for all time). These two prominent thinkers brought knowledge under question and enabled scholars of religion to uncover how what is and is not classified as 'religion' can benefit certain groups of people within society. Critical theory is thus not an abstract and disengaged way of thinking, but an active ethical responsibility for the world and the way we think about the world. It shows the link between ideas and political practices.

> 'Religion is a political force.'
> Michel Foucault

The end of phenomenology

Before critical theory, the study of religion often consisted of representing different religious traditions and understanding them according to their rituals, beliefs and practices. This is known as 'the phenomenology of religion' and is arguably still dominant in school and university programmes of study. Such an approach assumed that knowledge is neutral and that different issues can be presented without too much difficulty. It was also assumed by many scholars that one does not need a 'theory' or 'theoretical position' (a way of understanding knowledge and the world) to represent a religious tradition or a set of ideas. There was an assumption that language neutrally represented the external world according to a direct correspondence between the subject in representation (words) and the object in the external world (things), in this case 'religious' things. However, knowledge and the categories used to represent the world and religion are now seen to be carrying hidden assumptions, with implications for gender, society, politics, colonial history, race and

ethnicity. All knowledge is now seen as reflecting a particular viewpoint or bias about the world. The production and acquisition of knowledge is never neutral. Hence, after critical theory there is no neutral presentation of ideas about religion.

Critical theory is a way of thinking about how our dominant conceptions of religion come to be dominant or hegemonic. It seeks to identify the hidden positions within our knowledge and recognize that all ideas about religion hold a theoretical position about knowledge, even if that position is denied or not apparent. Critical theory is a way of exploring 'religion' through a set of critical questions about the world and the ideas under discussion. It is not limited to the study of religion, but applies to all ways of thinking about the world. It even questions the boundary between different disciplines of knowledge. Critical theory is not a sub-discipline of religious studies, like the sociology, anthropology or psychology of religion, but cuts across all these areas and questions all types of knowledge.

Critical theory questions the very idea of 'religion' as a Western – even Christian – category that assumes that belief is more important than how people live, which in turn is used to make assumptions about what people outside Christianity believe. This is seen as a distortion of other cultures. To correct such a view, critical theory considers traditions and cultures outside the bias of such an idea, which assumes there is something special and distinctive we can call 'religion' or 'religious'. For example, scholars question the Christian missionary interpretation of other cultures and question whether Hinduism is a 'religion' or the culture of South Asia. In turn, we may question whether Western capitalism is a culture or a religion. Critical theory draws attention to how knowledge is related to political ideas and questions the domination of Western ideas (particularly European–American ideas) over different ways of seeing the world in other cultures and periods of history. It explores the way ideas powerfully rule the world and the 'truth' people have about the world.

Religion, power and culture

Critical theory shows that the ways we think about religion are caught inside questions of power. Religious studies is now involved in exploring how the history and abuses of colonialism influenced the emergence of religion as an idea, how state power, political regimes and the globalized world of capitalism affect this process and how the mass media alter what we mean by religion, and uncovers those activities and groups within society not recognized as religious. Critical theory exposes the abuses of power in history and examines who benefits from thinking about the world in certain ways. It identifies those who are marginalized and unable to speak for themselves. By examining race, gender, sexuality and economic wealth one can see how ideas about religion often support those in power, usually the ruling educated elite of white, Western men. Thinking and writing about ideas from the position of the exploited radically changes the subject and the writing of history. Such a process questions the narrative of Christian history from its Roman-European bias and examines Christianity through its African, particularly Ethiopian, tradition and highlights the importance of Augustine as an African. It explores the involvement of Buddhist monks in political activism and uncovers how the Western media distort the understanding of Islam. Critical theory also identifies ways of life outside the mainstream traditions and explores the indigenous or local traditions around the world, which are suppressed by multinational business interests for land and oil.

Critical theory questions the boundary between religion and culture and argues that what people do, rather than what they believe, is more important in understanding. The distinction between the religious and the secular is seen as an ideological or political tool. According to this view, the category of 'religion' can be applied to all cultural activities, such as football, shopping, fashion, club culture and film. The historical roots of social institutions such as government, schools, hospitals and law are shown to carry ideas that can be classified as religious (even if they are not transparent). Critical theory radically alters the understanding of religion and shows the importance of the idea to world history. After critical theory the study of religion becomes a political activity, it becomes an account of how powerful organizations, in different parts of the world, shape the way we understand and classify the world.

Ritual and Performance

FIONA BOWIE

Ritual is patterned, formal, symbolic action. Religious ritual is usually seen as having reference to divine or transcendent beings or perhaps ancestors, whom the participants invoke, propitiate, feed (through offering or sacrifice), worship or otherwise communicate with. Rituals attempt to enact and deal with the central dilemmas of human existence: continuity and stability, growth and fertility, morality and immortality or transcendence. They have the potential to transform people and situations, creating a fierce warrior or docile wife, a loving servant or imperious tyrant. The ambiguity of ritual symbols and the invocation of supernatural power magnifies and disguises human needs and emotions. Because rituals are sometimes performed in terrifying circumstances, as in certain initiation rituals, the messages they carry act at a psycho-biological level that includes but also exceeds the rational mind. Symbols and sacred objects are manipulated within ritual to enhance performance and communicate ideological messages concerning the nature of the individual, society and cosmos. Rituals are fundamental to human culture and can be used to control, subvert, stabilize, enhance or terrorize individuals and groups. Studying them gives us a key to an understanding and interpretation of culture.

Anthropologists and religious studies scholars sometimes look at rituals in terms of what they do. For instance, Catherine Bell (b. 1953) distinguishes between:

● rites of passage or 'life crisis' rituals

● calendrical rituals and commemorative rites

● rites of exchange or communication

● rites of affliction

● rites of feasting, fasting, festivals

● political rituals

Another approach is to focus on their explanatory value. Mircea Eliade (1907–86) is interested in ritual as a re-enactment of a primal cosmogonic myth, bringing the past continually into the present. Robin Horton emphasizes the reality of the religious beliefs behind ritual actions. Using the Kalabari of Nigeria as an example, he insists that religious rituals have the power to move and transform participants because they express beliefs that have meaning and coherence for their adherents. Taking a lead from Durkheim (1858–1917), other scholars claim that rituals are effective because they make statements about social phenomena. Maurice Bloch, writing about circumcision rituals in Madagascar, makes the interesting observation that because a ritual is not fully a statement and not fully an action it allows its message to be simultaneously communicated and disguised. In some cases ritual symbols may be full of resonance, as Victor Turner (1920–83) demonstrated for Ndembu healing, chiefly installation and initiation rituals in Central Africa. In other cases the performance of the ritual itself may be what matters, the content or symbolism having become redundant or forgotten over time, as Fritz Staal has argued for Vedic rituals in India.

A key figure in the study of ritual is Arnold van Gennep (1873–1957), who distinguished an underlying patterning beneath a wide range of rituals. Whether we look at seasonal festivals such as Christmas, midsummer

A healing ritual in Benin.

or harvest, or 'life crisis' rituals that mark a change in status from one stage of life to another, such as birth, puberty, marriage or mortuary rituals, we see beneath them all the threefold pattern of separation, transition and reintegration. Van Gennep also noted that there is generally a physical passage in ritual as well as a social movement, and that the first time a ritual is celebrated it is usually more elaborate than on subsequent occasions as it bears the weight of change of status.

Victor Turner took up van Gennep's schema, emphasizing the movement from social structure to an anti-structural position in the middle, liminal stage of a rite of passage. In the middle stage, initiands often share certain characteristics. There is a levelling process – they may be stripped or dressed in such a way as to erase individuality, hair may be shaved or allowed to grow long. Neophytes are often isolated from the everyday world, and may undergo certain ordeals that bind them to one another and to those initiating them. Turner coined the term 'communitas' to describe a spontaneous, immediate and concrete relatedness that is typical of people in the liminal stage of a rite of passage. Liminality can also be institutionalized and extended almost indefinitely, as for instance in the military, monastic communities, hospitals or asylums.

Bruce Lincoln has criticized both van Gennep and Turner's models as more relevant to male than female initiations, pointing out that women have little status in the social hierarchy and therefore the middle stage of a woman's initiation is less likely to stress anti-structural elements. Rather than being brought low as a prelude to being elevated, her lowlier place within society is reinforced. A woman is more likely than her male counterparts to be initiated singly, and to be enclosed within a domestic space. Women are generally adorned rather than stripped,

and the nature of the knowledge passed on during initiation is likely to be mundane rather than esoteric. Rather than separation, liminality and reintegration, Lincoln proposes that for women initiation is more likely to involve enclosure, metamorphosis or magnification and emergence.

A ritual is a type of performance, but not all performances are rituals. Richard Schechner (b. 1934) has pointed out that whether a performance is to be classified as ritual or theatre depends on the context. If the purpose of a performance is to be efficacious, it is a ritual. If its purpose is to entertain, it is theatre. These are not absolute distinctions and most performances contain elements of both efficacious

intention and entertainment. At the ritual end of the continuum we are likely to have an active 'audience' who share the aims and intentions of the main actors. Time and space are sacred and symbolically marked, and it is the end result of the action that matters (to heal, initiate, aid the deceased or whatever it may be). In a theatrical performance the audience is more likely to observe than participate, and the event is an end in itself. It is performed for those watching and not for or in the presence of a higher power or absent other.

> 'No experience is too lowly to be taken up in ritual and given a lofty meaning.'
>
> Mary Douglas

Australian Aborigine boys decorated with face and body paint for their initiation ceremony.

RITUAL AND PERFORMANCE

The World's Religions

This map shows the approximate present-day distribution of the world's religions. In all areas, only the predominant religion has been shown.

- Indigenous religions (majority of population claiming to be adherents)
- Hinduism
- Buddhism (with Shinto in Japan)
- ☬ Sikhism
- 🦅 Zoroastrianism (Parsis)
- Judaism
- Christianity
- Islam
- The Religions of East Asia
- areas of low population (undifferentiated or tribal religions)

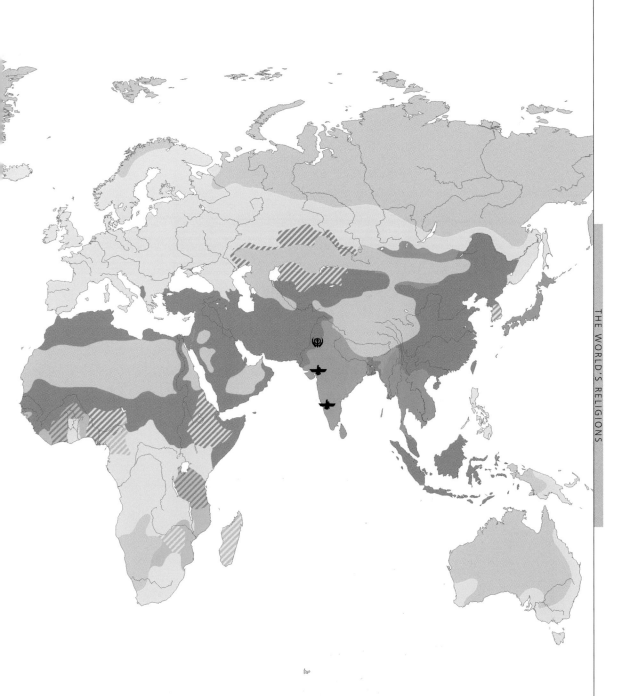

UNDERSTANDING RELIGION

	2500 BCE	2000 BCE	1500 BCE	1000 BCE	500 BCE
				OLMEC	
		SUMERIAN	AKKADIAN	BABYLONIAN	
			ASSYRIAN	ASSYRIAN	
		CANAANITE			
		HITTITE			
OLD KINGDOM	EGYPT	MIDDLE	HYKSOS NEW	EGYPT	
		MINOAN	MYCENAEAN		GREEK CITY STATE
					ROMAN REPUBLIC
		CHINA	SHANG	CHOU	
INDIGENOUS RELIGIONS					
VEDANTISM					
			ZOROASTRIANISM		
		ANCIENT ISRAEL			

Timeline of the World's Religions

Civilizations
of Antiquity

The Religions
of East Asia

	0	CE 500	CE 1000	CE 1500	CE 2000

MAYAN

AZTEC

INCA

PERSIAN

BYZANTINE

NORTHERN EUROPEAN

HAN   T'ANG   SUNG   MING   MANCHU

HINDUISM

JAINISM

BUDDHISM

SIKHISM

PARSIS

CHRISTIANITY

ISLAM

CONFUCIANISM

TAOISM

SHINTO

BAHA'I

Religions of Antiquity

PART
TWO

Religion Before History

ÅKE HULTKRANTZ

> 'There is nothing more ancient in the world than language. The history of man begins, not with rude flints, rock temples or pyramids, but with language. The second stage is represented by myths as the first attempt at translating the phenomena of nature into thought. The third stage is that of religion or the recognition of moral powers, and in the end of One Moral Power behind and above all nature.'
>
> Max Müller

Most religions are known to us through written sources. 'Prehistoric' means that we are dealing with the time before recorded history; that is, before there were written records about myths, rituals and beliefs.

Writing was developed in the ancient civilizations of the Near East, China and Central America. The literate era started about 3000 BCE in the Old World, and shortly after the birth of Christ in the New World. For the sake of convenience we may designate all religions before 3000 BCE as prehistoric.

BEFORE RECORDED HISTORY
The question of the origins of religion will not concern us here. Earlier evolutionists thought that there had been an original non-religious phase in human history. Their information has, however, proved to be false. All we can say is that some groups, for example the Maasai in Kenya, appear to lack a belief in life after death.

Some students of religion consider that religious consciousness was born during the time when humankind first appeared. Others find traces of 'religious' behaviour even in the animal kingdom. Despite some startling progress in animal-behaviour studies (ethology) and the study of early humankind (palaeoanthropology), nothing certain can be said about these alternatives. All that we know is that some early human cultures seem to have contained traces of religious orientation.

SILENT SURVIVALS OF THE PAST
The main difficulty in any approach to prehistoric religion lies, of course, in the absence of written sources from this extensive period in the history of humankind. The prehistorian is referred to silent survivals of the past: bone materials, stone arrangements, rough stone figures, rock drawings and similar materials. Such objects are difficult to decipher.

For example, it is difficult to tell whether a Danish bog find from the Iron Age – be it a well-preserved human body or a golden dish – was or was not used as a gift of offering, since there are no documents from that time to illuminate what really happened. (Some modern archaeologists even question whether Denmark, or even Scandinavia, had a religion during the Bronze Age!) We shall never know for certain what the people of those days thought.

However, there are means to come closer to an understanding of at least some general ideas of those distant times. Let us first see how the prehistoric source materials can be classified. The difficulty of such a classification is obvious: we cannot know if a particular type of artifact – an axe, say, or a wagon – ever had a ritual purpose. Nevertheless, a survey of materials which seem to qualify as connected with religion calls for a division along the following lines:

● burial places and burial finds

● deposition of offerings

● representations of deities, spirits and cultic figures (carved idols, reliefs, rock paintings, rock drawings, etc.)

● remains of constructions with religious associations, such as altars, temples, or foundations of world pillars

Archaeologists usually point out that this material can be interpreted only by analogy. The prehistoric material must be placed in a context which may suggest its original meaning. Of course, all such conclusions are hypothetical. The history of prehistoric research has seen a succession of interpretations. The methods of archaeological reconstruction have become more refined, comparisons with the world of the science of the peoples of humankind (ethnology) more restricted in scope, and ecological perspectives more decisive. Nevertheless, much of our reconstruction of prehistoric religion remains guesswork. Almost every interpretation of beliefs can be and has been contested.

Preliterate and literate religions

The prehistoric era of religion stretches from the beginning of humankind – probably about two or three million years ago – until approximately 3000 BCE. During all this time religious knowledge was transmitted through the spoken word (beliefs and myths) and through imitative behaviour (rituals). This somewhat restricted how much knowledge could be accumulated – although it is amazing how much tribal keepers of oral traditions are able to memorize.

In many prehistoric societies the fight for subsistence may likewise have precluded the growth of sophisticated religious thought (although there are examples of primal societies with a good deal of leisure time at their disposal). We therefore find some basic differences between representatives of preliterate and literate religions; for instance, the former value repetition in myth and ritual, the latter develop dogma and may go in for intricate speculations.

A DIFFERENT SOCIAL PERSPECTIVE
The main differences between prehistoric and historic religions are, however, that the former are organized around the perspectives of the hunter, food-gatherer, fisherman or early farmer, whereas historic religions, on the other hand, represent the world view of the developed civilizations, beginning with Egypt, Mesopotamia and China. In other words, prehistoric religions were at home in small-scale tribal societies where family or kin-groups meant more than other forms of social organization, and where the influence of natural forces had a tremendous impact on daily life and religion. Such primitive societies still linger on today, and it is possible to link the types of these societies with prehistoric periods.

HUNTERS, THEN FARMERS
The first period is the Palaeolithic, or Old Stone Age, during which people were hunters, food-gatherers and fishermen. Latter-day hunting societies have been organized along similar

lines, and the patterns of their religions are probably reminiscent of those of Palaeolithic times.

The Palaeolithic was followed by the Neolithic, or New Stone Age, about 10,000 BCE. This was the time when many hunters turned into primitive farmers. In the following millennia pastoral nomadism developed out of this agriculture in places where the cultivated lands met the grasslands and deserts. The world of the farmers and herdsmen is still with us. There is every reason to expect that their religious practices resemble those of their prehistoric predecessors.

These analogies between past and present are very rough and ready. Ecological, technological, social and historical differences may cast doubts upon their validity. But they do give us certain clues on which to base our interpretation.

Before 30,000 BCE
It is extremely difficult to tell from the finds at our disposal what religion was like during the long period called the Early or Lower Palaeolithic (before 30,000 BCE). This was the time of the pre-human members of the family of humankind, the early hominids such as *Australopithecus africanus*, *Homo habilis* (2,500,000 BCE), *Homo erectus* (1,600,000 BCE) and *Homo neanderthalensis* (100,000–30,000 BCE). Originating in Africa, perhaps – only Africa has the earliest skeletons and a continuous succession of species – the hominids spread to Europe (where they appeared before 1,000,000 BCE) and to Asia; Peking man and Sangiran man in Indonesia were both representatives of *Homo erectus*.

THE BEGINNINGS OF CULTURE
We have some information about the modest cultural achievements of early humankind. For instance, we know that two-and-a-half million years ago groups of hominids in East Africa used

> 'Religion in one or other of its many aspects is a universal phenomenon and it appears to be virtually as old as the human race itself.'
>
> E.O. James

choppers, scrapers and other stone utensils that they had shaped themselves. They practised division of labour between the sexes, and food-sharing.

However, their religious ideas if any, are unknown to us. This is what we might expect, for people's cultural capacity at this early time was crude and they did not express clear religious ideas that can be recognized as such by today's archaeologists. We have neither burials, drawings, nor stone monuments to guide our search. However, the toolmaking of these early individuals suggests that they had creative intelligence and therefore, very possibly, a form of religion.

'PEKING MAN'
Many prehistorians have assumed that the Peking representative of *Homo erectus*, who lived about half a million years ago, had some concept of religion or magic. The cave near Chou Kou Tien contained human skulls which were broken at the *foramen magnum*. This gives easy access to the brain, which it would seem was extracted and eaten. If this was the case (we can never be sure, of course), the motive was religious or magical rather than for food, for there were many animals to hunt. Such cannibalism, when practised in present-day primal societies, usually implies the incorporation of the dead person's vigour and power.

This is a very hypothetical interpretation, and, unfortunately, practically all finds from the Lower Palaeolithic that lend themselves to a religious interpretation are subject to the same difficulty.

Take, for instance, the discoveries of circles of mammoth skulls in Russia and the Ukraine. We are familiar with similar skull arrangements from North America in historical times, the circles of buffalo skulls on the plains which were important in worship. However, the Palaeolithic mammoth skulls may have served as weights on the tent-cloths instead of stones. In several instances there are bone circles surrounding fireplaces, and in these cases a religious purpose is probably out of the question.

'NEANDERTHAL MAN'

Almost all the early remains that may have religious significance are associated with 'Neanderthal man' and the last 50,000 years of the Lower Palaeolithic – the so-called Mousterian period.

Neanderthal people buried their dead with proper ceremonies, and seem to have believed in some kind of life after death. In the cave of Shanidar, northern Iraq, a dead person was buried under a heap of stones, resting on a bed of many flowers. At Techik Tach in Turkestan, a child was buried surrounded by five pairs of horns of the mountain goat, apparently placed in a circle. A cave at Monte Circeo in Italy contains a human skull within a small circle of stones; here is one of the so-called 'skull burials' that continue throughout the Palaeolithic period.

Grave gifts are common in many instances (for example, at La Chapelle-aux-Saints in France). Towards the end of the Mousterian period the dead were buried in a contracted position ('flexed burials') and painted with red ochre. Both these measures may reflect a belief in a future life: a return to the womb of Mother Earth, a continued existence in another world through the red 'blood'. Studies of certain modern peoples support these interpretations, but others are of course possible.

From this time also we have evidence of sacred objects: round fossils and pieces of iron pyrites. One round fossil from Tata, Hungary, is engraved with two lines, forming a cross; this could be the first clear evidence of the idea of a quartered universe, a concept widely represented in both Old and New World cosmology.

BEAR WORSHIP

Even in recent times some Arctic peoples have worshipped bears. It is quite possible that similar religious beliefs were represented in Central Europe (France, Switzerland and Italy) in Mousterian times. Thus, in the Drachenloch Cave in Switzerland, bear skulls have been found enclosed in a stone coffin covered by stone slabs. This looks like a regular bear burial. Some reputable scholars (Koby, Leroi-Gourhan, Kurtén) insist, however, that the bears in question – they are cave-bears – had died a natural death in their winter lairs. The apparent burial chests would then be due to natural rockfall from the ceiling of the cave. This is a plausible explanation, but the 'cultic' interpretation seems no less plausible. Finds from Dordogne in France and Weimar in Germany suggest deliberate burial of bears – brown bears in these cases.

The main idea behind bear ceremonialism is that the dead animal will return to life, or persuade its relatives to make themselves available to the hunter, provided it has received a correct burial. The pattern of burial has been taken from human burials.

HOMO SAPIENS

Neanderthal people belonged to Europe, the Middle East, North Africa and northern Asia. They were slowly replaced by another species, *Homo sapiens*, our own direct ancestors, who had already spread over the continents before the end of the Lower Palaeolithic: Siberian peoples entered the New World as early as 60,000 years ago, or perhaps even earlier, and Australia received its population from Indonesia more than 30,000 years ago. This is of some importance for our reconstruction of religious history. It means that the main structures of American and Australian hunting religions go back to the Lower Palaeolithic. And it may even imply that the totemism and high-god beliefs both appearing in these religions are just as old.

30,000–10,000 BCE

At the beginning of the Upper Palaeolithic period about 30,000 years ago, Neanderthal people had left the scene in Europe and modern humankind, *Homo sapiens*, took over. The main periods were the Aurignacian (from 30,000 BCE), the Solutrean (from 20,000 BCE) and the Magdalenian (15,000–10,000 BCE). It is now that the religious patterns, which we could glimpse in earlier periods, take a more discernible form. The world view is still that of hunting peoples, but it varies in different parts of Eurasia. The religious developments in Africa, southern Asia, Australia and America are as yet hidden from us.

The burial customs give evidence of a clear belief in life after death. For example, in some caves near Menton in south-east France some 'flexed' skeletons were found, stained with iron oxide, adorned with rows of pierced shells and bracelets, and equipped with quartzite tools and flint knives. Skeletons from Italy to Russia testify that the dead were buried with their most precious property. No doubt, they were thought to take it with them to another world.

THE MOTHER GODDESS

It is from this time that the famous sculptured 'Venus' figurines in ivory, bone and stone appear (Gravettian period, 25,000 BCE). They are distributed from France to eastern Siberia, and the best known of them all is the Venus from Willendorf in Austria. They all have characteristic, distorted features: the parts of the body which serve sexual and child-bearing functions – the breasts, the

A Palaeolithic female idol, the so-called 'Venus of Willendorf', c. 20,000 BCE.

hips, the buttocks, the private parts – are excessively enlarged, whereas little attention is paid to the face, the arms and the legs.

It has been suggested that these fat-rumped (steatopygous) figures are just representatives of mortal women, portrayed in the fashion of the time. This is scarcely probable, however. The emphasis on the sexual parts shows very clearly that these Venuses were supposed to represent deities of fertility, growth and fruitfulness. Here we have for the first time real representations of a deity, the mother goddess, conceived as one or many.

There is a seemingly puzzling question here. How could the mother goddess, forerunner of Ishtar, Cybele and Artemis, be such a prominent divinity in a hunting culture? The answer is simple. In recently studied northern Eurasian cultures, the women had similar birth goddesses protecting them during pregnancy and childbirth. Many Siberian tribes believed in a mother of the wild animals, a mistress who protects the wild creatures she has given life to. We also know that women played a very important role during the Stone Age as mothers, housekeepers and gatherers of roots and berries.

Do these figurines prove that the concept of a male god was introduced later than the concept of a goddess? Such a conclusion seems unwarranted. Before the emergence of the Middle Eastern city states, the Supreme Being was never represented in art as far as we can tell. A diffuse sky-god was not easy to picture.

We know that bull-roarers have been used to imitate the voice of the Supreme Being, or the voices of dead ancestors, in some modern primal hunting religions (in Australia, South Africa, Brazil and California). Some perforated, ornate stone slabs that have been found in Upper Palaeolithic caves may have been bull-roarers symbolizing the presence of the Supreme God, or

Prehistoric cave paintings at Lascaux, Dordogne Valley, France.

other supernatural beings. However, this is far from certain.

CAVE PAINTINGS
The most telling artistic creations from the Upper Palaeolithic are the engravings and paintings on cave walls. They first appear in the Aurignacian period, but receive their full development in the Magdalenian. Their focus is in southern France and northernmost Spain. The most famous and most numerous rock paintings stem from 15,000 to 11,000 BCE; this is the time of the caves of Dordogne (Lascaux), Ariége (Niaux, Les Trois-Frères, Montespan) and northern Spain (Altamira).

Four-fifths of the figures are animals, and of these most are horses and bisons, the hoofed fauna of the frost-bitten plains. Reindeer occur only at a late stage, at the same time as the glaciers made their last push forward. The composition of the beautiful, realistic animal scenes has been interpreted in various ways. In spite of some recent speculations in another direction, it seems quite reasonable to believe that the animals refer to hunting ritual and hunting magic.

Hunting was the major occupation of Palaeolithic man, and ceremonies to secure a successful hunt were most certainly part of the hunting craft, just as they have been among traditional hunters up to the present day.

Only 4 per cent of the pictured animals show arrows (or wounds resulting from arrows). Does this mean that they cannot be associated with hunting magic? Not necessarily. Among primal peoples hunting ceremonies are often very complicated, and real magic – indicating the anticipation of success in the hunt – is only part of a wider pattern. The mere representation of an animal form may lead to the kill – so it was believed.

Why did this animal ceremonialism take place in caves, often in the depths of scarcely accessible inner chambers? We do not know, but it may, perhaps, have something to do with the fact that in widespread tales, recorded even in this century, the animals are supposed originally to have come from underground, or to have once been secluded in caves. Some wall scenes depict human beings in animal disguise. They may represent ritual performers, perhaps magicians or ritual

'The prehistoric paintings discovered in southern France and in Spain reveal that our ancient ancestors were trying to decipher the meaning of life and the world from their primitive dwelling places.'

Joseph Kitagawa

RELIGION BEFORE HISTORY

dancers, or maybe mythical beings. Well-known is the 'sorcerer' of the cave Les Trois-Frères: a picture of a human being with reindeer antlers, long beard, bear's paws and a horse's tail. This figure has been interpreted as a shaman or a god of the cave, but his position in the picture over a great number of animals makes it more likely that he was a lord of the animals, a master of the game.

All these interpretations are of course tentative. There is a host of pictures which do not easily lend themselves to interpretation, such as pictographs of headless animals (there is even a sculpture of a bear without a head), of women dancing around a phallic man, and so on. However, such representations strengthen the general impression that Upper Palaeolithic European religion was concerned with the animals and sexual fertility – natural targets in a religion chiefly concerned with hunting. We can say the same about animal ceremonialism in Siberia in the same era: reindeer skeletons were carefully buried in anatomical order. Such hunting rites have survived in this area into the twentieth century. As in the bear rites, the aim has been to restore the animal to a new life in this world or hereafter.

From the end of the Palaeolithic, or the Mesolithic, we have evidence of what appear to have been sacrifices to the supernatural rulers of the reindeer in northern Germany. Reindeer were submerged in a lake close to present-day Hamburg, and weighted down with stones. It is less likely that these reindeer were caches for the hunters, as has been suggested.

10,000–3,000 BCE

The Neolithic period is, strictly speaking, the time when objects of stone were no longer chipped but ground and polished. More important, this is the age, from about 10,000 BCE, when people changed to producing rather than hunting or gathering their own food. The population of the world was probably then around 10 million. The climate had changed – the melting of the ice was in full flux – and the warmer weather made new inventions in subsistence possible.

FARMING AND VILLAGE LIFE

Agriculture was born, possibly as a consequence of the gathering of seeds by the women. This new way of life made it possible for a rapidly-growing population to settle in one place – to live in villages, and to practise pottery-making and weaving. Village life had a tremendous impact on religion, and so had the new food sources, the products of agriculture (or horticulture, as primitive agriculture is sometimes called).

The Neolithic period provides us with archaeological materials from the whole world. There are at least three independent centres where farming began. One is the Middle East, more specifically the mountain slopes of the Fertile Crescent. Wheat and corn were cultivated here, and dogs and goats were domesticated. The taming of animals slowly developed into pastoral nomadism on the outskirts of the area. In the north, where the grasslands were wide and open, horse riding was introduced in about 900 BCE.

Another centre of agriculture was South-East Asia, homeland of the cultivation of root-crops such as yams. Close by, in Assam, rice was introduced as a staple food that quickly spread to China and the surrounding areas.

A third centre was Central America, where the cultivation of maize began around 5000 BCE.

The religions of the Neolithic peoples were closely adapted to these three agricultural civilizations and spread with them. When pastoral nomadism appeared on the scene a new profile of religion was formed that changed the course of world religions.

'... in the deep reaches of the prehistory of Homo erectus, there are telltale signs of beliefs about the afterlife.'

Ninian Smart

DEATH AND BURIAL

If we now concentrate on the west Asian-Mediterranean Neolithic religions, it is easy to see how the archaeological finds fit in with this picture. People lived in villages and similar settlements; outside these, true cemeteries have been found (although in some cases the bodies were buried under the floors of the houses). Graves were provided with gifts and offerings, such as beads, shells, utensils like ivory combs, and female figurines – perhaps symbolizing servants for the next life, or protective goddesses.

The closer we come to the time of the developed civilizations, the more differentiated are the burials according to rank or class. Social distinctions (stratification) developed as the political organization based on kinship was succeeded by one based on territory, and a surplus of products made it possible for some to become relatively rich and important.

This development was reflected in the burial customs. 'Inhumation' was now common: the body was interred in the ground like the grain, to arise again in another world. Coffins became more commonly used as time went by. Towards the end of the Neolithic, cremation was practised here and there, perhaps associated with a more spiritual view of the afterlife.

In some early Neolithic burials the heads of the dead were removed and placed in a circle, facing the centre. This seems to be the last survival of an old Palaeolithic tradition. The beliefs behind this arrangement are hidden from us. Perhaps the circle as a symbol of the universe had something to do with it.

MALE AND FEMALE

Many female sculptures, fat-rumped and violin-shaped figures in bone, clay and terracotta, testify to the prominence of fertility cults. Figurines from Romania (5000 BCE) show a

The reconstruction of a Copper Age chieftain's grave at Varna, Bulgaria.

mother with her child, later a favourite motif in the Egyptian and Christian religions. In some places there are also phallic statuettes, most certainly representing the male companion of the fertility goddess. The female statuettes are, however, in the majority, no doubt reflecting the elevated position of the woman, and so also the goddess, in a matrilineal agrarian society. The functions of the mother goddess were now adapted to farming needs: she appeared as goddess of earth and vegetation.

Other fertility divinities were also portrayed, sometimes through animal masks, sometimes in sculpture. Serpentines around the goddess hint that she was a snake-goddess; in later Cretan culture the goddess raises her hands holding snakes. The snake was a fertility symbol in historical times in Europe, the Middle East, India and China (as the dragon).

Another divinity is probably represented in the bull effigies with human masks in the Balkan area. The cult of the bull, symbol of fertility, seems to have been distributed over the Mediterranean and Middle Eastern world. In historical times, it became associated with gods like Baal and

Dionysus, with the supernatural master of the bull figures in Zoroastrian religion, and Mithra is represented as killing the bull to rejuvenate the world. The bullfights in south-western Europe are probably reminiscences of ancient rituals in the worship of the bull-cult.

PRIESTS AND TEMPLES
This was the time when a form of priesthood evolved and temples of wood, stone and clay became common. The casual sacrificial places of the earlier nomadic hunting culture were succeeded by large buildings for divine service. Here were kept altars, vessels, inscribed objects, vases with paintings of ritual scenes, sculptures in clay and, later on, copper and gold. All these were used in the rituals.

In the Ukraine and surrounding areas archaeologists have found remains of temples, and clay models of temples. For instance, in the southern Bug Valley (now in Moldavia), Russian prehistorians have discovered a temple at Sabatinovka dating from about 5000 BCE. Built of wattle and daub, it occupied about seventy square metres. Its big rectangular room, with a floor plastered with clay, contained at the back a clay altar, upon which sixteen female figurines were found. They had large buttocks and were seated on horn-backed stools. Beside the altar was a chair of clay, perhaps intended for the high priest.

European and West Asian Neolithic developments are paralleled in East Asia, and are definitely connected with the Chinese Neolithic period. But the developments in South-East Asia are more difficult to follow. In America the fertility religion of the horticulturists was simply a transfer of the hunter's conceptual world to the planter's; agrarian rituals did not vary basically from hunting rituals in post-Columbian eastern North America. However, some mythological motifs connected with the 'maize mother' point to communications with Indonesia. In large areas of agricultural America the Neolithic period continued until the arrival of Columbus, and even beyond this date.

MEGALITHIC MONUMENTS
Towards the end of the Neolithic era structures composed of large stones, or megaliths, were erected in Europe. Perhaps most of them were burial structures: the striking tombs (dolmens) consisting of a large, flat stone supported on uprights, and the passage graves, found on the islands and shores of the Mediterranean and western Europe.

However, beside the megalithic tombs there are also huge stones in alignment, or menhirs, as at Carnac in Brittany. Their purpose is hidden from us; perhaps they marked ritual procession routes. Some large constructions, such as the Hal Tarxien stone buildings in Malta, were evidently temples. Chalk sculptures found in them show realistic human features and some kind of gowns, and may represent gods and goddesses and their priests.

Other megalithic structures give the

Stonehenge in England has been a focus of spiritual celebration for over three millennia.

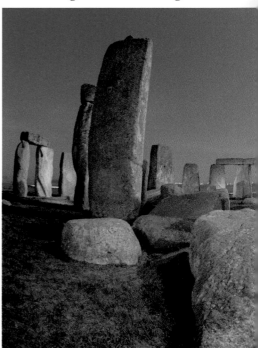

impression of having had astronomical functions. Perhaps they helped to determine the calendar and the agricultural seasons, always important to the farmer. Stonehenge, on Salisbury Plain in England, for instance, has a circle of sarsen stones; certain stones line up with the sunrise at midsummer. Whatever calendar purpose Stonehenge had, it was also a place of worship. Fertility-gods and goddesses were probably worshipped here, as has been suggested by archaeologists.

Megalithic monuments have been found from Britain in the West to Assam in the East, and reached South-East Asia, Polynesia and – according to some scholars – even the New World. Certainly, the Egyptian pyramids and the Maya pyramids in Yucatan do resemble each other, and in both cases they served as burial chambers. All over Eurasia and America, astronomers and prehistorians have identified stone constructions as observatories and megalithic calendars. If this is true, it is almost certain that astronomy was pursued within the frame of religious and ceremonial interests.

THE GREAT CIVILIZATIONS

The megalithic monuments are, like the Bronze-Age finds that date from approximately the same time, stepping stones to the era of the great civilizations, or 'high cultures'. The latter started on the river plains in Egypt, Mesopotamia and other Near Eastern areas around 3000 BCE. They introduce the age of history, that is, of writing. Living in towns, central political power, large economic surpluses and strict class differentiation are the characteristics of these new kingdoms. In the religious sphere they are distinguished by sacred kings, a priestly hierarchy, developed ritual, hecatombs of blood-sacrifices and imposing temple buildings. Their religious world is populated by great gods and goddesses (usually arranged in hierarchical order under a supreme god), their realm of the dead is stratified.

We have come a long way from the simple stone arrangements of the Palaeolithic peoples. Despite the 'Neolithic revolution', it is a continuous road that leads from the simple beliefs of Palaeolithic hunting groups to the polytheism of the great ancient kingdoms.

48

RELIGIONS OF ANTIQUITY

Holy Places, Sacred Calendars

HAROLD TURNER

The places where the gods are revealed or act, and the times when they do so, are central to religious experience.

The place of a vision, healing, miracle or sign tends to be set aside as a special holy space where the gods may be expected to act again. This may begin as a mere cleared circle in the grass, where people come with prayers and offerings. Symbolic objects representing the divinity, altars for the offerings and sacrifices, and buildings to protect both images and altars and to serve as a 'house for the god' may then be added. As the shrine is elaborated it

may become a vast temple space with massive structures.

Such sacred places have a symbolic significance. They may be regarded as the 'centre of the world' or 'navel of the earth', as the meeting-place between the gods and humankind, and the earthly replica of the heavenly realms. The inner cell where the image rests is the 'most holy place', often followed by a series of courts, with degrees of lesser holiness, to the entrances.

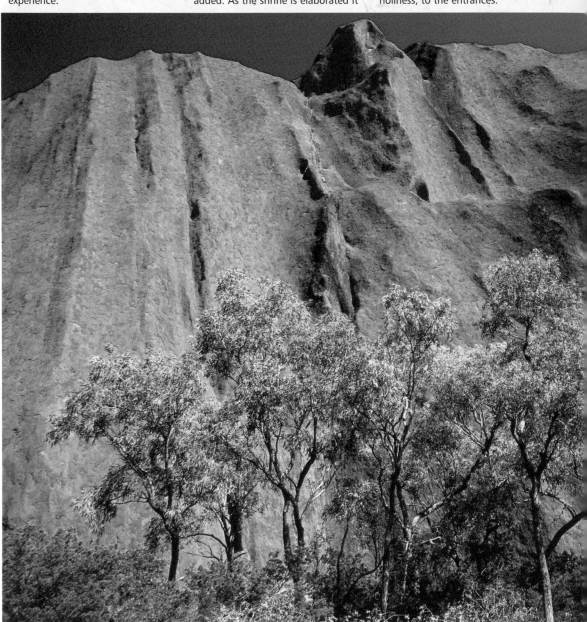

Ascent from the earthly to the heavenly realm is symbolized by vertical features – massive stairways, sacred pillars or trees, and sanctuaries on holy mountains. Similar ideas may attach to sacred caves, groves, healing wells, mysterious rock formations, or the tombs of saints or martyrs. Since divine power is more accessible at sanctuaries, these become places of pilgrimage.

The synagogues, churches and mosques of Judaism, Christianity and Islam, however, should be seen as meeting-places for the worshippers, not as sacred dwelling-places for God. They may have a historical or devotional value. But they do not possess a special 'holiness' because God is more active there than anywhere else.

Distance in time separates people from the divine creative acts of the past. In many religions this is overcome by regular recital of sacred myths, retelling what the gods did in creating the world, giving the land, and showing how to make fire, to hunt, farm, build and live together. The recital brings these foundation events to life again. Similarly, periodic rituals re-enact and so renew the actions of the gods.

Together myths and rites make up great religious ceremonies which are timed by the rhythms of the seasons or of the heavenly bodies. The most basic is the new year renewal rite when both human and earthly vitalities, which have been used up, corrupted or attacked by evil forces, are purified and given fresh life from the spirit world.

Calendars first developed as schedules telling when to be ready for the next renewal of divine blessing or power. Calendars, however, could not tell the right time to secure divine blessing on activities such as building a new village, making war, trading, travel, marrying or anything else of special importance.

For these, diviners sought to read the signs of divine approval in the position of the stars (astrology), the flight of birds, by casting lots, consulting oracles, and in many other ways. Divination is therefore important where people feel totally dependent on gods who do not otherwise disclose their will.

Religions with scriptures, such as Judaism, Christianity and Islam, have other means of revelation, and at their best have opposed divination. On the other hand, they have their calendars of times for renewal, whether in daily devotions, weekly worship or annual renewals of experience of the divine blessing.

The massive natural monument of Ayers Rock, Australia, is an Aboriginal sacred site.

Land of the Aztecs and Incas

GEORGE BANKES

'Pre-Columbian' America is a term generally applied to Central and South America before its conquest by the Spaniards in the sixteenth century CE.

In much of Central America, now mainly the modern states of Mexico and Guatemala, and the central Andes, largely modern Peru and highland Bolivia, high cultures with polytheistic religions developed. In both areas, however, there were two levels of religion. The common people had their local shrines at which offerings were made. But there were also the organized state religions with temples and systematic theologies.

What we know about these religions comes from archaeology, contemporary native documents such as the Aztec and Maya codices, and Spanish accounts. The origins of formalized religions in both Mexico and Peru can be traced back to temple structures with associated cults as early as 1200 BCE.

Central America

SACRED JAGUAR: THE OLMECS
Between about 1200 and 500 BCE a people, called the Olmecs by archaeologists, lived on the Gulf Coast of Mexico. They built ceremonial centres such as La Venta which were carefully planned temple communities. At La Venta a group of buildings was arranged symmetrically along one axis. At the south end was a clay pyramid, shaped like a fluted cone.

Olmec religion seems to have centred on the jaguar in various guises. At La Venta three identical mosaic pavements, made from blocks of green serpentine, were discovered. Each was laid out in the form of a stylized jaguar face, and as soon as it was finished it was covered up. These could have been some kind of offering to the beast.

On the lid of a stone coffin, or sarcophagus, at La Venta, a jaguar mask is depicted with feathers for eyebrows and a forked tongue of the type only found in snakes. This seems to show him as part bird and part snake, suggesting that he may be the ancestor of the Mexican god Quetzalcoatl, usually shown as a plumed serpent. It also suggests that in Olmec times different animals were combined to form one god, which is an idea basic to Central American deities.

The Olmec jaguar could also assume human characteristics. A carving from the site of Potrero Nuevo shows his union with a woman. This act was believed to have produced a race of creatures half human and half jaguar. The human element is generally childish, with a paunch and stubby limbs. Onto this are grafted the jaguar characteristics: fangs, sometimes claws, and a snarling mouth turned down at the corners. The heads are often cleft at the top. These hybrid creatures were probably deities, possibly of fertility.

THE MAYA
Successors to the Olmecs were the Maya, a Central American people who lived in the semi-tropical rain forest of the Guatemalan department of El Peten and the adjacent parts of Mexico and Belize. The Maya developed an elaborate state religion based on ceremonial centres or cities containing temples. Alongside this existed a native folk religion. The earliest temples were being built about 200 BCE at Tikal and Uaxactun. However, it was during the 'Classic Period', between CE 300 and 900, that Maya culture and religion

fully developed. After CE 900 the state religion largely collapsed, though the folk one has partially survived.

Maya religion was – and still is – a contract between human beings and their gods. The gods helped them in their work and provided them with food. In return the gods expected payment, usually in advance. Prayer was directed towards material ends such as obtaining rain to make the crops grow.

Before an important ceremony there seems to have been little difference, except in scale, between the preparations in the village and those at the ceremonial centre or city. Before all ceremonies there had to be sexual continence, fasting and usually confession. Continence involved husbands and wives sleeping apart for a specified period. If this was not carried out, both the ceremony and the guilty person might be endangered. In antiquity the body was painted black, the colour of unmarried men, during fasting.

Sacrifices in many forms played an important part in Maya religion. They could consist of one's own blood or that of human or animal victims. Also produce such as maize might be offered. Human sacrifice involved extracting the heart while the living victim was held down by the arms and legs. The rain-gods preferred small offerings, such as miniature corn grindstones, and in the case of human sacrifice the preferred victims were children.

In Maya theology there was no general assembly of gods. Maya deities usually only wanted recognition in the form of frequent offerings. Few of them were human in form, and most showed a blending of human and animal features. For example, the all-important *Chacs* or rain gods are shown in the Maya codices as long-nosed gods with snake features. In addition, gods like the *Chacs* were conceived of in fours, each one being associated with a compass direction and a colour. For example, there was one *Chac* for the east with the colour red.

These gods of the Maya had a dual character: both benevolent and malevolent. Also there was a sexual duality. The *Chacs* are generally masculine, but one is sometimes shown as female. The Maya indiscriminately marshalled their gods in large categories, and a god could belong to two diametrically opposed groups. The sun-god was mainly a sky-god, as one would expect. However, at night the god passed through the underworld on the way eastward from the point of sunset to that of sunrise. During this passage the sun-god became one of the nine lords of the night and the underworld.

THE GREAT CITY OF TEOTIHUACAN

Teotihuacan was a large city that flourished in the Valley of Mexico at much the same time as the Maya zenith, between CE 300 and 700. To judge from the number and size of the temples at Teotihuacan it appears to have been a theocracy. The city seems to have fallen to outside invaders about CE 700.

On Teotihuacan's temple walls, religious symbolism features strongly. The rain-god, called Tlaloc or 'the one who makes things grow', is frequently depicted, suggesting that the god was held in great esteem. One fresco shows him with a spectacle-like mask over his face and fangs protruding from his mouth. The other deity who features prominently at Teotihuacan is Quetzalcoatl. He can be seen on a temple facade bearing his name, where he is surrounded by sea shells and snail shells. He may have represented the waters of the earth.

A fourth-century sculpture of the Mexican god Quetzalcoatl.

THE TOLTECS

The Toltecs were a coalition of nations in north-central Mexico. They established their capital at Tula, about fifty miles/eighty kilometres north of Mexico City, about CE 980.

The fifth ruler of the Toltecs, the semi-legendary Ce Acatl, was a priest-king who took the name of the god Quetzalcoatl. Soon after his accession he was expelled by devotees of the god Tezcatlipoca and migrated with his followers to Yucatan, where he founded Chichen Itza. The two principal Toltec pyramids, the Castillo at Chichen Itza and the Temple of the Morning Star at Tula, illustrate how religious life had changed since the collapse of the theocracy at Teotihuacan. At the foot of the stairway of each pyramid was a large colonnaded hall. Here warriors could gather together at religious festivals to use their own altar platforms and sacrificial stones. Theocracy had been largely superseded by militarism.

Among the Toltecs Quetzalcoatl became a sky symbol instead of one of water. Another Toltec deity was a combination of the eagle and jaguar, representing the earthly warrior caste. The latter had the duty of feeding the sun and morning star with the hearts and blood of sacrificial victims.

Aztec religion traced several important elements back to Toltec times. Both Toltec and Aztec religion displayed a close connection between kingship and warriorhood on the one hand and fire, the sun and the morning star on the other. Also the Toltec method of human sacrifice was continued by the Aztecs. The victim was held down on a low stone block, the chest opened with a knife and the heart torn out.

RELIGION OF THE SUN: THE AZTECS

The Aztecs migrated into the Valley of Mexico in the late twelfth century and founded their capital city of Tenochtitlan about CE 1370. However,

An aerial view of the Pyramid of Kukulcan, Chichen Itza, Mexico.

LAND OF THE AZTECS AND INCAS

they did not start their political expansion until after CE 1430.

The Aztecs believed that two primordial beings originated everything, including the gods. They were Ometecuhtli, 'Lord of the Duality', and Omeciuatl, 'Lady of the Duality'. They lived at the summit of the world in the thirteenth heaven.

These two produced all the gods and also all humankind. However, by the time of the Spanish Conquest, the two primordial beings had largely been pushed into the background by a crowd of younger and more active gods.

The Aztecs believed that the gods in their turn created the earth. The most important act in this creation was the birth of the sun. The sun is supposed to have been born at Teotihuacan through the self-sacrifice of a little leprous god. The remaining gods followed his example of sacrifice to provide the blood needed to set the sun moving across the sky.

In order to keep the sun moving on its course it had to be fed every day with human blood. The Aztecs regarded sacrifice as a sacred duty towards the sun. Without this the life of the world would stop. Therefore constant human sacrifices – mainly of war captives – had to be provided. It is thought that more than 20,000 were slain each year.

There was a strong solar element in Aztec religion. Huitzilopochtli, the tribal god of the Aztecs, personified the sun at its height. He was the god of the warriors. In contrast there was the rain-god Tlaloc, who was the supreme god of the peasants. Tlaloc was rated equal with Huitzilopochtli, and their high priests were equal in status. This clearly shows how Aztec religion combined both ancient and modern elements in the form of the old rain-god and the later tribal one.

Aztec warriors who were sacrificed or died in battle were believed to join the sun in the sky for four years. Afterwards they were reincarnated as hummingbirds. When the peasants died they went to Tlalocan – a lush tropical paradise. Those who did not get to either of these places went to Mictlan, a cold, twilit underworld.

Central Andes

CHAVIN
Between 600 and 300 BCE a cult involving the worship of a supernatural feline being spread through northern, central and part of southern Peru. It appears to have emanated from a stone-built temple at Chavin de Huantar in the north Peruvian highlands.

The temple at Chavin is riddled with interior galleries. Some of these contained offerings of fine pottery, guinea pigs and llamas as well as sea shells. In the oldest part of the temple is a gallery containing a tall sculptured standing stone. Carved on this is a stylized feline – probably a jaguar – in human form. Snakes represent the eyebrows and hair. The upturned lips of this creature have earned it the name 'The Smiling God'.

Another version of the Chavin feline is the 'Staff God'. This is a standing feline figure with a large rectangular head and outstretched arms, holding a sort of staff in each hand. The fingers and toes have claws, while snakes represent the hair. This could have been a nature-god who was thought to live up in the sky with the eagles and hawks also carved on pillars at Chavin.

THE MOCHE
The Moche people revived the Chavin feline cult on the coast of north Peru during the first millennium CE. They made many pots showing fanged humans, often with snake belts. Frequently they are depicted fighting a monster, part human and part animal, which they generally defeat. Human prisoners were sacrificed to these fanged beings. There seem to have been a number of other animal deities,

> '... the central rites of the empire, presided over by the emperor himself, were human sacrifices in which the victim's chest would be opened and the still quivering heart torn out and presented to the gods.'
>
> Ninian Smart

such as one which was part owl and part human. The moon also was probably an important deity.

TIAHUANACO

The ruins of the city of Tiahuanaco are on the eastern side of Lake Titicaca, just in present-day Bolivia. Most of the buildings there are ceremonial and were erected during the period CE 200–500, when the city's influence was widespread.

The principal deity of Tiahuanaco appears to have been a standing figure carved on a monolithic gateway. In each hand he holds a vertical staff with eagle-headed appendages. His radiating headdress includes six puma heads. From his belt hang a row of trophy heads suggesting human sacrifice. This

The Inca ruins of Machu Picchu, Peru, rediscovered in 1911, are one of the most beautiful and enigmatic ancient sites in the world.

figure could represent Viracocha, the creator-god of Inca mythology.

THE CHIMU

The Chimu established a kingdom on the coast of north Peru between CE 1200 and their conquest by the Incas in the 1460s. Their greatest divinity was the moon. She was believed to be more powerful than the sun since she appeared by both day and night. The sun was believed to be an inferior supernatural being. Several constellations were highly regarded; Fur, or the Pleiades, was the patron of agriculture. The sea (Ni) was also very important. White maize flour and red ochre were offered to Ni with prayers for fish and protection against drowning. The feline cult of earlier times appears to have largely died out by this period.

THE INCAS

The Incas first established themselves in the Cuzco area about CE 1200. However, their conquest of highland and coastal Peru was not completed until about CE 1470, by which time their empire covered some 400,000 square miles (a million square kilometres).

In the Inca empire there were numerous local shrines which were allowed to exist alongside the state religion. Some of these were of great antiquity and a few, like the oracle at Pachacamac, were noted for their pronouncements. There were numerous Inca shrines round Cuzco which ranged from natural features such as hills to temple buildings.

The Inca state religion was largely concerned with organization, particularly that of the food supply, and ritual, rather than with mysticism and spirituality. Divination was essential before taking any action. Nearly every religious rite was accompanied by sacrifices. These were usually of maize beer, food or llamas, but were occasionally of virgins or children.

The Inca emperor Pachacuti instituted the worship of a creator-god called Viracocha (or Huiracocha). Viracocha created the sun, moon, other supernatural beings and all humankind. He was the theoretical source of all divine power, and had supernatural beings like the sun to help administer his creation.

The cult of the sun was very important to the Incas. He was thought of as a male god, Inti, who protected and matured the crops. Sun temples were established along with fields to support the religious officials. These temples also housed the images of all the other sky-gods like the thunder-god who was the servant and messenger of the sun.

In contrast to many Central American peoples, the Incas and their predecessors had a widespread ancestor cult. Elaborate offerings including food and drink were placed with the dead. The mummies of Inca emperors were preserved in their palaces and brought out at festivals.

The Incas believed that after death virtuous people went to live in the 'upper world' (Janaq Pacha) which was rather like earth. Sinners went to the 'lower world' (Uku Pacha) where they were cold and only had stones to eat.

THE SPANISH CONQUEST

At the height of its political power and cultural achievements, the Inca empire was destroyed by the Spanish invasion of 1532. Their ruler was deposed and killed, and within fifty years the last vestige of Inca resistance had ceased. Roman Catholic Christianity, imposed by force, displaced the old religion officially. However, it lingered on among the people, and some of its features are still recognizable in present-day indigenous beliefs.

Cradle of Civilization: The Ancient Near East

ALAN MILLARD

Mesopotamia is the Greek name for the land of the Tigris and Euphrates rivers, the area now ruled by Iraq and Syria. To the north the mountains of Turkey and to the east the Zagros range loom over the plains. On the west the steppe country reaches out to the Arabian Desert, while the two great rivers drain through marshes and lagoons to the Gulf in the south.

Mesopotamia was a region, therefore, that had no easily defensible frontiers. Throughout historical times fierce hill-folk raided from the east, and hungry herdsmen from the steppe overran the fertile lands from the west and south. This process began as soon as people realized the possibilities of cultivating the rich soil and harvesting the fish of the rivers. The northern part of Mesopotamia receives enough rain each year for farmers to grow grain and find pasture for their flocks. People have lived in the hills and near the rivers since the Neolithic age, about 12,000 years ago.

The south, ancient Babylonia, depends upon artificial irrigation by drawing the water from the rivers and carefully controlling it, in order to grow any crops. It appears that this skill was put into practice there about 5000 BCE. From then onwards we can trace a steady development of settled life until we find great cities flourishing by the rivers and canals during the fourth millennium BCE. From these cities traders and colonists spread up the Euphrates into Syria, eastwards into Persia, and south down the Gulf, carrying with them the inventions and ideas of their culture.

Amongst these was writing – one of the greatest inventions of all time. It was apparently the need to organize and administer the large settlements and their vital irrigation systems that stimulated the development of writing in Babylonia, and, at the same time – possibly by imitation – in Egypt. Without wide-ranging written documents relatively little can be learned about the life and religion of a long-dead society. The objects surviving from an ancient religion can be misunderstood very easily without the precise information that written texts can give.

THE SUMERIANS

The Babylonian cuneiform writing on clay tablets was produced for the dominant people of the south, the Sumerians. Their religious beliefs are the earliest we can learn about in Mesopotamia, but it is impossible to be sure that any feature is purely Sumerian because the land was always inhabited by a mixture of races. Indeed, apart

A Mesopotamian tablet containing mathematical text in cuneiform script and a geometric design.

from their language, there is very little that can be called distinctively Sumerian.

In Uruk, the city of about 3000 BCE best known from excavations by archaeologists and from the earliest texts, there were two main temples. One was for Anu, the supreme god, the king of heaven; the other was for Inanna, the great mother, goddess of fertility, love and war. Inanna was, undoubtedly, the principle of life worshipped from time immemorial, the goddess found depicted on paintings, carved in stone and modelled in clay in almost every prehistoric dwelling-place.

The temples employed large numbers of people, and owned large estates. Beside the farmers and herdsmen, there were craftsmen making fine objects for use in the temple services, weavers making clothes for the sacred statues and for the priests, and scribes keeping check on all the temple affairs. The priests had an important place in city life, the high priest sometimes being the king of the city. This seems to have been the normal structure of temple life in the Babylonian cities for many centuries. Each major city in the south was the centre for worship of a particular deity. During the third millennium BCE, beside Anu and Inanna at Uruk, there were Enlil, lord of the atmosphere, who was worshipped at Nippur, and was, next to Anu, the chief of the gods; Enki, ruler of the fresh waters that come from beneath the earth, who had his shrine at Eridu; the sun-god, Utu, whose home was at Larsa; and the moon-god, Nanna, who lived at Ur. In some places the chief deity was simply called 'Lord of the City X'.

Ancient theologians organized the relationships between the gods and goddesses. Each principal god had a family and servants, and they were honoured with temples and chapels also. Enlil's son, Ninurta, was lord of Lagash, for example. The less important deities had shrines inside the larger temples, but they were also revered in small shrines set amongst the houses of the citizens.

The temples dominated the cities. When a temple grew old, or was thought to be too small, a new one was built, often on top of the ruins of the previous one. Over the years, the temples came to be set up above the houses round about on the platforms that covered the earlier buildings. The most important part was the holy room where the statue of the god stood.

MYTHS OF THE GODS

Between 3000 and 2000 BCE Sumerian poets told stories about the gods, probably setting them to music. Some of these myths survive, a few in copies made about 2500 BCE, many in copies of around 1700 BCE.

The gods of the Sumerians were the powers of nature as revealed in the world. So the sun-god was the sun and the power within it. Just as human activities are limited, so were the gods each restricted to their own sphere. The myths show the gods acting in their own positions. They fight to hold their places against evil powers that want to break down their ordered way of life, they quarrel over their areas of influence, they engage in trickery and show every kind of human emotion and vice.

Like most people, the Sumerians asked why the world existed, why humankind was made. Several myths give answers. In one, Enlil separated the heaven from the earth. On the earth he made a hoe to break the soil. Out of the hole made by his hoe people sprang like a plant. Another myth tells how Enki and the mother goddess created humans. The gods were tired of the work they had to do, tilling the ground and digging canals to grow the crops for their food. Enki had the idea of making a clay figure which the mother goddess would bring to birth. This was done, resulting in humankind. Ever since, people have had to work the ground in order to grow food for the gods and for themselves.

The myth goes on to tell how the god and goddess drank too much beer in their celebration. They quarrelled, and the goddess boasted she could spoil their creation. Enki challenged her, boasting that he could find a place for any creature she made. The goddess produced all sorts of cripples and freaks, but Enki found each a place in society. So the story not only explained why human beings were made, but also offered a reason for the existence of the deformed.

Another topic the poets took up was the story of Dumuzi, later known as Tammuz. He was a shepherd who wooed and married the goddess Inanna. Afterwards, Dumuzi was carried off to the world of the dead. There is more than one version of the story. In the clearest, Dumuzi was the substitute provided by his wife who had dared to enter the realm of the dead in order to obtain her release. In other versions Dumuzi was captured by police from the underworld.

There follow in all the stories great lamenting for the dead god, and attempts to restore him to life. The idea that he did rise from the dead is hard to find in the Sumerian texts. It is very likely that the story arose from the cycle of nature when the fresh growth of spring dies in the summer heat. Certainly the story was significant for the Sumerians. In many cities it was retold each year as the king performed a symbolic marriage with a priestess in a rite aimed at securing prosperity for the year.

THE AKKADIAN EMPIRE

During the third millennium BCE Semitic peoples settled in Babylonia in increasing numbers. They mixed with the Sumerians, adopting their culture and their writing. From 2300 BCE they came to dominate Mesopotamia when Sargon of Akkad set up the first Semitic empire.

This was a time of high artistic achievement, and probably the time when the Sumerian stories began to be put into the Semitic language we call Akkadian. Semitic compositions, too, were recorded in writing. These Semites identified some of their gods with the Sumerian ones. Thus Anu was equated with El, the chief god; Inanna with Ishtar; Enki was known as Ea, a name that seems to mean 'living'; and the sun and moon became Shamash and Sin.

Sargon's dynasty fell to mountain raiders, then a new line of kings arose, at Ur, (in modern Iraq). There they built a magnificent temple-tower (ziggurat) for the moon-god, which still rises over the ruins. More invaders ended Ur's rule, and made the Semitic Akkadian or Babylonian language the normal one, ending the use of Sumerian outside of the schools.

It was in the schools that many of the Sumerian myths were copied out as writing exercises alongside a growing number of tales in Akkadian. Some of these were new compositions, some were new forms of the ancient Sumerian stories.

THE GILGAMESH EPIC

The most famous are those that tell of the great King Gilgamesh. He had ruled Uruk, there is now evidence to suggest, about 2700 BCE. Somehow he had captured the story-tellers' imaginations, and become a legendary figure. In Sumerian there are several separate stories about him; in Akkadian there is one long epic. Its basic theme is the problem of mortality. Gilgamesh did great deeds, but he was forced to recognize that he would die one day. He set out on a quest to gain immortality. After many adventures, he came to the place where there lived an old man, the Babylonian equivalent of the biblical Noah. This man, Ut-napishtim, was the only mortal who had won immortality. But Gilgamesh was disappointed, for the man was

Gilgamesh said: 'O barmaid, let me not see the death I constantly fear.' The barmaid said to him, to Gilgamesh: 'Gilgamesh, where are you wandering to? You will not find the life you seek. When the gods made mankind, They set death aside for men, But they kept life in their own hands. So, Gilgamesh, do you fill your belly, Be happy day and night, Take pleasure every day, Day and night dance and play. Wear clean clothes, Wash your head, bathe in water, Attend to the child who holds your hand, Let your wife be happy with you. This is what man's lot is.'

incredibly old and lay on his back doing nothing. Perhaps immortality was not so good after all!

He told Gilgamesh how he had reached his state. The gods had created humankind, but people disturbed them by their noise. Unable to quell the noise, the gods decided to destroy humankind by a great flood. Enki, who had made humankind in the first place, warned his particular devotee and told him to build a large boat in which he might escape. When the flood came, Ut-napishtim, his family and a variety of animals were safe. After the flood, the ship grounded on a mountain in the north-east of Mesopotamia, and the gods rewarded Ut-napishtim with immortality. But Gilgamesh could not have that experience.

Ut-napishtim told him how to get a plant that might make him young again. Gilgamesh found it, and was taking it home to Uruk to test on an old man, when he put it on the ground while he had a swim. A snake ate it, and went away sloughing its skin. The power of the plant was proved, but there was no other, and Gilgamesh could only go home with the thought that his noble deeds would live long after his death.

This story summarizes the basic outlook of the Babylonians. For them, life on earth was the main concern, life after death was a vague and shadowy concept. They thought of the world of the dead as a place of dust and gloom. Yet it was necessary for the dead to be properly buried; for if not, they would return to haunt their relatives. Offerings were made for the dead, too, partly to keep their memories alive.

What is believed to be a statue of Gilgamesh from the palace of Sargon II (722–705 BCE) at Korsabad, Iraq.

OMENS: THE FINGERS OF THE GODS

This present life was entirely under the control of the gods. To have success or happiness, it was essential to keep the gods in a good humour. There were special days of festival when the worshippers would attend ceremonies at the temple, or carry the statues through the streets. There were sacrifices that could be made to show devotion or ask for help. Ordinary people could not simply walk into the presence of a great god. They had to be introduced by an intermediary. This is the scene engraved on the cylinder seals current during the Third dynasty of Ur and following centuries. The owner of the seal would identify with the figure on it, and pray for the god's blessing. But the gods were unpredictable. The Babylonians could hope, but could have no assurance of divine favour. This led to the development of another aspect of Babylonian religion which is not yet extinct, the taking of omens.

The Babylonians, and the Sumerians before them, believed they could find out about the future from all sorts of strange happenings. In the birth of monstrosities, in the movements of animals, in the shapes of cracks in the wall, or of oil poured into a cup of water, they saw the fingers of the gods pointing to the future. If a man wanted to marry, or a king to go to war, the omens would be consulted. One common way was to examine the liver of a sacrificed animal. If the form was exactly as it had been once before then the events that followed on that occasion, if good, would suggest it was a good omen, or if bad, that the proposed action should not be taken.

A special class of priests was trained to take and interpret the omens, and they built up an enormous encyclopedia about them. In watching the skies they learned a lot about the stars, and became able to predict eclipses and to correct the calendar. They also originated fortune-telling by astrology.

THE ASSYRIAN EMPIRE

In northern Mesopotamia the state of Assyria grew strong about 1400 BCE, and, after an interval, became the dominant power in the Near East from 900 to 612 BCE. The Assyrian kings tried to copy the Babylonians, whose culture was much older. They worshipped the same gods, but the chief, identified with Enlil, was Ashur, the god of the original capital.

When the Assyrians conquered other lands, they did not interfere in the local religion, and, if the people were submissive, they allowed them to continue their own customs. If they revolted, then their gods might be taken away captive, to be set in the Assyrian temples. Usually they were respected, and were sometimes returned when a once-rebellious land was made to submit.

THE BABYLONIANS

The Assyrians fell to the Babylonians or Chaldeans, of whom Nebuchadnezzar is the most famous ruler. He rebuilt Babylon and the great temple of Marduk, the patron god of the city. Marduk had risen to prominence under Hammurabi of Babylon in about 1750 BCE, and was popular when Babylon's power was greatest. It was in his honour that the Babylonian creation story was written.

This describes the beginning of the world, when all was sea. The gods borne by the sea disturbed her, and she planned to destroy them. They chose a champion to fight her lieutenant, but he failed. Another was chosen and failed. Then Marduk, a god of no importance, offered a plan, and succeeded. His prize was the kingship of the gods. His gift to the gods was the creation of humankind, with the aid of his father Enki-Ea, to do the work they so disliked. The poem ends with a long list of Marduk's powers.

The Persians who conquered Babylon kept the local religion alive, and in a few centres it flickered on until the first century CE. Some of the gods and goddesses continued to be worshipped by local people until the coming of Islam to Iraq.

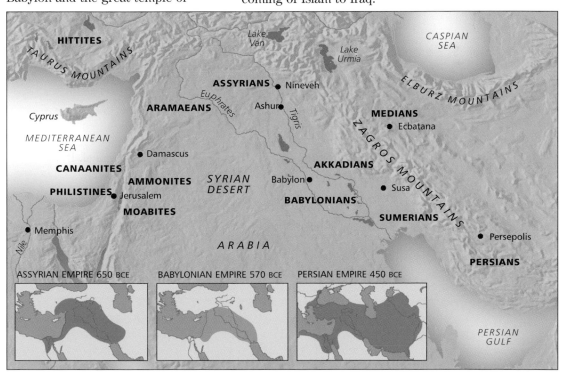

'Warrior Marduk,
whose anger is
like a flood,
Whose forgiveness
is like a loving
father's,
I am sleepless
through speaking
but not being
heard,
I am depressed
from calling but
receiving no
answer.
This has made
my heart grow
weak, And made
me bent like
an old man.
Great lord,
Marduk,
forgiving god,
Who among all
kinds of men,
Can understand
his nature?
Who has not been
at fault, who
is there who has
not sinned?
Who can know the
way of a god?
O that I were
careful not to sin,
O that I would
seek the places of
life always!
Mankind is set by
the gods on a
hapless course,
To endure what
the gods inflict
upon him.
If I, your servant,
have sinned,
If I have passed
the divine bounds,
What I did in my
youth, forget it,
whatever it was,
And absolve my
fault, remove
my wrong,
Lighten my
troubles, relieve
my distress...
Warrior Marduk,
let me live to sing
your praise!'

Part of a prayer to
Marduk

Canaan: gods of nature

Canaan was the name for the Holy Land from about 1800 to 1200 BCE. The people living there were a mixture of races, basically Semitic, with close relatives in Syria to the north. After Israel took control of the land, by about 1100 BCE, some of the Canaanites maintained separate states in the north, in the area the Greeks called Phoenicia (modern Lebanon). Their culture and religion continued to flourish there, and influenced the neighbouring lands.

Temples, religious objects and inscriptions that have been unearthed tell us something about the religion of the Canaanites and Phoenicians. Other information is given by Hebrew, Greek and Latin books. Ancient Israel was warned to avoid all contact with Canaanite religion, in fact, to wipe all traces of it from the land in which they were to settle (Exodus 23:23–33).

CANAANITE TEMPLES

Excavations have uncovered remains of many small temples in the towns of Canaan. They were single rooms with a niche opposite the doorway where a statue of the deity might stand. Other rooms in front of or beside the shrine could be for the priests or for storage. In a few cases, the thickness of the walls suggests there was an upper storey, and models in pottery show that some temples had towers. Presumably these were for special rites, perhaps for the worship of the sun or the stars.

Where the temple had a courtyard, it is likely that the worshippers stood there while the priests alone entered the sanctuary. A large altar may have stood in the courtyard, with a smaller one inside the building. Animal bones suggest the animals commonly sacrificed were lambs and kids, and at one place piglets had been slaughtered. Liquid offerings of wine and oil were made, and incense was burned.

In some temples stone pillars stood as memorials to the dead. Other pillars were symbols of the gods. They were objects of worship which were covered with fine cloth, and carried in procession for the faithful to see. Their ancient name, *bethel*, 'house of god', suggests that the god was supposed to live in them.

Statues of gods and goddesses were carved in stone or wood, or moulded in metal. They were overlaid with gold, dressed in expensive clothes and decorated with valuable jewellery given by the devotees. They have not survived, but there are many small bronze figures that are still to be seen, and they are probably copies of the larger images that stood in the temples. These small ones were made for the worshipper to offer at the temple, or to use in private devotions at home. When new, most of them were probably plated with gold or silver. The most common figures are cheap pottery representations of a naked female, thought to be the mother goddess, giver of fertility, which were used as charms.

WAR, LOVE AND POWER

To the north of ancient Canaan, but sharing much of the same culture, lay the merchant city of Ugarit. Excavations there since 1929 have yielded a lot of information about the local religion. In particular, clay tablets, written about 1200 BCE, have added an important dimension to our understanding of Canaanite thought, a dimension that could not be obtained from the material remains alone.

These texts from Ugarit contain stories about the gods, and instructions about their worship. We learn that the Canaanite gods were like many others of the Ancient Near East. They were the powers of the natural world. At their head was El, whose name means simply 'god'. He was the father of gods and humans. His wife was Asherah, the mother goddess. El appears in some of the myths as an old man, too old to act effectively, bullied by his wife and his children. In one story he is shown in a drunken stupor; in another he marries two girls who bear him two sons, Dawn and Dusk.

El had a daughter, Anat. She personified war. One poem tells how she slaughtered the people of a city, tied their heads to her waist, and waded up to her thighs in their blood, laughing with joy. Anat was also the goddess of love, and is described in some stories as the lover of her brother, Baal. He was the best known of the Canaanite gods. His name means 'master' or 'lord', and he was actually the god of the weather, Hadad, 'the thunderer'.

BELIEFS OF THE ORDINARY PEOPLE
It is difficult to discover what ordinary people believed, or how they worshipped. In offering sacrifices, the person could share in the meat at a cultic banquet with the priest and the god, the sacrifice being a sign of devotion, the payment of a vow, or an offering for pardon. Beside the chief gods there were many spirits and demons who had to be placated or warded off. Dead relatives, too, required regular commemoration to prevent their ghosts from haunting the living.

Many priests served at small shrines on hilltops, the 'high places', mentioned in the Bible, and in every town and village. These men, and others, cast spells and forecast the future, telling the anxious inquirer if it was a lucky day for a business venture, a war or a wedding. Divination was a skill Canaanites learned with the help of Babylonian manuals, and applied in every possible way.

According to Hebrew and Greek writings, popular worship included ritual prostitution and other excesses. Child sacrifice was believed by the Romans to be a custom of the Phoenicians, and the people of Israel were instructed not to 'pass their children through fire to Molech',

another form, apparently, of infant sacrifice (see, for example, Leviticus 18:21). Remains of such offerings have come to light in the ruins of Carthage in North Africa.

A happier side of Canaanite religion can be seen in the titles 'merciful' and 'gracious' applied to El. The main impression, however, is of gods and goddesses who were imagined as wilful and capricious, just like their human followers. Whatever the Canaanites might do, they could not be sure of divine approval or blessing, for they could not know their gods.

The gods of the nations

When the Israelites took control of Canaan, other peoples were settling in adjacent lands. Along the coast, in the south-west of Palestine, were the Philistines; eastwards, across the Jordan, were Edomites, Moabites and Ammonites, while the Aramaeans occupied Syria to the north.

The religions of all but the Aramaeans are little known, for these people have left very few inscriptions, and their cities have not been extensively explored. The Bible speaks of Chemosh as the national god of Moab, and a little more can be discovered about him from the famous Moabite Stone. This inscription, engraved about 830 BCE, describes Chemosh in much the same way as the God of Israel is depicted; he is angry with his land, so hands it over to an enemy, then he gives relief, and the enemy is defeated. Booty and captives were dedicated to him by the victorious king of Moab, Mesha (see 2 Kings), who set up the stone in a temple of Chemosh at Dibon. When under attack,

A guilded bronze figurine of Baal, from Ugarit, Syria, 14th–13th century BCE.

another king of Moab sacrificed his son in a bid to arouse Chemosh's aid (2 Kings 3:27). It was to Moab that the seer Balaam was brought to curse Israel (Numbers 22).

Clay figures of humans and animals, and especially of the 'mother goddess' type, are found in Moab, Edom and Ammon, just as in Canaan and Israel. From the little known of Moabite religion, similarities with Canaanite beliefs are evident, although the position of Chemosh as a national god is more like the position of Israel's deity. It is reasonable to assume that Edomite and Ammonite religions, of which even less is known, were very like the Moabite one. Edom's national god was Qaus, and his name formed part of personal names borne by Edomites (such as Qaus-gabbar, 'Qaus is mighty').

In Ammon (the name is preserved in modern Amman) the people worshipped Milcom. He may be identified with the Molech to whom Canaanites offered children. As for the Philistines, the Old Testament suggests that they adopted Canaanite gods (Dagon, Judges 16:23–24; Baal-zebub, 2 Kings 1:2), and a small temple uncovered at Tel Aviv is similar in design and furnishings to Canaanite shrines, except that it contained Philistine pottery.

THE ARAMAEANS

The Aramaeans of Syria also absorbed the religion of the people of the land. Hadad was revered as the chief god of Damascus, with the added title Ramman or Rimmon, 'Thunderer'. He was also called 'Lord of heaven' (Baal-shamen). Beside him was his consort Athtar. El continued to have worshippers, who gave him the title 'Creator of heaven and earth'. The 'Queen of heaven' was a name for the mother goddess. In course of time, these Semitic deities were identified with Greek and then with Roman gods, and some took over the attributes of

others. Under the Roman empire, magnificent temples were built for the gods at the main centres, and some still stand, most notably at Baalbek in Lebanon. There Baal-shamen was equated with Zeus and Jupiter, as the sun-god, while the goddess Atargatis, a fusion of Athtar and Anat, became Venus.

At Palmyra, the caravan city between Damascus and the Euphrates, a powerful state existed during the first century BCE and the first three centuries CE. Baal-shamen was important there, in addition to a triad of local deities, Bol, or Bel, Yarihbol, and Aglibol, the last two being the sun and the moon. Appropriately for a trading city, Gad, 'good luck', was prominent, too. The great temple of Bel still stands, its size and extensive outbuildings showing the wealth of the city and the number of staff employed in the cult.

The priests were organized in groups, the highest being the priests of Bel. They presided at the sacred meals following sacrifices. This was an ancient practice, followed by the Canaanites, when the priests, the offerers and the gods were all thought to eat and drink together. Wealthy citizens gave funds for the banquets to be held regularly, expecting to gain merit thereby. Admission was by small clay tokens bearing suitable pictures and inscriptions. As elsewhere in the Ancient Near East, the people of Palmyra buried their dead with care, recording their names so that their memory might not be lost.

Sun and storm: the Hittites

From about 2000 BCE until 1200 BCE most of the area of modern Turkey was controlled by an Indo-European people. They are called the Hittites although the name really belonged to another, non-Indo-European, group. A third people, the Hurrians, possibly related to the modern Armenians, mixed with the Hittites and influenced their religion and culture from 1450 BCE. After the end of Hittite power, the language and religious beliefs continued for a long time in parts of Turkey, being known to writers of the Roman period.

The country is mountainous, each town being distinct. As a result, each town had its own god or goddess, usually the deified elements, the sun, storm, and so forth, whom the citizens worshipped in the main temple of the place. A Hittite myth makes clear how the gods depended upon their human servants: when a disaster befell the land, the gods were starving because the sacrifices were interrupted! All sorts of other powers claimed attention: the spirits of earth, of grain, of fire, of seeing, of hearing. Magic spells were recited to win their aid or ward off their evil.

At the capital city, Hattusha, modern Bogazköy, the king led the cult of the storm-god and the sun-goddess, the national deities. The king was both high priest and deputy of the storm-god, and high priest of all the other gods. He was expected to attend the major annual festival of each god in that god's city. Elaborate rituals were performed to ensure that he was cultically pure for such occasions. If the king did not attend, or committed some other error, a catastrophe could overtake the land.

The causes of divine anger might be petty, as when the god's robe was worn out, or significant, the breaking of an oath. They could be discovered only by asking the god to give a sign through an omen of some sort. Only in such ways could people learn the mind of the gods, and hope to gain their goodwill.

Ancient Egypt: Land of the Priest-King

JOHN RUFFLE

Ancient Egypt is the name given to the civilization in the lower reaches of the Nile Valley, from about 3100 BCE to 30 BCE, when the Romans occupied Egypt. It covers periods of strength such as the Old Kingdom (about 2700–2200 BCE), when a line of powerful rulers left their pyramids as monuments, the Middle Kingdom (about 2000–1800 BCE), another time of strong central government with influence amongst Egypt's neighbours, and the New Kingdom (about 1550–1225 BCE), when Egypt was one of the dominant countries of the Near East. It also covers periods of weakness when Egypt was torn by internal strife and occupied by foreign powers.

Obviously such changes in political strength and economic fortunes over 3,000 years meant that philosophical and religious attitudes also changed, but there are enough consistent features for us to be able to talk about Egyptian religion as a whole.

The earliest period

Writing was not practised in Egypt until about 3100 BCE, when a single central government was established. What we know about Egyptian religion before then, therefore, has to be deduced from objects found by archaeologists. These take us back another 2,000 to 3,000 years and mainly consist of amulets, usually connected with hunting or fertility. Animal tusks worn as pendants were probably intended to protect the hunter and make him successful; earthenware figures of naked women were meant to ensure plenty of healthy children.

Some pictures painted on pots, or scratched onto rocks, seem to suggest religious rituals, but without a written explanation it is impossible to understand them fully. Sometimes they seem to refer to ceremonies or figures that we recognize from later periods, and it is fairly safe to assume that the basic beliefs and practices did not greatly change in the historical period.

Egyptian gods

The gods of ancient Egypt – as they are represented in the temples and tombs – present a bewildering complexity of strange forms, half animals, half human. In fact we know very little about Egyptian religious beliefs, since there are no studies of Egyptian theology made by the ancient Egyptians themselves.

Many of the Egyptian gods represented strong forces in the natural world. Egypt's prosperity depended on the daily reappearance of the sun and the annual flooding of the river, and these natural forces (with others) were thought of as gods needing to be cajoled and encouraged by sacrifice and worship. The Egyptians often portrayed them as animals. For example, they chose the hawk, which flies high in the sky, as a representation of the sun; and the cobra, which was often found basking on the hot threshing floors, as a symbol of the harvest goddess.

At an early stage other characteristics were associated with some of the gods. The ibis-headed god, Thoth, was thought of as the god of scribes and writing; Khnum, the ram-headed deity, was considered the creator of humankind on his potter's wheel, and so on. How these special attributes came to be given to particular deities is not clear, but they seem to be established in these roles at an early date.

The gods were often associated with particular cities. This probably dates back into the prehistoric period when Egypt was a series of individual communities. As these came together into larger political units, so their local deities gradually became important in the nation as a whole. For example, the god Amun from the city of Thebes was a kind of national god, protecting and leading the whole nation for a time during the New Kingdom while Thebes was the home city of the ruling family.

This was not exclusive, however. The town-folk of other communities would continue to worship their own local god or they would feel free to pray to any other god who might offer special favours. So a scribe who hailed from Denderah might accompany the king to the temple of Amun at Thebes after some notable victory, but would pay his respects to Hathor whilst at Denderah. He would also pray to Thoth, the god with a special interest in writing, for help in his career.

There are also references to 'God' or 'The God', who seems to have been an unnamed universal divine power who controlled the universe and upheld good against evil.

The 'reform' of Akhenaten

For a short while, from about 1375 to

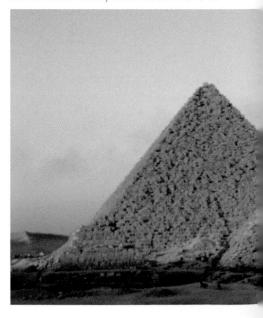

1350 BCE, there was an attempt to impose a form of monotheism. The pharaoh Amenophis IV, who is variously described as a visionary or a lunatic, gradually built up the worship of the Aten, or the sun's disk, until he was the only god whose worship was tolerated. The other gods were proscribed, their temples closed, their priesthoods disbanded and their names erased from all monuments where they could be found. The worship of Amun, in particular, was strongly attacked. The Aten was regarded as the source of all life. This gift of life was passed to the king, who changed his name to Akhenaten (which means 'the one who is beneficial to the Aten'), and to his family and thence to the people.

This 'reform' probably had some political cause, such as an attempt to stabilize and unite the nation, but was also influenced by Akhenaten's bizarre personality. It was apparently not popular; the priests would certainly have been against it since it deprived them of their living, and it survived only briefly after Akhenaten's death. The power of the priests of Amun could not so easily be destroyed. This period was exceptional, since normally the gods seemed happy to exist side by side even when ideas claimed on their behalf appear contradictory.

Other gods

As well as the 'mainstream' gods, other deities were adopted by the Egyptians. Some private individuals who had distinguished themselves in some way were deified. The king or pharaoh was also thought of as a god; he was referred to as 'The Good God', but it was a restricted idea of divinity because he was, plainly, mortal. Very few rulers actually had a statue placed in the temple shrine as an object of worship. The fact that the king could be both god and priest is an indication of some of the contradictions of Egyptian religion.

Sacred animals

Animals too form an interesting aspect of Egyptian religion. The actual practice varied according to the place and the time. In some cases all the animals of one species were regarded as sacred, and they were mummified and buried in huge numbers: baboons, crocodiles, ibises, and even cats and dogs, received this treatment on occasions. In other cases one individual animal was singled out as the

The pyramids of Giza, Egypt, c. 2525 BCE. From left to right: the Pyramid of Menkaure (Mycerinus), the Pyramid of Khafre (Chephren), and the Great Pyramid of Khufu (Cheops).

incarnation of a god. There were several places where a particular bull was selected, perhaps because it had some distinctive markings, and was then taken into the temple, pampered throughout its life and mummified and ceremonially interred at death.

Festivals and services

The festivals and daily services in the temples show that the Egyptians thought of their gods as having the same needs and instincts as themselves. The day began with a ritual in which the god was wakened by a choir. The night attire was then removed from the image of the god, which was washed, dressed and offered food and drink. After this the god might be called upon to receive visitors, deliver oracles or undertake some other duties. We may assume that his behaviour and his decisions would reflect the views and wishes of the priests who could claim to interpret them on his behalf. He would receive other offerings of food during the day, and eventually be put to bed for the night in his shrine.

The daily routine was broken by festivals. Some were short, involving only a special offering or a procession inside the temple. Others involved long journeys by river to the temple of another god. Amun, for example, went by boat from his great national temple at Karnak to the smaller shrine at Luxor which was regarded as his private home, where he stayed for several days with his consort, Mut, and then returned along the processional way. Hathor travelled nearly 100 miles by boat from Denderah on her annual visit to the temple of Horus at Edfu.

The festivals which involved processions along the river or in the town were treated as holidays by the people, who lined the route to cheer and wave at the god's shrine. Some travelled on long pilgrimages to attend. One writer records 700,000 pilgrims gathering for a festival. Some festivals

we know only by name; it is intriguing to try to imagine what happened on 'The Day of Smelling Onions'!

The actual images of the gods that were the centre of this worship have not survived. They may have been of stone or fine metal, probably richly ornamented. At festivals they were carried (hidden from public gaze) in ornate wooden shrines in a large model boat which was borne on the shoulders of several bearers. For the river journeys they travelled in special boats built of wood but shaped to resemble the early reed boats, a reminder that these festivals had their origin in very early times.

The priest who performed all the religious ceremonies was in theory the king. All the temple reliefs show him making the offerings, but in fact, of course, they would be made by his deputies. The priesthood was at first a duty taken on by the local dignitaries working according to a roster, but gradually a professional priesthood was set up. At certain periods when the king was weak, the high priest of Amun or another major god was the real ruler of Egypt.

In addition to the high priest there was a whole range of other clergy with carefully graded ranks and titles. Women served as priestesses, and of course there were numerous other people in the temple service, ranging from choristers and librarians to cooks and gardeners.

Born from water

There is no ancient Egyptian sacred book, equivalent to the Bible or Qur'an, which was accepted as a revelation of divine truth. The Egyptians had their myths like those of the ancient Greeks. The Egyptian myths told the story of the relationships between the gods, but very few have survived intact. All we have are short scattered references which can sometimes be pieced together to tell the whole story,

A detail of the Funeral Mask of Tutankhamun, c. 1320 BCE.

A detail from *The Book of the Dead of Maiherperica*. c. 1450 BCE.

though we cannot be sure that we have it correct.

Various creation myths abounded, for example. The Egyptians generally imagined the universe as originally filled with water, from which a hill arose on which life began. This was no doubt derived from what they observed each year as the Nile flood subsided. Thereafter the stories become extremely complex. Different gods were thought to have somehow emerged from the hill or the water, and in various ways to have created other gods. Many of the great temples were claimed to be built on this primeval hill.

An interesting claim was advanced by the priests of Memphis on behalf of their god Ptah. They declared that he was the great god who somehow was also the great watery universe from which the other gods were born, their acts of creation being simply the carrying out of his will.

As well as the myths there are prayers and hymns to the gods, which read very much like the Old Testament psalms. Books of wisdom are also known, which, rather like the biblical book of Proverbs, range from practical and moral advice to general theological reflections on the nature of life.

There are also many magical spells, which may be counted as religious since they invoke the gods and try to persuade them to give help and protection from all sorts of evils.

Living and dying well

Several of the wisdom books encourage their readers to live according to a moral and ethical code of personal piety. They urge this partly because it is the way to earn respect from one's fellows, partly because it is pleasing to 'the god'.

Living a good life was thought to be a way of ensuring a safe passage to the afterworld. There are many representations of a judgment scene in which the dead person's heart is weighed in a balance against a feather which represents truth. The result was recorded by Thoth, the scribe of the gods, in the presence of Osiris and those who failed were destroyed for ever. This judgment was not, however, a great incentive to piety, since the result could be influenced by correctly reciting an incantation in which the person denied ever committing a whole range of sins.

Journey to the next world

The Egyptians seem always to have had a belief in an afterlife. The very earliest

The journey to the afterworld was fraught with difficulty. All sorts of obstacles lay in the way, and demons were ready at every turn to seize the traveller. A successful journey was assured by possession of a papyrus roll containing a series of incantations which could be recited to allow the dead person to pass when an obstacle or demon was encountered. These books are usually called *The Book of the Dead*, although there are several different titles and versions. Copies were placed in the tomb with the dead, ready for use, or at different periods they were inscribed inside the coffin or on the tomb walls.

It was, of course, plain to the Egyptians that the physical body remained in this world and that it was the person's spirit that passed on. They thought that this spirit needed the body as a kind of base, and for this reason they made elaborate attempts to preserve the body by mummification. It was particularly serious if a body was lost at sea or destroyed by fire, although in extreme cases a statue or portrait of the departed might serve as a substitute.

The funeral ritual included a ceremony called 'The Opening of the Mouth', in which the mouth and other openings of the body were magically treated to ensure that the dead might continue to use their bodies to feed, see, hear and so on. The same ceremony performed over statues and paintings endowed them with a form of life in the afterworld.

tombs contain items of food and equipment, and, later on, the decoration of the tombs tells us how the Egyptians thought such a life would be. Generally it was thought to be similar to this world but better, with successful hunting and harvests, rich banquets and pretty girls.

The idea went through various stages of development. At first it was thought that the king would spend his afterlife alongside the sun-god Re (also known as Ra) on his daily journey across the heavens. Soon, however, his future became linked with the god Osiris, and each king in turn as he died became identified with him. Gradually this privilege was extended, first to the nobles and later to all classes, so that each person on their death somehow became identified with Osiris.

The story of Osiris himself was not recorded in full until the Greek writer Plutarch (about CE 100) recounted how the good King Osiris was murdered by his jealous brother, Seth. With the help of his wife, Isis, and other gods, Osiris eventually became the ruler of the afterworld and a symbol of continued life after death. There are several references to the story in Egyptian literature which make it clear that there were differing versions of this account.

Egyptian Temples: Houses of Power

JOHN RUFFLE

The outward appearance of an Egyptian temple was not particularly elegant. To those of us, whose ideas are coloured by Gothic cathedrals or Greek temples, they appear more like power stations than temples. This in fact reflects their purpose.

They were less concerned with telling people outside about the majesty and power of the god to whom they were dedicated, and more concerned with the ritual that went on inside. This ritual was intended to ensure that the gods would continue their favour towards Egypt and it was therefore the prime consideration in the design of the building.

The plan of the temple

The two main types of temple were the cult temple, dedicated to a particular god, usually the principal god of the city or area, and the funerary temple, dedicated to the memory of a dead king who was treated as a god. To all intents and purposes the plans of these two types were the same.

The temple was thought of as the house of the god, and its plan was similar to the houses of nobles and officials. These usually consisted of a number of reception rooms leading to the private family rooms and ultimately to the owner's bedroom. In the temples the same types of room were used, with large courts and halls corresponding to the reception room, and the shrine corresponding to the main bedroom. The chief difference was that the rooms of the temple were laid out in a straight line so that processions could pass from the main gate to the sanctuary without awkward bends.

Some temples were in use for several hundreds of years and were extended and altered, demolished and rebuilt during that time, but the same general arrangement was followed throughout. Even those cut in the rock cliffs of Nubia, like the temples of Ramesses II at Abu Simbel, kept to the same basic plan. A few exceptions occurred, as when, for example, two deities of equal rank occupied the same temple at Kom Ombo; a double aisle and twin shrines were provided.

The temples represented Egypt in miniature. The great monumental entrance was similar in shape to the hieroglyph which stood for the horizon or limits of the country. On the outside walls of this gate we see the king destroying his foreign enemies. Inside, the halls were decorated as huge thickets, the floors painted to represent water, and the ceilings painted with stars. Egyptian architects did not use vaulting, so the flat stone blocks that formed the ceilings had to be supported by closely arranged pillars which were based on plant shapes, usually with papyrus or lotus capitals.

Ritual protection of the temple

As far as possible the temple was cut off from the outside world to protect its ritual purity. At the foundation ceremony, a pit was filled with clean sand containing magic amulets which warded off any evil influence that might attack from below. The corners of the building were further protected by foundation deposits, consisting of animal sacrifices, groups of model tools and other items. A high wall protected the temple estate, and the building itself was erected within another wall and an ambulatory, or corridor, which formed a further protective layer around it.

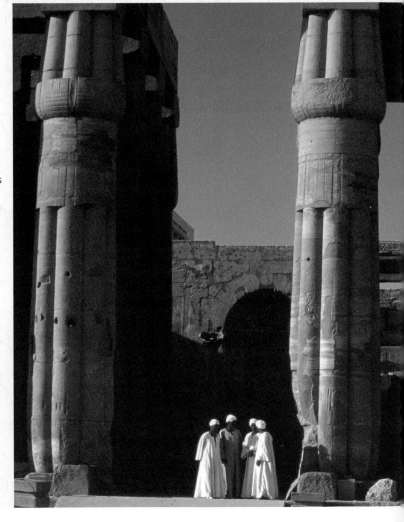

Elaborate precautions were even taken to remove rainwater from the roof, with a complex series of channels and huge gargoyles. The shrine itself was often constructed as a separate building within the main temple, complete with its own roof. So it was again separated from contact with the world outside.

Within the main building various rooms were set aside for special purposes. There would be a library for the papyrus rolls with the ritual texts, a vestry for the special clothing, and store-rooms for the chalices, censers and other vessels used in the rituals. Often, in addition to the main god who occupied the central shrine, there were other gods, perhaps members of the family, who shared the temple. Their images were kept in smaller shrines built around the central shrine in the sanctuary area.

Deepening mystery

The walls of the temple were decorated with relief carvings of scenes from the temple rituals. The words that were recited at the rituals were also inscribed on the walls. From the position of these carvings within the temple it is sometimes possible to tell the uses of the different rooms. These carvings were not just a large-scale service book; the ceremony that was performed when the completed building was formally presented to the god included an 'Opening of the Mouth' ritual by which all these carvings were given life and everlasting effectiveness. So the mere portrayal of the ritual supposedly guaranteed that it would continue for ever, even if the priests ceased to perform it.

As the worshippers moved from the temple entrance to the sanctuary the air of mystery gradually deepened. The size of the rooms was reduced in stages, the roof level became lower and the floor was stepped up. Daylight was also gradually excluded. From the open court one passed to courts lit by a clerestory or openings in the first wall which was sometimes only constructed half-way to the roof; the innermost rooms were completely cut off from daylight. It is easy to imagine how the flickering, leaping light of torches playing on the richly painted figures and hieroglyphs on the walls must have combined with the singing and incense to create a feeling of awe and wonder in the worshippers. The roof of the temple was also important. Some ceremonies, involving, for instance, the union of the divine image with the sun, were performed there. Special stairs with shallow steps were used so that the image of the god could be carried up to the roof in a small portable shrine. Small roof-top chapels were built for these ceremonies.

Shrines

Outside the main building of the temple, but within the enclosure wall, were many other buildings. These may still be seen in some temples, such as Karnak and Denderah. There are small shrines and chapels, often including one where a divine marriage and birth ritual was enacted. There was also housing for the priests, slaughter-yards and bakehouses where offerings were prepared, a well that provided holy water, and a sacred lake on which other rituals would be performed, rather like medieval mystery plays.

The Hypostyle Hall of Luxor Temple, Luxor, Egypt. The temple was built by New Kingdom Pharaoh Amenophis III (1391–1353 BCE) and was dedicated to the Theban Triad of Amun-Min, Mut and Khonsu.

The Ancient Religions of Greece and Rome

CLYDE CURRY SMITH

The ancient history of Greece covers some 6,000 years or more of development from the first permanent settlement based upon grain agriculture until Greece was absorbed by Rome. Within this immense period, only the last 2,000 years at most are definitely Greek by language.

The ancient history of Rome, by contrast, begins in the eighth century BCE and extends into the fifth century CE, and the Latin language is present over that whole span.

Minoan-Mycenaean civilizations

When barley and wheat entered the larger European and Mediterranean worlds, they were accompanied by those who understood their cultivation. These people's way of thinking included observing the seasonal cycle, and its ritual correlation with preparing, planting, weeding and harvesting, or breeding, pasturing, tending and milking. In this we see the base for all later development of religious ideas.

THE EARLY BRONZE AGE
For the earliest phase of the Bronze Age on the Greek mainland, objects of religious significance are minimal. There is much better evidence from the group of islands called the Cyclades. Best known of all Cycladic objects are the marble figurines. The two most common are the elongated female and the abbreviated 'fiddle-shaped' version, which emphasizes only the necklace and the sexually-explicit features. Although the figurines are usually less than twelve inches (thirty centimetres) tall, several life-sized examples exist. These were broken at the neck and knee to fit into the grave.

MINOAN CRETE
There is evidence of royal palace complexes. The palace rulers are said to be 'theocratic', because excavations have revealed no separate structures which can be called 'religious' within these palaces. But in 1979 during the excavation of a small site at Anemospilia, not far from Knossos, there was found the first example of a tiny Minoan temple, originally destroyed in an earthquake which simultaneously presented the apparent act of human sacrifice – a phenomenon unanticipated for this culture, but perhaps the desperate effort to propitiate the activity of the 'earth-shaker'.

The Minoans seem to have worshipped bulls and sacrificed them. There were 'bull-leapers', who performed dangerous acrobatics over a bull for religious purposes. This is often portrayed in wall-paintings, seals and the minor arts, bronze and terracotta. These ceremonial games took place in the large central courts of the palaces.

The palaces also contained 'pillar crypts', decorated with the double-headed axe, the chief Minoan religious symbol, possibly from its use in animal sacrifices. The double axe was a woodsman's tool rather than a weapon. Actual examples have been found, with other carpentry tools.

Storage magazines were sometimes connected with the pillar crypts. In the floor of one at Knossos were 'temple repositories' containing faience figurines handling snakes. Snakes were used as house-guardians, and so became the sacred animal of the household-goddess.

> 'We must dedicate to Poseidon... that he might take pity on us, and not pile up a huge mountain over our city.'
> Odyssey 13.180–83

> 'There is a land called Crete in the midst of the wine-dark sea, a fair country and fertile, seagirt, and there are many peoples, innumerable; there are ninety cities... and there is Knossos, the great city, the place where Minos was king for nine-year periods, and conversed with great Zeus.'
> Odyssey 19.172–74, 178–79

CITADELS OF THE MYCENAEANS

The Minoan epoch came to an end disastrously, probably when the volcanic island of Thera erupted with extreme violence in about 1450 BCE.

The Late Bronze Age or Late Helladic era belongs to the Mycenaeans, both on the mainland and the islands, including Crete. The Middle Bronze mainland had been dominated by Minoan cultural influence, but as the Late Bronze Age began we find the *tholos* tomb-builders. There are no surviving indications of the dwellings of these aristocratic warrior-rulers, though they may well have been built on the sites on which the Mycenaean palaces were to appear. The *tholos* tombs were underground beehive-shaped vaults, entered by way of a long, gently-sloping tunnel, and topped by an earth mound.

The Mycenaean palace complexes are neither towns nor houses, but fortified centres for developing valley communities. What most distinguishes these complexes from their Minoan predecessors is their location on high citadels, and their massive fortification walls. Five major sites on the mainland are known: Thebes, under the modern city; Athens, levelled for the fifth-century *acropolis*; Tiryns and Pylos, both well-preserved; and Mycenae, the best example, though part of the palace itself has collapsed down the slope.

The new ingredient in the Late Bronze Age is the earliest written texts, in a script called 'Linear B'. This was deciphered in 1952 and shown to be an archaic form of Greek.

The Linear B texts give a wholly new dimension to investigation. To date, tablets have been found only at Knossos, Pylos, Mycenae and Thebes. They include inventory lists of people and their occupations, livestock and agricultural produce, land ownership with some usage, textiles, vessels, furniture, metals and military equipment, and a grouping defined as 'proportional tribute and ritual offerings'.

It seems that commodities could serve as either tribute or offering, and that these were assessed seasonally according to fixed schedules, that receipts varied from assessments and, most important of all, that there were functionaries of all sorts, as well as deities known by name or title.

Poseidon is of considerable importance, as is 'the Lady' of different places. Zeus, Hera, Ares, Hermes, Athena, Artemis, Dionysus, and a few other classical deities are named. Among the great variety of functionaries which made up this administrative complex a 'priestess' or 'priest' is very occasionally mentioned.

THE EPICS OF HOMER

There is a gap at the end of the Bronze Age, with the destruction of the Mycenaean world. The palace bureaucracies disappeared.

Pottery remains from this period are very few. We have nothing which documents the religious response to reality – nothing, that is, except the 'epic interlude': the unsurpassed poetry of Homer, regarded by many later Greeks almost as sacred scripture.

The epic language is peculiar in that it was apparently not a spoken dialect, nor equivalent to any of the historic dialects found in inscriptions or subsequent literature. It was, however, designed to be recited.

The nearly 28,000 lines of Homer which form the *Odyssey* and the slightly longer *Iliad*, constitute the surviving bulk of this epic form with its strict metre.

THE HOMERIC GODS

The gods are portrayed in essentially human terms,

A Roman statue of Athena, goddess of wisdom.

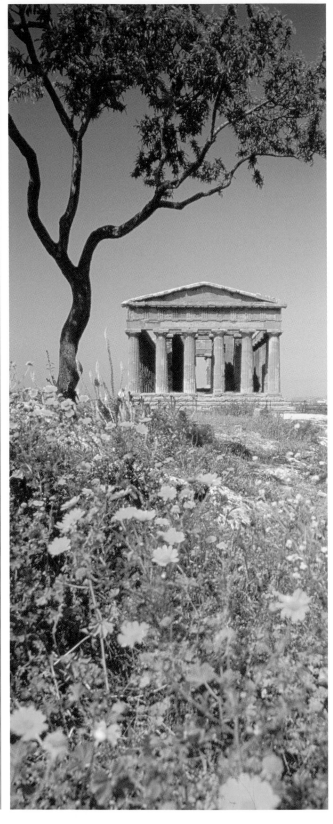

but they do not grow old, and they are immortal. The gods have power (*daimon*) to change their appearance, size and attributes beyond the bounds of the human form they may take.

Their awesome status prompted dread, fear, shame, or reverence. In response humans were impelled to pray, entreat, praise, take an oath, make sacrifice of a victim, or pour out a libation of grain or wine. Many of these activities can be tied quite naturally to daily domestic routine. The communication between gods and humans may be direct or via an intermediary (including the god in disguise as human friend), or by a dream. The gods may be consulted through an agent accomplished in the art of divining, most commonly through birds or the interpretation of dreams. Lightning, thunder or falling stars may also serve as omens. And places where there was an oracle, such as Dodona with its great oak tree at which people listened for the voice of Zeus, played a lesser role.

Life in Homer takes on some specific burden which humans must bear, sometimes even the delusion with which the gods affect them. The human characters tend to explain the course of events as the destiny imposed by the gods – even if, as Helen says to Hector, 'so that hereafter we shall be made into things of song for the men of the future'. With gifts and prayers these gods may be implored to change the situation. The god might sometimes do so, or might merely turn his head away in rejection, for these gods – even Zeus himself – are equally bound by fate. Whatever else may be granted, humans are not permitted to escape death, which is their final destiny. Within that framework all phenomena, religious as well as otherwise, are set. Although the gods manipulate human actions, they neither make nor change human nature.

THE HEROES

Heroes seek honour, glory and renown, believing that to obtain these is of much greater worth than life itself.

The burial of the dead is of great importance. They require that last honour, even though their souls go forth immediately to the underworld (Hades), lest they become the god's curse upon the living. In Homer, the funeral would seem to include cremation (if that of a warrior, dressed in his full armour) and some kind of interment of the burned remains accompanied by lamentations. A mound was heaped over the grave, with a stone indicating the dead person's profession. The funeral rites were commonly accompanied by athletic contests such as chariot-racing, boxing, wrestling, close-combat with sword and shield, weight-throwing, spear-throwing – and betting on all of these.

ANGER OF THE GODS

The other side of heroic life is an overbearing, presumptuous pride, violence and transgression. Although it cannot be shown that in any final sense, other than death, recompense is required for sin, there nevertheless are hints at some larger levels of justice and decency which the gods love in preference to cruelty, or to excessive glorification over slain men. Since fate determines all, the anger of the gods, like the anger of humans towards one another, must work out its destined course. Yet their full destructive anger may be averted by means of prayer, libation (a poured-out drink offering), and sacrifice. The gods may be offended by perverse judgments, refusal or neglect of funeral rites, brutal conduct in a host's home, and murder of a guest. Ultimately, the values of the society are vindicated by the gods.

Temple and city state

The Mycenaean age ended in destructive violence brought about by human efforts around 1100 BCE and, with it, not only palace and palace art but also the Linear B script pass into obscurity. The archaic phase of classical Greece opens on a new world with the coming of alphabetic writing. The fundamental factor is a devastating decline in total population. Whereas some 320 inhabited sites are known from the thirteenth century BCE, many of them large centres, only forty are known from the eleventh century, and all of these are small.

What remained intact through that major alteration, was a legacy of technology in the mundane matters of mixed farming, building, carpentry, boat-building, spinning, weaving, pottery and metallurgy. The simultaneous shift from bronze to iron carried with it the 'hateful strife of evil war', rather than healthy competition among hard-working neighbours.

Greece was divided among the Hellenes into at least twelve separate regions, and the Greek language into five major linguistic blocks. It is not surprising that Greece consisted ultimately of no fewer than 158 independent city states. Most were quite small, and were incapable of sustaining a total population above 10,000. By colonial expansion even more city states were founded throughout the greater Mediterranean basin.

URBAN RELIGIOUSNESS

By the sixth century BCE, to use Lewis Mumford's words, 'a new god had captured the Acropolis, and had, by an imperceptible passage, merged with the original deity'. What he had in mind was the city (*polis*) itself. Just as ordinary men insinuated themselves by warfare into political life, so the city assembly (*ekklesia*) insinuated itself into what religious structure was still considered relevant. This humanizing transition is evidenced by the

A ruined temple in the Valley of the Temples, Agrigento, Sicily.

'Since there are three brothers born by Rheia to Kronos, Zeus and I, and the third is Hades, lord of the dead, all was divided among us three ways, each given his domain: I, when the lots were shaken drew the grey sea to live in forever; Hades drew the lot of the mists and the darkness, and Zeus was allotted the wide sky, in the cloud and the bright air. But Earth and high Olympos are common to all three.'

Iliad 15.187–93

development in sculpture of the perfected human form, as well as by contemporary inscriptions and decrees.

Yet several major groups remained outside the pale of citizenship-participation: the women, the children, the large cluster of slaves descended from suppressed indigenous inhabitants or taken captive in war, and the resident aliens.

Official city religion is clearly manifest in the very layout and architecture of the city. The lofty citadel (*acropolis*) which had been the Mycenaean fortress and palatial residence was now abandoned – left for the gods alone. The new city lies within the plains whose agriculture supports its economy. The centre of life is the marketplace (*agora*), whose purpose reveals that economics is central to this renewed urban life, and whose architecture reflects the necessity for public access. Although public inscriptions bear witness of dedication and piety to the official religion, no gods dwell there. At some distance from the city centre, or perhaps on the old acropolis, decorative and elaborate temples were created and maintained, with more than a hint that a major function was as treasury for the wealth of the city.

The growth of temples typifies this new era of the growth of the city state and of law and order. The decorative arts were used to portray mythical events that expressed this sense of order. Victory over the great uncivilized forces was personified in the victory of lapiths against centaurs, or of their legendary ancestors against Amazons. The final form of Greek mythology is the end product of the creative formation of the Greek city states. Their nature is also reflected in the temple architecture with its basic patterns or 'orders'.

At the individual level of society from the Geometric period onwards come marker-stones (*stela*), especially those set up at graves. Thus names and titles, genealogies and deeds enter into history. Objects of all kinds were dedicated to the gods, but the funeral stele is fully human.

TEMPLE STYLES

The history of temple styles is summarized in three successive 'orders': Doric, Ionic and Corinthian. The columns of these orders are increasingly elaborate and more highly embellished. As Gisela Richter has stated: 'A central hall was provided with a columned porch, practically always in front and often also at the back; pilasters terminated the side walls of the central hall. Rows of columns were placed in front, at the back, and sometimes all around to form a colonnade; occasionally columns were added also in the interior to support the roof.' The pitched roof created triangular space at each end of the pediment, which came to be decorated often with a central mythological theme for the particular temple.

Even the largest temples are quite small: few exceed one hundred feet (thirty metres) in overall width, nor much more than twice that in length. The inner hall, being open only in one direction, could not have allowed easy access to many people at once. Clearly the major purpose was to provide a space for the great statue of the god who was worshipped.

PAINTING AND SCULPTURE

Vase-painting styles developed from the earlier black-figure to red-figure techniques. Athenian examples dominate both varieties. Some shapes in the black-figure style were exclusively intended for ritual use: as grave-offerings, or for other uses at funerals, or for use in marriage ceremonies.

Although the illustration focused on a god or myth, that is no guarantee of explicit religiousness. The world of

'I am Demeter the honoured, the greatest benefit and joy to undying gods and to mortals. But come now, let all the people build me a great temple and beneath it an altar under the steep walls of the city, above Kallikhoron, on the rising hill. I myself shall introduce rites so that later You may propitiate my mind by their right performance.'

Homeric Hymn to Demeter 268–74

vase-painting is basically secular, reflecting the structure of the city state. Yet, as well as maenads – the ecstatic female followers of Dionysus – with their attendant satyrs, with the onset of the red-figure phase, women of all sorts, increasingly in domestic scenes, are more often portrayed.

Temples are rare in these paintings; but altars with sacrifice are often shown. The deities invoked are rarely to be seen, and the attendants cannot be distinguished from those in domestic life. Since there was no explicit ceremony, marriage processionals indicate that event. Funerals show chiefly the laying out of the body, the women mourning – only the men approaching in ritual gesture. The strange phenomenon of the *herm* – that unhewn pillar, seldom with any other features than a human head and an erect penis, which stood everywhere throughout the city, outside the doors of ordinary houses – is illustrated in scenes beginning with its carving to the perfunctory act of worship made by passers-by. Similarly, the phallus-bearing celebrants in some revelry, often dedicated to Dionysus, are commonplace. Erotic scenes, both hetero- and homosexual, were considered appropriate subjects even on votive and funeral plaques.

THE GREEK WORLD VIEW

Although the fifth century BCE has often been interpreted as a crucial age for human civilization, its achievements were built on the whole period from the time of Homer. The boundary is not only the turn of a century but the life and death of one man, Socrates (469–399 BCE).

Before Socrates it was thought that all things were made out of one or more of the four basic ingredients: air, earth, fire and water. The one fully preserved example of pre-Socratic cultural inquiry is Herodotus (about 490–430), who divided the known world into five intellectual components.

An Attic red-figured kylix (shallow two-handled cup), showing Athena preparing the judgment of Paris, c. 490–480 BCE.

The Greek was set over and against the Egyptian, Libyan, Scythian and Persian, collectively considered as 'barbarian' – that is, incapable of Greek language and hence of civilized Greek thought. Pre-Socratic understanding turned on the assumed relationship between nature and custom, but this broke down in the crisis which accompanied the destructive half-century of war among the Greek city states.

The literary response to the Peloponnesian war is provided by two groups of Athenian writings. The first consists of plays, cast in metrical poetry. These portray the actions of the gods in relation to humans, especially in the growing horror of a world at war. Beginning with the self-esteem which all Greeks shared from their common resistance to the Persian invasions, all the cherished assumptions of Greek society were questioned by Aeschylus (525–456), Sophocles (497–405) and Euripides (485–406), as Athens, whose democracy had become imperialistic in regard to its allies, struggled with Sparta, whose militaristic regime championed the freedom of the other city states.

The second (prose) grouping came to be called 'Sophist'. They taught rhetoric, 'the art of persuasion'. The major surviving fifth-century author in whose work these ingredients are found is Thucydides (about 455–400).

Both analyses, poetic and prose, arrive at the role of the irrational in human affairs, and particularly in power politics. For in both Thucydides and Euripides we are introduced to the pathology of human nature under stress. Human affairs cannot ultimately be blamed on the gods, though perhaps some fortune or necessity controls the mysterious past which has produced the present disastrous situations at both the urban and the individual levels. When human nature is aroused to do something – anything – it is not possible to turn it aside, either by law or fear of punishment. Consequences cannot be anticipated. This somewhat sceptical approach was accompanied by a sense that the Olympian gods were remote – and scarcely model examples of ethical behaviour.

The Hellenistic world state

The ridicule of the gods in the plays of Aristophanes (about 450–385) received no apparent criticism at the time, although dedications to the gods continued to be made in the state's official inscriptions. But after the defeat of Athens in the war, the trumped-up charges against Socrates were said to be: not acknowledging the gods worshipped by the state, and introducing new divinities or an educational atheism which served to corrupt the young men from their attitudes as good citizens.

It is less than clear what, in their own times, either Plato (about 429–347) or Aristotle (384–322) contributed to religious thought. Aristotle's treatise format has a greater precision than Plato's dialogues. His discussion of fundamental substance as the basic constituent of reality served the growing sense of the nature of God, so that *Metaphysics* contains reference to the 'unmoved-mover' – God – as First Cause.

By the fifth century there was an unprecedented enlargement of religious vocabulary. From Herodotus comes a word for 'religious observance', almost 'religion' itself, and a verb 'to observe religiously' or to worship, to *do* religion. In contrast, by the time of Theophrastos (371–287), a word was in common use whose meaning, 'fear of' or 'reverence for' divinity, already had such negative overtones that it could designate the 'superstitious' person. Interestingly, the era produced no words for 'believing in' gods.

RULERS WHO BECAME GODS
Hellenization was taking place even before the advent of Alexander the

THE ANCIENT RELIGIONS OF GREECE AND ROME

'There was a time when undisciplined was human life, kindred to beasts, servant to brute strength; there was no reward for good, nor punishment for evil... Then it was, someone wise in intellect discovered for humans fear of gods, that awe might restrain evil ones, even those doing things in secret... So now, if you want to do some evil, even in secret, you will not escape these gods.'

Critias, *Sisyphus* fragment

Great (356–323), though it was his conquest of the vast Persian empire in the East which brought the process to fruition. Alexander founded some seventy cities on the Greek pattern, mostly named after himself, 'Alexandria'. With easy transport and communication within the empire, Greek being the common language, Hellenization opened up the Mediterranean world to Eastern influences, including religious beliefs. This era was one of conspicuous luxury among the rich and powerful, while inflated prices and lower wages were the lot of the poor.

At the very top of the society were the Hellenized rulers, who declared themselves to be divine. Alexander, whose heroic deeds could not be doubted, was believed to have been received among the gods on his death, like Heracles before him. This soon degenerated into automatic deification for the king.

MYSTERIES AND HEALING CULTS
The specific technical term 'the

mysteries' first occurs in Herodotus and the tragedians, though their usage had clearly grown out of urban ceremonial and temple festivals. By Hellenistic times, however, the process of initiation was open to all Greek-speaking people not ritually impure who could afford the initiation fee.

Ultimately, *the* mysteries, meaning those primarily of Eleusis near Athens (commonly called 'Greater'), must be said to lie in the initiate to whom something real is revealed, rather than in the ritual act or paraphernalia. The total complex included: 'things said', 'things shown' and 'things performed'.

Initiation promised happiness, perhaps simply in a glorious vision of the god. Although at first no particular good life was implied beyond death, the mystery religions were highly syncretistic and tended to absorb Eastern myths which hinted that this happiness continued into an afterlife, perhaps by a unification with the gods or by a deification of the human. But no kind of group association followed, and no moral demands were required for this bliss – except purity at the cult and silence ever after on 'the mysteries'.

The mythological and ritual complex at Eleusis, involving the goddess Demeter and her daughter, was tied to cereal grain. The processional and festival celebration, which was the context for initiation, took place in September-October – the ploughing season. Unlike other Greek temples, the one at Eleusis was meant for a large gathering and could hold up to 10,000 people.

THE WORD OF THE GOD

Herodotus tells us that the most ancient oracular site in all Greece, and the only one in his time, was that at Dodona with its great oak tree. Preserved inscriptions of questions asked of the oracle at Dodona reveal concern for health, including successful pregnancies. There were also oracles in Amphiaraus and Trophonius. In each case some kind of earth-fault or warm spring provides the context for belief in a divine presence and a cultic sacrifice. After this the inquirer, sleeping at the spot, received by dream an appropriate response to his or her inquiry. Individuals brought their own private concerns; officials consulted about matters of state.

DIVINE HEALING: ASCLEPIOS

The temple-cult of Asclepios, the god of healing, was set up principally in times of great need, especially by city states threatened by disease. It thrived because rich people who were healed rewarded the cult with wealth, though payment was not required from the poor. It became the most widespread of all the newer cults, with important centres at Pergamon and Corinth as well as Epidauros and Kos.

Apart from the environment of cleanliness and pure air, a combination of exercise, cold baths, rest, herbal prescriptions and diet were employed, along with dreams induced by suggestion. The god was understood to have visited the suppliant while he or she slept.

SYNCRETISM IN EGYPT

Two cults from Egypt provide an interesting illustration of further syncretism with the Ancient Near East. The cult of Serapis was created in Egypt under the Ptolemies as an intentional fusion of the Greek mysteries with the native Egyptian cult of Osiris, a funerary deity. The name itself was a compound of Osiris and Apis, the sacred bull. Serapis became a manifestation of the one god. Attached to his cult-centres were functionaries who proclaimed the power and mighty deeds of the god.

The second cult is that of Isis, originally the personification of the pharaoh's throne. In the ancient myth she became important as the king's divine mother in whose lap he sat, a 'madonna-and-child' image. She also became associated with the royal succession myth of Osiris and Horus, in which she was a deliverer.

Under the impact of Hellenistic syncretism these two cults of Isis and Serapis may be brought together. These deities had the power of deliverance from war, prison, pain, wandering, shipwreck, even death and were believed to guide humankind, for they saw the manifold deeds of both the wicked and the just. They were expected to grant to the righteous, where such righteousness is individual virtue, appropriate sacrifice, and a share of blessings received.

The Roman Republican expansion

Historically, the event which marked the beginning of actual Roman achievement was the sacking of the city of Rome in 387 BCE by those same marauding Gauls who helped eliminate the Etruscans. Until then the central Mediterranean had suffered rivalry among the Greeks of Magna Graecia in southern Italy, the Phoenicians centred on Carthage, and the Etruscans. The conflict focused on Sicily. It was the disruption of this balance of power which permitted Rome to move swiftly, deploying the sword, founding colonies and building roads, to bring all Italy south of the Po under their rule within a century.

The historical character of Rome, which took shape in the centuries between the two sackings of the city – by Gauls in 387 BCE and by Goths in CE 410 – is best described on two levels: the social institutions on which the structure of urban life rests, and the buildings, known to archaeology, in which the structure was contained. At the first level the focus of attention is on the army, the law, the populace and the religion. The architectural needs of each caused the city's buildings to be erected. Nothing was planned, it simply grew.

RELIGION OF HEARTH AND FIELD AND CITY

Just as the myth of Rome as the city of cities was to dominate the political aspect of Roman self-understanding, so the myth of their own religiousness was to dominate their personal and cultic insights. Cicero (106–43) put it clearly: 'If we compare ourselves with other peoples, in various things we appear equal or even inferior, except that of religion, meaning the worship of the gods, in which we are by far superior.' 'Religion' (*religio*) is a Latin concept; there was no exact equivalent in Greek.

Latin authors could speak of a person as having a 'religious nature free of superstition'; or affirm that 'it is proper to be religious but not to be superstitious', contrasting the positive and negative elements of belief. On the other hand, the late Republic came to be sceptical of older religious forms still practised. Authors, with the bondage of religious duties in mind, could affirm that religion is that from which the soul (Lucretius), or oneself and one's household (Livius), ought to be freed.

The documented evidence provides little knowledge of early Roman domestic religion. The structure of the laws, especially those relating to women and marriage, children and inheritance, bears out the links of household and hearth, with paternal domination expressed in religious custom and ritual. The 'Twelve Tables', the oldest law code, are strictly civil.

To the Romans, gods were functions. Irrespective of what myths might have been attached to a particular deity, the Roman concern was to assign the precise office, so that the office rather than the older personification received appropriate worship.

The communal religion was related to the basic agricultural economy, and

'Go proclaim to the Romans it is heaven's will that my Rome shall be capital of the world; accordingly they must cherish soldierliness, and they must be assured, and transmit to posterity the assurance, that no human power can withstand Roman arms.'

Romulus in *Livius* 1.16

so was dependent upon the Etruscans and others, for Rome developed too late to foster more than the mythology of her own creation. This religion was primarily that of the state, with the city personified as the chief deity. The Romans were aware of the need to accept some foreign gods, especially Greek, into their state-cult, and they modified these deities to fit their functional need. Livius (59 BCE – CE 17) claims that the first celebration in Rome of a public offering of a sacred meal to images of Greek deities placed on couches (*lectisternium*) took place in 399 BCE. In contrast to Greek pairing of such deities as divine couples, symbolizing sacred marriage, the Romans indiscriminately paired Apollo with his mother Larona, or Mercury with Neptune. It was not until 217 BCE that the traditional Twelve Olympians were appropriately paired, but with Latin names and given an *interpretatio Romana*, on pretence of confusing foreign deities with their own.

Three of the oldest deities – Jupiter, Juno and Minerva – were worshipped in an impressively large temple on the Capitoline hill. They are thus known as the 'Capitoline Triad'. The temple was dedicated to Jupiter the Best and Greatest (*Jupiter Optimus Maximus*): his was the central hall of worship, flanked by those of Juno and Minerva to the right and left.

Other deities followed in the remaining centuries BCE in response to various communal needs or crises such as the cult of Aesculapius (Greek Asclepios) to overcome pestilence in 293–291, or that of the Cybele to counteract Hannibal's military threat in 204. At the turn of the era Augustus (63 BCE – CE 14) could still be described as one who 'treated with great respect such foreign rites as were ancient and well-established but held the rest in contempt'. That distinction of old versus new in matters of religion was characteristic. Conservatism was maintained by the high priest, *pontifex maximus*; open-mindedness was fostered by the *viri sacrisfaciundis*, religious officials who were responsible for the introduction of a new idea precisely when it was most appropriate.

Foreign elements could be brought into Rome; and equally, those already present might be suppressed or driven out. The official Senate decree of 7 October 186 BCE severely limited the celebrations of the Bacchanalia and the number of its followers. This applied not only to Rome but also to its allies, and arose from the supposed threat of societies which meet in secret or conduct secret rites.

Among legitimate groupings within Rome were various associations of pontiffs, augurs and auspices; flamens or special priests for individual gods; and the vestal virgins.

BELIEFS AND PHILOSOPHY

Marcus Tullius Cicero wrote *On the Nature of the Gods* in 45 BCE in the form of a dialogue among several of the intellectual positions of his day: Sceptic, Epicurean and Stoic. Two important traditions are absent: the Peripatetic (if the Stoics were really different from Aristotle as he was by then understood) and the Cynic position which was merely described.

The importance of the various positions lies simply in the fact that religion until then had no explicit intellectual content. It hinged exclusively on ritual: right doing, not right thinking, and certainly not yet right believing. For until the first century BCE the vocabulary of belief was hardly coined. The value of this practical religion can be quite bluntly stated: 'Men describe Jupiter as best and greatest not because he makes us just or temperate or wise, but because he makes us healthy, rich and prosperous.'

For the relatively few who were caught up in the discussion or could read, or for the larger audience to whom the philosophical views were preached by itinerants, there began that transformation by which religion came to mean an intellectual consideration of god, gods and the world. The several philosophies ask essentially three questions: 'What is the nature of the world?', 'How do I know the world?', 'How am I to live in the world?' Although theologically they produced different systems in response, they began with similar assumptions in answer to these questions:

● Matter is the sole reality.

● Senses are the sole source of knowledge.

● Being untroubled and undisturbed is the nature of happiness or pleasure.

The Epicurean position was that gods exist but they have no concern for the world. The Stoic position was that the world is ruled by a divine rationality (*logos*), manifest as fate and providence, and closely related to human reason. Scepticism was a by-product of the Platonic Academy, sharing in the common assumptions. Its appeal was to the one who 'suspends judgment about things that are either good or bad by nature, or that are to be practised or not practised, and in so doing he resists the dogmatic tendency and follows without strong convictions either way the observances of everyday life', achieving thereby the desired untroubled state. Cynics are 'dog-like' (*kunikos*) because they substitute for a system a way of life blatantly rejecting all imposed values. They identified the ideal life with that of nature. Taking nothing but the beggar's knapsack and staff, delighting in flouting all standards of decency, they wandered about with a minimum of food or shelter, though often functioning as missionaries by preaching on the street corners.

Empire – the Roman world

When Virgil (70–19 BCE) wrote the *Aeneid* to honour the emperor Augustus by linking him with Rome's past, Augustus not only restored the Hut of Romulus, but absorbed into himself the whole religious tradition of the city by assuming the ancient office of *pontifex maximus*. A temple of Roma and Augustus at Ostia expresses the result. Throughout the time of the empire, even the older gods of the state cult, with the exception of the major deities – Jupiter, Juno and Minerva – gave way to the increasingly dominant cult of the imperial house.

DEIFICATION ROMAN-STYLE
Republican Rome, even with its dictators, had avoided constitutionally the absolute rule of Hellenistic kings. A precedent was set by the Roman Senate on the assassination of Julius Caesar in 44 BCE, when he was enrolled among the gods. The deification of his successor, Augustus, had been demanded in parts of the empire, especially the east, while Augustus was still alive, and divine honours were accorded him in some places. Though the Senate's action in proclaiming Augustus divine followed the precedent, Tiberius (42 BCE – CE 37), who succeeded him, stoutly resisted deification, and so much angered the Senate that he was not even acclaimed as a god upon his death. Thereafter, apart from Nero and the three unsuccessful military contenders for his position, all the early emperors received a place among the gods: even Gaius Caligula (CE 12–41), who had assumed it for himself while living, and Domitian (CE 51–96), who did likewise, though without reaffirmation by the Senate.

From the days of Augustus oaths of allegiance to the emperor were required from the Roman businessmen making money in the provinces. These show him as already 'son of a god' and express loyalty not only to him but 'to

'... there are many things in philosophy which have not yet been satisfactorily explained, particularly that most obscure and most difficult question concerning the nature of the gods, which is so extremely important both for a knowledge of the human soul and also for the regulation of religion.'

Cicero, *The Nature of the Gods* 1.1

his children and descendants'. From the coronation of Caligula, the oath includes Augustus between 'Zeus the Saviour' and 'the holy Virgin of our city' (Athena Polias). Such oaths were engraved in bronze (at the oath-takers' expense) and mounted for all to see.

THE RELIGIOUS MIX OF IMPERIAL ROME
The disastrous eruption of Vesuvius began on the morning of 24 August, CE 79, and by evening had buried the two flourishing cities of Pompeii and Herculaneum and the coastal resort of Stabiae. Martial asserted that 'even for gods this was going too far'. Many other cities of the ancient Mediterranean world have been destroyed and buried, but none so completely preserved in the process.

The religious evidence from Pompeii is of two principal forms. There are buildings: both official buildings, innumerable domestic shrines and wayside altars. We also have works of art, especially frescos, and inscriptions of all sorts, including graffiti, and, from Herculaneum, even a prodigious papyri library chiefly devoted to the religious philosophy of the obscure Epicurean Philodemus (about 110–40 BCE).

Family cults flourished. Nearly every house and workshop had its private shrine (*lararium*), normally housing busts of ancestors and other traditional household gods (the *Lares* and *Penates*). The simple rites at these shrines were part of daily life and under the care of the paternal head of the household, and would have included rituals for important family events such as the coming of age of the heir. Many plaques and statues have been found, representing various minor deities – Faunus, Silvanus, Flora, Priapus and so on. They are largely concerned with fruitfulness and reproduction, plenty and gain. Wreaths of fruit, or horns of plenty (*cornucopiae*) were commonplace. So too was the phallus, either alone or gigantically displayed on a little deity, often with scales to weigh its fullness.

Official cults were more elaborate

A *lararium* in Pompeii.

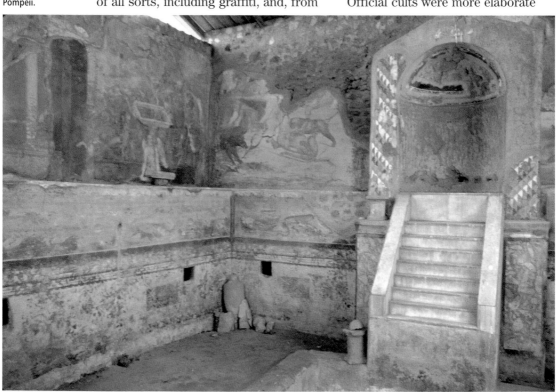

but their remains are fewer. Pompeii had ten temples, but three had been wrecked in the earlier earthquake of CE 62 and were still unrepaired at the time of their burial. One had been converted to the use of a private association; two were dedicated to the imperial cult, one to the most recently enrolled member, Vespasian (CE 9–79), who died just one month before the eruption, and the other to Fortuna Augusta. Graffiti bear out the people's nonchalant attitude towards this cult: 'Augustus Caesar's mother was only a woman!' Of the remaining four temples, only that dedicated to the cult of triune Isis, her consort, Serapis, and their divine child, Harpocrates, showed the signs of prosperity coming from popular support. Wall-size frescos indicate the religious life within this sanctuary as conducted by its white-robed, shaven-headed priests.

Apart from the buildings designed for religious use, we have the houses of rich and poor, in which were displayed not only wealth and varying aesthetic taste and styles, but also frescos or mosaics of religious themes. The most important of these is the sixty-roomed 'Villa of the Mysteries': one room presents on three walls twenty-nine figures nearly life-size, subdivided into ten group scenes, acting out a complex Bacchic ritual. This was entirely a woman's rite. It is impossible to say what place this great house or its spectacular scene played within the religious life of the city – perhaps somewhere in between the few great temples and the numerous little shrines.

The preserved ruins of Ostia, the port of Rome, show a different array within this religious mix, including (by the third century CE) not less than fifteen Mithraea – shrines devoted to Mithras.

PHILOSOPHICAL RELIGION
Roman religion was thus a complex mixture from varied sources. Later in the third century CE the mix was to receive a more systematic treatment blending the religious and philosophical elements into a form of Neo-Platonism. Plotinus (205–69) was its founder, and Porphyry (232–305) his expositor. This revived Platonism was a blend of elements from the traditions of Plato himself, Pythagoras, Aristotle, and the Stoics. World-mind, World-soul and Nature are the descending levels of reality between the Ultimate One, which is the ground of existence and the source of values, and Bare Matter. All these ingredients lie within human nature, whose purpose is to achieve unification in a kind of ecstatic union with the One. This rare union was believed to occur as a result of prolonged effort of the will and understanding. Plotinus makes little explicit reference to religious ritual or particular gods, though the writings of his followers do contain hymns to certain gods. The result is the philosophical equivalent of the 'mysteries'.

A CRUTCH FOR A TOTTERING STATE
Of the thirty-five Roman emperors from CE 192 to 284, only three reigned for more than ten years, and only one died a natural death. All the others died of unnatural causes at the hands of troops or counter-claimants, after a reign of less than a year in at least twelve cases. Consequently, few of these imperial figures lived long enough or died in such a way as to receive deification. Most of the emperors, even the stronger ones, preferred to rule under the aegis of some greater deity, since they had perceived that to be declared divine themselves hardly secured them a long life. The most important such god is Aurelianus's choice: *Sol Invictus*, the Unconquered Sun.

It was a mere matter of time before the one resilient religion would be imposed upon the state. This took place in the 'Edict of Milan' issued in

'It is hard to say whether the birthday of the most divine Caesar is more joyful or more advantageous; we may rightly regard it as like the beginning of all things, if not in the world of nature, yet in advantage. There is nothing that was decaying and declining to unfortunate state that he did not restore, and he gave a fresh appearance to the whole universe, which would have been content to accept its own ruin if there had not been born the universal blessing of all – Caesar Augustus. The birthday of the god was the beginning of the good news (evangelion) to the world on account of him.'

Roman Proconsul to Provincial Assembly of Asia, 9 BCE

313, jointly by Licinius and Constantine. Christian worship, like any other, was allowed to take place freely; and the Christian church, alone among the competitive cults, was singled out for 'compensation from our benevolence'. It was its organization that gave it an edge over all alternatives, from the authorities' viewpoint, for Christianity, as Arnold Toynbee has said, 'was singular in building up for itself a world-wide administrative organization, instead of letting each local group of converts go its own way'.

THE END OF ANTIQUITY

The remoulding of the Roman empire as Christian in all senses took more than a century, though Theodosius I had proscribed other religions by CE 381. The old forms, however, lingered on in several ways. Initially 'pagan' (*paganus*) had meant a rural in contrast to an urban dweller, and Christianity had made little headway in the former environment before it became the state religion. By this later date, the term came to designate civilians in general, over against soldiers, and thus took on its 'religious' connotation.

Several remnants of the older religion survived for a while. The short-reigned Julian (361–63) was the last non-Christian emperor.

The older traditions at the more subtle levels died out in the educational replacement of one mythos by another, but survived in terms of human nature and its response to the realities of the agricultural economy. At the level of fundamental assumptions little really seemed to matter, for as Sallustius said, there are 'universal opinions, by which I mean those in which all men, if rightly questioned, would concur; such opinions are that every god is good and impassive and unchangeable'.

Rome itself, however, had become less advantageous as the capital. Once it proved vulnerable to Visigothic

assault in 410, it was but a matter of time before the imperial government was withdrawn to a safer location.

The sacking of the city after 800 years precipitated a crisis of ideas for a state newly allied to the Christian religion. Augustine of Hippo (354–430) in his *City of God*, carefully sifted all the religiousness of the ancient city and its empire; what was worthwhile was baptized into Christ, the rest was to be put aside for ever. The city, now greatly reduced in dignity and size, became the Christian Rome. Its bishop became the sole remaining officer of rank when the imperial government of the West was transferred north to Ravenna, and then in 476 when the Western empire itself ceased to exist. Rome's change of hands is well illustrated when its bishop, Leo the Great, in office from 440 to 461, assumed the defunct urban title of *pontifex maximus* ('Supreme Pontiff'). The Christian church was the final successor to the ancient religion which was the city, and in such terms the primacy of the church at Rome came to be declared.

'Hence it is that throughout wide empires, provinces, and towns, we see each people having its own individual rites and worshipping the local gods... but the Romans one and all.'

Minucius Felix, Octavius 6.23

'Those who would learn about the gods need to have been well educated from childhood and must not be bred up among foolish ideas; they must also be good and intelligent by nature, in order that they may have something in common with the subject.'

Sallustius, Concerning the Gods and the Universe 1

The Old Gods: The Religion of the Celts

RONALD HUTTON

Thirty years ago scholars were reasonably confident about who the ancient Celts were and what could be agreed about their religion. They were a family of peoples speaking similar languages who occupied Europe north of the Alps and south of the River Elbe, with extensions into Mediterranean lands. They were warlike, with a ruling military aristocracy, creative, producing a marvellous art characterized by fluid lines and abstract figures, impetuous and emotional. They were also intensely spiritual, believing in a mixture of gods and goddesses, of whom the greatest was Lugh, identified with the sun, intelligence, skills and arts. Traces of his worship have been found from Ireland to what is now eastern Germany. This religion was dominated by a highly trained and learned priesthood, the Druids, who presided over ceremonies and had an important role as scholars, lawgivers and arbitrators. They taught that, when humans die, their souls pass into new bodies and are reborn into this world. At the same time they conducted large-scale human sacrifice by a range of cruel means, including the burning alive of victims in huge wicker images. Their most important festivals were on the days that opened the seasons, at the beginning of November, February, May and August, with the year starting on the first of these, the modern Halloween. They preferred not to build temples, but worshipped in natural groves of trees. All this information comes from a mixture of archaeological finds, the writings of the ancient Greeks and Romans, and the medieval literature of the Celtic peoples who became the Irish and Welsh: a varied group of sources, but one that can present a coherent picture.

The collapse of the traditional picture

The view of the subject that was dominant in the 1960s has virtually collapsed. Experts now recognize that the term 'Celts' was originally used by the Greeks as a vague label for barbarians living north of the Alps and Danube, and was not applied to types of language until the end of the seventeenth century. No ancient writer ever described Celts as living in the British Isles. It is now accepted that the distribution of Celtic languages does not seem to match the distribution of what has been called Celtic art, and neither matches that of material culture. None of these ranges seems to have any relevance to racial types. It seems as though ancient peoples living along the Rhine and Elbe who have traditionally been called Celtic had more in common with their neighbours across the rivers, whom scholars, following the Romans, have called 'Germanic', than with their remote linguistic relatives in places like Ireland or Spain. As a result, the term 'Celtic' is still valuable as a label for types of language, and therefore of literature, and for modern cultural politics. As a label for ancient societies and cultures, it is more or less dead, most experts now preferring the cumbersome but precise formula 'late pre-Roman Iron Age' to describe the groups to whom it was formerly applied.

Mostly propaganda?

So what was the religion of ancient north-western Europe in the 'late pre-Roman Iron Age'? Again, the old certainties have crumbled. It has been repeatedly noted that all of the sources of information that we possess are suspect. Some of the Greek and Roman writers who described that religion lived at the time when it was still active, but all may be accused of distortion intended for propaganda purposes. Those who hailed the Druids as philosophers and scientists tended to live at the opposite end of the Mediterranean world, and may have been making a romantic idealization of them with which to entertain and criticize their own society. The alleged Druidic belief in a form of reincarnation could be a projection of Greek ideas onto much simpler native traditions. On the other hand, those who wrote of the Druids' addiction to human sacrifice may have been seeking to destroy their reputation in order to justify the Roman conquest of their lands. Their identification with groves appears after that conquest and may simply reflect the fact that they had been reduced to a secret religion lingering in the woods. The medieval Irish and Welsh texts were all composed centuries after the conversion of those peoples to Christianity and may be fantasies about an almost-forgotten past, rather than echoes of it reliably preserved in oral tradition. The worship of Lugh seems to have been confined to Ireland and Spain, and apparent traces of his name further east could just be linguistic errors. There is no good evidence for generally worshipped, 'pan-Celtic', deities. As for the four festivals, they represent an Irish system that may not have been observed elsewhere, and there is no real proof that the New Year was celebrated at Halloween even in Ireland. There is plenty of evidence in the structure of monuments and in literature that at least as much importance was attached to the summer and winter solstices, all over northern and western Europe, as to the four quarter days.

The new consensus on religion

So what can be said with certainty?

> 'The most important doctrine that they seek to teach is that souls do not perish, but after death pass on to new bodies.'
>
> Julius Caesar

The best evidence consists of the inscriptions left by the native populations of the north-western provinces of the Roman empire, which express religious belief in a distinctively local way that does seem genuinely to reflect an older native tradition. These can be compared with the Greek, Roman, Irish and Welsh sources and other material remains. They show an intense localism in which every tribe, stream, hill and wood had its own deity or deities. Of 375 native gods identified by the 1980s in the Roman period of what is now France, 305 are recorded just once. Some were honoured across large regions – a cross-legged, antlered god in central and eastern France, a young horseman god in the east midlands of England – but none seems to have had a wider range than that. Certain stereotypes were very widespread, however, such as a god of smiths, a patron god who protected the people and land of a particular district, and a god of trading and communication. Goddesses were more closely identified with the natural world, being spirits of hills, rivers and woods, but there were still plenty of nature-gods and goddesses of human activities. Both sexes of deity were associated with war, although it is possible that gods were more identified with leadership in it, goddesses with its raw emotions.

What else remains?

It is certain that the Druids had a leading role in religion and society, although we cannot be exactly sure what it was or what they taught. It is very likely that worship was carried on in groves of trees; and springs, rivers and lakes were certainly considered sacred because offerings of precious metalwork were thrown into them. The earth itself was venerated, gifts of food and drink being deposited in the pits used for storing grain each time that one was taken out of use, as if to thank

The Gundestrop Cauldron, thought to be from the 2nd or 1st century BCE, may depict Celtic deities and animals.

the soil for its bounty. On the other hand, shrines and temples were certainly erected, ranging from huge circles of wooden posts in Ireland, and small rectangular huts, perhaps just houses for deities, in British settlements, to huge sanctuaries enclosed by ditches and ramparts in northern France, and stone-built temples with carvings and statues in Provence. Animal sacrifice was certainly practised, as it was all over the ancient world, and it is significant that the most popular victims were horses and dogs, which form the closest emotional bonds with humans: they would have been sacrifices in the modern sense of the word. The killing of humans is also likely, because it was found in many parts of the ancient world, and the Romans themselves had only banned it in 97 BCE. The number of human bodies, skulls or long bones found buried at settlements and fortresses, or displayed at the French sanctuaries, are probably the remains of the victims, although it is just possible that they had belonged to honoured warriors. The careful deposition of personal possessions in graves strongly suggests a widespread belief in a continuation of life after death.

That is all that can be said at present, although continuing archaeology may well resolve some of the mysteries and enable the development of more secure knowledge. What matters most is that, however accurate or distorted they may have been, the references to this religion in Greek, Roman, Welsh and Irish writings have shaped the self-image of Europeans and inspired the art and literature of later times. They have become part of the world's cultural heritage. The ancient reality has left little solid evidence of itself, but the dream of what it might have been has been one of the great inspirations of Western humanity.

The Norse Gods: The Religions of Scandinavia

MORTEN WARMIND

The period of the Norse gods is best narrowed down to the Viking Age, from roughly CE 800 until the arrival of Christianity around 1000 – a little sooner in Denmark and somewhat later in Sweden. There are signs of continuity from the Iron Age, at least from Roman times, but there is a clear change in the language used from around 800. It is therefore reasonable to consider the pre-Christian Viking Age on its own terms.

Sources for understanding religion in pre-Christian Scandinavia

The few sources from the period are especially informative and extremely important in that they confirm the existence of belief in indigenous gods before Christianity. Most of these sources are simply place names, which include references to the gods and inscriptions of personal names containing the names of deities or invoking a particular deity. There are also a few helpful non-Scandinavian descriptions. For example, an Arabic traveller describes a funeral in 923, in which deities and religious rites are mentioned, and a German monk writes of a temple (see below). Indeed, a large proportion of the most revealing sources for understanding pre-Christian religion in Scandinavia have come to us from Iceland, having been preserved by the Icelandic scholar Snorri Sturlusson (d. 1241).

The most informative artefacts are two series of poems in very different styles, which together provide the fullest account available of the beliefs of any pre-literate peoples. Unfortunately, the precise date of their composition is unknown – sometime between 800 and 1200. (Although the poems often do provide an author and a precise date, scholars now believe that these may have been forged at a later date.)

● One group is a collection of about thirty-seven poems about gods and heroes, traditionally called the *Elder* or the *Poetic Edda*.

● The other is a collection of writings known as Scaldic poetry. It mostly consists of praise poems to kings or short verses about everyday life.

Because these poems constantly allude to the gods, goddesses and rituals of Norse mythology, they provide a relatively good understanding of ancient Scandinavian religion.

A gifted writer with a keen sense of humour, Snorri wrote a handbook on Scaldic poetry, which he called the *Edda*. This is now referred to as the *Younger Edda* or *Prose Edda*. It contains a complete Norse cosmology (an understanding of the cosmos from the perspective of Norse religion) and many stories about the Nordic gods. Although it is the most popular source for understanding Norse religion, it is often forgotten that Snorri was a Christian thinker, writing in a medieval scholarly context, rather than a Viking writer in a pre-Christian context.

Another important source is provided by the Danish scholar Saxo (d. 1208). His Latin work, *History of the Danes*, contains much mythological material about deities and heroes, which, he claimed, he had learned from Icelanders. Although this is actually an older source than Snorri's *Edda* and it is clear that Saxo uses some of the same stories as Snorri, it is not used nearly as much by scholars. Other sources used to investigate pre-Christian customs and religious life can be found in the Icelandic Saga-literature. However, there is a widely recognized problem with this material. It was principally written in the 1200s and 1300s and it is evident that the (anonymous) writers had very limited knowledge of actual religion in pre-Christian Scandinavia.

Place names and other early sources

The early sources confirm the existence of deities that were both widely worshipped and also more localized. The distribution of belief in a particular god or goddess can be gauged, particularly, from their appearance in place names. For example, Ull, described by Snorri as a minor ski god, is found in place names in Norway and Sweden but not in Denmark (which is flat and thus not known for skiing). The god Thor, on the other hand, was worshipped all over Scandinavia. Several inscriptions in the memory of dead men invoke Thor with a prayer that he bless the memorial. (Indeed, it should be noted that Thor is the only god mentioned as a god in indigenous pre-Christian, Scandinavian sources.)

The German monk Adam of Bremen, who wrote around 1070, was told of a magnificent temple in the town of Uppsala, Sweden, where 'pagan' rites were still performed at this time. He describes three gods – Thor, Odin and Freyr – each with an emblem and a function. Thor has a sceptre and decides the weather; Odin has a spear and is a war deity; and Freyr, a fertility deity, has an enormous phallus. From later sources we know that Adam must have mistaken Thor's hammer for a sceptre, but this lends credibility to his description, which is evidently not based on mythological tales. Adam further relates that great festivals, which included human and animal sacrifice, took place at Uppsala every

ninth year of the vernal equinox. At these festivals participation was mandatory.

Northern cosmology

Much of what is known about ancient Norse cosmology comes from medieval sources. In Snorri and the Eddic poems, particularly a unique poem called the *Voluspá* (*The Prophecy of the Sibyl*), a strange story of the creation is told. First, there was only heat and cold. Where they met, an immense giant, Ymir, came into being. The different parts of Ymir's body could have children with each other. As a result, a race of giants was born. Ymir was fed by a cow, who licked the salty earth. Where the cow licked the earth a man came into being, named Bor. Bor begat a son, called Bur, who was the father of Odin, Vili and Ve. These three killed Ymir and made the cosmos from his body: his flesh is the soil; his blood the sea; his skull the heavens and so on. In the middle the gods fashioned Middle Earth for men. They live in Asgard and the giants live in Udgard. Eventually the gods, who became known as Æsir, battled another race of deities called the Vanir. They ended up exchanging hostages and three of the Vanir joined the Æsir – Njord, along with his daughter Freyja and his son Freyr.

The world in which we live is one of nine worlds, all of which are linked to an immense, self-renewing ash-tree called *Yggdrasil*. Adam tells of a great tree in Uppsala which probably represented *Yggdrasil*. It is said that *Yggdrasil* has a root in each of the different worlds. Our world, Midgard (or, as popularized in J.R.R. Tolkien's *Lord of the Rings*, 'Middle Earth'), is predominantly populated by humans. The other worlds are populated by giants, elves, gods, dwarves and so on. Often there is conflict between these worlds. Because *Yggdrasil* provides sustenance to the different worlds, because even the great god Odin had to hang in its branches to gain wisdom from it and to learn how to read the hidden runes, it seems to be greater than all the deities.

The Æsir

Odin is the king of the world of gods, sitting in his great hall, Valhalla (The Hall of the Slain), where he brings all the great warriors from humanity. Although he is the god who gives victory to warriors and leaders, he is a capricious deity who is just as likely to

A small bronze figurine of the Norse god Thor, from Reykjavik, Iceland, c. CE 1000.

take it away again. Odin is preparing for the fight at the end of the world. He is portrayed as the ideal aristocrat, feasting on an endless supply of pork and drinking mead. He is glib and treacherous and always on the lookout for wisdom. Indeed, he only has one eye, having surrendered the other for a single drink from the spring of wisdom and understanding owned by the giant Mimir. He is also a performer of *seid*, a ritual described as shamanistic. There are many stories and ideas associated with Odin, including notions of shape-shifting, heroic warfare, strangulation and death, as well as poetry and wisdom. Devotion to him perhaps explains grim stories of ritual killings by noose and spear.

Giants in Norse religion, such as Mimir and Suttung (whose mead Odin stole), represent the forces of chaos. Because they are so old, they are also very wise. Interestingly, wisdom itself is perceived as a chaotic force.

The most widespread devotion appears to belong to Thor, the slayer of giants. If the leaders and warriors looked to Odin as their patron, common people looked to Thor as their protector. He is the thunder-god, full of chaotic and destructive energy. In later Northern religion, the 'black Thor' (possibly so called because of the colour of his images) was understood to be the principal enemy of the 'white Christ'. His symbol, the hammer *Mjollnir* (The Crusher), was used at weddings and as a protective amulet. Stories speak of him going on adventures with his *Mjollnir* in order to protect humans. The most entertaining of the stories of Snorri describes Thor's battles with giants in order to protect humanity, often aided by the shadowy and enigmatic Loki.

● Loki is probably best understood as a trickster: he often sets a story in motion. It was Loki who, by a trick, secured the death of Balder, Odin's son and the fairest of the gods. Other gods of the Æsir are less prominent:

● Tyr is a god who seems to have been an important war god.

● Balder is a god who apparently does very little, apart from famously dying, according to Snorri, through the agency of Loki.

● Bragi is the deity associated with poetry.

The goddesses are less exciting and seem less important:

● Sif, the wife of Thor, has hair made of gold.

● Idun, the wife of Bragi, keeps the apples of youth.

● Frigg, the wife of Odin, is exceedingly wise.

Several groups of less personal 'forces' are referred to as female. Most famously the Valkyries (Choosers of the Slain) are said to help Odin collect the finest warriors from among the dead and to serve them mead in Valhalla.

The Vanir

Among the Vanir it is the goddess Freyja (The Lady) who stands out as a particularly dynamic deity. She is also a trophy, often desired by the giants, but she shows independence in her sexuality, which is proverbial; like Odin, in the Eddic poems she is significantly connected to death and shamanism. The fertility god Freyr (The Lord) is known chiefly because of a story where he falls in love with a giantess; so in love is he that he is in danger of dying; his servant Skirnir (The Shining) therefore coerces the maiden into sleeping with him. Finally, Njord is connected with the bounty of the sea.

Religious rituals and festivals

Religious life seems to have been made up of great feasts at significant times of the year, determined by the sun. All the people from a district met at a central place to sacrifice and eat and drink together. Formal oaths were sworn and contracts were made on holy ground. The leader of the feast seems also to have been the political leader. It is reasonable to assume that both human and animal sacrifice was part of the ritual. Adam of Bremen, for example, records that victims were hung in trees.

The Arabic account of an early funeral (923) provides a glimpse of such a sacrifice. The victim, a slave-girl significantly, volunteers. She immediately becomes a very important figure within the community and is treated with great respect. At the time of the funeral she is lifted up to look into the realm of the dead. She is brought to the ship with the dead man and given plenty of alcohol. Six men and the priestess in charge then sacrifice her. The men have intercourse with her and then hold her arms and legs while two men pull at a rope around her neck. While she is strangled, she is also stabbed in the ribs by the priestess.

A myth describes Odin as hanging in a tree, pierced with a spear as part of his quest for wisdom. Again, because this myth incorporates stabbing, strangling and hanging in trees, it further supports the theory that this was the preferred form of sacrifice.

Nomads of the Steppes

ÅKE HULTKRANTZ

Some 3,000 years ago the wide steppes of southern Russia were sparsely populated by Indo-European peoples: the Cimmerians west of the Caspian Sea, the Persians east of it. The northern Persians, or Scythians, developed into horse-riding nomads about this time or soon afterwards.

This had tremendous historical consequences. Not only did they, in the seventh century BCE, overrun the Cimmerian lands, so that their territory stretched from present-day Romania to Turkestan, they also opened communications between East and West, so that religious ideas and art forms ('animal style') streamed over the open steppes. Long after the disappearance of the Scythians, this road to China constituted a major link between Western (Christian) and Eastern religious ideas. The famous silk route (from the first century CE) partly followed the same way.

The Greek historian Herodotus (fifth century BCE) gives some interesting information on Scythian religion. The foremost divinities were the Sky Father, Papa, married to Mother Earth, Api. Among other deities, all apparently heavenly beings, were the fire- and war-gods. There were no images of the gods, altars or temples. The gods received animal sacrifices, usually horses. They were strangled, and their meat cooked over a fire that was made on their bones. A piece of the meat was thrown into the fire.

They had a war-god who was represented by an iron sword raised on a heap of brushwood. To him were sacrificed cattle and horses in large numbers, as well as prisoners of war;

their blood was poured over the god's sword. Herodotus also mentions diviners, who, however, were killed when they were unsuccessful.

When a king died his corpse was carried around on a wagon among the tribes of his domain, followed by his wives and servants in a long procession. He was finally buried in a wooden chamber together with several court servants (who were strangled), his horses and some golden bowls. An enormous earth mound was heaped over the burial place. The bereaved cleansed themselves by entering a tent filled with steam from hemp seeds that had been thrown on red-hot stones.

This is the first description we have of a religion of the horse nomads. Its essentials fit in rather well with what we know of later religions among equestrian pastoralists. The pattern of horse nomadism spread to the Mongol and Turko-Tataric tribes to the east of the Scythian area and on the plateaux of central Asia. Here the war-like religion of the plains joined the traditional hunting religions with master-of-the-animals concepts and shamanism, and formed a new type of religion.

The Mongols: a sense of wonder

A good illustration of this kind of religion is offered by the Mongols of central Asia. From tribal beginnings in north-eastern Asia they ousted the Turkish peoples of Mongolia and then built up an empire that stretched from the Amur River to the Volga and beyond – the greatest empire the world had seen (thirteenth and fourteenth centuries CE). Their primitive beginnings, nomadic way of life and stratified patriarchal society were all reflected in their religion.

TENGRI

The supreme god was Tengri, a name by which both the god and the blue sky were designated. Prayers were directed to him

A plaque in the form of a Scythian horseman brandishing a spear, 4th century BCE.

by lone supplicants bowing down on mountain-tops, and juniper incense was burned in his honour. Like other nomadic high gods, Tengri was not represented by pictures. He did not create the world. In all of central Asia the beginning of the world was referred to two creators, one a good spirit (but not Tengri), the other a devil. This story of creation was diffused from Europe to North America and was sometimes combined with the flood myth, sometimes with the myth of a primeval sea.

'Tengri' is, however, also a word for everything 'heavenly', wonderful or marvellous, and for ninety-nine tengri gods that in particular protect the herds. For instance, Ataga tengri gives luck in horse-breeding, another tengri protects the cows, still another the yaks. Manaqan tengri is the guardian of the wild game.

Landmarks like mountains, lakes and rivers were worshipped. In particular the mountains inspired great awe. Passes and mountain-tops were residences of spirits, and whoever passed by had to propitiate these spirits by throwing a stone on a pile of rocks, a so-called obo. The ground was sacred, and libations were poured out for Mother Earth.

GENGHIS KHAN

Dead princes and tribal ancestors had their own shrines. Chingis Khan – better known as Genghis Khan – the mighty ruler of the Mongols (d. CE 1227), was considered to be of heavenly descent. A statue representing him was raised on a wagon in the military camp, and horses were dedicated to him. Sometimes he was mentioned as Tengri himself, sometimes as a culture-hero who had initiated all cultural and religious institutions. Offerings were also given to other deceased great princes by their descendants: most often horses were impaled above their graves. The Mongols of the Golden Horde in southern Russia suspended horse skins upon poles over the graves of their great leaders.

At the entrance of their tents the Mongols placed house idols (*ongons*) to whom they offered milk. These *ongons* were made of felt.

One God in Heaven and the Khan on earth. The seal of the Master of the World.

The inscription on the seal of Genghis Khan.

There was a 'fire mother' to whom butter was offered regularly. At the end of the year she also received a bone from a sheep, and ritual hymns were addressed to her. Fire was supposed to have cleansing power.

SHAMANISM

The tribal leaders were also shamans, that is, experts who cured diseases and who divined hidden knowledge while in a trance. Shamanism, a heritage from very ancient times, was strongly integrated with ancestor-worship – the shaman's guardian spirits were his ancestors – and concentrated on the exorcism of evil spirits. Shamans performed many of the customary sacrifices.

Of the Mongol and Turkish tribes that invaded Europe during the first Christian millennium, the Huns were known for their belief in Tengri and the Magyars (Hungarians) for their high-god beliefs and their shamanism.

Slavic religions: gods of fear

From their ancient homes in Poland and White Russia the Slavs spread over Eastern Europe during the first millennium of the Christian era. They were organized in numerous tribes which, as time passed, formed themselves into larger groups. Of these only the western Slavs, formerly living east of the Elbe, and the Russians have left traces in the history of religions. What they believed is not at all clear, however, and interpretations differ widely among scholars.

THUNDER-GOD

Thus, we can only guess what the religion of the Russians was like before the emergence of the Russian grand duchy in the ninth century. The most well-known god seems to have been Perun, a god of thunder and lightning, and apparently a Supreme Being.

His position was probably reinforced when, in about 980, Vladimir the Great – of Viking descent – created two cultic centres for him, one in Kiev, the other in Novgorod. In Kiev, Perun was represented in wood on a hill outside the princely palace together with a few other gods. His image was adorned with a head of silver and a beard of bronze. Cattle and even human beings were sacrificed to this god. When in 988 Vladimir was baptized, the idol was dragged into the River Dnieper and the sacrificial grove destroyed. It is obvious that the cult of the thunder-god had developed under the influence of the cult of Thor in Scandinavia; Kiev was effectively a Viking colony.

Other Russian gods were Svarog and Dashbog, father and son, both representing the sun and the fire. The common element in their names, bog (compare the Indian bhaga) stands for 'richness' and also 'god'. Volos is mentioned as the god by whose name one swears solemn oaths. Perhaps he was a master of meadows and herds.

VAMPIRES AND WEREWOLVES

The folk beliefs in Russia, Poland and Yugoslavia have probably preserved traits of ancient Slavic religion. Best known are the vampires, dead people who suck the blood of the living, and the werewolves, human beings transformed into wolves. *Rusalki* are maidens who have suffered premature death. Bogs are the abodes of *bagnik* and *bolotnik*, old and dirty men. Very commonly referred to are river-maidens, *vila*, seen as beautiful and cunning.

WESTERN SLAVIC TEMPLES

In the western Slavic area the old religion continued until 1168, when the temple in Arkona on the River Rügen was destroyed by King Valdemar I of Denmark. Unlike the Russians, the west Slavs built temples to their gods, probably very late, and possibly influenced by Germanic peoples. The temple clergy seem to have enjoyed high prestige. In Arkona, for instance, only the priest was allowed into the temple where he made libations and, at the harvest, sacrifices of meat. He also performed divination; for instance, he took omens from the movements of the white horse dedicated to the chief god, Svantevit ('the sacred lord').

The west-Slavic gods were very warlike and all-knowing. The latter quality was expressed by their statues having several heads or faces. Thus, Svantevit's huge image had four heads, two looking ahead, two looking backwards. Triglav in Stettin (modern Szczecin) had three heads, Rugievit at Garz on the Rügen one head with seven faces (and seven swords hanging from his belt), Porsevit at the same place had five heads, and so on. The idea of multi-headed gods is truly Slavic. Even in late Serbian folklore there is a three-headed mysterious nightly rider, Trojan (probably called after Emperor Trajan).

The temples sometimes contained precious things. Triglav's statue was made of gold (but Svantevit's image in Arkona was a wooden idol, chopped up and put into the fire by the Christian king, Valdemar). In the temple belonging to the war-god Jarovit of Wolgast a shield was preserved which was brought forth every time they prayed for victory in battle. Sacred groves were next to the temples. In Stettin, Triglav had a sacred oak with a spring beneath. The god Proven who was venerated at the site of Oldenburg (north of Eutin) owned a grove of sacred oaks surrounded by a wooden fence. Here the prince executed his justice in the middle of his subjects, just as the Germanic kings did under an oak.

Baltic religions: a late survival

The old religions of the Baltic peoples – the Latvians, Lithuanians and the now-extinct ancient Prussians – lived on until very recent times. Thus, the sacred groves in Latvia were not felled until the eighteenth century, and the cult of Perkons (Perkunas in Lithuania), god of thunder and fertility, and closely related to the Slavic Perun, prevailed in Latvia until 1750. As a matter of fact, Lithuania did not turn Christian until the fifteenth century. Thus it was still possible to observe these indigenous religions until the end of the nineteenth century.

Baltic religions are of interest because they are supposed to have been very close to the original Indo-European religion in Persia and India. The heavenly god, Dievs, has his counterpart in the Indian Dyaus, and Perkunas is identical with the Indian Parjanya.

A characteristic feature of Baltic religions is that there are many female divinities (whereas Slavic religions are noted for their lack of goddesses). We find a host of 'mothers', among them Mother Earth (Zemes mate) and the Fire Mother (Uguns mate). The Sun (Saule in Latvia) is represented as a beautiful maiden with golden hair who rides in a wagon drawn by horses. Laima and Mara (St Mary) are important goddesses of fate, and guardians of human beings. Laima receives sacrifices of dogs, sheep and pigs and blesses the fields and the cattle.

Besides Dievs, who is thought of as a farmer with a family, there are other sky-gods, such as Usinsh. The latter is a god associated with the spring and is a patron of horses.

Among terrestrial gods should be mentioned the earth-god, Zemes dievs, who has developed into a lord of the farmstead, and the fertility-god Jumis, who is represented by a double ear of córn. Jumis is connected with the harvest feast in the autumn, when he is identified with the last sheaf of the cornfields.

Indigenous Religions

PART THREE

Understanding Indigenous Religions

GRAHAM HARVEY

Indigenous religions are the majority of the world's religions. They are as diverse as the languages spoken, the music made and the means of subsistence employed by the many and various people who find them meaningful and satisfying. The number of people who might be counted as members of indigenous religions may not account for the majority of the world's religious people – some of these religions exist only in one small village – but they are far from insignificant when considered altogether.

The following general overview is intended to improve approaches to, and understanding of, indigenous religions such as those discussed in the 'case studies' in this section. It is important to note that not all indigenous religions are the same. Just as there are hundreds of indigenous languages in North America or in Papua New Guinea, so there are many different ways of being religious.

Few indigenous languages have a word like 'religion' and some people have drawn the conclusion that it is inappropriate to speak of 'religion' with reference to indigenous cultures. But if we think of religions as particular ways of living in and particular ways of seeing the world, then we can find religion in the ordinary, everyday lives of many people who do not use the word. In fact, it is unusual for adherents of any religion to separate their 'religious beliefs and practices' from their everyday lives, so indigenous people are not so very different. It is also noteworthy that religions are not all about seemingly strange ideas and peculiar practices, but these are often the things that stand out when we encounter something new to us. There is nothing wrong with noticing 'strange things', as long as we also pay attention to the more everyday ways in which people speak of what makes their lives meaningful and interesting.

Tradition and change

As a result of the spread of transcultural or global religions (e.g. Buddhism, Christianity and Islam), some indigenous religions have been destroyed, rejected or abandoned. Some indigenous people have accepted the arriving religion on their own terms and slotted it into an indigenous understanding. Many indigenous religions have been adapted to the presence of more powerful or dominating religions and continued with considerable vitality and creativity. While many people are returning to their 'traditional ways', others are engaging in both indigenous and another, newer religion.

Such processes that keep religions continuously relevant are not only interesting in themselves, but they provide the most recent example of the quite ordinary fact that all religions continuously change. 'Tradition' does not mean nothing ever changes, rather it means that one generation sets standards by which the next might judge the value of an idea or practice before changing. Indigenous religions are not the fossilized remains of the earliest or first religions. They are rarely simple or simplistic and should not be mistaken for the basic building blocks from which 'more advanced' religions were built or evolved. Hence, earlier terms – such as *primitive religion* or *primal religion* – detract from a proper and respectful understanding of the vibrant ways in which people understand and engage with the world. Similarly, it is unhelpful to speak of groups that might include millions of people as 'tribes' and of their religions as *tribal religions*. Indigenous religions are not stuck in the past, nor do they only make sense when practised in their original homelands. Although indigenous religions are severely affected by colonialism, they continue to provide resources for people surviving and thriving in the new, globalized world.

Respect

The notion of respect is important in most of the books, websites and other discussions of indigenous religions. Elders continuously encourage younger people to show respect in particular ways to those who deserve it. Asking who is respected and how respect is shown can be quite revealing about what is of central importance. In many parts of Africa, for example, beer is offered to those one respects. Native Americans did not traditionally use alcohol and continue to give gifts of tobacco or sage to respected people. In some cultures it is appropriate to

A nun teaching the catechism to young African orphans at the Mission of the Fathers of Saint-Esprit in Tanzania.

be reserved when first meeting another person, in others it is permissible to act quite intimately. Knowing whether to touch someone else at all, and in what way, is important. Do you shake hands or press noses? Do you hand people gifts or place them on the ground in front of them?

A Dani chief displays the mummified body of a village elder, preserved to be honoured after death.

Significant persons

Important as these questions are, the more radical question is 'Who is a person?' Most cultures understand that humans are not the only kind of person. Christians, Jews and Muslims, for example, consider God and angels to be persons of considerable importance. Of course, this nicely illustrates the point that not all persons are the same and that there are different ways to approach particular persons. There are indigenous religions in which teachings about a God who created the world are significant. There are many more in which everything we see is the result of the creative activities of many other persons. Perhaps a single creator, or a creative process, started it all, but then life developed as each living being or person played their part. Trees separated sky and land, mountains

arose to shape the land, coyote or jaguar or a robin tamed fire, corn taught planting cycles and ceremonies, humans built towns, and so the world became the way it is. And similar processes continue to change the world, making it important that people learn to act responsibly and respectfully. All this is commonplace in a great variety of indigenous religions.

What needs more careful thought is the implication that there is a great variety of creative persons. Some of these might be recognized as being like the God monotheists acknowledge, others are more polytheistic deities who are often encountered in the kind of intimate everyday matters for which some academics use the word 'immanence' (the divine within the world and everyday experience). Many significant persons are humans: elders, priests, shamans, grandparents, rulers and so on. Although ancestors are important, it is important to note that among indigenous people this word typically refers to those from whom a particular person or family is descended. It rarely means 'all those who have died'. This can cause difficulties because some museum scientists consider that all human remains belong to 'humanity' universally. The difference between these 'scientific' and indigenous ways of speaking (and the resulting confusion) is illustrated in references to 'our ancestors' by those museum officials who reject requests for the return of particular remains to their places of origin. Such misunderstandings also illustrate tensions familiar from wider concerns about globalization.

If ancestors are pre-eminent among the community of human persons in many indigenous cultures, and deserve appropriate displays of respect, they are far from alone in being categorized as 'persons'. In many, but not all, indigenous cultures words equivalent to 'person' can refer to animals, plants, rocks, clouds and more. Having learned from Ojibwe people in southern-central Canada, Irving Hallowell (1892–1974) coined the influential term *other-than-human persons*. That is, in Ojibwe understanding the world is inhabited by a vast community of persons, only some of whom are human. There are human-persons, tree-persons, rock-persons, cloud-persons and so on. From a rock-person's perspective there might be 'other-than-rock persons', such as some humans with whom it is possible and even desirable to communicate. Many indigenous peoples have similar understandings of the nature of life and personhood.

Exchanging gifts

Children brought up in particular indigenous religions may have to be taught to distinguish between persons and objects, but religious education is rarely presented as lectures and lists. More commonly, children are taught how to act towards other persons. Just as they receive gifts from and give gifts to elder relatives, they learn that the process of giving and receiving is a vitally important element of the relationships that mark people as different from mere 'things'. Gifts are given as signs of respect and love to those more powerful or more esteemed than us. Gifts are received as signs of support, help and compassion from those more powerful or esteemed than us. Gifts initiate, maintain and further relationships between people. Gifts carry obligations and create ongoing relationships. Just as Ojibwe children might offer respected elders gifts of tobacco, elders might offer tobacco to respected rocks or eagles or to sage plants from which they wish to cut leaves. Gift processes thus demonstrate who are considered to be persons, who is expected to act personally towards other persons.

Power dynamics

Gift is also central to the dynamics of power. Understandings of power are also a common theme in discussions of indigenous religions. Although the history of Western scholarship contains misunderstandings of indigenous ideas about power, the theme is an important one. Some scholars have claimed that many indigenous people have 'primitive' and mistaken notions about mystical powers being something like electricity. Often these scholars have not listened attentively to their hosts, who have been explaining the social dynamics by which people interact. For example, social, not mystical, powers are usually at stake in Polynesian references to *mana* and Ojibwe references to *manitou*. Again, this usage is not alien to Westerners who are familiar with the language of 'empowerment'. There are more and less powerful persons. More power manifests itself as more ability to perform certain roles, e.g. making pots or speeches, and brings with it the responsibility to act respectfully and to the benefit of others.

Shamans and witches

Person, gift and power are also central to common problems to which indigenous religions proffer solutions. For example, some indigenous people understand that it is possible to cause harm by performing particular rituals, i.e. witchcraft and sorcery. Solutions might be found among some people by recourse to diviners, while others employ shamans. For the indigenous people, these specialists are adept at finding knowledge unavailable to others and require careful and sometimes frightening training for their role. In response to questions about whether such practices are superstitious, indigenous people might point to the fact that rather different questions are important in indigenous communities. The interesting question for them is not

'Mau e ki mai, he aha te mea nui? Maku e ki atu, he tangata, he tangata, he tangata.' (If you ask what is the greatest thing I will tell you it is people, people, people.)
Taitokerau Whakatauki (Maori)

UNDERSTANDING INDIGENOUS RELIGIONS

why a grain store collapsed: everybody knows that grain stores collapse because termites eat their supports away. The important question as they see it is why it collapsed when this person sheltered beneath it, rather than earlier or later. In indigenous religions talk of witchcraft arises in a personal and relational world where the person who shelters beneath a grain store may have previously insulted an ancestor or a witch and made himself or herself liable to disaster. Alternatively, a person aware of having incurred another's wrath might offer the kind of gifts commonly identified as 'sacrifices' to restore a more positive relationship.

Conclusion

Indigenous religions, like all other religions, may be considered to be ways in which particular groups of people seek the means of improving health, happiness and even wealth for themselves, their families and communities. Finding out what a particular group means by health, wealth and happiness, and how they go about improving these, will greatly enhance understanding of that group's culture. Indigenous religions have been of considerable importance in the Study of Religions and Anthropology and their adherents are now participants in rich and significant dialogues with members of other religions or none. The recognition that religion may be largely about the etiquette by which people relate to one another can be seen as one of the most significant gifts of indigenous people to understanding what it means to be human.

'À ńlọ wá ìmò, òtító, àti òdodo.'
(We are going in search of knowledge, truth, and justice.)
A line of Ifa divination text (Yoruba)

CASE-STUDY 1:

Indigenous Religions in Asia

BARBARA BOAL

Asian tribal peoples do not separate the sacred and secular. Their religious concepts are expressed in ritualized activities involving the community.

These concepts and actions do not result from verbal 'beliefs'. In this they differ from 'religion' as we know it in the world's major faiths.

The key to understanding Asian tribal world views is 'relationship': with gods and spirits; with fellow human beings; with nature.

These cannot be separated: they form one whole. Each group has religious practices appropriate to themselves and their environment, most often seeking to restore the good order that was created 'in the beginning'. So the practices of tribal groups stretching across Asia and the neighbouring islands vary widely.

The spirits

Shamans dominate religion in Siberia. They believe in a high god, beyond all good and evil. Chosen by the spirits from certain families, male and female shamans enter rigorous training. Their souls leave the body by ecstatic trances to communicate with the spirits. They bring back instructions to correct the erring and restore harmony between people, the spirit world and everything created. This harmony is fundamental to their beliefs. Similar beliefs are held by the Ainus of northern Japan, the mountain peoples of Taiwan and, to some extent, the Hakka of China.

Nomadic groups

Many people think the nomadic groups are descendants of Asia's ancient peoples who have preserved traditional ways down the ages. Today they live in small bands in remote, forested hill-country, where they were probably pushed long ago by more highly organized immigrants. They include very small tribes in west-central and south India and in Chota Nagpur. They are also found on the Andaman Islands and scattered in remote forest and swamp areas of coastal Cambodia. Better known, perhaps, are the small groups of Semang-Negritoes and their neighbours, the Senoi, inhabiting the jungle hills of northern and central peninsular Malaysia; also the Aëtas-Negritoes of Luzon, Mindanao and Mindoro in the Philippines. Other hunter-gatherer groups can be found wandering in central Kalimantang, the Celebes and eastern Sumatra.

Such groups may be made up of one elder and his family or several families. Scarcity of food dictates size. However much they roam, they usually keep within their own boundaries. Food is always shared equally – roots, tubers, leaves and fruits from the forest, possibly fish speared or trapped. Small game is hunted by bow-and-arrow except on the Malaysian peninsula, where Senoi blowgun and poisoned dart have also been adopted by the Semang.

Land and ritual

Their home area of land and its produce has great religious significance. However far they wander, they return repeatedly to the place they regard as their own. Many, such as the Malaysian Senoi hill-people – widely known as 'slave' (*Sakai*) – have changed to slash-and-burn cultivation for part of each year. They still live in very temporary shelters during food-collecting expeditions, but cultivation demands settled base camps at some

seasons. This changes their religious attitude to the land and to the spirits.

The Senoi, like other hill-cultivators, are surrounded by taboos and work restrictions as soon as they choose which trees to fell and fire to prepare a hill-plot. Through a series of rituals they seek the spirits' help in securing a good crop, until the final harvest celebration. These are performed by the whole community. For instance, all are in 'quarantine' on the first day of

A hunter from the Igorot tribe in North Luzon, Philippines.

planting. Similarly, one person's sickness involves everybody; for the person's soul has wandered out of the group and must be brought back. The shaman employs the power of certain herbs and plants disliked by the spirit world to drive away the evil and call back the wandering soul.

Taboo

In cases of serious illness the whole group is involved in taboos and ritual observances, perhaps in days and nights of music and spirit-possessed dance. Finally, when blood sacrifice has been offered, the spirit is driven out. If the patient dies, another set of pollution observances begins. Deaths, like births, are full of danger, and the group must isolate itself, both for its

'The elements of the taboo... are always the same: certain things, or persons, or places belong in some way to a different order of being, and therefore contact with them will produce an upheaval at the ontological level which might well prove fatal.'

Mircea Eliade

INDIGENOUS RELIGIONS IN ASIA

A woman from the Igorot tribe in North Luzon, Philippines displays the tattoos that give her spiritual protection.

Eastern Ghats of Orissa, India, and number over a million. Traditionally they supported themselves by slash-and-burn hill-plots, and by hunting and gathering during the dry 'hungry season'. Paddy-cultivation has now steadily increased.

In 1835 the East India Company first encountered the Kondhs' constant human sacrifices to satisfy the earth's demands. Kondh myths taught that only in return for this costliest form of sacrifice would the earth deity grant them fertility of crops, animals and healthy children.

Earth-goddess

The creator-god, Bura, formed the earth-goddess, Tari, as his companion, but found her sadly lacking in wifely attentions. She tried in vain to prevent his creating the world and humankind. All was paradise in the created world except for her growing jealousy. This led to a fierce conflict between the two. All the Kondhs except a small minority believed that the earth-goddess had won, though she let the creator keep second place. She taught the arts of hunting, war and cultivating only in return for human blood, 'her proper food'.

Buffalo now replace human victims. Though declining, this ritual continues. Strips of flesh are hacked from the victim and buried in the village and in neighbouring villages to release her gift of fertility. Many villages were formerly at war. Brief, strict peace-pacts are therefore made for each annual stage of this three- or four-year ritual, ensuring cooperation for the set few days. In some areas it is still annually celebrated in each district, also at certain farming seasons or when the health of the people or its livestock is affected. This binds the people together as Kondhs, when otherwise the strongest unit is the lineage group.

A number of myths and dialogues show how the Kondhs tried to avoid

own safety and that of its neighbours. If any member breaks the taboo, terrifying tropical storms will follow. These come from a supreme god, but the Senoi have little idea of a hierarchy of spirit beings. To them the presence of ancestor-spirits is vague and unwelcome. Safety and well-being depend on the unity and harmony of the living community.

Tribes with more complex social structures and more settled and advanced economic patterns develop a stronger pattern of rituals. These demand ritual specialists for proper celebration. Though certain rites may be performed for the individual they still involve the wider community. The Kondhs are an example.

Human sacrifice

The Kondhs – or Kui, as they call themselves – live in the jungle-covered the earth-goddess's demands:

'We will die rather than give you human beings!'

But breaking the relationship with her also involved breaking the relationship with the land – bringing drought and famine – and with humankind, bringing pestilence and death. Hence she always made them submit, as the means of recreating harmony and well-being.

Kondh rituals

The Kondhs try to use mystical powers in many other rituals to increase or restore relationship – thus strength and well-being – in the district, village, kin-group or household. Rituals:

● between the high god, humankind and the land. These follow the farming calendar, from ground preparation and sowing to reaping and threshing; also taboo-lifting rituals on hunting and gathering wild produce.

● to seek the blessing and help of the ancestors. These may involve other clans: such as marriage or the taking of a second wife, or the removal of an entire village with its ancestors, if problems and pestilences show the need.

● to guard against loss of well-being through pollution. Ritual impurity runs the full gamut from small household avoidances to incest, which pollutes the earth and everybody in the area.

All births and deaths pollute, but most serious for the Kondhs are deaths before due time, by tiger-mauling, in childbirth, or by hanging, falling from a tree or drowning. These place the entire village in 'quarantine', traditionally for a month, but nowadays for a shorter period, while priest and people undergo daily purification rites.

● to safeguard life. The danger may come from high-ranking spirits: gods of the hill, of smallpox, of boundaries, of iron (war), or hunting. These are stronger than spirits of springs, trees and lesser hills. Offence against them rapidly brings disaster. Also life-destroying is an overpowering belief in evil eye, sorcery and witchcraft. These powers, neutral in themselves, become evil and deeply feared when someone uses them against their fellow, for this reverses Kondh beliefs about community well-being. Counter-rituals by 'witch-detectives' may return the evil to its originator, but the victim may nevertheless fall sick or die.

Specialists

Seers communicate with the spirits through trances or divination to find out who caused the problem and why. Priests perform the rituals, sacrificing cocks, goats, pigs or buffalo. A spirit-chosen keeper of the village's shrine-stones performs many annual purification rituals. Many villages also have groves sacred to the hill-god or guardian spirit. The household head is priest for ancestor rites and some look after bronze emblems animals, reptiles or other household spirits.

One community

The ancestors, the unborn and the living are all one community. The same daily activities continue in the shade-world. Death in old age with a full funeral gives the best hope of passing peacefully to the ancestors. The dead are also rehabilitated into the bereaved home in the form of a spider, found near the funeral pyre. Sudden death in the feared forms mentioned earlier rules out being accepted by the ancestors. This results in unbearable loneliness for the now dangerous spirit. For the Kondhs, it is as necessary to live in community after death as before it. The manner of death, not good or evil behaviour in this life, decides the future life.

'Taboo is a sort of warning: "Danger! High voltage!" Power has been stored up, and we must be on our guard. The taboo is the expressly authenticated condition of being replete with power, and man's reaction to it should rest on a clear recognition of this potent fullness, should maintain the proper distance and secure protection.'

Gerardus van der Leeuw

'Being chosen by the spirits, taught by them to enter a trance and fly with one's soul to other worlds in the sky or clamber through dangerous crevasses into subterranean worlds; being stripped of one's flesh, reduced to a skeleton and then reassembled and reborn; gaining the power to combat spiritual enemies and heal their victims; to kill enemies and save one's own people from disease and starvation – these are the features of shamanic religions in many parts of the world.'

Piers Vitebsky

INDIGENOUS RELIGIONS IN ASIA

CASE-STUDY 2:

The Foe of Papua New Guinea

JOAN RULE

In the tribal religion of the Foe in the Southern Highlands of Papua New Guinea, there is an awesome, seldom-named being, Siruwage, and a chief spirit, Ama-a Hai Ta-o ('Old Man in East'), but neither is earth's creator and there is no creator worship.

There are, in addition, three groups of spirits who live in fixed places:

● the evil things (*maame gai*)

● the *hisare*

● the *hibu yii*

Certain men in each village make a special relationship with one of these groups of spirits, and others pay them to make an offering on their behalf.

The evil things

The 'evil things' inhabit a clump of trees, a big rock or some unusual natural feature. For example, in about 1967, on a point of land on the south-eastern side of Lake Kutubu, in a swampy area of wild bamboo, a man named Igare from Gese village found a small area with red cordyline shrubs growing neatly. This, all agreed, must be a spirit house, so it was regarded as a place of the 'evil things'. Those who made a relationship with the evil things, and who had the right spells for them, were in their favour and would not be harmed. But those who roused their anger would get swollen legs or a swollen stomach.

Children whose parents had garden-houses in the area were warned not to go near or to make a noise, for fear of making them angry.

Further up the lake, some *hisare* spirits live. In the waters of the lake live a number of fearsome water spirits, the *guruka*. Men who make a relationship with the *hisare* spirits also make contact with these *guruka*. After the *hisare* people have danced with the *hisare* spirits, the *guruka* will come up from the water and dance. They will bring cassowary feathers or perhaps human bones and present them to the *hisare* people, acting for the spirits. According to the gift, the following month a cassowary will be caught, someone will die, or some similarly appropriate event will occur.

The *hibu yii*

Hibu yii men built a house in their village and at secret ceremonies the *hibu yii* spirits appeared to them. In many villages this is no longer practised.

Wandering spirits

Other spirit beings wander from place to place. The *soro* are spirits of the air who wander here and there at will, always on the lookout for some harm to do to humans. Children are afraid of the spirits of the air, being sure that they could carry them off or do dreadful things; but adults make it plain that they must work in company with the spirits who live within the living (*baisese*). A pair or group of *baisese* must work with at least one spirit of the air. If someone has an enemy, their spirit will go out, find another person's spirit, find a spirit of the air and then go to do damage. For example, in about 1960 a stone was thrown into a man's sleeping area. He realized that his spirit was leaving him, pressed into service by a fellow villager's spirit. He said 'There'll be a man harmed at Hegeso village,' naming the man. Two days later the man was dead.

Spirits of the dead

Most feared of all are the spirits of the dead. These include the spirits of men slain, mostly in inter-village fighting, and the spirits of those who have died from other causes. Both can cause harm and serious illness, entering into a person's body in the form of stones and wood which will cause death.

The spirits of the slain (*bauwabe*) are the most potent. These spirits live 'up above' and are always painted all over with red. People who make offerings to a spirit of the slain find that their spirit appears to them in a dream or vision, guaranteeing success and help. But if a man and his kinsmen are enemies of a man who is slain, his spirit appearing to them means trouble. If a person has a bad ulcer or abdominal pain, this is clearly the work of the spirit of the slain.

The spirit of someone who has died in any other way (*amena denane*) goes 'east', but wanders back and hovers around, at least for a time. It can cause sickness, but not death. An exasperated mother may say to a child, 'If you don't stop, the spirit will come with a bamboo, collect your tears and drink them, and if they're sweet cause you lots of harm.'

Medicine men

Medicine men once claimed to be able to 'suck out' the stones and sticks implanted by the spirits. They were paid in strings of cowries or with a pig. This cult died a natural death. The prices charged were high, and the number of cures not impressive. At the local health centres, on the other hand, drugs such as penicillin and chloroquine produced dramatic cures free of charge.

Certain medicine men would also for a fee chant away a spirit said to be causing sickness. This practise also appears to have been largely discontinued.

Bamboo and sorcery

The sorcerer is greatly feared. In a group of two or three hundred people, complete and electric silence resulted as a well-known sorcerer produced a small bamboo of sorcery material bought from sorcerers in the west to produce the death of named men. Foe sorcerers have three main methods.

The first, 'hitting the skin with a stick', is the most potent; the man will die in one or two days. Sorcery material from the bamboo, generally a fine, white, powdery substance, touches the skin of the doomed man, either by means of a stick, or by being shaken on him while he is asleep. If it can be put into his bamboo of water or his food, it works just as well.

In the second method, pieces of the man's belongings – a fragment of his cane leg-band, or of the leaves or cloth covering his buttocks – are put in the bamboo of sorcery material which is placed in the fork of a tree, where it wears slowly away. Or it may be placed in a large ant-mound on a tree trunk, or in a small running stream. As the friction or the eating takes place, the man will sicken and die over a period of four or five months.

The third method, white sorcery, is done with a set of small white stones. The sorcerer obtains a tree gum, and says his spell as he rubs it into the stones. This also causes death.

CASE-STUDY 3:

Australian Aboriginal Religions

LYNNE HUME

Australia is a vast continent that was peopled sparsely by its indigenous inhabitants before the advent of Europeans. When Europeans did arrive, they found a very different land from the one they had left and an indigenous population that held religious views and lifestyles they found almost impossible to comprehend. The archaeological record of human life on the continent reaches back at least 40,000 years, white colonization little more than 200 years.

Land and creation

Central to Aboriginal beliefs are stories that tell of their relationship to the land, of totemic ancestors that once lay beneath the land and who, in the creative period or founding drama, gave form to the formless and instituted unchangeable laws that humans were to follow for all time. The ancestors gave shape to an existing, yet formless world; they were self-created and creative, possessing special powers that could be used for good or harm. When they rose up from beneath the land, they journeyed across, under or over it, leaving tangible expressions of their essence, or power, in the land itself. Where they stopped to urinate, for example, one might find a waterhole; where they sat, one might find a shallow depression; where they slept might be a rock; where they bled, ochre deposits were left; where they dug in the ground, water flowed and springs formed; where they cut down trees, valleys were

formed. These primordial beings, the ancestors of living Aborigines, instituted tribal laws for their progeny to follow, and, when they completed their travels, they returned into the land whence they had come. Because all things share a common ancestral life force that is sacred, everything is interconnected, the living to the non-living, the sentient to the non-sentient, within a sacred geography that provides visual evidence of ancestral presence.

Aboriginal beliefs about the origins of the universe and the place of humans in that universe are conveyed in stories to do with the ancestors and relayed through ceremonial performance, art, dance and song. Songlines consist of a number of songs that follow tracks of land pertaining to particular ancestors and their associated journeying, and those areas of land are associated with particular species of animals, birds and other phenomena, and their connections to humans. Everything is linked in an all-encompassing system of interrelatedness and a network of tracks that cover the continent.

The Dreaming

When Frank Gillen and Baldwin Spencer encountered the Arrernte Aborigines in central Australia in the late nineteenth century, they tried to understand what they referred to as their *Altyerrenge/Alcheringa* – the fundamental religious concepts that permeated every aspect of Aboriginal life and death. The closest translation that these two white men could arrive at was 'Dream times', because it seemed to them that the Arrernte were talking about a past period of a vague and 'dreamy' nature, yet one that was still present. They realized that the *Altyerrenge* was of great importance to Aboriginal culture, but also that 'Dream times' (which later became *the Dreaming* or *Dreamtime*) did not adequately convey the meaning of the Aboriginal term. W.E.H. Stanner

An Aboriginal rock painting depicts figures from the Dreaming (c. 23,000 BCE).

described the Dreaming as 'everywhen' to convey the sense of a non-linear, ever-present aspect to the Dreaming. Other Aboriginal language groups throughout Australia talk about similar concepts, and so the term 'Dreaming' came to have a universal application. Aborigines are more likely to give specific language names to the concept, or to call it their 'Law'. T.G.H. Strehlow aptly described it as 'eternal, uncreated, sprung out of itself'.

Dreaming stories and songlines

Since different parts of the landscape were created by particular ancestral beings, there is a plurality of Dreamings. Access to the Dreaming can come about through various means: participation in ceremonial performance, song, dance or ritual and via dreams and other methods. The significance of Dreaming stories is conveyed through these means and according to an individual's position in the scheme of sacred knowledge. For example, a song might have several layers of meaning: at the basic level, men, women and children have access to the public nature of a story conveyed in the song; at another level a sacred meaning would be conveyed; and at a secret-sacred level only those who have undertaken a specific initiation in either 'men's business' (knowledge about the Dreaming pertaining to men) or 'women's business' (knowledge about the Dreaming pertaining to women) would be privy to the deepest levels of meaning. Similarly, paintings also have layers of meaning, from public to esoteric knowledge, that is held by only a few senior people. The most secret, restricted knowledge is owned or known by senior men who are experts in 'men's business' and by senior women who are experts in 'women's business'.

The concept of 'ownership' only has relevance to knowledge, not ownership of land.

> 'I am not painting just for my pleasure; there is the meaning, knowledge and power. This is the earthly painting for the creation and for the land story. The land is not empty, the land is full of knowledge, full of story, full of goodness, full of energy.'
>
> Marika, quoted in Wally Caruana and Nigel Lendon, *The Painters of the Wagilag Sisters' Story 1937–97*

● Ownership of knowledge extends to everything that is non-material: the right of someone to paint certain designs, to sing a song or to tell a story. The expression 'keeping up country' means that the people who come from a specific area (or 'country') and are associated with it through the Dreaming must look after it in the form of stewardship or custodianship – by continuing the rituals, following the songlines and maintaining a proper relationship with the ancestors of that 'place'.

● Legal recognition of traditional ownership is an ongoing concern for Aboriginal people, many of whom were displaced from their original lands after colonization. This is a major issue for Aboriginal people, still under debate in courts of law throughout Australia.

Aborigines and Christianity

After 200 years of colonization and Christianization through missionary influences, a great many Aboriginal people are now Christian or combine tenets of Christianity with indigenous beliefs and practices. Their stories of the Dreaming, their displacement, their sometimes traumatic experiences as a consequence of European presence, are all depicted in their distinctive art which now consists of traditional methods such as dot paintings and abstract designs, Christian influences, and political statements about their lived experiences.

CASE-STUDY 4:

Melanesia

CARL LOELIGER

Melanesia is the area of the Pacific Ocean from the western end of New Guinea (Irian Jaya) to Fiji in the east, from the northernmost islands of Papua New Guinea to New Caledonia in the south, and includes Irian Jaya, Papua New Guinea, the Torres Strait Islands, the Solomon Islands, the New Hebrides and New Caledonia. There are no fewer than 1,200 vernacular languages among its roughly 5 million inhabitants.

More than a century of close contact with foreign cultures and Christianity has changed Melanesian indigenous religion, but has not everywhere reduced its vitality and pervasiveness.

World view

Melanesians make no distinction between the 'religious' and the 'secular', between the 'natural' and the 'supernatural'. Their religion can be seen as a particular view of the universe, and a set of relationships with it, including people, gods, spirits, ghosts, magical powers, totems, the land and features of the landscape, living creatures, trees, plants and all physical objects, all of which are in some sense potential sources of power.

Relationships with people and ancestral spirits are universally the most important, for at the centre of life is the community of people and spirits. This community, along with clan and extended family, and links with a particular piece of land, give a person identity and security, a reason for living, a sense of history and an approach to the future. All rituals of birth, initiation into adult life, marriage and death are directed towards maintaining these relationships.

Melanesian indigenous religion aims at life, fertility, prosperity, harmony, control and balance in all relationships between people and spirits, and in this world rather than the next. However, as with many other religions, not all its activities match these ideals.

Narrow concern with family and clan, suspicions and hostility between and within groups, and in some areas between the sexes, have helped foster seemingly harsh and inhuman practices.

Myths and stories

Melanesian indigenous religion features a range of migration and other stories, legends and myths, songs, prayers and incantations all transmitted orally. Parts of this repertoire are known only by initiated males, or adult women or by specialists such as priests. Especially sacred knowledge is restricted to elderly initiated people. There is a variety of creation stories, but little speculation about the origins and nature of the universe. Many people believe that important parts of culture – social, economic and political life – were created for, or given to, the people by gods.

Gods and spirits

Not all Melanesian peoples have believed in a god of the whole universe, or in a powerful god or gods, or that the god or gods are interested in human activities. But some believe gods to be creators who continue to care for the world. Many believe in a variety of spirit beings, including evil 'ghosts', demons and witches (not widespread), many of which can harm or kill people. Ancestral spirits are important everywhere; some societies look forward to the return of the dead, others fear it. Some societies regard the spirits of the recent dead as dangerous; others think they are friendly towards the living. They believe that elaborate rituals in honour of the dead – mourning, food offerings, dances,

'If a stone is found to have supernatural power, it is because a spirit has associated itself with it; a dead man's bone has with it mana, because the ghost is with the bone; a man may have so close a connection with a spirit or ghost that he has mana in himself also, and can so direct it as to effect what he desires.'

R.H. Codrington

'A man is a good fighter, not because of his own strength or resources but because of the strength he gets from the mana of some dead fighter; this mana may lie in the little stone amulet hanging around his neck, in some leaves fastened to his belt, or in some spoken formula. The fact that a man's pigs multiply or his garden thrives is due to his possessing certain stones containing the particular mana of pigs and of trees'.

Mircea Eliade

MELANESIA

exchanges of pigs, food and valuables – will ensure that the dead will protect the living. Where beliefs in totems occur, the totems – animals, birds, fish, trees, plants – are sometimes seen as ancestors, sometimes simply as emblems.

Ritual and magic

Rituals vary from simple acts linked with everyday activities (hunting, gardening, fishing) to complex rituals, festivals and festival cycles lasting days, weeks, even months and years. In the major activities initiated men take the central role; women and juniors have only minor roles. The pig figures in many of these rituals and festivals. Food, drink and sexual taboos accompany most important rituals. Some peoples believe rituals force the spirits or gods to act; others believe the gods are free to act as they will.

Magic has a place in most societies. The sorcerer is an important person in many Melanesian societies; deaths are often credited to his activity, since a death is usually regarded as being caused by someone. Every Melanesian society includes people with special ritual responsibilities, temporary, permanent or hereditary.

For Melanesians, sacred places can include features of the landscape, such as caves, pools, streams and rocks, but also artificial constructions varying from simple structures to large elaborate buildings such as the Sepik ancestral spirit houses.

Conduct

In some societies ethics and religion seem to have no connection; in others the spirits and gods are clearly concerned with behaviour. Ethical conduct is the particular interest of the god Datagaliwabe among the Huli people of the Southern Highlands of Papua New Guinea.

A decorated human skull from the New Hebrides, Melanesia, that has been plastered and painted, probably as a form of ancestor worship.

CASE-STUDY 5:

South American Indigenous Religions

ANDREW DAWSON

This overview concerns the religious world views of the indigenous peoples of Central and South America, focusing upon those disparate and diverse communities whose tribal practices and geographical remoteness have until relatively recently helped to preserve much of a cultural heritage that predates European 'conquest' (1492–) by a very substantial margin. Because of the linguistic and cultural diversity of these communities, examples have been interspersed from as many different contexts as possible (with indigenous sources cited regarding their most popular name). The majority of examples relate to peoples inhabiting the forested highlands and forested lowlands of northern/central South America, with broader representation gained by referring to assorted groups in Tierra del Fuego and Patagonia in the south and the Central American isthmus to the north. A proper appreciation of the practices and belief systems of these indigenous groups requires an awareness of an overarching world view consisting of an enormously complex interaction of situated socio-cultural processes and localized economico-political dynamics.

Time and space

Conceiving time as linear rather than cyclical, these indigenous peoples make sense of the present with reference to the foundational events of a primordial past. Here, a mythical period of momentous upheavals engenders an

Caracas

Guajiros

Kógi

VENEZUELA

Winikina-Warao

Georgetown

Arawak

Paramaribo

Bogotá

Pemon

GUYANA

Cayenne

Wakuénai

SURINAM

Taulipéng

Arecuna

FRENCH
GUIANA

COLOMBIA

Tukano

Baniwa

Waiwai

Quito

ECUADOR   Siona

Putumayo

Shuar (Jívaro)

Matsigenka

PERU

Kayapó

Kagwahiv

Tapirapé

Ashaninka
(Campa)

Arua (Jívaro)

BRAZIL

Lima

Bororo

La Paz

Brasilia

BOLIVIA   Chiquitanos

Ayoreo

Chamacoco (Ishir)

PARAGUAY

Toba

Asuncion

Ava-Chiripá

Toba

Guarani

CHILE

Guarani

URUGUAY

Santiago

Buenos
Aires

Montevideo

ARGENTINA

The approximate
locations of most
of the indigenous
groups mentioned
in this article.

Tehuelche

Falkland
Islands

Ona   ● location of tribe

increasingly variegated world in which flood, fire and violence mould and reshape the cosmos. Indigenous mythologies represent the world as the intended product of pre-existent deities (such as Temáukel of the Ona) or as an unintended result caused by their godly and semi-divine offspring (as with Kumai of the Baniwa). The transition from mythical pre-history to human time is often effected through the foundational practices of mythical cultural heroes (such as Elal of the Tehuelche). Within this period of momentous change and unfolding differentiation, tribal traditions are established and classificatory systems formulated – the ambiguities, contradictions and maladies of which continue to find their basis in the primeval period. The recalcitrant disorder of the present is framed by the ambivalent discontinuities of a mythic past.

The indigenous cosmos is spatially divided into a series of overlapping tiers, some of which are further subdivided. The number of strata differs from culture to culture, with the Kógi having as many as nine divisions, the Siona and Waiwai five, the Tapirapé and Baniwa four, and the Toba, Matsigenka and Pemón three. At its simplest, the universe has the earth sandwiched between the heavenly terrain of the gods above and the subterranean world below. With the Baniwa the heavenly realm comprises a lower 'Other World', adjacent to the earth, and a more distant 'Other Sky'. The underworld can also be layered, as with the Campa's partition of it into two. Although any particular stratum may be divided laterally, the earthly tier is most commonly subjected to such treatment, with prominent environmental features (such as mountains, lakes and dense parts of the forest) and mythical places (such as the Avá-Chiripá's 'land without evil') accorded extra-special status.

> 'Myth is... a constant by-product of living faith, which is need of miracles; of sociological status, which demands precedent; of moral rule, which requires sanction.'
>
> Bronislaw Malinowski

The physical mirrors the supernatural

The physical space and moral environment of indigenous peoples is ordered to reflect mythico-cosmic space-time. The Kayopó village, for example, both in its design and external orientation to the surrounding forest, exemplifies physical space as a microcosm upon which temporal heritage and spatial hierarchy write themselves through individual lives and social processes. As with the village, so too the human individual is held to mirror the cosmic order of things. The indigenous self is seen in a wide variety of ways. The Waiwai, certain Guaraní groups and the Toba talk of the self as having two principal elements (rendered 'souls' by most scholars). The Avá-Chiripá, Matsigenka and other Guaraní groups understand the self as comprised of three primary components. Whatever the structure, indigenous conceptions of the self and its constituent parts serve at least two basic functions:

● As within many other mythico-religious systems, they allow for continuity in the face of spatio-temporal change. Whether awake or asleep (as with the nocturnal roamings of the Matsigenka 'free soul' and the Toba 'image soul'), alive or dead (as with the post-mortem ascension of the Waiwai 'eye-soul' to Kapu), in this world or another (as with the 'soul flight' of shamanic ecstasy), partitioned conceptions of the self help to preserve a continuity of personal identity.

● They help to situate the individual amidst a multiple configuration of mythical, temporal and spatial reality. Whether unified, dualistic or tripartite, these views of the self serve generally to articulate an understanding of the individual as constituted through the continuous interplay of its divine origins, base corporeality and personal-social processes. They thereby allow for relations with other spheres of existence (both in this life and the next), ground the individual in the corruptible materiality of this world and preserve a personal identity which is derived from more than its heavenly-physical origins. The indigenous self exists as a nodal point at which mythical, spatial and temporal dynamics intersect.

Supernatural beings

Alongside humankind and the flora and fauna surrounding it, the indigenous universe is populated by a broad array of supernatural beings. Whilst taxonomy differs from people to people, the following categories are generally representative.

● Inhabiting the higher strata of the cosmologies, often remote from everyday human activity, are (for some tribes) uncreated/pre-existent deities such as Kóoch of the Tehuelche, Ñanderuvusú of the Guaraní and Nanderú Guazù of the Avá-Chiripá.

● These divine beings are accompanied by a pantheon of lesser deities whose origins and characteristics are usually connected with celestial, climatic, totemic and otherwise routine phenomena, as with Gidosíde (the Ayoreo moon goddess), Karuten (the Tehuelche god of thunder), the black monkey of the Arawak or the tiger of the Goajiros, and Pel'ek of the Toba (the owner of the night).

● Although indigenous deities involve themselves in the general ordering of human affairs, and are at times difficult to differentiate from the more numerous category of 'spirits', it is the latter who most directly influence day-to-day affairs. Usually occupying the lower strata of the cosmos, the spirits of animals, plants and elementals (e.g. of water), along with those of deceased human beings, are regarded as primary causal forces potentially influencing every facet of personal well-being, interpersonal relations and social reproduction.

The shaman is the key figure in human-supernatural interaction.

● Experienced through dreams or visions, encountered at night in the village or by day in the forest, the spirits of the indigenous world view are central to the dynamics of a human world which is, after all, nothing but a pale imitation of the 'real world' they inhabit. Whilst benevolent and malevolent forms exist, within the indigenous mindset spirits are by and large morally ambivalent in their dealings with humans. However, with adequate inducements and the appropriate opportunities they are quick to make their ubiquitous presence felt. The prevalence of widespread supernatural causality demands constant and careful handling and most indigenous peoples turn to ritualized activity, managed by the local shaman, to limit or coordinate the impact of the spiritual upon the material.

Shamanism

Although intended (as opposed to accidental and undesired) engagement with indigenous spirits is not restricted to formal shamanic activity, the shaman is the primary agent in human-supernatural interaction. Selected by way of heredity (as with the Putumayo) or shamanic preference (as with the Avá-Chiripá), shamans undergo rigorous and prolonged training. Lasting anywhere from less than five years (as with the Matsigenka, Siona and Chiquitano) to more than ten (as with the Kógi, Arecuna and Taulipáng), shamanic apprenticeship comprises an extended period of isolation and instruction, coupled with numerous ordeals and disciplinary regimes. In effect, literal marginalization, sexual abstinence, emetically induced purgation and narcotically managed disruption to sleep and hygiene patterns reconstitute the shamanic novice as one who is to live and function at the personal and spiritual margins of everyday life. Yet, to borrow

a phrase, the shaman is an 'outsider within'. For the overwhelming role accorded supernatural causality entails that the shaman's place is thoroughly intertwined within the warp and woof of daily routine.

The Tapirapé, for example, hold shamanic activity to be central to biological reproduction, believing the shaman to be responsible for the safe transit from other realms of the souls of those newly conceived. Like many other indigenous communities, the Baniwa regard serious illness to be a direct result of spirit assault. Whether induced at the behest of other (usually shamanic) human beings or resulting from the breaking of any number of food, hygiene and social taboos, an attack by spirits can only be properly dealt with through recourse to one trained in the arts of the supernatural spheres. In addition to the almost daily routine of preventing, diagnosing or curing serious illness, the shaman is a focal point of communal festivals (such as harvest), rites of passage (such as female menarche and male coming of age), socio-economic reproduction (such as successful hunting) and political processes (such as assuaging internal discord or inter-tribal dispute). Differentiation of shamanic specialisms is a varying phenomenon among indigenous peoples. The Jívaro and Wakuénai distinguish two classes of shaman, whereas the Ishír, Winikina-Warao and Desana have three types. The grounds for such differentiation differ from tribe to tribe, with the most popular distinctions related to abilities to heal or injure, the frequenting of different supernatural realms or the relationship with particular spirits (often relative to the use of specific hallucinogenic agents).

Whatever his (the indigenous shaman is overwhelmingly male) title, role or place in society, the shaman executes his responsibilities by drawing upon a vast range of knowledge acquired through initiation, apprenticeship and practice. In addition to memorizing the structures of the numerous cosmic realms, the shaman must master the techniques of ecstasy, dream and vision through which other worlds are visited and the services of their supernatural inhabitants engaged. The shaman thereby provides a heavily ritualized service, the execution of which demands combining a vast cosmological knowledge with gruelling physical regimes, diagnostic lore with curative techniques and socio-economic practices with religious performance.

Central to successful shamanic practice are the alliances forged by the indigenous shaman with spiritual forces from other worlds. Generally occupying the higher strata of the cosmos, 'guardian spirits' serve as powerful allies to the shaman, offering protection from supernatural assault and information as to the probable causes of individual malady and social disturbance. Visiting their domains in person, a shaman communicates with his guardian spirits by transporting his soul through the media of naturally occurring, ritually induced and narcotically stimulated dreams, trances and visions. Complementing the overarching support of a particular shaman's set of guardian spirits may be any number of auxiliary spirits (principally of animals and plants). Resident within the shaman himself, auxiliary spirits play a diagnostic role, but come into their own as active agents in the curative techniques called upon in shamanic practice. The principal relationship between a shaman and his auxiliary spirits is one of mutually beneficial exchange. Here, the resident spirits get to enjoy whatever hallucinogenic agents are used in ritualized shamanic activity in return for their aid in resolving problems. In this instance narcotics such as tobacco and ayahuasca (*Banisteriopsis caapi*) are not simple hallucinogens but commodities of a highly ritualized exchange forming the central component by and around which other forms of shamanic performance (such as chant and dance) are ordered.

The shaman's ability to persuade, co-opt, suborn and manipulate agents of the spirit world, subsequently exploiting these alliances and relationships for the betterment of his community, furnishes a practical corollary to indigenous belief in widespread supernatural causality. Triadic in nature, shamanic activity is

● mimetic, in that its recapitulation of received tradition reappropriates for the present the powerful forces of primordial times;

● restorative, in that these forces align current practices with primeval order;

● creative, in that the correlation of past and present staves off disorder and assures futurity.

Integral to the indigenous world view, shamanic practice exemplifies indigenous existence as a nodal point through which a multiple configuration of mythico-religious forces write themselves upon human space-time.

CASE-STUDY 6:

Native North Americans

J.W.E. NEWBERY

A Plains shield cover showing the divided circle, a symbol of the twoness of life and nature.

Contrary to popular belief, indigenous religions are today reviving in many parts of the world. The superior attitude, which spread European civilization over the globe, spurred on by Western Christianity and materialism, has been discredited in the twentieth century. Native faith-ways – scorned, forbidden, almost destroyed – reached their lowest point at the end of the nineteenth century. Their flame was extinguished.

But today the disregard for the earth, for community, for spirituality, have brought the whole human enterprise into jeopardy. Arising like the phoenix from the ashes, tribal peoples are gathering again in their ceremonial circles, remembering discarded teachings, renewing the traditional ways. As they do so, perhaps they are laying the foundations for what they themselves are calling 'the fourth world', and a hope for a new beginning on the earth.

Life is one

Wisdom, for such people, is found in the past, in the long experience of the race, in tradition. A very frequent expression in their ceremonies is, 'it is said…' The teaching of the ancients is meant. The teachers are the Elders. They are closest to those things of the past that are important. For tribal people, life is one. The sacred is very real – and specially real in some times and places. But the sacred is not divided off from times and places called secular. All life is sacred. All things are 'indwelt' to some degree. The whole range of life is open to spirit.

The One Great Spirit

The tribal peoples of North America proclaim the One Great Spirit. Their thought and action is governed by the circle, which they see as basic in nature: the shape of moon and sun, the wheeling stars above them, the rotating seasons, the actions of birds and animals. 'Everything tries to be round.' This form is evident in everything they do – in myth, ceremony, art and community organization.

Essential to the circle is its centre. From that point it is created. This is the symbol of the Great Spirit. It is reflected in all the dances around the fire, drum or pole, and in ceremonies such as the sacred pipe.

Two realities

Tribal people also reflect upon the two-ness of life and nature. Native North Americans symbolize this by a divided circle, as in the Plains shields and many forms of art and craft.

Nature presents itself in pairs: dark and light, cold and hot, male and female, good and bad and so on. These are not contradictory but complementary. They are depicted in native North American shields as mirroring each other. This twoness is also expressed in the myths, such as that of the two sons of Mother Earth, in the totems of the west coast such as Sisutl of the Kwakiutl, the two-headed serpent which punishes and protects; in the Thunderbird, threatening and caring, or in ceremonies such as the forked pole of the Sundance.

But the *two* are always seen as aspects of the one: the circle. They are different, but they appear in balance, in *harmony*, the overriding virtue. Contentment is found not by conflict, but by coming to terms.

An example of this are the native Arctic-dwellers, the Inuit. Intruding whites complain about a harsh, cruel environment, and insist when they go north on taking with them all manner of technologies to beat the climate. The Inuit, on the other hand, live face to face with nature and, when untouched by the intruder, are happy. They have found harmony with their surroundings, and treat the ice and snow as friends, not enemies.

Threefold action

Give and take is the basis of all healthy relationships. It can be symbolized as a triangle on a circle.

Tribal people search for the support that will make their ventures succeed. This help is obtained in the *ceremonies*, whose action is three-sided. For example, a Mohawk community is threatened by drought. The corn withers in the fields. Help lies with the Thunderbeings; the rain must be sought by their aid. The thing to do is the rain dance. The community gathers in the fields. The drum and shaker sound. The dance begins. Prayer is sung. Water is sprinkled. The rains come.

'When we killed a buffalo, we knew what we were doing. We apologized to his spirit, tried to make him understand why we did it, honouring with a prayer the bones of those who gave their flesh to keep us alive, praying for their return, praying for the life of our brothers, the buffalo nation, as well as for our own people.'

John Lame Deer (Twentieth-century Sioux shaman).

NATIVE NORTH AMERICANS

The same give and take, between human need, heavenly power and particular action is found in all ceremonies for healing, guidance and power.

The four powers

Native peoples in North America, as elsewhere, tended to see the structure of the world, and of the powers that control it, as four-sided. The symbol they used for this is a circle, with four points on the circumference.

Lame Deer, a present-day Sioux, explains: 'Four is the number that is most sacred [*wakan*]. Four stands for the four quarters of the earth… the four winds… seasons… colours… four things of which the universe is made (earth, air, water, fire). There are four virtues which a man should possess… We Sioux do everything by fours…'

Into this structure of fours is gathered and classified all life's variety. It is made one (the circle) through the 'great law of sacrifice', in which each part depends upon and contributes to all the others. 'One dies that another may live.' The 'wheel' is the pattern of all ceremonies, because it symbolizes the variety of life in the wholeness of life.

This concept of unity in variety and variety within unity is basic to the goal of harmony and balance in life, seen by tribal people as the foundation of all health, peace and well-being in the world.

The seven 'Grandfathers'

A 'mystery of sevens' lies at the root of ancient wisdom and is found among indigenous cultures in all parts of the world. We find this same feeling about seven among the tribal people of North America. We hear of the seven sacred rites of the Sioux, the seven prophecies (or fires) of the Ojibwa Midewiwin and the seven stopping-places in their ages-long migration westward. We hear of cycles of seven years and seven-times-seven years, we hear of the seven Grandfathers.

The seven Grandfathers are found in Ojibwa mythology. They are symbolized in the teaching staff hung in the centre of the ceremonial circle. The staff is made up of three straight sticks bound together at their centres. These sticks have six points standing for the four directions, plus the 'above' power (sky) and the 'below' power (earth). There is a seventh, at the crossing-point.

It is the 'here' place of power, the *self*, the power within. This is not to say that the individual is the centre of all, but that all the powers are available to and are flowing through individuals. The powers come to them in visions and dreams, and work through them in teachings and ceremonies.

The quartered circle

Finally, there is the simple quartered circle, the symbol of wholeness. When taking part in the ceremonies, as the sweet grass is burned, the water drunk, the pipe smoked, one hears from each worshipper the words 'All my relations'. All are *related* to each and each to all. Participants are conscious that the whole universe is around them, sharing in their need and their prayer.

'Every object in the world has a spirit and that spirit is wakan. *Thus the spirits of the tree or things of that kind, while not like the spirit of man, are also* wakan. Wakan *comes from the* wakan *beings. These* wakan *beings are greater than mankind in the same way that mankind is greater than animals. They are never born and never die… Mankind can pray to the* wakan *beings for help… The word* Wakan Tanka *means all of the* wakan *beings because they are all as if one.* Wakan Tanka Kin *signifies the chief or leading* wakan *being which is the Sun. However, the most powerful of the* wakan *beings is Nagh Tanka, the great Spirit who is also Taku Skanskan.'*

Sword, a Dakota Native North American

CASE-STUDY 7:

Inuit

JAMES COX

Inuit cultures extend from the Pacific coast of Alaska to the Siberian and Alaskan sides of the Bering Sea and from there thousands of kilometres north and east along Canada's Arctic coast and into Labrador and Greenland. The population of the Inuit people within this vast region is put at around 125,000. (Many scholars persist in lumping Inuit peoples under the generic term 'Eskimo' – originally a term of ridicule meaning 'eaters of raw flesh'. The word 'inuit', which is used now as a term of self-designation, means 'real people'.) The Inuit claim a common ancestry in eastern Siberia and Asia, probably appearing in Alaska little more than 2,400 years ago, and spreading eastward rather rapidly. The Inuit economy was characterized by the manufacture of harpoons, skin clothing, oil lamps, and skin-covered boats (kayaks or umiaks), the Inuit hunting sea mammals along the coasts and seas or in more inland regions hunting caribou or fishing.

Despite the natural resources available to the Inuit, because of the extreme climate and in many places the barrenness of the land, a fragile relationship with nature existed. The people depended on their skill and ingenuity in hunting and fishing to ensure adequate supplies of food and materials. This tenuous relationship with the land explains why, in the traditional world view, life, spirit or soul (inua or personhood) was attributed to the animals and fish which provided the primary sources for sustenance. Spirits were thought also to inhabit the instruments used in hunting and fishing

An Ituko Inuit hunter in north-west Greenland with a seal caught in a net.

INUIT

and to be connected to the weather, particularly the winds blowing from the cardinal directions which brought quite distinct climatic conditions.

The shaman, who acted as a mediator between the spirit world and the human community, was the central religious practitioner. Some traditional stories relate that the world was originally thin and permeable, hardening since its creation by the mythic Raven and thus making communication between the human and spirit worlds more difficult. As the earth thickened, the need for shamans to cross over the boundaries between the spirit and human worlds became imperative. The role of the shaman was to gather under his control various spirits which could be utilized to ensure that the needs of the community were met. The shaman would go into a trance in rituals, often leave his body, travel to other worlds in the sky, such as the moon, or beneath the earth or under the sea, and return having persuaded the spirits of the animals or fish to cooperate during the annual hunting and fishing seasons.

Inuit indigenous religions were suppressed in many parts of the circumpolar region, under the anti-superstition programme of the former Soviet Union, under the direction of government-appointed missionary teachers in Alaska and since the eighteenth century by Danish missionaries in Greenland. In some places Inuit culture was virtually eradicated, including language and of course the practice of shamanism. Today, a revival of Inuit culture is occurring in some areas, with younger people learning the indigenous languages, participating in traditional dances and affirming cultural values such as honouring elders, fostering a reciprocal relationship with animals and re-establishing subsistence patterns of life.

'Subsistence is our spiritual way of life, our culture.'

Old Inuit woman testifying to Canadian Judge Thomas Berger

'The single biggest fear that we Inuit have is the fear of losing control of our own lands.'

Jimmy Stotts, Inuit from Barrow, Alaska

CASE-STUDY 8:

Norse Shamanism

VEIKKO ANTTONEN

Shamanism is a socio-religious system in which a religious functionary called 'shaman' plays a central role. Shamans have ritual mastery over spirits, which are believed to inhabit human beings and nature. They are skilled practitioners of a technique which induces a state of trance in order to create a connection between the human and the non-human worlds. In short, 'shaman' is the name given to the specialist in spirits whose domain of expertise comprises both the visible and the invisible world.

Shamanism is practised in small-scale societies in which hunting and agriculture are dominant forms of subsistence. As a cultural phenomenon, shamanism is most commonly associated with the traditions of the Arctic and Subarctic zones and of Central and East Asia. In the geographical area of so-called classical shamanism in the Eurasian north, from Greenland to the Bering Straits, in the Arctic and Subarctic zones, the shaman is a person who possesses the necessary technical competence, traditional knowledge and psychic tendency to go into an ecstatic trance and establish contact with the spirit world (as defined by the particular religion). By falling into a trance and separating the spirit from the corporeal body, the shaman is believed to cure the sick, escort the souls of the dead to the underworld, foretell the future, and transcend time and space as well as the boundaries between the living and the non-living, in order to find something lost or to assist hunters in tracking down prey.

Bronze Age petroglyphs of a solar chariot, near Brastad, Sweden.

In Old Norse the term *seidr* was used to denote witchcraft. In Norse shamanism *seidr* can denote both natural rock or stone formations and man-made wooden columns around which ritual actions are organized. Most *seidr* objects are stone formations, erratic boulders, weathered rocks or conspicuous, anthropomorphic stones on the banks of a river or a lake. Salient natural features and locations have been perceived as boundaries, edges, crossroads, openings and fissures: as places where a channel from this world to the other can be opened up. Places which shamans employ to exit and re-enter the world of ordinary reality are holes and openings in the ground, caves, and fissures between rocks.

Seidr stones contain cracks, hollows, excrescences and flat 'shelves' caused by weathering. These have functioned as altars, on which reindeer, deer and fish were sacrificed. Likewise the indigenous Saami gods were believed to have their abode on the *seidr*. The *seidr* sacrificial sites were closely connected with economies based on reindeer pastoralism, hunting and fishing. Depending on the specific location in the territory of the individual Saami groups, observances at the *seidr* sites were performed either by several reindeer-herding communities (*sii'dâ*), by members of a family or by individuals. The motif of the world tree (*Yggdrasil*) is a salient feature, which is represented in shamanistic practices not only among the peoples of the North, but also among the ancient Germanic tribes. A mythical world tree was believed by some to support the heavens.

'Culture is man's major mode of adaptation at the same time that culture alters, and to a degree provides, the ecological situation to which we adapt; and religion, as a part of culture, is one kind of cultural adaptation, and a rather special one. All the religions, perhaps, began as crisis cults, the response of society to problems the contemporary culture failed to resolve.'

Weston LaBarre

NORSE SHAMANISM

CASE-STUDY 9:

African Indigenous Religions

JAMES COX

The continent of Africa covers over 11.5 million square miles (30 million square kilometres) and has a population of over 700 million. The diversity of religions in such a vast region is immense and extremely complex. Islam has been present in most of North Africa since the seventh and eighth centuries CE and, following the spread of European colonialism in the eighteenth and nineteenth centuries, Christianity has been growing rapidly throughout the sub-Saharan regions. As a result, it is accurate to say that no 'indigenous' religion exists in Africa today, if we mean by the term 'indigenous' that which is original, archaic or unchanging.

In fact, the religious expressions of African peoples have always been dynamic, changing just as societies have changed, and taking different forms as contact is made with other African peoples and as economic modes and power structures have evolved. Indigenous, therefore, is not a term referring to some original African religiosity: it designates what we are able to know historically about the religious life and practices of particular African societies prior and subsequent to extensive encounters with Islam and the colonial West, and through a study of those practices which persist among contemporary African peoples. The indigenous religions of Africa thus are known through a wide combination of methodologies including the study of historic documents, analysis of oral traditions, archaeological evidence, phenomenological classifications and anthropological fieldwork.

Characteristics of African indigenous religions

Although wide variations exist, most scholars of African indigenous religions have identified eight characteristics that practitioners hold in common, particularly those living in the sub-Saharan regions.

● Because African indigenous religions are coextensive with their societies and based largely on kinship relationships, religion cannot be separated from other cultural practices. Society, in its widest sense, is thought to include not only the living, but what the community understands to be a variety of spiritual forces, foremost the ancestors.

● The impossibility of segregating the religious from the social means that to outsiders the visibility of African indigenous religions is low. What people in the West typically regard as secular, such as planting and harvesting crops, is connected closely to religious understandings in Africa.

● The multi-stranded nature of thought that is used to explain misfortunes, illnesses and catastrophes, which commonly afflict communities, can appear unsystematic and unanalytical to an outsider. For example, if the remedy prescribed by a traditional healer or diviner fails, other diviners are consulted, who may offer quite opposing solutions. Sometimes explanations relate to violations of social norms that occurred long before the present generation was alive and thus cannot be remembered by the living. These ways of resolving human crises are not thought by the participants to be irrational, since the multi-stranded nature of thought means that many (apparently contradictory) explanations are believed and acted on at the same time.

● Rituals are performed primarily to guarantee tangible benefits in this life only. African indigenous religions are pragmatic, concerning themselves with securing and maintaining largely material advantages, which promote the well-being of the community as a whole. Communication with a variety of spirits in rituals is intended to achieve this end.

● Reciprocity between the community and the spirits defines the primary way such tangible benefits are acquired and maintained. Generally this means that the community must provide gifts to the spirits, usually in the form of sacrificed animals, as a sign of respect and remembrance. In return the spirits provide protection and material gains for the community.

● Beliefs are not articulated, but remain implicit. Hence, there are no doctrines, theologies, claims to truth or factional disputes between sects. African indigenous religions are non-missionary in their intent.

● African indigenous religions readily adopt ideas, beliefs and practices from other religions. They have an open mind, importing their deities and rituals readily and integrating them into their own complex systems.

● African indigenous religions are adaptive. They are able to accommodate to new factors, including modernization. In the modern religious scene in Africa, most believers have expanded their original religious perspectives to include that of an imported religion, usually Christianity or Islam. The widespread popularity of African-founded churches, often referred to as African Independent or African-initiated Churches, confirms the process of adaptation of traditional beliefs and practices to missionary religions.

The content of African indigenous religions

Although it is possible to outline the substantive features or general content of the religiosity of African peoples, summarized in the following six points, it must be kept in mind that these do not constitute a coherent doctrinal system or a kind of 'African systematic theology'.

● Reality is regarded as dynamic. Centres of power are located in natural phenomena, animals and humans. Some societies may acknowledge one source of power behind these, but the overriding concern is to ensure that such power enhances the quality of human life, rather than diminishing it. An example of the positive use of power is when ancestors provide ample rain to ensure the abundance of crops and the health of the cattle. Witchcraft is always identified with a power that diminishes the quality of a community's life.

● African indigenous religions can be called a form of humanism, because religious activity focuses on how positive benefits for society can be enhanced. Forces seen as spiritual, whether deities, ancestor spirits or nature spirits, are understood primarily in connection with their ability to guarantee human well-being.

● This humanism is a communal humanism and is not individualistic. Fulfilment comes for individuals as they participate in family and community relationships.

● Because religion focuses on communal well-being, Africans are concerned with the present moment and not with a future existence after death. There is no sense of the past

'The African is notoriously religious.'
J.S. Mbiti, Kenyan theologian

AFRICAN INDIGENOUS RELIGIONS

moving through the present to some future event; the past and the future find their meaning in the present. Hence, distance from the present is more important than the direction time takes.

● Maintaining good health defines a dominant concern for African societies. When good health fails, methods for healing must be identified and employed. Healing has to do with the preservation and/or restoration of human vitality in the context of the community as a whole. Ultimately, health depends on right human relationships and harmony with the spirit world, particularly the ancestors.

● The fundamental concerns of African societies with health and well-being are expressed primarily through ritual activity. Festivals, feasts, dances and artistic expressions celebrate communal existence, both of the living and the dead.

Characteristics and content exemplified

Taken together, the characteristics of African indigenous religions and the basic content within the African way of life lead to the following core definition:

African indigenous religions are localized, kinship-based, non-missionary religions with inarticulate, multi-stranded and pragmatic beliefs aimed at securing optimal material health for the community, primarily through ritual activity.

This definition is exemplified vividly by an interview the present author conducted in Zimbabwe in 1992 with a traditional healer and diviner (*n'anga*). In this case, the *n'anga* was a woman of about fifty who was the chosen medium of the spirit of her deceased father.

When the interview began, the *n'anga* was seated outside her hut with her daughter and granddaughter, wearing a simple dress and a sweater. She explained that the people in the region come to her with many different problems such as sickness, poor crops, death, infertility and problems at school. She indicated that her deceased father speaks to them through her and tells them why they are having problems and what to do about it. She started doing this about three years before, following a long illness no one had been able to cure. During a special ritual prescribed by a *n'anga* she became possessed by her father. She recovered completely. Since then, she has helped other people.

A series of questions then seemed to confuse her. When asked how her father takes control of her, she replied simply: 'He does.' Asked if her father (as an ancestor spirit) has special knowledge that he did not have when he was alive and whether he was in communication with other ancestors, she began to appear uncomfortable, turning away and shaking a little. Further questions followed: 'Does your father carry messages to higher ancestor spirits, and even to God? Do any people come to you who are victims of witchcraft?' The woman muttered something to her daughter, let out a very loud belch and began to shake. Her daughter announced that she was now possessed and needed to put on her clothes. They then entered the nearby hut from which a deep voice could be heard asking, 'Who are these people? Why are they asking my daughter such hard questions?'

The *n'anga* returned from the hut no longer dressed in simple village attire, but wearing a skirt of animal skins, a hat of eagle feathers, a black cloth draped over her shoulders and

Traditional practitioners in bright traditional dress dance vigorously to drive the power of a spirit from Gemsbokspruit village, South Africa.

around her waist. She had rattles tied on the side of her legs. She was holding a dark walking stick, about three feet (a metre) in length with designs on the top. She walked with heavy steps, like a man, and spoke in a deep voice. She was then asked the same questions that had been posed earlier. The reply was: 'These are questions that cannot be answered.' Then a practical problem was raised and the atmosphere suddenly became quite relaxed. The present writer indicated that he had lost his wallet somewhere in his travels around the region. He asked if the woman, now possessed and acting as the medium for her father's spirit, could help to retrieve it.

What followed was a dramatic presentation and explanation. The medium said that on the way to the Chief's home, at a local shop, someone in the crowd spotted the wallet and said to himself: 'Ah, *murungu* (white person)! I will be rich.' He slipped the wallet out of the back pocket and left the shop. When he looked in the wallet, however, he was extremely disappointed, because there was very little money in it. He threw it in some red soil beside the road. Another person came along and spotted it. He also thought, 'Ah, I will be rich!' When he found no money in it, he threw it back into the red soil. That is what happened, said the spirit medium, and the wallet will never be found. During the whole time that she was telling this story, she was acting it out. She showed how the man had slipped the wallet out of the back pocket, how he hurriedly left the shop, how he opened it and expressed disappointment before throwing it by the road. When the medium finished, she sat down again with her legs crossed like a man. She then stood up and announced: 'I am returning to a mountain near Great Zimbabwe.' At that, the woman re-entered the hut, appearing shortly afterward in her simple dress and sweater. When asked if she remembered being possessed by her father, she said she did not remember anything.

For the spirit medium, the purpose of the possession had nothing to do with revealing knowledge of the other world or with constructing a systematic diagram of the relationships between ancestor spirits. Its purpose was entirely practical, to alter directly the enquirer's experience, if possible, in favour of health and well-being. This does not mean that her reactions to the analytical questions posed were simplistic; indeed, she illustrated the type of rationality characteristic of the indigenous religions of Zimbabwe. Her responses were pragmatic, concerned with the present, never speculative in a cosmological sense, and employed the spirit world only to influence experience in the here-and-now material existence.

Conclusion

If the definition of African indigenous religions presented and exemplified in this article accurately captures their essence, we would expect to detect these emphases to a lesser or greater extent in all forms of African religions, including Christianity and Islam. By identifying these central characteristics and core elements, therefore, the student of religions in Africa is provided with key concepts for analysing the multiple, complex and often bewildering expressions of religion found throughout this immense and culturally diverse continent.

CASE-STUDY 10:

The Bangwa

FIONA BOWIE

The Bangwa of Lebialem Division, South-West Province, Cameroon, occupy a mountainous region that stretches from the grassfield plateau of Eastern and North-West Provinces, to the Cross-River Basin in the south-west. An entrepreneurial people with origins both in the lowland forest zone and the grassfields, they have linguistic, cultural and historical links to surrounding groups. Evidence from ancestral skulls suggests that most of those who belong to one of the nine Bangwa chiefdoms (or 'villages') settled in the mountains during the eighteenth century, intermarrying with resident pygmoid people known as the 'owners of the land' (Beketshe). The Bangwa are traders as well as farmers and hunters. European contact was first made at the beginning of the twentieth century, and there has been a permanent mission presence in Lebang (Fontem), the largest of the Bangwa villages, since the mid-1960s.

Traditional religious practices focus on *belem* (sing. *ndem*), used to translate both 'gods' and 'ancestors'. There is a hierarchy of sacred places (*fuandem*), such as waterfalls or other natural features, where a chief or sub-chief makes offerings for the fertility and well-being of the land. Most people live in scattered compounds (extended family homes), the larger of which will have a 'house' (*ndia ndem*) for the household or threshold god or gods (*ndem bo*), at which a compound head can make offerings of food and drink on behalf of his family. Ancestral skulls are exhumed and kept by a man's successor and, less formally, women's skulls might pass to women. They are kept in a special house in the compound and are 'fed' and consulted about important decisions using various forms of divination.

The Nweh language makes no distinction between witches, sorcerers, animal and spirits (*lekang*). Everyone has a witch animal or spirit in the stomach that remains dormant unless sent out either consciously or unconsciously. Chiefs and other powerful individuals can use their ability to transform themselves into wild animals through witchcraft to confront their enemies or fight other witches.

Around 10 per cent of the population of Lebialem are baptized Christians, mostly Roman Catholics. Many Bangwa now live outside their home area in the larger towns of Cameroon, in Europe and the USA, most regarding themselves as Christian. The first-generation emigrants retain strong emotional and kinship links with their home villages and value their language and culture. Both Christians and non-Christians take the performance of traditional ceremonies, such as the wake (or 'cry die') very seriously, and will try to travel back to their natal or parental villages for a funeral celebration. Polygyny remains common and, in terms of Church membership, problematic. Because of their marital status, many fervent Christians cannot be baptized or are excommunicants, while the widespread baptism of children in mission schools produces what are disparagingly referred to as 'baptized pagans'. What we see with the Bangwa is a people bringing their traditional world view into their Christian practice and vice versa in a dynamic and creative process of transformation.

Bangwa carved post, Azi Palace, Lebang, Cameroon.

THE BANGWA

CASE-STUDY 11:

The Zulu

AXEL-IVAR BERGLUND

Recent studies on African traditional beliefs have shown quite convincingly that African ideas and religious convictions are not primitive in an evolutionistic sense. Nor are they 'backward' and without sense. Quite the contrary! Thoughts and beliefs, expressed in rituals and in life-attitudes, make sense and are fully logical, if they are seen from the angle of those who live these thought-patterns.

Zulu, who live on the east coast of South Africa and belong to the Nguni family of Bantu-speaking people, are a good illustration of how an African traditional religion can adapt and accommodate itself to new ideas and symbols.

Traditional healers, or diviners, have become popular once again among both urban and rural Zulus. A rural Sangoma priest gives a diagnosis to an elderly man suffering from stroke-like symptoms. Kwabaadaza, Kwa-zulu, Natal, South Africa.

The Lord-of-the-Sky

Early literature on Zulu religious ideas, dating back some 100 years, seems to indicate that Zulu of that time hardly entertained thoughts of a god in the sky. The preoccupation was with the shades.

Due chiefly to the presence of, and challenge by, Christian missions, there has developed among traditional Zulu an idea of the Lord-of-the-Sky, *iNkosi yezulu*.

This Lord is believed to be the eternal from whom flows power and might. The Lord-of-the-Sky is the source of both good and evil, is both kind and generous, but also erratic and unpredictable. In times of crisis such as drought or childlessness, Zulus turn to him; but he also sends lightning that will strike 'the one he wants to be his slave up there in heaven'. He will cause barrenness 'because the woman has irritated him, sometimes by talking too much, sometimes because the Lord-of-the-Sky is fretful'.

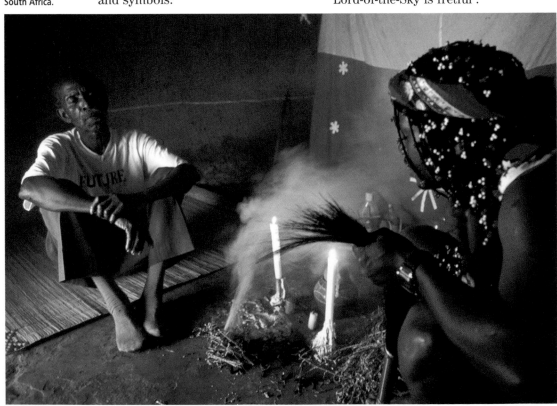

The chameleon is linked with the Lord-of-the-Sky. It, too, is unpredictable. It continually changes colour! It has five legs (the tail is said to be a leg because it coils around branches), and has eyes that look in different directions at the same time! 'How could such a thing as a chameleon be created? There can be no sympathy with the one that made such a creature as this.'

Although the Lord-of-the-Sky can be approached, he must be avoided lest you become insane. Only on special occasions should he be approached, and only after long preparation. Certain well-known hills in Zululand are recognized as his. On these no cattle graze, and people rarely ascend them.

'Only when we plead for rain will we go up this mountain. First there must be fasting and much prayer. When everybody is ready and the set day arrives, we gather at the foot of the hill. Everybody is quiet. We climb with awe, looking down and walking humbly. Then prayer is offered by the rain-doctor. We kneel or lie down when he speaks to the Lord-of-the-Sky. When he has finished we return, without speaking. We do not talk, for the one in whose presence we are is fearful.'

The brooding shades

In the lives of the Zulu people the shades play an all-important role. But in times of crisis the shades brood over their descendants 'as a hen broods over her chickens'. The chief occasions are childbirth, puberty, marriage, death and burial. Diviners are constantly brooded over by the shades, but because they 'eat the right medicines, they do not become mad. All other people would have gone mad long ago, if they had been in the same situation.'

When a hen broods over her eggs, the chickens eventually hatch.

Likewise the brooding of the shades heralds the emergence of a different person.

'It is like this. There is the bride. She is one kind of person. At marriage, when the shades brood, she becomes another person. She is now the wife. When they brood again, she changes from the childless to the mother of a child.'

A world reversed

Zulu diviners claim they see things upside down. Shades are believed to be pale-coloured; in the world of the shades, dark stands for light and light for dark. Shades are said to like gall 'because gall to them is sweet as honey'. People work during daytime, the shades are active at night. The right hand is left, and the left is right in the world of the shades. So diviners, servants of the shades, often use the left hand when divining. Up stands for down and down for up!

These reversals and opposites make sense in the context of a flat earth viewpoint (and the global concept is, after all, relatively recent, even in Europe). If Zululanders believe we live on top of a pancake-like world, it follows that those who live on the other side are opposite. On the top, people walk with their heads upward and feet downward; in the underworld they move upside down.

When it is night on top it is daytime underneath! Hence people were buried at night, not to avoid the grave-site being known to thieves and evil-minded people, but so that the deceased can reach the land of the dead 'at a time when he can see in this new country'.

'A man may suffer from his mother's discipline, but a Zulu son would never accuse his mother of bewitching him. And although some modern Zulu men have accused their fathers of witchcraft, this is regarded as a sign of the degeneration of modern times.'

Geoffrey Parrinder

THE ZULU

Hinduism

A Historical Overview

MAYA WARRIER

The term 'Hinduism' as we understand it today refers to the majority religion of the Indian subcontinent. The present understanding of Hinduism as a world religion, has come about only since the nineteenth century, when Hindu reformers and Western orientalists came to refer to the diverse beliefs and practices characterizing religious life in South Asia as 'Hinduism'. Hinduism has no single historical founder, no unified system of belief, no single doctrine of salvation and no centralized authority. In this sense, it is different from other 'world religions'. Diversity is a characteristic feature of Hinduism, yet most scholars would agree that there are unifying strands that run through the diverse traditions that constitute it. Although the term Hinduism is recent, the diverse traditions that it encompasses have very ancient origins that extend back beyond the second millennium BCE.

The Indus Valley civilization
The earliest traces of Hinduism can be found in the Indus Valley civilization which flourished from 2500 to about 1500 BCE along the banks of the River Indus, which flows through present-day Pakistan. Archaeological excavations in this area have revealed evidence of what appears to be a highly developed urban culture with sophisticated water distribution, drainage and garbage disposal technologies and well-developed systems of farming, grain-storage and pottery. Little is known about the religion of this civilization. The large number of terracotta figurines unearthed through excavations suggest a continuity between the iconographic features of these images and those of such later Hindu deities as Shiva and the mother goddess. Given the lack of systematic evidence for such continuity, however, scholars are inclined to be cautious. Archaeological evidence suggests that the Indus Valley civilization declined rather suddenly between 1800 and 1700 BCE, perhaps because of flooding or inadequate rainfall.

The Aryans and early Vedic society
What followed is a matter of considerable controversy. Some maintain that the Indus Valley civilization came to be replaced by the culture of the Aryans, Indo-European invaders or migrants from the Caucuses region, who moved south and settled in the Indian subcontinent. Others believe

the Aryan civilization developed from within the Indus Valley culture and was not introduced from outside. Whether Aryans came from outside the subcontinent or not, the history of Hinduism as we understand it today is the history of the next 2,000 years of Aryan culture, often interacting with, but always dominating over, non-Aryan cultures in the area.

The language of the Aryans was Sanskrit. Knowledge of the early Aryans derives primarily from early Sanskrit compositions, the Vedas, a corpus of texts compiled over hundreds of years. Many Hindus today regard the Vedas as timeless revelation and repository of all knowledge, seeing these texts as a crucial marker of Hindu identity. The Vedas constitute the foundation for most later developments in Hinduism.

The earliest Vedas were mainly liturgical texts used primarily in ritual. The Vedic rituals were rituals of sacrifice addressed to such early gods as Agni (the fire god) and Soma (the plant god). The central act was the offering of substances (often animals, but also such items as milk, clarified butter, grain and the hallucinogenic soma plant) into the sacrificial fire. The ritual was usually initiated by a wealthy sponsor (*yajamana*) and conducted by ritual specialists. These specialists were the most highly ranked in Vedic society which followed a fourfold system of hierarchical classification. Below the priests or ritual specialists (Brahmans) came the warriors or rulers (Kshatriyas), followed by the commoners (Vaishyas). These three classes (*varna*) were known as 'twice-born' (*dvija*) because their male members underwent initiation which confirmed their status as full members of society. This initiation rite separated them from a fourth class, the servants (Shudras), who because of their 'low' status were debarred from perpetuating Vedic ritual traditions.

In due course Aryan culture came to be well established in northern India. Brahmanical ideology became central to social and political life and was concerned with the ritual status and

Brahman procession in Chidambaram, India.

duties of the king, the maintaining of social order and the regulation of individual behaviour in accordance with the all-encompassing ideology of duty or righteousness (*dharma*). Dharmic ideology related to ritual and moral behaviour and defined good conduct according to such factors as one's class (*varna*) and one's stage of life (*ashrama*). It operated simultaneously at several levels: the transcendental and therefore eternal (*sanatana dharma*), the everyday (*sadharana dharma*) and the individual and personal (*svadharma*). Neglecting *dharma* was believed to lead to undesirable social as well as personal consequences.

The later Vedic Period

Alongside the performance of Vedic ritual, speculation arose about its meaning and purpose. These speculations were developed in the later Vedic texts – the *Aranyakas* and *Upanishads* – which tended to see the observance of ritual action as secondary to the gaining of spiritual knowledge. Central to this approach was the *karma-samsara-moksha* doctrine:

● all beings are reincarnated into the world (*samsara*) over and over again;

● the results of action (*karma*) are reaped in future lives;

● this process of endless rebirth is characterized by suffering (*dukkha*);

● liberation (*moksha*) from this suffering can be obtained through minimizing action and gaining spiritual knowledge.

Gaining spiritual knowledge thus came to assume central importance and the self-disciplining and methods of asceticism necessary for gaining it were developed in Hinduism's traditions of yoga and world renunciation. Ascetic groups known as strivers (*sramanas*)

Intricate carvings cover the exterior of Kapaleeshwara Temple, Madras, India.

'Hinduism is a living organism liable to growth and decay and subject to the laws of nature. One and indivisible at the root, it has grown into a vast tree with innumerable branches.'

Mahatma Ghandi

were formed during this period, seeking liberation through austerity. Buddhism and Jainism, both of which rejected the authority of the Vedas, originated in these groups. Whereas monastic institutions developed in Buddhism from its inception, similar institutions appeared within the Hindu pale only later, possibly in the eighth and ninth centuries CE when according

The last episode of the 'Mahabharata' depicted in a Kamasan-style painting by Nyoman Mandra, 1990s, Indonesia.

to Hindu belief the theologian Shankara (c. CE 788–820) founded monastic centres in the four corners of India and instituted the first renunciatory order of the Dasanamis.

Alongside early Hinduism's elaboration of systems of ritual and its teachings about liberation/salvation involving yoga and meditation, there developed highly sophisticated philosophical systems, the *darshanas*, comprising mainly Samkhya and Yoga, Mimamsa and Vedanta, and Nyaya and Vaisheshika. These in turn generated a multitude of metaphysical positions, and traditions of rigorous philosophical debate, within the parameters of Vedic revelation and the doctrine of liberation. One of the most important of these Indian philosophical traditions today is the philosophy of non-dualism (*advaita vedanta*), propounded by Shankara, the most famous of Indian philosopher-theologians.

Devotionalism and sectarian worship

Through much of the first millennium CE, sectarian worship of particular deities grew and flourished in India. Vedic sacrifice came to be increasingly marginalized, giving way (though never disappearing completely) to devotional worship or *puja*. *Puja* is a ritual expression of love or devotion (*bhakti*) to a deity, often a personal god or goddess with whom the devotee establishes an intense and intimate relationship. Corresponding to the growth of Hindu theism and devotionalism, Sanskrit narrative traditions grew and flourished, the most important of which were the Hindu epics or *itihasas* (the *Ramayana* and the *Mahabharata*), the Puranas (devotional texts containing among other things mythological stories about the gods and goddesses and treatises on ritual worship) and devotional poetry in several Indian regional languages, most notably Tamil. One of the most important developments at this time was the composition of the *Bhagavad Gita*, the 'Song of the Lord' contained in the *Mahabharata*. This work, perhaps the most famous of the Hindu scriptures, expresses in narrative form the concerns of Hindu orthodoxy: the importance of *dharma*, responsible action and the maintenance of social order and stability, combined with the importance of devotion to the transcendent as a personal god.

Temple cities grew and flourished in this period, serving not only as commercial and administrative hubs of kingdoms, but as ritual centres with the temple located at the heart of the town and, therefore, of the kingdom. Kings sought to derive legitimacy for their rule through their royal patronage of these ritual sites, dedicated to one or the other of the major Puranic deities. Large temple complexes stood testimony to a king's dharmic rule over his kingdom, which was often modelled on the ideal of divine kingship symbolized by the great god Vishnu. Sectarian devotional groups emerged dedicated to the worship of Vishnu (*Vaishnavas*), Shiva (*Shaivas*) and the goddess Devi (*Shaktas*).

Hinduism during British colonial rule

The above theistic traditions continued to flourish, to lesser or greater degrees, through much of the following period, when large sections of the Indian subcontinent were conquered and ruled by Muslim rulers. The rule of the last Muslim emperor in India came to an end in the eighteenth century, and British forces, initially in the form of the East India Company and later the British crown, stepped in to assume power. By the middle of the eighteenth century, British power was at its peak. Hindu traditions, which had tended to be relatively insular in the intervening period, now responded actively to the British and, more importantly, Christian presence in their midst. Hindu reform movements arose, led by such figures of historical significance as Ram Mohan Roy (1772–1883), Dayananda Sarasvati (1824–83) and Vivekananda (1863–1902), all seeking to restore the perceived glory of Hinduism's ancient past. It was at this time that Hinduism came to be defined in the terms by which we understand it today – a world religion with a distinct identity. These reform movements, often collectively referred to as the Hindu renaissance, absorbed Christianity's rationalist elements and paid particular attention to social and ethical concerns. Most of these movements were closely linked with the increasingly strident Indian nationalist movement, which brought about the end of British colonial rule and established India as an independent nation state in 1947.

Religious nationalism in contemporary India

Though India defined itself as a secular state on gaining independence, it has experienced a resurgence of religious nationalism, particularly since the 1980s. Hindutva, the ideology of Hindu nationalists, manifests itself today as an organized and militant form of religious supremacism whose proponents call for the setting up of a Hindu Raj – a state in which civic rights, nationhood and national culture would be defined by Hinduism. The politicized, activist religious nationalism of the present has considerable precedent in various movements of organized Hinduism which arose in British India. Today the Sangh Parivar, a so-called 'family' of social and political organizations, works to propagate Hindutva, with its political wing, the Bharatiya Janata Party (BJP), winning enough support in India's general elections in 1999 to head a five-year coalition government.

Among the most significant acts of religious violence in recent times was the destruction of the Babri mosque in Ayodhya in 1992, by supporters of Hindutva demanding the setting up of a temple dedicated to the Hindu deity Rama at the site, which they believe to be Rama's birthplace. There have been several incidents of violence and rioting between Hindus and Muslims precipitated by this temple–mosque controversy. Hindu supporters of the highly organized campaigns of violence justify these by arguing that Muslim rulers destroyed Hindu temples in the past, thereby damaging Hindu pride. They see incidents like the demolition of the Babri mosque as crucial for recovering a sense of Hindu dignity and asserting Hindu pride.

Hinduism beyond India's frontiers

Running counter to these narrowly chauvinist and violently exclusivist forms of Hinduism, other forms of Hindu belief and practice have emerged which adopt a more inclusive, universal orientation, emphasizing values such as social justice, peace and the spiritual transformation of humanity. Some recent manifestations of Hinduism, especially in the form of Indian gurus addressing Western and/or multicultural audiences, have transcended nationalistic boundaries in their teaching and philosophy. Hinduism has also transcended national boundaries in another sense. While Hinduism has long flourished beyond the Indian subcontinent in places such as Java and Bali, in the last century the Hindu diaspora has spread markedly, establishing communities in host cultures across the globe. This geographical transcendence of boundaries does not always parallel ideological dispositions and orientations, however. Religious nationalism often strikes deep roots in diaspora communities, such that India as a geographical entity comes to be perceived in the imagination of Hindus abroad as their sacred or holy land, which they identify with conceptions of a Hindu religious polity and therefore a Hindu nation state.

Philosophy

TINU RUPARELL

Hindu philosophy, the oldest continuing tradition of Indian thought, stretches back to sacred texts written 900–400 BCE known as the *Upanishads* (literally 'to sit beneath', as at the feet of a teacher). These texts are reflections on the deeper meaning of the rites, hymns and ritual prescriptions found in earlier Vedic writings. However, they were soon regarded as a genre of Vedic literature in their own right and it is here that we first encounter a developed theory of *karma* (action, making; law of cause and effect) and *moksha* (liberation from the cycle of rebirth).

The *astika* schools

Hindu philosophy developed through debate between schools of Hindu thought and, importantly, with Jain, Carvaka (materialist) and Buddhist thinkers. During the classical period of Hindu philosophy (100 BCE to CE 1000) the six *astika* schools ('orthodox' in accepting Vedic authority) condensed and cemented their distinctive views. These are usually paired:

● Purva-mimamsa – Vedanta

● Samkhya – Yoga

● Nyaya – Vaisheshika

It should be noted that these pairings bring together a larger number of schools and are less to do with Indian philosophical schools themselves and more the result of the way Indian thought has been studied in the West since the nineteenth century.

Central presuppositions

While it greatly oversimplifies historical Indian thought to impute consensus, it is useful to isolate a few central notions which serve as building blocks for the six 'orthodox' philosophical perspectives (*darshanas*) above. A key philosophical question in Indian thought, addressing, among other issues, being (ontology), knowledge (epistemology), morality (ethics), God (theology) and even beauty (aesthetics) is 'Who are we?' To understand the various responses, we need to consider three central presuppositions of Hindu thought:

● the cyclical nature of time

● an essential connection between micro-cosmic and macrocosmic levels of reality

● a principle of causality

In Hindu philosophy the universe has neither beginning nor end. It issued forth from *Brahman* (the ultimate, divine 'ground of Being') and will eventually return to *Brahman*, only to repeat the cycle again. If time itself revolves in an endless cycle, then all of creation also exists in a cyclical way. So life is followed by death, giving rise to a new life and so on. This cycle of birth and rebirth (*samsara*) is deducible from any observation of the natural world and is an example of how events at the microcosmic level of individual lives, seasons and generations are seen to be intimately connected to the macrocosmic level of the great ages of history (*yugas*), the cosmic creations and dissolutions and indeed time itself. Furthermore, the causal principle of *karma* connects each event in *samsara*, so that events in this cycle affect events in subsequent cycles, just as they themselves are already affected by events in previous cycles. Time, causality and the micro–macrocosm are linked: what one does and how one chooses has a necessary, if miniscule, effect on the entire universe.

Dharma and moksha

The three presuppositions inform two other primary concepts: *dharma* and *moksha*.

● *Dharma* ('to uphold') is understood to be the moral and metaphysical foundation of the universe. Acting in accordance with one's *dharma* (which is not always easy to determine) connects one's activities and life to one's social structure and environment. Fulfilling one's dharmic duties is necessary but not sufficient for *moksha*.

An eighteenth-century Indian miniature depicting a yogi sitting cross-legged on an animal skin.

● To attain *moksha* (ultimate liberation, the goal of human existence) is to attain complete freedom from the samsaric cycle of birth and rebirth and all of the dissatisfaction, suffering and death – as well as the joys and pleasures – which go with it.

The Samkhya–Yoga school sees *moksha* as one's return, through yogic discipline, to an original, blissful state of pure spirit (*purusha*) separated from matter (*prakriti*). For the Nyaya–Vaisheshika school, more interested in logical reasoning and the right understanding of reality, *moksha* is gained through right understanding of the universe and of one's real nature as a simple collection of material and non-material qualities: it means returning to an undifferentiated state of being, free from change and suffering (a vision harshly criticized by the Mimamsa–Vedanta school, which compared it to the existence of a stone). This last school saw *moksha* as the fulfilment of one's dharmic duty, resulting in the cessation of rebirth and the realization of one's true relationship with *Brahman*.

A continuing debate

Only Vedanta now commands a large following. Of the dozen or so Vedantic schools, three are of particular interest:

● *Advaita* (non-dualism)

● *Vishishtadvaita* (non-dualism of particulars)

● *Dvaita* (dualism)

> *'The wise call him a man of learning whose every activity is free from desire and specific intention; his actions are consumed in the fire of knowledge.'*
>
> Bhagavad Gita 4:19

The great Hindu philosopher–saint Shankara (c. CE 788–820) expounded an austerely non-dualistic (*advaita*) system. In his short life he established monasteries in the four corners of India and a monastic order of ten divisions and was held by some of his followers to be an incarnation of the Hindu deity Shiva. He has had inordinate influence on modern Hinduism through such Neo-Vedantic exponents as Dayananda Sarasvati (1824–83), Swami Vivekananda (1863–1902) and even Gandhi (1869–1948). *Advaita* holds that one's true self (*atman*) is literally identical to *Brahman*. Whereas Judaism, Christianity and Islam are dualistic, maintaining a strong distinction between God and the human soul, between God and the world and between the individual and the world, for Shankara's *advaita vedanta* all is one and any perceived dualism is the result of ignorance. We are working within a beguiled interpretation (*maya*) of the world, but through hearing and study of the Vedas (particularly the *Upanishads*, the *Bhagavad Gita* and the *Brahmasutras*) we can come to a correct and liberating knowledge of the world and our own true nature as identical with *Brahman*.

Ramanuja (1077–1157) is often compared with Thomas Aquinas (1225–74), such was the depth and subtlety of their respective systems. Ramanuja revered the South Indian poet–saint traditions of the *Alvars* and proposed that, although identical to *Brahman*, the individual *atman* retains its particular qualities just as a unified body retains its particular parts (*Vishishtadvaita*). He recognized that simultaneous unity and difference (*bheda-abheda*) is essential in a monotheistic tradition which claims ultimate unity between God and the devotee but also values devotional love towards God.

Madhva (c. 1197–1276) wrote commentaries on a number of sacred texts and established a new, dualistic interpretation of Vedanta. The *dvaita vedanta* school maintains that the perfect *Brahman* could not be identical to the imperfect, created *atman*. There must be a fundamental distinction between the individual self and God. One can only talk of such identity in the way one talks of the relationship between a devoted lover and his or her beloved. A Vaishnavite, Madhva took both the evidence of our senses and the reality of difference seriously. Any view which claimed real unity with the divine threatened the transcendence of God and undervalued our own experience.

There was and remains lively debate. The question of who we ultimately are provided for Hindu philosophers a gateway into profound discussions of the nature of reality, knowledge, truth and goodness which continue to guide and instruct today.

Sacred Writings

THEODORE GABRIEL

Hindu scriptures comprise a vast corpus of literature dating from 1300 BCE to modern times. Most of the scriptures are in Sanskrit (a word meaning 'refined'), a classical Indian language now used only by scholars. There is also a considerable amount of religious literature in regional Indian languages and there are variants of the original texts, which emphasize a particular aspect of Hindu belief. For example, the *Adhyatma Ramayana* is a version of the popular epic *Ramayana* that stresses devotion (*bhakti*). What follows does not exhaust the many diverse categories of Hindu sacred writings, but rather it outlines the major elements of a vast array of texts dealing with various aspects of belief, ritual and tradition in Hindu society.

Sruti and *Smriti*

Hindus generally divide their scriptures into two categories: heard or revealed (*Sruti*) and remembered (*Smriti*). *Sruti* scriptures are believed to be communicated directly by God to ancient Indian sages. *Smriti* scriptures, on the other hand, are less authoritative and consist of texts such as the Hindu epics (the *Ramayana*, and the *Mahabharata*), the Dharma Sutras (books of law, concerned with customs and correct conduct) and Puranas (mythology).

The Veda

The Hindu canon is usually termed Veda (from the root *vid*, meaning 'knowledge'). The Vedas comprise four main types: The Vedic *Samhitas*, *Brahmanas*, *Aranyakas*, and *Upanishads*.

● The Vedic *Samhitas* (classified as the *Rig*, *Sama*, *Yajur* and *Atharva* Vedas) are the earliest known Hindu religious literature (1300–200 BCE), mainly consisting of praises to various deities of ancient Hinduism led by Indra, king of the gods.

● The *Brahmanas* stipulate the details of and explain the significance of rituals (*yaga* or *yajna*), especially the fire ritual, in which oblations were poured out or cast into fire to be conveyed to the gods. The prominence

A Hindu fire ritual in Calcutta, India

of Agni, the god of fire and of the Brahman priest in these texts indicates the growing importance and complexity of the fire ritual in early Indian religion.

● The *Aranyakas* ('forest books') provide analysis and interpretation of the fire ritual whereby a correspondence is drawn between the ritual and the cosmos. The ritual, moreover, is understood to have an intrinsic power by which the gods are to some extent bypassed. Indeed, the *Aranyakas* also represent a transition from the ritualistic *Brahmanas* to the far more contemplative and philosophical themes of the *Upanishads*, tending to move away from the polytheism of the *Samhitas* towards a more philosophical, monistic or pantheistic understanding of reality, in which despite appearances all is one. Hence, the *Aranyakas* and the *Upanishads* mark a growing resistance to the ritualism of the fire sacrifice and a preference for more contemplative and spiritual forms of worship.

● The *Upanishads* (*upa* = alongside, *nishad* = set) are commentaries and elaborations of the ideas encountered in the Vedic *Samhitas* and the *Brahmanas*. Four major themes can be identified: internal sacrifice, the idea of the *atman* (similar to 'soul' or 'self'), *Brahman* (non-personal divine being) and monistic theology (which equates the *atman* and indeed the whole cosmos with *Brahman* – everything is *Brahman*). The previous emphasis on the importance and intricacy of the fire ritual is overshadowed by an emphasis on personal spiritual development. In religious terminology, *tapas* or *pranagnihotra* – sometimes described as the oblation of one's body in the fire of one's breath – is shown as much more efficacious and powerful than the external *yajna*. The *atman-Brahman* identification has tremendous implications for the Hindu's understanding of the nature of God, the cosmos and the liberation (or 'salvation') of the individual.

Of the Dharma Sutras (literally: aphorisms relating to duties), the most important is the compendium of law known as *Manava Dharma Shastra* (The laws of Manu). These stipulate the duties, laws and regulations binding on all categories of Hindus, whatever their caste (*varna*), stage of life (*ashrama*) or gender. Because ideas of salvation in Hinduism involve adherence to these laws, regulations and duties, it is vital for Hindus to know and understand them. In other words, devout Hindus seeking release from *samsara* (the cycle of lives, deaths and reincarnations) need to obey the Dharma Sutras.

The Epics

Perusal of the two epics of Hinduism, the *Ramayana* and the *Mahabharata*, is deemed a sacred duty and helpful in progressing towards liberation/salvation (*moksha*) from the cycle of worldly life.

These epics, allegedly written by the ancient sages Valmiki and Vyasa (respectively, 'one covered by an anthill' and 'compiler') are deemed by scholars to be compilations of folk tales, songs sung by minstrels and heroic stories composed in honour of kings. However, the editing of these scriptures was highly skilful and, in spite of their complexity and bewildering multiplicity of themes, they seem to point to a central theme of salvation of the world and the continual war between good and evil in the universe. The stories are threaded into a central theme of a world slowly but inexorably declining to an age of destruction. The Battle of Kurukshetra is a climactic event in the *Mahabharata*, for instance, marking the beginning of the age of evil (*Kaliyuga*) and witnessing the gradual decline of honour, compassion and chivalry during its denouement. In the *Ramayana* the war between Rama and

Ravana symbolizes the confrontation between the forces of good and evil in the world. In both the principal characters are either gods or demigods and demons. Although the gods ultimately win, they have to compromise and often resort to devious stratagems to achieve their victory. The end result is that of a tainted world in which even the gods are not entirely free of unethical actions.

Both epics have common features: a righteous prince excluded from kingship and exiled; a climactic battle between forces of good and evil; the intervention of God on behalf of the good; in spite of many reverses, the ultimate triumph of good over evil. The epics present many ideals and heroic role models to Hindus. They are generally Vaishnavite, extolling the god Vishnu.

The *Bhagavad Gita*
The *Bhagavad Gita* ('song of the Lord') is a small part of the epic *Mahabharata*. Nevertheless, it is a highly influential scripture within Hinduism, which has acquired almost an independent standing of its own. It is a discourse between Krishna, the incarnation (*avatar*) of the god Vishnu, and his devotee Prince Arjuna (the greatest warrior in the *Mahabharata*). The discussion is obviously an insertion into the epic and many scholars consider it to be an *Upanishad*.

Above all, the *Bhagavad Gita* is an irenic scripture which seeks to unite the major theological strands of Hinduism. It says that all ways (*margas* or *yogas*) to salvation are equally valid: the way of enlightenment (*jnana*), the way of altruistic righteous action and progression through the caste hierarchy (*karma*) and the way of devotion (*bhakti*). However, it argues that the way of devotion (*bhakti*) is the highest of all paths and, for the first time in Hinduism, it reveals that the devotee is greatly loved by a gracious God. Consequently, it also proposes a radical rethinking of traditional Hindu concepts of salvation (*moksha*), in that it argues that it is open to all castes and to women.

The Puranas
The Puranas ('ancient stories') are, once again, a vast body of literature. Traditionally there are eighteen Puranas which have been classified as associated with the gods Vishnu, Brahma and Shiva, as well as many which are associated with minor deities and with holy places, such as particular temples or sacred sites. The contents are wide-ranging, including, for example, genealogies, law codes,

A late eighteenth-century depiction of Rama and Lakshmana wandering in search of Sita (from the *Ramayana*).

descriptions of rituals and pilgrimages to holy places. They are not merely a collection of old tales, as the name Purana seems to suggest, but narratives that highlight a particular theological stance and vision.

Beliefs

ANNA S. KING

A sculpture of
Vishnu at Perumal
Temple, Singapore.

A statue of Brahma.

What we now know as Hinduism –
partly because it has no single founder,
sacred book, hierarchy or creed – has
developed into a rich pluralist religious
culture with a great variety of customs,
forms of worship, gods and goddesses,
theologies, philosophies, stories, art
and music. Many Hindus believe that
its essential teachings remain the same
down the centuries. However, diversity
within Hinduism has led some scholars
to talk of Hindu *religions* rather than
a single Hindu *religion*, 'Hinduisms'
rather than 'Hinduism' or even to
abandon the term 'Hinduism' altogether.
Moreover, many different Hindu voices
and traditions compete globally to
define the essential beliefs of Hinduism.

What are Hindu beliefs?
Hindus accept that they share
common beliefs, principles and
structures. For many, however,
Hinduism is not so much a system of
beliefs as *a way of life*, a religious
culture, a spiritual and intellectual
quest and an intense identification
with the myriad ways in which the
sacred is present in India. If asked
about their beliefs, they often begin by

talking about ethical teachings:
kindness and truth; hospitality to
the guest; respect for the family and
particularly for elders and parents.
They may go on to consider beliefs
in particular gods or goddesses, the
authority of important sacred texts, the
merit of pilgrimage or the doctrine of
karma. Some (not all) may accept the
social hierarchy of the four *varnas*
(caste system) and certain principles
of purity and pollution. Any study of
popular Hindu beliefs begins with the
gods and goddesses of Hinduism.

God, gods and goddesses
Hindus may be polytheistic,
monotheistic or monistic (believing
that all reality is actually one). There
are even orthodox Hindus who are
atheistic. Many Hindus believe that
there is one God (*Brahman*) who can
be worshipped in many forms. God can,
for example, appear as a baby, a friend,
a king, a mother or a lover. God can
manifest as male or female or in non-
human form, be worshipped as without
form (*nirguna Brahman*) or with
form (*saguna Brahman*), appear
through icons and images (*murti*)
or in human shape as a living saint
or guru. Some Hindu gurus, such as
Vivekananda (1863–1902), have even
taught that God is embodied in the
form of the universe and in all sentient
beings. Hence, in serving others we are
quite literally serving God.

Sometimes God is understood in
a threefold way, as *Trimurti*. The
Trimurti consists of Brahma (the
creator), Vishnu (the sustainer) and
Shiva (the destroyer). However, not
only is Brahma seldom worshipped,
but nowadays, the *Trimurti* is often
replaced by a group of five gods
(Vishnu, Shiva, Devi, Surya and
Ganesha).

● The two pre-eminent gods,
worshipped by Hindus everywhere, are
Shiva and Vishnu. Vishnu is principally

associated with the preservation of the cosmos and its proper order. He is, therefore, linked to kingship and to the maintenance of *dharma* (law, order, righteousness). He is probably most frequently worshipped in his incarnations (*avatar*) as Rama and Krishna.

● Shiva, 'the auspicious' is both the lord of *yogis* (ascetics), depicted with matted hair a body smeared with ashes and meditating in a cremation ground, and also the divine lover. He is worshipped most commonly in the form of the phallus (*linga*). He has two sons, Ganesha, the elephant-headed god, and Skanda or Murugan. Shiva reveals the ultimate nature of reality, the polarities of life and death, creation and destruction, the ascetic and the erotic, on whose interrelationship the whole of life depends.

Vaishnavism (devotion to Vishnu), Shaivism (devotion to Shiva) and Shaktism (devotion to the Goddess or Devi) are the best-known traditions within Hinduism. However, Hindus often have a chosen deity (*ishtadev*) who, for the devotee, can take on the aspects of the ultimate god. Such gods and goddesses are worshipped both as distinct beings with their own stories and iconography, and as forms of the one ultimate reality (*Brahman*). Hindus may worship many gods but they also believe that all gods are one.

Goddess worship is one of the most distinctive traditions of Hinduism, going back to prehistoric times. *Shakti* (power, strength, force) is a term used to refer to the power of any deity and is also the activating energy incarnated in goddesses.

● All goddesses can be seen as distinct deities or as diverse forms of (Maha)devi, *the* (Great) Goddess. The Goddess (*Adyashakti*) is worshipped

> 'To see the universal and all-pervading Spirit of Truth face to face one must be able to love the meanest of creation as oneself.'
>
> Mahatma Gandhi

as the Supreme Being but also as the consort of a male god.

● The consorts of the three great gods are Lakshmi, Sarasvati and Parvati.

● Sometimes scholars draw a distinction between independent goddesses who are dangerous and 'hot' and wifely goddesses who are restrained and 'cool'. For many Hindu women Sita (the wife of Rama) is the model Hindu wife whose resolute integrity and courage are today emphasized by the Indian women's movement.

● The land of India itself is worshipped as 'Divine Mother' (*Bharat Mata*) and is further sanctified by *Shaktipithas* (centres of Goddess worship) and by great rivers like the Ganges which are worshipped as bestowers of prosperity and liberation.

Avatars

Avatars are manifestations (literally 'descents') of God. They periodically intervene to fight evil and ensure that the universe functions in accordance with *dharma* (see below). The best loved are Krishna and Rama (*avatars* of Vishnu).

● Krishna is worshipped as a child, as the god of erotic mystical love and as the hero of the epic *Mahabharata*. While the youthful Krishna with his flute entrances the world with his play (*Krishna-lila*), in the *Bhagavad Gita* Krishna reveals himself as the great teacher and supreme god (Vishnu).

● Rama is worshipped as the ideal ruler and the restorer of *dharma*. Always popular in northern India, Rama, has latterly become the principal god of Hindu nationalism. His reign (*Ram Rajya*) is invoked as a golden period of justice, harmony and prosperity.

Image worship

While many Hindus acknowledge that *Brahman* is the ultimate reality, the vast majority also worship divine beings and images. Many believe that the power (*shakti*) of a deity is actually present in that deity's image (*murti*). Therefore, in worshipping before an image, worship is offered to the deity whose power is *in* the image and also to the deity *as* an image. When an image is consecrated, the ceremony transforms images of stone, metal and wood into embodiments of God. Hindus go to the temple for *darshana*, the 'sight' or 'vision' of the deities. It is believed that *darshana* brings good fortune, grace and spiritual merit. It also makes possible an intimate, loving relationship between deities and their devotees. During ritual worship (*puja*) the gods are served and cared for as honoured guests by the offerings made to their images.

Dharma

Hindus today often refer to Hindu beliefs and practices as *sanatana dharma* (eternal religion) or Vedic *dharma* (Vedic religion). *Dharma* may mean the social order, it may mean the cosmic order, but equally it can refer to personal behaviour and attitudes. At the simplest level it means the individual's religious and social duties according to status and stage of life. The *Bhagavad Gita*, for example, teaches that it is better to do one's own duty imperfectly than that of another well.

Samsara

Many Hindus, particularly those in the higher castes, believe in the endless cycle of rebirth (*samsara*). Efforts to bring the cycle to an end are at the core of many Hindu religious practices. The picture of a world as a place where the eternal soul is perpetually reincarnated has dominated the Indian imagination for over three millennia.

Karma

Central to the teaching about reincarnation, *karma* is the taken-for-granted belief that one's actions determine one's condition in this life and rebirth in the next. Every action has its inevitable fruit or consequence. *Karma* is thus inseparable from *dharma* and *samsara*. To summarize the belief: good deeds result in good *karma*, which produces good fortune in this life and a good birth in the next life; bad deeds result in bad *karma* which may lead to much less desirable rebirths in the next life as a human lower down the social hierarchy – or as an animal or even as an unfortunate soul suffering the torments of one of the many hells.

There are ways in which *karma* may be overridden. Devotion to a deity is perhaps the most potent. Religious rituals and meritorious action may also cancel past sins. Some Hindus withdraw from the world and practise non-engagement. However, the *Bhagavad Gita* teaches that adherence to one's duty combined with internal renunciation of attachment to, or desire for, the results of one's actions can lead to liberation (*moksha*) from the cycle of *samsara*.

Karma can lead to either fatalism or ethical activism. It can be seen as an uncontrollable, impersonal determinant of the human condition or can encourage people to feel responsible for their own fate and promote a dynamic view of action in the world.

The Three Paths

The three paths (*margas* or *yogas*) to spiritual fulfilment are: *jnana* (knowledge, insight, wisdom), *karma* (action) and *bhakti* (ecstatic devotion). Some Hindus consider that each of the three paths requires exclusive concentration and is sufficient for liberation. However, many modern teachers and gurus teach a *yoga* of synthesis, arguing that the three paths

'Just as a person casts off worn-out garments and puts on others that are new, even so the embodied soul casts off worn-out bodies and takes on others that are new. Weapons do not cleave the Self, fire does not burn the Self. Waters do not drench the Self, winds do not parch the Self. The Self is the same forever: unmanifest, unthinkable, still.'
Bhagavad Gita II, 22–25

BELIEFS

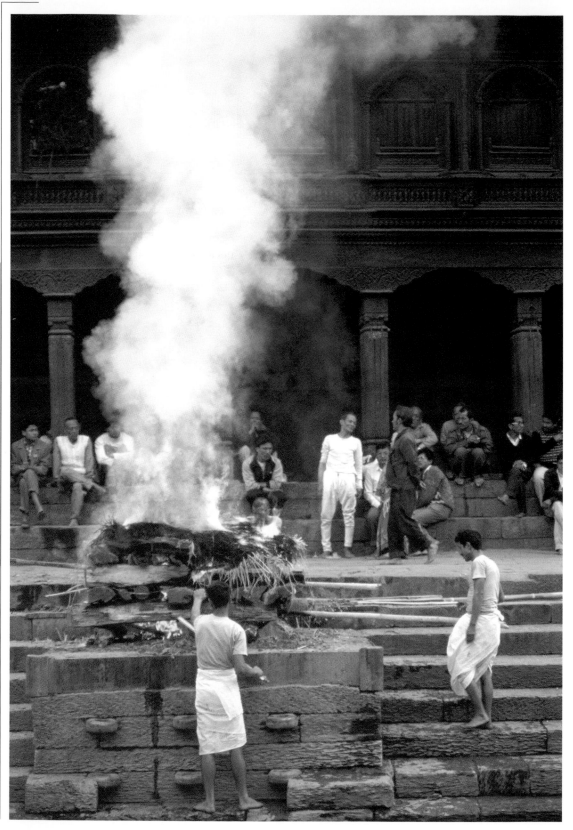

are linked and liberating knowledge may be obtained through all.

● *Jnanayoga* (the path of wisdom/knowledge) liberates from *karma* and rebirth and indeed from sickness, old age and death. It leads to the overcoming of ignorance and the realization of *Brahman*. The pursuit of wisdom implies religious practice, meditation, self-purification and above all study of the scriptures. The Vedas and particularly the *Upanishads* provide knowledge of *Brahman* and of our true condition. Indeed the famous teaching of the *Upanishads* is that in spirit (*atman*) humans are identical with *Brahman*. According to some Hindu schools, if humans realize this truth they can be liberated-in-life (*jivan-mukta*).

● *Karmayoga* (the path of work) enables ordinary people everywhere to give spiritual meaning to their everyday lives. It is associated for many with the *Bhagavad Gita*'s teaching that action can be a positive means of personal transformation if people perform their duty selflessly and act without the desire for status or reward. Gandhi reinterpreted *karmayoga* by equating it with social commitment and struggle. He found in the *Gita* authority for his philosophy of non-violence and peaceful resistance to British rule.

● *Bhaktiyoga* (the path of loving devotion) is characterized by an intense personal relationship between the deity and devotee. Selfless love of God consumes past *karma* and results in a state of intimate, blissful and loving communion with the deity. Vaishnavas often speak of *prapatti* (complete self-surrender in love) to Vishnu. God-intoxicated saints are depicted as immersed in blissful devotion. Today many busy Hindus follow the path of *bhakti*. Their spiritual discipline (*sadhana*) may vary, but is broadly characterized by selfless service and loving devotion to God.

The Four Goals
Hinduism offers four legitimate goals (*purusartha*) for human beings which, taken together, are believed to ensure spiritual and social harmony.

● *Artha* (worldly wealth and success) is a proper goal if pursued without desire, anger and greed. Kautilya's *Artha Shastra*, written in the third to fourth century BCE, argues that prosperity is the basis of a well-ordered state and people need *artha* if they are to practise religion. Thus pursuing an occupation, accumulating wealth, governing and so on are justified if they do not violate *dharma*.

● *Kama* (pleasure, desire) is also a legitimate goal if it accords with *dharma*. This is the pursuit of pleasurable activities, including sexuality, play, recreation, the arts and literature. The *Kama Sutra*, written in the third or fourth centuries CE, deals at length with erotic techniques, the arts of pleasure and seduction.

● *Dharma* (virtue, morality) has two levels. It is both one's own particular set of duties (*svadharma*) and the absolute morality, valid universally. When profit and pleasure are pursued for themselves, outside of *dharma*, they lead to social chaos.

● *Moksha* (spiritual liberation) is the ultimate Hindu quest. It is release from the bondage of suffering and rebirth (*samsara*).

Some Hindus believe that these goals are interconnected and that no goal is primary. Others believe they form an ascending hierarchy with *moksha* transcending and even opposing the other three. Whatever one's understanding, this system of the four

A Hindu cremation in Kathmandu, Nepal.

BELIEFS

goals implicitly recognizes the complexity of human drives and aspirations.

Death and the afterlife

Hindu beliefs about the afterlife are complex. Most Hindus believe that they will be reborn into another body according to their *karma*. However, *moksha* (salvation or ultimate spiritual fulfilment) may be understood in different ways: as final union with *Brahman*; as a perfectly blissful state; as communion with God; as liberation in some heavenly realm or paradise. Many Hindus may find the concept of salvation or liberation after death a very distant ideal.

Moreover, very ancient understandings of the afterlife persist. Vedic views are implied in the death ritual. Funerary rites of passage and memorial rituals for the dead indicate a belief in the continued existence of ancestors (*pitr*) who are benefited and pleased by offerings made by their descendants. There are also popular beliefs about the journey of the soul after death; the multiplicity of heavens and hells and the role of the god of death (Yamraj or Dharmaraj) as judge; restless or malicious ghosts (*pret*, *bhuta*) who may possess or disturb the living.

The Four *Yugas*

Hindu, Buddhist and Jain beliefs about the vastness of time and the age of the universe in some senses coincide with modern scientific understanding. The classical Hindu view is of gradually deteriorating conditions until finally the world is destroyed by fire and returns to chaos. The world itself perpetually undergoes cycles of evolution from a state of non-differentiation through a series of ages to its dissolution (*pralaya*) back into the unevolved state, from which the cycle starts again. This process of evolution and dissolution is a 'day of Brahma':

> 'To conquer the subtle passions seems to me harder far than the physical conquest of the world by force of arms.'
>
> Mahatma Gandhi

● each day of Brahma divides into the fourteen 'periods of the Manu'

● each of the fourteen periods of Manu divides into four great ages

● each of the four great ages divides into four *yugas*

The passing of the *yugas* is marked by progressive moral and physical deterioration. We are now in the middle of the last and worst age, the *Kaliyuga*. Hence, that there is apparent moral decline, suffering, famine, and war is no surprise to Hindus. Indeed, the orthodox view is that life will get worse as we progress through the *yuga*.

Gurus

The *guru* (spiritual teacher) is a figure of the greatest importance in Hinduism, the object of *darshan* and worship, and comes in all shapes and sizes, traditions and orders. Some may assert their status by virtue of their charisma, others are initiated into a long-established lineage (*sampradaya*). Many have carried their spiritual message to the West, helping to extend the bounds of Hinduism (see *New Religious Movements*). One of the best known gurus alive today is Sathya Sai Baba, worshipped as an *avatara* of Sirdi Sai Baba and also of Shiva and Shakti. There have also been women gurus, such as Sarada Devi (widow of Ramakrishna), Mira Alfassa (the Mother of the Aurobindo organization), Ananda Mayi Ma and Amritanandamayi Ma.

Worship and Festivals

MAYA WARRIER

In early Vedic times, worship usually took the form of a sacrificial ritual (*yajna*) addressed to nature gods such as the sun god (Surya), the rain god (Indra), the god of fire (Agni), or the Soma god (believed to reside in a probably hallucinogenic plant of the same name). These rituals involved the sacrifice of animals such as goats and cows or the pouring of oblations of such items as clarified butter, honey and milk into a sacrificial fire, accompanied by the chanting of Vedic hymns and prayers. The early Vedas are liturgical texts which set out in great detail the method of ritual observance. These rituals were intended to please the gods through worship, and to ensure the well-being of the sponsor or patron of the sacrifice (the *yajamana*) and his family.

Puja

Yajnas are something of a rarity in the contemporary Hindu world. The form of worship that is far more commonly observed is *puja*, a ritual of devotional worship regularly conducted at temples, usually by Brahman priests, and often observed privately at household shrines. *Puja* may be addressed to any of the manifold gods and goddesses in the Hindu pantheon. Important among these are the great gods Vishnu and Shiva and the goddess Shakti, all of whom appear in myriad forms and aspects in Hindu mythology and across the contemporary Hindu sacred landscape.

Temples dedicated to the different Hindu gods and goddesses usually contain a sanctified image of the deity, and it is to this image that the ritual of *puja* is addressed. During *puja*, the priest ritually purifies himself and the shrine, invokes the presence of the deity in the image and then worships the image by ritually bathing and adorning it, feeding it symbolically and waving a flaming lamp in a circle around it in a ritual of light. This is usually accompanied by the chanting of Sanskrit mantras, the blowing of conches and the ringing of bells. In Hindu households, the householders usually observe an abbreviated form of this ritual.

The relationship between the image and the divine presence is, in the Hindu world view, often a complex one. For most Hindus, the image is *symbolic* of the divine presence, but equally, for many, it also *is* the divine presence manifesting itself in tangible form. Moreover, Hindus are seldom agreed on the importance of *puja*. While some see it as an act of great religious significance, others see it as a largely unnecessary, outward expression of religious piety and prefer instead a more inward-oriented mode of spiritual development. Besides *puja*, other modes of worship commonly practised in Hindu society include *bhajana* or the singing of hymns, and the recitation of the *sahasranama*, the thousand names of the gods and goddesses.

> '*Whatever you do, or eat, or give, or offer in adoration, let it be an offering to me; and whatever you suffer, suffer it for me.*'
>
> Bhagavad Gita 9.26

A priest performs a *puja* as women burn incense, offer flowers and pray to their gods at an open-air, circular temple with relief carvings of the 64 *yoginis* (or female consorts to Hindu deities).

Pilgrimage and conceptions of the sacred

In the Hindu scheme of things, the sacred is ubiquitous, contained not only in temples and sacred images, but also appearing in nature – in stones, trees, mountains and rivers. Every once in a while the sacred 'manifests' itself in the form of a mysterious rock or a stream or spring, and the site of such manifestation becomes a place of worship. Pilgrims flock to such places during auspicious months of the Hindu calendar, and mythological stories grow about the miraculous nature of the pilgrimage site. Particularly important in the Hindu cosmology are sacred rivers, and holy towns and cities situated along their banks. These are seen as places of crossing (*tirtha*) between the mundane and the sacred, and also between the worlds of the living and the dead. The water of the Ganges in North India is believed to be especially potent in this respect, and a single dip in the river is believed to earn untold spiritual merit for the worshipper.

The sacred often manifests itself in living things too. The cow, the monkey and, in some parts of India, even the snake and the rat are believed to be sacred and therefore worshipped.

Even more common is the worship of men and women believed to be holy and therefore capable of performing

Devout Hindus bathe to wash away their sins in the Ganges River, Varanasi, India.

miracles which can transform the lives of devotees and ensure their well-being. Many such holy figures attract an extensive following and head vast spiritual empires extending across regional and national boundaries.

Festivals
The Hindu (lunar) calendar year is punctuated by a series of religious festivals. Temple festivals are usually marked by processions when worshippers carry the deity's image through the temple town or village, offering devotees a chance to glimpse it in all its glory. Other festivals, which celebrate landmark events in Hindu mythology, include:

● *Janmashtami* (July–August): the celebration of the birthday of the popular Hindu god, Krishna.

● *Ganesh Chaturthi* (August–September): a festival dedicated to the elephant-headed god, Ganesh, the remover of obstacles.

● *Dussehra* (September–October towards the end of the monsoon): marking the victory of Rama and his monkey army over the demon-king Ravana. It encompasses *Navaratri* (also known as 'the festival of nine nights'), which in Bengal culminates in a grand celebration dedicated to the worship of the goddess Durga.

● *Diwali* (October–November): the festival of lights, following shortly after *Dussehra*. Hindus throughout the world illuminate their homes with lamps and exchange gifts.

● *Shivaratri* (January–February): a festival during which Shiva is worshipped.

● *Holi* (February–March): a spring festival, during which people drench one another in water and coloured powder.

Besides these, there are several localized festivals observed in different parts of the Hindu world. The *Kumbh Mela*, perhaps the most popular of these, attracts pilgrims in vast numbers to its four sites in North India (Hardwar, Nasik, Ujjain and Allahabad) where it is celebrated on a rotational basis once every three years. The *Purna Kumbha Mela*, which takes place once every twelve years in the holy town of Allahabad, has, in recent times, earned the distinction of recording the single largest gathering of people in one place in all the world.

'I am the same to all beings, and my love is ever the same; but those who worship me with devotion, they are in me and I am in them.'
Bhagavad Gita 9.29

WORSHIP AND FESTIVALS

Festivals of Hinduism

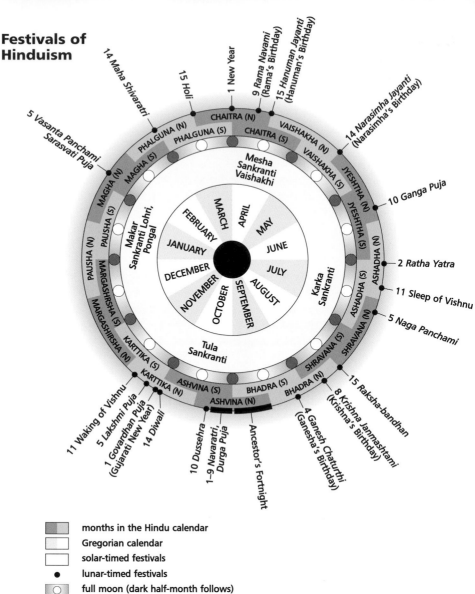

14 Maha Shivaratri

15 Holi

1 New Year

9 Rama Navami (Rama's Birthday)

15 Hanuman Jayanti (Hanuman's Birthday)

14 Narasimha Jayanti (Narasimha's Birthday)

5 Vasanta Panchami Sarasvati Puja

10 Ganga Puja

2 Ratha Yatra

11 Sleep of Vishnu

5 Naga Panchami

15 Raksha-bandhan

8 Krishna Janmashtami (Krishna's Birthday)

4 Ganesh Chaturthi (Ganesha's Birthday)

Ancestor's Fortnight

1–9 Navaratri Durga Puja

10 Dussehra

14 Diwali

1 Govardhan Puja (Gujarati New Year)

5 Lakshmi Puja

11 Waking of Vishnu

CHAITRA (N)
CHAITRA (S)
VAISHAKHA (N)
VAISHAKHA (S)
JYESHTHA (N)
JYESHTHA (S)
ASHADHA (N)
ASHADHA (S)
SHRAVANA (S)
SHRAVANA (N)
BHADRA (S)
BHADRA (N)
ASHVINA (N)
ASHVINA (S)
KARTTIKA (N)
KARTTIKA (S)
MARGASHIRSHA (N)
MARGASHIRSHA (S)
PAUSHA (N)
PAUSHA (S)
MAGHA (N)
MAGHA (S)
PHALGUNA (N)
PHALGUNA (S)

Mesha Sankranti Vaishakhi

Karka Sankranti

Tula Sankranti

Makar Sankranti Lohri, Pongal

MARCH
FEBRUARY
JANUARY
DECEMBER
NOVEMBER
OCTOBER
SEPTEMBER
AUGUST
JULY
JUNE
MAY
APRIL

months in the Hindu calendar

Gregorian calendar

solar-timed festivals

• lunar-timed festivals

○ full moon (dark half-month follows)

● new moon (bright half-month follows)

month in new-moon system (North)

month in new-moon system (South)

A multitude of oil lamps surround one large one at the *Diwali* festival, Kathmandu, Nepal.

Family and Society

MAYA WARRIER

Caste and joint family are often seen as the central features of traditional Hindu social organization. The caste system orders Hindu society hierarchically such that different social groups are ranked in a relationship of superiority/inferiority to each other in terms of their levels of purity. Every Hindu is born into the caste of his/her parents. Traditionally, caste groups were by and large occupational groups and the nature of one's occupation determined one's level of purity. Ritual, worship and scholarship in sacred texts, seen as the purest pursuits, were the preserve of the 'purest' and 'highest' of castes, the Brahmans. At the opposite end of the hierarchy were the so-called 'untouchables' who, by virtue of the 'impurity' attaching to their occupations (scavenging, tanning leather and the like) were considered too polluting to be incorporated into mainstream society and were therefore excluded from everyday social life. Between these two extremes there ranged a vast and varied spectrum of caste rankings. In traditional Indian village society, caste determined most aspects of one's life – where one lived, with whom one could legitimately interact, with whom one could share food, and whom one could marry. As a result, social mobility, especially for those at the lowest rungs of society, was highly restricted.

The joint family system
Just as caste determined one's place in society, so also status within the joint family determined one's place within the household. In the joint family system, two, often three or even four generations of a family lived together as part of the same household, sharing common living space and kitchen facilities, drawing from a common pool of financial resources, and sharing responsibilities for the upkeep of the family home. The head of the household was usually the oldest male member of the family. In the traditional Hindu family system, family property passed down the male line. The women of the family seldom owned or controlled family property. Indian epic narratives, such as the *Mahabharata* and *Ramayana*, dwell at great length on familial roles and duties as husband, wife, father, mother, son, daughter, brother and so on, thus providing traditional models for good conduct in familial contexts.

Marriage
Traditionally a woman derived her identity from the male authority figures in her life: usually her father before her marriage, her husband after marriage and her sons in her old age. Marriage was, and remains to this day, a central institution ordering and regulating the Hindu social system. Conventionally, marriage is seen not as the formalizing of a romantic relationship between the individuals concerned but as an arrangement between families of the same or similarly ranked caste groups within the caste hierarchy. The bride, seen in most Hindu communities as a 'gift' from her parents to the family of the groom, often brings wealth in the form of dowry to the groom's family. Her parents, in popular belief, derive spiritual merit by gifting their daughter to the groom's family. Although in some instances it is permissible for the woman to 'marry up' into a family of higher social standing than her own, the reverse, where the woman marries someone from a lower caste, is considered taboo.

'For the sake of the family, one may abandon an individual. For the sake of a village one may abandon a family. For the country's sake, one may abandon a village. For the sake of the soul, one may abandon the world!'
Mahabharata 2.55.10

Family and society in the contemporary world

While the institutions of caste and joint family still prevail in contemporary Hindu society, they have undergone vast changes, mainly due to changes in economic organization. The status of women in society too has undergone some measure of change, although several traditional ideas regarding the woman's role in the family prevail to this day. In modern Hindu society, one's caste need no longer determine one's occupation, income or social status. Particularly in urban contexts, where modern occupations and workplaces afford employees some degree of autonomy from caste restrictions, caste often ceases to be the all-important marker of one's identity. The joint family system likewise worked best when occupations were hereditary and different generations of a family derived their income from the same source of livelihood. With urbanization and industrialization generating new and more numerous job opportunities, and modern educational institutions imparting new skills to recruits from diverse backgrounds, it has been possible for younger generations not only to break away from their hereditary familial occupations and move into new kinds of employment, but also to set up independent nuclear families of their own. With more and more women entering educational institutions and the employment sector, they too need less support from the male members of their families. They are thus, to some degree, able to assert their independence and autonomy from the traditional family structure.

While in several instances the nuclear family has come to replace the joint family, the idea of the joint family continues to retain a powerful hold over the Hindu imagination. Families tend to be closely networked across generations and older members of the family, although they may not live in close proximity to younger members, continue to exercise considerable authority over the latter. Parents continue to have a major say in determining (same-caste) life partners for their sons and daughters, even though the concept of the 'love marriage' as opposed to the 'arranged marriage' is gaining increasing popularity in the contemporary Hindu world. Families come together on occasions such as birth, wedding and death ceremonies, reinforcing a sense of solidarity as a group. Hindu epic stories such as the *Mahabharata* and *Ramayana*, which are often retold today in the form of television serials and dance dramas, also serve to bolster the ideal of the joint family in popular thinking.

A bride and groom at a Hindu wedding at Tunapuna, Trinidad and Tobago.

I am a Hindu

NAREN PATEL

I was born in a village in Gujarat, India – a few years after India gained independence – just outside the town of Dandi, which is famous for Gandhi's Salt March protest against the British colonial government. I came to England when I was eleven because my father was employed in a car factory in Coventry. Although I had attended school in India from the age of five, I found schooling in England difficult, mainly because I knew little English. However, I quickly learned the new language and settled in.

At sixteen I joined a local engineering company and began an apprenticeship. After five years I successfully concluded it and was encouraged to apply for a place at Sussex University. I was awarded a BSc Honours degree in Mechanical Engineering, returned to the company I had joined after school, and over the years I have worked my way up to become one of their chief engineers, which has led to my travelling to various parts of the world.

As a Hindu, I believe in one God who has many incarnations (*avatars*). I believe in all these gods but, like many Hindus, focus on a particular God who has become special to me, Krishna, a very popular God within Hinduism. I am particularly moved and helped by the many stories about Krishna. My belief in God has encouraged me to be a helpful, contributing member of society. For instance, I assisted in starting a cricket club for young people and I have been its secretary for thirty years. I did this because, as a Hindu, I wanted to put something back into the community from which I have benefited so much. I believe that if I lead a good life, helping others and worshipping God, as a result of reincarnation I will be reborn into a better life.

I do not believe that it is necessary to visit the temple every day in order to keep in touch with God. God is with me every hour of the day. I pray to God in my thoughts wherever I am and I reflect on my beliefs and whether what I am doing is good for me or for other people. I do this, not only because they are good things to do in and of themselves, but also because they will contribute to a good reincarnation. That said, I like to be in the temple whenever I can, serving my community. I find that regular attendance helps my religious life by expanding my thoughts and helping to make me less selfish and see the best in others. This is what faith means to me. It is a faith I learned particularly from my mother, a traditional Hindu. She has been the greatest influence on my religious upbringing.

When we moved to Cheltenham, we were the first Hindu family and there was no temple. We had a shrine in our house but had to return to Coventry for important festivals, celebrating there as we had done in India, if on a smaller scale. Finally, in 1975, the growing Hindu community in Cheltenham established their own temple, an occasion of much rejoicing and celebration.

In 1976 I returned to India, where I met my wife, a traditional Hindu from Gujarat. Already a devout Hindu, shortly after our marriage I became even more involved in the activities of the temple. I became the secretary and am now the treasurer. Because of my work, I do not participate in worship in the temple every day, but I do attend at least three times a week. When I retire I will certainly attend worship in the temple far more regularly.

In our home, we have a temple-like shrine at which my mother and my wife perform *puja* every day. After bathing in the morning, I also pray there for a short time. I observe fasting on special occasions, but I am not too particular about my diet. My wife and my mother are far more traditionally Hindu in this respect. Actually, my faith is more interior than exterior, in that I am less concerned about outward symbols such as dress than I am about what I think and do. That said, although I do not believe in wearing any specific clothing on a daily basis, I do often wear traditional Indian dress for *puja* and other religious functions.

Again, I do not have time to attend formal scripture study regularly. Once or twice a year I attend scripture reading and exposition in Coventry. I would like to go regularly to a local reading of Hindu sacred texts, but none is available locally. Having said that, scholars from the Hare Krishna temple in Watford are sometimes invited to explain Hindu texts to the local community. I have gone to these sessions quite a few times and have made contacts in the Hare Krishna temple. They are very knowledgable and I enjoy listening to them.

I visit India most years and whenever I go I make a point of visiting places of pilgrimage or particular temples. My aspiration is to visit and see most of the temples and sacred places in South India. These temples, I believe, are the original Hindu temples. My goal as a Hindu is eventually, when I have retired, to devote my life to seeking inner peace through prayer and meditation.

My wife is a more devout Hindu than I am and observes all the Hindu calendar events. Hence, my family life is firmly based on Hindu religion and culture. My faith has certainly helped to strengthen my relationship with my wife, mother and sisters. Together we observe all the Hindu festivals and religious celebrations, such as *Navaratri* (the 'nine-nights festival' celebrating the sowing of the winter crops) or *Janmashtami*. We also observe key ceremonies (*samskars*) such as cyclical funerary rites (*sraddha*). I took my father's ashes to India to scatter in rivers and on the land, especially the land in our hometown.

As a Hindu community we are very close-knit. We all get to know about the sickness, death, and other problems faced by other Hindu families. The close friendships we have mean that we are always ready to support each other in times of need.

Hinduism in the Modern World

THEODORE GABRIEL

Hinduism, the most ancient world religion, has been subject to many changes in the course of its long history. The rise and fall from prominence of some ancient gods such as Indra (King of gods) and Varuna (god of the sea), the decline in importance of the fire sacrifice, the rise into popularity of the *bhakti* (devotional) tradition in the sixth century CE are some instances of this. At the turn of the twentieth century Hindu reformers such as Vivekananda (1863–1902), Ram Mohan Roy (1772–1833), Mohandas (Mahatma) Gandhi (1869–1948) and Sarvepalli Radhakrishnan (1888–1975) advocated a particular ethical form of Hinduism which campaigned against social practices such as *sati* (the self-immolation of widows in their husbands' funeral pyres) and child marriage, and displayed the distinctive influence of Western values during this period of Western colonization. In contemporary times Hinduism has moved away from this puritanical type of religion, which decried many ancient beliefs as superstition, and has come back with full vigour to traditional Hinduism.

Astrologers, gurus, new religions and the West

A large number of Hindus now defend traditional Hindu mores and practices. Contemporary Hindus are not as apprehensive about being labelled 'superstitious' as they once were, but openly consult astrologers and gurus. Indeed, this latter practice is a very popular phenomenon, and among the increasing number of Hindu gurus some are even of Western provenance, such

Mahatma Gandhi on the Salt March, 1930. He led a 200 mile march to the sea to collect salt in symbolic defiance of British rule in India.

as the American guru Da Avabhasa.

This increase of individual practices and veneration of gurus has given rise to the cultic phenomenon in modern Hinduism. That is to say, some of the more prominent gurus, such as Swami Prabhupada, Bhagavan Rajneesh, and Satya Sai Baba, have established enormously popular new religious movements that have spread beyond India, attracting considerable attention from Westerners. This has happened even though, technically, conversion into Hinduism is impossible, because, strictly speaking, Hindus are – as a result of their *karma* (actions) in a previous life – those who are born into Hindu families and into a particular caste. Non-Hindus do not have a caste identity. Hence, traditionally Hindu missionary activity was aimed at recovering Hindus who had lapsed into Christianity or Islam (and required a purification ritual or *shuddi*). However, in the modern world, new cults and movements have emulated Christians by engaging in mission to non-Hindus and many of these new Hindu movements have been very successful in recruiting Westerners into the Hindu fold.

The impact of Indian independence
One of the most striking developments has been the politicization of Hinduism and a rising level of militancy among some factions, perhaps a natural consequence of the emergence of Hindu nationalism in a country so long under the yoke of Muslim and Christian powers. Independence for India in August 1947 ended about 400 years of such rule and, although the Indian leaders of the time opted for a secular or religiously neutral nation, the fact remains that the vast majority of the population is Hindu. This numerical superiority becomes highly significant in a democratically constituted nation. With the passing of time, the secular ideals of Jawaharlal Nehru (1889–1964) – the first Prime Minister of the republic of India – and Gandhi have become somewhat less cherished, and today many right-wing Hindus view India as a Hindu rather than as a secular multi-religious nation.

This shift toward Hindu nationalism may be seen in the context of a rise of Muslim nationalism in the subcontinent and the perennial dispute over Kashmir, a Muslim-majority state located between the two nations. It is, however, less than salutary that Hindu nationalistic parties such as the RSS (Rashtriya Swayam Sevak Sangh/National Self-Service Association), The VHP (Vishwa Hindu Parishad/World Hindu Organization) and the BJP (Bharatiya Janatha Party/Indian People's Party) have evoked the concept that India is a Hindu state and Hindu religion, ideology and values should predominate. This has exerted pressure on the religious minorities and created a divide. The actions and pronouncements of more militant sections of Hindu nationalistic organizations, such as the Bajrang Dal (described by some as 'the storm troopers of the VHP') have been decried by Hindu and other Indian intellectuals. They describe it as totally uncharacteristic of Hindu religion and culture, with its image of tolerance and its willingness to absorb beliefs and practices from other religions and philosophies. These parties operate on an ideology based on Hindutva ('Hindu-ness'), which immediately raises problems for the religious minorities and raises the spectre of a Hindu theocratic state in India that will alienate many millions of non-Hindus in the nation.

What worries many contemporary commentators is that in many places the Indian electorate has voted them into power and, in reality, the central government of India was until recently led by just such a right-wing party, the BJP. Although the contemporary appeal

A Hindu couple celebrate *Diwali* at their home shrine at Chandigarh, India.

of the Hindu nationalistic ideology is more evident among the less literate and rural sections of the Hindu community, it is they who constitute the vast majority of the Indian populace. This dangerous combination of political power and militant religious nationalism has led to great tension in some areas of India where several faith communities live alongside each other. The massacre of Muslims in Gujarat in June 2002 had been, allegedly, condoned and even abetted by the Hindu nationalist government of the state.

Hindu nationalists seek the Hinduization of Indian polity, culture and even education. This trend (usually termed *saffronization*, saffron being a colour religiously associated with Hinduism) is growing stronger, although it is opposed by the Indian intelligentsia. They argue against the politicization of religion, its identification with the nation and the growing hostility to other faiths. It is, they insist, difficult for a national identity to coalesce with the identity of one religion, however preponderant it may be demographically, in such a religiously pluralistic nation as India. The concern is that such a project will lead, not only to a lack of unity among the Indian people, but also to an increase in internecine conflict.

Hindu diaspora in the West

A significant development in Hinduism has resulted from the migration of many Hindus to the West. As a result of these diaspora communities being in a minority situation, a defensive, more fervent type of Hinduism has emerged. For example, in the USA, especially where there is a strong conservative Christian culture in the south, Hindus have challenged what they see as the distortion and misrepresentation of Hindu concepts and practices in, for example, school textbooks. The VHP has been particularly vocal.

Westernized Hindu ideas, when imported back to India, have been responsible for an increased awareness of mystical traditions, sacred sites and some esoteric forms of Hindu spirituality. There has been, in recent times, a burgeoning of interest in pilgrimage to sacred shrines, such as the Shabarimala Temple in Kerala or

Hardwar and great festivals such as the *Kumbh Mela*. There has also been an increase in those visiting gurus or 'god men' in search of miracles for health, wealth and power, through what are often erroneously referred to as 'Tantric' practices.

The caste system

Another feature of modern Hinduism is the strengthening of the caste system. At the turn of the twentieth century the campaign by Hindu reformers such as Dayananda Sarasvati (1824–83), Vivekananda and Gandhi had sought to reform what they saw as the evil chauvinism and discrimination of the caste system. Caste did not disappear but was felt to be out of date and incompatible with modern egalitarian ideals. For some, the conversion of 'untouchables' (those deemed to be spiritually polluted by birth outside the caste system, and thus relegated to engaging in 'unclean' occupations such as scavenging, working on animal skins and preparing liquor) to Christianity, Islam and Buddhism seemed to be a threat to the predominance of Hinduism in the subcontinent. Under Gandhi's influence the Indian constitution and laws guaranteed privileges to the untouchables in education and employment. In recent years this has faced opposition by the 'forward communities' who state that positive discrimination policies have undermined the economic status of their own communities. In some areas there have been caste wars between the *savarnas* (those belonging to the *varna* or caste system), and the *avarnas* (those outside the caste system, the untouchables). Both the untouchables and the *savarnas* have now organized into vote banks in order to achieve political influence. As a result, increasingly, politicians dare not offend the different caste configurations.

There is a reversionary thinking, which emphasizes the positive side of the caste system. Even practices such as *sati* have been extolled by fundamentalists, despite the growing feminist movement within Hinduism. On the other hand, there is a remarkable phenomenon termed 'sanskritization', which sees the untouchables and tribal people of India attempting to Hinduize their religious practices. Although present-day Hindutva organizations claim these people to be within the Hindu fold, the fact is that they have their own distinctive religious beliefs and practices. Having said that, some of the untouchable and tribal groups are beginning to abandon their traditional deities and practices to build temples and worship Hindu deities such as Vishnu and Shiva. This may be an effort to absorb themselves into the Hindu fold or an effort to gain higher status for their community. The Indian constitution has made restriction of

Women from the Dalit caste removing human waste from residential dry latrines and emptying the buckets into nearby gutters and streams, in Ranchi, India.

entry of untouchables to Hindu temples illegal. Nevertheless, these groups wish to have their own places of worship and rituals in the Hindu style, rather than make use of this legal provision. In a way this is a reaction to the still prevalent emotional opposition to the entry of untouchables to caste Hindu temples. Some untouchables have taken to Hindu theological training and have demanded priesthood on successful completion of their training, even in *savarna* temples.

Interestingly, other untouchable and tribal groups have retained their traditional pantheon and ritual praxis, but sought to identify their deities and practices with Hindu gods and worship by a reinterpretation of their mythology and ritual proceedings. Thus through an exegetical process they wish to gain status and identification with Hinduism while still retaining most of their indigenous practices. The leaders of the Muttappan cult of northern Kerala, for example, have reinterpreted the Muttappan deities as Vishnu and Shiva. (Originally, the Muttappan deities were tribal gods of the forest dwellers of the region, and had nothing to do with Hinduism.) Some of these tribal religious practices have become popular even among the *savarnas*.

The status of women in modern Hinduism

At personal risk, nineteenth-century and twentieth-century social reformers spearheaded efforts to achieve the liberation of women. Ram Mohan Roy's campaign against *sati* resulted in the banning of the practice. Ishwar Chandra Vidyasagar married a widow to set an example of ameliorating the lot of people virtually treated as dead. (Widows lived in seclusion, were not allowed to remarry, had to forgo all adornments and were looked down on as inauspicious.) Gandhi, for the first time in modern India, brought Indian women to the public arena in his campaign for independence. Women took part in public demonstrations and in the civil disobedience movement. The momentum gained has not been lost in modern India and the traditional image of the Hindu woman, domesticated and subservient to father and husband, is rapidly changing. Women are well represented in the

employment sector and in government. There has been a move to set quotas for women members of the *Lok Sabha* (parliament). A Vanitha Commission (Woman's Commission) is functioning in Kerala State to look into women's grievances, including their molestation or 'eve teasing' in public places, discrimination in employment and position in the family.

Traditionally the role of women was in the home serving their husbands and nurturing children. Hindu mythology often emphasized this image. Female figures such as Sita (the virtuous and long suffering wife of Rama) and Savithri (who pleaded successfully to Yama, the god of death, for the life of her husband) were held up as paradigms of womanly behaviour. Modern Hindu women are not adhering to these norms. They are out in public competing against men in all fields, even in occupations traditionally viewed as exclusively masculine (such as law, engineering and the police and armed forces). Feminist groups such as the Working Woman's Forum are very active in trying to achieve equality. Film directors, particularly Mira Nair and Deepa Mehta with *Monsoon Wedding* and *Fire*, have made films highlighting the aspirations of Indian women and the problems they face, provoking controversy among right-wing Hindu groups. Indeed, the production of Deepa Mehta's film *Water*, which challenged traditional Hindu values, had to be discontinued.

Jainism

A Historical Overview

EMMA SALTER

Jainism originated in India. Its name is derived from the term *Jina* (conqueror). Jinas are also called *Tirthankaras* (the terms are synonymous), meaning 'ford-makers'. The Jinas or Tirthankaras are religious teachers who, Jains believe, have attained enlightenment and omniscience by conquering *samsara* (see 'Jainism: Beliefs'). Their state of omniscience means their teachings have indisputable authority and can provide Jains with a crossing or ford (hence 'ford-maker') from *samsara* to liberation.

Early in its history Jainism split into two main sects: Digambara Jainism predominates in South India, Shvetambara in North-West India. Some scholars suggest that the difference in beliefs and practices emerged gradually, the sects bifurcating after the Council of Valabhi at Saurashtra in the fifth century CE, during which the Shvetambara canon was fixed in the absence of any Digambara representation. Today Jainism has many different branches, most of them associated with either Digambara or Shvetambara Jainism.

Twenty-four Jinas

Twenty-four Jinas are born and preach during the third and fourth phases of each half of the cosmic cycle (see 'Jainism: Beliefs'). Jains of the Digambara sect believe all twenty-four Jinas of the last cosmic cycle were men; Shvetambara Jains believe the nineteenth Jina, Mallinath, was a woman. The twenty-fourth and most recent Jina was called Mahavira. Jain tradition states that just a few years after Mahavira's death the cosmos entered the fifth phase of its regressive half-cycle, which will last for approximately 21,000 years. The first Jina of the next group of twenty-four will not be born until the third phase of the next progressive cycle. Historians of religion sometimes associate Jainism's point of origin with the birth of Mahavira. Jains themselves subscribe to a timeless history in which Mahavira is one of a perpetual cycle of spiritual masters. Textual evidence verifies Mahavira as a historical figure who was contemporary with the Buddha. Evidence also supports the historicity of the twenty-third Jina, called Parshva, who lived in Varanasi about 250 years before Mahavira.

Religion in India during Mahavira's lifetime

Mahavira lived towards the end of the Vedic period when religious culture centred on rituals to preserve the health and prosperity of individuals, as well as cosmic equilibrium and political stability. Rituals, which sometimes involved animal sacrifice, were commissioned by high-caste householders, but performed by members of the priestly caste (Brahmans), who monopolized religious authority and had an important status in Indian society. From about the seventh century BCE a number of 'renouncer' traditions (*shramana*) emerged. Breaking with Vedic culture, they shifted the emphasis of their religious practice from external ritual to renunciation and asceticism. Jainism and Buddhism are two examples.

Mahavira's life story

Mahavira lived and preached near Patna, in the state of Bihar. He died aged seventy-two. Historians date his death at around 425 BCE. Digambara Jains believe he died in 510 BCE, Shvetambara Jains in 527 BCE. Jains celebrate five auspicious moments in his life: his conception, birth, renunciation, enlightenment and final spiritual liberation (*moksha*). These five auspicious events, which occur in the lives of each of the Jinas, are thought to authenticate the Jina's identity as a Jina.

Mahavira's life story and teachings are recorded in Jain scriptures. The *Kalpasutra* describes how, after Mahavira's previous incarnation as a celestial being, Indra (the king of the gods) arranged for Mahavira to be transported to his mother's womb. Shvetambara Jainism tells how Mahavira was mistakenly delivered to a Brahman woman before reaching his intended mother, Trisala, who was the wife of King Siddhartha. Jinas are always born into the caste of warriors and noblemen (in contrast to Vedic culture, in which holy men were always Brahmans). The impact of Mahavira's renunciation is enhanced by the luxurious lifestyle he left. Trisala had a series of auspicious dreams during her pregnancy, which were interpreted as predictions that Mahavira would be a

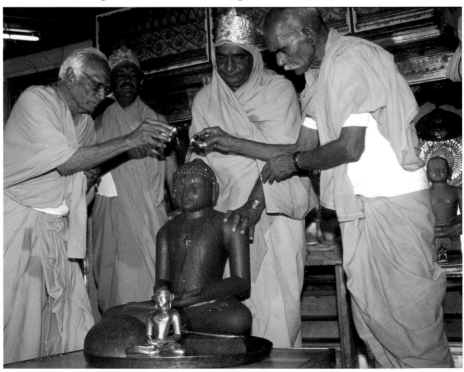

Jains bathing a statue of Lord Mahavira with milk and water.

great political or spiritual leader.

Humans and gods rejoiced when Mahavira was born. Indra took the infant to Mount Meru at the centre of the universe were he was anointed and consecrated. Mahavira was originally named Vardhamana ('increasing') because his family had prospered during his mother's pregnancy. Much later he was given the name Mahavira ('great hero') in recognition of the strict asceticism he practised as an adult.

Shvetambara tradition recalls that when Mahavira was a young man he married Princess Yasoda, who bore him a daughter. Digambara tradition denies this. When Mahavira was thirty, the gods beseeched him to pursue his destiny as a Jina. Heeding them, Mahavira initiated as an ascetic, the gods officiating at the ceremony. As part of his initiation Mahavira renounced all his possessions and even pulled the hair from his head. Novice Jain ascetics still pull the hair from their heads during their initiation ceremonies.

For the rest of his life Mahavira wandered homeless and without possessions. Digambara tradition states that he was naked from the outset. Shvetambara tradition tells how his white robe caught on a bush, but that Mahavira was too deep in contemplation to notice its disappearance. He depended on alms from villagers for sustenance, although the people he encountered often abused him. He practised non-violence, undertook extreme fasting and meditated continually on the nature of the soul. After twelve and a half years Mahavira attained enlightenment and omniscience.

Mahavira's enlightenment is a vital moment in Jain history because it was from this point that his career as the twenty-fourth Jina began. The assemblies (*samavasarana*) at which he preached are depicted frequently in Jain art. Mahavira took the central position surrounded in concentric rings

Leaders and enlightenment

Indrabhuti Gautama and Sudharman were the only two of Mahavira's eleven closest disciples to survive him. Tradition tells how Indrabhuti Gautama's enlightenment was obstructed by his supreme attachment to Mahavira. He was initially distraught by Mahavira's death, but his passion ceased within a few hours when he realized the truth of Mahavira's *moksha* and he became enlightened too. Jains celebrate the combined events of Mahavira's *moksha* and Indrabhuti Gautama's enlightenment during a festival in November called Dipavali.

Sudharman led the ascetic community until he too achieved enlightenment and was succeeded by his disciple Jambu, who also attained enlightenment. Early in the Common Era Jains started to believe that, since Jambu, enlightenment was no longer possible during the current cosmic era. This protects Jainism's claim that its spiritual leaders were omniscient, because no living person's omniscience can be tested.

by his congregation, who consisted of gods, humans and animals. Mahavira faced east, but so that the whole congregation could hear and see him the gods replicated his image to face each cardinal point. According to Digambara Jainism Mahavira's body emitted a divine sound (*divyadhvani*) during his sermons which his disciples translated for the congregation.

During his life Mahavira is believed to have established a Jain community of 36,000 nuns, 14,000 monks, 318,000 laywomen and 159,000 laymen. His first disciples were three Brahman priests: Indrabhuti Gautama and his two brothers, Agnibhuti and Vayubhuti, who converted after Mahavira defeated them in debate. They were soon joined by a further eight Brahman converts, bringing the total of Mahavira's closest disciples to eleven. These eleven disciples had hundreds of disciples of their own, who also converted to Jainism.

'On reaching the most excellent asoka tree, he [Mahavira] ordered his palanquin to be placed beneath it. Then he came out of the palanquin. Thereafter, with his own hand, he took off his wreaths, fineries and ornaments. Having taken them off, he himself tonsured his head in five handfuls.'
Kalpasutra verse 116

'Still in meditation, [Mahavira] attained the supreme knowledge and faith, kevala by name, unsurpassed unobstructed, unlimited, complete and full. "Then Sramana Bhagavan Mahavira became the venerable, victor, omniscient, all-knowing, all observing."'
Kalpasutra verses 120 and 121.

A HISTORICAL OVERVIEW

Mahavira's eleven closest disciples all attained enlightenment under his guidance.

Ascetic and lay communities
Soon after Mahavira's death the community of Jain ascetics began to branch into groups. Having taken a vow of non-possession, they depended for survival upon alms from a laity who shared their values of non-violence and vegetarianism, and lay communities probably developed in tandem quite early. Inscriptions describing donations by tradesmen and artisans date from the beginning of the Common Era. By the fifth century CE alms giving had escalated from food offerings into the construction of ascetics' dwelling halls. By the eleventh century CE numerous ascetic communities existed that were supported by a lay following. Each ascetic community was led by a religious teacher (*acharya*). In Shvetambara Jainism an *acharya*'s religious authority was, and continues to be, authenticated by a lineage traced back to Mahavira's disciple Sudharman.

The spread of Jainism in India
Jains soon began to migrate from the north-east to other regions in India, ascetics to uphold their vows as wandering mendicants, the laity to pursue mercantile opportunities. Some followed a western caravan route towards Delhi, Mathura and finally Gujarat; others followed the southern caravan route towards Orissa, Chennai and Mysore. Mathura was an important Jain centre for trade and culture from about 100 BCE to CE 100, perhaps even earlier: an inscription dated CE 157 at a Jain shrine here implies the shrine was already of considerable antiquity by that date. By about the fourth century CE pressure from the ruling Gupta empire and international trading opportunities led some Jains to travel further west to Valabhi, which became an important centre of Shvetambara Jainism.

Jain presence in South India is confirmed from about the second century BCE by inscriptional evidence at Kalinga. Digambara Jainism continued to be a major religious and cultural influence in South India for almost a millennium. By the sixth century CE Jains were largely divided by geography and sect: Shvetambara Jains in the west, Gujarat, Rajasthan and Punjab; Digambara Jains in the south, Maharashtra and Karnataka. Very few Jains remained near Mahavira's homeland in the north-east.

Royal patronage
The development of Jainism benefited from periods of royal support. King

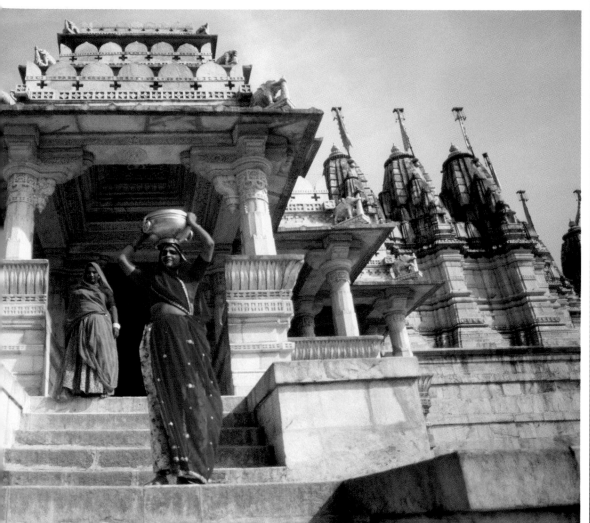

Female worshippers at the Jain temple at Fatehpur Sikri, India.

Srenika, who ruled in Bihar during the period that Mahavira preached, was sympathetic to Mahavira's message. The pro-Jain Nanda dynasty followed by the Chandragupta Maurya dynasty ruled in Bihar until the third century BCE. In Gujarat, King Vanaraja, who had been raised by a Shvetambara ascetic, established Jainism as the state religion from CE 746 to 806. Jain ascetics sometimes forged links with royal patrons, such allegiances affording protection to Jain communities and helping to promote Jainism. Acharya Hemacandra (b. 1089) was court scholar to Jayasimha Siddharaja (King of Gujarat 1092–1141) and to Siddharaja's heir, Kumarpala, who ruled until 1165. With Hemacandra at his side, Kumarpala employed Jain values in the running of his kingdom. He took Jain lay vows, practised vegetarianism, outlawed animal slaughter and erected Jain temples – for example, at Taranga Hill in Gujarat.

Digambara Jains in South India enjoyed almost seven centuries of political stability under the rule of the Ganga dynasty in Karnataka, which came to power in CE 265 with the assistance of a powerful ascetic called Simhanandi. Two other southern dynasties that supported Jainism were the Rashtrakutas in the Deccan between the eighth and twelfth centuries CE and the Hoysalas in

Karnataka between the twelfth and fourteenth centuries. During periods of royal patronage Jainism in North and South India grew in wealth and political influence. However, by the thirteenth century, this influence began to wane under increasing Muslim rule and the Hindu *bhakti* movement.

Heresy and reform

By about the fourth century CE the spiritual ideal of wandering Jain ascetics was jeopardized by ascetics

Part of a column with carvings of dancers in the temple of Dilwara, Luna Vasahi Temple, Mount Abu, Rajasthan, India.

who lived permanently in monasteries. In Shvetambara Jainism these sedentary mendicants were called *caityavasi* (temple-dwellers). Temple-dwelling ascetics questioned the religious validity of perpetual wandering and argued that their presence preserved Jainism by keeping Jain temples active. However, their behaviour was challenged by reformed Jains who upheld the value of non-possession and who regarded sedentary

mendicants as lax and irreligious. In 1024 a reformed ascetic called Jinesvara Suri defeated in debate a temple-dwelling ascetic at the royal court in Patan, Gujarat. During the mid-fifteenth century a famous layman from Gujarat called Lonka Shah established the Lonka Gaccha. These Jains sought to return to Mahavira's teachings, which, according to Lonka Shah's interpretation, meant no *caityavasi* and no use of temples and images during worship.

During the twelfth century an institution of clerics developed within Digambara Jainism. *Bhattarakas* ('venerable ones') underwent minimal ascetic initiation. They managed temple ritual and temple-dwelling ascetics, supervised vow taking by the laity, maintained libraries and oversaw lay religious education. *Bhattarakas* also acted as emissaries between Jain communities and other religious and political authorities. In this role they often wielded significant political influence. *Bhattarakas* are credited with negotiating political protection for Jains and for promoting Jainism through the spread of education and publications. However, as an institution *bhattarakas* are regarded retrospectively as an emblem of spiritual decline in Jainism because their claim to religious authority was not verified by the moral authority of ascetic renunciation. By the early twentieth century most of the thirty-six *bhattaraka* seats in India had become obsolete.

Sacred Writings

EMMA SALTER

Jain sacred writings are not a tidy affair. Jainism has no single textual equivalent to, for example, the Christian Bible. Throughout Jainism's history a variety of religious texts has become regarded as sacred. Some are ancient texts, but many reflect the teachings of relatively recent saints. In Jainism the sacredness of a text is not judged necessarily by its antiquity, but by the religious value of its content and by its use during worship. Jains may regard as sacred writings both an ancient scripture written by an illustrious ascetic and a nineteenth-century hymn written by a pious layman.

Ancient scripture

It is not known when ancient Jain scriptures (*agamas*) were first written down. Early texts were written in Ardhamagadhi (a form of Prakrit) and later in Sanskrit. Jainism's ancient scriptural tradition began orally. Each of Mahavira's disciples is said to have compiled an oral recension of Mahavira's teachings, known collectively as the *Twelve-limbed Basket*. The current extant Jain canon was not written by a single person at a single point in history, although it is accepted by Jains as a reflection of Mahavira's teachings.

Digambara and Shvetambara Jainism do not refer to the same canon. Shvetambara Jains believe their scriptures descend directly from the *Twelve-limbed Basket*, whereas Digambara Jains believe this early literature to have been lost by the second century CE and therefore question the authority of the Shvetambara canon. Nevertheless, some Digambara ascetics accept the authority of some Shvetambara scriptures. Perhaps the migration to South India dislocated Digambara Jains from their early scriptural tradition (see 'Jainism: A Historical Overview'). Some scholars suspect their rejection of Shvetambara scripture was a strategy to establish a clear division between the two sects. Evidence suggests that both scriptural traditions have the same roots.

The Digambara canon

The oldest text accepted by Digambara Jainism is the *Scripture of Six Parts*. It originated with the recollections of the ascetic Dharasena, who lived during the second century CE. Soon afterwards another ascetic, Gunabhadra, composed the *Treatise on the Passions*. These are the only two texts that Digambara Jains accept as belonging to the ancient scriptural tradition. Both discuss the nature of the soul and its liberation from *samsara* (see 'Jainism: Beliefs').

Over the centuries texts written by revered Digambara ascetics have been collated into a corpus of literature that has acquired canonical status. This is organized into four groups known as the *Expositions*.

● One of the most famous texts in the first group is the *Universal History*, which describes among other things the origins of Jainism and society and the lives of Mahavira and the other Jinas. The *Universal History* was written during the eighth century by an ascetic called Jinasena and his pupil Gunabhadra. (Shvetambara Jainism has its own version of the *Universal History*.)

● The second exposition includes texts about cosmology.

● The third exposition includes texts about codes of behaviour for ascetic and lay Jains. Some of the most important texts in this group were composed by a famous Digambara *acharya* called Kundakunda, whom some historians place in the eighth century CE, although Digambara tradition places him several centuries earlier.

● The fourth exposition includes a broad range of metaphysical works and devotional hymns.

The Shvetambara canon

The Shvetambara canon was formed during three councils at which senior Shvetambara ascetics, but no Digambara ascetics, recited what they could remember of the oral tradition. Their recollections were recorded and collated into textual scripture. The first council was held in Patna one hundred and sixty years after Mahavira's death. The second council occurred eight hundred and twenty-seven years after Mahavira's death. It was held simultaneously at Mathura, in the north, and at Valabhi, in the west. This led to some discrepancies, but Shvetambara Jains generally accepted the Mathura version as the first official canon. The third council, at which the Shvetambara canon was finally closed, was held at Valabhi during the first half of the fifth century. The problem for scholars attempting to reconstruct the early Shvetambara canon is that no lists of the texts accepted at any of these councils remain.

The Shvetambara canon is organized into three groups. First are the *Purva*, the tradition of lost scripture that Digambara and Shvetambara Jains accept as authoritative. Next are the Twelve Limbs, of which the twelfth text is lost. The third group is divided into five categories of subsidiary texts that do not originate with Mahavira's disciples, but with later ascetic teachers.

This is a broad and inclusive outline of the Shvetambara canon. Not all Shvetambara Jains accept all of the texts as authoritative. For example, two branches of Shvetambara Jainism,

'The enlightened world-view, enlightened knowledge and enlightened conduct are the path to liberation.'

Tattvarthasutra by Umasvati verse 1.1.

Sthanakvasi Jains and Terapanthi Jains, reject texts that advocate image worship.

Tattvarthasutra

One important text that is accepted by both Digambara and Shvetambara Jainism is the *Tattvarthasutra*. It was written during the fourth or fifth century CE by the ascetic Umasvati, about whom little is known, although Digambara and Shvetambara Jains both claim he belonged to their sect. The *Tattvarthasutra* was the first significant Jain text to be written in Sanskrit and the first text to organize the main aspects of Jain doctrine into a single volume. The opening verse of the *Tattvarthasutra* identifies the essence of Jain doctrine as correct faith, correct knowledge and correct conduct. This triad became known as 'the three jewels of Jainism'.

Attitudes towards scripture

Historically, only ascetics were allowed to study scripture. Laypeople were precluded because they could not read the non-vernacular language of the texts and because scriptural study without the qualification of ascetic rigour was considered dangerous. The laity encountered sacred literature at religious lectures delivered by ascetics and through their devotional practices. Partly as a result of this, Jainism lays claim to a substantial quantity of devotional texts written by laypeople in their vernacular languages. More recently, attitudes have changed. Edited editions of some sacred Jain texts have been published, which has widened access for lay Jains and non-Jains. However, a vast corpus of sacred literature remains within the exclusive domain of ascetic communities.

Beliefs

EMMA SALTER

Much of Jain doctrine is concerned with the nature of the soul and its liberation from bondage. Every living being has a soul that is trapped in *samsara* (the continuous cycle of birth, death and rebirth that binds a soul to its worldly existence). A soul bound in *samsara* is believed to be suffering, even if the body in which it is incarnated enjoys a happy life, because bound souls are unaware of their true nature, which is omniscience and absolute bliss. Omniscience is pure and simultaneous knowledge of all things. Once a soul becomes fully aware of its true nature it is released from *samsara* and becomes a liberated soul (*arhat* or *kevalin*) that endures no more incarnations and suffers no further worldly entrapment. The Jinas were *arhats* who were distinguished by their vital roles as religious teachers.

When the physical body in which a liberated soul is incarnated dies, the liberated soul attains *moksha* (a state of absolute purity and perfection) and is called *siddha*. *Siddhas* do not have physical bodies. They reside at the topmost part of the universe, where they exist in a constant state of omniscience and bliss, and have no further dealings with mundane, worldly affairs. The soteriological goal of Jainism is to attain *moksha* and become *siddha*.

Bondage

Souls are trapped in *samsara* because of the effects of *karma*.

● In Jainism *karma* is believed to be physical matter that permeates the entire universe, but which is so fine that it is imperceptible. Under certain conditions *karma* 'sticks' to the soul and obscures the soul's knowledge of its true, pure nature. Imagine how dust on a mirror prevents the mirror from giving a clear reflection. A soul generates energy by motivating the body to perform mental, verbal or physical actions. This energy attracts free-floating *karma* towards the soul.

● *Karma* is unable to stick to the soul of its own accord. For this to happen, *kashaya* (which translates loosely as 'passion' and includes feelings of anger, pride, deception and greed) needs to be present. The soul produces *kashaya* in response to attachment, of which there are two types: attraction to an event or a thing, and aversion to an event or a thing.

● Eventually *karma* 'stuck' to the soul matures and produces an effect (a mental, verbal or physical action usually reflecting the activity by which it was attracted) before falling naturally away. That is why Jains sometimes refer to the circumstances of peoples' lives as resulting from their *karma*.

● *Karma* sometimes produces unpleasant results, sometimes pleasing results, but as all *karma* traps the soul in *samsara* it is anomalous to describe any *karma* as 'good'. The action *karma* induces the soul to take generates energy that attracts more *karma* towards the soul. The soul's response of attraction or aversion to the action causes more *karma* to stick to the soul and so the cycle continues.

Thus, *karma* traps the soul in *samsara* because it deludes it of its own pure nature, and because it entangles it in a perpetual cycle of action and reaction. A soul has to be reincarnated over and over again to expel the *karma* it has accrued, whilst at the same time it continues to accrue more *karma*. The type of *karma* accrued determines the soul's next incarnation.

> 'The five causes of bondage are: deluded world-view, non-abstinence, laxity, passions and the actions of the body, speech and mind. Because of its passions, the soul attracts and assimilates the material particles of karmic bondage. The result is bondage.'
>
> Tattvarthasutra by Umasvati verses 8.1 to 8.3.

BELIEFS

Liberation

Jains state that the binding effect of *karma* is not the same as predestination (in which a person has no free will to affect the events of her or his life) because the soul is an intellectual force that exerts free will by the way it chooses to respond to life's events. Jains aim to control the type and quantity of *karma* attracted to their soul through their religious practices (see 'Jainism: Worship and Festivals'). Strategies for overcoming the mechanism of bondage therefore provide a moral framework for Jains to live by.

Jains do not depend upon an external figure of salvation, but have to take personal responsibility for their liberation. Mahavira's teachings describe how Jains can cleanse their souls of *karma*, but Mahavira cannot undertake the process for them. The path of religious practice leading to liberation (*moksha marg*) is charted by the *gunasthanas*, fourteen stages of purity through which a soul has to pass on its way to *moksha*:

● The fourth stage is a vital turning point in a Jain's spiritual journey because it is at this stage that a Jain experiences *samyak darshana*, true insight. Jains interpret the experience of *samyak darshana* differently. For some it is a deep personal commitment to their religion, for others it is religious commitment coupled with a spiritual experience of communion with their soul.

● The *anuvratas* (lay vows) are taken at the fifth *gunasthana* and the *mahavratas* (ascetic vows) are taken at the sixth *gunasthana* (see 'Jainism: Family and Society'). Jains believe that only ascetics can attain liberation. Shvetambara Jains believe that women ascetics can attain liberation, whereas

A worshipper places gifts and anoints the feet of Gomatesvara, the 'Colossus of Mysore', erected in CE 983 at Shravana Belagola, Karnataka, southern India.

Digambara Jains believe liberation can only be achieved by men.

● At the thirteenth *gunasthana* all deluding *karma* is finally dispelled and the soul attains omniscience.

● At the moment of death all *karma* associated with embodiment is exhausted and the liberated soul attains *moksha*. This is the fourteenth *gunasthana*.

Jains believe that in this part of the universe, during the current cosmic era, it is not possible to progress beyond the seventh *gunasthana*.

God and divinity
Jains do not believe in a creator-God, so Jainism is sometimes described as atheistic. This is a misrepresentation. In Jainism liberated souls are venerated as divine beings and it is these, but most

specifically the Jinas, whom Jains worship. The hierarchy of beings worthy of veneration is expressed in the *Panch Namaskara Mantra*:

I bow before the arhats
I bow before the siddhas
I bow before acharyas
I bow before ascetic teachers
I bow before all ascetics
This fivefold salutation
Which destroys all sin
Is pre-eminent as the most
auspicious of all auspicious things.
ADAPTED FROM P.S. JAINI, *THE JAINA PATH OF PURIFICATION*

The recital of this, the most popular and widely used mantra in Jainism, is incorporated into most patterns of worship and it is accepted, with small variations, by all Jain sects. The *arhats* – embodied, liberated beings – are the first to receive veneration because they perpetuate Jain teachings. *Siddhas* have attained *moksha* and so no longer engage in worldly affairs.

The Nature of the Soul
Physical bodies consist of matter: they cannot act, think or respond to the world unless 'inhabited' by a soul, which is their sentient force. The soul is the only type of substance in the universe that has the capacity for consciousness, which is its fundamental quality. Two other qualities of the soul are energy and bliss. Only liberated souls can fully experience bliss.

Jains believe that all living beings have a soul. They also believe that the entire universe is permeated by infinite, minute life monads that exist alongside more substantial life forms such as plants, animals, humans, celestial beings and hell beings. When a living being dies, its soul is immediately reincarnated into another body, although not necessarily of the same type. For example, a human being may not necessarily be reincarnated as

'Morality is perfect forgiveness, humility, straight forwardness, purity (freedom from greed), truthfulness, self-restraint, austerity, renunciation, detachment and continence.'

Tattvarthasutra by Umasvati verse 9.6.

BELIEFS

another human being. Although souls are not material, they expand or shrink to fit precisely the size and shape of their current corporeal form. Just as the light from a lamp will fill different sized rooms, so a soul will fill different sized bodies.

Souls are eternal, which means they can be neither created nor destroyed and every soul is likely to have experienced every conceivable embodiment millions of times over. Jains therefore generally adopt an attitude of respect to all living beings in the belief that one may have been similarly incarnated in a previous life and that most beings have the potential of becoming *siddha* in a future incarnation.

Jains believe that all living beings, no matter how small, have the capacity for suffering because all living beings have a soul and are therefore conscious. Causing harm to another soul is believed to generate an influx of *karma* to one's own soul. For this reason Jains take great lengths to avoid harmful behaviour. Non-violence is Jainism's principal ethical value and the emphasis Jains give to it has earned them a reputation for compassion and tolerance. Their commitment to non-violence, combined with their belief in the ubiquity of life, has resulted in many of Jainism's characteristic religious practices, such as vegetarianism (see 'Jainism: Worship and Festivals'). Jainism's doctrine of non-violence is said to have inspired Mahatma Gandhi in his peaceful protest for India's freedom from British rule.

Cosmology

Jains believe the cosmos is uncreated and eternal. It is dualistic, consisting of consciousness (determined by the presence of souls) and that which is not conscious. That which is not conscious includes both matter and aspects which are neither material nor conscious, for example, space, time, motion and non-motion.

Matter has shape, colour, taste, smell and density. From a philosophical perspective Jainism regards matter as both permanent and temporary. It is permanent because the physical atoms that make up material substances are constant, they can be neither created nor destroyed. At the same time matter is temporary because substances with particular qualities and modes are formed when atoms combine, but when the combined atoms dissipate the substance they have formed is destroyed. Atoms then rejoin in different combinations to form new substances with different qualities and modes.

The structure of the Jain cosmos is finite in size, but vast beyond human imaginings. Its shape is sometimes described as two drums balanced on top of each other or as a human figure standing legs apart and hands on hips. At the base of the cosmos are seven realms of hell, inhabited by hell beings who suffer hideous tortures as a result of the bad *karma* they have accrued during previous incarnations. Above the seven realms of hell is a middle

As wandering mendicants, these Sthanakvasi nuns do not reside for more than two or three days at any one place.

realm, *madhya loka*, the smallest cosmic realm and the domain of human habitation. Above *madhya loka* are seven celestial realms, which are inhabited by celestial beings who live in great luxury and splendour as a result of the meritorious *karma* they have accrued during previous incarnations. At the very top of the cosmos is *siddha loka*, also known as *isatpragbhara* (the slightly curving place), where liberated souls, those free from *karma*, reside in a state of *moksha*.

From a soteriological perspective *madhya loka* is the most significant cosmic realm because it is where humans live. Liberation is only possible from a human incarnation, and then only as an ascetic. *Madhya loka* undergoes perpetual cyclical phases, like a wheel constantly rotating. There are six phases of ascent during which *madhya loka* becomes increasingly more spiritual and human suffering decreases. This is followed by six phases of descent during which spiritual purity declines and suffering increases. Twenty-four Jinas are born and preach

in *madhya loka* during the third and fourth phases of each half cycle. It is only possible to attain *moksha* during these phases, because during the other phases society is either in such a state of suffering that it cannot accept the possibility of liberation or in such a state of contentment that it cannot accept the necessity for liberation. Jains believe that our world entered the fifth phase of the descending cycle soon after Mahavira's death. Only one region in *madhya loka*, called *mahavideha*, is immune to the cycle of ascent and descent. Here a Jina (currently Simadhar Svami) is always preaching and so *moksha* can be attained at any time. The structure and mechanism of the cosmos explains why liberation is not currently possible in our world, but encourages religious effort by the opportunity of rebirth in *mahavideha*.

Family and Society

EMMA SALTER

There are over three million Jains in the world, the majority of whom live in India. Digambara Jains live predominantly in the Deccan, Delhi, East Rajasthan and neighbouring Madhya Pradesh. Shvetambara Jains live predominantly in Mumbai, Delhi, Rajasthan, Gujarat and Madhya Pradesh. There are also Jain communities in East Africa, Europe and North America.

Jain religious society is organized into a fourfold structure of female ascetics, male ascetics, laywomen and laymen, a pattern said to have been established by the first Jina, Rishabha (also called Adinatha), and re-established by the subsequent twenty-three Jinas. The inclusion of ascetic and lay communities in Jain religious society indicates that both communities share the same goal of spiritual liberation.

There are numerous Jain sects, most of which are associated with Digambara or Shvetambara Jainism. Most have their own ascetic and lay communities. The origin of different sects often lay with reformers who established a new ascetic lineage after a reinterpretation of doctrine or practice. For example, the seventeenth-century reformer Lavaji founded the Sthanakvasi branch of Shvetambara Jainism when he broke from the Lonka Gaccha because they had returned to the practice of image worship.

Ascetic communities

Ascetic communities are hierarchical. Novice ascetics are at the bottom of the hierarchy. The spiritual head and leader of an ascetic order is called an *acharya*. *Acharyas* and other senior

ascetics may have many lay disciples as well as their ascetic followers. Throughout Jain history far more women than men have taken ascetic initiation. Despite this, they are usually regarded as subordinate to their male counterparts, even if they are older or have been an ascetic longer. Much earlier in Jain history children sometimes took ascetic initiation. In modern times only adults are allowed to become ascetics and only after they have been granted permission by their next of kin.

Before initiation is permitted, a Jain layperson has to progress through eleven stages of renunciation (*pratimas*) under the supervision of an *acharya*. This includes taking five lay vows (the *anuvratas*) which are a less rigorous version of the ascetics' vows. The ceremony at which a novice ascetic is fully initiated is called *diksha*. Lay and ascetic communities come together to celebrate and perform ascetic initiation. During the *diksha* the novice wears luxurious clothes, similar to wedding finery, and is treated like royalty. This final extravagance emphasizes the material sacrifice the novice makes as she or he renounces all possessions and association with worldly life, including familial contact. The novice takes five ascetic vows (the *mahavratas*):

● non-violence

● truthfulness

● not taking anything that has not been given freely

● celibacy (fidelity for the lay Jain)

● non-attachment to worldly possessions (restriction of wealth and possessions for the lay Jain)

Finally the novice ascetic plucks the hair from her or his own head as a symbol of commitment to the ascetic way of life. Then the new initiate undertakes a period of fasting, which is broken the first time she or he seeks alms.

To uphold their vows of renunciation ascetics have no permanent home and are permitted to spend only a few days in any one place. In small groups they walk between towns and villages, where they receive donations of food from Jain laypeople. They take shelter in lodging halls (*upashraya*) built exclusively for them by the lay community. Their vow of non-violence means they are only allowed to travel on foot, because motorized transport may harm insects and other small creatures, and they cease their wanderings temporarily for the monsoon season (approximately July to October) when travelling would risk breaking their vow of non-violence because of the proliferation of insect life. It is during this period that they have a sustained period of contact with the lay community. For this reason many Jain festivals in which ascetics and laypeople take part occur during the monsoon season.

Mutual Benefit

Jain ascetics renounce all worldly attachments, but they do not live in solitude. Instead, ascetics are public figures who are under more or less constant scrutiny by their lay followers. They have no money and are not allowed to prepare food themselves, so they have to maintain contact with lay communities, on whom they are dependent for their material needs. Lay Jains depend on ascetics for their spiritual needs. Ascetics deliver sermons to the laity, usually from the local *upashraya*, they counsel laypeople in religious matters and administer vows of fasting and other austerities. Laypeople also accrue spiritual merit for providing ascetics with food and shelter. Lay Jains regard ascetics as worthy of veneration because they embody Jainism's doctrinal message as living paradigms of the religious ideal.

Lay Communities

Jain lay society is divided by sect and caste. Interaction and intermarriage between Jains of different sects in India is rare, although this is more frequent amongst diaspora communities because of a greater need for solidarity. In India intermarriage between Jains and Hindus of the same caste is not uncommon. The Jain marriage ceremony and funeral rites are similar to their Hindu equivalent. Jains believe that religious qualities are judged by a person's conduct, not by their birth status, so caste division is restricted to a secular societal role. However, in practice many Jain sects prohibit low-caste Jains from taking ascetic initiation. Sthanakvasi Jainism is an exception.

Jain commitment to non-violence means they are prohibited from entering professions associated with causing harm to other living beings. For example, a Jain would never operate a slaughterhouse or trade in leather goods. Apart from this restriction Jains enter all types of professions. In India many are traders or financiers.

In modern times it is rare for lay Jains to take lay vows unless they intend to initiate as mendicants in the future. Nevertheless, the practice of non-violence is a strong influence in their daily lives. Jains are vegetarian. Many also avoid eating potatoes, which they believe to contain millions of tiny life-forms, and root vegetables because harvesting them may cause harm to earth dwelling creatures. Jain households tie small muslin bags over their taps to filter their water. This is to avoid ingesting water bodies and harming them. (Jains living in countries where tap water is not fit for drinking boil and re-filter their water for health purposes). Non-violence also extends to proactive endeavours, such as charitable donations.

'The universe is peopled by manifold creatures who are, in this round of rebirth, born in different families and castes for having done various actions... Sometimes they become nobles or outcasts and untouchables, or worms and moths, or... ants.'

Uttaradhyayana Sutra

FAMILY AND SOCIETY

Worship and Festivals

EMMA SALTER

In Jainism worship is directed towards ascetics, because their commitment to renunciation and non-violence is thought to represent the religious ideal taught by Mahavira and the other Jinas. Lay Jains venerate ascetics, and ascetics venerate their superiors. The *Panch Namaskara Mantra*, which is recited by ascetic and lay Jains, venerates all ascetics, from the novice to the liberated soul (see 'Jainism: Beliefs'). Ascetics are believed to have progressed further along the path of liberation (*moksha marg*) than lay Jains, and have therefore attained a higher level of spiritual purity.

Veneration of ascetics

Whenever a lay Jain meets an ascetic, whether at a public sermon or a private interview, she or he performs a rite of veneration (*guru-vandan*), bowing twice to the ground in front of the ascetic and reciting a short prayer of veneration. Often the ascetic will then offer a blessing. Devout Jains visit ascetics' lodgings daily to perform *guru-vandan*. Theoretically lay Jains do not personalize their veneration towards one particular ascetic, because all Jain ascetics are equal representatives of Jainism's religious ideal. In practice they sometimes revere a particular ascetic as their special guru.

Veneration of the Jinas

The twenty-four Jinas were perfect, liberated ascetics who taught the path of liberation and attained *moksha* and are thus the principal focus of worship. Jains worship the Jinas during rituals called *puja*. They also express their veneration of them in a rich tradition of devotional songs.

Shvetambara Jains of the Terapanthi and Sthanakvasi sects and Digambara Jains of the Taranapanthi sect do not use images of the Jinas during worship. They do not believe the practice was sanctioned by the Jinas. Ascetic and lay Jains who belong to these sects perform their worship in plain halls, usually attached to the ascetics' lodgings, venerating the Jinas through *mantra* chanting, meditation and scriptural study. If available, a senior ascetic teacher may provide a focal point; otherwise a scriptural text may be used as a substitute. In either case it is the Jinas' teachings that are the central focus of veneration.

Other Shvetambara and Digambara sects use images of the Jinas during their worship. Usually crafted in marble or metal, they depict the twenty-four Jinas as identical to each other; with robust male physiques, broad shoulders and narrow waists and always meditating, either sitting or standing. A symbol carved at the base of each image identifies which Jina it represents: for example, images of Mahavira are identified by a lion. Images of Parshvana, the twenty-third Jina, have a canopy of cobra hoods. Digambara images are plain and naked, depicting the Jinas in their ascetic role. Shvetambara images depict the Jinas as nobility, before they became ascetics, and so are bejewelled, dressed in royal regalia and adorned with gold or silver crowns. A Digambara or Shvetambara temple is often very ornate and beautiful and is usually dedicated to a single Jina, an image of whom is the focal point. Large temples may also house images of other Jinas and associated deities.

Most ritual worship in the temple is non-congregational. One simple ritual (*darshan*) means gazing upon the image of a Jina with a feeling of devotion and humility. Another ritual (*aarti*) is usually performed in the evening and involves placing five small candles – representing five different types of knowledge – on a special tray. Worshippers then wave the tray in clockwise, circular motions before the image while singing devotional hymns. Another ritual that many Jains perform

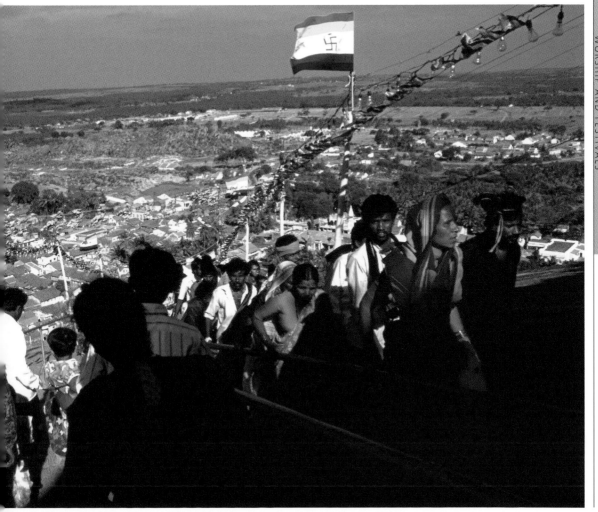

Pilgrims climb up the stairs towards the Vindhyagiri Hill shrines at Shravana Belagola, Karnataka, southern India.

daily is the *'puja* of eight substances' (see panel).

As liberated beings who have transcended worldly affairs, the Jinas take no reciprocal role during worship. Worship does not appease them and they do not respond to it by granting favours. Despite this, Jains feel immense love and devotion towards the Jinas.

The most important aspect of Jain worship is the devotional sentiment of the worshipper, regardless of ritual patterns or whether or not an image is present. For this reason Jains have to perform their own worship, no one else can do it on their behalf. Substances used during rituals are not offerings from the worshipper to the Jinas (who have no use for them), but gestures of renunciation on the part of the worshipper. This is one reason why ascetics cannot perform temple rituals; they own nothing and therefore have nothing to renounce.

Festivals

Festivals are a time when lay Jains worship collectively and are often a time when lay and ascetic communities come together. Most Jain festivals celebrate an aspect from the lives of the Jinas: for example, *Mahavira Jayanti* in March/April celebrates Mahavira's birthday. Jains share some festivals with Hindus and in mid-October celebrate *Diwali*. For Jains, however, *Diwali* signals the start of a new ritual and commercial year and celebrates Mahavira's transcendence to *moksha* and the enlightenment of his disciple Gautama.

Paryushan (abiding) is an important Shvetambara festival because it closes the old year. It occurs in August/September and lasts for eight days:

● Jains may attend the temple more often than usual.

'Micchami dukkadam' ('May my improper actions be inconsequential').

John E. Cort

● Some perform fasts leading up to *Paryushan*, culminating on the last day of the festival when there is a celebratory feast. Fasting is an important and frequently performed religious practice amongst Jain laity. It is usually women who fast, men often claim to be restricted by their professional obligations. In addition to having spiritual benefits, the completion of an arduous fast may also improve the social prestige of the family of the person fasting.

● Particularly pious lay Jains may stay at the mendicants' lodgings, having taken temporary vows of asceticism.

● Some may make a pilgrimage to a holy site, such as Mount Shatrunjaya in Gujarat or Shravana Belagola in Karnataka.

● Ascetics deliver sermons daily for the first three days of *Paryushan* and twice daily for the remaining five days. On the fourth to seventh days this involves a public reading of the *Kalpasutra*, a Shvetambara scripture that contains histories of the twenty-four Jinas. The description of Mahavira's birth, on the second day of the reading, is accompanied by an elaborate ritual and great celebration.

● On the final day Jains perform *pratikraman*, a congregational ritual that is a communal statement of atonement and repentance for any harmful actions that may have been committed during the year. For more pious Jains *pratikraman* is also a daily practice.

● At the end of *Paryushan* many Jains send cards or emails to relatives and friends, seeking forgiveness for any wrong doing. A sincere Jain carries no grudge or quarrel over into the new year.

The *'puja* of eight substances'

This ritual varies slightly between Jain communities. It is usually performed in the morning after bathing.

■ Upon entering the temple the worshipper bows before the Jina image while saying *'nisihi'* (abandonment) signifying that she or he has left the mundane world and entered the sanctity of the temple.

■ The worshipper then circumambulates the image three times clockwise.

■ Shvetambara Jains anoint the image (with milk mixed with water) and while reciting special prayers use the third finger of their right hand to apply camphor and sandalwood paste to nine parts of the image in the following order: left and right big toes, right and left knees, right and left wrists, right and left shoulders, crown, forehead, throat, chest and navel. Digambara Jains do not touch their Jina images, so for this part of the ritual they sit before the image pouring water (or a mixture of milk and water) from one vessel into another and reciting prayers.

■ Shvetambaras and Digambaras place a fresh flower by the image and in a circular motion waft incense followed by a camphor lamp.

■ The worshipper then performs a joyous dance before the image while waving a yak-tail fan.

■ Next, the reflection of the Jina's image is observed in a hand-held mirror.

■ The worshipper then places a handful of dry rice on a special plate, forming it into the shape of a swastika (representing four possible incarnations: human, animal, celestial being or hell being). Some food (usually sweets, fruit or nuts) and sometimes a small amount of money, is placed on top of the rice swastika.

■ At the end of the ritual the worshipper says *'nisihi'* again, perhaps spends some time in spiritual contemplation, and usually sounds a bell upon departure.

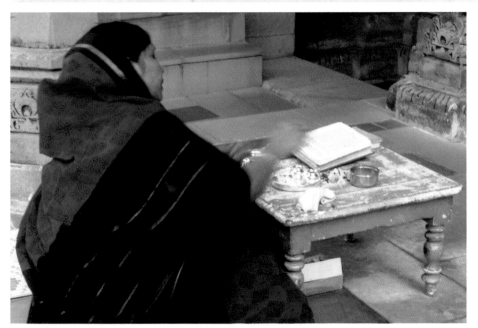

Jain worshipper performing the daily ritual of the *'puja* of eight substances'.

The equivalent Digambara festival is called *Dashalakshanaparvan* (Festival of Ten Religious Qualities) and lasts for ten days:

● The ten chapters of the *Tattvarthasutra* (see 'Jainism: Sacred Writings') are recited publicly, with laypeople taking an active role because there are relatively few Digambara ascetics.

● Towards the end of the festival a special *puja* with flowers is performed to Ananta, the fourteenth Jina.

● On the last day rites of atonement are performed, similar to those of *Paryushan.*

Ascetic practices

By taking ascetic initiation a Jain dedicates her or his life to spiritual progression. Therefore, every activity an ascetic performs might be described as a form of devotion, observance or worship. The vows of renunciation ascetics take mean they no longer have a secular role in society. Their worldly possessions are replaced with those things necessary for their ascetic lifestyle. For Digambara ascetics this is a broom made from naturally shed peacock feathers and a water pot. They do not wear robes, Digambara literally meaning 'sky-clad' (i.e. naked). It is socially unacceptable for women to be 'sky-clad', which is one reason Digambaras (unlike Shvetambaras) do not accept that women can attain liberation. Shvetambara ascetics receive a set of simple white robes, a bowl for collecting alms and a broom made from naturally shed cow-tail hair. As well as relinquishing worldly possessions, renunciation also means giving up anything that may be pleasing to the senses, such as tasty food or comfortable living quarters.

Of the five ascetic vows, the most famous is commitment to non-violence: not harming any creature, however small or seemingly insignificant, by action, speech or thought, and not condoning such actions by others. Ascetics use their broom to gently sweep the ground before them free from insects, so that they do not tread on them. During the rainy season they do not travel, because the risk of harming creatures is too great. Terapanthi and Sthanakvasi Shvetambaras wear cloth mouth-shields to protect tiny airborne creatures from being harmed by their breath. During alms collection donations are accepted only if they meet the ascetics' strict ethical requirements, food being inspected for insects and other impurities prior to consumption. Collecting or eating alms after dark is prohibited because cooking fires may lure insects to their deaths. Jain commitment to non-violence also includes honesty, respect and

compassion towards others.

● The first three matrices of doctrine are restraint of mind, body and speech (not using these faculties for frivolous or irreligious activities). The other five help to avoid harm to living beings by imposing carefulness while walking, speaking, alms collecting, picking up and putting down objects and going to the toilet.

● The six obligatory actions woven into the ascetic's daily routine are concerned with internal attitudes: meditating to achieve equanimity (*samayika*); praising the twenty-four Jinas; venerating senior ascetics (*guru-vandana*); repenting harmful actions (*pratikraman*); abandoning bodily needs during lengthy meditation (*kayotsarga*); and performing specific austerities (*pacckkhana*).

Ascetic practices, which can be internal or external, are believed to 'burn off' *karma* already attached to the soul. Internal practices develop spirituality and are met by the six obligatory actions. External practices involve enduring physical hardships. The most frequently performed is fasting, which includes total abstinence from food for a designated period, reduction – for example, eating every other day – or denial of certain types of food. The most dramatic form is *sallekhana* (elective fasting until death). The ascetic meditates throughout, to maintain a state of equanimity, which is believed to result in a meritorious rebirth. Ascetics are permitted to perform *sallekhana* only if they are already facing death by terminal illness or old age, and the process must be overseen by a senior ascetic. Few perform *sallekhana*, but those who do are highly celebrated.

A revered Jain *acharya* with a book of his teachings.

'The observer of vows should cultivate friendliness towards all living beings, delight in the distinction and honour of others, compassion for miserable, lowly creatures and equanimity towards the vainglorious.'

Tattvarthasutra by Umasvati chapter 7 verse 6.

I am a Jain

SAMANI CHARITRA PRAJNA

Om. Without spirituality there is no meaning to life.

I am a Jain nun and have been practising Jainism for nineteen years. I joined my monastery when I was eighteen. Jain ascetic life is very simple: I have two sets of clothes; I eat pure vegetarian food in handmade wooden bowls; I have no monetary assets (no property, no bank balance etc); I have given up family attachments; and I am happy, having no desires for material possessions.

I did not become a nun because I was unhappy. I had incredibly happy moments with my parents, my two sisters and brother. I was born in Chennai, in southern India. My father is a physician and radiologist, my mother a housewife. We always said prayers and meditated for an hour on Sunday. The inspiration of my family and the religious environment in which I was brought up made a deep impression on me and developed within me. My parents are not only followers of the Jain religion, but have applied Jain principles throughout their lives. Their deep spirituality and religious commitment influenced me a lot.

Eventually I started to learn more about Jainism by discussing and spending time with many Jain monks and nuns who visited Chennai. Their simple way of life appealed to me. After finishing my education at high school, I sought the permission of my parents to join the training institution for nuns. I had to wait for a couple of years to convince my parents of my commitment to the religious life: they needed to be sure this was what I really wanted. I wanted a life that was peaceful, purposeful, productive and progressive. I wanted something special that gave me a feeling of contentment and fulfilment. Finally, I chose this path. In the Jain training centre I read not only the holy scriptures but also comparative studies of different religions, philosophies and ideas. I studied for a Masters degree in comparative religion and philosophy at the Jain Vishwa Bharati Institute at Ladnun in Rajasthan. This period of study helped me to understand my beliefs and values with more clarity.

After six years of training, my spiritual gurus Acharya Tulsi and Acharya Mahaprajna initiated me in August at a gathering of thousands of people. It was a deeply spiritual celebration. I took vows of non-violence, truth, non-stealing, celibacy and non-possession. It is a lifelong commitment with self-discipline and self-control. That day I was so happy – my dream was coming true. I was at the feet of my guru receiving blessings for this new journey of spiritual enlightenment. I was dressed in a white robe. My head was shaved. I was named 'Samani Charitra Prajna'.

Acharya Tulsi and Acharya Mahaprajna established the Saman Order in 1980. Their vision was to propagate and reinforce the message of non-violence, peace and harmony throughout the world. In Jainism we believe that water, air, fire, earth and plants are living beings. Although it is not possible to be completely non-violent, we try to prevent unnecessary violence by our actions, words and thoughts. Acharya Tulsi established a new form of monastic life. The lifestyle of a *saman* or *samni* is very similar to that of a monk or nun in other Jain monastic communities, but there are differences. For example, we use transport in order to educate and enhance human life and values at the global level.

As a *samni* my lifestyle is totally different from that of a secular person. I spend four to five hours a day in meditation, prayer, chanting and reading the holy scriptures. Twice a day, before sunrise and after sunset, I recite a special prayer known as *pratikraman*, in which I ask for forgiveness from and give forgiveness to all living beings; if I have committed sins or violated any kind of vows I repent and resolve not to repeat them. I freely admit my flaws and mistakes and seek to improve myself.

I observe *preksha* meditation every day. A very scientific technique, it is aimed at transforming my inner personality; it is known to have a great impact on the endocrine system by changing the biochemicals and balancing the hormones. It helps me a lot, enabling me to eliminate negative emotions and regenerate the positive qualities. It benefits me by relaxing me and giving me peace of mind. Also as a *samni* I do not eat and drink before sunrise and after sunset. This religious ritual has a basis in science, in that it has been shown that sunlight is needed for good digestion.

Along with the daily practice of meditation and prayer, once a year I celebrate eight special days of spiritual enhancement and upliftment of my soul. This is called *paryushan* ('being closer to your soul') and is practised not only by monks and nuns, but the whole Jain community. We listen to sermons, fast day and night and practise living simply with detachment from the material world and self-control. The last day of *paryushan* is considered very important, because this is the day we recall all our past mistakes and sins and ask for forgiveness from those against whom we have sinned and give forgiveness to those who have sinned against us.

Jainism emphasizes a process of self-purification. All my efforts are focused on freeing the soul from the bondage of *karma*.

Being a *samni*, ten months a year I travel extensively in India and overseas to lecture at universities, at colleges, at national and international conferences and to various associations. I have often participated in interfaith dialogues and discussions. I have conducted many camps, workshops and seminars on stress management, anger management, the science of living and ailments (e.g. diabetes, high blood pressure, anxiety, obesity, allergies and heart attacks). I often receive an overwhelming response from people of all ages because it helps to alleviate their physical, mental and emotional ailments. The rest of my time I spend in the presence of my guru. His holy presence itself clarifies many doubts and queries.

I am very happy to have dedicated my whole life to a good cause and to be a follower of the message of non-violence and a soul-oriented religion that emphasizes human values.

Jainism in the Modern World

EMMA SALTER

Jainism is a dynamic religion, remaining relevant in the modern world by responding to social change and to scientific and technological innovations. Some Jains embrace modernization, others prefer to uphold established traditions, and the different points of view have sometimes led to tension within the Jain community. The estimated one hundred thousand Jains living outside India face additional challenges, in that Jain ascetics play a vital role in the religious practices of Jain laypeople yet are allowed to travel only on foot and are not permitted to travel outside India.

Social change and modernization

Changing social values have influenced traditional Jain practices. For example, most Jain sects no longer allow children to take ascetic initiation. Jains sometimes attempt to demonstrate the validity of Jain doctrine by reference to current social issues, such as associating vegetarianism with healthy living or associating non-violence with cultural tolerance. In 1992 L.M. Singhvi published *The Jain Declaration on Nature*, which promotes the ecological and environmental benefits of Jainism. These modernist perspectives on the Jain doctrine of non-violence are accretions to the traditional doctrinal meaning that intend to appeal to contemporary society.

Jainism has also had to respond to scientific discoveries. Some Jains have suggested that science proves the truth of Jain doctrine and, therefore, the authority of the Jinas, because Jain teachings about the formation of matter from particles correspond

with scientific discoveries about atoms. Where science and doctrine are not reconciled, as with the structure of the cosmos, Jains have to decide whether to accept scientific discovery and reclassify their doctrinal beliefs as mythical or reject scientific discovery and hold fast to their doctrinal beliefs.

Technological advances have presented Jains with new ethical dilemmas. Some progressive mendicants use microphones during their sermons to ensure the entire congregation can hear them. Other mendicants refuse to use electrical equipment out of concern that electricity may harm tiny airborne creatures. Advances in printing and publishing and information technology have made Jain literature increasingly accessible to a broad readership that includes lay Jains and non-Jains. Some Jains hope that this will further the understanding of Jainism. Others are concerned that sacred texts may be misinterpreted or treated irreverently. Modernization also obliges Jains to rethink the motivation behind certain religious practices. For example, today most lay Jains live in houses or apartments where it is no longer appropriate to suggest that eating after dark increases the risk of harming insects. If they do not eat after sunset, they have to justify this as exercising discipline and respect for tradition, rather than as an act of non-violence.

Today many Jains are well educated and intellectually sophisticated, with enquiring minds. Religious rituals that appear to hold little meaning beyond tradition may not satisfy them. However, numerous independent educational programmes are being established in India and abroad to teach lay Jains about Jainism and revitalize their commitment by explaining the doctrinal reasons for their religious practices. The first Jain university was established in 1970 at Ladnun, Rajasthan, under the direction

Modern leaders

Shrimad Rajachandra (1867–1901) was a Jain layman and saint from Gujarat who taught, amongst other things, the importance of devotion to an authoritative guru for achieving liberation. His followers turn to spiritual laypeople instead of to ascetics. As lay gurus have no travel restrictions placed upon them, the Shrimad Rajachandra movement has transferred well to diaspora communities.

Kanji Swami (1898–1980), also from Gujarat, was initiated as a Sthanakvasi ascetic in 1913. He later relinquished his ascetic status to become a Digambara layman, although he never married. Kanji Swami attracted a huge following, which is one of the most successful movements in modern Jainism. Like the Shrimad Rajachandra movement, the Kanji Swami Panth is a lay organization that places little emphasis on the role of ascetics and therefore has an important place among diaspora Jains.

Acharya Mahaprajna (b. 1920), who succeeded Acharya Tulsi as the spiritual leader of Terapanthi Jainism, instigated numerous reforms and established a class of 'semi-ascetics': partially initiated men and women who may travel abroad to teach and administer to lay Jains.

Chitrabhanu (b. 1922) was a Shvetambara ascetic in India who relinquished his status and settled in North America in the 1970s, establishing an extensive community of lay followers who regard him as an authoritative guru.

of Acharya Tulsi (1914–97). The Federation of Jain Associations in North America (JAINA) is one of several organizations making educational resources about Jainism available on the Internet.

Jain diaspora

Towards the end of the nineteenth century many Indian people emigrated to East Africa where they established homes and businesses. By 1926 a Jain temple had been built in Nairobi. Another temple was constructed in Mombassa in 1963. Temple construction indicates a religious community's growth in stature and economic prowess. However, during the late 1960s and 1970s Indian people were persecuted by East African political regimes. Many fled to Britain and North America where they took up citizenship while endeavouring to establish a communal identity. In 1973 British Jains of the Shrimali and Oshval castes established an association to provide a community centre for Jains living in Leicester. This evolved into the 'European Jain Association'. During the 1980s it built a temple in Leicester that has Digambara and Shvetambara shrines, as well as shrines where the followers of Shrimad Rajachandra and Kanji Swami can worship (see panel).

To Jains who do not live in India the absence of ascetics presents a significant difficulty. Ascetics have religious authority and play a vital role in the religious practices of Jain laypeople, offering instruction, administering vows, performing initiation and consecration ceremonies and giving laypeople the opportunity to gain spiritual merit through alms giving. Some diaspora Jains travel to India, either regularly or occasionally, to be in the presence of ascetics. However, family, work and financial restraints make such trips difficult for many. The difficulty is compounded by ascetics being peripatetic for eight months of the year.

Some modern movements have, consciously or not, addressed the problem of ascetic absence. Terapanthi Jainism, the followers of Chitrabhanu, Shrimad Rajachandra and Kanji Swami all have different organizational structures, but each is an example of progressive and modernized Jainism.

'Jain bono na bano, good man bano.' *(It doesn't matter if you become a Jain, aspire to become a good man, a moral person.)*

Acharya Tulsi

Buddhism

PART SIX

A Historical Overview

PAUL WILLIAMS

Buddhism is the '-ism' that is named after the Buddha. 'Buddha' is not a personal name. It is a title meaning 'the one who has awakened'. *The* Buddha was a historical individual who lived and died some centuries BCE, although it is difficult to be very precise about his exact dates. Recent scholarship is only prepared to say that the Buddha lived in North India probably sometime in the fifth century BCE. His name is held to have been Siddhartha Gautama (in Sanskrit) or Siddhattha Gotama (in the Pali language in which many early Buddhist works are written).

'Buddhism' is an English name for a religion that its followers often simply refer to as the *Dharma* (Pali: *Dhamma*). This word can be taken as meaning here both 'the teaching' and 'the way things are'. It was discovering this and teaching it that made Siddhartha Gautama 'the Buddha'. Notice, therefore, that whereas Western discussions tend to stress the importance of its founder (Buddha + ism, no doubt on the model of Christ + ianity), Buddhists prefer to emphasize not him but rather *what he*

taught. For Buddhists the obvious place to start is the teaching. This teaching, they say, leads people to understand how things *truly* are, and thence to a radical reassessment of their lives. The Buddha simply awakened to this truth and taught it. In this he was not unique, for (it is said) others had awakened before him and there will be many, many after him too.

Who was the Buddha?

To start with the life story of the Buddha is 'our' Western tradition. And even if we start with it here too, this life story should be read not as historical fact. We can reasonably take it that Siddhartha Gautama lived and died. He was considered by his followers to have achieved the fullest possible understanding of reality, an understanding that is true freedom. The historicity of the rest is difficult to assess. Some of it we know is very unlikely to have happened. But Buddhism itself has always been more interested in the ways in which the life story illustrates Buddhist teachings than in its literal historical truth.

Siddhartha Gautama is said to have been born a prince who grew up cosseted and protected from all knowledge of the nasty things of life – specifically old age, sickness and death. He married and had a son. But the shock of his subsequent discovery of old age, sickness and death led to his renouncing the world of kingship and family. Siddhartha took to the life – not uncommon in India then as now – of a wandering seeker. He sought the final truth that would lead to complete freedom from suffering. It was a harsh life of meditation, study and asceticism. Food, and very little of it, came from asking for alms. But eventually Siddhartha, looking within, in deep meditation, reached the truth he sought. He came to 'see it the way it really is'. This truth set him free. He was now the awakened one, the Buddha. The Buddha gathered around him a group of disciples and he wandered northern India teaching all who would listen. Eventually, in old age, the Buddha died. But for him death was nothing. For he was now free from death, as he was free from all other forms of unpleasantness, imperfection and frustration. And after death? On a Buddha after death there is nothing more to say.

What did he teach?

The very life story of the Buddha is all about things appearing one way and really being another. The Buddha taught that 'seeing things the way they really are' is the way to overcome every sort of unpleasantness, imperfection and frustration. These are all classed under the expression (in Pali) *dukkha*, a term which in the everyday context of the time meant quite literally 'pain' or 'suffering'. He taught that when we look deeply we can see that all our lives are, one way or another, at root simply *dukkha*. The Buddha was uninterested in the question of God; and Buddhist tradition has been unanimous that a creator-God in the sense in which he is thought to exist by Christians, for example, simply does not exist. Suffering, for Buddhists, is the result of our ignorance, not understanding the way things really are, and we all live our lives in the light of that failure in understanding. The central dimension

of such misunderstanding lies in our not appreciating that everything in our experience by its very nature is *impermanent*. All such things change, ourselves most of all. Suffering results from holding on, trying in our experiences and in our lives to 'fix things' so that they do not break up and cease to be. Clearly we are doomed to failure. We need to learn to let go, but this letting go has to occur at a very deep level indeed since we have been confused, and suffering, in this manner for infinite lifetimes.

For Buddhists, we each consist of a

The head of the statue of the Buddha at Waikaloa, Hawaii, USA.

flow of consciousness, with associated mental contents such as feelings and intentions, and a body that is ever changing as well. Any further unchanging element called a 'self' (Pali: *atta;* Sanskrit: *atman*) would appear to be unnecessary. Indeed it could lead to a dangerous form of self-grasping, the very opposite of letting go. As such, Buddhist tradition teaches 'not-self' (Pali: *anatta;* Sanskrit: *anatman*). At death the body ceases, but the ever-flowing continuum of consciousness and its mental accompaniments continues and 'spins', as it were, another body in accordance with one's good or bad deeds (*karma*). Such 'reincarnation' means that one is yet again subject to suffering (old age, sickness, death and so on). This process ceases only with letting go at the deepest possible level, attained through meditation. It is a letting go that springs from seeing things as they truly are and completely reversing one's almost instinctive and frantic patterns of grasping after things. That cessation Buddhists call 'enlightenment' (Pali: *nibbana;* Sanskrit: *nirvana*).

Monastic traditions and doctrinal schools

Central to the Buddha's vision of the way forward was an order of monks and nuns, surviving on alms and expressing in their state of renunciation their commitment to the radical transformation we all need. This order is known as the *Sangha*. In time monasteries were established together with a monastic rule to regulate the conduct of the *Sangha* and promote the peace and harmony necessary in order to follow the Buddha's path. The Buddha did not appoint a successor. He reportedly declared that the teaching, the *Dharma*, should be his successor. But after his death, with time, disagreements occurred. Initially this was over the monastic rules. Such disputes were viewed very seriously indeed. Where disputes over the rule could not be reconciled, monks in the minority were required to depart. They thus formed their own groups with variant sets of the monastic rule. Eventually, a number of different monastic traditions were formed. The best known of these, and the only one of the early Indian Buddhist monastic traditions to survive to the present day, is the 'Way of the Elders' (*Theravada*), found nowadays in, for example, Sri Lanka, Thailand, Cambodia, and Myanmar (Burma).

Technically, 'schism' (*sanghabheda*) in Buddhism is a matter of monastic rule, not doctrinal disagreement. Doctrinal disagreement is relatively less serious. Nevertheless, as time passed, there also evolved different doctrinal positions, sometimes followed by identifiable schools. An example here might be the school(s) known as *Pudgalavada* ('Teaching the *pudgala'*). The point of contention here was that of the 'person' (*pudgala*). Advocates urged that although the Buddha taught 'not-self', there still exists something (albeit difficult to specify what) called the *pudgala*, as something in some sense really there 'in' us. Others viewed this *pudgala* as just a self in disguise, and an abandonment of a central part of the Buddha's teaching. Further issues of debate involved who or what exactly the Buddha himself was. Some urged that a Buddha is really much more extraordinary than people realize. For example, although he seems to teach, really he is permanently in meditation. He has no need to sleep, to defecate or even to eat. He only does these things in order to act in accordance with the expectations of the world. Many such topics were debated in early (and even later) Buddhism, as the Buddha's followers sought to put his teaching into practice and also to explain it clearly to others. Indeed, also discussed was the relative importance of practising the *Dharma* for one's own freedom from all suffering, as opposed to compassionately teaching it to others.

What is Mahayana Buddhism?

To understand early Buddhist history it is thus necessary to distinguish doctrinal dispute and debate (that is, doctrinal *schools*), from behavioural disharmony and schism (monastic *traditions*). Different again, and appearing in the literature from about the first century CE, is the greatest internal development within Buddhism, the growth of *Mahayana* (the 'Great

Buddhist monks on the morning alms round at Kyaiktiyo, Myanmar (Burma).

Vehicle' or perhaps the 'Vehicle that leads to the Great'). Mahayana Buddhism is not a doctrinal school. Within Mahayana there are many doctrinal schools. Moreover Mahayana is to be distinguished from a monastic tradition. There is no such thing as a proper, comparable set of Mahayana monastic rules (*vinaya*). For example, monks in India holding to the Mahayana perspective would be ordained and live in accordance with any one of the sets of monastic rules that had already developed. Such monks were sometimes to be found in monasteries with others that did not hold to the Mahayana perspective.

Hence it makes no sense to speak of two 'schools' of Buddhism, Theravada and Mahayana. Theravada is a monastic tradition. Mahayana is not. They are not comparable phenomena. There could (in theory) be a Theravada follower of Mahayana. This is because Mahayana can best be thought of as *a vision*, of what Buddhism is really, finally, all about. Mahayana appears first in texts, writings (known as Mahayana *sutras*) claiming controversially to be the word of the Buddha himself. Crucially, what gradually emerges in these writings is a distinction between simply being free

from all suffering (in other words, enlightened), and actually being a Buddha. A Buddha is spiritually more than just free from his own suffering. A Buddha is also perfectly *compassionate* as well. Thus to be a Buddha is better than simply being enlightened. This is not only because of a Buddha's great compassion, but also because of the many marvellous – indeed miraculous – abilities a Buddha possesses in order to help others. But it takes many, many lifetimes of spiritual striving to become a Buddha. Thus, those who aim for the highest goal should not seek just their own freedom from suffering and rebirth. Rather, they should vow to follow the long path to Buddhahood. This path is to be followed over very many rebirths, willingly taking on their attendant sufferings, in order eventually as a Buddha better to be able to help others.

The Mahayana, in a nutshell, is the way of those who aspire to become perfect Buddhas. This is said to be for the benefit of all sentient beings (that is, all those with consciousness). Those who vow to do this are known as *bodhisattvas* (perhaps originally meaning 'one who is capable of awakening'). Mahayana sources go into great detail on the stages of the path that a *bodhisattva* must follow in order eventually to become a Buddha.

With time, Mahayana also elaborated more fully on the ways in which a Buddha is superior to someone who has simply put an end to his or her own suffering. Developed further here is the idea that a Buddha is really much more than he appears to be. Even his death was really just a show put on in order to give a 'skilful teaching' of impermanence. For Mahayana the Buddha – indeed infinite Buddhas – are still around, living on higher planes ('Pure Lands'). From there, through their great compassion combined with miraculous powers, the Buddhas are available and willing to help those who have need of them. With them are advanced *bodhisattvas* who too are full of compassion and

able to help others. Some of these Buddhas and 'celestial' *bodhisattvas* are named, such as Avalokiteshvara, a *bodhisattva* who is said to be the very incarnation of compassion, or Mañjushri, likewise the very incarnation of wisdom and insight.

The spread of Buddhism beyond India

Significant to the history of Buddhism in India was the conversion of the great emperor Ashoka (third century BCE). This gave the religion important imperial patronage, although scholars now discount the view that he attempted to make Buddhism the state religion. From the time of Ashoka, Buddhism began to migrate further afield and according to tradition it reached Sri Lanka at this time. It subsequently spread into South-East

Novice monks contributing to a *mandala*, or sacred circle, Bhutan.

Asia. The religion reached China along the Central Asian trade routes during the early centuries CE, spread to Korea and other countries of East Asia, and reached Japan in the sixth century CE. It came to Tibet from various directions, including India and China probably from about the seventh century. In India, however, for various reasons that are not as yet fully understood (but may be partly related to the rise of devotional theistic forms of Hinduism, as well as the impact of Islam on India), Buddhism eventually declined. It all but ceased to exist in India from about the fourteenth century. It has revived in recent centuries, and Buddhism has also now taken on a global dimension. Perhaps the most well-known contemporary Buddhist is the Dalai Lama of Tibet, who is also a former winner of the Nobel Peace Prize, as is another Buddhist, the Burmese opposition leader Aung San Suu Kyi.

It is common, although misleading, to speak of the Buddhism of, for example, China, Japan and Tibet as Mahayana, contrasting it with the Theravada Buddhism of, for example, South-East Asia. To repeat, these are not comparable phenomena. Nevertheless many Mahayana scriptures were transmitted to, and given in the main unquestioning authority in, China, Japan and Tibet. Unlike in South-East Asia, Buddhists in those countries could be expected, if asked, to express adherence one way or another to the Mahayana vision as embracing their highest and final aspirations. Particularly characteristic of East Asian Buddhism is the tradition known in Japan as *Zen*. Zen (the very word is related to 'meditation') is well known for stressing direct, non-verbal, intuitive insight, expressing itself through the arts such as painting, but also employing sometimes humour and shock tactics to bring about awakening. This awakened 'Buddha-nature', it is urged, is really already present within all of us if we did but realize it. Also important in, for example, Japanese Buddhism is the tradition of Shinran (thirteenth century CE). For Shinran the awakening of a Buddha is really quite beyond unenlightened capabilities. Only by completely letting go even of reliance on ourselves, and relying instead on trust in the Buddha's salvific ability, can the already-enlightened nature of the Buddha (a Buddha known here as *Amitabha*) shine forth. According to this teaching, humans have to let go, completely, of even the subtle egoism that encourages them to think they can achieve anything spiritually worthwhile, including enlightenment, through their own efforts. Being a monk or nun, even meditating, is finally irrelevant, a distraction and a possible source of egoistic attachment.

What is meant by *Tantra* (and *Vajrayana*)?

The final important development to mention is *Tantra*. Buddhists from the beginning, in common with their wider environment, accepted magic. Magic entails bringing about desired results through manipulation of hidden forces, usually by ritual means such as sacred circles (*mandalas*), utterances of power (*mantras*), visualizations and so on. As well as teaching, among the services that Buddhist monks and nuns might be required to perform for the lay communities that supported them would be magical rituals – for crops, for health, for children or whatever. Although employment of this technology was not their main theoretical interest as Buddhists, its appropriateness (as an act of caring) or efficacy was not questioned. From quite early on, Buddhist ritual texts were produced. In some circles such texts were (again controversially) attributed to the Buddha himself and were often called *tantras*.

Also controversial was the development, from perhaps the seventh

'Hatred is never quenched by hatred; by non-hatred alone is hatred quenched. This is an Eternal Law.'

Dhammapada, v. 5

A HISTORICAL OVERVIEW

century CE or earlier, of certain *tantras* claiming that one could even become a Buddha through the use of such magical means. Secret initiations were required, with unquestioning devotion to the teacher (*guru*), in order to learn their use. Yet more controversial were *tantras* that explained the possibility of this supreme attainment through the employment and manipulation of a sort of subtle, psycho-physical body everyone is said to possess within them. In this, the ritual use of sexual intercourse was also held to be a particularly powerful technique. And, since an awakened Buddha is beyond all worldly entanglements and confusions, recommended as well – expressing humanity's awakened nature – are not only sexual activity, in ways and with partners usually considered outside the socially accepted norm, but equally other behaviour surprising to the unenlightened. These developments, often associated with the expression *Vajrayana* (Way of the Thunderbolt, Way of the Diamond), produced also a genre of literature detailing the unexpected exploits of certain awakened tantric 'persons of magical power' (*siddhas*).

Not surprisingly, such developments within Buddhism were (and still are) highly controversial. One should add that with time, subjected to more orthodox and particularly monastic control, the more controversial dimensions of Tantric Buddhism were 'tamed' and absorbed into the wider Mahayana spiritual context of great compassion and wisdom. It is in this form that one finds nowadays the widest and most well-known presence of *tantra*, in the Buddhism of Tibet.

> '*Let none deceive another, not despise any person whatsoever in any place. Let one not wish any harm to another out of anger or ill-will... Let thoughts of boundless love pervade the whole world: above, below and across, without any obstruction, without any hatred, any enmity.*'
>
> From the *Metta Sutta*, the *Sutta* on Loving Kindness, the *Sutta Nipata*, vv. 6 & 8

Sacred Writings

PAUL WILLIAMS

The Buddha himself wrote nothing. He simply taught. He taught sometimes his vision of the world, humanity's place within it and the spiritual and moral way to freedom – eventually complete freedom – from incompleteness, frustration and suffering. At other times he engaged in settling disputes among his followers and legislating for the best sort of life to live in order to attain this complete freedom. According to Buddhist tradition, it was soon after the Buddha's death that those monks who had achieved the goal – enlightenment (Pali: *nibbana;* Sanskrit: *nirvana*) – met together in order to recite what they remembered of the Buddha's discourses. This was the First Buddhist Council. It is often stated in books that there were three such councils in classical times, although actually only two are accepted by all Buddhist traditions. The emphasis from the beginning was on *memory* and *recitation*, employing the same method as, for example, the Hindu transmission of their basic scriptures, the Vedas.

Oral transmission

Thus, for the first few centuries the Buddhist scriptures were handed down orally (which partly explains the importance in Buddhism of the *oral transmission* from teacher to pupil) rather than in written form. Different groups of monks specialized in the preservation of different texts or collections of scriptures and – contrary to what might be expected – as far as we can tell, transmission through oral recitation in groups proved to be a very effective way of preserving the Buddha's word. It was at least as accurate as preservation through writing, since interpolation of additional and perhaps controversial material – or, for that

卧 子 眾 礼 已 乘 臣 謹 摩 堪 臣 子 人 言
未 恒 畫 又 具 而 擇 奉 訶 此 並 年 語 極

A detail showing men with oxen from the *Sutra of Past and Present Karma*.

matter, omission – is much more difficult in the case of group recitation. It would obviously be immediately noticed. According to one Buddhist tradition the scriptures were first written down in the first century BCE. The decision to use writing was perhaps partly due to a fear in times of social and political stress that the teachings might become lost through the death of disproportionate numbers of important reciters by disease, war or famine. This seems to have happened, for example, with some of the scriptures of Jainism.

The Buddhist canon

The texts recited at the First Council form the basis of the Buddhist scriptural canon. They are divided into:

● *sutras* (Pali: *sutta*) – the general discourses of the Buddha and, sometimes, the teachings of his authorized followers

● *vinaya* texts – texts relating to the structure and discipline of the monastic order.

With time a further section of the canon was added, the *abhidharma* (perhaps 'higher', or 'more precise', teaching'). This section consists in the main of works developing an elaborate description of how the psycho-physical world looks when seen 'as things really are' by an enlightened person, rather than through everyday unenlightened vision. The canonical *abhidharma* texts probably date from after the death of the Buddha but one way or another all claim direct origin from him. These three sections together form the 'Three Baskets' (Pali: *Tipitaka;* Sanskrit: *Tripitaka*), which are themselves subdivided. For example, in the Pali Canon (see below) the *sutra* 'basket' is divided into four sections (plus one supplementary section) known as *Nikayas*. The best known of these is perhaps the 'Collection of Long Discourses' (*Digha Nikaya*).

It was some centuries before the canon became more or less closed such that (at least in theory) no more works could be added to it and given the prestige of 'coming directly from the Buddha himself'. One should also add there are some Buddhist texts that have all the authority of canonical scriptures but which are technically not part of the canon at all (such as the monastic

> *'To be attached to a certain view and to look down on other views as inferior – this the wise man calls a fetter.'*
>
> Sutta Nipata

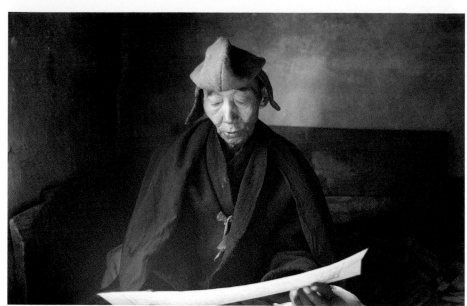

A Buddhist monk reading scripture, Ladakh, India.

rule, still recited regularly by monks and nuns).

Different versions

There is a tradition that the Buddha specifically recommended preserving and transmitting his teachings in local languages rather than Sanskrit, the pan-Indian language of education. Hence, from quite early times Buddhist scriptures were in a number of languages and also underwent translation. Moreover, as Buddhist monastic traditions and doctrinal schools were formed, eventually somewhat different versions of the canon appeared. They were often also in different Indian languages. Nowadays the comparative study of different canonical versions of recognizably the same text forms a fruitful area for scholarly research.

Scriptures require some sort of authoritative body to preserve and transmit them down the ages. In Buddhism, particularly in the Indian world, this has always been the monastic order (the *Sangha*). As mentioned in the previous article, the only Buddhist monastic tradition originating from the early centuries to have survived to the present day is the 'Way of the Elders' (*Theravada*). Correspondingly, the version of the canon preserved by the *Theravada* is the only version surviving effectively in its entirety and still in its ancient Indian language. This is known as the 'Pali Canon', because the language in which it is written is called *Pali*. But, although old and of inestimable importance for the study of Buddhism, the Pali Canon is still only one of a number of Buddhist canons that existed in ancient times. Other individual canonical works, or collections, have survived. They are either in other Indian languages or in ancient translations, for example into Chinese or Tibetan, made as part of Buddhist missionary activity.

With time, and with greater reliance on writing than oral transmission, certain Buddhist traditions and schools within India started to preserve their scriptures in Sanskrit. This is why Buddhist technical terms are often given in both their Sanskrit and their Pali forms. Usually they are very similar: for example, *nibbana* (Pali), *nirvana* (Sanskrit). As Buddhism spread across India, using just one language made sense, rather than relying on different translations in different areas. Educated people would all be familiar to some extent with Sanskrit, and a monk with a text in Sanskrit could take it anywhere without needing to have it translated. He could explain what the text meant in the vernacular to less educated people as part of his teaching mission. This changeover to the use of Sanskrit can actually be seen occurring in the greatest post-canonical scriptural development in Indian Buddhism, the appearance of the Mahayana *sutras*. A number of the early Mahayana *sutras* show signs of having been translated into Sanskrit out of other Indian languages in which, presumably, they were originally composed.

Apocryphal scriptures: Mahayana *sutras* and the *Tantras*

The earliest form in which we know of Mahayana Buddhism is that of its scriptures. Indeed scriptural support for Mahayana appears to be older by some centuries than archaeological evidence for *followers* of Mahayana! Mahayana *sutras* are apocryphal, and their ideas often seemingly new and radical. As apocryphal *sutras*, although they claim to be the words of the Buddha himself, this claim is hotly disputed within Buddhism; and it is true that the extant versions of these *sutras* cannot possibly be that old. There is some reason to think that elements of at least some early Mahayana *sutras* may have originated in inspiring, meditative visions and revelations, held to be from a Buddha who was thus thought to be still accessible to us on some sort of 'higher plane'. Although there may have been attempts to add some such *sutras*, they are not included as part of any official Canon preserved by an identifiable Indian monastic tradition.

Apocryphal *sutras* were not only created in India. For example, there are many Mahayana apocryphal *sutras* that were composed in China and were unknown in India in classical times.

Even nowadays, outside areas usually associated with Mahayana, in, for example, the monastically Theravada world of Sri Lanka, apocryphal Buddhist *sutras* are still being produced, claiming to spring from some sort of special revelation, but clearly not accepted as canonical by the mainstream, local, Buddhist monastic order.

It has been suggested that the very origins and survival of Mahayana as a movement required the existence of writing. Religions often produce controversial texts claiming to be the words of, or in some sense inspired by, that religion's founder. Such works, however, disappear unless they are taken up and preserved down the ages by enthusiasts. In Buddhism, canonical works are preserved and transmitted to future generations by the *Sangha*, as an institution. But the *Sangha* is unlikely to preserve apocryphal texts, certainly not texts like the early Mahayana *sutras* that were inclined sometimes to be critical of the existing monastic hierarchy. Hence, so long as the canon was transmitted orally the preservation of significantly new perspectives such as that of Mahayana, claiming the authority of the Buddha, was all but impossible. Effectively, it was the writing down of the scriptures that enabled the preservation and transmission of apocryphal works and perspectives. A *written* text could survive providing there was someone – just one person – willing to preserve it.

The other major corpus of apocryphal, scriptural literature in Buddhism claiming the authority of the Buddha himself consists of the *Tantras*. *Tantras* are texts associated with the use of ritual magic. Their origins in Buddhism (they are also found in, for example, Hinduism and Jainism) are obscure, and the earliest *Tantras* are certainly some centuries later than the earliest Mahayana *sutras*. The literature is very large. To practise the ritual prescriptions of these texts, that in time came to include techniques for attaining enlightenment as well as more mundane magical activities, requires initiation, close instruction from a teacher (a *guru*) and vows of secrecy. Tantric texts involve in particular the use of, for example, magical diagrams, utterances (*mantras*) and visualizations. *Tantras* have become linked with, and in some cases (notably in Tibet) assimilated into, Mahayana; but recent research has indicated the genre of tantric literature in countries such as Myanmar (Burma) or Cambodia, not normally thought of as associated with Mahayana perspectives.

Exegetical treatises

In addition to scriptures – those accepted by all as canonical and those of disputed authority held by some or even many as apocryphal – Buddhist literature also includes a vast number of exegetical treatises, often known generically as *shastras*. They have been produced by the great scholars of the Buddhist traditions and schools with the intention of clarifying difficult points of interpretation; or defending their understanding against rivals and alternatives; or perhaps, like the 'Treasury of Abhidharma' (*Abhidharmakosha*), they were written to serve as great critical compendia of the Buddhist doctrine and path. Such exegetical treatises have been produced in each country in which Buddhism has been established, and are enormously important for the study of Buddhist doctrinal history.

> 'Asked by some citizens of Kalama for guidance, the Buddha said: "Be not led by reports or tradition or hearsay. Be not led by the authority of religious texts, nor by mere logic or inference, nor by considering appearances [...]. But, O Kalamas, when you know for yourselves that certain things are unwholesome (akusala) and wrong and bad, then give them up... And when you know for yourselves that certain things are wholesome (kusala) and good, then accept them and follow them."'
>
> Anguttara Nikaya
> Text ii, 167–68

Beliefs

ELIZABETH J. HARRIS

A disciple of the Buddha, Malunkyaputta, complained that the Buddha had not answered some of the most important questions of life. Is the world eternal? Is the soul the same as the body? And so on. The Buddha replied with a story.

'A man is wounded by an arrow thickly smeared with poison. His friends and relatives brought a surgeon to him. The man said, "I will not let the surgeon pull out this arrow until I know whether the man who wounded me was a noble, a brahman, a merchant or a worker. I will not let the surgeon pull out the arrow until I know the name and clan of the man who wounded me... until I know whether the he was tall or short or of middle height... until I know whether the bow that wounded me was a longbow or a crossbow... until I know whether the bowstring that wounded me was fibre or reed or sinew or bark..."

All this would not be known to the man and he would die.'

ABRIDGED FROM THE *CULAMALUNKYA SUTTA* WITHIN THE *MAJJHIMA NIKAYA* OF THE PALI CANON

So, the Buddha added, will those who insist they must know the answers to speculative questions about the nature of reality before starting to live the holy life. For such questions are not beneficial to the real task, which is the cessation of suffering.

This story points to the heart of what Buddhism is about. Buddhism is less a set of beliefs than a path, leading from suffering to the cessation of suffering, from ignorance to compassion and wisdom. The Buddha's first invitation to those who wished to follow him as monks or nuns in the fifth century BCE was: 'Come, live the holy life in order that you make an end of suffering.' The only credal statement in Buddhism, therefore, is this:

I go to the Buddha for refuge;
I go to the Dhamma *for refuge;*
I go to the Sangha (the Buddhist community) *for refuge.*

These are the 'Three Jewels' or 'Three Gems'. Anyone who can place them at the centre of life is a Buddhist. The *Dhamma* (Pali; Sanskrit: *Dharma*) is what the Buddha 'awoke to' at his enlightenment and what he taught for forty years after. Literally, the word means 'that which constitutes'. For Buddhists, it is the truth about the nature of existence; the truth that upholds the cosmos; the truth that all Buddhas have taught. It is 'the way things are'. Across the different schools of Buddhism the *Dhamma* is expressed in a variety of ways. However, there are elements that all schools hold in common.

Living the holy life
Living the holy life in Buddhism involves a way of seeing reality and a way of acting. The way of seeing begins with experience rather than metaphysics: the experience that something in life is dislocated, flawed, unsatisfactory and full of suffering, and the realization that one reason for this is that everything is impermanent. We are separated from loved ones. We lose our strength. We grow old, sicken and die. Everything we cherish – youth, strength, possessions, relationships – passes away. Buddhism speaks of three defining characteristics of existence: impermanence (Pali: *anicca*; Sanskrit: *anitya*), unsatisfactoriness (Pali: *dukkha*; Sanskrit: *duhkha*), and not-self (Pali: *anatta*; Sanskrit: *anatman*). The characteristic of not-self arises

when the concept of impermanence is applied to the self. As with all external phenomena, everything in our bodies and minds is changing. Everything is conditioned. There is no unchanging 'self', 'soul' or ego. Mahayana Buddhists use the word 'emptiness'. All things, the self included, are 'empty' of their own nature.

This is the start of the Buddhist view of existence, but it is not the end. The message of the Buddha was that the suffering or unsatisfactoriness of life is not haphazard, random or immovable. It has a cause, as all other phenomena have a cause, and if this cause is eradicated, suffering will not arise. The cause that the Buddha identified was 'craving': self-centred craving for sensual pleasures and life itself. Remove this craving and suffering will cease, giving way to the liberation of *nibbana* (Sanskrit: *nirvana*). It is this 'view' that forms the first three of the Four Noble Truths:

● The Noble Truth of *Dukkha*: that there is an incompleteness and unsatisfactoriness at the heart of existence;

● The Noble Truth of the Origin of *Dukkha*: that the cause is craving or thirst (Pali: *tanha*; Sanskrit *trsna*), the thirst for sensual pleasures, the thirst for continued existence and the thirst for annihilation;

● The Noble Truth of the Cessation of *Dukkha*: that there is an end, based on the law of cause and effect (that is, if craving is destroyed, *dukkha* cannot arise);

● The Noble Truth of the Path to the Cessation of *Dukkha*: the Eightfold Path (see below).

The Buddhist view of the world is, therefore, of a world dis-eased (i.e. ill

> 'Whatever harm an enemy may do to an enemy, or a hater to a hater, an ill-directed mind inflicts on oneself a greater harm.'
> *Dhammapada, v. 42*

BELIEFS

at ease), a world entrapped in craving, where *dukkha* reigns supreme because people have not seen the *dhamma*, the truth about existence. It is a world where people are trapped in mental prisons of their own making. But it is a world where liberation waits for all who can change the way they look at the world and work towards freedom from the craving that is rooted in ignorance and expressed through greed and hatred.

The way to liberation

The Noble Truths are the 'house' into which everything else fits in Buddhism. The Fourth Noble Truth is the Noble Eightfold Path, the way to the ending of suffering:

● right view

● right resolve

● right speech

A depiction of the Buddhist Wheel of Life. In the centre are a pig, a bird or cock and a snake, representing ignorance, attachment or greed, and aversion or hatred. The next circle shows people going upwards because of their good actions (white path) and downwards because of their bad actions (black path). The six sections of the next circle represent the six realms into which one can be reborn (see page 202). The twelve sections of the outer ring depict the stages through which rebirth happens again and again, according to the law of cause and effect, beginning with ignorance. The whole thing is carried by the Lord of Death. In one corner, a Buddha points to the sky, showing there is a way out of this.

- right action

- right livelihood

- right effort

- right mindfulness

- right concentration or meditation

This is often reduced to just three categories: morality (Pali/Sanskrit: *sila*); concentration or meditation (Pali/Sanskrit: *samadhi*); and wisdom (Pali: *panna*; Sanskrit: *prajna*). Or sometimes this verse from the *Dhammapada*, a text known and loved throughout the Buddhist world, is quoted:

'The avoidance of evil, the undertaking of good, the cleansing of one's mind; this is the teaching of the awakened ones.'
DHAMMAPADA, V. 183

Morality

Morality is the bedrock of the Buddhist path. It involves 'the avoidance of evil, the undertaking of good'. Without moral discipline, the holy life cannot be lived. Most lay Buddhists place the following five precepts at the centre of their life:

- to abstain from harming any living being

- to abstain from taking what is not given

- to abstain from sexual misconduct

- to abstain from false speech

- to abstain from anything that clouds or intoxicates the mind (such as drugs and alcohol)

Many would insist that these precepts involve not only an abstention, but a cultivation. A commitment not to harm involves the development of loving kindness and compassion. The commitment to abstaining from taking what is not given involves recognizing the dignity and worth of other people, as does abstaining from sexual misconduct. Abstaining from false speech involves cultivating honesty and integrity.

An ancient text in the Theravada tradition, the *Karaniyametta Sutta*, describes loving kindness in the following way: 'Just as a mother would protect her only child at the risk of her own life, even so cultivate a boundless heart towards all beings.' One way to do this is to meditate on loving kindness (*metta*). The first step is to imagine oneself surrounded by loving kindness. Then this loving kindness, sometimes imagined as a white, warm light, is thrown further and further outwards into the world. First of all those dear to the meditator are brought to mind. Then the radius widens, eventually reaching those who are disliked or even hated. It is a transformative practice that spills into everyday conduct.

Morality, for many Buddhists, is also linked with the law of action, the law of *karma* (Sanskrit; Pali: *kamma*), that moral action will produce good fruit and unwholesome action bad fruit. This does not mean that Buddhist morality is essentially selfish. Rather, self and other are seen to be interconnected. What is good for others is good for self. What would not be done to oneself would not be done to another.

Meditation

The task of meditation is to cleanse the mind. It ties in with the heart of the Buddha's message: that the cause of our dis-ease lies in our craving, in the three unwholesome roots of greed, hatred and delusion. Since it is our minds and hearts that generate this craving, according to Buddhism, the only way to uproot craving is to work

A monk meditating in a temple in Matsushima, Japan.

'Monks, there are to be seen beings who can admit freedom from suffering from bodily disease for one year, for two years, for three, four, five, ten, twenty, thirty, forty, fifty years; who can admit freedom from bodily disease for even a hundred year. But, monks, those beings are hard to find in the world who can admit freedom from mental disease even for one moment, save only those in whom the asavas ('corruptions' such as ignorance) are destroyed.'

Anguttara Nikaya
Text ii, 143

on the mind and heart. Buddhism offers numerous meditation methods, but these can be reduced to two main practices: tranquillity meditation (Pali/Sanskrit: *samatha*) and insight meditation (Pali: *vipassana*; Sanskrit: *vipasyana*).

Tranquillity meditation is not unique to Buddhism. It is a method through which an object of meditation is used to concentrate the mind and gain one-pointedness. The most popular object is the breath. Some Buddhists watch the breath as it enters and leaves the nostrils; others watch the rising and fall of the abdomen. The meditator sits with the back upright. In some traditions the eyes are closed; in others they remain partly open. When the mind wanders away from the object, it is brought back, gently and non-judgmentally, to the breath. Traditionally, there are forty other meditation objects that can be chosen under the direction of a teacher. It is this kind of meditation that may lead to what Buddhists call 'meditative absorptions' or *jhanas* (Pali; Sanskrit: *dhyanas*), which are basically refined states of mental and spiritual awareness.

Vipassana means 'seeing clearly': seeing the body and the mind clearly. It is unique to Buddhism and has nothing to do with altered states of consciousness. Its aim is direct verification of the *Dhamma* through a watching of the body and the mind. Many exercises have been developed within the Buddhist tradition to aid this. One method that is used widely is 'bare attention' or 'choiceless awareness', a form of mindfulness that emphasizes the present moment. Whatever arises in the mind and the body becomes the object of meditation, of awareness. It may be a reaction of attraction or aversion to an external noise. It may be a feeling of pain in the legs. Or it could be thoughts of hatred, jealousy or love. Nothing is judged good or bad. Nothing is clung to. Everything is watched, noted and

allowed to pass. Their impermanence and not-self is seen. The greed, hatred and delusion in them are seen, as well as what triggers these. Each period of meditation, in fact, becomes a voyage of discovery into the way the mind and body function.

Meditation is the means, Buddhists believe, through which greed, hatred and delusion or ignorance can be uprooted and transcended. Central to 'delusion' (Pali: *moha*) is the belief that we have an unchanging 'I' or ego that has to be placed at the centre of all things, to be protected, promoted and pampered. Meditation shows that much that we believe to be 'self' – our feelings, our thoughts, our pain – is impermanent and empty.

The goal

Buddhists stress that there is continuity after death, but that the ultimate goal of religious practice is not an after-death state. The term most often used is 'rebirth'. Most Buddhists prefer this term to 'reincarnation', since they do not believe that there is an unchanging soul to reincarnate, but rather an ever-changing process of cause and effect. Death is believed to lead continually to rebirth after rebirth until greed, hatred and delusion are eradicated. For the Theravada Buddhist, one can be reborn into any of five realms: (1) the hells; (2) the animal world; (3) the realm of the hungry ghosts; (4) the realm of humans; and (5) the realm of the gods. Mahayana Buddhists have added another heavenly realm: (6) that of the demi-gods. Each realm is linked to a particular emotion or characteristic. They are in fact states of mind as well as states of being. So one who is in the grip of hatred and anger is, in one sense, already in the hell realm.

The goal of the Buddhist path is to go beyond all of these realms by attaining *nirvana*, through eradicating greed, hatred and delusion. Some Buddhists would see this as an

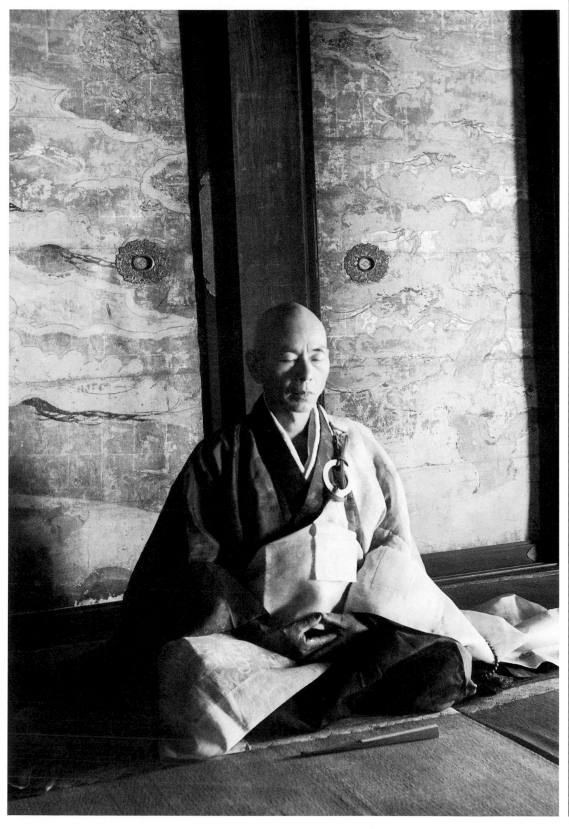

impossible immediate goal. For them, rebirth in a heavenly realm (through following the five precepts and developing loving kindness) is goal enough. Others insist that *nirvana* is possible in this very life. Whether it is seen as possible now or in the distant future, all Buddhists speak of it with joy and wonder. *Nirvana* is the end of suffering and rebirth. It is attained when the fire of craving is put out. It is the highest ethical state, but also beyond all human ethical constructs. It is defined by wisdom and compassion, yet is beyond anything the unenlightened person can conceive. It is absolute security and bliss. It is liberation. Mahayana Buddhists link it with realizing one's Buddha nature. Theravada Buddhists speak of reaching the state of the *arahat*. What happens after death to those who have realized their Buddha nature or have reached the state of the *arahat* is left open. The message of the texts is that it is beyond all human language.

Some Buddhists in the Mahayana tradition have an additional goal: the liberation of all beings. These take what is known as the *bodhisattva* vow, which is an aspiration to achieve enlightenment not for oneself alone but for the sake of all beings. This is sometimes envisaged as a commitment to stay within the realm of birth and rebirth until all beings have been liberated.

Family and Society

ELIZABETH J. HARRIS

The original call of the Buddha was: 'Come, live the holy life in order that you make an end of suffering.' Some who heard this renounced home and family to become celibate monks and nuns (Pali: *bhikkhus, bhikkhunis*; Sanskrit: *bhiksu, bhiksuni*). Others remained within their family as lay followers. A clear division emerged between the two, summed up in the verse from the Pali Canon (see 'Buddhism: Sacred

Writings') about the peacock and the swan.

The Fourfold Society

Put simply, those with no responsibilities to their families were believed to be on the fast track to *nirvana*, because they could more easily free themselves from attachments and from the attraction and aversion attachments generate. Laypeople generally speaking were on the slower track, forced into wealth creation and worries about survival. However, that did not mean laypeople were unimportant or that they could not reach high levels of religious purity. The canonical texts contain many examples of strong, spiritual laypeople. Early Buddhism spoke about the 'Fourfold Society' – monks, nuns, laymen and laywomen – with a relationship of interdependence between them:

● The monks and nuns were dependent for food and other requisites on laypeople.

● The laity were taught the *dhamma* (Pali; Sanskrit: *dharma*) by the ordained and gained a 'field' for the making of merit (Pali: *punna*; Sanskrit: *punya*).

The concept of merit derives from the law of action (Pali: *kamma*; Sanskrit: *karma*), according to which good action produces good consequences (see 'Buddhism: Beliefs'). Monks and

> *'The blue-necked peacock which flies through the air never approaches the speed of the swan. Similarly, the householder can never resemble the monk who is endowed with the qualities of a sage who meditates, aloof, in the jungle.'*
>
> Sutta Nipata, v. 221

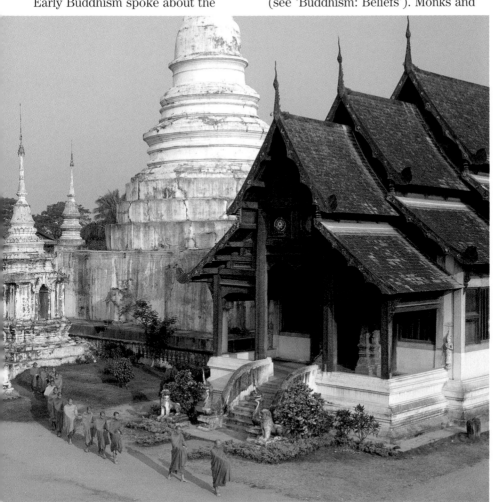

The Wat Phra Singh, Chiang Mai's largest and most important temple. The smaller building to the left is the temple's most important shrine, the Phra Wiharn Lai Kam, which houses the Phra Singh Buddha.

A young woman rings chimes above a statue of the Buddha to make merit at the Sule Pagoda, Rangoon, Myanmar (Burma).

'Just as a mother would protect her only child at the risk of her own life, even so cultivate a boundless heart towards all beings.'

From 'The Discourse on Loving Kindness', *Sutta Nipata*, v. 149

nuns were a 'field' for merit-gaining, because good consequences were ensured for any who were generous to them.

This fourfold system still exists in many Asian countries with a Buddhist majority. The order of nuns was lost in countries such as Sri Lanka and Myanmar (Burma), but action by Buddhist women in recent decades is bringing it back. In the twentieth century, Buddhist movements without ordained orders of monks or nuns developed. This is true, for example, of Rissho Kosei-kai and Soka Gakkai in Japan, and the Friends of the Western Buddhist Order in Britain. However, the last distinguishes between 'members' – *Dharmacari* and *Dharmacarini* (male and female 'followers of the *Dharma'*) who follow a limited rule of discipline – and 'friends'. It is still true to say that the majority of Buddhists operate in a system in which there is a clear distinction between those who renounce family ties and the laity.

Having said that, when Buddhist societies are compared to each other, there is a tremendous variety. As Buddhism spread from India, it became rooted in diverse cultures. Buddhism in Japan and China, for instance, feels very different, culturally, from Buddhism in Sri Lanka. In the present, globalizing forces and the entry of Buddhism into the West are causing more changes, as Buddhists adapt, innovate and sometimes retrench. To generalize about family and society within Buddhism is therefore difficult.

Family

In all Buddhist communities the family is most important. In most traditional Buddhist societies, however, marriage is a secular matter. It is linked with the worldly and takes place without the presence of a religious officiant. There is no concept of sacred vows made before God, since Buddhism is not a theistic religion in the strict sense of the word. For the same reason, divorce in some Buddhist communities, at least before the period of European colonialism, was a straightforward, mundane matter that gave rights to the wife that Western women could only have dreamt of at the time. Under the influence of colonialism, Christianity and globalization, changes have occurred. Some Buddhist brides in Sri Lanka, for instance, now wear white, a colour that is traditionally linked with funerals and sterility. Religious verses are sung during the ceremony and occasionally monks are involved. And divorce has become much more difficult.

Children are greeted with joy. Although there is recognition that the love and attachment connected with parenting has a cost and is a cause of pain (*dukkha*), positive images of parenthood permeate all schools of Buddhism.

Because of the Buddhist belief in rebirth, children are seen as coming into the world with a history. They are not the parents' 'possession', for they have had previous lives. Added to this is the belief that human life is tremendously precious, a not-to-be-missed opportunity to progress spiritually. In the Tibetan tradition especially, focusing on the preciousness of human life is part of meditation practice.

Family relationships, according to one ancient Theravada text, the *Sigalovada Sutta*, are to be regulated according to reciprocal sets of duties that almost touch on the modern concept of human rights. Wives are to offer hospitality to the extended family, show faithfulness, look after the goods brought by their husbands and carry out their duties with skill. Husbands should in turn show respect, courtesy and faithfulness, give authority to their wives and provide 'adornments' such as clothing and jewellery. Servants are to do their work well and rise before their employers, but employers in turn are to assign their employees work according to their strength, look after them in sickness, supply them with food and wages and give them leave. Times have changed since this discourse was written, but its underlying ideals remain influential in Buddhist families and in the wider society, particularly in Theravada countries.

Society

The traditional Buddhist image of the state is of a monarch, influenced by the *Dhamma* and advised by the monastic *Sangha* (community), creating well-being in society through a wise legal system and economic justice – ensuring the poor have a means of livelihood, for instance. The spread of democratic models has changed this, although in some countries the monastic *Sangha* still sees itself as an adviser to the State. It could be argued, however, that Buddhism has always had a democratic model to offer – the monastic *Sangha*, inspiration for which could have come from some of the more republican models of governance in the Buddha's own society. Today Buddhism is practised within a number of different political models.

One stereotype of Buddhism is that it encourages withdrawal from society, because of the emphasis on non-attachment. This is a misleading stereotype. For the Buddhist non-attachment is non-attachment to all that plays havoc in society: selfishness, greed, hatred, anger, violence and jealousy. It has nothing to do with lack of compassion or apathy. In fact, one of the contributions Buddhism can offer to the world is its emphasis on the compassion and loving kindness that can flow when greed and hatred, jealousy and competitiveness, are controlled and transcended. One of the first steps in this is the ability to empathize with others:

'All tremble at violence; to all life is dear. Comparing (others) with oneself, one should not kill nor cause others to kill.'
DHAMMAPADA, V. 130

'To those in the Kingdom who are engaged in cultivating crops and raising cattle, let Your Majesty distribute grain and fodder; to those in trade, give capital; to those in government service assign proper living wages.'

Advice given to a king troubled by lawlessness; from the Kutadanta Sutta, Digha Nikaya, I 135

The Cao Dai and the Hoa Hao

BARBARA BOAL

In the late nineteenth and early twentieth centuries Vietnamese nationalism was firmly, sometimes harshly, repressed by colonial French occupiers. The intellectuals who traditionally led nationalist movements began in the 1920s to profit financially from the situation and to enjoy privileged status like the French. Organizations therefore arose under new forms of nationalist leadership, seeking to end French domination and to establish a republic. Some of them followed Communist principles, but three were under the religious leadership of monks and priests: the Cao Dai and the Hoa Hao and, less important, the Binh Xuyen. All three feared and hated things foreign. They were products of local education and aimed not only at expelling foreigners but also establishing local rule by religious leaders – something quite new to the Vietnamese pattern of rule by the privileged.

Political melting-pot
During the next decade the Communist Party of Indo-China (CPI) began to gain sympathy abroad. At this point the three religious movements began armed opposition to the French colonial troops. The Cao Dai held the Mekong Delta, the Hoa Hao the border of Cambodia and the Binh Xuyen the Saigon area.

From 1941 until the end of World War II, Japanese military commanders directed the French colonial forces for the Vichy government in France. For a brief period in 1941 the combined French and Japanese all but defeated the local troops, but for the remainder of the war the latter gained strength. After the final defeat of the Japanese, the USA, in the grip of its anti-colonial convictions, aided the Communist-controlled Viet Minh, led by Ho Chi Minh (1890–1969), and independence was declared on 2 September 1945.

Because American and French interests in Vietnam were at variance, a decade of confused political, cultural and religious action and reaction resulted. It led finally to the Geneva Accord of 1954 and the partition of North and South Vietnam. The Communist Viet Minh held the North while the South was under the nationalist government of Ngo Dinh Diem (1901–63). Close on a million refugees from North to South added to the confusion. The French, as part of their opposition to Diem, had supplied arms to the Cao Dai, Hoa Hao and Binh Xuyen, but by 1956, with American aid, Diem had smashed the military strength of the three sects. Their followers, numbering about a quarter of the total population, were resentful but remained active in a less military context.

Out of the maze of political aims, cultural diffusion and varied religious beliefs that form the background to twentieth-century Vietnam, four principal religious groups have emerged to play a significant part in more recent years. These are the Buddhists, the Roman Catholic Church, the Cao Dai and the Hoa Hao.

The Cao Dai
The Cao Dai sect arose from a seance communication received by Ngo Van Chieu (1878–1926), an administrator for the French in Cochin China, in 1919. In 1926 it was formally organized by a wealthy compatriot and Mandarin, Le Van Trung (d. 1935). Cao Dai means 'Supreme Palace' or 'High Altar' and denotes the name of the supreme God.

Strikingly syncretistic, Cao Dai is also known as 'The Third Amnesty' of God. It was preceded by a first (eastern) amnesty with Buddha and Lao-tzu and a second (western) amnesty with Moses and Jesus Christ. Cao Dai is the third and unsurpassable manifestation of God in the historical process of revelation; it requires no human representatives; God communicates directly through trance to certain devotees. In its characteristic hierarchical structure it follows the pattern of the Roman Catholic Church, with its own pope

dwelling in a village outside Tan Ninh city near Saigon, where an ornate cathedral was built in 1937 at the foot of a high mountain. Its dignitaries include a full ranking-list of priests, bishops and cardinals.

In addition to Catholicism and Buddhism, it combines Confucianism, Taoism and traditional cults of spirits and ancestors. Spiritualistic elements have a striking importance, especially contacts with the dead. Amongst a host of additional figures revered in its pantheon are Victor Hugo, Sun Yat Sen, Joan of Arc, Louis Pasteur and Jean Decoux, the French Admiral of World War II who administered Vietnam for the Japanese. Its breadth thus appeals to the integrated view of peasant peoples; they have become its followers in entire village communities. The wealthy Le Van Trung had, like Buddha, renounced the luxurious life; but for villagers to whom poverty is nothing new, it is the magical elements that prove attractive.

Its ethic is based on the underlying concept of the transmigration of souls. Cao Dai revived traditional Buddhist rules regarding vegetarianism, attitudes towards animals and rules for social behaviour. Fraternity and charity, however, are much stronger than in Buddhist ethics and practice. There is also a strongly marked temple cult with numerous rites. Prayers, incense offerings, meditation and exorcisms are of great importance. Female celebrants are permitted, and matrilineal descent is important.

The religious symbol of the community is Cao Dai's eye over the globe. Its initially rapid expansion led to struggles for leadership. Despite splitting into several sects, Cao Dai has continued to grow, and its numbers are claimed to be over 5 million.

The Hoa Hao
This neo-Buddhist sect was started by Huynh Phu So in the village of Hoa Hao in Vietnam near the Cambodian border. Born in 1919, he was the son of a leading Roman Catholic peasant in the local community. He received religious training as a young man in

the hope of improving poor health. In 1939 he experienced a violent nervous spasm from which he emerged not only cured but with great power to preach and teach a new religion.

By claiming to be the incarnation of several past heroes, he set this religion on a supposedly ancient foundation which also indicated a political role for himself and his followers. He combined a revised form of Buddhist rituals with a teaching that no intermediary or holy place is necessary for direct prayer to the Almighty.

There are four main precepts in his sect's teaching:

■ honouring one's parents

■ love of one's country

■ respect for his interpretation of Buddhism

■ love towards one's fellows

Not in temples, but in teaching-centres spread over former South Vietnam, his teachings were communicated in forms attractive to the peasant population. These sometimes had nationalistic overtones and strangely predicted the coming of Americans two decades ahead of their arrival. Viewed in the 1940s as a 'living Buddha', his reputation rapidly drew followers to the sect. The French, however, saw him as a centre of political unrest and detained him in a psychiatric hospital, then later under house arrest. This enhanced his reputation, and from his home he taught continuous groups of pilgrims. A few days before a French plan to exile him to Laos could be put into action, his followers, aided by Japanese secret police, removed him to Saigon. There he was kept out of French hands.

Later it became obvious that the various nationalist movements, including Cao Dai and Hoa Hao, would each be seeking their own supremacy in the power struggle. By the late 1960s increasingly disillusioned nationalist urban intellectuals joined the Hoa peasants' religious movement, though it remained fundamentally of rural appeal.

By the time Huynh Phu So was murdered by Communists in April 1947, sub-sects had arisen which were far more active and united within themselves than were the sub-sects in the Cao Dai. They utterly rejected the bribery and betrayal that discredited some Cao Dai leaders – who also suffered disunity and decline after the death of their pope in 1959. The vigorous teaching activities of Hoa Hao continued to appeal to the large rural population in the Mekong Delta, and the sect has remained a powerful force in southern Vietnam.

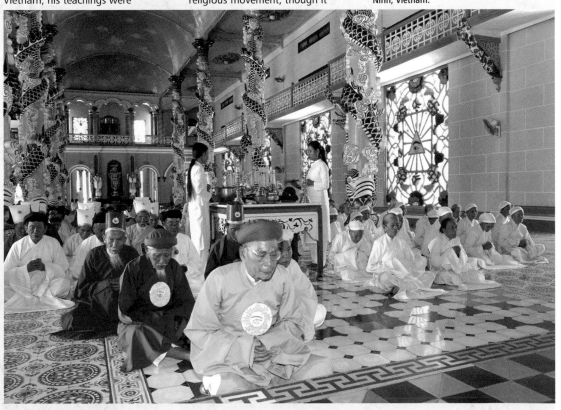

Members of the Cao Dai sect at prayer in Tay Ninh, Vietnam.

I am a Buddhist

PAUL SETO

I was born in Brisbane, Australia, into a Roman Catholic family. (I have Japanese, Irish and English ancestry.) For seventeen years I strove to be a good Catholic boy, until the time of the Vietnam War. All the Christian religious teaching I had received included as a central premise the commandment: 'Thou shall not kill.' I was therefore confused when I learned that Australia had introduced conscription for seventeen-year-old boys. This seemed to me to be hypocrisy and made me question the religion I had taken for granted. Eventually, I decided to explore my Japanese heritage.

I had already become interested in the martial arts of judo and karate. However, as I pursued my interest, I learnt that *karate* means 'empty hand' and that *judo* means 'the gentle way', that it is not violence and coercion that lead to success, but rather becoming so developed and aware that one cannot be hurt. However, much training is required to remain focused and alert. There is a saying concerning being attacked by a sword: 'The beginner can only see where the sword is, and cannot move. The master sees everywhere that the sword is not, and quietly moves there.'

Later I discovered the calm, smiling, accepting faces of the Buddha statues, which attracted me strongly. Here, in front of them, was a place where I could sit and no one was going to criticize me, where I could let my guard down and just be a boy – relaxed and happy. Over the years the Buddha faces became more real as I began to meet Buddhist monks and nuns, people who could explain in great detail why and how they looked so peaceful. In essence, it was because they had given up worrying. 'If something can be done, then do it. Do not worry. If something cannot be done, then it cannot be done. Do not worry.'

This is one of the most valuable things I have discovered as a Buddhist. It is always possible to do something useful in every situation. No matter how difficult or impossible something might seem, there is always an explanation and always something to do next. For example, if I fail at a task and feel awful, Buddhist teaching instructs me to examine who I think I am. Am I just a collection of other people's judgments, good or bad? Or do I truly have a reality and an essence that is already complete and whole, yet is at the same time developing with everything, good or bad, that I do? This deep understanding helps me to move forward in life. If suddenly there is a mountain in front of me, either literally or figuratively, I can either sit down defeated or start climbing upwards step by step. It is only by climbing a mountain that one becomes a good mountain climber. The same is true of every human situation. I can only become a more compassionate person by acting compassionately, a good leader by leading well, a good follower by learning to give loyalty to those who have been appointed to lead.

My Buddhist teacher tells me I must learn to love problems like chocolate! He means that problems provide opportunities to develop the wisdom to see the best way forward in every situation. Although the experience of happiness should be fully enjoyed, it is impermanent and constantly changing – just like problems. Nothing lasts forever.

After many years I have learnt that, if my heart and my mind are truly in a compassionately wise state, the results will usually be effective and useful to myself and other people. To this end, I start each day with prayers and readings from the Buddhist lineage that I follow (which is the Tibetan Gelugpa lineage of His Holiness the Dalai Lama). I try, as my teacher advises, to sit in formal meditation for at least forty-five minutes a day. In this way I can set my motivation and focus for the coming day, which on a 'normal' day is full of competing demands on my time, energy and attention. Although I have a formal time of meditation, I seek to stay in a 'meditative state of mind' all day, which is the goal of all spiritual practice: to live the faith in the 'real world' and thereby show that it is alive and well.

In the evening I briefly review what has happened during the day and determine to try to be even more mindful during the following day. Also, I pray that the Buddhas and gurus will watch over me throughout the night and teach me in my dreams. This is a way of reaching through the limited conceptual mind into the core being of who I really am, and why I am really here, not the collection of public facades that I have to wear for my various roles and positions.

There are four special days of the Buddhist year on which I fast: (1) *Wesak*, (2) the Descent to teach in this world, (3) the day of the Buddha's first teaching (the Four Noble Truths), and (4) Tibetan New Year. I also try to fast on all full moon days (many Buddhists still use a lunar calendar). During the two weeks when the moon is waning I practise reducing my negative activities, and in the two weeks of the waxing moon I practise developing my positive qualities.

Over Christmas I often go on a retreat and fast for forty-eight hours, drinking just a little fruit juice or black tea. I find it relatively easy, especially if I do it in a Buddhist centre, with no television, radio or music to distract me. I am not a strict vegetarian, although some Buddhists are. As one who follows a Tibetan tradition I am not required to be. The Tibetans, because of their environment, are not vegetarian: not many crops grow above the snow line, and yak meat is very warming in a stew. That said, the overall emphasis in Buddhism is always to try to reduce harm with every thought, word and deed.

Every week I go to my local temple to hear my teacher discuss his views on the scriptures and how to apply them in modern life. This keeps me in touch with 'real reality', rather than the reality of the newspapers and television.

Buddhism in the Modern World

ELIZABETH J. HARRIS

What can Buddhism offer to the contemporary world? In what ways is it challenging society? In what ways is it reinforcing the traditional? To answer these questions it is first necessary to look at some of the forces that have influenced the development of Buddhism in the last two hundred years.

Nineteenth century European colonialism

Sri Lanka (Ceylon) was the first predominantly Buddhist country to be affected by European colonialism. When the British occupied Colombo in 1796, Sri Lanka had already known two colonial powers: the Portuguese and the Dutch. Both ruled only part of the island. The British brought the whole under foreign rule by bringing down the previously independent Kandyan Kingdom in 1815. Myanmar (Burma) was the second. In 1795, the Burmese authorities allowed a British Resident in Yangon (Rangoon). Three Anglo-Burmese wars followed, until in 1885 all of Myanmar came under British rule. Independence for both countries came in 1948. Cambodia, Laos and Vietnam were the third areas, coming under French rule. For Cambodia, the process began in 1864. By the 1890s the French had almost complete control over the internal running of the country. Significant also was Western penetration into China. Between 1839 and 1865 the West, through military action and forced treaties, gained rights of residence and, in some parts of the country, jurisdiction.

This imperialistic movement affected Buddhism in two main ways. Firstly, Western visitors to these countries started to study Buddhism and interpret it to the West, working in tandem with European-based orientalists. In the early years of the nineteenth century, some drew on oral sources in Asia, but, as the century progressed, the texts took precedence, leading to an increasingly textualized interpretation of Buddhism in the West. Secondly, Asian Buddhism itself underwent revival as it attempted to resist the Christian missionary activity that accompanied colonialism. In Sri Lanka, for instance, archival records suggest that Buddhists at first sought coexistence with Christians. They were willing to procure Buddhist texts for them and to teach them the language of the texts, Pali. When they discovered, however, that the missionaries would use their knowledge to undermine Buddhism, hospitality turned to confrontation and to the development of 'Protestant Buddhism': a form of Buddhism that both 'protested' against Christianity and borrowed elements from it, from the *Young Man's Buddhist Association* and hymns to Protestant Christianity's emphasis on the texts and the devaluing of ritual. Myanmar witnessed a similar revivalist development, influenced by Sri Lanka. And in both countries revival movements and independence movements gave strength to each other. At the beginning of the twentieth century, Chinese Buddhism also underwent revival, again in response to the impact of the West, although its impact was lessened by the growth of secular ideologies.

Secular ideologies and authoritarianism

In the middle years of the twentieth century, Buddhism in Cambodia, China, Korea, Laos, Tibet and Vietnam was adversely affected by secular ideologies, Communism in particular. Communist leaders in China, after the

> *'The monk's vow: I shall eat whatever is given to me with appreciation.'*
>
> From the Monastic Code of Discipline, Vinaya IV 189

establishment of the Chinese People's Republic in 1949, simply expected Buddhism to die away. When it did not, particularly from 1966–76, the years of the Cultural Revolution, there were violent attacks on Buddhist leaders and religious buildings.

It was the British withdrawal from India that gave Communist China the opportunity to invade Tibet. The process began in 1950 and culminated in 1959, when China imposed direct rule on the country and the Dalai Lama fled. Systematic suppression of Tibet's Buddhist heritage followed: the looting of monasteries; the destruction of libraries and religious images; the execution of some monks; and the torture and imprisonment of others. In the late 1970s, there was some relaxation of this almost genocidal policy leading to a limited renewal of Buddhism in the country.

Cambodia gained its independence from the French in 1953. In 1975, Phnom Penh fell to the Khmer Rouge under Solath Sar or Pol Pot. Although before victory the Khmer Rouge had seemed to praise Buddhism, after 1975 Buddhism was systematically dismantled together with everything else that evoked Cambodia's former culture. Almost all Buddhist temples were razed. Buddhist monks were either killed or given degrading labour. Buddhist libraries were gutted. In the Buddhist Institute in Phnom Penh, for instance, forty thousand documents were destroyed. When the Vietnamese defeated Pol Pot in 1979, the country was in ruins, and there was only a handful of Buddhist monks left.

Since 1979, Cambodia has painstakingly, in the context of ongoing violence and war, attempted to rebuild its Buddhist heritage, gaining help from countries such as Sri Lanka, Japan and Germany. The first priority was to rebuild the temples. After this came teachers and books. In 1992, the Buddhist Institute was re-opened.

A deeper challenge than any of these, one that continues into the present, has been to spark an interest in spiritual values in those Cambodians who had only known violence.

Buddhism's entry into the West
One consequence of China's invasion of Tibet was that thousands of Tibetans fled from the country. Most went to India, Nepal and Bhutan, but some travelled to Europe and America, internationalizing the Tibetan story and spreading Tibetan forms of Buddhism. For instance in 1967 two Tibetans, Chogyam Trungpa Tulku Rinpoche (1939–87) and Dr Akong Tulku Rinpoche (b. 1939), founded Kagyu Samye Ling monastery near Eskdalemuir in southern Scotland. Samye Ling has now become the largest Tibetan Buddhist centre in Europe, attracting numerous Westerners, a good number of whom have become monks and nuns.

Tibetan Buddhism, however, was not the first kind of Buddhism to enter the West. In the nineteenth century, Buddhists came to British universities from countries such as Sri Lanka and Myanmar. Then, in 1893, the Anagarika Dharmapala (1864–1933), a key figure in the Buddhist Revival in Sri Lanka visited Britain, although his principal goal was to attend the World's Parliament of Religions in Chicago (1893). He returned in 1896 and 1907. The first formal Buddhist mission to Britain, however, came from Myanmar in 1908, led by the second British person to become a Buddhist monk, Venerable Ananda Metteyya (Allan Bennett 1872–1923), who was then living in Myanmar. The Buddhist Society of Great Britain and Northern Ireland was formed to welcome him. Allan Bennett had come to Buddhism through theosophy and Edwin Arnold's poem on the Buddha, *The Light of Asia*, published in 1879. The poem's presentation of the Buddha as compassionate hero drew on both Theravada and Mahayana textual sources and attracted countless readers.

The history of Buddhism in Britain and the West between 1908 and 1959 is a complex one. In 1924, the work of the Buddhist Society of Great Britain and Northern Ireland was taken over by a lawyer, Christmas Humphreys (1901–83), who combined it with a Buddhist centre he had started within the Theosophical Society to form the Buddhist Lodge. In 1943 this was renamed The Buddhist Society, London. Today it continues as the Buddhist Society. One of the inspirations for Christmas Humphreys was Daisetz Teitaro Suzuki (1870–1966), the Japanese Zen master who did more than any other person to bring Zen Buddhism to laypeople in the West. As a young man, he lived in La Salle, Illinois. In 1921 he became Professor of Buddhist Philosophy at Otani University in Tokyo. Following World War II he resumed contact with the West, influencing a generation of Westerners. He produced over thirty volumes on Buddhism and Zen in English.

In the West now, almost all schools of Buddhism are present and new Buddhist organizations are emerging to meet the needs of Westerners. In Britain, for instance, Theravada Buddhism has a strong presence, with monasteries and educational centres catering for Buddhists from Sri Lanka, Thailand, Myanmar and Western converts. The Japanese Mahayana schools are represented – Zen, Pure Land, Tendai – and also newer lay movements such as Soka Gakkai, with its many Western followers, and Rissho Kosei-kai. The different Tibetan schools have taken root. And there are movements such as the one founded in 1967 by the British Buddhist, Sangharakshita (b. 1925), the Friends of the Western Buddhist Order, which aims to offer a Buddhism to Westerners

that combines the best of all schools. Never in the history of Buddhism has one area of the world received so many forms of Buddhism within the same time span.

The globalization of capital

Asian countries such as Thailand and Japan have been particularly affected by the internationalization of capital, and the individualism and consumerism that has followed in its wake. Since the mid-twentieth century, both countries have experienced phenomenal economic growth. On the one hand, this has led to an undermining of Buddhism's emphases on non-greed and community. On the other, new counter-cultural Buddhist voices have emerged, challenging forms of Buddhism that place individual well-being above the health of the whole community.

Contemporary challenges

Conditioned by forces such as those mentioned above, Buddhists are entering many contemporary debates. Their contribution falls into two broad categories: the dynamics of social engagement; the benefits, and indeed necessity, of meditation as a way of preventing hatred, anger and violence.

Buddhism and peace

In Cambodia, after the fall of Pol Pot, in a situation of ongoing violence, a remarkable Buddhist movement, The Coalition for Peace and Reconciliation, grew up under the leadership of Maha Ghosananda (b. 1929), a monk who escaped the Pol Pot regime because he was in Thailand in 1975. During the 1990s, annual peace walks or Pilgrimages for Truth (*Dhammayietras*) were held, passing through areas still torn by conflict. Monks and nuns, laywomen and men, took part, sometimes risking their lives as they walked through crossfire. Such costly witnesses for peace have

'Thus, from the not giving of property to the needy, poverty became rife, from the growth of poverty, the taking of what was not given increased, from the increase of theft, the use of weapons increased...'

From the *Cakkavatti-Sihanada Sutta, Digha Nikaya*, III 68 – referring to the duty of the state to provide economic justice characterized Buddhism in the modern world. However, Buddhists have not stood for non-violence in all situations.

Buddhism and war

Japanese Buddhists aligned with, or at least did not resist, the militarization of

A Buddhist monk burning in flames as a form of protest in Saigon, South Vietnam, 1963.

Japan in the middle years of the twentieth century, an attitude criticized by Buddhists born later in the century after the horror of Nagasaki and Hiroshima. In Sri Lanka, some Buddhist monks and laypeople have supported a military solution to the ethnic war that ravaged the country after 1983, arguing that defence of Buddhism is justified if Buddhism is seen to be threatened. Other Sri Lankan Buddhists have utterly rejected this stance.

Buddhism and women

In the Buddha's time, women received higher ordination and became nuns (Pali: *bhikkhunis*; Sanskrit: *bhiksunis*). This higher ordination was lost in Sri Lanka and Myanmar and never transmitted to countries such as Tibet and Thailand. Even without higher ordination, however, women have left their families to become nuns but have not officially been able to follow the complete *bhikkhuni* rule of discipline. This began to change after the founding in 1987 of Sakyadhita ('Daughters of the Buddha'), an international organization of Buddhist women. At Sakyadhita conferences, fully ordained nuns from Mahayana countries such as Taiwan and Korea met 'contemporary

nuns' from countries such as Sri Lanka. This eventually led to ordination ceremonies at which nuns from countries such as Taiwan, together with sympathetic Theravada monks, ordained nuns from countries that had no higher ordination. It is a story still in process.

Giving back to all Buddhist women the opportunity to gain higher ordination is not simply about regaining lost 'rights'. It is about affirming what women can contribute to Buddhism. Whether all Buddhist women gain the option to renounce as fully ordained nuns or not, Buddhist women are now coming together with urgency to meditate together, to co-operate in joint projects and to share their vision of a world transformed by the Buddha's teaching.

Engaged Buddhism

In 1989, the International Network of Engaged Buddhists was formed. The founders included Sulak Sivaraksa (b. 1933), a lay Buddhist from Siam (he will not call himself Thai) and Thich Nhat Hanh (b. 1929), an exiled monk from Vietnam, who had founded the Order of Interbeing in 1965. It asserted that Buddhism was not only about individual peace and liberation, but also about creating a better world now. Drawing on the Buddhist concern for the elimination of suffering and the concept of interconnectedness, it sought to draw attention to the fact that the causes of much oppression, poverty and suffering lay in unjust structures and the corporate greed of the rich. Engaged Buddhist movements are now found throughout the world. The members of the Amida Trust in England, for instance, draw inspiration from the Pure Land Tradition of Japan (which emphasizes that rebirth in the 'Pure Land', from where it will be easy to attain *nirvana*, is possible through relying on the compassion of the Buddha Amitabha), but direct this towards working for a 'Pure Land' here

Buddhist nuns pray during festivities to celebrate the Buddha's birthday. Seoul, South Korea.

and now, a task they link with the original message of the Buddha.

Meditation

Engaged Buddhists insist that meditation and social engagement go hand in hand, in line with the Buddha's message that we need to know how our minds and hearts work if we are to act with wisdom rather than with greed and hatred. A growth of meditation centres catering for laypeople in Asia and the West is now putting this message across strongly. In traditional Asian Buddhism, meditation practices, except for the most elementary, were linked with monastic life. Now, whether it is Sri Lanka, Thailand, the USA or Europe, meditation is becoming an important part of life for laypeople as well.

Interfaith relations

Although mistrust of Christianity can be found in countries such as Sri Lanka, where Buddhists have experienced aggressive Christian missionary activity, many Buddhists across the world are involved in building bridges of understanding between faiths. Rissho Kosei-kai, for instance, a Japanese Buddhist lay movement founded in 1938, was one of the founders of the World Conference on Religion and Peace in 1970, a pioneering international interfaith organization. In 1987 the USA-based Society for Buddhist–Christian Studies was formed and in October 1997 the European Network of Buddhist–Christian Studies.

Conclusion

What is certain is that Buddhism is changing and part of this is due to the interpenetration of Western and Eastern forms of Buddhism. The result is that Buddhism has become a positive, dynamic force in the world; and one of the insights it can offer the world is that social engagement and compassionate action must go hand in hand with work on self, the work of meditation, the work of wisdom.

Sikhism

PART SEVEN

A Historical Overview

CHRISTOPHER SHACKLE

The major sites of Sikhism in the Punjab, divided since 1947 between India and Pakistan.

The history of Sikhism has always been closely linked to the Punjab, the land of its origins, because of its situation in the north-west of the Indian subcontinent, always the first region of the fertile northern plains to be exposed to successive conquests by invaders crossing the great mountain boundaries through such routes as the Khyber Pass. The first such cultural inroads recorded were those of the Aryan tribes in the Vedic period which initiated the beginnings of the Hindu tradition. The last were the invasions mounted by Muslim sultans from Afghanistan and Central Asia from early in the first millennium CE, which resulted not only in the establishment of centuries of Muslim rule over the Punjab, but also in the presence of substantial numbers of Muslims in Punjabi society, largely the product of peaceful conversion.

When Sikhism first emerged, some five hundred years ago, it appeared in a society already religiously divided. It would be quite misleading to think of Sikhism as a mechanical combination of Hindu and Muslim elements, since from its beginnings it has been self-defined as a new and independent third way. Equally, its evolution needs to be understood as a complex process of the ongoing relationship, within the Punjab and beyond, of a vigorous minority community to the two numerically larger traditions of Hinduism and Islam.

Guru Nanak

Nanak (1469–1539) is revered by all branches of the religion as the defining first Guru of the Sikhs (Punjabi for 'disciples'). He was by birth a Hindu

(Map showing the region with labels: AFGHANISTAN, Kabul, Kandahar, Quetta, Sukkur, Karachi, HINDU KUSH, Gilgit, CHINA, Srinagar, Islamabad, PAKISTAN, HIMALAYAS, Lahore, Amritsar, PUNJAB, Multan, Sutlej, Chandigarh, Delhi, Ganges, Bikaner, Yamuna, INDIAN DESERT, INDIA, Indus. Scale: 0–400 km, 0–300 miles)

Guru Nanak (1469–1539) founder of Sikhism and the other nine Gurus. Guru Nanak was born in Narkana Sahib in present day Pakistan. The nine successive Gurus all manifested the same divine light during their guruships:
Guru Angad (1539–52)
Guru Amar Das (1552–74)
Guru Ram Das (1574–81)
Guru Arjan (1581–1606)
Guru Hargobind (1606–44)
Guru Har Rai (1644–61)
Guru Har Krishan (1661–64)
Guru Tegh Bahadur (1664–75)
Guru Gobind Singh (1675–1708)

of the Khatri caste (professionals with strong hereditary links to the administration). His father was a village accountant. Nanak himself was married with a family and had a career as an administrator working for a local Muslim nobleman. But his true mission began when he was around the age of thirty with a transforming experience of the divine reality, granted to him when he entered the river to bathe. Mysteriously hidden from the view of his companions, he emerged after three days uttering the words 'There is no Hindu, there is no Muslim,' taken as the inaugurating formula of the new religion. Nanak then embarked upon an extended series of travels, before returning later in his life to the Punjab where he established a settled community of the first Sikhs.

Guru Nanak's teachings are embodied in his verses, hymns and longer poetical works which now form a substantial collection at the heart of the Sikh scriptures. In their broad thrust, these teachings are similar in content to those of other North Indian teachers of the medieval period from lower castes, such as Kabir and Ravidas. They all preached that salvation was dependent upon devotion not to a divine incarnation, such as Krishna, but to the undifferentiated *Formless One*; and that to observe caste practices and Brahmanical authority was as futile for those who wished to be saved as obedience to the alternatives officially promulgated by Islam. But the subsequent, successful, independent development of Sikhism itself shows that Nanak was much more than just another teacher in this dissenting tradition of medieval Hinduism, called *nirgun bhakti* (devotion to the Formless).

Nanak's hymns combine a remarkable beauty and power of poetic expression with an equally distinctive coherence and ability for systematic exposition, which is perhaps to be related to his professional background. Their contents embrace repeated praise of the divine order presided over and permeated by its creator, the one and only Immortal Being (*Akal Purakh*), with a penetrating analysis of the human condition which is condemned through egotistical self-will (*haumai*, literally 'I-me') to the mechanical succession of suffering and endless rebirths in blind unawareness of that order. In place of the false claims to offer true guidance offered by the religious specialists of the day, whether Brahmans, yogis or Muslim clerics, Nanak sets out his own prescription for human salvation. This explains the necessity of inner transformation

'Great Guru whose encounter brought the Lord to mind! With his teaching as their salve, these eyes survey the world. Attached to the other, some traders left the Lord and roamed. How few have realized the Guru is the boat, Which delivers those he favours safe across.'

Adi Granth 470

through listening to the voice of the True Guru within the heart and meditating with love upon the Divine Name. Only thus may freedom from self be gained and escape from the

The *Khalsa*

On *Baisakhi* day in 1699, the tenth Guru founded the institution of the *Khalsa*, the community of initiated (*amritdhari*) Sikhs. The nucleus of this dynamic community is popularly known as the five beloved ones (*panj-piare*) who volunteered to sacrifice their lives for the sake of the Guru on that historic day.

Thereupon the Guru prepared *amrit* (water of immortality) – popularly known as *khande di pahul* (water of the double-edged sword) – for the initiation ceremony; the five volunteers who belonged to different caste groups drank *amrit* from the same bowl, signifying their entry into the casteless fraternity of the *Khalsa*. The next most important innovation was the change in their names. All five volunteers, like the Guru, had traditional Hindu names before the initiation ceremony. Now they were given a new corporate name: 'Singh'. Afterwards, the Guru received *amrit* from the *panj-piare* and changed his name from Gobind Rai to Gobind Singh. He also admitted women into the *Khalsa*, who after the initiation received the name 'Kaur'.

According to tradition, Guru Gobind Singh prescribed a new code of discipline for members of the *Khalsa*. It includes the wearing of five emblems collectively known as *panj kakke* (five ks), because each begins with the letter '*kakka*' of the Gurmukhi script:

- *kes* (uncut hair)

- *kangha* (a small wooden comb worn in hair)

- *kirpan* (a sword, nowadays a small one)

- *kacha* (a pair of knee-length breeches)

- *kara* (a steel bracelet worn on the right wrist).

It is believed that Gobind Singh also declared that members of the *Khalsa* must not smoke or chew tobacco or consume alcohol. They should not eat meat slaughtered according to Muslim custom, and they must not molest a Muslim woman. Although a turban (*pag*) is not one of the prescribed emblems, it has far greater significance for Sikhs than any other head-covering. A male Sikh is required to wear the turban in public as a symbol of honour.

cycle of transmigration be achieved, so that the liberated soul may at last join the company of saints in their eternal singing of praises at the court of the Immortal Being.

There is, however, nothing automatic about access to the path of salvation which Nanak describes. His hymns repeatedly emphasize that a righteous life is no guarantee of salvation, since

A Sikh makes ritual ablutions in Anandpur Sahib, India.

the coming of the inner True Guru to any given individual depends on the favour of the Immortal Being. For this to happen, it is equally a necessary condition that the individual should have prepared him or herself for the True Guru's coming through living properly. Such a life certainly does not entail the practice of elaborate rituals or extreme asceticism, which are both frequently stated to be quite pointless. What is important is rather the discipline of living a normal life in this world, practising loving meditation on the divine reality and supporting others through an honest existence, as summed up in the triple formula of 'the Name, giving, and keeping clean' (*nam dan isnan*).

The later Gurus and the scriptures
As has been repeatedly demonstrated throughout history, the successful establishment of a religion depends not just upon the teachings of its founder but also upon how the community created by them is subsequently organized. Besides being a teacher of outstanding force and insight, Guru Nanak was evidently a most capable organizer of his followers. He laid the foundations of some of the defining practices of the subsequent Sikh tradition, notably the establishment of daily offices of prayer (*nitnem*) and the practice of congregational assembly to hear the hymns of the Guru. Himself married with two sons, Guru Nanak went outside his family in selecting a disciple to succeed him as the second Guru of the Sikh community or *Panth* (path, way).

From the time of Guru Nanak's death the Sikh Panth was led by a line of living Gurus until the death of the tenth Guru in 1708. While rejection of the Hindu caste hierarchy was symbolically reinforced by the third Guru, Amar Das – through the institution of the *langar*, the temple kitchen offering food to all irrespective

of caste – all the Gurus were from the same Khatri caste as Nanak; and from the fifth Guru onwards the succession became hereditary within a single family. Initially the centre of the community shifted with each Guru, until Guru Arjan founded the great temple at Amritsar known as the Golden Temple (*Harimandir*), which since its inauguration in 1604 has been the focal point of Sikhism.

At the same time, Guru Arjan undertook a project of still greater importance in providing a unifying object of devotion for the Sikh Panth, through his codification of the Sikh scriptures, issued with the Guru's authority as the *Adi Granth* (original book). This is an enormous hymnal, filling 1,430 pages in the standard modern edition, and having a central place in the ritual of the Sikh temples, which are called *gurdwara* (gate of the Guru). Besides the compositions of Guru Nanak, the *Adi Granth* also contains those of the next four Gurus – who each used the same poetic name 'Nanak', in keeping with the belief that the transmission of the light of the guruship blended them into a seamless line of 'light blended into light'(*joti jot samai*). Guru Arjan himself is the largest single contributor, accounting for about one third of the whole. Its contents also include hymns by non-Sikh authors such as Kabir and Ravidas, and the Muslim Farid, collectively referred to as 'devotees' (*bhagats*). The language of most of the scripture is a mixture of Old Punjabi and Old Hindi, written in the special Sikh script, Gurmukhi. The elaborate arrangement of several thousand hymns, itself an outstanding achievement of editorship, is not primarily by author but by the mode (*raga*) in which they are to be sung. While no other early Sikh literature has the same canonical authority as the *Adi Granth*, popular devotion has always been fostered by the prose hagiographies of Guru Nanak called *janamsakhis* (birth-witnesses) which were first produced during this period.

Guru Gobind Singh and the *Khalsa*

The Panth grew significantly in numbers and membership during the time of the early Gurus, which closely overlapped with the reign of the great Mughal emperor Akbar. But the strategic location of the Punjab inevitably embroiled the Gurus in imperial politics, and Guru Arjan became the first Sikh martyr when Akbar's less tolerant successor ordered his execution. During the seventeenth century the Panth expanded from its initial largely professional and commercial membership to embrace increasing numbers of Sikhs from the Jat farming caste. At the same time, an increasingly militant policy was reflected in the proclamation under Arjan's son Guru Hargobind of claims to secular (*miri*) as well as to spiritual authority (*piri*). Continuing conflict with the Mughals came to a further head with the execution in Delhi of the ninth Guru, Tegh Bahadur.

This led to a radical new formation of the community under the martyred leader's son Guru Gobind Singh, the tenth and last Guru. Guru Gobind consciously adopted the role of a ruler as well as that of guru in his court at Anandpur in the Punjab. His most important innovation was the re-establishment of the Guru's authority over the Panth through the foundation of a new order called the *Khalsa* (the Guru's elite) (see p. 218).

While the Sikh Panth has always continued to contain many followers of Nanak and the gurus who choose not to become baptized members of the *Khalsa*, it is the latter who have led the Panth since the time of the last Guru. Gobind Singh's own sons were all killed in the course of his struggles against the forces of the Mughal emperor Aurangzeb, and he was himself killed by a Muslim assassin. After his death, the line of living Gurus came to an end, and their authority was henceforth vested in the scripture, expanded by the addition of Guru Tegh Bahadur's hymns to Guru Arjan's collection, and since revered as the *Guru Granth Sahib*.

Compositions by Guru Gobind Singh, some of which form part of the daily liturgy, and many more by others associated with him were assembled in another volume of lesser canonical status, the *Dasam Granth (Book of the Tenth One)*. A further influential set of extra-canonical Sikh religious literature also came into being at around this time in the form of the *Rahitnamas*, simple manuals prescribing various rules of conduct (*rahit*) for the Sikhs of the *Khalsa*.

During the eighteenth century the Punjab was fought over between the declining Mughal empire and new Muslim invaders from Afghanistan. This was the heroic age of the Sikh Panth, which was organized into local guerrilla bands who mounted a spirited resistance to both sets of Muslim armies, and who even in defeat are still remembered for their glorious acts of martyrdom (*shahidi*). Led and manned by the Jat Sikhs who had now become the dominant group in the community, the *Khalsa* forces achieved complete political success with the capture of Lahore, the provincial capital which became the centre of a powerful Sikh kingdom under Maharaja Ranjit Singh (1799–1839), whose generous patronage is responsible for the splendid appearance of many of the great Sikh temples today. But Ranjit Singh's weaker successors proved unable to resist the pressure of the British, who after two hard-fought wars finally incorporated the Punjab into their Indian empire in 1849.

'Surrounded, with no choice, in turn I too attacked with bow and gun. When matters pass all other means, It is allowed to take up arms.'
Dasam Granth 1391

A HISTORICAL OVERVIEW

Sacred Writings

SEWA SINGH KALSI

One of the unique features of the formation of the Sikh scripture is the way it emerged under the leadership of human Gurus, and finally, culminated in having ultimate authority within the Sikh tradition.

Sri Guru Granth Sahib

The principal scripture of the Sikhs is the *Adi Granth* (eternal book or original collection of compositions in a book form). In everyday Sikh usage, the *Adi Granth* is reverentially referred to as the *Sri Guru Granth Sahib* which implies an affirmation of faith in the scripture as Guru. The words *Sri* (Sir) and *Sahib* (Lord) are honorific titles, indicating the highest authority accorded to the scripture. The *Adi Granth* opens with the basic creed (*Mul Mantra*) which affirms the fundamentals of the Sikh faith. It begins with the phrase '*Ek Onkar*' (one God) which signifies the oneness and unity of God. Thus it affirms that the Supreme Being or God is 'One without a second'.

The *Adi Granth* was compiled by the fifth Guru, Arjan, in 1604. It contains the compositions of the first five Sikh Gurus alongside the writings of Muslim and Hindu saints of the medieval period some of whom belonged to the lowest caste group (Shudra), such as Kabir, Ravidas and Farid. The entire collection is recorded in script 'from guru's mouth' (*Gurmukhi*) that is also used for modern Punjabi. Because of its association with the Gurus and the scripture, *Gurmukhi* acquired a sacred status within the Sikh community.

The contents of the *Adi Granth* are respectfully referred to as *bani* (voice) and as *gurbani* (utterance of the Guru). Sikh Gurus also applied the phrase '*dhur ki bani*' (utterance from the beginning, eternal utterance) which refers to its perceived divine origin. Guru Nanak clearly affirms the divine origin of the *bani*. He says: 'As the *bani* of the Lord comes to me so do I proclaim its knowledge' (*Adi Granth* 722). The Guru is, in a primary sense, the 'voice' of God. Guru Nanak further clarifies the distinction between the

The *Guru Granth Sahib* is read to the congregation.

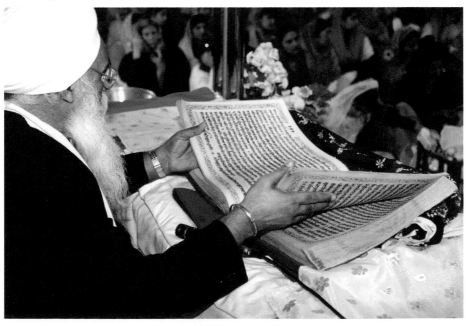

Divine Guru and the human Guru. He regarded himself as the minstrel (*dhadi*) of God (*Akal Purakh*) who openly proclaimed the glory of the divine Word (*Shabad*).

The process of identification of the *bani* with the Guru (*God*) had begun with Guru Nanak and it was further extended by his successors. For example, the third Guru, Amar Das, proclaimed: 'Love the *bani* of the Guru. It is our support in all places and it is bestowed by the Creator himself' (*Adi Granth* 1335). Similarly, the fourth Guru, Ram Das, says: 'The *bani* is the Guru, and the Guru the *bani*, and the nectar (*amrit*) permeates all souls…' (*Adi Granth* 982). The scripture concludes with Guru Arjan's hymn *Mundavani* (seal) which summarizes the essence of Sikh faith:

*'In the platter are placed three things, truth, contentment and wisdom, as well as the nectar of the Lord's Name [*amrit-nam*], the support of all.'*

The *Adi Granth*, on its completion, was accorded the utmost sacred and authoritative status in 1604 when it was installed by Guru Arjan in the newly built Golden Temple (*Harimandir*) at Amritsar. Guru Arjan says: 'The book [*Adi Granth*] is the abode of the Supreme Lord.' From the time of Guru Nanak, the Sikh community began to use the *gurbani* in devotional singing (*shabad kirtan*) as part of congregational worship. Currently the original copy of the *Adi Granth* is in the possession of the Sodhi family at Kartarpur in Jullundar district, Punjab.

From the *Adi Granth* to *Sri Guru Granth Sahib*

According to Sikh tradition, the tenth Guru, Gobind Singh terminated the line of human Gurus by bestowing guruship on the *Adi Granth* to which he had added the compositions of his father, the ninth Guru, Tegh Bahadur. The ceremony of the transfer of personal authority to the scripture is believed to have taken place before Gobind Singh's death in 1708. Since that moment the *Adi Granth* has been revered as a human Guru, and is respectfully addressed as the *Sri Guru Granth Sahib*. It is always placed on a high platform under a canopy and a ritual fan (*chauri*) is waved over it while a service is in progress. Moreover, the presence of the *Guru Granth Sahib* is regarded as mandatory on almost all ceremonial and domestic occasions, such as weddings, initiation ceremonies and naming ceremonies.

The *Dasam Granth*

The *Dasam Granth* is the second scriptural book of the Sikhs. It contains the compositions of the tenth Guru, Gobind Singh, and other poets. The contents were collected by Mani Singh after the death of Gobind Singh; it was completed in 1734. The *Dasam Granth* is not installed in all *gurdwaras*, but is found at the two historic *gurdwaras* of Hazoor Sahib and Patna Sahib, popularly called *Takhat* (Throne of the Immortal Being) (two of the five centres of temporal authority in Sikh society); however, some of its compositions are recited during the preparation of *amrit* (water used for the initiation ceremony) and other acts of worship.

The compositions of Bhai Gurdas

Bhai Gurdas was the scribe who wrote out the *Adi Granth* under the direction of Guru Arjan. The collection of his writings is called *varan* (ballads). These are popularly known as 'the key to the *Adi Granth*' and are normally sung and quoted by Sikh musicians and preachers at the *gurdwaras*.

Reflecting on the concept of *dhur ki bani*, Guru Arjan, the compiler of the *Adi Granth*, wrote: *'This utterance has come from the beginning. It has effaced all anxiety from my heart. The Supreme Being is kind and compassionate… The Lord has revealed the truth.'*

Adi Granth 628

SACRED WRITINGS

Beliefs

SEWA SINGH KALSI

The central teaching in Sikhism is the belief in the oneness of God. The Sikh scripture begins with the phrase 'Ek Onkar' (one God). According to the concept of the oneness of God, all people – irrespective of caste, creed, colour and sex – emanated from one divine source. In their compositions, Sikh Gurus have applied a number of terms from Islamic and Hindu traditions for God, including Allah, Qadir, Karim and Paar Brahma.

The diversity in God's creation is perceived as a divine gift, with all religious traditions regarded as equally valid and capable of enriching the spiritual and cultural lives of their believers. According to Sikh teachings, all human groups evolved and developed their modes of worship and religious institutions within the context of their social environment. Reflecting on the essence and universality of religious truth, the tenth Guru, Gobind Singh, wrote: 'Recognize all humankind, whether Muslim or Hindu as one. The same God is the Creator and Nourisher of all. Recognize no distinction among them. The temple and the mosque are the same. So are Hindu worship and Muslim prayer. Human beings are all one' (Dasam Granth).

In Sikhism, the nature of God is clearly manifested in Guru Nanak's first composition, the basic creed popularly known as the Mul Mantra, and his first utterance: 'There is no Hindu, there is no Muslim.'

The opening phrase of the Mul Mantra summarizes the fundamental belief of the Sikhs. The words 'Ek' (one) and 'Onkar' (God) emphasize the oneness of God. God is also believed to be the creator, from whom the universe has emanated. God is

'Firstly God created Light and then by His omnipotence, made all the world. From the One light has emerged the entire universe. Then who is good and who is bad? O, men, my brethren, stray ye not in doubt. Creation is in the Creator and the Creator is in Creation. He is fully filling all places.'

Adi Granth 1349–50

beyond the qualities of male and female. They are attributes of the creation, not the creator. Nanak says: 'The wise and beauteous Being is neither a man nor a woman nor a bird' (Adi Granth 1010). As God is believed to be ajuni, he/she does not experience birth or die. God having no particular gender further signifies the unity and equality of humankind.

Sikhism is strictly monotheistic. Belief in God's incarnation and the worship of idols is strongly disapproved of. Since God is without any form, colour, mark or lineage, God cannot be installed as an idol. God is regarded as eternal truth (ad sach) without beginning and without end, whereas everything else in this universe, including the sun, moon, stars and earth, will perish. The notion of permanence only applies to God, who will remain the divine truth forever.

Hukam (divine order)

The term hukam (order, command) entered the Sikh/Punjabi vocabulary from Arabic. In the Islamic tradition, God is perceived as one who gives orders, a commander (Hakam). In Sikhism, hukam is perceived as the divine order and everything in this universe is believed to be working according to God's hukam. The Sikh gurus extensively applied the concept

The Mul Mantra

Ek Onkar	There is one God
Satnam	Eternal truth is his/her name
Karta Purakh	Creator of all things
Nirbhau	Without fear
Nirvair	Without enmity
Akal Murat	Timeless, immortal, never incarnated
Ajuni	Beyond the cycle of birth and death
Saibham	Self-created, self-existent
Gurparsad	Known by the grace of the Guru

(Guru Granth Sahib – 1)

of *hukam* in their compositions to describe the nature of creation, the universe and human life. Nanak refers to *hukam* as the divine hand behind the functioning of the universe as well as the daily lives of human beings.

Although human beings are unique in God's creation, alone endowed with the qualities to discriminate between good and evil, the most significant aspects of human existence, such as birth and death, are beyond their control. Human life (*manas janam*) is a divine gift; both birth and death occur according to *hukam*. For example, at Sikh funerals death is explained as eternal reality; it occurs according to the *Alahi Hukam* (divine order, Allah's order). Therefore, mortals must submit to God's will without any doubt or questioning. Guru Nanak reflects on the concept of *hukam* by posing a question: 'How may a man purify himself? How the veil of falsehood tear aside? This is brought about by living in accordance with God's command or will' (*Hukam Adi Granth* 2).

The concept of *hukam* raises a fundamental question. Are mortals helpless creatures in God's kingdom? Sikh teachings reject this view and proclaim that all human beings are endowed with qualities to determine their own destiny. As the Sikh Gurus have strongly emphasized, if someone commits evil deeds, he or she will suffer accordingly: that which one sows, that one shall reap. Ultimately, falsehood or evil will be destroyed and truth shall prevail. For the attainment of truth one needs to engage in righteous deeds.

Mukti (spiritual liberation)

The word *mukti* is the Punjabi version of the Sanskrit term *moksha* (to be free from, to release). As a religious concept, it denotes the final release or spiritual liberation of the soul from human existence, leading to merger with the Supreme Soul (*Parmatma*). According to the Sikh teachings, the soul (*atma*) is immortal while the body in which it resides is perishable. After death the body is cremated and the *atma* either merges with the Supreme Soul or passes from one form of life to another, depending upon one's *karma* in this world.

As a religious concept, the term *karma* (literally: deeds, actions) denotes one's preordained destiny. Although the Sikhs believe in the doctrine of *karma*, they do not regard human beings as helpless creatures. The notion of *jivan-mukta* (see below) transcends the limitations of *karma* and transforms it into a dynamic force. As Guru Nanak says: 'Let deeds be the soil, the seeding God's Word; let Truth be the water you daily apply. Let faith be the crop which you grow in your field, for thus you will learn of both heaven and hell' (*Adi Granth* 1245)

For the cycle of birth and death the Sikhs Gurus used the term *awagaun*, which is based on the doctrine of *karma* and the transmigration of souls. According to traditional Hindu belief, there are 8,400,000 forms of existence before one is reborn as a human being. Those who are sinful and engage in evil-doing keep going through the cycle of birth and death which is regarded as the most degrading state: *narak* (hell). At a Sikh funeral, the officiant recites the final prayer (*antam-ardas*) invoking God's forgiveness for the departed soul and saving him or her from *awagaun*.

In order to overcome the ultimate punishment of *chaurasi* (cycle of birth and death), Sikhs are required to conduct themselves according to the teachings of the Sikh Gurus. They must work towards becoming Guru-oriented (*gursikh*) as opposed to self-oriented (*manmukh*). A Sikh is taught to lead a life of an honest householder, a true believer in the oneness of God and equality of humankind while earning a

Swami Peer Zindigi performs his daily meditation rite in New Delhi, India.

living by honest means (*kirat karna*) and sharing it with others (*vand chhakna*).

A Sikh who succeeds in attaining the status of *gursikh* is called *jivan-mukta*, one who is liberated from worldly temptations such as lust (*kaam*), anger (*krodh*), greed (*lobh*), attachment (*moh*) and false pride or ego (*ahankar*). Another attribute of a *jivan-mukta* is his or her faith in *gurbani* to earn *mukti* now rather than after death. A *gursikh* transforms into a *jivan-mukta* by leading a life of detachment from worldly temptations while actively engaged in the social and cultural enrichment of society or *seva* (voluntary service). A *jivan-mukta* Sikh is like a lotus which remains clean despite living in muddy water.

Dharmsal (the practice of righteousness)

The term *dharmsal* is composed of *dharm* (religious, moral and social obligations) and *sal* (a place of abode). Guru Nanak describes the earth as *dharmsal* (a place to practise righteousness) established by God within the universe. In this *dharmsal* human life is regarded as the highest and most precious form as well as the divine gift. Moreover, the earth and everything which stands on it is believed to carry the divine stamp.

According to Sikh teachings, Sikhs are not passive spectators or recluses in this world; they are expected to be active participants in the drama of human affairs and be truly Guru-oriented (*gursikh*). The concept of *dharmsal* implies faith in the oneness of God and the equality of humankind. Guru Nanak severely reprimanded Hindu ascetics (*yogis*) who advocated the path of renunciation by abdicating their social obligations. Apart from Har Krishan, who died aged eight, all Sikh gurus were married men who by personal example demonstrated their faith in their

> 'In pride, man is overtaken by fear. In utter commotion he passes his life. Pride is a great malady because of which, he dies, is re-born and continues coming and going [caught in the cycle of birth and death].'
>
> Adi Granth 592

adherence to the householder's state (*grihsth-ashrama-dharma*). For a Sikh, there is no place for the renunciation of society and the aimless pursuit of God in the forest by giving up all social responsibilities.

Gurparsad (grace and blessing)

The term *gurparsad* is composed of *gur* (from *guru*) and *parsad* (from Sanskirt for grace, blessing, boon), which is also applied to the sanctified food offered to the congregation at the culmination of a Sikh service. *Gurparsad* is the concluding word of the *Mul Mantra*. Here the word *gurparsad* does not stand for any personal Guru but for the eternal Guru (God). In fact, the term *gurparsad* affirms the Sikh belief and the way God can be realized.

The Sikh Gurus have used several terms for elaborating the essence of the concept of *gurparsad*, such as *karam*, *mehar*, *nadar* and *kirpa*. The word *karam* is derived from Arabic, *mehar* and *nadar* from Persian and *kirpa* from Sanskrit. The Arabic word *karam* should not be confused with the traditional Hindu and Sikh concept of *karma*, which denotes actions or deeds done in one's previous life. It is believed that everybody's destiny is preordained according to his or her *karma*, and ultimately one is responsible for its consequences.

The concept of *gurparsad* seems to override the law of retribution. As Guru Nanak says: 'Through good actions comes the human incarnation, through grace is reached the Door of The Divine' (*Adi Granth* 145). Guru Nanak gives an analogy to illustrate the ultimity of *gurparsad*; he says that as one spark of fire may burn away huge stocks of firewood, so acts of devotion and love of God may annul the consequences of bad *karma*. The Sikh Gurus repeatedly affirm that divine grace is the fruit of sincere devotion to God.

Worship and Festivals

SEWA SINGH KALSI

Namsimran (meditating on God's name)

The concept of *nam* (name) is one of the key doctrines in Sikhism. It symbolizes the eternal truth or God and occurs many times in the *gurbani* (*Adi Granth*). The word *simran* is a noun from the verb for 'to meditate'. In everyday usage the concept of *namsimran* is applied to the discipline of daily meditation undertaken by devout Sikhs. It is a common practice to use a rosary during the *namsimran*. Normally the words *Waheyguru* and *Satnam* are repeated too. Many Sikhs participate in the *namsimran* sessions organized at *gurdwaras*.

The Sikh Gurus extensively applied the concept of *nam* to affirm their faith in the omnipresence of God and impressed upon their disciples the necessity of the discipline of *namsimran*. They also assert that *nam* is the creator of everything. Through *nam* comes all wisdom and light; *nam* extends to all creation; there is no place where *nam* is not.

The doctrine of *nam* also provides insight into the *Guru–sikh* relationship. Two most popular terms, '*nam laina*' and '*nam dena*', are applied to signify this sacred bond (*laina* meaning to receive or be blessed and *dena* meaning to bestow). Many Sikhs desire to become disciples of renowned saints (*Sants*); in this process a devotee expresses his or her devotion through the ritual of *nam laina*; the *Sant* communicates the *gurmantra* (sacred word or formula) '*Waheyguru*' to the initiate; from that moment the *Guru–sikh* relationship is established. Normally, a devotee would make an offering of money to the newly adopted *Guru*. The devotee is instructed to rise early in the morning and to take a bath before engaging in the ritual of *namsimran*. It is believed that by repeating the *gurmantra* one's ego is destroyed.

In popular Sikh usage the act of worship means reading from the scripture and reciting a selection of hymns (*path-karna*). In individual or congregational worship the central focus is on the utterances of the Gurus in the *Adi Granth* (*gurbani*). Sikh festivals, which are both religious and cultural celebrations, fall into two categories: *gurpurb* (an anniversary when a Guru is remembered) and *mela* (a fair). The most popular *melas* are *Baisakhi*, *Diwali* and *Hola*.

Individual worship

The pattern of individual worship is prescribed in the Sikh code of discipline (*Rehat Maryada*) approved by the Supreme Gurdwara Management Committee (*Shiromani Gurdwara Parbandhak Committee*) in 1945 and published in 1951. The daily routine (*nitnem*) comprises texts from the *Adi Granth* and rules for personal cleanliness:

● A Sikh should rise early and take a bath, then recite the hymns of Japji, Jap and Ten Sawayyas.

● At sunset he or she should recite the hymn of *Rahiras*.

● Before going to bed he or she should recite the hymn of *Sohila*.

● At the conclusion of each recital, the Sikh prayer *ardas* (petition) is recited.

Worship can be undertaken anywhere in peace and quiet, and most Sikh

> *'Whosoever calls him/herself a disciple of the True Guru should rise in the early morning and meditate on God's name. He/she should endeavour to take a bath in the Pool of Nectar in the early morning. By repeating God's Name under Guru's instructions, all his/her sins are washed off. Then at sunrise he/she should sing gurbani (Guru's word) and meditate on God's Name whilst working or resting.'*
> Adi Granth 305

WORSHIP AND FESTIVALS

households have a selection of hymns normally recited during worship (*gutka*), wrapped in a cloth and kept in a safe place. Many devout Sikhs also have a copy of the *Guru Granth Sahib* at home, respectfully kept in a special room usually located on the top floor. Although any building where a copy of the *Guru Granth Sahib* is installed qualifies to be called a *gurdwara*, a family *gurdwara* is strictly a private shrine and not open to the general public.

Congregational worship

Congregational worship takes place at the *gurdwara*, one of the central institutions in the Sikh tradition. There is not fixed day, but in the diaspora most services take place on a Sunday. The term *gurdwara* is composed of *guru* (denoting the *Guru Granth Sahib*) and *dwara* (gate or house) and is attributed to the sixth Guru, Hargobind, who is believed to have built *gurdwaras* at sites associated with his predecessors. During the period of the first five Gurus, a Sikh place of worship was known as a *dharmsala*. According to tradition, Guru Nanak established the first at Kartarpur as a place where a congregation (*sangat*) of men and women of all caste groups would gather for communal worship and hymn-singing (*shabad kirtan*) followed by a communal meal (*langar*). The institutions of *sangat*, *shabad kirtan* and *langar* emerged as the most distinguishing features of the Sikh tradition.

Historic *gurdwaras* have been built on sites linked to important events in the development of Sikhism: for example, *Gurdwara Kesgarh* at Anandpur, where the tenth Guru, Gobind Singh, established the Khalsa in 1699 (see panel on p. 218) and *Gurdwara Sis Ganj* in Delhi, built on the site where the ninth Guru, Tegh Bahadur, was beheaded by the Mughal

authorities. Community-based *gurdwaras* are autonomous institutions, established by local Sikh communities and run by locally elected management committees which are answerable only to their local *sangat*.

There is a general pattern of Sikh service that is observed at all *gurdwaras*. It begins with the recital and singing of *Asa di var* in the morning followed by more hymn-singing from the scripture. The service concludes with the recital of *ardas* by the *granthi* (reader of the scripture) while members of the *sangat* stand silently with folded hands. After the *ardas*, a randomly chosen hymn from the scripture is read out to the congregation, called *hukam-nama* (divine order for the day). The service ends with the distribution of sanctified food (*karah parshad*) to the members of the congregation, symbolizing Sikh belief in the equality of humankind.

The way a Sikh expresses his or her reverence for the scripture may create the impression that the Sikhs are idol worshippers. For example, as soon as a Sikh enters the congregational hall he or she approaches the *Adi Granth*, makes an offering and bows. In fact, the devotee is showing devotion towards the *Guru Granth Sahib*, which is regarded as the living Guru.

Gurpurbs

The term *gurpurb* is made up of *gu* (short for *guru*) and *purb* (a sacred or auspicious day). There are four main *gurpurbs* celebrated by Sikhs throughout the world:

● the birthday of Guru Nanak: 26 November

● the birthday of Guru Gobind Singh: 5 January

● the martyrdom anniversary of Guru Arjan: 16 June

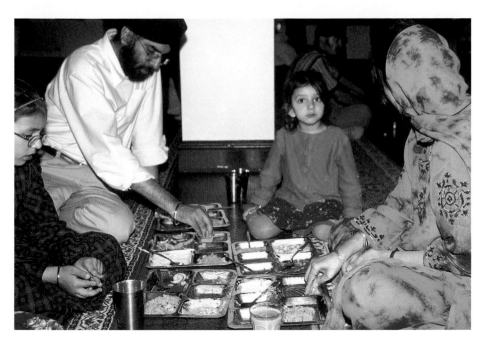

A Sikh family in London eating *langar* after Sunday worship in the *gurdwara*.

Festivals of Sikhism

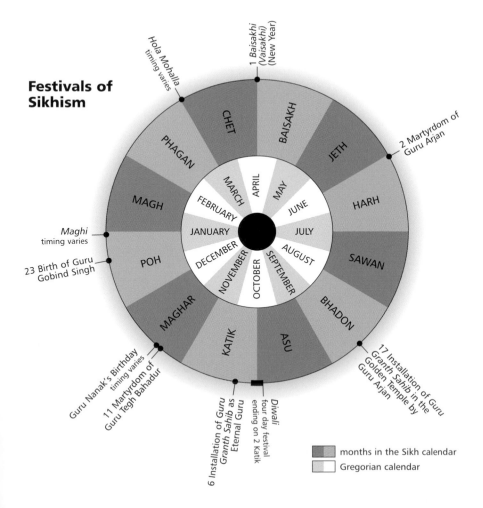

Hola Mohalla
timing varies

1 *Baisakhi* (*Vaisakhi*) (New Year)

2 Martyrdom of Guru Arjan

CHET

BAISAKH

PHAGAN

JETH

MAGH

HARH

Maghi
timing varies

23 Birth of Guru Gobind Singh

POH

SAWAN

MAGHAR

BHADON

17 Installation of Guru Granth Sahib in the Golden Temple by Guru Arjan

Guru Nanak's Birthday
timing varies

11 Martyrdom of Guru Tegh Bahadur

KATIK

ASU

6 Installation of Guru Granth Sahib as Eternal Guru

Diwali
four day festival ending on 2 Katik

MARCH

APRIL

MAY

FEBRUARY

JUNE

JANUARY

JULY

DECEMBER

AUGUST

NOVEMBER

SEPTEMBER

OCTOBER

months in the Sikh calendar

Gregorian calendar

● the martyrdom anniversary of Guru Tegh Bahadur: 24 November

In India, *gurpurbs* are celebrated by taking the *Guru Granth Sahib* in processions around towns and villages. In villages the scripture is placed in a decorated palanquin (*palki*). A procession is led by five initiated (*amritdhari*) Sikhs carrying swords, symbolizing the 'five beloved ones' initiated by the tenth Guru in 1699.

Baisakhi

The festival of *Baisakhi* is celebrated on the first day of the month of Baisakh in the Punjabi calendar and nowadays it has a special importance for the Sikhs. It is celebrated as the birthday of the *Khalsa* (see 'Sikhism: A Historical Overview'). In Punjab, the farmers begin harvesting the wheat crop after the *Baisakhi* celebrations. Apart from religious ceremonies, a

number of cultural activities are organized, such as *kabadi*, football, hockey and wrestling. Traditional *Bhangra* dancing (when dancers dress up in colourful Punjabi costumes) is the climax of the celebrations.

Hola

Hola takes its name from the traditional Hindu festival of *Holi*, which is celebrated by communal singing, dancing and throwing colours on people irrespective of caste, gender and status. Guru Gobind Singh disapproved of the nature of the *Holi* festival, regarding it as a wasteful and degrading exercise. He summoned his followers to Anandpur to celebrate the festival of *Holi* in a quite different way. Instead of indulging in merrymaking, he organized mock battles between two groups of Sikh volunteers and trained them in martial arts, thereby giving them a new purpose in life. The title

The Golden Temple at Amritsar was built by Arjan, the fifth Guru of Sikhism, at the end of the sixteenth century.

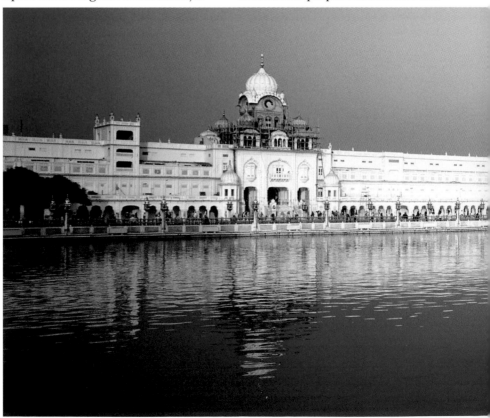

The Golden Temple

DOUGLAS DAVIES

The Golden Temple (*Harimandir*) can serve as a symbol of the Sikh religion, and a visual aid to our understanding of its spiritual meaning, and of how the past has influenced the present. For Sikhs this temple is the court of the Lord (*Dharbar Sahib*). In its precincts are to be found peace and the possibility of access to God.

The Hindi and Punjabi hymns of the early Gurus, together with those of some non-Sikh mystics, were collected together in the *Gurmukhi* (mouth of the Guru) script and first installed here by Arjan in 1604. Later editions of this volume, which include the devotional poetry of the later Gurus, constitute the focal point of devotion and meditation.

The hymns are sung from morning to night at the temple, and a constant stream of visitors and pilgrims comes to listen to the words, which confer a blessing on their believing hearers.

The whole temple site consists of an outer paved area with shaded cloisters surrounding the large pool or tank from which Amritsar (pool of nectar) takes its name. At the centre of the pool lies the beautiful Golden Temple itself, in which the sacred book is placed early in the morning.

This temple has served as the basis for many interpretations of the religious life. It is, for example, like a lotus plant growing from the murky water of life, yet producing a beautiful flower of devotion and good works, teaching people to reach above the evil of the world which would choke their higher desires. The outer courtyard possesses four entrances, unlike the single doorways of Muslim and Hindu shrines. This expresses the universality of Sikh truth, which is open to all.

Another gold-topped building stands in the outer area, facing the long walkway to the inner holy place. This is the *Akal Takhat*, a political and community centre where important pronouncements are made concerning the life of Sikhs. Built by the sixth Guru, it indicates the rise of political and social awareness among Sikhs as they sought to establish a code of conduct for themselves and a way of organizing their relations with other groups. Here in the temple area religion and politics are clearly distinguished.

There are, in fact, four other major *Takhats* (or thrones) and many other important temples, but Amritsar provides a clear demonstration of the great unity of social and religious life which has emerged in Sikh culture.

WORSHIP AND FESTIVALS

A celebration at Amandas Raggis Gurdwara, Southall, London.

The Guru's arrival in Amritsar was celebrated by the illumination of the whole city by his followers. Nowadays special *Diwali* services are conducted at the *gurdwaras*, signifying the release of Guru Hargobind and affirming a distinct Sikh identity. *Gurdwaras* and private houses are decorated with candles, and firework displays are organized. The tradition of illuminating the Golden Temple (*Harimandir*) marks the climax of the *Diwali* festivities.

them a new purpose in life. The title of the festival was changed to *Hola* and the tradition of martial arts remains associated with it.

Diwali

Diwali is one of the traditional festivals of India, popularly known as the festival of lights. Its origin is traced to the homecoming of Lord Rama from exile. Hindus illuminate their homes and temples and exchange gifts of sweets with friends and relatives. The festival has another significance for the Sikhs. It is associated with the release of the sixth Guru, Hargobind, from the Gowalior Fort where he was imprisoned by the Mughal emperor Jahangir.

Guru Hargobind's release

According to Sikh tradition, Guru Hargobind was imprisoned by the emperor Jahangir in the Gawalior Fort on the suspicion that he had raised a large army to fight against the government. There were 52 Hindu princes already imprisoned in the fort. After several years the authorities ordered the Guru's release, but he refused to go until the other princes were set free. The emperor agreed to the Guru's demand and said that he would release as many princes as could come out holding the Guru's garment and hands. On hearing this condition, the Guru ordered a special cloak which had many strips of cloth, and in this way all 52 princes came out of the fort holding the Guru's garment and hands. Thus the Guru became popular as *Bandi Chhod* (deliverer of prisoners).

Sangrand

The first day of every month in the Hindu lunar calendar is called *Sangrand* (from the Sanskrit word *sangkrant*, denoting the entrance of the sun into a new sign of the Zodiac). In Sikhism it is regarded as the most auspicious day of the month and is observed in a special service (*diwan*) at *gurdwaras*, with the name of the new month ritually announced from scripture. Guru Arjan composed the 'hymn of twelve months' (*Bara Maha*). Each of its twelve parts illustrates the stages of life and the journey of the soul, while directing the Sikhs to conform to the prescribed code of discipline during each month.

Before setting off to work on this festival day, Sikhs visit *gurdwaras* to invoke divine grace for the general well-being of their families and the whole of humankind. Listening to the recital of the name of the new month is perceived as a most meritorious boon. The festival of *Baisakhi* occurs at *Sangrand* in the month of Baisakh (usually 13 April) and the ceremony of replacing the old covering of the flagpole with a new one (*Nishan Sahib*) takes place at the *gurdwaras* on this day.

I am a Sikh

RESHAM SINGH BHOGAL

I was born in a Sikh village called Talhan in the state of Punjab, India. It had its own large temple (*gurdwara*), which was over ninety years old. Every year the residents of the village and the surrounding areas celebrated the important religious festivals and took part in processions. With the other children I joined in. My early nurturing in the Sikh traditions took place within my family and this village community. I knew the basic beliefs of Sikhism at a very young age.

In 1968 my family moved to Leeds, England. I was only nine and this was quite an experience for all of us. None of us could speak any English. We found it hard to socialize and everything around us was so different. We were fortunate to have a very helpful English family next door. They had two daughters the same age as myself. We used to play together and their father took me to school on my first day because my parents could not speak English. This helped us to settle in our local primary school and made us feel at home in Leeds. At school we began to learn English. We were very keen and worked hard, attending extra English classes for Asian children (mainly from the subcontinent). We made lots of friends. At that time there was only one *gurdwara* in Leeds – simply called 'the Sikh temple'. Although it was a three-mile walk from our house, we attended regularly on Sundays. I also attended Punjabi classes there.

Attending the *gurdwara* on a regular basis for prayers in the presence of the congregation (*sangat*) and listening to hymn-singing (*shabad kirtan*) helped me to understand the meaning of 'the oneness of God.' I began to take part in voluntary serving (*seva*) in the community kitchen (*langar*). Food is served to everyone attending, including visitors from other faiths and backgrounds. Importantly, all are served the same meal, as this shows equality.

Soon after we arrived in Leeds, my elder brother and I had a haircut. In our new surroundings we were embarrassed to have long hair. When I moved to secondary school, I met a young Sikh who wore a turban. I was impressed and soon began to grow my hair again and wear a turban. Although I am not an 'initiated Sikh', I wear a turban in order to identify myself as a follower. I also wear a steel bracelet (*kara*) on my right wrist. My middle name is Singh, a name given to all male Sikhs by the tenth Guru. I do not cut my hair or trim my beard. I do not drink or smoke – both of which are against Sikh teachings.

My religious discipline is based on Sikh teachings, central to which is the belief that there is only one God. My daily commitments include meditation on God's name (*nam japna*), sharing with others (*vand chhakna*), voluntary service (*seva*) and earning my living honestly (*kirat karna*). These are most important for every Sikh.

Every morning before breakfast I say the Morning Prayer, the *Mul Mantra*. My mother taught me this when I was young and since she passed away, over twenty years ago, I have said it daily. I regularly participate in religious activities

and festivals at the *gurdwara*, such as *Baisakhi*, *Diwali*, the Gurus' birthdays and other celebrations. These bring the community and the families together, enabling the younger generation, including my children, to learn more about Sikhism.

Gradually, my involvement at the *gurdwara* has increased, as has my commitment to helping others. As Sikhs, we also take part in the activities of Leeds Concord (multi-faith fellowship). Recently my youngest daughter lit the candles at the Peace Service on behalf of the Sikh community. I regularly contribute (*vand chhakna*) towards the religious activities. This includes, for example, donations towards the upkeep of the *gurdwara* and the community kitchen (*langar*).

My job as a Technical Liaison Officer involves a lot of travelling. I come into contact with people of different backgrounds and faiths. With my turban, my beard and so on, I openly represent my commitment to my faith.

I greatly enjoy my work and, as I do it, I apply my faith's teaching about equality and truthful living (*kirat karna*).

My wife came from India in 1983 and, having completed her postgraduate studies, became a well-respected primary school teacher in Leeds. We have three daughters, one in a primary school and two in a high school.

Because of my cultural tradition I had an arranged marriage, conducted at the *gurdwara* in the presence of the Sikh holy book (*Guru Granth Sahib*) and the congregation. Verses from the *Guru Granth Sahib* were read out and sung by the priest. Not only did I marry a person of the same religion, but we also bring up our children within the faith. Both my wife's and my own influence on the children has encouraged them to speak Punjabi as well as English and attend the *gurdwara* on a regular basis. I hope that, by learning the value of prayer, by understanding the importance of helping and respecting others and by learning the Gurus' teachings, my children will follow me in the faith and commit their lives to God.

As a family we have visited India. As well as seeing the tourist attractions, we visited many *gurdwaras* in the Punjab and New Delhi. Our visit to the famous Golden Temple at Amritsar (built by Guru Arjan, the fifth Guru) was most exciting and gave me a greater understanding of my religious tradition.

I have enjoyed music from an early age, particularly *shabad kirtan*. I can listen to *shabad kirtan* in the morning before going to work as well as in the evening. I find this very helpful in my quest to learn more about the Sikh faith. It is also helpful for my children. However, we don't listen to religious music alone. We also enjoy traditional Indian music, folk music and *bhangra* dancing.

I think that the teachings of the Sikh faith have made me a better person. I thank God who has given me so much and, in return, I want to give back to God as much of myself as I can by committing myself to the Sikh faith.

Family and Society

SEWA SINGH KALSI

The Sikh movement emerged in the context of a caste-ridden Indian society in which occupation and status were ascribed and determined on the basis of one's birth into a particular caste group (Jat). There was no significant social interaction between members of different caste groups. Sikh Gurus were acutely aware of the destructive impact of the caste system on the social, religious and cultural fabric of Indian society. They strongly rejected the Hindu doctrine of *varnashramadharma* (laws of social classes and stages of life) which they saw as based on caste exclusiveness and institutionalized inequality.

Although Sikh teachings reject the doctrine of caste, it remains an important factor within the Sikh society. The notion of caste in its widest sense provides a general framework by which members of various caste groups organize their behaviour in relation to each other. The joint family or the extended household is the basic unit within Punjabi Sikh society; it has a traditional occupation, such as Jat (farmer), Tarkhan (carpenter) and Chamar (leather-worker). All households belonging to one occupational group are collectively known as a 'band of brothers'. The Punjabi Sikh social structure is based on patriarchal and patrilineal principles in which the head of the family, who is male, exercises authority.

Several domestic rites provide insight into the dynamics of interaction between religious and social customs, such as marriage, birth and death.

> Rejecting the falsehood of caste status, Guru Nanak writes:
> *'Worthless is caste and worthless an exalted name. For all mankind there is but only one refuge.'*
> Adi Granth 83

Marriage

Marriage is regarded as the bedrock of Sikh society. Sikhism rejects the notion of celibacy and renunciation. All Sikh Gurus, except Guru Har Krishan who died at the age of eight, were married men. They strongly advocated that Sikhs should lead a worldly life as householders (*grihasthi*) recognizing their duties to parents, wife and children and the wider society.

A Sikh marriage has far greater significance than the simple unification of man and a woman; it is regarded as an alliance between two families of compatible social and caste status. The scriptures consider marriage to be a spiritual bond and emphasize the concept of one spirit in two bodies (*ek jote doye murti*). The fourth Guru, Ram Das, says: 'They are not man and wife who have physical contact only. Only they are truly wedded who have one spirit in two bodies' (*Adi Granth* 788). Moreover, the marital relationship is perceived as a relationship preordained by God (*sanjog*) and not a social contract; it cannot therefore be dissolved. No wonder there is no term for divorce in Sikh and Hindu usage!

The selection of spouses is based strictly on the rules of caste endogamy and exogamy according to which partners can be found only in one's own caste group. For example, members of the Tarkhan group must marry carpenters. The rules of caste exogamy require that in choosing a partner the families avoid four *gotras* (clan or sub-caste): father, mother, mother's mother and father's mother. Secondly, the Sikhs strictly observe the custom of village exogamy by marrying out of their own village as well as outside the mother's village. The practice of caste endogamy and exogamy ensures the perpetuation of caste solidarity. Since the institution of marriage plays an important role in maintaining boundaries between caste groups, inter-caste marriages are strongly disapproved of; partners in such alliances are treated as outsiders and a stain on the family honour (*izzat*).

A registry wedding is regarded only as a legal requirement by Sikhs, who place a high value on their traditional rituals:

● The engagement ceremony (*kurmai*, *mangni*) is conducted in the presence of male relatives and members of one's *biradari* (kinship group) and begins with the recital of a prayer (*ardas*). A special hymn of *kurmai* is recited from the *Adi Granth*, a *hukamnama* is read out for God's blessing, then the girl's father performs the offering (*sagan dena*) by putting one dried date (*chhuara*) in the boy's mouth, which confirms the relationship.

● The customary meeting of the heads of both families (*milni*) begins with the recital of *ardas* by the *granthi*, who prays for God's blessing on the alliance of the two families. Then the bride's father formally greets the groom's father and makes a gift of one turban and some money.

● The guests move to the *gurdwara* for the wedding ceremony (*anand karaj*). The presence of the scriptures is mandatory, and bride and groom sit in front of the *Adi Granth*. The most popular colour for brides to wear is red. The bride usually wears a *lengha-suit* (tunic and long skirt) made of the same material, but some wear a sari or trouser suit (*salwar kamiz*). The bride does not wear a veil, but covers her head with a long scarf (*chuni*). The groom may wear a red turban as well as a long red scarf.

● The *anand karaj* begins with *ardas* followed by the ritual joining of the couple with the groom's scarf (*palla pharana*), which is performed by the bride's father and also called *kanyadan* (the gift of a virgin).

● At this stage the religious musicians (*ragis*) sing *palley taindey lagi*, a hymn from the *Adi Granth* which stresses the sanctity of the marital bond. The essence of this hymn is a pledge by the bride: 'Praise and blame I forsake both. I hold the edge of your garment. All else I let pass. All relationships I have found false. I cling to thee my Lord.'

● There are four wedding hymns, collectively called *lavan*. After each one, the couple walks around the *Adi Granth* in a clockwise direction, the bridegroom leading the bride.

● The *anand karaj* concludes with the recital of the hymn *anand sahib* and *ardas*.

The bride and the groom sitting in front of the scripture.

FAMILY AND SOCIETY

Divorce and remarriage

The Hindu Marriage Act of 1955 provides for divorce of Sikhs. However, Sikh marriage is regarded as a spiritual relationship with no place for the breaking of the bond created in the presence of the *Adi Granth*. The rate of divorce among Sikhs is very low and divorce continues to be regarded as a stigma, particularly on the honour of a woman and her family. A divorced woman is called *chhadi hoyi* (discarded woman) whereas there is no such pejorative term for a divorced man.

The remarriage of divorcees and of widows is acceptable. However, a divorced woman is not entitled to a religious wedding (*anand karaj*) because she cannot be given as a *kanyadan*. A male divorcee is free from any customary restrictions.

Children's customs

The birth of any child is regarded as a divine gift (*waheyguru di dat*). However, the arrival of a daughter remains a comparatively quiet affair, whereas the birth of a son is greeted with rejoicing, the distribution of sweets (*ladoos*), the festival of *Lohrdi* and the ceremony of *chhati*. Punjabi Sikh society is patriarchal, all inheritance is through the male line, and it is a son who performs the funeral rites to save his parents' souls.

Traditionally, children were given names by their grandparents or their father's sister. Nowadays most Sikh families visit the *gurdwara* and ask for an *akhar* (a letter from the scripture). Usually, this is the first letter on the page where the *Adi Granth* is opened and a name is chosen that begins with this. As well as their first name, Sikh boys get the name-title *Singh* (lion) and girls the name-title *Kaur* (princess).

Although a turban (*pag*) is a symbol of honour, there is no specific Sikh injunction concerning the age at which a Sikh boy starts wearing one. Usually, he will be eleven or twelve and thus able to look after it. A turban may be of any colour. Normally, it is made of muslin and is 15 feet (nearly five metres) long.

Death

In India, funerals usually take place soon after death or on the next day depending on the time of death. The body is ritually bathed and dressed in new clothes, a ritual of purification of the body before cremation. It is the duty of a son to light the pyre. In the absence of a son one of his male relatives performs the ritual of lighting the pyre. Before this, a *granthi* recites *ardas* for the departed soul. Women are prohibited from helping to carry the bier and lighting the pyre. At the death of a married woman (*sohagan*), her shroud is provided by her paternal family and she is dressed as a bride.

In the Punjab, the ashes are collected after three days and deposited either in the River Ganges at Hardwar or at Kiratpur. After the funeral, the deceased's family organize the reading of the *Adi Granth* either at their residence or the local *gurdwara*. Usually after thirteen days of mourning a big feast (*akath*) is held for relatives and members of one's *biradari*.

If the deceased was a man, the ritual of *pagri* (transfer of paternal authority) takes place at this time. The ceremony involves the chief mourner who sits in front of the *Adi Granth* and receives a turban and some money from his maternal uncle. He wears the new turban in the presence of the relatives and members of the new *biradari*, discarding the old one. Then a senior member of the *biradari* reminds him of his new status and responsibilities. Having been accepted as the head of his family, he joins the elders of the *biradari* for a communal meal. The social function of the rite of *pagri* is to facilitate the gradual incorporation of a son into the role of his father.

Sikhism in the Modern World

CHRISTOPHER SHACKLE

The evolution of Sikhism has remained closely involved with political and social developments in the Punjab, throughout a century of British rule and since 1947 in independent India. Like many other Asian religions, Sikhism first experienced the challenges of modernity at the same time as those of nineteenth-century European colonialism. A Sikh reform movement proved remarkably successful in articulating for much of the twentieth century a reinforced Sikhism, which survived the community's traumatic experience of the partition of Punjab between India and Pakistan in 1947. More recent decades, however, have been marked by tensions between the politicized expression of Sikhism which grew out of the reform movement and an Indian political leadership increasingly identified with Hindu majoritarianism. The same period has also seen the establishment of substantial Sikh diasporas in Britain and North America, where the challenges of adapting Sikhism to the very different circumstances of the international, twenty-first century, English-speaking world are being most acutely faced.

The Sikh reform movement
In the heyday of colonial rule in the later nineteenth century the leaders of all sections of Indian society, including the Sikhs, had to confront the linked implications of British political dominance and their dominant Victorian world view with its strongly Christian emphasis. A path of total resistance to modernity was chosen by a few, like Baba Ram Singh (1816–84),

but his self-proclamation as Guru confined his support to the Namdhari Sikh sect which he founded.

The mainstream leadership realized, however, that a more complex process of accommodation to the new order was required for the successful survival of the Sikh community. The Sikhs' distinct religious identity was seen to be doubly threatened: by the dismantling of state-supported Sikh political institutions after the British conquest of Ranjit Singh's kingdom and by the threat of assimilation into a resurgent Hinduism. The latter threat was forcefully articulated in the Punjab by the modernist *Arya Samaj* organization, founded by Dayananda Sarasvati (1824–83), whose doctrine of all truth being found in the Vedas was found offensively dismissive of the teachings of the Sikh Gurus.

To combat these challenges, a number of reformist associations (*Singh Sabhas*) were founded in the main cities of the Punjab. Through these associations, and making full use of the new communication systems established by the colonial state, a number of gifted lay leaders, often honoured with the title *Bhai* (Brother), came to formulate a redefinition of Sikhism which has remained the dominant orthodoxy to the present day. Like most reformers, the *Singh Sabha* activists saw the contemporary plight of Sikhism as the consequence of a falling away from the pristine ideals of an earlier age. They diagnosed an increasing reversion to Hinduism in both religious and social practice as the cause of what had gone wrong and preached the necessity of return to the glorious age of the Gurus, marked by an uncompromising monotheism and the adoption of a simple and devout lifestyle untainted by superstition. The title of the most famous of the many tracts through which their message was disseminated, 'We are not Hindus' (*Ham Hindu Nahin*, 1898) – by Bhai

'Although many of our brethren regard themselves as Sikhs of the Khalsa *they accept the Hindu tradition. They imagine that it is actually harmful to observe the teachings of gurbani by acknowledging that the Sikh religion is both distinct from the Hindu religion and superior to it. The reason for this is that they have neither read their own scriptures with care nor studied the historical past.'*

Bhai Kahn Singh Nabha

Khalsa members parade in Anadpur to commemorate the tercentenary of the founding of the Khalsa brotherhood by Guru Gobind Singh.

Kahn Singh Nabha (1867–1938) – points to the cornerstone of the reformists' programme, their strenuous efforts to distinguish the Sikhs of the *Khalsa* as a community quite separated from its Hindu origins and traditionally close ties with Hinduism.

The reformists often justified their definition of Sikhism in relation to Hinduism by an analogy between Protestantism and Roman Catholicism. Fitting well with imperial policies of 'divide and rule', it found particular favour with the British as a way of ensuring the separate loyalty of their Sikh troops, who were recruited as a reliable minority out of all proportion to their numbers in the population, and army regulations specified strict adherence to *Khalsa* practice in the Sikh regiments. At the same time, a remarkable cultural transformation was being effected within the Sikh community itself through the literary and scholarly activity of leading reformers such as Bhai Vir Singh (1872–1957). Developing Punjabi in the Gurmukhi script as a vehicle for modern communication, they produced new editions of the scriptures with extensive commentaries and an impressive body of creative writing which often drew upon the mythic power of Sikh history to drive home the reformist message.

The political expression of Sikhism in India

By the end of World War I, the reformists had given the Sikhs the confidence and coherence to engage with the nationalist politics of the late colonial period. A new activist phase was launched with the *Akali* movement, which was established to push through the transfer of control over the major *gurdwaras* from their hereditary guardians, who administered their vast endowments often for private profit. A programme of mass demonstrations, producing violent conflicts and fresh martyrs for the cause, eventually resulted in government sanction for the Sikh Gurdwaras Act of 1925. This gave control over the great *gurdwaras* of the Punjab to an elected committee of male Sikhs, the Shiromani Gurdwara Prabandhak Committee (SGPC), which was henceforth to be the single most important voice within Sikhism and through its resources supports the *Akali Dal*, the main Sikh political party.

For the next decades, the leaders' chief energies were devoted to the pursuit of a political settlement which would guarantee the position of the Sikhs as a distinctive ethno-religious minority which was always felt to be under threat from larger groups. The approach to Indian independence was marked by increasing polarization between Hindus and Muslims. With no realistic chance of achieving their own country, the Sikhs' lot was cast with the Hindus in 1947, when the partition of the Punjab between India and Pakistan was effected at the cost of a massive ethnic cleansing. Although this uprooted that half of the community which found itself on the Pakistan side, its resettlement in Indian Punjab in place of the departed Muslim population also had the effect of consolidating the Sikh population territorially for the first time.

From this base, and building on the Sikh identification with Punjabi versus the cultural attachment of the Punjabi Hindus to Hindi, the *Akali Dal* launched the '*Punjabi Suba*' (Punjabi state) campaign with the purported aim of establishing within the Indian Union a linguistically defined state with a 'Punjabi-speaking', that is, Sikh majority. Although this goal was achieved with the separation of a truncated Sikh-dominated Punjab from the Hindu-majority state of Haryana in 1966, this did not halt the dangerous religio-political momentum which had been set in motion. By the early 1980s, the Punjab became a battleground between armed Sikh activists inspired by the ideal of establishing Khalistan as an independent Sikh country and the Indian security forces. This culminated in the notorious events of 1984 at Amritsar, when the Indian prime minister, Indira Gandhi (1917–84), ordered the Indian army to storm the *Harimandir* – which had been occupied by the followers of the charismatic young preacher Sant Jarnail Singh Bhindranvale (1947–84) – and when her own later assassination by her Sikh bodyguards provoked anti-Sikh pogroms in many parts of India, killing thousands. While the separatist cause eventually lost the support of most Sikhs in India, there has yet to emerge a motivating alternative to a mainly defensive position centred upon the reformist formulation of Sikhism.

Organization and authority

The rules of reformed Sikhism are set out in the official *Guide to the Sikh Way of Life* (*Rehat Maryada*), first issued as a pamphlet by the SGPC in 1945. It defines a Sikh as any person

● whose faith is in one God, the ten Gurus and their teaching and the *Adi Granth*

● and believes in the necessity and importance of initiation (*amrit*)

● and does not adhere to any other religion.

The first section of the *Rehat Maryada* deals with the daily offices, before defining the proper pattern of *gurdwara* rituals. It emphasizes the central place of the *Adi Granth* and the respect to be paid to the scripture, and the particular importance of the congregational recitation of the *ardas*, the prayer which invokes divine protection of the *Khalsa* in the name of the Gurus and of all the Sikh martyrs.

Separate paragraphs deal with singing of scriptural hymns (*shabad kirtan*); the common practice for special occasions of a continuous complete reading in relays of the vast scripture (*akhand path*) which takes some 48 hours; and the preparation and distribution of the ritual mixture of flour, ghee and sugar (*karah parshad*). All these emphasize the prohibition of any caste distinctions and the inclusion of any practices identified with Hinduism.

A shorter section then deals with miscellaneous regulations for individual living, including a few basic ethical commandments. Stress is laid on the fundamental *Khalsa* rules, especially the distinctive bans on the cutting of hair and the consumption of tobacco (far more generally observed than the similar ban on alcohol), and on the reformed rituals of birth, marriage and death from which Hindu practices are eliminated in favour of the ceremonial use of the *Adi Granth*. A final section deals with importance of Sikh community service (*seva*), including work in the communal kitchen (*langar*) as well as the general maintenance of *gurdwara* activities.

Sikhism is a religion without priests, so authority in the larger *gurdwaras* rests with the lay committees which run them, not with the 'keepers of the scripture' (*granthis*) whom they employ. The final part of the *Rehat Maryada* is a brief summary of the rules of discipline as ultimately vested in the headquarters of the community as the *Guru Panth*, which are situated in the *Akal Takhat*, which faces the entrance to the *Harimandir*.

The Sikh diasporas

Like all successful reforms, the necessarily rather rigid redefinitions of Sikhism first formulated by the *Singh Sabha* leaders in the late nineteenth century are beginning to be perceived as in need of adjustment to meet the

'An unbroken reading of the Guru Granth Sahib may be held in time of distress or to mark an occasion of particular joy. During unbroken readings the participants' enunciation should remain clear and the text should be correctly read. The reading should not be conducted at such a speed that hearers are unable to follow its meaning, a condition which amounts to disrespect for the sacred scripture. Every letter and symbol should receive its due attention, thus ensuring a clear and accurate reading. This should be done even if it means that the intended time will be exceeded.'

Rehat Maryada

A member of the Sikh community in France, Jasdev Singh Rai, ties a traditional turban for his two-year-old son, Damanpreet Singh. Jasdev believes it is important that his son maintains his cultural identity.

changed circumstances of the twenty-first century. With the failure of the long pursuit of solutions through political means in India, there are already signs that the chief impetus for such a reformulation may come rather from the increasingly confident and well-established diaspora communities now settled for over a generation in Britain, Canada and the USA. These total about one million, even numerically quite significant in relation to the fifteen million Indian Sikhs.

The Sikh diasporas remain closely linked to the Punjab, through family ties, through the rituals of the *gurdwara* and the great Sikh festivals (*gurpurbs*), and through the regular practice of pilgrimages to the great shrines associated with the Gurus. But they are also directly exposed to their Western environments and relatively free from the constraints felt within an increasingly Hindu-dominated India. These factors are encouraging the emergence of a new intellectual leadership, based within Western universities and elsewhere and using English rather than Punjabi as its prime medium of expression.

Several emerging trends may be signalled as pointers. A new critical attention is being given to very sensitive topics, notably the study of the formation of the scripture and the interpretation of key mythic episodes of Sikh history, such as the foundation of the *Khalsa*. There is also a revaluation of the importance of the many other traditions within Sikhism which were marginalized by the triumph of the reformed *Khalsa* to whom the SGPC *Rehat Maryada* almost exclusively refers, neglecting the many who follow the teachings of Guru Nanak and his successors but do not observe the full *Khalsa* discipline. And women's voices are starting to be articulated in a religious tradition which has been so powerfully dominated by the bearded male presence. These and other trends have yet to coalesce, but it seems certain that traditional authority will become subject to increasing challenges as Sikhism, like all other religions, grapples with an ever-changing modern world.

Zoroastrianism

A Historical Overview

JOHN HINNELLS

The story of Zoroastrianism begins in the third millennium BCE with the Indo-Europeans. Somewhere to the east of Europe about 3000 BCE a group of tribes began to split up.

Some travelled south and settled in Greece and Rome, others went north and settled in Scandinavia, and others went east to Persia (now Iran) and India. It is because of this common descent that the ancient languages of these countries have a similar pattern. The important group for Zoroastrian studies is the third one, which settled in India and Persia. These people are called the 'Indo-Iranians' by scholars. They referred to themselves as the 'Aryas' (Aryans), 'the noble ones'. They travelled eastwards in two main waves. The first, in approximately 2000 BCE, passed through northern Persia, leaving only a few settlers there, with the main body carrying on into North-West India, where they gradually overthrew the Indus Valley civilization. The second wave of Indo-Iranians settled in Persia about 1500 BCE.

Natural powers

The religion of the Indo-Iranians provides the background to Zoroastrianism just as ancient Israelite religion does to Christianity. The Indo-Iranians were nomads, travelling from pasture to pasture on foot with their herds, not staying long enough to build temples, travelling light so that they did not have statues of the gods.

Theirs was a religion of the mountain-top, with the dome of the sky for their temple, using the ordinary household fire as the focus for their ritual offerings. Their imagery was drawn from wind and storm, from sun and rain. Their gods were not thought of in human form, but as the forces which surround humankind.

The prophet Zoroaster

Zoroaster is the name by which the West knows the prophet of ancient Persia, more correctly called Zarathushtra. It was usual to date him about 600 BCE, but the evidence of language is persuading more scholars nowadays to date him about 1200 BCE, which means that he lived when Persia was emerging from the Stone Age. This would make him the first of the great prophets of the world's religions.

Zarathushtra's life

Zarathushtra was a descendant of the first wave of Indo-Iranians. His people had become settled agriculturalists who were threatened by the second wave of Indo-Iranian settlers. We know little of the prophet's life. He was a priest (interestingly, the only one of the great prophets who was); he was married and had several children.

At the age of thirty he had the first of a series of visions which inspired him to preach a new message. His teaching was at first rejected, and he suffered persecution, being forced to leave his home. It took ten years before he made his first convert, his cousin. Then his message found favour with a local king, Vishtasp, and Zarathushtra's religion became the official teaching of a small kingdom somewhere in north-east Persia, in what was formerly part of southern Russia (the precise location is not known). Zarathushtra's religion in time spread throughout Persia and became the official religion of what was, for 1,000 years, one of the major world empires.

Zarathushtra's teaching

Zoroastrians believe that their prophet is the one chosen by God to receive his unique revelation. This is contained in seventeen hymns, the *Gathas*. Obviously the prophet gave more teaching than this, but all that has survived is a fragment cast into verse-form to help memorize the words in an age and region where writing was unknown. These hymns are now the central part of a major act of worship (*yasna*).

The great choice

Perhaps *the* characteristic feature of Zarathushtra's teaching is his emphasis on personal religion, inspired presumably by his conviction that God had called him and appeared to him personally. All men and women (both sexes have the same duties in Zoroastrianism) have a personal responsibility to choose between good and evil. On the basis of their exercise of their free-will, they will be judged in the hereafter. Those whose good thoughts, words and deeds outweigh the evil will go to heaven, regardless of their social status; those whose evil thoughts, words and deeds outweigh the good will go to hell, again regardless of their social status.

A similar prophetic emphasis can be seen in the badge Zarathushtra took for the religion. For the Indo-Iranians a sacred cord was the symbol of priesthood, as it still is with the Brahmans in India. Zarathushtra made this and a sacred shirt (made of white cotton rather like a vest) the symbolic armour which all believers should wear

A relief of the god Ahura Mazda on the facade of the Old Majilis building in Tehran, Iran.

at all times after initiation, to remind them of the battle they must fight against evil.

Good and evil

God, Zarathushtra taught, was the wholly Good Creator of all things, of sun, moon and stars, of the spiritual and material worlds, of humans and of animals. The Wise Lord (Ahura Mazda) is the bountiful sovereign, the friend not only of Zarathushtra but of everyone.

He is in no way responsible for evil in the world; this comes from the Destructive Spirit (Angra Mainyu) whose nature is violent and destructive. It was he who created the demons, who rules in hell and who has opposed God from the beginning. In Zoroastrianism the 'Devil' is not a fallen angel, for that would make the Good Creator ultimately responsible for evil – an inconceivable idea for Zoroastrians. The world is the battleground in which the forces of good and evil do battle. The world and humankind were created by God to aid him in this battle.

He also created a number of heavenly beings. Foremost among them were the Bounteous Immortals (Amesha Spentas), the sons and daughters of God, as they became known. In some ways they resemble the Christian idea of archangels (which belief some scholars think was influenced by Zoroastrianism). But like the gods of the Indo-Iranians there is an important abstract dimension to their nature, as their names show. They are: Good Mind (Vohu Manah); Righteousness (Asha); Devotion (Armaiti); Dominion (Kshathra); Wholeness and Immortality (Haurvatat and Ameretat). These are not only heavenly beings, they are also ideals to which the righteous should aspire. So by sharing in the good mind, by a life of devotion and righteousness, people share in God's dominion and attain wholeness and immortality.

Each of the Bounteous Immortals is thought to protect, and be represented by, one of the seven creations which together constitute the Good Creation of God: the sky, waters, earth, plants, animals, man and fire. At important acts of worship, a representative of each creation, and therefore of the Bounteous Immortal, is present so that the earthly and heavenly worlds are both symbolically present.

Zarathushtra taught that the world was essentially good, but spoiled at present by the attacks of evil. He looked forward to the day when the battle with evil would reach its climax, when good would triumph and the world would be restored to the perfect state its Creator gave it. At the last the dead will be raised and judged, the wicked will go to hell, and the righteous dwell with God in perfection for eternity.

The spread of Zoroastrianism

The first 700 years after the death of the prophet are shrouded in mystery. There simply are not the sources to reconstruct Zoroastrianism's early history. It appears to have spread across the Persian plateau, largely through the movements of tribes and through tribal battles. The Medes came to power in western Persia in the seventh century BCE, and the Persians in the sixth century. By that time Zoroastrianism was evidently a power in the land.

THE PERSIAN EMPIRE

Persia really emerges into the light of history in 559 BCE, when Cyrus ascended the throne of a small Persian kingdom called Anshan in the south-west of the country. In 550 he seized the throne of the Medes, then captured the fabulously wealthy king of Lydia in distant Anatolia (modern Turkey). Then in 539 the mighty Babylonian empire capitulated before him. So in twenty years he rose from being the ruler of a petty kingdom to emperor over what was

'This I ask Thee. Tell me truly, Lord. Which man in the beginning was the father of truth during the creation? Which man did fix the course of the sun and of the stars? ... Through whom does dawn exist, along with midday and evening, [all of] which remind the worshipper of his purpose? ... Which man, O Wise Lord, is the creator of the good mind...? By these [questions], O Wise Lord, I am helping to discern Thee to be the Creator of everything.'

Yasna 44:3–5, 7

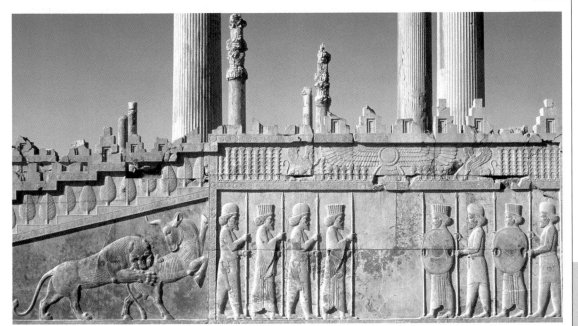

Part of the relief on the grand staircase at Persepolis (fifth century BCE), the chief royal palace of the Persian Achaemenid kings.

A HISTORICAL OVERVIEW

then the world's largest empire.

In capturing Babylon, Cyrus liberated the Jews from their exile, an act which the biblical book of Isaiah ascribes to the powerful guidance of God, who specially chose Cyrus to accomplish his purposes. No other foreign king is spoken of in such glowing terms in the Bible. Cyrus established for himself a considerable and widespread reputation for tolerance and justice. The dynasty which ruled Persia after him continued to uphold these ideals. It also spread Zoroastrianism throughout the realm.

The people largely responsible for its propagation were the Magi, the priestly tribe of the Medes who continued in office throughout all periods of the Zoroastrian history of Persia. The Magi acted as royal chaplains, and travelled with all important delegations, whether on military or diplomatic missions. They also lived in the many Persian settlements in various parts of the empire. So when Matthew's Gospel refers to wise men (Magi) visiting the infant Jesus, his readers would know well the significance of that. The later Christian legend that they were kings is wrong.

ALEXANDER 'THE VANDAL'

The Achaemenid empire was brought to an end by Alexander in 331 BCE. In Persian history he is known not as 'Alexander the Great' but as 'Alexander the accursed', because he killed priests and burned down the royal palace of Persepolis. He said he wanted to unite the cultures of Persia and Greece, but he and his successors, the Seleucids, are remembered as the foreign interlopers who intruded into Persian life.

THE PARTHIAN EMPIRE

A native Persian dynasty gradually expelled Seleucid power from the land in the middle of the second century BCE. They are known as the Parthians, because of the region in Iran from which they came. They did not bring an advanced technology with them from this remote region, so in the early part of their rule they took over certain Hellenistic features such as coin-types and some architectural styles. But their own feudal Persian culture is better reflected in the surviving minstrel tales and epic legends. It was during the Parthian period that the first moves were made to collect together the ancient traditions and sacred literature which made up the Zoroastrian holy book, the *Avesta*.

The Parthians have not received the attention they deserve, mainly because the archaeological and written sources are so few. Yet they ruled Persia for about 400 years, with an empire as

The Sasanian monarch Shapur I receives homage from defeated Roman emperors Philip and Valerian, c. CE 241–72. Like their Achaemenid and Parthian forebears, the Sasanian monarchs ruled over an empire stretching from India to the shores of the Mediterranean. For over 1000 years, Zoroastrian Iran was the major power in the known world.

large as that of their more famous Achaemenid forebears stretching at times from North India to what is now Turkey. They were the largest power to confront the might of Rome. They had good relations with Israel; invading the land in 40 BCE, they deposed the hated Herod and put a Jew in his place. The Romans returned two years later and restored Herod.

It is interesting to speculate how different history would have been if Israel, at the time of Jesus, had been under the sway of the tolerant Parthians instead of the widely hated Romans. What is not generally realized is that at the time of Jesus, the Parthians had made Zoroastrianism the most powerful religion of the then known world.

'CHURCH AND STATE'
In CE 224 the ruler of a province in the south-west of Persia rebelled against the Parthians. The new dynasty was named after a legendary ancestor, Sasan. The Sasanians ruled Persia until the Muslim invasion in the seventh century. They left behind a wealth of material splendour and a number of writings, creating the impression that

this was the most glorious epoch in the history of Zoroastrian Persia.

The high priest was a major power behind the throne, determining much of imperial policy. After Constantine and his successors made Christianity the official religion of the Roman empire, providing a religious basis for its unity, a comparable unity was necessary in the major Eastern empire. Zoroastrianism had always stressed the unity of church and state, and this was developed to the full in Sasanian times.

The Islamic conquest

The Arab armies of the new Muslim religion entered Persia in CE 633, only one year after the death of Muhammad. At first they came for booty, but later battles were aimed at permanent conquest. The intention was primarily to enforce submission to the rule of Islam. In theory religions which the Muslim authorities recognized as 'people of a book', that is, those who had received a revelation from God (mainly Jews and Christians), were allowed to continue their religion, subject only to the imposition of an extra tax.

But the position of Zoroastrianism as a religion of a book was less clear, and as the new world empire took hold, the position of Zoroastrians in their own land became increasingly threatened. Education, promotion, equality before the law, all were denied to the followers of Zarathushtra. Gradually they were forced to retreat into the obscurity of desert villages. So the religion of the land became associated with poverty and backwardness.

PERSECUTION
Zoroastrians, as the oppressed poor, were often the subjects of vicious attacks from Muslim 'bully boys'. Even in the twentieth century under the protective Pahlavi dynasty, 'infidel-baiting' was common in the remote villages far from official gaze. Any

Zoroastrian venturing alone into a Muslim quarter could expect verbal and often physical abuse.

Persecution, oppression, poverty, injustice, isolation – these have been the conditions which Zoroastrians have faced in their own land for nearly 1,400 years of Muslim rule. It is an enormous tribute to their courage, determination and faith that there are any followers of Zarathushtra left in present-day Iran. They are mainly in Tehran, and in the villages of the Yazdi plain. Altogether there are about 25,000 (although government figures are much higher) still following the religion of ancient Persia.

THE PARSIS AND IRANIANS

The population of the Parsi and Iranian Zoroastrians is reckoned to be no more than 115,000 all over the world. The main base of the religion today, in numerical terms, is in India, among the Parsis and Iranis, with a population of around 65,000 people. (The term Irani is used for those Zoroastrians who fled Iran because of increasing religious persecution between the eighteenth and twentieth centuries and settled in India). In the tenth century CE a small band of the faithful set out to seek a new land of religious freedom, preferring to leave Persia rather than give up the religion of their forefathers. In India they have lived in peace and security, in time even achieving a position of wealth and power which they used to campaign for and support their co-religionists back in the homeland.

Beliefs

JOHN HINNELLS

The tenth century was not only the time when the 'Pilgrim Fathers' of Zoroastrianism set out for India, it was also a time of literary activity among the Zoroastrians of Persia. A number of texts were produced to encourage, inspire and instruct the faithful, in the contemporary language known as Pahlavi or Middle Persian. The holy book, the *Avesta*, was in a language which only a few learned priests understood. Translations, summaries and explanations were produced, as well as defences of the faith against Muslim, Christian and Hindu teachings. Although they were written in the ninth and tenth centuries, they can be taken as the definitive statements of traditional Zoroastrian thought. These Middle Persian texts codify, elaborate and systematize the teaching of Zarathushtra himself, from which they stem.

Creation

The Middle Persian forms of the names of God and the 'Devil', ancient Ahura Mazda and Angra Mainyu, are Ohrmazd and Ahriman. Ohrmazd, it is taught, dwells on high in perfect goodness and light, whereas Ahriman dwells for eternity in darkness below in the abyss. Battle between these two primal spirits was inevitable, so Ohrmazd created the heavenly and material worlds to aid him in the battle. First he created the heavenly beings, then the world in purely spiritual form, that is, invisible and intangible. In Zoroastrian belief the material world is not evil or corrupt, rather it is the visible, tangible manifestation of the spiritual creation. It is the creation of God, therefore it is good.

The essential characteristics of evil are violence, chaos and the will to

'Then I recognised you, O Mazda, in [my] thought as being the beginning and the end...'

Yasna 31:8

BELIEFS

destroy. When Ahriman saw the Good Creation of God, he tried to destroy it, afflicting it with misery, suffering, disease and death. None of these evils, therefore, came from God, nor were they part of his plan for creation. They are unnatural afflictions wrought by a wholly independent 'Devil' who seeks to ruin the perfection of the divine creation.

In the myth of creation it is said that Ahriman defiled all parts of creation: the ordered creation was afflicted with chaos; the round, flat earth was shaken so that valleys were opened up, and mountains raised; the sun was dislodged from its ideal noonday position; fire was afflicted with smoke; the archetypal man and bull were afflicted with suffering and death. Ahriman was apparently triumphant. Then a miracle occurred: the dying bull and man emitted sperm; from the bull's seed grew cattle, from man's came a plant whose leaves grew, separated and formed the first human couple. In Zoroastrian thought human beings are literally at one with their environment.

The cosmic battle

Then Ahriman sought to escape from the world, but found he was trapped within it. Thus the cosmic battle between good and evil is now fought out in the arena of world history. For the first 3,000 years after Ahriman's attack, the two forces were reasonably evenly balanced in what is known as 'the period of mixture' (that is, of good and evil). Then the prophet Zarathushtra was born. With the revelation of the Good Religion the defeat of Ahriman was assured. From this time on, the defeat of evil began. But in Zoroastrian thought it does not come suddenly and unexpectedly like a thief in the night, it is a further 3,000-year conflict as Ahriman makes a desperate bid to destroy all that is good. This final fling is in vain. At 1,000-year intervals three saviours are born: each born of a virgin

who had been impregnated with the prophet's seed preserved in a lake where the maidens bathed. They are, therefore, of the line of the prophet, though born of a virgin. A part of the evil creation is destroyed by each of them, until the third saviour raises the dead and introduces the last judgment. From this, humanity will return to heaven and hell for a limited period before they re-emerge to pass through a stream of molten metal – the final ordeal before all dwell in total perfection with Ohrmazd.

During these cataclysmic events the heavenly forces will have been engaged in the final battle with the demonic powers, finally overcoming them. The molten metal which had already restored the earth to its original state by reducing mountains and filling up the valleys, and which finally tested humankind, now fills up hell. So Ahriman is rendered powerless for eternity. For the first time Ohrmazd becomes all-powerful. Evil is wiped out. So, in the myth, the earth ascends to the moon, the heaven descends to the moon – neither is done away with. Zoroastrians do not speak of 'the end of the world', for that would be the end of what God made. Instead they look forward to the 'renovation of creation', the time when heaven and earth join together to make what is literally the best of both worlds.

The nature and destiny of humankind

In Zoroastrian thought the individual faces two judgments. One comes after death when his or her thoughts, words and deeds are weighed in the balances. If good outweighs evil, then the person's own conscience guides him or her across the Bridge of the Separator (Chinvat Bridge) to heaven. If evil predominates then his or her conscience leads him trembling to the bridge from which he or she falls into the abyss of hell. The second judgment is after the resurrection. Whereas

'Yes, there are two fundamental spirits, twins which are renowned to be in conflict. In thought and in word, in action, they are two: the better and the bad... When these two spirits first came together they created life and death, and how, at the end, the worst existence shall be for the deceitful, but the best thinking for the truthful person... Of these two spirits, the deceitful one chose to bring to realization the worst things. [But] the very bounteous spirit, who is clothed in the hardest stones, chose the truth...'

Yasna 30:3–5

Christianity has no explanation for the belief in two judgments, Zoroastrianism has. There are two sides to human nature, the physical and the spiritual. Both are the creations of God. The individual must be judged, rewarded or punished in both aspects of his or her being. The first judgment after death is evidently one in the spirit because the body can be seen to remain on earth. But hell is not eternal in Zoroastrian belief. The purpose of punishment, they believe, must be corrective. However 'eternal' is defined – whether as everlasting or absolute – eternal hell cannot involve corrective punishment. In hell, Zoroastrians believe, the punishment is made to fit the crime, so a cruel ruler who tortures or starves his people is himself tortured and starved in hell. But at the resurrection all return from heaven or hell to face their second judgment, this time in the body; and again they return to heaven or hell as appropriate so that they may be physically rewarded or corrected.

The purpose is that the whole person, body and soul, should be so corrected that he or she may dwell, in the perfection of a united being, with God. Man and woman are a divine creation, intended to be fellow-workers with God; their final destiny must be with God. During their earthly life they have complete free-will to act as they choose, to support the forces of good or evil. They can live contrary to their nature, but they cannot, in eternal terms, change that nature. Through judgment, heaven and hell, they are corrected and rewarded, for their part in the great battle between good and evil.

Body and soul

A person's foremost duty is to make his or her body the dwelling-place of the Bounteous Immortals; as we have seen, people's lives are to be determined by the Good Mind of Righteousness and Devotion directed towards divine Dominion, Wholeness and Immortality – and to reject the demons such as Violence, Greed and the Lie. They should seek to reflect the bounteous creative spirit of God and reject the negative path.

In doing this they must keep the spiritual and material sides of their

Fire temples

Fire has been the focus of Zoroastrian rites and devotions from earliest times. The nomads used the household fire as the centre of their rites, having the sky as their dome, not a man-made temple. Temples were first introduced into Zoroastrianism by the Achaemenid monarch Artaxerxes II (404–359 BCE), probably in imitation of Babylonian practice. He also introduced the cult of statues, but this was too radical a break with tradition for it to succeed. Instead of man-made statues, Zoroastrians placed the divinely created 'icon' of fire at the centre of their holy buildings. Temple worship was, then, a late entry into the religion.

There is no set time of day for temple worship, nor any fixed ritual to perform. For the laity it involves essentially a personal pilgrimage.

Before entering the temple worshippers wash and then offer prayers, so that they are clean physically and spiritually. The prayer room itself is very simple. Against one wall there is the sanctuary, marked off by ceiling-high walls, with a door for the priest to enter and windows for the faithful to see through. The sacred fire is kept burning in a large vessel, sometimes as much as 6 feet/2 metres high. Ordinary worshippers approach the door of the sanctuary, touch the ground with the forehead, leave an offering of wood for the fire, and take a pinch of ash from a ladle left by the priest. They then stand to offer their prayers in private. There is no congregational worship; prayer is offered by each person directly to God.

Fire temples have an enormously powerful sense of the holy. The prayer room is bare of all decoration, so that attention is focused exclusively on the fire, the living image of God, 'the pure flame of the fire symbolizing him who is himself eternal light', as a Parsi has said. No artificial lights must shine, lest they dim the glory of God's own creation. The priests are expected to undertake many important 'higher' ceremonies on behalf of laypeople, but the ordinary Zoroastrian's duty is primarily the life of good thoughts, words and deeds; the daily prayers, the practice of rituals and the inspiration of a personal pilgrimage to the temple.

The Dakhme-ye Zartoshi (at Yazd, Iran), also known as the Towers of Silence, was used by the Zoroastrians to expose the dead to birds of prey.

nature in balance. So people have a religious duty to expand God's material creation as well as to support his spiritual creation. A man should marry and have children, he should seek to expand his herds and the natural environment through agriculture. To remain celibate is sinfully to refrain from this duty. On the other hand, he should not abuse the divine gift of marriage through lechery. In Zoroastrian belief a monk is as great a sinner as a lecher – both deny what God wills. Similarly a man should not fast so that the spirit is exalted over the body, nor should he be gluttonous and exalt the body over the soul. The health of body and soul are interdependent and should be cared for equally.

The world is God's Good Creation, and it is people's religious duty to care for and enjoy that creation, for Zoroastrians believe that 'misery drives away the divine'. There is no belief here of a spiritual self imprisoned in an alien material universe, as there is in some religions. Indeed, it is practically the reverse – the 'Devil' is a spiritual being trapped in what is to him an alien good universe. The spirit of happiness permeates not only Zoroastrian ethics, but also their rituals, (see 'Zoroastrianism: Family and Society').

If evil is associated with death and decay in the material world, then people have a duty to avoid contact with any matter that aids these evils. Dirt, rotting and dead matter are places where death, and therefore evil, is present. The housewife cleaning the home, rites associated with birth, marriage and death, standards of personal hygiene – all are concerned with the great cosmic battle between good and evil. In this way each individual, the fellow-worker with Ohrmazd, seeks to wipe out evil and restore the world to its God-created perfection.

Personal responsibility

Zoroastrianism is a religion which is concerned with the Good God, the Good Creation and the goodness of humankind. The term its followers often use of it is 'The Good Religion'. It has no doctrine of original sin, nor of one man dying to save all. Everyone is responsible for his or her own part in the cosmic battle, and for his or her own destiny. It is a religion of stalwart determination – which is perhaps what has enabled it to survive for so long, despite a millennium of oppression.

Family and Society

KHOJESTE MISTREE

The Parsis of India and the Zoroastrians of Iran are small minorities in their countries. Generally a small community generates its own socio-religious dynamics. Much of it arises from the community having a distinct ethno-religious identity. In the case of Zoroastrians, followers of one of the oldest credal faiths in the world, the community membership is limited to two groups, identifiable as being either Parsi or Irani, as of race. Ethnicity is an important criterion to be a Zoroastrian and so the religion throughout its entire history has been ethno-focused, linked to the cultural milieu of the ancient Iranians. Moreover, the Parsis and Iranis have always followed a patrilineal or an agnatic socio-religious order within their family structure.

Small, close, dynamic

While the men may be seen as the dominant patriarchs of the family, it is the women who wield greater influence and power within the family structure. Not only are they educated and career-minded in today's world, but in many instances they rival their male counterparts. In most Parsi homes the women go out to work and are involved in bringing up their children. Parsi mothers tend to be overprotective and indulgent with their sons and appear to be tougher, emotionally, with their daughters. The children, even if grown up, normally continue to live with their parents until they marry and often even longer.

Amongst the Parsis and Iranis the family units are close-knit and the feeling of belonging to a small community is strong and cohesive, as safeguarding the community's unique religious identity is of paramount importance to most Zoroastrians. Coming from a small community gives the average Parsi or Irani Zoroastrian the drive of wanting to excel and do well in life, as otherwise they may be left behind by the majority community from the ladder of economic success. The Parsis in India and the Zoroastrians of Iran have community welfare organizations, known as Punchayets or Anjumans, which act as the apex bodies of the community wherever pockets of Zoroastrians live, often providing heavily subsidized housing and financial support to those who require it for education, medical attention or the alleviation of poverty. The welfare system within the Parsi and Irani Zoroastrian communities is on the whole excellent, particularly as the corpus of funds has been built up over a long period of time. Not only is a Zoroastrian encouraged to make money, honestly, but he or she is enjoined to donate generously. The promotion of charity is a central tenet of the faith and is crucial for the well-being of the soul in the hereafter.

In the case of the Parsis there is near 100 per cent literacy, with over 70 per cent of Parsis graduates. If the economic barometer of the community in India is healthy, the same economic standards are not found in Iran. Unlike the Parsis, the Iranian Zoroastrians have unfortunately not had equal opportunities to study and excel in their careers. However, the global state of the community is prosperous and the educational attainments are impressive and creditable.

The role of a Zoroastrian

The religion is a 'this-worldly' faith, in which one is taught to spread happiness and harmony in the world by learning to be happy within oneself. It is a religion which abjures monasticism, fasting, celibacy, asceticism and all forms of denial which affect the material well-being of man. Spirituality is to be achieved through affirming all that is good and beneficent in this world which is not seen as an impediment or a prison for the soul. A Zoroastrian is taught to promote the Truth and fight the Lie, for the promise given by prophet Zarathushtra is that, through an ethical awareness of knowing what is right and proper, the soul will achieve a place in the house of song (Heaven); whereas if the soul directs a person to follow an unethical path by doing what is wrong and improper, as a result of freewill and choice which the soul enjoys, then it falls into the house of darkness (Hell). Man is the maker of his own destiny and the role of every Zoroastrian is to promote the joyous, light-filled world of Ahura Mazda (Lord of Wisdom) and reject the unhappy dark world of Angra Mainyu (the evil spirit).

Transmission of the faith

The reliable transmission of the beliefs and practices of the faith are quintessential to the well-being of the community from a religious point of view. A small community has to be anchored within a strong religious framework and hence the Parsis chose to leave Iran a thousand years ago (CE 936) and set sail to the warm shores of India, in order to preserve their religion, culture and way of life. If the early Parsi settlers had shown any flexibility at all in their religious beliefs and practices, then very little of what is Zoroastrian would have survived to today. The rich religious heritage which the Parsi and Iranian Zoroastrians have managed to preserve, and in some cases even strengthen, has enabled the community to maintain its strong religious presence and identity intact. Clearly, there is great merit in striving to uphold the time-tested traditions of the faith. In pockets where Zoroastrians have shown flexibility either in marrying

out or in changing ritual practices under the guise of moving with the times, the consequences seem to have been quite disastrous. The religious identity over a period of time has weakened and in some cases been lost as a result of a slow process of socio-religious assimilation with the host culture.

The Importance of Personal Purity

Dualism is at the core of the Zoroastrian value system, which recognizes that a Lie can never be seen as good and that which is intrinsically good can never be turned into a Lie. From an early age a Zoroastrian child is taught to recognize this reality and his or her mind is imbued with the laws of purity and cleanliness. For example, a child is not encouraged to walk barefoot, as dirt is seen as a manifestation of evil. An orthodox Zoroastrian will never drink or eat from somebody else's unwashed glass or cutlery, as that is seen to be dirty and ritually impure. Likewise, an orthodox Zoroastrian will never have a tub bath, as that is seen as wallowing in one's own dirt. Similarly tidiness is seen as part of the world of Ohrmazd (or Ahura Mazda), whilst untidiness or chaos is deemed to be an affliction of Ahriman (or Angra Mainyu). Clearly, the laws of purity include bodily cleanliness and anything that thwarts this state: may it be a bleeding wound or the cycle of menstruation, both are conditions which are seen to be impure from a ritual point of view. As a result, during such times no religiously minded Zoroastrian will seek an audience with the sacred fire in the fire temple or for that matter touch a prayer book or light an oil lamp for religious purposes.

In a traditional Zoroastrian household a special area is maintained where the prayer table is kept upon which an oil lamp burns perpetually. On this table a prayer book and an incense burner are also placed with a photograph or photographs of those who have passed away. This area is normally not touched by any non-Zoroastrian in order to maintain a level of religious sanctity. As fragrance is seen as being part of the world of Ahura Mazda, twice a day, in the morning and in the evening, the ignited incense burner is taken around to each room of the house, so that the fragrance of frankincense may remain in each room as a symbolic daily blessing. Likewise, in a traditional Zoroastrian home the paring of nails and the cutting of hair also entail certain ritual injunctions. Nails are normally pared in the bathroom and flushed down the toilet and any cutting of hair is done in the same area with similar ritual precautions. After nails are pared or hair is cut, a Zoroastrian is expected to take a bath in order to be in harmony with the world of Ahura Mazda.

Three levels of ritual purity

There are three levels of enhancing religious purity within the world.

● The first level is the untying and retying of the sacred cord (*kusti*) five times a day with an appropriate formula of prayers.

● The next level is the *nahn* ceremony, in which a Zoroastrian undergoes a ritual purification by way of a special bath under direct instructions of an ordained priest who keeps a safe distance from the bathing area. The *nahn* comprises the chewing of three pomegranate leaves to give the celebrant spiritual immortality, the sipping of a holy libation (*nirang*) three times for the purification of both the body and the soul, and finally the celebrant's special bath. Some holy libation is rubbed on the body by the celebrant and then water is poured to cleanse the body. While this is happening, the priest maintains a prayer vigil standing a few paces away from the bathroom door. The *nahn* is undertaken before an initiation ceremony, before a wedding, forty days after giving birth to a child or when a layperson has touched a corpse.

● The highest level is when the priest undergoes the *bareshnum* ceremony within the precincts of the fire temple for nine days and nights, under austere and strict conditions administered by a pair of priests who themselves have to be in a high state of ritual purity.

The rites of passage

The main rite of passage is *navjote*, the ceremony at which an ordained priest initiates a child, between the ages of seven and nine, into the Zoroastrian faith. The child is given a white cotton undervest (*sudreh*) and a sacred tubular cord woven from lamb's wool (*kusti*) which circumvents the waist three times. To an appropriate set of prayers the cord is tied with two reef knots, one in front, one at the back. The sacred *sudreh* and *kusti* are worn by a Zoroastrian throughout life, as it is believed that wearing them gives a Zoroastrian a unique identity as well as offering a level of spiritual protection in the physical world.

Marriage is seen as a righteous act that even makes the earth feel joyous and happy. All Zoroastrians, including members of the clergy, are encouraged to marry; and the advice of Zarathushtra, to both the bride and the groom, is that 'Marriage should be based upon the Truth, as it shall be of good gain to each' (*Yasna* 53.5). The nuptial bond is seen both as a contract and a sacrament which, when enacted through the Zoroastrian marriage ritual, brings together the couple in both the physical and spiritual worlds. The marriage benediction is chanted by two priests who ask Ahura Mazda to grant the couple sons and grandsons and many opportunities to develop strong bonds of friendship. The priests also exhort the couple to uphold and follow the practices of the Zoroastrian religion based upon a righteous life so as to

> 'It is suffering and death that destroys the body, not the Creator whose will is good, and who preserves and maintains the body.'
>
> Shkand-gumanig Vizar 8:64

seek everlasting spiritual happiness. Upon the formal completion of the wedding benediction the bride and groom exchange rings.

The final rite of passage is the funeral ceremony, performed in order to give the soul solace and comfort in its new environment. Death, in Zoroastrianism, is seen as the temporary triumph of evil and therefore the Parsi Zoroastrians in India normally do not bury, burn or drown their dead, as all these modes of disposal are seen to be agents of pollution and therefore evil, which is not acceptable from a theological point of view. The bodies are exposed, naked, in a *dakhma*, a circular, stone tower which is open to the sky and is known in English

into dust as the pit is lined with layers of natural lime and black salt. Where traditional *dakhmas* do not exist or are not in use, Zoroastrians are permitted to use alternative modes of disposal.

It is said that the soul of a Zoroastrian is judged on the dawn of the fourth morning. Depending upon the life it has chosen to lead, the soul is rewarded if its good thoughts, words and deeds are greater than its bad thoughts, words and deeds during its earthly sojourn. If the reverse is true, then the soul through its own earthly misdeeds relegates itself to hell, where it remains till the end of time, when it is promised that the final resurrection will take place. The afterlife ceremonies for the soul of the deceased

Parsi priests lead a boy and a girl in the *navjote*, the ritual tying of the sacred thread, or *kusti*, around the body.

as a 'Tower of Silence'. The bodies are placed in this tiered structure and devoured by birds of prey. The skeletal remains are allowed to dry, as the body is exposed to the natural rays of the sun. Subsequently, professional corpse bearers respectfully move the remains into a circular pit in the middle of the tower, where over a period of time they turn

are very important, as the rituals and all the accompanying prayers give the soul comfort and solace in its new spiritual environment. In Zoroastrianism, it is the living who protect the souls of their near and dear ones with the performance of monthly ceremonies for the first year, followed by ten days of daily rituals which are done by the priests before the end of the Zoroastrian calendar year. Ceremonies for the dead should be performed for at least one generation which means a period of between twenty and thirty years.

The *yasna* ritual is performed to invoke a pantheon of spiritual beings known as the Yazatas. During the liturgy, 72 chapters of the *Yasna* are recited and the Yazatas are enlisted to battle against the forces of darkness. It is done for the protection of the physical and spiritual world and is the re-enactment of the larger cosmic battle between the forces of good and evil and celebrates the promised triumph of Ahura Mazda. In the ritual a sacred bread is consecrated and a holy libation is made.

Pollution – the work of evil

As purity is linked intrinsically to Ahura Mazda, it follows that impurity is the temporary triumph of Ahriman (the evil spirit) in the physical world. Moreover, in the classical tradition pollution is seen as the work of evil, whose sphere of influence extends to all the seven creations of Ahura Mazda: namely the sky, waters, earth, plants, animals, man and fire. It is said in the Zoroastrian story of creation, that Ahriman pierced the sky and polluted it, sullied the waters, defiled the earth, killed the plants, animals and man and finally created smoke and polluted the seventh creation, fire. A Zoroastrian is taught to be conscious and responsible towards all the seven creations of Ahura Mazda. Each of the creations are seen to be living and are deemed to be embodiments of Ahura Mazda in the physical world. Hence, a Zoroastrian celebrates the birthdays of all the seven creations when the calendar month and day names coincide.

The sensitivity towards nature which modern man calls ecology has thus been practised by the Zoroastrians for thousands of years. Likewise, Zoroastrians cannot take part in the wanton destruction of nature nor are

they permitted, doctrinally, to indulge in any form of excess or deficiency which is attributed to the wiles of the evil spirit. Moreover, Zoroastrians cannot participate in any rituals and/or eat a food offering consecrated through any other religious tradition. Nor can a Zoroastrian show allegiance to any other faith, as a Zoroastrian swears allegiance to being a follower of Wisdom through the teachings of prophet Zarathushtra exclusively (*Av. mazdayasno ahmi mazdayasno Zarathushtrish*).

In conclusion, a Zoroastrian grows up in a family with a value system which is largely based upon the precepts and practices of the faith. The paradigm of 'the good life' is part and parcel of following the path of Truth as well as living well through the honest generation of wealth; the creation of wealth is seen as a great Zoroastrian virtue. This wealth must also be shared amongst fellow human beings and so charity is central to the mindset of a Zoroastrian. Great merit accrues to the soul in the hereafter for the one who does charity in this world. The coming together of the physical and spiritual worlds as a harmonious reality in the daily life of a Zoroastrian is what a worshipper seeks by way of self-realization. This realization leads to the promotion of the right thoughts, words and deeds creating happiness in the world (*ushta*), which forms the basis of prophet Zarathushtra's vision and revelation.

> *'He is a generous man who takes from his own and who gives to good people... for the fondness of the soul.'*
>
> Denkard Bk VI, E 6

FAMILY AND SOCIETY

I am a Zoroastrian

FIROZA PUNTHAKEY MISTREE

I was born and brought up in Karachi, Pakistan, where the Parsi Zoroastrian community survives as a small but significant minority. Having been born into a priestly family that can trace its lineage back thirty-three generations, I experienced a way of life at home that was a constant reassertion of the basic tenets and practices of the faith. Some of my earliest memories are of visiting the fire temple on special days, attending congregational prayers and the ceremonies in memory of the dead every month. This was in addition to the many initiation, thanksgiving and wedding ceremonies we regularly attended. Although I grew up with little understanding of the significance of rituals, ours was a traditional family steeped in rituals as a way of life.

My early religious instruction came from my father, who as a deeply religious man believed that his children should be brought up as devout Zoroastrians, attentive to the everyday practice of the religion. For me, the sonorous drone of prayers being recited by priests, their mysterious ritual actions, the dancing flames of the sacred fire, and the fragrance of incense and ritual food cooked for the spirits of the dead, all had a mesmeric quality when I was growing up.

Our family prayer table was kept in a secluded corner of the house and was laid out with pictures of my grandparents and close family members who had died. Every morning and at night my father prayed before it. There was always a small beaker of water and of milk, fresh flowers, an oil lamp and a small fire urn, fed with hot burning coals, sandalwood pieces and incense. At sunrise and in the evening at sunset, the fire urn, fragrant with burning incense, was taken to each room in the house and to family members who paid their respect to the fire, which was seen as the house fire.

Being part of a traditional family meant there were rituals and precise ways to do the ordinary things in life. For example, I was only allowed to cut my nails in the bathroom. Nails were carefully trimmed on a newspaper and then flushed down the toilet bowl. We were careful to ensure that none were left to fall on the floor as this was seen as polluting the home. Similar injunctions were followed for a haircut. Hair was never cut at home. After a haircut I was immediately sent home for what was termed a head bath. This was a Parsi euphemism for a 'full bath' which required washing of the hair. Only after such a bath could one touch anything in the house, as one was seen to have re-established a state of ritual purity. Everything that was worn during the haircut was washed.

Having lost both sets of grandparents before my initiation into the faith, I was sent to our *Panthaky* (the equivalent of a parish priest) to learn by rote the prayers necessary for me to be initiated into the faith. Every Saturday and Sunday, with prayer cap and book in hand and a long piece of cord to practice the ritual of untying and re-tying the sacred cord, I was sent along with my brother to the priest to learn prayers in the sacred languages of Avestan and Pahlavi. This was done by constant repetition and in retrospect I am amazed at how quickly and easily my infant tongue learned these very old languages.

My initiation ceremony was not performed in my home town of Karachi. My brother and I were taken across the border into India to the most sacred fire temple, known as the Iranshah, in the dusty village of Udwada some 110 miles (180 kilometres) north of Mumbai, along the western coastline of Gujarat. The Iranshah has been continuously burning for over a thousand years and my father felt strongly that we should receive the blessings of this great fire. Again a priest was employed to teach us our prayers and we were also inducted into the legendary travails of the warriors Rustom and his son Sohrab. These tales of courage, strength and truth from the *Shahname*, *The Book of Kings*, were to prepare us for life after the all-important initiation ceremony.

Initiation meant having to undergo a ritual cleansing, a topic of much debate amongst friends. Was it really bulls' urine? Or was it a sacred libation as explained to us by our elders? Whatever, we all sipped the libation during the ceremony and were none the worse for it. After my initiation I was presented before the sacred fire, to receive its blessings and to attend a ritual to enthrone the fire, especially in honour of my initiation. These cumulative experiences were like religious icons painted on my soul and in later times I drew on these images.

The last ten days of the year, before the onset of the Parsi New Year, all the Parsis of Karachi gathered every morning for congregational prayers in memory of the souls and spirits of the dead. Attendance for us as children was mandatory. We had to rise early in the morning, have a quick bath, wear our 'fire temple clothes', which were kept separate from everyday wear, and be at the community hall before seven in the morning for congregational prayers. We were made to join in the singing of verses from the *Gathas* and then an explanation was given in Gujarati. This was followed by a fifteen-minute inspirational lecture in English on some aspect of the religion and its history. During those ten days we also went to the fire temple every morning, where rooms were specially maintained with tables laden with flowers in shining silver vases, a fire burning in a large fire urn, priests praying and oil lamps lit on each table. I was told simply that the souls and spirits of the dead came down to earth to taste the consecrated food, take in the fragrance of incense and hear the prayers offered by the living. The spirit beings in turn, we were promised, would bless us for the year. It seemed to me like a wonderful system of reciprocity that guaranteed us blessings of good health and prosperity from the spirit world. These blessings were very important to me as a child. The food consecrated in the ritual was carefully brought home and shared only by Zoroastrian members of the house.

New Year's Day was a joyous time. It meant new clothes, gifts and a special breakfast. The lintels of doors were decorated with garlands; we woke up early to mark the thresholds of the house with designs made with powdered chalk; flowers were put everywhere; family members and relatives came for lunch or dinner. But the day began with a visit to the fire temple and it was a wonderful experience to see the enormous leaping flames of the sacred fire fed with hundreds of pieces of sandalwood, offered by the crowds of Parsis visiting the fire temple on New Year's Day.

My marriage to Khojeste Mistree, a well-known religious scholar of the community, was a turning point in my life. My exposure to Zoroastrianism, which until then had been purely a sensate experience of rituals and traditions, took on a new meaning as I gained greater understanding of my religious roots and culture. I was introduced by my husband to the theology and philosophy of the faith and was trained intellectually in the religion. With this learning I developed a deep passion for Iran, the ancient homeland of the Zoroastrians.

Traditions and practices followed assiduously at home tend to become a way of life. So, just as in my childhood I had seen my mother celebrate the birthday of the waters or the birthday of the creation of fire, or new moon day, I too continued these practices in my home as part of my family life. These became special days for the family and all our activities were linked to propitiating the divinity of the day as well as cooking special food as part of the celebration.

Although both my children were born in America, all the rituals associated with pregnancy were performed. On our return to India many months later, our first act was to undergo a special purificatory bath in order to re-establish our ritual purity. It was only after this that we were able to visit the fire temple. It would have been unthinkable for us to have done so otherwise.

Our children have grown up in an environment in which the ritual practice of the faith and an understanding of the religion has been paramount. They adhere to the Parsi Zoroastrian way of life by always wearing the sacred shirt and cord and participating actively in all religious events and festivals. This has, I believe, given them pride in the religion and anchored them in the community. Therefore it has, for instance, been easy to induct my daughter into the Zoroastrian approach to menstruation, in its more practical and simple form, of never touching anything holy and sacred, maintaining a separate sacred vest and cord for that period of time, and having a complete 'head bath' at the end of each menstrual cycle. Thus in my own children I have promoted the thought that they must live and act as per the will of Ahura Mazda and deviation from it can lead one onto the wrong path.

In our family our faith is central to our lives and ritual practices offer a dimension of security in this uncertain world. When my mother died I felt an immense ebbing of grief once the death rituals began. It was as if one was relegating the care of the soul to a higher force. I found solace in having rituals performed as exactingly and precisely as possible, as if I were conforming to a hauntingly old pattern of life. My family, including my children, spent four days after my mother's death in seclusion in the grounds of the Tower of Silence complex, away from the outside world, and this too helped us to come to terms with the loss of my mother.

In today's world the community and the religion are constantly subjected to pressures of change and, as a

One of the Zoroastrian shrines of Yazd.

people steeped in ancient practices, we struggle to maintain our way of life, so my focus in life is to extend an understanding of the faith to young Zoroastrians across the globe. As part of my duty and because I enjoy teaching, I take four classes a week teaching the theology and ritual practice of the faith to Parsi schoolchildren. I also conduct an adult class every week on the history of ancient Iran.

My most spiritually fulfilling experiences have been during visits to the Zoroastrian stronghold of Yazd in Iran. Zoroastrianism is practised in a different way in Iran. There is sacredness in almost every aspect of creation: the great cypress trees, the sacred springs, the fires of the faith, old men and women with wisdom of the past, small fire temples hidden in inconspicuous mud structures with ever-burning fires so bright that their radiance fills the heart. Together, these experiences transport me into another world. The fire shrines, hidden deep in the mountains and dedicated to family members of the last Zoroastrian king, symbolize for me hope and renewal. My pilgrimages to the sacred shrines and fires of Yazd connect me to my past and, although we Zoroastrians are a nation-less people, when I visit Iran I truly feel that I am in the land of my forefathers, where our kings ruled, where our people once lived and walked, and where it all began.

Zoroastrianism in the Modern World

KHOJESTE MISTREE

It is with the coming of the British to India that the Parsis were first exposed to the Western mindset, culture, and methodology on a sustained basis, resulting in major changes in perception, particularly on religious issues. Among the Indian communities the Parsis were the first to avail themselves of a Western education. This meant being exposed to an Anglican value system founded upon Western ethics rooted in Christianity. In 1829 the Reverend John Wilson came to India with the sole aim to proselytize the 'natives' and that included the Parsis. He questioned the importance of dualism, the laws of purity and the relevance of the Zoroastrian 'Story of Creation'. He also sowed the seeds of doubt with regard to the role and importance of religious rituals, as he himself came from a low church Anglican background as opposed to the high church of the Roman Catholics, where rituals are celebrated with greater pomp and majesty. Western education, particularly in the secular sphere, ushered in the age of inquiry and reason within the community. The Parsis were exposed to, and quickly adopted, a British way of life that meant a change from the insular lifestyle they had lived for centuries. This change was important if the Parsis were to conduct business and negotiate trade agreements with the British rulers and with other foreign traders based elsewhere.

The advent of trade and the weakening of the faith

Until the advent of the British in India, it was only the priestly class who could read and write and therefore the clergy formed a natural leadership within the community. In the eighteenth century many Parsi families grew phenomenally rich through general trade, ship building, ship chandelling, setting up cotton mills, trading in cotton, moneylending and acting as general agents for the British government. A professional class of entrepreneurs, businessmen, doctors, lawyers, engineers and accountants emerged in the nineteenth century, and this in turn led to a shift in the balance of power between the clergy and the laity. The clergy who were not able to keep pace with the changing times found themselves marginalized, particularly once the process of industrialization had taken root in India, and leadership within the community shifted to the wealthy merchant classes. These wealthy traders built many fire temples and became the main employers of the priests. As trustees of these fire temples, the merchants asserted extensive control over ecclesiastical and social matters and through this new-found power they were able to flout their wealth, gain control over community matters and reposition themselves in society.

Religious and social changes

This change in the social and economic power base of the community resulted in the laity rejecting the ecclesiastical knowledge base of the priests and religious injunctions were set aside, as being irrelevant to changing times. The age of reason had arrived on the shores of India, leading Parsis to question the need for and efficacy of performing complex religious rituals, as science and its application in an emerging India were seen as the 'new temples' of the future. Unfortunately, Zoroastrian priests in those days were not trained adequately to be able to answer with conviction and reason the questions asked by an increasingly educated laity. They were unable to explain the beliefs, practices and customs of the faith rationally.

A good education in the nineteenth and early twentieth century meant that young Parsi men and a handful of women went abroad for further studies, mainly to the UK. This resulted in a loosening of their ties within the community and as a result they distanced themselves even further from the beliefs and practices of the religion. By interacting with persons outside their faith, both professionally and socially, they soon bonded with partners outside their own fold. In some ways this was caused by the fact that women among the Zoroastrians of the time were poorly educated and rarely moved outside their homes or social circles. Intermarriage brought with it an exposure to other cultures and faiths and this in turn over the decades has led to a weakening of the Parsi-Zoroastrian identity. Increasing secular influences have encouraged some Parsis to adopt a rational, ecumenical approach and this has promoted an amorphous amalgam of eclectic beliefs and practices within this group. The reasons for the Parsis moving away from a classical traditional base and thereby weakening the Parsi-Zoroastrian identity are manifold. Religious education has not kept pace with secular studies within the community. The understanding of the religion has weakened due to the worshipper not comprehending the ancient languages of the liturgies. Only a handful of Zoroastrians have studied the Avestan and Pahlavi languages, so that the prayers and rituals performed are done so blindly. English has become the mother tongue amongst the majority of Zoroastrians, making the daily recitation of prayers and the performance of rituals meaningless for some within the community. Parsis see no reason to pray in a medium which they do not understand and to participate in rituals which they perceive as antiquated and devoid of any content or spirituality.

This new thinking was combated by those living in India who sought to uphold the traditional beliefs and customs of the community. Conservative and orthodox Parsis felt strongly that misplaced liberalism and reform would bring about the downfall of the community in more ways than one. Nevertheless, their opponents continued to see merit in promoting religious rituals apparently supported by scientific theories, seeking to rationalize rituals through the world of science. In the 1920s an indigenous Parsi movement started, known as Ilm-e Khshnum (Knowledge of Joy), the Khshnumists believing in a hidden world of Zoroastrian men, women and children living secretly as spiritually advanced souls under Mount Demavand in Iran, a mountain of importance and holiness to the Zoroastrians. Even today the Khshnumists and the Theosophists promote a faith-based, pseudo-scientific ideology steeped in ritual traditions. This has resulted in a schism within the community which has weakened the religious position even further, with no leadership coming from within the ranks of the clergy or from any other group within the community.

Additional outside influences weakening the faith

In the early twentieth century some groups of educated Parsis rejected the need to wear the sacred vest (*sudreh*) and cord (*kusti*) which every Zoroastrian is enjoined to wear. Several adopted new faiths such as Christian Science, Vedanta, Vegetarianism or the cult of babas and swamis with their own teachings which were and indeed are quite alien to classical Zoroastrianism. These conflicting beliefs have proliferated within the community and growing numbers of Zoroastrians have rejected the importance of performing high inner rituals by espousing a form of humanism. Their code of conduct then was to generate good thoughts, good words and good deeds and to be of service to all human beings. The roots of secularism were well and truly reflected within the belief paradigm of this group. But the most pervading religious thought was that of Christianity and to some extent this is apparent even today. Christianity, and Christian thought, appears to have influenced the Zoroastrians living under

Parsi priests in London performing a thanksgiving ritual in the presence of a sacred fire as part of the Zoroastrian New Year celebrations.

British rule and this was reflected by the fact that in the mid-twentieth century most Parsis could quote the Bible and sing church hymns and carols more fluently than they could their own scriptures and religious songs.

Since the end of the empire, Hinduism has made huge inroads into the religious mindset of the Parsis. Hindu concepts such as the omnipotence of God, reincarnation, vegetarianism, death being the work of God, celibacy, fasting and asceticism have crept into the belief paradigm of some Parsis, who see these beliefs as the signposts of true 'Zoroastrian' spirituality. In classical Zoroastrianism, these perceptions are nowhere to be found and are in fact seen as heresies and sins which are to be rejected in the one physical life which a Zoroastrian is deemed to live. In fact, living 'the good life' and promoting happiness and harmony among others in the physical world are central tenets of the Zoroastrian faith.

The fusion of religious beliefs in modern times has meant that some Parsis have sought solace in other religious traditions, believing that God is one and that all religions lead up to the same mountain top, which in turn offers a common reality. What this group does not seem to realize is that each religion gives a uniquely different spiritual experience and therefore the perception of the oneness of God, or of a common reality on the figurative mountain top, is going to be different for each religious group.

A light in darkness

However, there is a growing religious awareness amongst the younger generation of Zoroastrians. Many more religious classes are being held today than a generation ago. Likewise, there is a greater number of publications available in English in the present times than in the past, which in turn has resulted in the spreading of religious knowledge for those who want to understand and experience the beliefs and practices of the faith. Community-based organizations such as Zoroastrian Studies in Mumbai (formerly known as Bombay) have introduced structured courses on Zoroastrianism at different levels for the community. Ongoing classes, newsletters, books, workshops and seminars have contributed to a growing awareness of the religion and its practices. Moves are afoot through community resources to establish a professorial chair in Zoroastrianism at the School of Oriental and African Studies, University of London, where a few years ago a post for senior lectureship was created with an aim to promote the study of the ancient faith. There is a greater interest in the performance of rituals today and more young people visit the fire temples (where the sacred fire burns continuously) than a generation ago. This shows that the religious health of the community is strong and vibrant and this augurs well for the future. Another important, relatively recent development is that young priests are being trained in the performance of high, inner rituals of the faith. With the establishment of the Athravan Educational Trust in Mumbai, full time priests serving the fire temples have the opportunity to continue their study of theology, history and ritual practices by attending regular classes structured to their needs and requirements. Interfaith work in recent times has also increased, as Zoroastrians are often being called to represent their faith at international religious conferences. A short while ago the Zoroastrian religion as a world faith was welcomed into the fold by the Alliance of Religions for Conservation (ARC).

The unfolding of the religion in the UK and Europe

For a century or more Zoroastrians have moved away from their home bases in India and Iran and settled in many different parts of the world. In the early twentieth century young Parsis went mainly to England to pursue their graduate studies and then settled in the UK where a sizeable community of Parsis has been living continuously since. The Parsi Zoroastrians of the UK formed an association in1861 and today the Zoroastrian Trust Funds of Europe (ZTFE) is the premier Zoroastrian organization in the UK and in Europe. There is a settled community of nearly four thousand Parsi Zoroastrians living in the UK, mainly in the north-western suburbs of London. The community comprises mainly Parsis and Iranis from India and Pakistan but there is also a sizeable number of Parsis and Iranians who have come from East Africa, Zanzibar, Aden and Iran since decolonization. By and large the community's religious beliefs and practices are traditional and efforts have been made to preserve both the practices of the faith and a Zoroastrian way of life. The office bearers of ZTFE have sought to promote religious classes and workshops and community get-

togethers to celebrate all the important religious festivals at their centre in north-west London. They are also very active in the interfaith movements representing their small but dynamic community in the multicultural milieu of Europe.

The unfolding of the religion in North America

Since the independence of India in 1947 the USA has become a haven for Parsis who went initially to further their graduate studies and then settled. Canada too has accepted Parsi and Irani immigrants from India, Pakistan and Africa. Its thriving community of Zoroastrians accounts for about half the estimated 15,000 Parsi and Iranian Zoroastrians living in North America, where the community is by and large educated, prosperous and well assimilated, celebrating some festivals, holding classes and producing a glossy community journal under the auspices of their apex body, the Federation of Zoroastrians of North America (FEZANA).

The trend in North America is to move away from the ritual component of the religion and promote the teachings of Zarathushtra as a mere philosophy for living the good life. Zoroastrianism has been inverted into a form of modern humanism, shorn of its time-tested continuity and ritual majesty. There are no properly consecrated houses of worship or fire temples in North America despite the economic wealth of the community, and so an entire generation of Parsis and Iranian Zoroastrians are growing up with no spiritual experience of the sacred fire or its worship.

It would seem that the North American Zoroastrians are on the horns of a dilemma so far as their religious identity is concerned. There are over twenty-three Zoroastrian associations, but none has sought to define who is a Parsi/Iranian Zoroastrian. With nearly 50 per cent of the North American

Zoroastrians marrying out of the faith, they have sought to reformulate the ancient ethno-religious identity to include as members anybody professing to be a Zoroastrian. The Parsis in India and the Iranian Zoroastrians, by contrast, have maintained a traditionally defined ethnic identity within a socio-religious framework.

The unfolding of the religion in Iran

The urban Zoroastrians of Iran in the late 1960s took the path of shedding their rich ritual heritage, claiming that the ritual practices were man-made and created by the Sasanian clergy (CE 224–651) to further their own ends. This misplaced thinking, coupled with efforts to synchronize beliefs and practices with the dominant culture of Islam, has meant that over a period of time all the rituals appertaining to the sacred fire in a fire temple and the performance of many other associated rituals have been discouraged by the Zoroastrian leadership in Iran and hence all the high inner rituals have fallen into disuse. The process of assimilation of religious beliefs and practices between Islam and Zoroastrianism has taken root. In Iran the priests do not tend the sacred fire five times as is enjoined in the classical Zoroastrian texts. In India and Pakistan, trained priests serve the sacred fire five times a day in all the fire temples, and both the high inner and outer rituals continue to be performed by the younger members of

Zoroastrians pray during their annual pilgrimage in the shrine of Pir-i Sabz, popularly known as Chak Chak, in the central province of Yazd in Iran. Thousands of followers of Zarathushtra travel every year from all over the world to pray in the temple built in the side of the rock.

the clergy specially trained in the performance of complex religious ceremonies. However, because of the constraints of living in an Islamic country, the Zoroastrians of Iran seldom marry out and thereby seem to have retained their ethno-religious identity far better than their co-religionists living in many other parts of the world.

The unfolding of the religion in Australasia and the Middle East

Around the turn of the twenty-first century, over two thousand Parsis mainly from India, Pakistan and the Middle East settled in Australia and New Zealand. It is too early to ascertain the direction the community will eventually take. In the Middle East

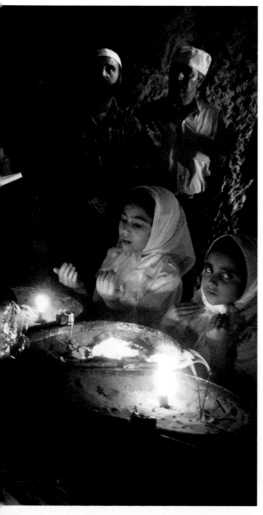

there are likewise about two thousand Zoroastrians, but with no form of religious infrastructure available to them. They do however celebrate the Zoroastrian festivals discreetly and in particular they observe the festival of *Hamaspathmaedya*, associated with the souls and spirits of the dead. The community in the Middle East resides there for economic betterment, thus their stay is temporary and their religious links and bonds continue to be strong, mainly to their home countries of India and Pakistan.

The unfolding of the religion in China

The Parsis of India had for many centuries traded with the Persian Gulf, the cities along the Red Sea, the Straits of Mallacca and East Africa. Their expanding long distance trade links brought them into contact with China in the mid-eighteenth century. Parsi merchants constituted a significant trading group in Canton, Shanghai and Hong Kong. The earliest Zoroastrian association was started in Canton in 1845 and by the late-nineteenth century, Parsi trading families had set up home in China and Hong Kong. The community played a major role in establishing banks, business houses, hospitals, clubs, the Hong Kong University and even the racecourse. Today descendants of these families continue to live in Hong Kong, a large number coming from the conservative ecclesiastical town of Navsari on the west coast of India. The affluent Parsis of Hong Kong have a tradition of sharing their wealth with the community in India and their large charities support hospitals, community housing, and the poor in India. They celebrate Parsi festivals, invite scholars for lectures and remain in constant touch with their home country, India. A few Parsi traders also settled in Singapore where there is an active Parsi association. The first Parsi who arrived in Singapore was commissioned by the British to help build the docks. He stayed in Singapore and went into business. Over a period of time several Parsi families settled there, trading in commodities or setting up shops and other businesses.

Has Zoroastrianism changed significantly?

As time moves on a linear scale, it is inevitable that the process of change affects every community and the Zoroastrians are no exception to this global phenomenon. The world is a global village and information technology enables one to access data more or less instantly. All forms of religious issues are discussed on the Internet and numerous web sites have been created to cater for a plethora of different shades of opinions, particularly with regard to the doctrine and practices of the faith. The technological revolution has led to the authority of the priesthood being weakened further, as laypeople promote what they perceive Zoroastrianism to be. The religion is being further shorn of its sacredness as they challenge the inviolability of the ritual and theological understanding of the faith. This, in turn, has exposed the community to a plethora of religious controversies. The clergy in India have been marginalized from most discussions appertaining to the religious well-being of the faith, while differing points of view are being circulated globally, causing even greater confusion within the community. However, the ritual practices have in the main remained the same in India, although a shortage of priests has meant that the clergy cannot cope with a greater demand for the performance of rituals by the laity.

In Iran the tradition of Zoroastrians going on pilgrimage to the six important shrines (*pirs*) in the environs of the province of Yazd has in fact grown, allowing a number of Zoroastrians to interact socially, at a family level, whilst on pilgrimage.

Communal meals (*gahambars*) are also quite popular, as are the many festivals, but unfortunately the high inner rituals of the faith have all but ceased to exist owing to a breakdown of the ritual tradition coupled with an acute shortage of trained priests. This has resulted in a qualitative loss from an experiential point of view of Zoroastrian spirituality amongst the younger generation living in Iran, where they have been introduced to Zarathushtra's teachings abstracted away from the ritual and devotional life of the faith. However, in recent years groups of Parsis from all over the world have been going on religious pilgrimages to Iran in order to experience their roots and heritage by way of a reaffirmation of their faith. This has resulted in greater bonding between the Parsis of the diaspora and the rural Iranian Zoroastrian communities, which have always shown great warmth and hospitality towards the Zoroastrian pilgrims visiting them.

Despite these different schools of thought, most Parsi Zoroastrians in India and Pakistan remain traditional, recognizing the wisdom of promoting Zoroastrianism in its classical form. This understanding permeates the minds and hearts of many young Zoroastrians who are today taking an active and keen interest in learning more about the precepts, practices and cultural heritage of the Zoroastrian faith.

Judaism

PART NINE

A Historical Overview

GEOFFREY COWLING

A religion continually develops over ages of time. Whatever historical point we look at, religion always has links with the past. Rabbinic Judaism sees itself today as a direct development from the time of Moses, the giver of the Torah, over 3,000 years ago.

To understand the developing beliefs and practices, we need to know something of the social and political events which affected the Jewish communities. We also need to observe the ideas of their neighbours, to see the influences of the cultures with which they came into contact. Greek thought, Christianity, Islam, medieval philosophy, charismatic movements, all have affected the intellectual activity and popular customs of Judaism.

The exile and after: 539–333 BCE

The story of Judaism begins in the late sixth century BCE. In the years 539–333 BCE, the Persian empire was dominant. And it was in this period that Judaism consolidated as a religion based on the Bible.

In 586 BCE, Jerusalem was destroyed by Nebuchadnezzar II and the people taken captive to Babylon.

In July 539 the army of Cyrus II ('the Great') of Persia, commanded by Gubaru, in turn captured Babylon. Cyrus thus gained nominal control of the whole Babylonian empire. Fourteen years later Egypt was captured by Cyrus's successor. Ezra 1:3 says that Cyrus permitted the Jews to return from exile and to rebuild their Temple in Jerusalem.

In both Babylon and Egypt there were communities of people who still considered themselves Judeans. These communities consisted largely of mercenary soldiers or prisoners of war and their families. The Judeans were agents of the ruling power, and privileged for that reason. In Egypt this caused much resentment, and the Judeans remained separate, following the religion (which was not strictly biblical) and customs they brought with them. In Babylon, biblical religion appears to have been dominant among the Judeans, though we know very little about their life there.

As soon as Cyrus made it possible, the priests returned to Jerusalem and the city was established as a Temple community, led by the priests. There was a strict separation between Judean (Jew) and non-Judean in Judah which, the Bible records, was enforced by Ezra and Nehemiah. This separation was

'I was glad when they said to me, "Let us go to the house of the Lord!" Our feet have been standing within your gates, O Jerusalem! Jerusalem, built as a city which is bound firmly together, to which the tribes go up, the tribes of the Lord, as was decreed for Israel, to give thanks to the name of the Lord. There thrones for judgment were set, the thrones of the house of David. Pray for the peace of Jerusalem! "May they prosper who love you! Peace be within your walls, and security within your towers!" For my brethren and companions' sake I will say, "Peace be within you!" For the sake of the house of the Lord our God, I will seek your good.'

Psalm 122

marked by circumcision, observance of the *Shabbat* (the Jewish Sabbath, which runs from Friday evening to Saturday evening), the Sabbatical year, recognition of the Law (Torah) of Moses and obligations to the Temple in Jerusalem. The rigorists also required that marriage arrangements should be made only between Judeans.

THE TEMPLE AND THE SYNAGOGUE
The Judeans believed that there must be only one Temple. The Temple was the only place where the Jewish religious sacrifices could be carried out. And this belief, enforced by Persian authority, had far-reaching consequences. When all Judeans lived in Judah, it was possible for them all to make the pilgrimage to Jerusalem. When Judeans

A detail of Alexander the Great from a Roman mosaic depicting the Battle of Issus.

lived abroad this was out of the question – though the Jews of the Dispersion made great efforts to visit Jerusalem in obedience to the Torah. The priestly regulations in the Torah became a dead letter, and a new form of religion had to emerge for the ordinary Jew. This form culminated in the setting up of 'synagogues', where prayer, singing, reading, discussion and teaching (but not sacrifice) took place.

In the Temple at Jerusalem the old religion continued. And here the procedure was governed by written regulations, by a book. The book began to create its own ambience over and against – even in opposition to – the rituals of the priests.

Some time in this period the first scribes appear. Their home is the synagogue. Their job is to understand the Torah and to interpret its rules for the contemporary situation. They are also the bearers of tradition and of conduct. With hindsight, we can see how this 'guild of scholars' evolved into the rabbis of rabbinic Judaism. But at this time they were only one strand among many in Judaism.

The Hellenistic kingdoms: 333–63 BCE
The victory of Alexander the Great at Issus in 333 BCE began a new era, an era of much greater prosperity. Cities, founded on the Greek pattern, began to grow rapidly in size. In Egypt, Alexandria became the leading city within a few years of its foundation. The Judean community there was substantial, and Greek, instead of Aramaic, became their language. Government by democratic rule by a small nucleus of citizens (who were, or considered themselves to be, Greek) brought new political ideas to the East. The Greek language rapidly spread. People even tried to look Greek.

After the death of Alexander, his empire broke up into smaller units. The principal kingdoms were Macedonia (Greece), Egypt (ruled by the Ptolemies), and the Seleucid kingdom. (Seleucid kings did not rule Phoenicia or Judea at the beginning.) In the third century BCE, the Parthian empire rose to power. The Seleucid kingdom was gradually reduced to the Syrian region only and Babylon came under Parthian control. The Jews in Babylon became somewhat cut off from all other Jewish communities. Aramaic remained the language of Babylonia – so a barrier of speech was added to the barrier of politics.

These communities inevitably developed differently. But they were still united through having a common Bible, and also through their emphasis on Jerusalem, and the Temple in particular. The priests were still undisputed leaders. The high priest was the glory of the city, powerful both politically and economically.

TENSION AND REVOLT

In 191–190 Antiochus III of Syria was defeated by the Romans, who were now turning their eyes toward the East. Prisoners of war from these battles were probably the founders of the Jewish community in Rome. Jews also settled in Antioch in Syria, and in Asia Minor (modern Turkey). The Romans imposed tribute on Antiochus. This meant increased taxes. It seems that tension between rich and poor in Jerusalem and Judah became extreme at this time. This factor, added to political and cultural differences (those for and against the Greek way of life) made for an explosive situation.

The explosion came in the reign of Antiochus IV. When the Jews resisted his nominee for the high priesthood, he sent troops to sack Jerusalem. He established pagan practices in the Temple and attacked the Jewish religion. Some Jews gave in. But those who loved the Law, especially the Hasidim ('The Pious') endured great suffering. Eventually there was full-scale revolt, led by the family of the Hasmoneans.

In 165 BCE Judas Maccabeus won peace with the Syrians, marched into Jerusalem, and the desecrated Temple was solemnly cleansed. (The victory is still celebrated today in the Festival of Lights or *Hanukkah*.)

The Maccabee family began a line of rulers – the Hasmonean dynasty. Ironically the Hasmoneans became typical Hellenistic despots. But they won a real measure of freedom for the Jewish realm before the Romans, under Pompey, annexed Judea in 63 BCE.

Under the Roman empire: 63 BCE – CE 200

Judea was now a vassal of Rome. The current Hasmonean king was confirmed as the nation's leader and high priest, but the Romans would not recognize him as king. Successive Roman governors kept a firm hold on Judea.

In 40 BCE, following a Parthian invasion of Syria and Judea, the Roman Senate gave Herod the title 'king of the Jews'. Although Herod's personal life was disastrous, the country prospered under his rule. Herod is remembered as a builder – of cities (Sebaste, Caesarea), of fortresses (Masada, Herodium), of palaces, theatres and amphitheatres, of the temple in Jerusalem and pagan temples abroad. Those who opposed Rome and the Greek way of life hated him.

During the Roman period the Jewish hope of a messiah (a king of David's line, for some a priest-king) came to the fore. He would rescue his people from the Romans and restore the Judean state.

There were several revolts in Judea during the time of Herod and his successors, and many 'prophets' drew large followings. The most serious threat to the Jews came in the time of the emperor Caligula (CE 37–41). He demanded that all his subjects worship him, and ordered a statue of himself (as Zeus) to be placed in the Temple.

THE TEMPLE IS DESTROYED

Judea became more and more unsettled. Conflict between Greeks and Jews was constant in the coastal cities. Conflict between the Roman governors and the people increased. Finally in CE 66 the Jews rose in a general revolt against Rome. Initial success was followed by crushing defeat. Jerusalem was taken and the Temple destroyed in CE 70.

The destruction of the Temple was decisive for the future of Judaism. The Temple and the high priesthood and the council (Sanhedrin) were finished. No longer could Jerusalem, as centre of pilgrimage, be the unifying force within Judaism. Jewish communities were now simply descent groups within larger communities. Although they remained

'By the rivers of Babylon we sat and wept when we remembered Zion. There on the poplars we hung our harps, for there our captors asked us for songs, our tormentors demanded songs of joy; they said, "Sing us one of the songs of Zion!" How can we sing the songs of the Lord while in a foreign land? If I forget you, O Jerusalem, may my right hand forget its skill. May my tongue cling to the roof of my mouth if I do not remember you, if I do not consider Jerusalem my highest joy.'

Psalm 137:1–6

A HISTORICAL OVERVIEW

The sacking of Jerusalem in CE 70. A detail from carvings on the Arch of Titus (c. CE 81) in the Forum, Rome.

distinct, they were inevitably affected by the culture of the city or nation in which they found themselves. Unless something took the place of the Temple, the scattered communities would grow apart.

It was a seemingly insignificant event which provided the new direction for Judaism. Jochanan ben Zakkai founded a school at Jamnia. The Romans made no objection because this act had no political implications. At this school the mode of address *rabbi* (master) became a formal title. The teachers were 'rabbis'. Jochanan may not have been a Pharisee, but his successor, Gamaliel (?grandson of Hillel) was. The ethos of the school was essentially Pharisaical: and this gave the tone to emerging rabbinic Judaism.

This school at Jamnia came to exercise the function of a council, and even to adopt the name Sanhedrin. Jochanan fixed the calendar for the Jews abroad, once the prerogative of the high priest. Jews began to look to this council for advice and judgments. The extent of the influence of the council is impossible to determine. As happens so often, the writings which came from the council were even more influential than the council itself. The rabbis of this early period are known as *Tanna* (plural *Tannaim*: teachers). Their earliest surviving works are the 'sayings' in the *Pirqe Avot* and the second-century commentaries, or the laws, written in Hebrew.

Most other varieties of Judaism died out gradually. Jewish Christianity survived into the second century CE, even though the rabbis tried hard to exclude Jewish Christians from the synagogues after about CE 90. In the

the Romans now gave the country) were now Romans of a much higher rank. Aelia Capitolina was completed and Jews were forbidden to enter the city. Galilee now became a centre of Jewish life and various towns successively became the seat of the council.

Judaism was not banned, but since the circumcision of the converts was forbidden, conversion was made difficult, if not impossible. Many Jews in Palestine still hoped for a Parthian invasion to free them from the Romans.

Simeon II, son of Gamaliel II, became 'patriarch' of the Jews with – at least in theory – authority over the Jews of the Roman world. Simeon's son, Judah I ('the Prince') appears to have exercised considerable political power. He was a considerable scholar, and in his time the Mishnah was codified and published.

The patriarchate declined in power after this, but rabbinic discussion continued in Palestine, Babylon and Rome.

In Babylon (from 223 BCE a part of the Persian empire), the recognized rulers of the Jews were the 'exilarchs' or princes of the captivity. They enjoyed a status perhaps higher even than that of Judah I and certainly much greater than that of their contemporaries in Galilee.

Israel and abroad: CE 200–640

Within the land of Israel the patriarch was almost always a descendant of Hillel. The patriarchate was abolished by the Romans in 429, but the council, the Sanhedrin, continued until 640.

The conversion of Constantine to Christianity in 313 was not auspicious for Jews. Although Judaism was never made illegal it became very difficult to be a Jew. Many, perhaps most, Christian leaders, writers, monks and bishops hated the Jews.

In Egypt, the Jewish communities began to recover, though numbers were never the same as they had been in

Greek world Christians broke entirely with Judaism, all too often becoming anti-Jewish.

PERSECUTION CONTINUES

Jewish revolts were widespread and they were brutally put down. The Judean revolt of 132 may have been sparked off by the establishment of the new Roman city of Aelia Capitolina on the ruins of Jerusalem. (The Old City of present-day Jerusalem is the linear descendant of this Roman town.) This revolt was led by Simeon ben Koseba, who claimed to be the messiah, and he was supported by the greatest rabbinic scholar of the day, Rabbi Akiba, then an old man. The attempt was hopeless. Though considerable casualties were inflicted on the Romans, this only made the final defeat more disastrous.

The governors of Palestine (the name

earlier centuries. Greek culture was on the wane, and with it Hellenistic Judaism. Relations between the Jews and the Persian authorities became less amicable from the fifth century onward. The Jews there were thus ready to welcome the Arab conquerors. Similarly, in Palestine, the harshness of the Byzantine rule caused the Jews to look for redemption abroad. They aided the invading Persian forces in 614, but in 617, uprisings among the Jerusalem Jews were subdued by military force. The Byzantine army re-entered Jerusalem and the Jews were once more expelled from the city.

The age of the Gaons: 634–1096

The Muslim conquests were spectacular. In 634 the Byzantine army was defeated. Syria and Palestine were conquered. Persia fell in 637. Egypt followed soon after. Spain was invaded in 711, and an independent Muslim state was set up there around 750. The armies reached France, but were driven back to the Pyrenees.

Within 100 years, many Jews came under Muslim rule. The general conditions of life for most improved considerably. The Jews shared in the great intellectual ferment of the Arab world. Great advances were made in mathematics, astronomy, philosophy, chemistry and philology. Some Jews in the enlightened Spanish area rose to influential positions in the courts of the rulers. The tenth and eleventh centuries in Spain were especially a 'Golden Age' of literary achievement. The type of Judaism known as 'Sephardic' developed in Spain with its synagogue rituals and its own Spanish–Jewish dialect, Ladino.

The rite of the other Jews in Europe, especially in Germany, is known as the 'Ashkenazi', with its own language – the German–Jewish dialect, Yiddish.

In Christian France the Jews were relatively well-treated in the ninth century. But from then on hatred of the Jews and riots became common. The crusading armies marched to 'The Holy Land', looting and slaughtering the Jews in particular as they went. The capture of Jerusalem hailed throughout the Christian world as a great triumph, merely meant death to the Jews there – burnt in the synagogues. Life in Christian Europe became harsh for Jews.

The Jews saw these deaths as martyrdom, the ultimate form of witness, or 'sanctification of the Name' (*kiddush haShem*). Some committed suicide rather than renounce their faith. It became clear that the authorities, even when sympathetic, were helpless before the Christian mob. The rules of conduct (*halakhah*) stated plainly that while laws could be broken when life was at stake, there were times when death must be preferred, to avoid the guilt of idolatry, incest or murder, or to 'sanctify the Name'.

THE INFLUENCE OF BABYLON

In Babylon, the authority of the exilarch continued under the Muslims. At this time the authority and importance of the heads of the Babylonian academies (the Gaons) grew immensely. It was these men who ensured that the Babylonian Talmud was accepted throughout the world. A gaonate was established in Palestine in the ninth century which was recognized as authoritative by Jews in Spain, Egypt and Italy. Under the Gaons collections of Talmudic laws were made, synagogue poetry was written, prayer-books were drawn up, the text of the Bible was fixed and annotated. Most influential of all the work of the Gaons were their Responsa: questions on matters of practice were sent to the Gaons, these were debated in the academies and an answer was sent out in the name of the Gaons.

There were variants from rabbinic Judaism. In the eighth century Anan ben David, and the Karaites of the tenth century, rejected the Talmud and all forms of oral law, taking their stand on the Bible only. The Karaites seemed likely to divide the Jewish world, but their movement soon became merely a sect. It still survives today (like the Samaritans), but in small numbers (perhaps 5,000 in the former Soviet Union, 7,000 in Israel and 1,000 or so in Egypt).

The Western teachers: 1096–1348

From the middle of the eleventh century scholars in the schools of the West became more significant than the Gaons. One French scholar is outstanding. Rabbi Solomon ben Isaac (known, from his initials, as Rashi) produced standard commentaries on the Bible and Talmud. His commentary on the Bible was used by Nicholas de Lyra, whom Luther often consulted, and his interpretations were frequently adopted in the translation of the Authorized King James Version of the Bible. Rashi's commentary and the additions of his successors are printed in the Talmud today.

Rabbi Moshe ben Maimon (see 'Developments in Judaism') in his Mishneh Torah presented a code containing all the *halakhah*, all the rules and laws that ever applied to Judaism. Other scholars applied themselves to this task after him: mostly Sephardim (after the expulsion from Spain).

MASSACRES IN EUROPE

In this period Jewish communities continued to be founded in new areas and communities which had been decimated by massacres were re-established. Jews entered England in the eleventh century, but were expelled in 1290, not to return until after 1650. A new round of massacres began in the late thirteenth century. The Jewish communities in southern Italy were almost wiped out between 1290 and 1293 and many forced conversions were made. Jews were expelled from France in 1306 and further massacres occurred in 1348. The great achievements of Jews in medieval France came to an end. Jews were falsely accused of poisoning wells and causing the Black Death which killed off a third of the population of Europe in 1348. From Spain to Poland Jews were massacred.

At this time two ghastly lies were current: the so-called 'blood libel' and the 'libel of desecration of the host'. The blood libel, which claims that Jews are guilty of ritual murder, using the blood of Christian children during Passover, is still used by neo-Nazis and other anti-Semites to whip up hatred against the Jews.

The Golden Age of Spain had come to an end in this period. In the twelfth century Christians tried to recapture Spain from the Muslims. In response, fanatical Muslim tribes, 'Almohades', from North Africa poured into Spain. These Muslims did not show the usual tolerance towards Jews and drove them northwards. Christian leaders welcomed these Jews at first, but their tolerance did not last long.

Jewish survival: 1348–1517

When massacres, the expulsions and the plague had ceased, the Jews were allowed to return to their cities. With other means of livelihood closed to them many Jews became moneylenders. Now the rulers needed their expertise; the new economy demanded their help.

In Christian Spain attacks on Jews reached a peak in 1391. Many Jews professed conversion, and were known by the insulting name of *Marranos* (swine). Jews left Spain in large numbers. In 1492 Jews were offered the choice of converting or leaving. Many converted, but thousands fled.

Wherever they went, in Europe and beyond, from Amsterdam to Safed in Galilee, the exiles had an enormous impact.

'This God is one. He is not two nor more than two, but one. None of the things existing in the universe to which the term one is applied is like unto his unity.'

Moses Maimonides

> 'All things that are, are in God, and must be conceived through God, and therefore God is the cause of the things which are in himself. This is the first point. Further, no substance can be granted outside God, that is, nothing which is outside God exists in itself; which was the second point. Therefore God is the immanent, but not the transcendent, cause of all things.'
>
> Baruch Spinoza

Moses Mendelssohn, founder of the humanist movement, *Haskalah*.

Europe in ferment: 1517–1700

In the sixteenth and seventeenth centuries, the Muslim Ottoman (Turkish) empire was in the ascendancy. The Ottomans captured Palestine in 1515, Egypt in 1517, and expanded into Europe until they were halted in Vienna in 1683. During these centuries, the greatest number of Jews lived in countries of the Ottoman empire, or else in Christian Poland–Lithuania.

Christian Europe was also in ferment. The Protestant Reformation on the whole favoured Jews, though Luther's personal attitude changed over the years from tolerance and defence to rabid anti-Jewish fulminations. Anti-Jewish riots continued to occur, but the authorities tended to protect the Jews, who were seen as useful. The massacres of 1648 and 1649 came as a severe blow to the Jews in the Ukraine and Poland. The Jewish writers claim that all those 'who could not flee were slain and were martyred with unnaturally cruel and bitter deaths'.

Looking more closely we see that these massacres were more than just a matter of ignorant peasant superstition. The Jewish leaders were seen to be on the side of the Polish overlords of the Ukraine, both economically and politically. It is the tragedy of history that Jews have often had the skills most appreciated by a ruling class. They have also often been forced into such occupations as moneylending, and therefore greatly resented by the lower classes.

In Italy, severe penalties were inflicted on the Jews. In the Ottoman empire conditions were generally better, but they were subject to the arbitrary and capricious actions of the rulers.

THE HOPE OF A MESSIAH
In the late seventeenth century a number of messianic movements arose. No doubt these were partly a product of the insecurity of Jewish life. The most important was centred on Shabbetai Zevi (1628–1716) and his prophet, Nathan of Gaza. They found acceptance and a following throughout the world.

Nathan behaved very much as a latter-day John the Baptist. He called for deep repentance, with severe ascetic practices and mortification of the body. Fasting, bathing in freezing water and constant prayer were called for and practised.

Shabbetai was imprisoned in Gallipoli in 1665–66, and in 1666 he yielded to threats and converted to Islam. Jews were devastated: 'The paradox of a traitorous Messiah is far greater than an executed Messiah,' wrote Gershom Scholem. The Shabbeteans who continued to exist were viewed with deep suspicion and inevitably the general result was a great disillusionment with Messianism.

A pointer to the new times coming was Baruch Spinoza (1632–77). A great philosopher, he ceased to be a Jew without becoming a Christian – or a member of any other religion.

Enlightenment and persecution: 1700 to the present day

From the beginning of the seventeenth century, Jews gradually began to move outwards from Poland and the Ottoman empire into the new cities of the West. There was a growing realization of the value of Jewish commercial activity and Jews began to be associated with the most developed social and economic systems. In the nineteenth century, for example, large numbers of Jews migrated to America.

Those who opposed all religion, or all revealed religion, still found Judaism a convenient target, but generally there was a growing tolerance. In the nineteenth century 'equal rights' were eventually obtained, though often with very great difficulty.

The possibility of emancipation was based on the separation of church and state. Judaism was regarded as a religion only. The Jew in England, say, or in Germany, was to be a loyal English or German citizen, differing only in religion.

The Jewish enlightenment

At the same time, there were important new directions in Judaism. The so-called Jewish enlightenment, the *Haskalah*, was a humanist movement. The founder, Moses Mendelssohn (1729–86), was a practising Jew, though many of his followers were not. Mendelssohn advocated the separation of church and state, so that religious bodies should not be able to compel, only persuade. He emphasized the universal principles of religion within Judaism, and encouraged the use of German by translating the Torah into German. After his death the members of this movement, now led by Leopold Zunz (1794–1886), began to be more radical. They rejected the Talmud and traditional ideas – even the idea of revelation. Modern Jewish studies began.

The dark counterpoint to increasing tolerance was modern anti-Semitism, based on spurious pseudo-biology and a belief in the 'soul' of a people. A sharp contrast was drawn between the 'Semite' nature (in practice only Jews) and the 'Aryan' or 'Slavonic' nature. The strong anti-Semitic movements began in Germany and France in the 1880s.

The direct consequence of all this, in 1939–45, was the 'elimination' of six million breathing human beings merely because they were Jewish. European Jewry almost ceased to exist. One-third of all the Jews in the world were killed. The blow this dealt to security, sanity and faith is incalculable. The Holocaust, and the sorry role played by most governments and Christian leaders, is a central fact in all relations between Jews and non-Jews today.

Branches of Judaism

MARVIN WILSON

The majority of Jews throughout the world today are descendants either of the Ashkenazim or the Sephardim. The Ashkenazim came from central Europe, notably Germany ('Ashkenaz' means Germany) and France, and later moved to Poland and Russia. Ashkenazic Jews developed Yiddish (medieval German) as their language. Around it they produced a rich culture in art, music and literature.

Sephardic Jews ('Sepharad' means Spain) created the language of Ladino (a mix of Spanish and Hebrew). Before being driven from Spain in the Inquisition of 1492, the Sephardim became closely involved with the Muslim world. This enabled them to develop a unique intellectual culture. The wide difference in cultural background between the Ashkenazim and Sephardim is especially evident in Israel today where each supports its own chief rabbi.

Clearly the Jews are not a race. And Judaism is not an unchanging institution. Due to intermarriage, conversion, and dispersion among the nations, there has been a 'branching out' over the centuries. Wide cultural differences between Jews have resulted. For instance, the difference between the black Falasha Jews of Ethiopia and the Indian Jews in Mexico is immense.

In addition to these cultural groupings, several religious branches can be distinguished within Judaism today. Modern Judaism is rooted in rabbinic (Talmudic) Judaism, and both evolved from biblical Judaism.

Orthodox Judaism – submission to the Law

Orthodox Judaism regards itself as the

'The deeper you dig into the Torah, the more treasures you uncover. Without the Torah the world would not exist. With the letters of the Torah, God has created heaven and earth.'

Isaac Bashevis Singer

only true Judaism. During the first half of the nineteenth century it developed into a well-defined movement. It sought to preserve traditional (classical) Judaism against the emerging Reform movement in East Europe.

Orthodox Jews are characterized by a 'Torah-true' approach to life. They teach that God personally and decisively revealed himself in giving the Torah at Sinai. The words of the Torah are therefore divine and hence fully authoritative. They are the changeless revelation of God's eternal will.

Every aspect of the Orthodox Jew's life is to be governed by the commandments (*mitzvot*). Daily, Jews are to study the Torah and conform their lives obediently to its propositions and rituals, including the strict rules of *Shabbat* observance, dietary laws and prayer three times a day. In short, Orthodox Judaism is 'mitzvahcentric'.

The East European Jews at the start of the nineteenth century lived in a close-knit community known as a *shtetl*. In this stockaded culture they were shut off from the secular world. Toward the end of the century, however, a new orthodoxy slowly began to emerge. As large numbers of Jews started to emigrate to the United States, Orthodox leaders like Rabbi Samson Hirsch encouraged Jews to involve themselves in the contemporary culture of the Western world, pursue secular university education and develop philosophical minds. Today, most Orthodox Jews believe that adjustment to the modern world is essential so long as it does not conflict with the teachings of the Torah.

Orthodox Jews maintain a high regard for the rabbi as teacher and interpreter of the Torah. They place a strong emphasis upon education, particularly day schools where traditional learning can be acquired. Most Orthodox Jews are Zionistic and support the state of Israel. Many hope for a personal messiah, an ideal man who will one day fully redeem Israel.

Of all the branches of Judaism, Orthodox Judaism places the greatest demands on its adherents.

Reform Judaism – response to change
Reform Judaism had its beginnings in Germany. The Enlightenment of the eighteenth century had stressed reason and progress. The Emancipation in the following century opened the Jewish people to new freedoms, to equal rights as citizens and to new opportunities to explore secular society.

The mood of the day was geared to change and growth, scientific inquiry and critical evaluation, and Jews quickly began to adapt to this new age. To stem this tide away from Jewishness, certain changes occurred within European Judaism. Abraham Geiger (1810–74) was one of the powerful forces in this movement.

Influenced by the spirit of the age, Geiger and others taught that scientific people could no longer accept the revelation of the Torah as factual and binding. Hence changes in ritual law and worship were encouraged. Dietary laws were abandoned. Prayers were translated from Hebrew into the vernacular. Synagogue worship changed: the organ was introduced; services were shortened; the 'family pew' replaced segregation of sexes. Some even began to worship on Sunday rather than the *Shabbat*.

In the USA, dynamic leadership in the Reform movement was provided by Isaac Wise. After founding an organization of Reform congregations, in 1875 Wise established Hebrew Union College, the main seminary in the USA today for training Reform rabbis.

Reform Judaism represents the most progressive main branch of modern Judaism. Liberal (Reform) Judaism is still evolving, since revelation is thought to be a continuing process. It seeks to keep current with each new generation by using reason and experience to establish the relevance or truth of a proposition. This means that the ethical teachings of the prophets are emphasized rather than the ritual Law. Reform thus provides an approach to religion which is highly individualized and non-authoritarian. A law is observed not because God said so, but because it is meaningful to modern religious experience.

Today the Reform movement remains dynamic and innovative. It has been aggressive in the area of dialogue between faiths. In the 1970s Hebrew Union College began to ordain women rabbis.

Conservative Judaism – the preservation of the people

Many European Jews were uncomfortable with the radical changes introduced by Reform Judaism. Conservatism arose as a new movement at the end of the nineteenth century. It sought to emphasize the positive historical elements of the Jewish tradition.

In the USA, Solomon Schechter (1847–1915) became a leading figure as president of the newly founded Jewish Theological Seminary. He stressed the need for commitment to tradition, but with adjustment if necessary. Schechter urged that preservation of the Jewish people was the way to achieve both tradition and change. Correspondingly, Conservativism has maintained a strong emphasis on the people of Israel and modern Zionism. Laypeople have considerable influence, particularly in instituting change. Some congregations, for instance, permit the use of an organ; others reject it. Some stress keeping dietary laws; others do not.

Other branches

The Hasidim are the Ultra-Orthodox wing of Judaism. Living in isolation from the Gentile world, these Jews maintain a strict commitment to the Torah in every phase of life. They are characterized by their distinctive style of dress (including black coats and ear locks) and their joyful form of worship (song and dance). The movement was

Hasidic Jews are easily distinguished by their distinctive dress.

founded in Europe by Israel Baal Shem Tov (1700–60). The Hasidim have many sects around the world, each led by its own *rebbe*. In the United States, the sects of the Lubavitch and Satmar are especially influential.

A younger branch of Judaism is known as Reconstructionism. It was founded by Mordecai Kaplan (1881–1983) who stressed Judaism as an evolving religious civilization. It gives equal importance to religion, ethics and culture.

Recent developments

The collapse of the Soviet Union led to a rapid acceleration of Jewish immigration to Israel. Due to the earlier Soviet restriction of religious freedom, however, many of these immigrants came to Israel severely limited in their understanding and practice of Judaism. Unemployment, housing needs and political unrest among Israelis and Palestinians created additional hardships associated with return to the Land.

The increased secularization of society has continued to threaten Jewish religious and community life through assimilation and intermarriage. To help counter these and other challenges, Reform Jewry in the USA has made efforts to strengthen its ranks through an outreach programme aimed to make converts among non-Jews who are religiously unaffiliated. At the other end of the continuum, the Hasidic movement, largely held together by its deep ties to religious tradition and separatist community life, appears strong and growing, relatively undaunted by the array of challenges posed by modern secular society. (See 'Judaism in the Modern World'.)

Developments in Judaism

GEOFFREY COWLING

When Judeans abroad adopted Greek as their mother tongue, a change in outlook inevitably followed. The Greek language was the medium by which Greek ideas, attitudes and ways of reasoning were passed on. These ideas were not necessarily terribly profound. The riches of classical Greek culture had been diluted, mixed and to a degree cheapened. But it was still a powerful, exciting and stimulating experience. People who could read Greek – especially those living in Alexandria – might have had a chance to read the great philosophers in the original. But it seems that the Greek-speaking Jews were not drawn away from their customs as much as some feared they would be. They still regularly visited Jerusalem to celebrate the festivals in the Temple, for example.

Hellenistic Judaism

The home of Hellenistic (Greek-speaking) Judaism was the Roman empire, and there were also branches in Palestine. The most important effect of Greek thought was the conscious use of logical rules of thinking. Instead of relying on personal charisma in their teaching, the rabbis drew up rules to prescribe what methods of biblical interpretation would be accepted as valid. As well as drawing from Greek ideas, Hellenistic Jews attempted to influence Greek thought in return. But it seems that they largely failed; non-Jewish writers of the period show great ignorance of Judaism.

Philo of Alexandria sought to explain the Bible from the point of view of Greek philosophy. Philo himself was a preacher and commentator rather than a profound philosopher. He explained the great events of Israel's history as allegories of eternal truths and adopted the Stoic idea of Reason (Logos), which he called a 'second God', an intermediary between God and the world.

Many Jewish works, such as the *Book of Wisdom*, were written with an eye to convincing Greek readers. Their critique of Greek ideas never went very far – the greatest gulf they saw between the Jewish and the Greek world was the worship of idols – and as propaganda they were useless.

COMMUNITY LIFE
The life of the ordinary Jew in Greek-speaking areas was centred on the synagogue. Both worship and practical matters of community life were conducted there. Strangers were lodged, the poor helped, discipline enforced, public gatherings held and children taught in the synagogue. The authority was in the hands of the 'ruler of the synagogue'.

Associated with the synagogue was the 'house of study'. Here the Bible was studied and there was a library for scholars.

The synagogue was the first Jewish centre of worship which had no rite of sacrifice. Worship consisted of prayer, singing and reading of scripture. Visiting preachers might give a sermon, but the resident scholars probably did not.

THE TALMUDS
The Talmud (see 'Judaism: Sacred Writings') is a vast collection of writings which contains the teaching of the rabbis. Its basis is the collection of rabbinic teachings made by Judah the Prince (the Mishnah). But the Gemara, the collection of discussions of the Mishnah, forms the larger part of the Talmud. In fact there are two Talmuds, the Palestinian and the Babylonian. The former is a record of the discussion in the rabbinic schools of Galilee,

especially Tiberias, during the fourth century CE. The latter records the views of Babylonian schools and was not completed until the seventh or eighth century.

We have to be very careful about taking any opinion in the Talmud as 'the teaching of Judaism'. The Talmud records all authoritative minority views and therefore it is necessary to discover who said what, how authoritative it was, whether it was accepted by the later authorities and what later commentaries said about it!

It took centuries for all the communities even to know about, let alone accept, the Talmuds. The Babylonian Talmud gained much dominance, since Judaism flourished strongly in the Muslim empire, in which Babylonian Judaism was dominant. The Palestinian Talmud was most influential in Italy and in Egypt, places which had close links with Palestine.

Jewish philosophy
It was thanks to the Arab empire that Jewish philosophy blossomed in the ninth to twelfth centuries. The Arab empire gathered the wealth of thought of past civilizations, translating into Arabic the learning of Greece, Persia and even China and India. Much of their most original work in philosophy, science, mathematics and medicine was done by Jewish scholars. And many of these were concerned with religious philosophy.

One of the greatest Jewish philosophers – Saadiah Gaon (882–942) – was concerned with the problem of 'faith and knowledge', discussing proofs of God's existence.

The most influential philosophers after Saadiah lived in Muslim Spain. Until the eleventh century the greatest influence on them was Neo-Platonism. This philosophy considers that God is separated from the world by a descending series of 'emanations'.

The Jewish philosophers had an

impact beyond Judaism. The work of Solomon ibn Gabirol was translated into Latin and made a profound impression on Christian thought. His influence can also be seen in the Jewish mystical tradition known as the Kabbalah. Judah Halevi of Toledo (1085–1140) wrote a fictional dialogue between a Jewish scholar and the king of the Khazars (a Turkish tribe converted to Judaism). He showed how philosophy could prove the existence of God, but revelation was then necessary to know more of him.

TACKLING ATHEISM

In the eleventh century there was a shift in philosophical thought: Aristotle became more important than Plato. Aristotle's science seemed to leave no room for religion, and Jewish scholars set about tackling the problem of whether his philosophy could be reconciled with biblical religion.

Ibn Daud (active c. 1180) was the first, but the greatest thinker of this time was Rabbi Moshe ben Maimon (1135–1204, known as Maimonides in English). Exiled from Spain to Egypt, he brought the thought of Spain to the East. His great philosophical work was *The Guide for the Perplexed*. As the title suggests, he was concerned with the difficulties Aristotle's philosophy gave to the believer. In contrast to many Jewish scholars, Maimonides saw 'right belief' as of great importance. He met great criticism for this at the time.

Maimonides drew up thirteen 'roots' of Judaism, the 'Thirteen Principles of the Faith', (see panel).

A century later, the Christian philosopher Thomas Aquinas also tackled the problem of Aristotle's philosophy. He was deeply indebted to Maimonides, frequently quoting him as 'Rabbi Moyse'.

The Jewish philosophers were not concerned with the concept of 'the chosen people'. It does not appear in Maimonides' thirteen roots (except

The Thirteen Principles of the Faith

● Belief in the existence of a creator and of providence

● Belief in his unity

● Belief in his incorporeality

● Belief in his eternity

● Belief that worship is due to him alone

● Belief in the words of the prophets

● Belief that Moses was the greatest of all the prophets

● Belief in the revelation of the Torah to Moses at Sinai

● Belief in the unchangeable nature of the revealed Law

● Belief that God is omniscient

● Belief in retribution in this world and in the hereafter

● Belief in the coming of the messiah

● Belief in the resurrection of the dead

perhaps to some degree in the idea of the messiah). They were much more concerned with universal truths. This may partly explain why, when Spanish Jews were persecuted in the fifteenth century many of the philosophers yielded and converted, while the ordinary people (with more to lose) resisted to the death. This led to a suspicion of philosophy.

Jewish mysticism

Mysticism forms an important strand of Judaism. It is the belief in some kind of direct 'vision' of divine things, a way to experience things and events otherwise than through our ordinary senses. Mysticism may deal with the same ideas as philosophy, but it claims to rely not on argument or thought but on mystical experience.

The Kabbalah, a Jewish mystical tradition, developed in Spain. It brought together many earlier traditions, such as ideas from the Talmud and the 'Book of Creation' (*Sefer Yetsirot*), which emphasized the mystical meaning of the letters in the Hebrew alphabet and the philosophy of Neo-Platonism. Direct from Neo-Platonism came the idea of how God related to the world. In the Kabbalah, God was known as the 'limitless' (*En Sof*). From him came the ten aspects of God (*Sefirot*), ways in which he is manifested or made known. They are 'emanations' of God, intermediate between the *En Sof* and the world.

The most important work of Kabbalah is the *Zohar*. It was attributed to Rabbi Simeon bar Yohai (second century CE), but in reality was written in thirteenth-century Spain. The final editor author was probably Rabbi Moses de Leon. This is a book of extreme historical importance. It is the Talmud of Jewish mysticism. After the Jews were expelled from Spain it became known to the West, producing the school of 'Christian Kabbalists', and still attracts those interested in the occult today.

The study of the Torah is still central in Kabbalah, but the aim is to find hidden, secret meanings. The *Zohar* expounds the Torah by literal, allegorical and expository techniques and, most important, by mystical insights. Astrology is bound up in the *Zohar* as well: each day is under the influence of one of the ten *Sefirot*.

After the expulsion from Spain, Safed in Galilee became the centre of Jewish mysticism. Here Rabbi Isaac Luria (1544–72) gave a new twist to the Kabbalah. His work, which, like the *Zohar*, made much of erotic imagery, had great influence on later movements such as Hasidism. In Luria's view, when the *En Sof* created the universe he withdrew from it. The *Sefirot* are vessels which contain the 'divine light'. But the last six *Sefirot* could not contain the light, and shattered. Some of them sank, trapping sparks of the divine light within them. This is the origin of evil; and redemption will come when these sparks are returned to their source.

Hasidism

Hasidism arose in Poland in the eighteenth century. From the start it was a popular movement. It gave hope and interest and excitement to people who were frightened, deprived and confined. The Shabbetai movement had led to disillusionment, and the 'worship through study' of rabbinism offered them no consolation. But Hasidism was a movement with emphasis on emotion and devotion. It may be paralleled with many similar movements of the time, such as the rise of Methodism in England and Wales.

The key figure in this movement was Israel ben Eliezer (1700–60), known as the Baal Shem Tov. He was a dynamic, charismatic figure, widely known as a miracle worker. Baal Shem Tov means 'Master of the Good Name', which reflects the belief in his powers. His teaching contained much from the Kabbalah, especially the *Zohar*.

Many legends are told about him, and much popular belief, indeed superstition, was caught up into the movement. But the essence was a passionate devotion to God, expressed in ecstatic prayer, singing and dancing. From the outside, Hasidic life may seem a narrow existence, but within it is sustained by the Hasidic 'joy' – a genuine religious 'high'. In fact, from its early days asceticism was played down.

Unlike rabbis, the leaders of the Hasidic groups were more gurus than scholars. The leader, the *rebbe* or *zaddiq*, is a man who is able to live the life of devotion and thus act as intermediary between his followers and God. The leader's word is absolute: his followers leave their families to be with him, they even contend to get a share of the food he has touched. Various

A Hasidic Jewish rabbi in Safed, Israel.

The Covenant

ROBERT BANKS

At the heart of the Jewish religion lies the existence of a covenant between God and the people. The term 'covenant' signifies an agreement made between two parties and must be distinguished from related ideas such as 'testament' and 'contract'. Unlike a testament, a covenant involves a personal response on the side of the second party to make it effective. Unlike a contract, however, it is not a mutually negotiated affair but is offered unilaterally by one side to the other.

The covenants we are concerned with are those forged between God and humankind, especially Israel. But investigation of purely civil treaties from the adjacent Hittite culture of the fifteenth and fourteenth centuries BCE has provided interesting insights. These treaties between king and people always included amongst other things, three elements:

■ a historical prologue describing the deeds of the maker of the treaty;

■ a list of obligations binding the lesser of the two parties;

■ a list of punishments and rewards.

The Jewish covenants generally reproduce this pattern. They are grounded in certain divinely ordered events; they contain a set of stipulations; and they are concluded with a list of 'woes and blessings'.

God's chosen people

The first covenant referred to in the Jewish scriptures is that between God and Noah (Genesis 9:8–17). The basis for this lies in God's preservation of Noah and his family during the flood. Through Noah, a promise is made to humankind and the animal world that this disaster will never be repeated. The promise has its sign, the rainbow, which is to act as a reminder, both to God and to all living creatures, of this undertaking.

The covenant with Noah provides the basis from which the later, more specialized commitment to Israel

follows. To begin with there is the covenant between God and the great patriarch of Israel, Abraham. God first promises to make Abraham the ancestor of a great nation (Genesis 12:1–7) and to give him and his descendants the land of Israel (Genesis 13:14–18). The covenant itself (Genesis 15 and 17) begins with a historical introduction, stating that God is the one who brought Abraham out from Ur of the Chaldees (in Iraq). It then outlines obligations about living righteously and justly, which are elaborated in later books. Circumcision becomes the sign of this covenant.

Over 600 years later, this covenant is reaffirmed and extended at Mount Sinai, with all the people who have come out of Egypt (Exodus 19–20). This covenant recalls God's historical deliverance of them from Egypt and the accompanying promise that Israel will be God's special possession among all the nations. There is a series of obligations in the form of the Ten Commandments, and the people's acceptance of their responsibilities is also indicated.

This covenant, therefore, is again an expression of both God's grace and demand. Even the instructions are as much a gift as an obligation, for they show Israel how they may appropriately respond to God's choice of them. And since God later maintains both sides of the covenant, even when certain elements within Israel fail to obey, the fact that the covenant is based on God's grace remains transparent.

These things are nowhere clearer than in the biblical book of Deuteronomy. Deuteronomy is the record of Moses' farewell addresses to Israel, on the eve of their entry into the promised land. Deuteronomy 5 recounts the Sinai covenant; Deuteronomy 7 refers to the covenant with the patriarchs of Israel, and Deuteronomy 29 is a renewal of the covenant with the whole people. Throughout the book, insistence on God's continued gracious maintenance of the covenant, despite Israel's failure to fulfil its conditions, is a prominent theme.

In the later historical books a still

more specialized covenant is recorded – that with David and his descendants and, associated with this, with the Levitical priesthood (1 Chronicles 17:7, 28:4). Here again there are the standard elements:

■ the prologue reminds David that it was God who turned him from being a shepherd into a victorious king;

■ the outlining of conditions indicates that God's blessing is not automatically guaranteed (1 Chronicles 22:11);

■ the promise tells of God's commitment to establish David's descendants upon the throne forever.

A renewed covenant

So naturally did the people take the covenant on which their nation was based, that the great prophets (except Hosea and Jeremiah) rarely referred to the Sinai agreement. It was only after the exile had shattered Israel's confidence that the later prophets were less reticent about the covenant (Zechariah 9:11; Malachi 2:4). The later historical writings also speak of significant covenant renewals (Ezra 9; Nehemiah 9).

Most significant in a number of these writings is the promise of a new covenant to replace the broken one for which Israel had been punished (see, for example, Jeremiah 31; Ezekiel 16). The decisive difference between the two is that the new covenant will have its obligations inscribed on the wills of the people rather than existing merely as external obligations which the people must seek to observe. When this happens, Israel will receive back all that they have lost and more.

In the post-biblical writings, further changes in the understanding of the covenant take place. The idea of a new covenant either drops away altogether, or becomes simply a reiteration of the old one (Baruch 2:30).

In the apocryphal writings the word for covenant refers, much more frequently than before, just to the obligations within it. This pushes the Torah into a more prominent position and the covenant in a more contractual direction, though these are only tendencies, not full developments. Meanwhile the covenant with the Fathers comes to be regarded as irrevocable, leading to the use of the term for the Jewish nation itself (Judith 9:13).

The apocalyptic writings preserve the same emphasis and the term for covenant is used more often than previously for its sign, circumcision (Jubilees 15:13–14). The Torah is now said to precede the covenant, moving into a position of greater prominence (Ecclesiasticus 24:6; 44:19).

The Qumran and rabbinic writings maintain this perspective. The former do take up the idea of the new covenant made with its community, but this is basically a reaffirmation of the old covenant. The rabbinic writings occasionally suggest that God's covenant with Israel rests upon their obedience as much as God's free choice.

The well-known Rabbi Schneersohn reads from the Torah in a New York synagogue (early 1990s).

leaders have created the different branches of Hasidism today.

Women played a much more prominent role in the beginnings of the movement than they do today. Generally, Hasidism is a man's world. Women are responsible for the survival of the community but they lead separate lives.

OPPOSITION

The Hasidic movement met strong opposition from the establishment of the Jewish communities. There was something of a class struggle, as the *rebbes* replaced the rich and learned. Excommunication was used as a weapon against them by their opponents.

One of the most hostile, certainly the most influential, was the 'Gaon of Vilna', Elijah ben Solomon (1720–97). The emphases of Hasidism were anathema to his ascetically orientated intellectualism. In his time the excommunicated were even betrayed to the hostile authorities.

It was Shneur Zalman (1745–1813), the philosopher of Hasidism, who enabled the movement to be accepted. Under his influence Hasidism, or at least his branch of it, was reconciled to Talmudic study.

Sacred Writings

ERIC S. CHRISTIANSON

For as long as Judaism has been a significant religious force in the world its texts have been central to its life and culture. This can be seen in many expressions. In the Torah, Deuteronomy 30:14, we read: '… the word is very near to you; it is in your mouth and in your heart for you to observe' (literally: for you *to do*). Psalms and wisdom also hint at the centrality of texts. For example, the psalmist proclaims: 'I treasure your word in my heart, so that I may not sin against you… Your word is a lamp to my feet and a light to my path' (Psalm 119:11, 105). More specifically, in the reign of Josiah (c. 639–609 BCE; see 2 Kings 22–23), it is the discovery of the 'book of the Law' (an early form of Torah, see below) that inspires Josiah's reforms, and again renewal in the time of Nehemiah (c. 450 BCE; see Ezra–Nehemiah). From the late biblical period through classical rabbinic Judaism, the scribe (from the copyist to the 'maker' of scrolls or books) has been regarded as something of a hero, often on a par with a sage or, eventually, a *reb* or rabbi.

A Jewish legend further reflects the sacredness of texts. It tells of a Roman soldier who defaced a Torah scroll in the first century CE. The authorities were forced to put him to death to avoid insurrection. At least since the watershed of the destruction of the Temple in CE 70 and the final revolt against Roman authorities (Bar Kokhba, CE 132–35), sacrifice and pilgrimage to the Temple was gradually replaced with the study of Scripture and other sacred texts, prayer and works of piety.

The study of texts made Judaism a portable tradition. Decentralized from the Temple, Jews of the diaspora (or exile) were able to worship God anywhere, and study of sacred texts became capable of fulfilment anywhere. Today the sacredness of texts is expressed in other ways as well. Since the advent of printing, Jewish writers and publishers have been at the forefront of the book industry. Modern *halakhot* (observances) even cover stipulations regarding the proper treatment of books. In sum, Judaism has always exhibited a remarkable love of the word, of manuscripts and of books; and in what follows, the three major textual traditions will be discussed:

● Tanakh (Hebrew scriptures)

● Mishnah (tractates and regulations on the Law)

● Talmud (exposition of the Mishnah and Torah)

Tanakh

It is worth noting first that in Jewish practice and theology the term 'torah' is used in three basic senses:

● the first five books of the Scriptures, traditionally ascribed to Moses;

● the whole of the Jewish Scriptures (*written* torah);

● ethical teaching of the rabbis (*oral* torah).

This article only uses the term in the first sense, referring to the first five books. In referring to the whole of Hebrew scripture we can quite rightly use the term Tanakh. The term derives from the tradition, since late biblical times, of dividing the Hebrew scriptures into three distinct sections.

Much debate surrounds the question of how and why particular books of the Jewish canon came to be included and in what particular order. Certainly the order is significant. For example, in the Christian canon, the book of Ruth lies between Judges and Samuel (Ruth begins, 'In the days when the judges ruled…'). In the Jewish canon it lies in the Writings: it belongs to a group of five books (the *megillot*) that are read cyclically at festival times, Ruth being

> *'There is one way to salvation: to go back to the sources of Judaism, to Bible, Talmud, and Midrash; to read, study and comprehend them in order to live them… the seekers after knowledge will go back to the ancient fountains of Judaism, Bible and Talmud and the one effort will be to obtain the concept of life out of Judaism.'*
>
> Samson Raphael Hirsch

SACRED WRITINGS

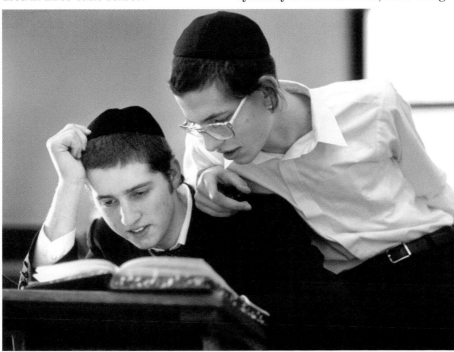

Two students discuss a point of law at an Orthodox Jewish *yeshiva* in Philadelphia, Pennsylvania, USA.

Divisions of the Hebrew scriptures

Torah: Genesis to Deuteronomy

Nevi'im (Prophets):
FORMER: Joshua, Judges, Samuel, Kings
LATTER: *major:* Isaiah, Jeremiah, Ezekiel
minor: the book of the twelve (Hosea, Joel, Amos, Obadiah, Jonah, Micah, Nahum, Habakkuk, Zephaniah, Haggai, Zechariah, Malachi)

Ketuvim (Writings): Psalms, Proverbs, Job, Song of Songs, Ruth, Lamentations, Ecclesiastes, Esther, Daniel, Ezra, Nehemiah, Chronicles

read at harvest. The canonical position of a book, then, says a great deal about its value to that faith community – Ruth primarily as history for Christians, as liturgy for Jews.

In Judaism the notion of canon itself has evolved over the centuries. One thing is clear from the earliest records: what mattered was the pragmatic nature of texts. Early rabbinic debate focused on value. Which texts manage, somehow, to speak beyond the context of their composition and speak with immediacy to the ongoing life and identity of a faith community? Once identified, those texts are 'biblical'. They are texts that, for whatever reason, accrued existential value for the community who used them.

Mishnah

The Mishnah is a collection of tractates consisting of *halakhot*, regulations that span every conceivable area of Jewish daily life and ritual purity. Its first tractate, the sayings of the fathers (*Pirqe Avot*), begins by laying down some principles for interpretation and for practice. The first verse sets the tone: 'Moses received Torah from Sinai and passed it on to Joshua, and Joshua to the Elders, and the Elders to the Prophets; and the Prophets passed it on to the men of the Great Assembly.

They said three things: 'Be careful in giving judgment, raise up many disciples, and make a fence around the Torah.' In other words, like Jewish writers after them, the authors of the Mishnah saw themselves as part of an unbroken chain of tradition. Furthermore, Jews who fulfilled the ordinances of the Mishnah would in turn be fulfilling the Torah, building a hedge around it in a mutually beneficial exchange – guard the Torah and it will guard you. The Mishnah became the key reference for decision making among the diaspora Jews from its inception (c. CE 200). However, within 50 to 100 years large portions of it were thought to be terse and obscure, and an explanatory companion soon evolved.

Talmud

The Talmud (literally: 'teaching') is big. The Mishnah is about half a million words long. The Babylonian Talmud (composed and 'practised' in exile) is about four million words long. In it the opinion of over a thousand rabbis is cited over seventeen successive generations (c. CE 200–650). There

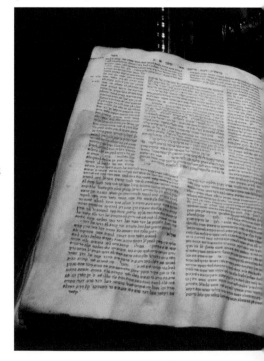

is a shorter Palestinian Talmud as well (composed in Palestine, often referred to as the Jerusalem Talmud). Within those words appear all kinds of literature. Solomon Schechter (1847–1915), an outstanding nineteenth-century scholar of Talmud, described it as 'a work too varied, too disconnected, too divergent in its elements, to be concisely defined at all, or to be even approximately described within the limits of an English sentence'. The Talmud arose in the rabbinic academies of diaspora Judaism from continued debate over the significance and implementation of the Tanakh (especially the Torah) and the Mishnah, with tractates and groups of tractates gradually becoming authoritative through use.

The range of topics that the Talmud covers is truly astounding. Hyam Maccoby's engaging anthology of Talmud, *The Day God Laughed*, organizes its material in the following categories (among others): Enjoying Nature; Against Asceticism; Physical Beauty; Eating and Drinking; Rejoicing; Studying; Tall Stories; The Value of

Argument; Arguing for Pleasure; Arguing with God; Privy Etiquette. That list gives not only a hint of the breadth covered by Talmud, but also the nature of some of its most memorable passages. The Talmud is at pains to blur any distinction between holy and profane. Even more striking is that it is not concerned with answers. It is far more concerned with questions and with the *process* of answering them. One of its most celebrated passages brilliantly captures this tendency and is worth citing at length:

On that day, Rabbi Eliezer put forward all the arguments in the world, but the sages did not accept them.

Finally, he said to them, 'If the halakhah is according to me, let that carob-tree prove it.'

He pointed to a nearby carob-tree, which then moved from its place a hundred cubits, and some say, four hundred cubits. They said to him, 'One cannot bring a proof from the moving of a carob-tree.' ...

[Two more miracles were performed by Rabbi Eliezer in a bid to have his argument accepted.]

Then said Rabbi Eliezer to the Sages, 'If the halakhah is according to me, may a proof come from heaven.'

Then a heavenly voice went forth, and said, 'What have you to do with Rabbi Eliezer? The halakhah is according to him in every place.'

Then Rabbi Joshua rose up on his feet, and said, 'It is not in the heavens.' [Deuteronomy 30:12 – he goes on to explain that since the Torah has already been given on Sinai, we do not need to pay attention to a heavenly voice.]

Rabbi Nathan met the prophet Elijah. He asked him, 'What was the Holy One, blessed be He, doing in that hour?'

Said Elijah, 'He was laughing, and saying, "My children have

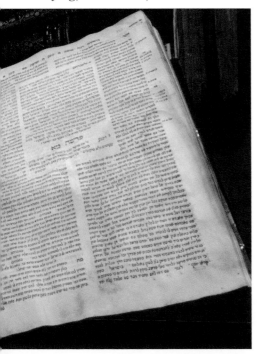

A 300-year-old copy of the Talmud, printed in Italy.

*defeated me, my children have
defeated me.'"*
BAVA METSIA 59B

In other words, God's children are
grown up enough to argue with him.
For the rabbi it is even a responsibility.
In this sense, the Talmud captures
something essential not just of the
historical period and contexts it
emerges from, but also of the ongoing
life of Judaism: God is in the argument,
and he may well be found in the delight
of vigorous human discourse.

The Textual Balance
In some sense it is true that for
modern Judaism generally the Tanakh
is not the most important text. In
matters of practice, the texts of
classical rabbinic Judaism, of its
subsequent commentators – such as
the biblical *Targums* (paraphrases)
and medieval figures such as
Maimonides, Rashi and Ibn Ezra and of
a whole range of popular prayer books
and guides to Jewish life, including
The Zohar (c. late 1550s) and *Shulhan
Arukh* (c. 1565) – are often the first
port of call. Having said that, it remains
that for the composers of the Mishnah,
Tanakh was the foundation (not just of
the laws being composed, but of life
itself); and for the Talmud, Mishnah
and Tanakh were foundational.

Judaism's sacred texts, then, can be
envisaged as concentric circles. The
innermost three circles are the Tanakh,
and centremost is its most vital element,
Torah (followed by *Nevi'im* [the
prophets] and *Ketuvim* [the writings]).
After Tanakh, Mishnah and Talmud
follow to the outermost circle, *Midrash*
(meaning 'commentary'). *Midrash*
refers to the ongoing tradition of
commentary and critique, a potentially
never-ending circle that includes all
texts that manage to become, in some
way, of existential worth to the Jewish
community.

Beliefs

DAN COHN-SHERBOK

In the Hebrew Bible, the Israelites
experienced God as the Lord of history.
The most uncompromising expression
of his unity is the *Shema* prayer
(*shema* meaning 'hear'): 'Hear, O
Israel, the Lord our God is one Lord'
(Deuternomy 6:4–9). According to
Scripture, the universe owes its
existence to the one God, the creator
of heaven and earth, and since all
human beings are created in his image,
all men and women are brothers and
sisters. Thus, the belief in one God
implies for the Jewish faith that there
is one humanity and one world.

God and creation
For the Jewish people, God is conceived
as the transcendent creator of the
universe. That is to say, God is
'transcendent' in that he is distinguished
from that which he has created. God is
above and beyond the world. He is
'wholly other' than anything that is not
God. Unlike creation, God is uncreated
and does not depend upon anything for
his existence. Thus in Genesis 1:1–2
he is described as forming heaven and
earth: 'In the beginning God created the
heavens and the earth. The earth was
without form and void, and darkness
was upon the face of the deep; and the
Spirit of God was moving over the face
of the waters.'

Throughout the Bible this theme
of divine transcendence is repeatedly
affirmed. The prophet Isaiah proclaims:
'Have you not known? Have you
not heard? Has it not been told you
from the beginning? Have you not
understood from the foundations of the
earth? It is he who sits above the circle
of the earth, and its inhabitants are like
grasshoppers; who stretches out the
heavens like a curtain and spreads them

like a tent to dwell in' (Isaiah 40: 21–2).

Despite this view of God's remoteness from his creation, he is also viewed as actively involved in the cosmos. In the Bible the belief that he is always omnipresent is repeatedly stressed. In the rabbinic period Jewish scholars formulated the doctrine of the *Shekhinah* to denote the divine presence. As the indwelling presence of God, the *Shekhinah* is compared to light. Thus the *Midrash* paraphrases Numbers 6:25 ('The Lord make his face to shine upon you, and be gracious to you'): 'May he give thee of the light of the *Shekhinah*.' In the medieval period the doctrine of the *Shekhinah* was further elaborated by Jewish thinkers. According to Saadiah Gaon (882–942), the *Shekhinah* is identical with the glory of God, which serves as an intermediary between God and human beings during the prophetic encounter. Judah Halevi of Toledo (1085–1140) argued in his *Kuzari* that it is the *Shekhinah* rather than God himself who appears to prophets.

Time and eternity

In addition to his transcendence and immanence, the Hebrew Bible depicts God as having neither beginning nor end. This teaching was elaborated by the rabbis. According to the Talmud, there is an unbridgeable gap between God and humans: 'Come and see! The measure of the Holy One, blessed be he, is unlike the measure of flesh and blood. The things fashioned by a creature of flesh and blood outlast him; the Holy One, blessed be he, outlasts the things he has fashioned.' In midrashic literature, God's eternal reign is similarly affirmed. Yet the rabbis discouraged speculation about the nature of eternity. Such reluctance is reflected in the Mishnah's dictum: 'Whoever reflects on four things, it were better for him that he had not come into the world: What is above? What is beneath? What is before? and What is after?'

Despite such teaching, in the Middle Ages Jewish theologians debated this issue. In his *Guide for the Perplexed* Rabbi Moshe ben Maimon (1135–1204) – known in English as Moses Maimonides – argues that time itself was part of creation. Therefore when God is described as existing before the creation of the universe, the notion of time should not be understood in its normal sense. This concept of time as part of creation was later developed by Joseph Albo in his *Ikkarim* (fifteenth century). He maintains that the concepts of priority and perpetuity can only be applied to God in a negative sense. That is, when God is described as being 'before' or 'after' some period, this only means that he was not non-existent before or after that time. However, these terms indicating a time span cannot be applied to God himself.

According to other Jewish thinkers God is outside time altogether. On this view, he does not live in the present, have a past or look forward to the future: he lives in the 'Eternal Now'. Hence, God is experiencing every moment in the past and future history of the created world simultaneously and eternally. What for us are fleeting moments rushing by are a huge tapestry for God, of which he sees every part continually.

Omnipotence and omniscience

Allied to this belief about God's eternity is the Jewish conviction that he is all-powerful and all-knowing. From biblical times the belief in God's omnipotence has been a central feature of the faith. Thus in Genesis when Sarah expressed astonishment at the suggestion that she should have a child at the age of ninety, she was criticized. Similarly, when Jerusalem was threatened by the Chaldeans, God declared: 'Behold, I am the Lord, the God of all flesh; is anything too hard for me?' (Jeremiah 32:27).

In the Middle Ages, however, Jewish thinkers wrestled with the concept of

'Whither shall I go from thy Spirit? Or whither shall I flee from thy presence? If I ascend to heaven, thou art there! If I make my bed in Sheol, thou art there! If I take the wings of the morning and dwell in the uttermost parts of the sea, even there thy hand shall lead me.'

Psalms 139:7–12

BELIEFS

A statue of Jewish philosopher Maimonides in the Jewish quarter of Cordoba, Andalucia, Spain.

divine omnipotence. Maimonides, for example, argues in his *Guide for the Perplexed* that, although God is all-powerful, there are certain actions that he cannot perform because they are logically impossible: 'That which is impossible has a permanent and constant property, which is not the result of some agent, and cannot in any way change, and consequently we do not ascribe to God the power of doing what is impossible.'

Regarding God's omniscience, the Bible proclaims: 'The Lord looks down from heaven, he sees all the sons of men... he who fashions the hearts of them all, and observes all their deeds' (Psalms 33:13, 15). Following the biblical view, rabbinic Judaism asserted that God's knowledge is not limited by space and time. Rather, nothing is hidden from him. Further, the rabbis declared that God's foreknowledge of events does not deprive human beings of free will. Thus, in the Mishnah, the second-century sage Akiva declares: 'All is foreseen, but freedom of choice is given.' In his *Guide for the Perplexed* Maimonides claims that God knows all things before they occur. Nonetheless, human beings are unable to comprehend the nature of God's knowledge because it is of a different order from theirs. It is similarly not possible to understand how divine foreknowledge is compatible with free will.

The election and mission of Israel

The Bible asserts that God controls and guides the universe. The Hebrew term for such divine action is *hashgahah*, derived from Psalm 33:14 – 'From where he sits enthroned he looks forth on all the inhabitants of the earth.' Such a view implies that the dispensation of a wise and benevolent providence is found everywhere: all events are ultimately foreordained by God. Such a notion was developed in rabbinic literature. God is depicted as the judge of the world, who provides

for the destiny of individuals as well as nations on the basis of their actions.

In this connection Jews affirm that God chose the Jews as his special people: 'For you are a people holy to the Lord your God: the Lord your God has chosen you to be a people for his own possession out of all the peoples that are on the face of the earth' (Deuteronomy 7:6). Through its election Israel has been given a historic mission to bear divine truth to humanity. God's choice of Israel thus carries with it numerous responsibilities: 'For I have chosen him, that he may charge his children and his household after him to keep the way of the Lord by doing righteousness and justice' (Genesis 18:19).

The Torah

To accomplish this task, God revealed both the oral Torah and the written Torah to Moses on Mount Sinai. As Maimonides explains: 'The Torah was revealed from Heaven. This implies our belief that the whole of the Torah found in our hands this day is the Torah that was handed down by Moses, and that it is all of divine origin. By this I mean that the whole of the Torah came unto him from before God in a manner which is metaphorically called "speaking"; but the real nature of that communication is unknown to everybody except to Moses.'

In rabbinic literature a distinction is drawn between the revelation of the Pentateuch (the first five books of the Bible – Torah in the narrow sense) and the prophetic writings. This is frequently expressed within Judaism: the Torah was given directly by God, whereas the prophetic books were given by means of prophecy. The remaining books of the Bible were conveyed by means of the holy spirit rather than through prophecy. According to the rabbis, the expositions and elaborations of the written Law were also revealed by God to Moses on Mount Sinai. Subsequently they were passed from generation to generation, and through this process additional legislation was incorporated. This process is referred to as 'the oral Torah'. Thus traditional Judaism affirms that God's revelation is twofold and binding for all time.

According to tradition, God revealed 613 commandments to Moses. These *mitzvot* are recorded in the Five Books of Moses and classified in two major categories:

● statutes concerned with ritual performances characterized as obligations between human beings and God;

● judgments consisting of ritual laws that would have been adopted by society even if they had not been decreed by God.

All these laws, together with their expansion in rabbinic sources such as the Mishnah and Talmud, are binding on Jewry for all time.

Obedience and sin

Any deviation from the commandments as interpreted by rabbinic sages is viewed as a violation of God's word. Rabbinic Judaism teaches that there are two tendencies in every person: the good inclination (*yetzer ha-tov*) and the evil inclination (*yetzer ha-ra*). The former urges individuals to do what is right, whereas the latter encourages sinful acts. At all times a person is to be on guard against the assaults of the *yetzer ha-ra*.

Eschatology

Eschatology is teaching about the 'last things', such as the end of time, the afterlife, heaven and hell. Traditional Judaism asserts that, at the end of time, God will send the messiah to redeem his people and usher in the messianic age. In Scripture, such a figure is depicted in various ways, and as time

passed the rabbis elaborated the themes found in the Bible and Jewish literature of the Second Temple period. In the *midrashim* and the Talmud they formulated an elaborate eschatological scheme divided into various stages. First there will be the time of the messianic redemption. According to the Babylonian Talmud, the messianic age will take place on earth after a period of decline and calamity and will result in the complete fulfilment of every human wish. Peace will reign on earth; Jerusalem will be rebuilt; and at the close of this era the dead will be resurrected and joined with their souls, and a final judgment will come upon all humankind. Those who are judged righteous will enter heaven (*Gan Eden*) whereas those deemed wicked will be condemned to everlasting punishment in hell (*Gehinnom*).

Changing beliefs in modern times

From biblical times Jews have subscribed to a wide range of beliefs about the nature of God and his action in the world. In modern times these have been increasingly called into question. In the nineteenth century Reformers sought to reinterpret this belief system for modern Jews. In their view, it no longer made sense to believe in the coming of the messiah and the entire eschatological scheme as outlined in rabbinic sources. Subsequent movements, including Reconstructionist and Humanistic Judaism, rejected the supernaturalism of the past, calling for a radical revision of Jewish theology for the contemporary age. In more recent times, the Holocaust has raised fundamental questions about the belief in a supernatural God who watches over his chosen people. Today there is widespread uncertainty in the Jewish world about the central tenets of the faith.

'Before the mountains were brought forth, or ever thou hadst formed the earth and the world, from everlasting to everlasting thou art God.'

Psalm 90:2

BELIEFS

Family and Society

DAVID HARLEY

According to Orthodox Jewish law, a Jew is one born of a Jewish mother, although it is possible to become a Jew by conversion. On the eighth day after his birth, a Jewish boy will be circumcised. This is a religious rite performed by a *mohel*, a trained and registered circumciser. When he is circumcised, the boy receives the Hebrew name which will be used at his *Bar-Mitzvah*, at his wedding and on his gravestone.

During his early years his mother is responsible for his religious education. As soon as he can speak, he is taught the words of the Shema. At about the age of five he is sent to a synagogue religion class which is held after school

A Jewish boy celebrates his *Bar-Mitzvah* at the Western Wall in Jerusalem.

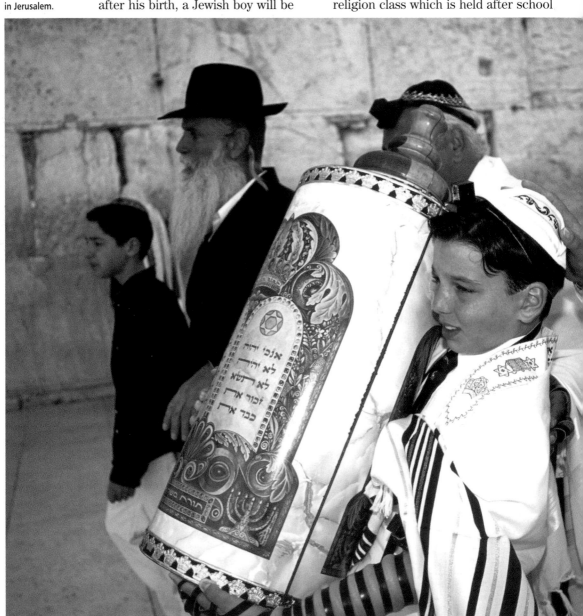

hours on weekdays and also on Sunday mornings. One of the main activities of the religion class is to learn Hebrew and study the sacred books. For a girl it is also particularly important to learn how to keep a Jewish home.

At the age of thirteen a boy becomes *Bar-Mitzvah* (son of the commandment); on the *Shabbat* after his birthday he reads from the scroll of the Torah during the synagogue service for the first time. After the service there is usually a party for family and friends. From this point on he is regarded as a responsible person. He is expected to fulfil all the duties of a Jew and may count as one of the ten who are required to make a quorum for public prayer (*minyan*). A Jewish girl automatically comes of age at twelve and is considered to be *Bat-Mitzvah* (daughter of the commandment). It is increasingly becoming the custom to hold a ceremony to mark the occasion.

Prayer

A devout Jewish man prays three times a day – morning, afternoon and evening – either in his home or in the synagogue. When he prays he covers his head with an ordinary hat or a skull-cap (*yarmelka* or *kippah*). In the morning he wears a prayer-shawl (*tallit*) which has tassels or fringes at the four corners in obedience to the command found in the Torah. On weekdays he may also put on phylacteries (*tephillin*). These are black leather boxes containing four passages of scripture: Exodus 13:1–10 and 11–16; Deuteronomy 6:4–9 and 11:13–21. They are strapped to the forehead and left upper arm.

A *mezuzah* attached to the doorframe of a Jewish home.

When he goes out, the Orthodox Jew may continue to cover his head as a mark of reverence towards God in whose presence all life is lived. By the front door he passes the *mezuzah*, which is another reminder of his religious obligation to God. The *mezuzah* consists of a tiny scroll of parchment on which are written in Hebrew the opening paragraphs of the Shema: Deuteronomy 6:4–9 and 11:13–21. The scroll is housed in a wooden or metal container and fixed to the upper part of the right-hand doorpost of the front door. A similar *mezuzah* is fixed to the doorpost of every other living-room in the house.

Kosher **food**

It is the duty of a traditional Jewish housewife to safeguard the religious purity of the home, and one of her many responsibilities is to make sure that the food eaten there is *kosher* (fit or clean according to Jewish dietary laws).

Meat and dairy products must not be served at the same meal. If meat is eaten, there can be no butter on bread or milk in coffee. To avoid any possibility of mixing meat with milk the traditional Jewish housewife uses two sets of dishes, one of which is only used for meat, the other only for milk foods. In addition she may use two bowls for washing-up and two sets of tea-towels. In *kosher* hotels there are two separate kitchens.

Only certain kinds of meat may be eaten in a Jewish home. These are listed in Leviticus 11 and Deuteronomy 14. Lamb, beef and chicken are among those permitted; pork and shellfish among those that are not. The animals must be slaughtered by a trained and ordained *shochet*, who follows carefully prescribed regulations which cause the blood to drain quickly from the body and ensure the minimum of pain. After the animal is properly slaughtered, the meat must be soaked in cold water and salted to remove all the blood that remains.

Jewish people vary a great deal in the degree of their observance of these dietary laws. Some do not observe them at all. Some abstain from food that is expressly forbidden but are not so particular about the details of keeping a *kosher* kitchen. However, Orthodox Jews will follow these regulations meticulously as an act of religious obedience, whereby the taking of food is sanctified and the family table becomes an altar. Before each meal a traditional blessing is recited, and though this may vary according to the food that is being eaten, the most common words are, 'Blessed art thou, O Lord our God, King of the universe, who brings forth bread from the earth.'

The *Shabbat*

The *Shabbat* is considered to be the most important of all the Jewish religious festivals. It commemorates both the creation of the world and the deliverance of the people of Israel from Egypt. It has played a significant role in the preservation of Judaism. It is a day with a special atmosphere of joy and peace, and as such is thought of as a foretaste of the age to come.

The beginning of the *Shabbat*, sunset on Friday evening, is marked by the lighting and blessing of the *Shabbat* candles by the mother. The father attends synagogue, often with his children, and on his return blesses his children and praises his wife with the words of Proverbs chapter 31. The family then enjoys a *Shabbat* meal together, which begins with the blessing over bread and wine. The bread is a special plaited loaf called *challah*. Usually two loaves are used, in memory of the double portion of manna that fell in the wilderness on the day before the *Shabbat*.

No work is permitted on the *Shabbat* and Orthodox Jews have to be employed in occupations which allow them to be home before sunset on every Friday throughout the year. This often means that they will be self-employed, work in a Jewish firm or trade in Friday and Saturdays for work on other evenings, Sundays and Christmas.

No fires may be lit on the *Shabbat* though a fire which was lit before the *Shabbat* may be left alight. Many install time-delay switches to avoid forms of work not permitted to Jews on the *Shabbat*.

No long journeys may be undertaken on the *Shabbat*, though those on board ship do not have to get off. Orthodox Jews will live within easy walking distance of their synagogue since they must not drive on the *Shabbat* or use public transport.

These restrictions, far from being a

Guests at a traditional Jewish wedding in West Jerusalem lift the bride and groom up on chairs as they hold together a shared square of fabric.

burden, are seen by religious Jews as a means of releasing them from the ardours of the daily round. It is a day when they can rest completely from their ordinary work and be spiritually renewed.

At the close of the *Shabbat*, the family again gathers for a brief ceremony. Blessings (the *Kiddush*) are recited over a cup of wine and a box of sweet spices. The spices speak of the fragrance of the *Shabbat* day, which, it is hoped, will be carried over into the new week.

Marriage and divorce

In Judaism marriage is considered to be a holy covenant between the bride and groom. Before the ceremony the bridegroom signs the marriage document (*ketubbah*) in which he pledges himself to his bride. During the service the couple stand under an embroidered canopy supported by four poles, which represents their future home. The ceremony ends with the breaking of a glass under the bridegroom's foot. This symbolic act is thought by some to represent the idea that even times of great joy need to be balanced by moments of serious

reflection. Others see it as a reminder of the destruction of the Temple of Jerusalem, a theme which constantly reappears in Hebrew prayers.

In the event of the breakdown of a marriage, the local community tries in every way possible to reconcile husband and wife. If this is not possible, a *get* (bill of divorce) may be issued by the Jewish religious court if both partners agree. This document, written in Aramaic and signed by two witnesses, is handed by the husband to the wife. It frees her from all her marital obligations to him. In most countries a civil divorce is required first, and then the issuing of a *get* serves as a religious ratification of the divorce.

Death and resurrection

The last words uttered by religious Jews when they are dying – or said on their behalf if they are too weak – are the words of the Shema which they first learned as children: 'Hear, O Israel, the Lord our God is one Lord…' At the funeral, close mourners make a small tear in their clothes as a mark of grief. The funeral service, which is characterized by simplicity even among wealthy families, is

> *'Hear, O Israel, the Lord our God is one Lord. Love the Lord your God with all your heart and with all your soul and with all your strength. These commandments that I give you today are to be upon your hearts. Impress them on your children. Talk about them when you sit at home and when you walk along the road, when you lie down and when you get up. Tie them as symbols on your hands and bind them on your foreheads. Write them on the door-frames of your houses and on your gates.'*
>
> Deuteronomy 6:4–9

arranged as soon as possible and preferably within twenty-four hours of death. No prayers for the dead are offered but *kaddish* (a prayer of praise to God) is recited in their memory. It is the particular responsibility of children to say *kaddish* on behalf of deceased parents.

After the funeral the close relatives return home for a week of private mourning. This period is known as shivah or the seven days, during which those who have been bereaved sit on low stools or even on the floor. On the anniversary of the parent's death, the children light a memorial candle and recite the *kaddish* at the end of the synagogue service.

The doctrine of the resurrection is not found in the Torah and it is considered by some as a foreign import from Christianity. However, the idea of life after death can be traced back within Judaism at least 2,000 years, and it is expressed in Maimonides' 'Thirteen Principles of the Faith' (see 'Developments in Judaism') in the words, 'I believe with perfect faith that there will be a resurrection of the dead at a time when it shall please the Creator.' Yet it remains true that Judaism is concerned primarily with this life rather than the next, and with obeying the Law of God in the present rather than speculating about the future.

Worship and Festivals

LIZ RAMSEY

The annual cycle of worship and festivals gives Judaism its distinctive form. There is a major or a minor festival in almost every month of the year. Beginning with *Rosh Hashanah* (New Year's Day) on the first day of Tishrei and proceeding to the period of penitence that begins in the twelfth month, Elul, Jews are able to express and celebrate their identity through the regular re-enactment of stories that explore life's meaning and purpose. High and low points of the Jewish story are remembered.

The heart of Judaism
Rabbi Moshe ben Maimon (1135–1204) – known in English as Moses Maimonides – set out 'Thirteen Principles of the Faith' (see 'Developments in Judaism'). These help to define Judaism and lie at the heart of the Jewish Prayer Book, the basis of Jewish worship. They were not intended to become a creed – indeed, Judaism is based more upon practice than belief – and can be summarized in the three great themes that underpin the Jewish religion: *creation, revelation* and *redemption.*

At the heart of Judaism is the profound idea that human beings can bring God into the world through everyday actions and interactions. Although Judaism acknowledges a huge distance between the infinity of God and the limitations of human beings, it believes human beings are called to be partners with God in the task of creation. This understanding of the divine–human relationship can be traced back to the Babylonian Talmud

(*Shabbat* 10a, 119b, *Sanhedrin* 38a). The supreme moment of revelation was when the people received the commandments at the foot of Mount Sinai. Hence, Jewish religious expression or worship occurs when *mitzvot* (the commandments) are being followed – when one practices *halakhah* or 'walking in God's way'.

Home and synagogue

The holiest object in Judaism is a scroll of the Law, a *Sefer Torah*. It is a very moving moment when the Torah scroll is taken out of 'the ark' in the synagogue in the course of a service of worship and held up before the people. The synagogue is important as a meeting place, a focus for prayer and a house of study. Nonetheless, it is not the only significant place of worship in the sense in which a mosque or a church may be. Jews will often refer to the synagogue simply as *shul* (school).

The home is a focus for many of Judaism's most sacred institutions: *Shabbat*, the festivals and the dietary laws, as well as education across the generations (see 'Judaism: Family and Society'). The role of women is considered crucial to the future of Judaism in terms of the active contribution women can make towards creating a spiritual and educative environment in the home.

Every effort is made to involve children in the celebration of the major festivals. It is a child who asks the questions concerning the specialness of 'this night' at the *Seder* celebration during *Pesach* (Passover). It is children who enjoy drowning out the sound of Haman's name whenever it is mentioned during the reading of the book of Esther at *Purim*. It is children who are given the honour of the best places in front of the lights of the *menorah* (candelabrum) at the festival of *Hanukkah*.

The three pilgrim festivals

Three of the most popular Bible-based festivals are known as 'pilgrim' festivals. These recall the three annual occasions when Jews made the journey to worship in Jerusalem in the time when the Temple played a central role in Jewish life. They are the eight-

> '*Judaism begins not with an idea but with a community... going through the experience of Egyptian slavery and miraculous liberation from slavery. Out of that shared experience and the subsequent encounter with God at Mount Sinai, we shaped a religion... But throughout it all, it is the participation in the community that defines us as Jews; the creeds and rituals are secondary.*'
>
> Rabbi Harold Kushner

A Yemenite family celebrates the Passover *Seder* meal in a *moshav*, an agricultural settlement, in Israel.

day festival of *Pesach* (Passover), *Shavuot* (Pentecost) and *Sukkot* (Tabernacles). Together, they form an annual re-enactment of the special events, which forged the relationship between the Jews and their God.

● *Shavuot* (6 Sivan) marked the bringing of the first fruits in the days of the Temple and celebrates the giving of the Torah by God to Moses on Mount Sinai.

● *Sukkot* (15–20 Tishrei) commemorates the time when God protected the people in the desert.

● *Pesach* (15–21/22 Nisan) remembers the exodus from Egypt under the leadership of Moses and celebrates the passing over from slavery to freedom. The highlight is the first evening, with the observance of the *Seder*. Around the table in the home, Jews relive the story (*haggadah*) and reflect on how it must have felt to be a slave in Egypt (Exodus 13:8).

In many ways, the story of the exodus from Egypt did not end with Moses gaining freedom for a small group of people many centuries ago. The theme of Passover gives a context for exploration of the fundamental issues of freedom and slavery, with the accompanying themes of risk, choice, hope, disappointment, leadership, hardship and sacrifice. Moses has inspired many people who have

> 'The three Pilgrim festivals have in common the theme of joy in God's presence: "And you shall rejoice on your festivals" (Deuteronomy 16:14–16). ... The festive joy is traditionally expressed in feasting with meat and drink, and with the purchase of new garments for the women. It is a joy which is only complete when allied with concern for the needy; as the verse continues, "with... the strangers, orphans and widows among you."'
>
> Rabbi Norman Solomon

Festivals of Judaism

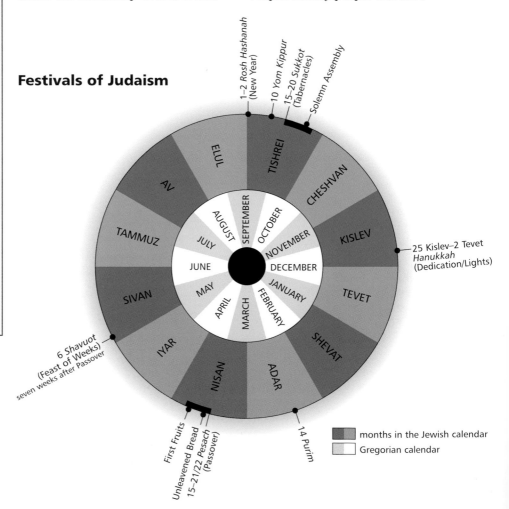

months in the Jewish calendar
Gregorian calendar

struggled to gain freedom from prejudice and oppression. Issues of marginalization and possibilities for liberation in the contemporary world are often discussed during the *Seder* meal.

Rosh Hashanah (1–2 Tishrei)

The new year festival of *Rosh Hashanah*, as in many traditions, is a time for making resolutions regarding the future. However, it is a serious occasion. A month earlier a forty-day period of penitence begins – 'The Days of Awe' (*yamim noraim*) – and *Rosh Hashanah* marks the beginning of the last ten of these. The foods eaten at the meal on New Year's Eve symbolize sweetness, blessings and plenty. Bread is dipped into honey (rather than the usual salt) and the following prayer is said: 'May it be

Seder meal

Through the ritual and symbolism of the *Seder* meal, Jews tell the story of how their ancestors left Egypt. The foods placed upon the often beautifully decorated *Seder* plate are symbolic and comprise: three *matzot* (wafers of unleavened bread) to symbolize the bread eaten by the Israelites when they left Egypt in a hurry (Exodus 12:39); bitter herbs (*maror*) to recall the experiences of slavery in Egypt (Exodus 1:14); a sweet paste (*haroset*), made from almonds, apples and wine, to represent the mortar used for building in Egypt as slaves and symbolize both the toils of slavery and the sweetness of redemption and freedom; a bowl of salt water to represent the bitter tears of slavery, with parsley used for dipping; a roasted bone as a reminder of the Paschal lamb and a roasted egg as a reminder of the offering brought to the Temple for the festival with the Paschal lamb, these last two items being left on the *Seder* plate during the meal, not eaten. It has also been the custom, since Rabbinic times, to drink four cups of wine during the *Seder* to represent the four stages of redemption, from the exodus to the future coming of the messiah.

your will to renew for us a good and sweet year.' Prayers at the morning service the following day, which lasts up to six hours, focus on the characteristics of God as creator, king and judge: the God who will show mercy and compassion to those who sincerely turn towards him (*teshuva*). The sounding of the *shofar* (ram's horn) regularly through the service is literally 'a wake-up call' to the people (see Amos 3:6).

Jacov Adar blows the *shofar* on *Yom Kippur*. The inscription on the side of the ram's horn reads 'Happy are the people who understand the sound of the *shofar*'.

Yom Kippur (10 Tishrei)

Yom Kippur (Day of Atonement) is a fast day that marks the end of 'The Ten Days of Awe' and is the holiest day in the Jewish liturgical year. It is the day on which Jews solemnly review their record of behaviour and literally turn to face a new year.

The whole day is spent in prayer for forgiveness and for a good year ahead. Synagogues are full to overflowing for at least part of the day. It marks one of the most emotionally charged times of the Jewish year. The theme is *teshuva* ('return' to God) – a major religious theme within Judaism, involving a renewed commitment to walk in the right path. *Kol Nidrei* forms the beginning of the synagogue service, sung to a profoundly moving melody and setting the tone as the congregation gathers before God in a spirit of awe.

Work is forbidden, as on *Shabbat*. There are five further prohibitions (*innuyim*) or forms of self-discipline. Jews must abstain from eating and drinking, anointing with oils, sexual relations, washing (for pleasure) and wearing leather shoes.

Ne'ilah (The Closing of the Gates) is the final service as the fast ends, and emphasizes the importance of the last hour in which the gates of heaven remain open for a returning to God. *Avina Malkenu* ('our father, our king') is chanted to express the congregation's commitment to the unity of God. A final blow is sounded on the *shofar* with its haunting expression of human grasping at goodness and worth.

Minor Festivals

The most popular of 'the minor festivals' are *Hanukkah* (25 Kislev – 2 Tevet), *Purim* (14 Adar) and the New Year for Trees, *Tu biShevat* (15 Shevat).

● *Hanukkah* celebrates the rededication of the Temple in about 165 BCE after its defilement by the Greeks. On each of the eight nights of the festival, a light is lit to commemorate the 'miracle of the oil'. The Hasmoneans, seeking to

rededicate the Temple, could only find one cruse of oil, enough to keep the Temple *menorah* burning for a day. Yet it lasted for eight. This is interpreted as a sign of God's creative action in the world.

● Between the destruction of the first Temple and the building of the second, many Jews were killed on account of Haman's scheming with Ahasuerus, the king of Persia. Queen Esther and her uncle Mordechai were used by God to avert catastrophe. *Purim* is celebrated with parties and sending gifts of food to people in need, and the *Megillah* (scroll of the book of Esther) is read in the synagogue.

● In these days of concern for ecology and responsible stewardship of the world's resources, Judaism's celebration of a new year for trees, *Tu biShevat*, is attractive. It has become a popular festival with the 'return to the Land' (Israel) in modern times. In Israel it is marked by a school holiday and tree-planting ceremonies.

Other fast days

Yom Kippur is a major fast day. Of the other fast days the most important is 9 Av (*Tishah b'Av*) when the destruction of the two Temples (in 586 BCE and in CE 70) is usually commemorated, as well as other tragedies of Jewish history. Reform Jews tend to use the day to commemorate the Holocaust.

On *Yom Kippur* and on *Tishah b'Av* people fast for twenty-five hours, instead of the twenty-four hours required for other fast days. Nothing is eaten or drunk during this time unless there is a practical reason for *not* undertaking this discipline.

'Secular' Judaism

Many Jews who describe themselves

Judaism is a very practical and also a very joyful religion. "Happy are we! How good is our lot! How pleasant is our destiny! How beautiful our heritage! Happy are we who, early and late, evening and morning, twice each day declare: Hear O Israel, the Lord is our God, the Lord is One!"

The Jewish Prayer Book. Extract from the Morning Service.

as 'secular' nevertheless experience a sense of belonging to the wider Jewish community at times such as *Pesach* or *Yom Kippur*. Official Israeli holidays can also strengthen the links between communal identity and liturgy:

● *Yom HaShoah*/Holocaust Day (27 Nisan) remembers the Holocaust and the six million Jews who were murdered.

● *Yom HaZikaron*/Memorial Day (4 Iyar) remembers the soldiers killed defending the state of Israel.

● *Yom Ha-Atzma'ut* /Independence Day (5 Iyar) marks the anniversary of the coming into existence of the state of Israel (in 5708, CE 1948).

● *Yom Yerushalayim*/Jerusalem Day (28 Iyar) commemorates the reunification of the city of Jerusalem (in 5727, CE 1967).

The Israeli Declaration of Independence (proclaimed on 14 May 1948), is celebrated with social activities, both in Israel and throughout the world, and special psalms and prayers are said in the synagogue. Yet it is somewhat controversial, both for religious and political reasons. The anti-Zionist group, *Neturey Karta*, does not celebrate. It observes the day as one of mourning and fasting.

A young woman reads before the lighted candles of the *menorah* during the festival of *Hanukkah* in Maryland, USA.

I am a Jew

DAVID ARNOLD

My paternal grandparents immigrated to Western Europe from Lithuania at the turn of the twentieth century to escape the combined effects of anti-Semitism and grinding poverty. My mother was born and brought up in Frankfurt am Main, Germany. She fled Germany at the end of June 1939, a refugee from Nazi persecution. She and her father were the only members of my maternal line to survive, the rest of the family are numbered among the millions of Jews murdered in the Holocaust. We live in a predominantly secular world, where religion and spiritual values are often assigned a very low priority. But, for me, my Jewish faith and family history have shaped and defined my identity. I attach great value to the traditions of democracy, freedom of speech and equality before the law. I also feel a personal responsibility to contribute to building a better understanding and harmonious relations between the Jewish community and the non-Jewish majority among whom we live.

I also think I am incredibly lucky to be Jewish. I draw inspiration from the courage and fortitude with which my mother confronted both the difficulties of her childhood and the humiliation and poverty of being a refugee. No less inspiring is the example of friends who are Holocaust survivors. They are often the sole surviving members of their families, whose homes and communities were completely destroyed. Their suffering and loss is unimaginable. They were brutalized and terrorized solely because they were born Jewish. Yet despite all this, so many of the survivors have chosen to renew and rebuild their lives firmly rooted in the Jewish faith and tradition into which they were born. This, for me, is proof of the eternal and enduring nature of their Jewish faith. The triumph of their humanity is truly inspiring.

Many of those murdered in the Holocaust were condemned in part because of the failure of so many countries, including the Western democracies, to take in Jewish refugees. So for me and most Jews living in the diaspora (i.e. Jews who live outside the borders of Israel) Israel represents a life insurance policy, a place of safety to which we can go if we feel we are once again endangered by anti-Semitism. Israel is, therefore, very important for the worldwide Jewish community. I have visited Jerusalem twice. It is at the heart and geographical centre of the Jewish world. Synagogues around the world are all built facing Jerusalem. The festival of *Hanukkah* and the fast days of *Tevet*, *Tammuz* and *Av* have their origin in the sieges of Jerusalem and the desecration of the Temple. Each time I prayed at the *Kotel* (formerly known as the 'Western Wall' or 'Wailing Wall') I sobbed uncontrollably, such was my emotion.

For me Judaism is not just a religion, but a complete and distinctive way of life. It defines my relationship with God, my relationship with other people, Jewish and non-Jewish, and my obligations as a human being. The central and defining principal of Judaism is the belief in a single God who is responsible for the creation of the universe and everything in it. The foundation of Judaism is the Torah, also known as the Five Books of Moses. I remember as a five-year-old schoolboy going after school to *cheder* (the Jewish equivalent of Sunday school) where I was taught to read Hebrew. At school I had to attend assembly each morning for Christian prayers, while at home, at the synagogue and at *cheder* I was expected to follow Jewish religious practice and traditions. For a few years I found this mixture of Jewish and Christian teaching all very confusing, especially when one day at school I was beaten up because, according to my accuser, I had 'murdered little Lord Jesus'!

The Torah contains not only the Ten Commandments but a total of 613 laws which are obligatory. These include the obligation to study of the Torah, observation of *Shabbat* (day of rest) and the festivals and the dietary laws. The whole of the *Tanakh* (known to Christians as the Old Testament) is sacred for Jews. There is also a vast library of Jewish scholarship, upon which many Jewish practices are also based. The most important of these other sacred writings is the Talmud, which comprises both the Mishnah and the Gemara.

Every Jew is obliged to obey the law of the land, to do all they can to preserve human life (*pikuach nefesh*) and give to charity. This includes not only donations of money or goods, but acts of kindness, the promotion of education, and caring for the sick, needy, elderly.

The dietary laws are complex, precise and exacting. Only certain kinds of fish and meat are permitted. Only meat and poultry killed by the Jewish humane method of animal slaughter, known as *Shechita*, is permitted. Milk and meat foods may not be eaten together – dairy and meat foods must be cooked, prepared and served separately using different utensils, plates and pans.

On *Shabbat* Jews are obliged to refrain from all forms of work: using machines, operating mechanical or electrical equipment, cooking, handling money and travelling in a vehicle. For me, *Shabbat* is the one day of the week to which I always look forward. It is truly a day of both physical and spiritual renewal.

The Holocaust

DAN COHN-SHERBOK

Traditionally, the term 'holocaust' refers to a burnt sacrifice that was offered to God in the ancient Temple. Today, however, 'the Holocaust' is widely used to refer to the destruction of Jewry under the Third Reich (1933–45), when bodies of victims were burnt in crematoria. Many Jews consider the term *Shoah* (catastrophe) more appropriate, as this is devoid of any religious connotations.

The rise of Nazism

At the end of World War I Germany became a democratic republic, based on a constitution drafted in Weimar. The regime faced opposition from the extreme right and left, and during 1922 to 1923 there was massive economic inflation. An interlude of stability and intellectual and cultural development was unfortunately followed by the Great Depression: over 6 million were unemployed between 1930 and 1933. As a consequence both the Communists and their fascist rivals, the NSDAP (*Nationalsozialistische Deutsche Arbeiterpartei*, better known as 'the Nazi Party'), gained considerable support. The Nazis, who linked Jews to Communism, were backed by leading industrialists. To cope with the unstable situation, the government began to rule by presidential decree. After several ineffectual conservative coalitions President Hindenburg (1847–1934) appointed Adolf Hitler as Chancellor on 30 January 1933.

Once in power, the Nazi Party suspended the constitution. In the course of 1933 other political parties were eliminated, strikes were outlawed, book burnings took place and trade union leaders were imprisoned along with dissident scientists, scholars and artists. In 1934 the role of Hitler's elite security forces (SS) was expanded. Under Heinrich Himmler (1900–45) SS troops took over many of the functions of the police, as well as the running of the concentration camps.

The persecution and extermination of Jews

After Hindenburg's death Hitler became the head of state and he required civil servants and members of the armed forces to swear an oath of loyalty to him. Jewish academics lost their jobs, Jewish shops were boycotted. In September 1935 all sexual liaisons between Jews and non-Jews were criminalized. In 1938 Jewish communal bodies were put under the control of the *Gestapo* (secret police) and Jews were forced to register their property. On 9 November that year the NSDAP organized an onslaught against the Jewish population, killing, looting and setting fire to homes, schools, shops and 250 synagogues. This 'night of broken glass' (*Kristallnacht*) was a prelude to the terrors of the death camps.

The first stage of the Nazis' plan for European Jewry began with the invasion of Poland in 1939. In every conquered town and village the Germans forced Jews to clear rubble, carry heavy loads, hand over jewellery and scrub floors and lavatories with their prayer shawls. Religious Jews had their beards and sidelocks cut off with scissors or torn from their faces. When the Jewish population was forced into what Hitler referred to as a huge Polish labour camp, a massive work programme was initiated.

The second stage began with the invasion of Russia in 1941, which was designed to destroy what the Nazis called the 'Jewish Bolshevik conspiracy'. At first mobile 'task forces' (*Einsatzgruppen*) – murder squads of 500–900 men under the supervision of Reinhard Heydrich (1904–42) – began the slaughter of Russian Jewry. Of the 4,500,000 Jews who resided in Soviet territory more than half fled before the German invasion. Those who remained were concentrated in large cities making it easier for Heydrich's troops to carry out their task. Throughout the country the *Einsatzgruppen* moved in, demanding from the rabbis or Jewish councils a list of all Jewish inhabitants. The Jews were then rounded up in market places, crowded into trams, buses and trucks and taken to woods where mass graves had been dug. They were then machine-gunned to death.

Other methods were employed. Mobile gas vans were sent to each battalion of the *Einsatzgruppen*; and their killing operations were supplemented by the use of fixed centres, the death camps. Two of these were at Chelmno and Auschwitz in the Polish territories and four at Treblinka, Sobibor, Majdanek and Belzec in the Polish 'General Government'.

Construction of this mass murder industry began in 1941. Two civilians from Hamburg went to Auschwitz to train the staff to use Zyklon-B gas. In September 1941 the first gassing took place in Auschwitz Block II; then work began in Birkenau, the killing centre in Auschwitz.

By September 1942 Germany had conquered most of Europe. Yet as the murder of Jews continued, resistance spread. The Jews of the White Russian town of Korzec set the ghetto on fire and a partisan group was formed. In Kaluszyn near Warsaw, the chairman of a Jewish Council collected money from Jews assembled in the main square expecting to use it to ransom the community. When he discovered the deportation would take place, he shouted: 'Here is your payment for your trip, you bloody tyrant.' Tearing the money into shreds, he slapped the German supervisor in the face and was shot on the spot.

In the same month a former soldier in the Polish army escaped from a prison camp in Lublin with seventeen more Jews and formed another partisan group. In the Warsaw ghetto, the Jewish Fighting Organization prepared itself for action. In October one member killed the commander of the Jewish police in the ghetto. Some months later the Jews in Warsaw learned that the ghetto was to be destroyed. They determined to fight. As the Germans entered the ghetto, they attacked. The German soldiers shelled buildings and burned apartment blocks, yet the Jewish fighters continued their battle. By the end of the first week of May 1943 the last 120 fighters were trapped in a bunker. For two hours the entrance was bombarded, then the Germans used gas. Street by street the ghetto was eliminated: 7,000 Jews lost their lives in the fighting and 30,000 were deported to Treblinka.

The murders continued without pause. By the summer of 1944 the last deportation took place. More than 67,000 were deported from the Lodz ghetto to Birkenau. Most were selected for the gas chamber, but some were chosen for medical experimentation. By the end of World War II over 6 million Jews had lost their lives in the most terrible circumstances imaginable.

Questions and Memorials

In the years since, the Jewish community has struggled with the religious perplexity of the Holocaust. Where was God at Jewry's time of dire need?

These terrible events are commemorated today on Holocaust Memorial Days as well as in Holocaust Museums (such as Yad va-Shem in Israel) which seek to ensure that the murder of millions of Jews and others is not forgotten.

A memorial to the victims of the Holocaust at Yad va-Shem, Jerusalem. The stone pillars with their tops apparently snapped off represent children who were murdered in the death camps.

THE HOLOCAUST

Israel/ Palestine: A Testing Ground for Three Faiths

COLIN CHAPMAN

As the conflict between Israel and the Palestinians has intensified in recent years, religion has become even more inextricably tied up with politics. Issues that might appear to be essentially *political* take on a strongly *religious* dimension as religion is used, especially by Jews and Muslims, to undergird claims to sovereignty.

Jews were banished from Jerusalem by the Romans in CE 135, but continued to live as small communities in a number of towns in Palestine. From the fourth century the majority of the population were Christians. Then Islamic rule was established in CE 636 and continued – apart from the period under the Crusaders in the twelfth and thirteenth centuries – until the end of the Ottoman empire in 1918.

The first seeds of the modern conflict were sown in the 1880s when the Jewish community amounted to 5 % of the total population. Fleeing anti-Semitism in Eastern Europe, Jewish immigrants started to settle in Palestine in the hope of establishing a Jewish homeland – or even a Jewish state. When the Palestinian Arabs realized that the ultimate objective of the Zionist movement was to create a Jewish majority and win political power, they became much more openly hostile to the new immigrants.

Britain played a decisive role by supporting the idea of a Jewish homeland in the Balfour Declaration of 1917. At the same time, however, it was making promises of future independence to the Arabs in order to win their support against the Ottoman Turks. Under the British Mandate from 1922, the Jewish community grew steadily and consolidated itself, and both Arabs and Jews resorted to violence to further their cause. When Britain found in 1947 that the problem was insoluble, it handed it over to the United Nations, whose Partition Plan led to the establishment of the state of Israel in 1948. A quarrel that might have been purely local had thus turned into a major issue affecting the peace of the whole region – and of the world.

This conflict has at every stage presented profound challenges to Jews, Muslims and Christians, to which they have responded in a variety of different ways.

A test for Judaism

While the vast majority of Jews throughout the world welcomed the establishment of the state of Israel, some have been very critical of its policies in recent years, and a small minority believe that the very existence of the state represents a betrayal of the traditional values of Judaism. A recent book, *Jewish Fundamentalism in Israel* by Israel Shahak and Norton Mezvinsky, describes the major divisions over religious issues among Israeli Jews:

■ Approximately 25–30 per cent of Israeli Jews are *non-religious* or *secular*, having little to do with the synagogue and little respect for religious institutions.

■ Around 50–55 per cent are *traditional* Jews, who keep some of the more important commandments and ignore others.

■ The remaining 20 per cent are *religious* Jews who faithfully observe the commandments of their religion. They can be divided into two quite distinct groups: (a) the *Haredi*, who are sometimes known as pre-modern, Orthodox or Ultraconservative, are estimated to be around 13 per cent, and have been strongly opposed to the establishment of the secular Jewish state; (b) the Modern Orthodox or National Religious constitute around 7% and could be described as 'fundamentalist'. They strongly assert Jewish claims to the whole land, and some of them look forward to the day when the Dome of the Rock and the Al-Aqsa Mosque will be destroyed and a Jewish temple built in their place.

Secular governments in recent years have not always been able to restrain the settlers on the West Bank, many of whom are motivated by religious beliefs. A significant rift exists between Jews who are sympathetic to Jewish fundamentalism and those who are not. Jews throughout the world are deeply divided in their reactions to the policies of recent Israeli governments, and some observers believe that these policies have contributed to the recent rise in anti-Semitism in Europe.

A provocation to Islam

When Islam extended its rule across North Africa and the Middle East from the seventh century, Jews and Christians were accepted as protected communities paying a special tax and allowed to practise their religion. They suffered from time to time from the whims of individual rulers and the passions of discontented mobs, and in the course of about three centuries many converted to the religion of their conquerors.

The establishment of the Jewish state in 1948 profoundly altered the situation for both Jews and Muslims. The Jews, who for centuries had been powerless minorities living under Islamic rule, had now created a Jewish state in the heartlands of Islam. The Palestinians, however, most of whom were Muslims, were thrown into confusion, unable to destroy the new state (as they attempted to do in 1948) or to establish their own Palestinian state (as they could have done in accordance with the UN Partition Plan).

The very existence of Israel has therefore been seen by many Palestinians, Arabs and Muslims as a kind of cancerous growth or as an organ transplant that is rejected by the host community. While most Palestinians, however, now accept the existence of the state of Israel, others hope that just as the invading Crusaders were ultimately driven out, so before long a modern-day Saladin will rally the Arabs and destroy Israel. When they feel let down by their own leaders, the Arab world, the United Nations and the West, some turn to Islamic concepts of Holy War (*jihad*) and martyrdom (*istishhad*) for motivation in continuing the struggle against the Zionists.

The fundamentalist fervour of the Jewish settlers on the West Bank has inevitably stimulated a similar Islamic fundamentalism, while the more secular approach of Yasser Arafat (b. 1929) and the Palestinian Authority has failed to produce enough political gains to win the support of ordinary Palestinians. Many of these issues are focused on the question of sovereignty over the Temple Mount in Jerusalem, which came under Israeli authority during the Six Day War in 1967. Quite apart from issues of human rights and international law, Muslims all over the world find it intolerable that the Dome of the Rock (their third most sacred site after Mecca and Medina) and the Al-Aqsa Mosque should be under Jewish rule. They hope that any final settlement will enable the creation of a meaningful and viable Palestinian state which has sovereignty at least over East Jerusalem.

Offra, the first Jewish settlement in occupied territory, on the West Bank.

A dilemma for Christians

Most Christians recognize that their attitudes to the conflict must be based not only on historical and political considerations but on the person of Jesus of Nazareth, who died and was raised from death in Jerusalem. They therefore tend to have very mixed feelings about the Crusaders' violent attempts to win the holy places back from Islamic rule.

Less than 2 per cent of the total Palestinian community in Israel and the West Bank are Christians, and the vast majority identify strongly with Palestinian nationalism. In recent years, however, they have challenged its more Islamist expressions, and have felt caught in the middle between extremist Muslims on the one hand and extremist Jews on the other. A further problem for them is that while many Jews and Muslims base their claims to Jerusalem on scripture and tradition, Christians do not feel they can use the same kind of religious arguments that Jews and Muslims use to justify their attachment to the city.

These problems for Christians in Israel/Palestine are compounded by the influence of Christian Zionism in

the West, especially in the USA. Between 25 and 50 million fundamentalist Christians there believe that the Jews have a divine right to the land and that the establishment of Israel is an important sign pointing to the imminence of the Second Coming of Christ. They are therefore strongly supportive not only of the state of Israel but also of the policies of recent right-wing governments, and add to the weight of the Jewish lobby in influencing American government policy. The Middle East Council of Churches, which represents the majority of Christians in the Middle East, has repeatedly distanced itself forcefully from the views of Christian Zionists.

In 1994 the leaders of the historic churches issued a Memorandum entitled 'Significance of Jerusalem for Christians', which concluded: 'Jerusalem is a symbol and a promise of the presence of God, of fraternity and peace for humankind, in particular, the children of Abraham: Jews, Christians and Muslims... We invite each party to go beyond all exclusivist visions or actions, and... to give back to Jerusalem its true universal character and to make of the city a holy place of reconciliation for humankind.'

Facing the future together

The test therefore for Jews, Muslims and Christians at the present time is

whether, in asserting their own different visions of 'the Holy Land' and 'the Holy City', they can allow each other to hold their visions, and whether they can encourage political leaders both inside and outside Israel/Palestine to reach a negotiated agreement which enables all the different communities to share the one land to which they all lay claim.

Judaism in the Modern World

LIZ RAMSEY

Jewish communities can be found in most parts of the modern world. This means there are great cultural and social variations as well as religious diversity within Judaism. Out of a worldwide total of around 13 million Jews the largest groupings live in Israel (5,000,000 or 78.7 per cent of local population) and the USA (5,700,000 or 2.1 per cent of local population). Although Jews account for no more than 0.25 per cent of the world's present population, it would be hard to find another group of people who have had so much influence on the world in so many ways over such a long time. There is little sign of this influence lessening in spite of the challenges facing Jewish survival. In the context of the technological and scientific developments of the modern age, Jewish knowledge and expertise have a high profile, from medicine and genetic engineering to art and architecture. Jews are also prominent in the worlds of entertainment, law and politics. It is amazing how influence on this scale has been

Theodor Herzl, writer and Zionist politician.

maintained despite the appalling loss of people and centres of learning that took place between 1933 and 1945 (see 'Judaism: The Holocaust').

Who is a Jew?

This question is hotly debated within contemporary Judaism. The Orthodox insistence that a Jew must be born of a Jewish mother (or convert according to Orthodox criteria) is largely disregarded by Reform Jews, but can lead to painful situations concerning identity and status for partners and children. The Reform view is that a person is a Jew if one parent is Jewish. Moreover, conversion to Reform Judaism is a much simpler process. However, the term 'Judaism' does not only refer to a religion. Over one half of all Jews in Israel today call themselves 'secular'. One half of all Jews in the USA do not belong to a synagogue or a temple. Jews are better described as a 'nation' or a 'people'.

The land of Israel

Since its establishment in 1948, the state of Israel has been the focus of the Jewish world. In this tiny strip of land, only twelve miles wide in places, Jews from over a hundred cultures mingle. All Jews, inside or outside Israel, feel an obligation to assess their relationship with it. Within Israel there are serious tensions between 'secular', Orthodox and Ultra-Orthodox Jews concerning their attitudes to it.

There are groups of Orthodox Jews who do not support the existence of a Jewish state at all. They consider the militarism involved in preserving the state to be a contradiction of fundamental Jewish values.

● The Zionist movement, dating back to Theodor Herzl (1860–1904), includes many supporters who prioritize the preservation of the Jewish people over the preservation of the Jewish religion. Herzl's dream was

Jewish population figures by continent in 2004

Continent	Jewish Population
Africa	87,900
Asia	5,047,300
Europe	1,577,000
North America	6,114,500
South America	365,500
Oceania	103,000
Total	13,295,200

simply to establish a Jewish homeland after centuries of exile.

● A common Israeli view, shared by Jews outside, is that Israel needs to be strong in order to provide a safe haven for Jews all over the world, to provide a feeling of security and, perhaps even more importantly, hope for the future.

● A group such as Gush Emunim (Bloc of the Faithful) represents a very small minority. This fundamentalist group, founded in 1974 in the wake of the Yom Kippur War, claims a divine right to the settlement of the West Bank, the Gaza Strip and the Golan Heights (and sometimes as far as the Euphrates), as part of Israel. The majority of Israelis reject such views.

Jewish religious life

Religious Jews pray and study Torah. They observe the dietary laws, keep the Sabbath and the festivals, and try to apply Jewish ethics in a global context of commerce and business. Jews are keen to observe the religious regulations that emphasize the importance of the family and marriage. They are also aware of the responsibilities involved in being members of a community that is international as well as local, including praying together, providing welfare support, sharing in times of sadness and joy and becoming involved in the cycle of rituals and festivals. In so doing, the religious Jew receives a glimpse of what heaven on earth might be like.

The rabbinic tradition largely bonded the Jewish people from the first century CE onwards. Now there are more Jews studying in the rabbinical seminaries than at any time since the great Babylonian academies. But following the rabbinic tradition is only one way of being Jewish.

Committed Jews remain faithful because the continuing story of Judaism depends on such commitment. Traditionally, Jews have shared a strong sense that there is a divine purpose for humanity and that they have a special role in achieving it. The covenantal relationship between the Creator and creation described in the Torah, means that together God and human beings may embark on the task of *tikkun olam* ('repairing' or 'mending the world').

Jews and Judaism have shown an amazing capacity to adapt to changing times and circumstances while preserving the vital traditions central to the faith. This capacity is closely linked to a strong emphasis on interpretation as well as revelation. For many Jews do not view revelation solely as something that happened once and for all in the distant past. There are different layers of meaning of Torah that have to be rediscovered and interpreted in the light of contemporary contexts and needs.

At the core of Jewish life is an immense store of moral energy. Statistics demonstrate that 'social justice' is much the highest scoring factor that Jews (in the USA) give as relevant to what being Jewish involves. The restless drive to 'perfect the world under the sovereignty of God' remains long after other practices have been abandoned. Judaism puts a high value on the dignity and responsibility of human beings. It is this emphasis that can provide the stimulus for creative dialogue and shared action between Jews, Muslims and Christians with regard to the responsible stewardship and management of the world's resources. There may never be more than an agreement to differ as far as theological issues are concerned. However there is much common ground to be worked.

Diversity within modern Judaism

The Jewish world reflects the pluralistic nature of the wider society in which Jews live. All Jews, along with members of all religious denominations today,

'Lo alecha ha-mamlacha ligmor,' *says the Mishna. 'It is not incumbent on you to complete the work (of repairing the world), but neither are you free to evade it.'*

Avot 2:16

JUDAISM IN THE MODERN WORLD

contend with conflicting influences. One option is to cut off as far as possible from modern influences and seek refuge in tradition. Another is to abandon Judaism. The path that young Jews are increasingly choosing goes beyond the fractiousness between and within different groups with regard to authority, Torah, the role of women, modernity and cultural change and the state of Israel, and seeks to transform Judaism.

These differences of opinion and lifestyle date from the Jewish enlightenment (or *Haskalah*) and the figure of Moses Mendelssohn (1729–86), a primary influence on the radical reinterpretation of Judaism in the light of general knowledge and secular learning. Judaism was transformed by the *Haskalah* from a placing of Torah study at the centre of learning to a valuing of Torah study in addition to a major focus upon secular learning. It is still possible to distinguish groupings within Judaism today by their position on the continuum of Torah study/secular learning.

It is a mistake to define modern movements within Judaism as if they were sects, or even denominations. Judaism is not like that. It is more accurate to use the term 'schools of thought'. There is a saying among Jews that is often quoted, 'Where you have two Jews you will have three opinions.'

THE REFORM MOVEMENT
Many Jews claim that the Reform movement is now the most creative component within Judaism. Young Jews no longer feel their Judaism is defined by suffering and persecution. They are exploring the boundaries of cultural experience and convey a sense of expectancy with regard to a new age of Judaism.

CONSERVATIVE JUDAISM
Conservative Judaism has roots in Orthodoxy and in Reform and

combines the ideals of both. It preserves traditional Jewish practices but generally takes the view that Jewish law can, and should, be reinterpreted in the light of modern views and trends. The findings of modern historical criticism are accepted. Conservative Judaism is possibly the largest single Jewish grouping in north America. In Israel and Britain, where it has been a more recent development, it is known by its Hebrew name, *Masorti*.

ORTHODOX JUDAISM
Few would accept the divine authority of the Torah these days, the old test of 'Orthodoxy'. Indeed, it is not

Israeli flags fly near the Western Wall of the Temple Mount in Jerusalem.

uncommon for Jews to belong both to Orthodox and Progressive or Liberal synagogues. The term 'Orthodox' was initially used as a label for traditionalists who opposed radical change. Now there are many shades of Orthodoxy as the energy inspired by the Reform movement influences most Jewish groupings.

ULTRA-ORTHODOX JUDAISM

The Ultra-Orthodox Jew can symbolize the total separation of Judaism from the modern world. Yet the spiritual ideas rooted in mysticism, such as *tikkun olam*, kept alive by ultra-orthodoxy, now provide

inspiration for the social and political agenda of Reform. So the Ultra-Orthodox can be said to provide the 'spiritual dynamo' that will ensure Judaism's survival.

RECONSTRUCTIONIST JUDAISM

Reconstructionist Judaism is theoretically an outgrowth of conservative Judaism, and is based on the work of the scholar Mordecai Kaplan. However, the twenty-first century is seeing a realignment of trends and ideas within Judaism and the old 'containers' are becoming outmoded and inadequate. Reconstructionist Judaism certainly

> 'To be a Jew means first belonging to the group... Judaism is an evolving religious civilization.'
>
> Mordecai Kaplan

does not fit neatly into the traditional/liberal, observant/non observant continuum. Although there are few organized groups outside the USA and Israel, Reconstructionist Judaism has had a considerable influence upon Judaism generally. It has contributed to a reappraisal of such fundamental concepts as God, Israel and Torah. Since its inception in the late 1960s, it has been a leading influence in the developing use of inclusive language and has encouraged women to be fully involved in liturgical practice. People with one Jewish parent have been accepted as Jewish. Reconstructionists are actively involved in developing liberal Judaism in Israel.

HUMANISTIC JEWS

Humanistic Judaism can be traced back to 1965. Nowadays the principal organ of Humanistic Judaism is the International Federation of Secular Humanistic Jews. Many of the beliefs within traditional Judaism are rejected or reinterpreted. For example, the movement denies supernatural beliefs and treats the Exodus from Egypt as a myth. Consequently, Humanistic Jewish worship is quite different from traditional worship. It often does not, for example, include the word 'God'. Again, unlike traditional Judaism, they 'welcome into the Jewish people all men and women who sincerely desire to share Jewish experience regardless of their ancestry.

The Future

The continuity of Judaism cannot be taken for granted. People are freer to be Jews than at any other time in history. They are also freer not to be. There is real concern about the continuation of the Jewish faith when statistics (in the USA) suggest that one in two Jews either does not marry or marries out of Judaism. The long and painful history of anti-Semitism has understandably made some people

uncertain about wanting their children to be overtly Jewish. There are examples of people changing their name in order to hide their Jewishness. A new generation of Jews is expressing a desire to be free of the burden of memory that has traditionally been the hallmark of being Jewish. In complex, pluralist and multicultural societies, some argue that Jewish identity has become superfluous. However, Jews and Judaism have an incredible capacity to survive.

There is also today a greater confidence in the continuation of the story that is Judaism than there has been since the Holocaust. Jewish people have managed to outlive a succession of oppressors. At the same time, they have successfully increased the depth and richness of Jewish spirituality. More non-Jews find inspiration from the study of Judaism than ever before, as it has become a feature of the curriculum in institutions of higher learning. The people of Israel will flourish as long as they can retain their sense of peoplehood, their humour in the face of adversity and, above all, hope.

With rising levels of anti-Semitism across the world, the need for education and dialogue is acute. Never has it been more important for Judaism, Christianity and Islam to listen to one another and to hear one another's pain. Contrary to many people's perceptions, Judaism combines universalism with the exclusivity of an ethnic religion. Jewish ideas of salvation extend to the non-Jewish world. Neither Christianity nor Islam would be conceivable without Judaism. Since the Holocaust, many Christians have begun a more positive exploration of their Jewish roots. The monotheistic religions share a distinctive ethical focus that can inspire greater efforts on the part of human beings to work together to perfect the world.

Christianity

A Historical Overview

ALISTER McGRATH

Christianity rapidly spread beyond its original geographical region of Roman-occupied Palestine into the entire Mediterranean area. Something of this process of expansion is described in the Acts of the Apostles (in the New Testament). For example, it is clear that a Christian presence was already established in Rome itself within fifteen years of the resurrection of Christ. The imperial trade routes made possible the rapid traffic of ideas, as much as merchandise.

The early church
Three centres of the Christian church rapidly emerged in the eastern Mediterranean region. The church became a significant presence in its own original heartlands, with Jerusalem emerging as a leading centre of thought and activity. Asia Minor (modern-day Turkey) was already an important area of Christian expansion, as can be seen from the destinations of some of Paul's letters, and the references to the 'seven churches of Asia' in the book of Revelation. This process of expansion

in this region continued, with the great imperial city of Constantinople (modern-day Istanbul) becoming a particularly influential centre of mission and political consolidation.

Yet further growth took place to the south, with the important Egyptian city of Alexandria emerging as a stronghold of Christian faith. With this expansion, new debates opened up. While the New Testament deals with the issue of the relationship of Christianity and Judaism, the expansion of Christianity into Greek-speaking regions led to the exploration of the way in which Christianity related to Greek philosophy. Many Christian writers sought to demonstrate, for example, that Christianity brought to fulfilment the great themes of the philosophy of Plato.

Yet this expansion was far from unproblematic. The 'imperial cult', which regarded worship of the Roman emperor as determinative of loyalty to the empire, was prominent in the eastern Mediterranean region. Many Christians found themselves penalized as a result of their insistence on worshipping *only* Christ. The expansion of Christianity regularly triggered off persecutions. These were often local – for example, the Decian persecution of 249–51, which was particularly vicious in North Africa. Christianity was not given official recognition as a 'legitimate religion'

St Peter's Basilica in Rome is probably the most famous church in the world and is at the heart of Roman Catholicism.

by the Roman state until 313 (when Constantine, a recent convert, was joint emperor). From that point onwards, Christianity became not merely a recognized faith, but the official religion of the Roman state.

This period of Christian history was marked by a series of controversies over the identity of Jesus Christ and the Christian doctrine of God. A series of councils was convened to resolve these differences, and to ensure the unity of the Christian church throughout the empire. The most important of these was the Council of Chalcedon (451),

which set out the definitive Christian interpretation of the biblical witness to the identity of Jesus Christ as 'true God and true man'.

The fall of the Roman empire – traditionally dated to 476 – led to widespread insecurity within the Western church. In the East the church continued to flourish, as the Eastern empire, based at Constantinople, was largely unaffected by the attacks from northern European invaders which eventually ended Roman power in the West. The removal of Rome as a stabilizing influence, however, gave a new role to the church in the West, and particularly its monasteries. The founding of the first Benedictine monastery at Monte Cassino around 525 is widely seen as a landmark in this process. The increasingly important role of the pope as a political force also began to emerge during this period.

The major disruptions within the Roman empire in the fifth century led to a growing rift between the Western and Eastern churches. Increasing tension over political as much as theological issues led to the 'Great Schism' of 1054. By this stage, the influence of the Eastern church had extended as far north as Moscow. While the story of Christianity in Eastern Europe at this time is important, most attention focuses on developments in the Western church.

The Middle Ages and Renaissance

Christianity underwent a major renaissance in Western Europe during the period 1000–1500. This era (often referred to as the 'Middle Ages') saw the renewal of church life at every level. It was a period of consolidation of the political and social influence of the church, with the personal authority of the pope to intervene in political disputes of the region reaching unprecedented levels. The form of theology known as 'scholasticism' began to develop around this time, with thirteenth-century writers such as Thomas Aquinas and Duns Scotus achieving new levels of theological sophistication.

Yet scholasticism was not universally acclaimed. The European Renaissance, which began to become a major

Martin Luther nailing his 95 Theses to the door of the castle church in Wittenburg in 1517. Painting by Hugo Vogel (1855–1934).

cultural force in Western Europe during the fourteenth century, emphasized the importance of returning to the roots of Christendom through the simple language and imagery of the New Testament. The humanist movement, linked with the Renaissance, believed that it was essential to study the Bible in its original languages, rather than in unreliable Latin translations, such as the Vulgate. This created irresistible pressure for new Bible translations. Yet it became clear that some medieval theological ideas were ultimately based

on translation mistakes in the Vulgate. It became clear that some form of review of teachings would be necessary, in the light of the new biblical scholarship.

The rise of Islam in the seventh century had a significant impact on Christianity in North Africa and Palestine. However, its influence seemed poised to reach new levels in 1453, when Islamic armies finally managed to take Constantinople. This city was widely seen as the gate to Europe. By the early sixteenth century, Islam had become a significant presence in the Balkans, and was poised to enter Austria. Martin Luther (1483–1546) believed that it was only a matter of time before Europe became an Islamic sphere of influence. In the event, a series of decisive military defeats limited this influence to the Balkans. By this stage, however, western Europe was being convulsed by new controversies, as the movement we know as 'the Reformation' gained momentum.

The age of Reformation

The sixteenth century gave rise to a major upheaval within Western Christianity, usually referred to as the 'Reformation'. This movement had its origins in the Renaissance, especially its demand to return to the 'original sources' of Christianity in the New Testament. Alarmed at what they perceived to be a growing disparity between apostolic and medieval visions of Christianity, individuals such as Martin Luther and Huldrych Zwingli (1484–1531) pressed for reform. For Zwingli it was the morals and institutions of the church that required reform. Luther, however, judged that a deeper level of reform was required. The teachings of the church had been either distorted or inflated during the Middle Ages and needed to be brought back into line with Scripture. For Luther the whole question of how we enter into a right relationship with God (technically referred to as the 'doctrine of justification') needed radical revision in the light of the biblical witness.

Although the need for reform was widely conceded within the church, such reforming agendas proved intensely controversial. In the end, both Luther and Zwingli found themselves creating reforming communities outside the mainline church, instead of reforming that church from within as they had hoped. By the time of John Calvin

such as Luther found objectionable were eliminated. Nevertheless, significant differences remained between Protestantism and Catholicism. In many ways, the Reformation debates defined the contours of modern Christianity, and many remain live to this day.

The modern period

A period of political uncertainty developed during the eighteenth century, with major implications for

The Arrival of the Pilgrim Fathers in America, c.1864, by Antonio Gisbert (1835–1901).

(1509–64) and his reformation of the city of Geneva, Protestantism had emerged as a distinct type of Christianity in its own right, posing a very significant threat to the Catholic Church.

In the late 1540s the Catholic Church itself began a major process of reformation and renewal, often referred to as the 'Catholic Reformation', sometimes as the 'Counter-Reformation'. The religious orders were reformed, and many of the beliefs and practices which reformers

the future of Christianity in the West. Growing hostility towards the church in France was one of the contributing causes to the French Revolution of 1789, which saw Christianity publicly displaced from French society. Although the French Revolution did not achieve the permanent removal of Christianity from the nation, it created an atmosphere of instability. Revolutionary movements throughout Europe sought to repeat the successes of their French counterparts, creating serious difficulties for the Catholic Church in

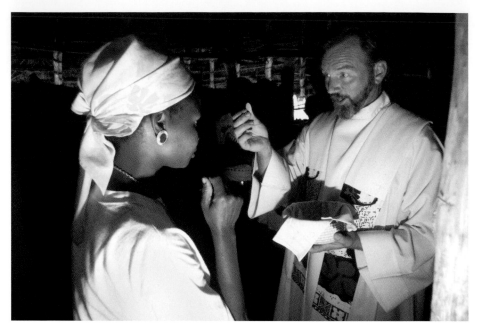

The celebration of Mass in Mugume, Tanzania.

many parts of Europe, especially Italy.

Christianity also faced new challenges in the West. During the 1840s, the German philosopher Ludwig Feuerbach (1804–72) argued that the idea of God was simply a projection of the human mind. Karl Marx (1818–83) declared that God was invented by people to console themselves in the face of social and economic hardship: all that was necessary for the elimination of religious belief of any kind was the radical alteration of the social conditions which brought it into being in the first place. Sigmund Freud (1856–1939) argued that religion was simply an illusion, a 'wish-fulfilment'. By about 1920, many had concluded that Christianity was intellectually untenable.

By then, other difficulties had arisen. Perhaps the most important of these was the Russian Revolution of 1917, which led to the establishment of the world's first explicitly atheist state. The Soviet Union actively sought to eliminate religion from public and private life, especially during the 1930s. The Allied defeat of Nazi Germany in World War II led to large areas of Eastern Europe coming under

Soviet influence and the state adoption of explicitly anti-religious policies. With the fall of the Berlin wall in 1989, a new openness towards religion developed throughout the former Soviet sphere of influence, with Christianity (especially in its Orthodox forms) and Islam experiencing a major renaissance. Yet by this stage, as we shall see, the epicentre of Christianity had moved away from this region altogether.

Worldwide expansion

The sixteenth century saw the beginnings of a process which would have a decisive impact on the shaping of Christianity. During the Middle Ages, Christianity was primarily a European religion. Although it was present in parts of India and the Middle East, its numerical strength was heavily concentrated in Europe. The discovery of the Americas opened up new mission fields and led to a new interest in spreading the gospel abroad. The Society of Jesus (the Jesuits), founded by Ignatius Loyola in 1540, took the lead within the Catholic Church and sent missionaries to the Americas, India, China and Japan. (See 'Contemporary

Christianity in the Non-Western World'.)

Protestant missionary activity was later in developing. There was a surge of missionary activity from England during the closing years of the eighteenth century. The Baptist Missionary Society (founded in 1792 and initially known as 'The Particular Baptist Society for the Propagation of the Gospel'), the London Missionary Society (founded in 1795 and initially known as 'The Missionary Society') and the Church Missionary Society (founded in 1799 and originally known as 'The Church Missionary Society for Africa and the East') all played a major role in planting Christianity in Africa, India and Oceania. American missionary societies also played important roles in establishing Christianity in various regions of the world, especially Korea.

Yet Christianity expanded by other means. One of the most important was large-scale emigration from Europe to North America, beginning in the late sixteenth century. Initially, the immigrants were primarily Protestant refugees from England; however, these were later joined by Lutherans from Scandinavia, Anabaptists from Germany, Calvinists from Holland and Catholics from Ireland and Italy.

Today, Christianity is primarily a faith of the developing, rather than developed world. Although European and American missionaries played a significant role in planting Christianity in regions such as Asia and Africa, these are now largely self-sufficient. The implications of this massive shift from the West to the developing world have yet to be fully explored. It is nevertheless clear that a new phase in the history of the Christian church has begun, with momentous implications for the future.

Jesus

RICHARD FRANCE

Christianity is founded on the worship of Jesus Christ ('Jesus the messiah') as Son of God, the unique self-revelation of God to the human race. At the same time it remembers this same Jesus as a real historical figure, a man of insignificant social standing who during his life was unknown outside the obscure corner of the Roman empire where he lived and died.

Almost all we know about Jesus comes from the four accounts of his life (Gospels) which we find in the New Testament. The account that follows is based on those Gospels. Although scholars disagree at some points about the historical value of the Gospel records, the following general picture is widely agreed.

Looking for liberation

Born just before the death of Herod the Great, king of Judea, in 4 BCE, Jesus lived for a little over thirty years, scarcely travelling outside Palestine throughout his life.

The Jews were a subject people, living either under local princes appointed by the Roman emperor or under the direct rule of Rome itself. A priestly party, the Sadducees, accepted Roman rule, to which they owed their influence. The Pharisees, who later became the dominant party, were mostly less concerned with politics, and concentrated on the study and application of the Old Testament Law. Some stricter Jews, Essenes, opted out of Jewish society and set up isolated communities – such as Qumran – where they could devote themselves to preserving their religious purity. But there were many Jews who resented Roman rule, and from time to time revolts broke out leading eventually to the disastrous Jewish War of CE 66–73.

The Jews had long hoped for 'the day of the Lord', when God would act to save his people. There were several different hopes of a 'messiah', a saviour, whom God would send, and such hopes ran high at the time of Jesus. Some saw the messiah in more spiritual terms, as a priestly or prophetic figure, but in popular expectation he was to be a political liberator, and there were occasional messianic movements centred on popular leaders. Galilee was known as fertile ground for such movements.

Jesus was born at Bethlehem in Judea, but was brought up in Galilee and most of his public activity was in that region. Judean Jews regarded Galilee as an uncultured, half-pagan area: Jesus' distinct northern accent would have been conspicuous in Jerusalem.

His family was respectable, if not affluent: he was a carpenter, or general builder, an important figure in village life. But Nazareth was an obscure village, and Jesus' background was remote from urban culture.

The Beatitudes

'Happy are those who know they are spiritually poor;
the Kingdom of heaven belongs to them!

Happy are those who mourn;
God will comfort them!

Happy are those who are humble;
they will receive what God has promised!

Happy are those whose greatest desire is to do what God requires;
God will satisfy them fully!

Happy are those who are merciful to others;
God will be merciful to them!

Happy are the pure in heart;
they will see God!

Happy are those who work for peace;
God will call them his children!

Happy are those who are persecuted because they do what God requires;
the Kingdom of heaven belongs to them!

Happy are you when people insult you and persecute you and tell all kinds of
evil lies against you because you are my followers.

Be happy and glad, for a great reward is kept for you in heaven.
This is how the prophets who lived before you were persecuted.'

From Jesus' Sermon on the Mount in Matthew's Gospel

The birth and early life of Jesus

Despite its provincial obscurity, Jesus' family had an honourable pedigree. So his birth took place in King David's town of Bethlehem. Owing to the overcrowding of the town for the Roman census, however, the circumstances were not very regal; Luke's account of the baby, cradled in a manger in a stable, visited by shepherds, has become one of the best-known stories in the world.

But, along with the very down-to-earth circumstances of his birth, the Christian Gospels record that it was far from ordinary. Angels proclaimed him the promised saviour, and it was maintained that he was not conceived by human intercourse, but by the power of God. This bringing together of earthly poverty and obscurity with a miraculous birth is typical of the Gospels' portrait of Jesus, as truly human but also uniquely the Son of God.

Virtually nothing is known of Jesus' life from his infancy until about the age of thirty. He clearly received a sound education in the Old Testament scriptures, presumably in the local synagogue school. However, his upbringing was not in academic studies, but in the practical work of a carpenter. The event which launched Jesus on his public ministry was the mission of his relative, John 'the Baptist', down in Judea. John called Israel to return to God, and baptized those who responded in the River Jordan. He attracted a large following, and Jesus joined him, was baptized, and himself began preaching. When John was put in prison, Jesus moved back to Galilee, and continued to preach in public.

Healing and preaching

The Gospels summarize Jesus' activity as preaching, teaching and healing, and that is how he would have appeared to his contemporaries during the three years or so of his public ministry.

He and his closest followers

deliberately adopted a wandering and dependent style of life. They had no permanent home, but moved around as a group, accepting gifts and hospitality when offered. Jesus spoke frequently of the danger of becoming preoccupied with possessions, and called his followers instead to an almost reckless generosity.

As a preacher he drew large crowds, who followed him constantly. He taught with a vivid simplicity and an authority which contrasted sharply with other Jewish religious teachers. We shall consider the content of his preaching later.

Jesus was clearly well known as a healer from the beginning of his public activity. The Gospels record his curing many different types of illness and deformity, usually by a simple word and a touch, sometimes by a word alone. There is no elaborate ritual, nor any search for patients; rather a power which responded to physical need as he met it. He is also recorded as an exorcist, driving out demons by a word of command. It was apparently as much for his healing power as for his teaching that he was sought out by the Galilean crowds.

Most of Jesus' recorded miracles are healings, but a number of incidents are recorded where he displayed a supernatural control over nature. Again these were in response to actual needs, not mere arbitrary displays of power, as when he multiplied a little food to feed a hungry crowd, or calmed a dangerous storm on the lake by a command. The Gospels present him as one who did not go out of his way to gain a reputation as a miracle-worker, but whose personal authority extended beyond his words to a practical control over nature which inevitably made a deep impression on those around him.

Like many other Jewish teachers Jesus quickly gathered a group of committed followers, known as his 'disciples'. He demanded of them an absolute commitment to the ideals he preached, and to himself personally, and a total dependence on God to supply all their needs. They acted as his spokesmen, going out on preaching and healing missions of their own. An inner group of twelve disciples were his constant companions. An increasing amount of time was spent in teaching his disciples privately, preparing them to

'The Healing of the Paralytic', from *The Golden Gospel Book* of Henry III, c.1050.

continue his mission. He told them that he would soon be killed, and expected them to be the focus of the new community created by his work. He taught them to see themselves as distinct from other people, and to make it their aim to win others to be his disciples.

Opposition

While Jesus was, at least at first, popular with the ordinary people of Galilee, he very quickly aroused the opposition of the leaders. His attitude was in many respects unconventional, and he posed a threat to the Jewish religious establishment.

He refused to recognize the barriers which divided people from one another in society. His habit of mixing with the ostracized classes, and even of eating with them, earned him the name of 'friend of tax-collectors and sinners'. Women held an unconventionally high place in his following, and not all of them were very respectable. He seemed to delight in reversing accepted standards, with his slogan: 'The first shall be last, and the last first.'

He did not share the general Jewish disdain for Samaritans – a despised minority of mixed blood. He even made a Samaritan the hero of one of his most famous stories, at the expense of respectable Jewish clerics. Although he seldom travelled outside Jewish territory, he welcomed the faith of a non-Jewish soldier and a Syrian woman, and declared that non-Jews, the Gentiles, would even displace Jews in the kingdom of God. As for economic barriers, Jesus deliberately gave up a secure livelihood, and made no secret of his contempt for affluence. It is no wonder that the establishment found him uncomfortable.

On religious questions he was equally radical. He clashed with the religious authorities because of his free attitude to the observance of the Sabbath, the day of rest, and his declaration that ritual purification mattered less than purity of heart. His bold reinterpretation of the Old Testament Law moved consistently away from an external keeping of rules to a deeper and more demanding ethic. He declared the will of God with a sovereign assurance which cut through centuries of evolving tradition, and set him on a collision course with the scribes and Pharisees whose heartless legalism he denounced.

Nor could he please the Sadducees, the priestly rulers. He taught that the Jewish nation was ripe for God's judgment, and predicted even the destruction of the Temple on which their national religion was centred. In a symbolic gesture he 'purified' the Temple by violently expelling the traders whose presence the priests encouraged. Moreover his enthusiastic popular following threatened to upset the delicate balance of their cooperation with Rome. All this, we may be sure, did not diminish Jesus' popularity with the ordinary people, who soon came to see him as the expected deliverer, and even on one occasion tried to force him to be their king in rebellion against Rome. But Jesus made it clear that his idea of salvation was not a political one. So gradually his popular following dwindled, as those who wanted a military messiah became disillusioned. Even one of his twelve closest disciples betrayed him in the end, and none of them understood his real purpose until after his death.

Death and resurrection

The opposition to Jesus came to its climax at the Passover festival in Jerusalem. Jesus rode into the city in a deliberately messianic gesture – though on a peaceable donkey, not a war-horse – and was enthusiastically welcomed by the crowds, who probably expected him now to declare himself their national leader. Instead he carried out his demonstration against the temple regime, and engaged in a series of increasingly bitter exchanges with the religious authorities; but he showed no

"'I'm ready to accept Jesus as a great moral teacher, but I don't accept his claim to be God.' That is the one thing we must not say. A man who was merely a man and said the sort of things Jesus said would not be a great moral teacher. He would either be a lunatic – on a level with the man who says he is a poached egg – or else he would be the Devil of Hell. You must make your choice. Either this man was, and is, the Son of God; or else a madman or something worse. You can shut him up for a fool, you can spit at him and kill him as a demon, or you can fall at his feet and call him Lord and God. But let us not come with any patronizing nonsense about his being a great human teacher. He has not left that open to us. He did not intend to.'

C.S. Lewis

sign of acting against Rome.

Eventually he was arrested by the Jewish leaders with the help of Judas, his disillusioned disciple, and was tried according to Jewish law on a charge of blasphemy, because he claimed to be the messiah and the Son of God. A death sentence was passed, but a Roman conviction was required to make it effective. This was secured by a charge of sedition, pressed upon the Roman governor by the religious leaders with a show of popular support. So, ironically, the Jesus who had

Christ on the Cross by Diego Rodriguez de Silva y Velazquez, 1632.

forfeited his popular following by his refusal to take up arms against Rome was executed by Rome as a political rebel, 'the king of the Jews'.

He was executed by crucifixion, the barbaric method reserved by Rome for slaves and rebels. Some highly placed followers obtained his body and buried it in a nearby tomb.

The cross has rightly become the symbol of Christianity. In that death, with all its cruelty and injustice, is the focus of salvation, and Jesus had already taught his disciples to see it that way, little as they had yet understood him. But the cross alone could have no such significance. It was the sequel that gave it meaning.

Two days later his disciples found the tomb was empty. Their failure to understand this is not surprising – there was much about Jesus they had not understood. But the meaning of it was brought home to them by a series of encounters with Jesus himself alive and real, though no longer bound by the limitations of time and space (he could appear and disappear suddenly even inside a closed room).

For a few weeks they met him in a variety of situations, sometimes one or two alone, more often in a larger group. He explained to them again the meaning of his life and death, and the mission he had entrusted to them. Then he left them, and they began to preach to the world that Jesus, triumphant even over death, was Lord and Saviour. It was the resurrection of Jesus which formed the focus of the earliest Christian preaching, it was the risen Lord whom they worshipped.

What Jesus taught

The Gospels sum up Jesus' preaching in Galilee in the challenge: 'The time has come; the kingdom of God is near. Repent and believe the good news!' This summary is a convenient framework for setting out some of the main points of his message.

> *'For God loved the world so much that he gave his only Son, so that everyone who believes in him may not die but have eternal life.'*
>
> John 3:16

> *'The Father and I are one.'*
>
> John 10:30

● 'The time has come': The Old Testament pointed forward to God's great work of judgment and salvation, when all Israel's hopes and the promises of God would be fulfilled. Jesus saw his mission as this time of fulfilment. In other words, however little he shared popular ideas of a political deliverer, he saw himself as the messiah, come to save God's people. He called himself the Son of man, echoing a figure in the Old Testament book of Daniel who represented the ultimate deliverance and triumph of the true people of God.

● 'The kingdom of God is near': The kingdom of God (more accurately the 'reign of God'; it is an activity, not a place or a community) is central in Jesus' teaching. It means that God is in control, that his will is done. So he called people to enter God's kingdom, to accept his sovereignty and to live as his subjects. He taught them to look forward to the day when this kingship of God, already inaugurated by Jesus ('Yours is the kingdom'), would find its fulfilment when everyone acknowledged God as king ('Your kingdom come'), when Jesus himself would return in glory, and share the universal and everlasting dominion of his Father.

● 'Repent': Jesus' call was issued primarily to his own people, Israel. He called them to return to their true loyalty to God. He warned them of God's judgment if they refused. There was an urgency in his appeal, and as it was increasingly rejected he spoke of God calling others to be his people instead. Finally, after his resurrection, he sent his disciples to call all nations into the kingdom of God. God's demands are absolute, and disobedience or disloyalty would not be overlooked.

● 'Believe the good news': Now was the time for deliverance. Jesus preached this not in a political sense, but in terms of the restoration of a true relationship with God. Those who repented would find forgiveness and a new life. And as Jesus predicted his own suffering and death, he saw this as the means of restoration; he was the servant of God whom Isaiah had foretold, 'by whose wounds we are healed'. So he came 'to give his life as a ransom for many', to institute 'the new covenant in my blood', a new people of God redeemed from sin, as Israel had been redeemed from slavery in Egypt, to be God's special people. This was the focus of Jesus' teaching, the call to repentance, to membership of a new people of God, forgiven and restored through his atoning death. His famous ethical teaching takes second place, for it is primarily an ethic for disciples, for those who have thus entered the kingdom of God.

For them life is new. It is focused on God, their king, but also their Father, for Jesus taught his disciples to depend on God with a childlike trust. Their relations with one another were to be those of members of the same family, inspired by an unselfish, uncalculating love. In this new community many of the world's standards would be reversed, and a concern for material security and advancement would be swallowed up in an overriding longing to see God's kingdom established. It is an other-worldly ethic which has profound this-worldly implications. Jesus expected his disciples to be clearly different, the 'light of the world' showing the world what life was meant to be like. They were to be like God their Father.

Who was Jesus?

He was hailed as a prophet, a man sent by God. In his preaching, teaching and healing he matched up to that role, and as such he is one of a long and noble sequence of God's people before and since. But Christians believe, and his own life and teaching suggest, that he was much more than that.

In his appeal to Israel there was a clear note of finality. This was not just another prophetic warning, but God's last call. Its rejection would spell the end of Israel as God's special people; its acceptance would create a new people of God in whom all God's purposes would reach their climax.

The criterion was not only the response to Jesus' message, but the response to Jesus himself. He called for faith in and loyalty to himself, and presented himself as the final arbiter of people's destiny. He not only proclaimed forgiveness and salvation: by his own life and suffering and death he achieved it. He is the messenger but he is also the heart of the message. He calls people to God, but he is also himself the way to God.

During Jesus' earthly life his disciples only dimly understood all this though they understood enough to make them tenaciously loyal to him. But after his resurrection they quickly came to speak of him as more than just a man, and to worship him as they worshipped his Father. And even during his earthly teaching Jesus had prepared the way for this by speaking of himself as the Son of God in a unique sense, and of God as his Father in an exclusive relationship quite different from the sense in which his disciples could use the term. 'All things have been committed to me by my Father. No one knows the Son except the Father, and no one knows the Father except the Son and those to whom the Son chooses to reveal him.' The worship of Jesus the man as the Son of God did not have its origin in some fanciful piety long after his death, but in the impression he made on his disciples during the three years of his ministry. His resurrection deepened that impression and confirmed it. Without in the least doubting his real humanity, they believed that they had been walking with God.

'I am the bread of life. He who comes to me will never be hungry.'

'I am the light of the world. Whoever follows me will have the light of life and will never walk in darkness.'

'I am the gate for the sheep... whoever comes in by me will be saved.'

'I am the good shepherd, who is willing to die for the sheep.'

'I am the resurrection and the life. Whoever believes in me will live, even though he dies; and whoever lives and believes in me will never die.'

'I am the way, the truth and the life; no one goes to the Father except by me.'

'I am the vine, and you are the branches. Whoever remains in me, and I in him, will bear much fruit; for you can do nothing without me.'

Jesus' great statements about himself, from John's Gospel

Branches of the Church

MICHAEL SADGROVE

The New Testament is proof both of the vision that the church should be one, and of the reality that it is not. The history of Christianity since then is, for the most part, a history of fragmentation. Only in the present century have serious attempts been made to seek reconciliation between churches separated by centuries of misunderstanding and mistrust. The various branches of the Christian church owe their existence to three historic crises. The first was the splintering of Eastern Catholic Christendom in the fifth century. The second was the so-called 'Great Schism' between East and West, usually dated at 1054, that resulted in the division between 'Catholic' and 'Orthodox' Christianity. The third was the Reformation in the sixteenth century, which, together with its seventeenth- and eighteenth-century aftermath, left as its legacy Protestantism in its various forms.

This article deals only with the principal branches of the church as they have emerged in the history of Christianity.

The Eastern Churches

These include the Orthodox Churches, together with those that share with them in a spiritual and cultural ethos that derives from the Byzantine empire. The church in the East suffered its most serious divisions following the councils of Ephesus (431) and Chalcedon (451), called to determine the orthodox Christian teaching on the relationship between the deity and the humanity of Christ. The Nestorian Church, centred historically on Persia, and the Monophysite Churches, such as those of Syria, Egypt and Ethiopia, date from this period.

The final separation of the Eastern churches from Western Christendom lay both in their conflict with Rome over the papal claim to supreme authority, and in their rejection of the *Filioque* clause, added by the Western church to the original text of the Nicene Creed, in which the Holy Spirit is said to proceed 'from the Son' as well as the Father. The Orthodox Churches extend across Eastern Europe, the Slav nations and the eastern Mediterranean. The patriarchates of Constantinople, Alexandria, Antioch and Jerusalem are given special honour, but authority belongs to the whole church, whose rich liturgical life and icon-based spirituality is seen as the living embodiment of divine love on earth. It is estimated that there are over 250 million Orthodox Christians today.

The Roman Catholic Church

Numbering around 960 million members, the Roman Catholic Church is the largest single Christian grouping. Roman Catholics (or simply 'Catholics') trace their lineal descent from the Western Catholic Church of the Middle Ages. They acknowledge the primacy and authority of the Supreme Pontiff, the bishop of Rome, who is traditionally regarded as Christ's representative (or 'Vicar') on earth, and the successor of St Peter. When speaking with full authority (ex cathedra) and defining matters of faith or morals, the pope's utterances are regarded as infallible and binding on Catholics.

The Second Vatican Council (1962–65) resulted in far-reaching reforms, including greater emphasis on the role of bishops acting as an episcopal college, more open relationships with non-Catholic churches, and the simplifying of the liturgy. Along with the Orthodox Churches, Roman Catholicism recognizes seven sacraments: baptism, confirmation, marriage, ordination, penance (the sacrament of reconciliation), extreme unction (anointing of the sick), and, at the centre of the sacramental system, the Mass. Especially in developing countries, Roman Catholics are often prominent in supporting the struggles of the oppressed and in the pursuit of justice and peace generally.

The Churches of the Reformation

THE ANGLICAN CHURCH

The Anglican communion is a worldwide family of autonomous churches in communion with the Archbishop of Canterbury, who has presidential status amongst the heads of other Anglican Churches. Largely anglophone, its members number around 80 million. The parent Church of England has its roots both in the Celtic Christianity of the earliest Britons, and in the Roman form of the faith brought to England by Augustine of Canterbury.

The Anglican Church claims to be both Catholic and Reformed. It has adhered to the Catholic threefold ministry of bishops, priests and deacons, but with a conservatively reformed liturgy: *The Book of Common Prayer* of Archbishop Thomas Cranmer (1489–1556) retained many of the texts of the medieval church while recasting them in a clearly Protestant direction. Nowadays, Anglicanism is an inclusive church embracing members of at least three persuasions: Anglo-Catholic, Liberal and Evangelical. For this reason, it is often seen as a 'bridge' church between Protestantism, Roman Catholicism and Orthodoxy.

THE LUTHERAN CHURCHES

These represent the chief Protestant presence in Germany and Scandinavia, as well as being a significant worldwide Christian denomination that speaks through the Lutheran World Federation. Following the teaching of the German reformer Martin Luther (1483–1546), the doctrine of justification by faith is its central tenet, embodied in the Augsburg Confession. Some Lutheran Churches have retained the Catholic threefold ministry, while others are more presbyterian or congregational in government. Like Anglicanism, Lutheranism adopted a conservative attitude to liturgy, although the preaching of the sermon has always been central. Music has always played an important part. Lutherans worldwide number around 66 million.

THE REFORMED CHURCHES

Protestantism in France, Switzerland, the Low Countries and Scotland at the time of the Reformation shared many of the central tenets of Lutheranism, but following the principles of John Calvin (1509–64), applied them in a more thoroughgoing way. The authority of the Bible is paramount and the preaching of the Word central to its liturgy. There are two principal forms of church organization: presbyterian (local churches grouped together under the government of a regional synod of ordained presbyters and lay elders) and congregational (local churches as independent congregations, responsible for their own life and order).

THE FREE CHURCHES

These all derive from the various churches of the Reformation as a result of movements in subsequent centuries.

The Baptist Churches are a worldwide family of independent congregations. They reject the baptism of infants, claiming that baptism is a sign of an adult profession of faith. Worship tends not to follow set liturgical forms. The Southern Baptists of the USA are a particularly influential conservative evangelical grouping. There are around 43 million across the world.

The Methodist Churches originate in the Evangelical Revival of the eighteenth century, and in the preaching of John Wesley (1703–91). Historically indebted to Anglicanism (which Wesley never renounced), congregational hymn-singing is one of its distinctive contributions to the church at large. Social action is emphasized. Methodists are especially strong in the USA. Their worldwide number is around 70 million.

The Society of Friends, or **Quakers**, was founded by George Fox (1624–91). It rejects all liturgical forms (including the sacraments), ecclesiastical structures and definitions of faith. Members meet for silent worship to attend to the 'inner light'. Quakers have a strong commitment to radical involvement in justice and peace issues. They number 300,000 in all.

The Salvation Army was founded by William Booth (1829–1912) as a mission to the poor of London. Now a worldwide movement, it gives equal place to the preaching of the gospel and to social action amongst the needy. Worship is informal and Bible-centred: the sacraments are not observed. Organization is along the lines of the armed forces. There are around 1.1 million Salvationists.

The Pentecostal Churches

(numbering around 38 million, amongst them, the Assemblies of God) date from the early twentieth century. Charismatic renewal is strong in Latin America and Africa. The gifts of the Spirit, ecstatic experience, healing, and speaking in tongues, are central to church life and worship.

The Charismatic movement

This has profoundly influenced churches in most denominations (including the Roman Catholic Church).

The **African Independent Churches** are vigorous (and fast growing) communities of black Christians for whom the black experience is crucial to their self-understanding. In various degrees, they are influenced by liberation theology (as a people whom have known oppression), charismatic renewal, and the indigenous religion of their ancestors.

The **House Churches** or **New Churches** are a growing phenomenon within the conservative evangelical movement. 'Restorationists' reject the institutional church with its ordained ministry, returning instead to what is seen as a New Testament pattern of worship in members' homes. Worship is informal, and often charismatic in style.

The Ecumenical Movement

The Ecumenical Movement (from the Greek *oikoumene*, meaning 'the inhabited world') is the product of the twentieth century. It has been increasingly realized that Christian witness in the world is severely compromised by the deep historic divisions between the churches. While organic unity, or even inter-communion, between the churches remains a long way off, the churches now recognize the validity of one another's baptism. The mutual recognition of ministries (especially by Roman Catholics of non-Catholic ministries) remains problematic. All the mainline denominations are publicly committed to the task of reconciliation between Christians.

The World Council of Churches was constituted in 1948 as a fellowship of churches united in their loyalty to Jesus Christ 'as God and Saviour'. The Council exists to enable the churches to debate matters of common concern, and where possible, to speak and act as one. It has been particularly vigorous (sometimes controversially so) in development work, in education, and in taking up the cause of oppressed minorities. Assemblies of the Council meet every seven years. Councils of churches exist in many places, enabling local congregations to worship, work and study alongside one another. More formal ecumenical agreements enable sharing of buildings and ministries to take place on a regular basis.

Sacred Writings

RICHARD FRANCE

The word 'Bible' comes from the Greek *Biblia*, meaning simply 'the Books'. The plural is significant: the Bible is a collection of books written over a period of more than 1,000 years, in widely differing cultural and historical situations and in a rich variety of styles and language.

Yet this collection has come to be regarded by Christians as a single unit, 'The Bible', as its books have been recognized as standing apart from other books.

The Old Testament

There are two unequal parts to the Bible. The first and by far the larger, called by Christians 'the Old Testament', is simply the Hebrew (and Aramaic) scriptures of Judaism. They present the history and religious thought of the people of God up to the time when Jesus came as the Jews' messiah.

Christians have always regarded themselves as the legitimate heirs to the religion of ancient Israel, and so accept the books of the Hebrew Bible as fully 'canonical', or part of scripture. Without them, the specifically Christian scriptures could hardly be understood.

A number of later Jewish works (in Greek) are included in Roman Catholic editions of the Old Testament, sometimes distinguished as 'deutero-canonical', of lesser importance than the Hebrew scriptures. Protestant Bibles do not include these works, which Judaism did not accept as canonical, in the Old Testament; but they are sometimes printed after the Old Testament as a separate section, known as 'the Apocrypha'. Protestant Christians may read them for their interest and profit but do not accept them as Scripture.

The Codex Sinaiticus, 4th century codex of the Bible in Greek. The page illustrated is from the Gospel of John.

The New Testament
The specifically Christian books of the Bible, known as 'the New Testament', comprise twenty-seven writings by Christians of the first century CE, mostly quite short. While most of the writers were of Jewish origin, the books are in Greek, which was the common language of the Roman empire.

They consist firstly of four 'Gospels' setting out from different points of view the life and teaching of Jesus, together with the 'Acts of the Apostles' which is a continuation of the Gospel of Luke to tell the story of the first thirty years of the Christian church. There are then thirteen letters by Paul, the great missionary leader, to churches and individuals; eight other letters by early Christian leaders; and the 'Revelation of John', a visionary work cast in the mould of Jewish apocalyptic literature.

The New Testament writings, although produced within a relatively short period compared with the many centuries of the writing of the Old Testament, are mixed in style and content; even the literary quality of the Greek varies widely. The different interests and personalities of the writers are clear on even a quite superficial reading.

The inspiration of the Bible
Yet Christians have regarded these varied writings of both the Old and New Testaments as a unity, often called the 'Word of God'.

They have spoken of the Bible as 'inspired', meaning by this not merely that it is great literature or that it brings spiritual enlightenment but that it comes from God. It is not that its authors were merely passive channels for a divine revelation independent of their own thoughts; the stamp of the writers' personalities on their books is clear. But the classic Christian belief is that what they wrote in their own language, and in their own historical setting, was directed by God so that the result was no less his word than theirs.

So while the biblical books must be interpreted with proper attention to their background and literary form, what they declare is, Christians believe, God's word to his people.

This is why the Bible, for all its variety, is treated by Christians as a unity, progressively revealing not only God's acts, but his mind and will.

The authority of the Bible
In theory, therefore, all Christians accept the Bible as authoritative, both in guiding their actions and in forming their beliefs.

In practice, however, Christians have differed on this. The Protestant Reformation aimed to restore the Bible to a place of authority above the pronouncements of the leaders of the church and the traditions which had grown up. Within Protestant Christianity, the Enlightenment of the eighteenth century led to a new confidence in human reason as the ultimate guide to truth, and the Bible was treated only as a record of human religious development, not as a divine revelation.

Today, while evangelical Christianity accepts the Bible as its supreme authority, more liberal Protestantism increasingly questions its importance. In Roman Catholicism, since the Second Vatican Council, there has been a remarkable resurgence of interest in the Bible.

Any recognizably Christian faith must be based on the Bible. That is why Bible translation is a major concern of the Christian churches. Teams of translators are at work all over the world, making the Bible available in the mother tongues of even quite small ethnic groups. Today the whole Bible is available in some 414 languages, and translations of Testaments in 1068 more, while translation is in progress in a further 873.

'The Holy Scripture is the only sufficient, certain, and infallible rule of all saving knowledge, faith, and obedience...'
Second Westminster Confession (1677)

'A sermon is not an essay in which you give utterance to your views and impressions of life... It is not a theological lecture, though it will contain some theology, and the sounder the theology the better... It is God's great activity of redemption in history, in the world of persons, focusing itself in challenge and succour on 'these persons here present'...
H.H. Farmer

SACRED WRITINGS

Beliefs

HOWARD MARSHALL

The Christian faith is directly descended from the religion of the Jews. At the time of Jesus this had the following characteristics, as taught in the sacred book of the Jews, the Old Testament:

● Belief in the existence of one God (monotheism), the Creator and Lord of the universe who is sovereign over all.

● Belief in the fact that human beings are made in the image of God, but have rebelled against their Creator and stand in danger of judgment.

● Belief that God, who is the righteous judge, is also gracious and merciful. He has provided a way for people to be set free from judgment by the penitent offering of sacrifices.

● Belief that God revealed himself to the nation of Israel and called them to be his people.

● Belief that God would some day establish his rule in a sinful world, setting his people free from their enemies, and appointing his chosen agent, the messiah, to rule over them for ever.

● The practice of a moral life under the guidance of the Law given in the Old Testament; the maintenance of a religious ritual based on the Temple and involving the offering of sacrifice.

The significance of Jesus

These beliefs were decisively affected by the coming of Jesus, his followers' confident reports of his resurrection from the dead, and their receiving of the gift of the Spirit of God at Pentecost. There remained a basic similarity with the Jewish religion, but there were some fundamental changes.

The most important of these changes was due to the Christian understanding of Jesus. From a very early date, the Christians began to realize that the Jewish hope of God's chosen agent coming to set up his rule had been fulfilled in Jesus. He was the messiah whom the Jews awaited. It is the rejection of this identification by Jews that constitutes the decisive difference between them and Christians. For Christians the coming of Jesus means that God's future plan, announced in the Old Testament, has already begun to happen. God's rule is being established in a new way.

But the way in which it has happened is different from what the Jews had come to expect. They thought that God's rule would be achieved by the military overthrow of their enemies and would lead to their own establishment as the dominant nation. But Jesus did not speak out against the external enemies of the Jews; rather he proclaimed the need of everybody for a change of heart. The rule of God advances by the conversion of individuals to a new way of life, and the way of violent revolution is firmly rejected.

The death of Jesus

God's action in Jesus was also seen as including sacrifice. The death of Jesus was understood as a means of cancelling sin, provided by God himself and displaying his love for sinners. Sinfulness must inevitably bring separation from God, or death. But Jesus died this death himself. A variety of pictures – drawn from the slave market, the law court, the Temple, and personal relationships – are used to express the fundamental belief that the death of Jesus is the means of reconciling God and human beings and freeing them from the fear of judgment.

The effect of this understanding was to bring to an end the system of animal sacrifices. They were understood as

'I believe Christ's teaching; and this is what I believe. I believe that my welfare in the world will only be possible when all men fulfil Christ's teaching.'

Leo Tolstoy

Believers are baptized in the sea off Durban, South Africa.

pictures pointing forward to the spiritual sacrifice of Jesus and now made obsolete by the offering of the perfect sacrifice. Christian worship was no longer a matter of offerings in a temple. Rather it was the expression of gratitude to God for *his* provision of a sacrifice.

At the same time the coming of Jesus was seen as bringing to an end the ritual Law of the Jews which regulated the Temple worship and a host of other matters. The ethical principles which lay behind the Law, seen especially in the Ten Commandments, were not abolished, but the detailed ritual and other observances were no longer needed.

In practice, the Jews had come to regard the observance of the Law in minute detail as the means of gaining and maintaining a good relationship with God and obtaining his favour. It was Paul who insisted that God's favour could not be gained by keeping the Law: all have sinned and come short of God's glory. So the proper relationship of human beings with God can only be that of faith, the grateful and obedient trust which comes to God on the basis of what *he* has done, in contrast to the approach of works which insists that the *individual* must do something to merit God's favour.

Though Christian worship abandoned the Temple, it was deeply influenced by the synagogue, the Jewish meeting-house in which the teaching of the Law was central. But the rejection of the Law as the means of salvation led to a shift in the understanding of the Old Testament. Interest turned more to its prophetic character as a book which looked forward to the coming of Jesus, and it was studied more and more for what it taught about him. At the same time, other writings were increasingly placed alongside it as equally inspired and authoritative scriptures. The writings of the infant church, the letters written by its leaders and the accounts of the actions and preaching of Jesus in the Gospels, were seen as a corpus of scriptures alongside the Old Testament. The whole collection became the Bible of the Christian church.

The recognition that observance of the Jewish Law was no longer binding on Christians, together with the simple fact that almost from the beginning non-Jews, the Gentiles, were attracted by the message, led quickly to the development of a community composed of both Jews and non-Jews. Despite initial uncertainties it was recognized that non-Jews did not need to adopt the practices of the Jewish Law, especially circumcision and the observance of Jewish holy days, in order to become Christians. Christianity, which might have remained a Jewish sect, was thus poised to become a world faith, open to everyone on the basis of belief in Jesus.

The characteristic rites of the new faith, which roughly parallel the Jewish rite of circumcision and the festival of the Passover (which celebrated the deliverance of the people of Israel from slavery in Egypt), were baptism and the Lord's Supper. Baptism was a ritual washing with water which signified cleansing from sin, the reception of God's Spirit, and the dedication of the baptized persons to God and their entry into the new people of God. The Lord's Supper, or Eucharist ('thanksgiving'), was a token meal of bread and wine – elements used by Jesus at his Last Supper before his death to point to his self-sacrifice and the shedding of his blood to open up a new covenant or agreement between God and his people.

The resurrection of Jesus
Alongside the death of Jesus, belief in his resurrection was the crucial thing

Romanian women pray in the church at Maramures.

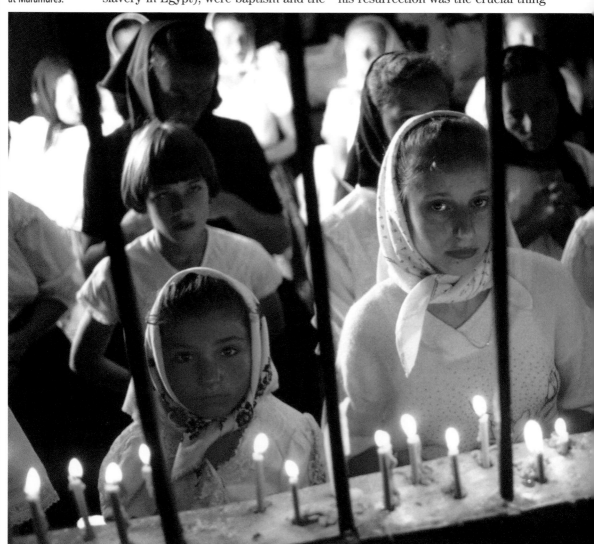

for the development of Christianity. Christians saw it as God's vindication of Jesus after he had been rejected by the Jewish leaders and put to death. It was the confirmation of his claims to be God's agent, and above all it demonstrated that he was triumphant over the power of sin and death. The resurrection was seen as the decisive stage in the ascent of Jesus to share the throne of God in heaven (to use the picture-language of the New Testament). This belief had several important consequences.

● First, it confirmed the Christian belief that God would act again in history

through the return of Jesus at the end of the world. The exaltation of Jesus meant that he was the agent appointed by God to carry out final judgment and to bring in God's eternal reign in peace and justice.

● Second, it led to the conviction that Jesus was to be seen as divine. Already in his lifetime he had displayed a unique consciousness that he was God's Son and that God was his Father. After the resurrection, Christians recognized increasingly that all the functions of God were exercised through Jesus and that he shared in the rule of God. He was to be regarded as the Son of God, who had 'come down' into the world in human form and then 'ascended' to be with God. The consequences of this belief were shattering. Jews and others who believed that there was one God could not accept the Christian claim. Christians for their part had to revise their ideas about God and recognize that, though God is one, alongside the Father there was also the Son; they were each divine in nature, yet in such a way that the Son could be regarded as dependent on the Father. The earthly Jesus was the Son of God made flesh, 'incarnate', become a human being.

● Third, now that Jesus has been exalted to heaven he remains active and living in the same way as the Father is the living God. Sharing the status of the Father, Jesus is now the Lord, so that the relation of the Christian to him is not simply one of belief and trust but also of obedience and commitment. To be a Christian is to make the confession 'Jesus Christ is Lord', a confession that he is both the Lord whom the believer obeys and also the one to whom the whole universe will one day bow the knee.

Such faith and obedience is part of a spiritual relationship between Christians and Jesus. Christians can be said to be united with Jesus, a whole

'All things are possible to him that believes, more to him that hopes, even more to him that loves, and more still to him that practises and perseveres in these three virtues.'

Brother Lawrence

BELIEFS

variety of metaphors from the language of personal relationships being used to express the reality of this link. The new life which they begin when they believe in Jesus is the reproduction of the life of Jesus in them. They die to their old way of life and rise again to a new God-centred and divinely inspired life, in the same way as Jesus died and rose again by the power of God. The Christian community is a vast organism or body through which the spiritual life of Christ flows.

The gift of the Holy Spirit and the birth of the church

After the resurrection came the third decisive event which determined the character of Christianity. The Jews already believed in the communication of God's power and guidance to particular individuals, especially the prophets, by the activity of the divine Spirit. The birthday of the church is reckoned from the day of Pentecost, when all the believers in Jesus became conscious of the gift of the Spirit given to each one personally. So universal is the gift that a Christian can be defined as a person who has received the gift of the Spirit. The initial experience can be spoken of as a second, spiritual birth, bringing the new life of Jesus to the believer. The Spirit works in the Christian community by giving different abilities to different individuals to enable them to lead and help the church as a whole. He also acts in the life of each Christian to foster the qualities of love and freedom from sin which were seen in Jesus himself.

Thus the Spirit can be seen as the personal agent of God in the lives of individuals and the Christian community. This meant a further development in the understanding of God. The Spirit was recognized as being divine in the same way as the Father and the Son, so that the Christian concept of God had to recognize a fundamental 'three-ness' or 'Trinity' in the nature of God as one

'I believe in God almighty, and in Christ Jesus, his only son, our Lord...'

Basis of the Apostles' Creed, from Marcellus of Ancyra

being who exists in three persons. Thus the understanding of God as Trinity, which in this form is peculiar to Christianity and sharply differentiates it from other religions in the same Judaic tradition (Judaism and Islam), sums up the distinctive and vital elements in Christian faith.

Christian belief takes the holiness and judgment of a righteous God seriously. This is seen in the character of the Christian message which includes the warning that all people are sinners who have rebelled against God and therefore face judgment. It is only against this background that the Christian message makes sense as 'gospel', as good news that the same God is merciful and longs for the salvation of all, he has provided the way of forgiveness and life in Jesus. Thus the gospel faces everyone with the alternatives of judgment or life.

Variety and error

The Christian message has naturally been subject to fresh thinking and reformulation down the ages as theologians have tried to express the biblical teaching in ways that are philosophically acceptable and logically coherent. It is not surprising that there have been differences in understanding in different times and places, and that some expressions of Christianity have veered away from the biblical witness.

Thus the doctrines of the Trinity and the incarnation have caused particular difficulty. Since the nature of God, who is infinite, lies beyond the scope of our finite understanding, attempts to explain his nature can lead to dangerous misunderstandings and one-sided statements. This has led to a variety of attempts to simplify the doctrine of God, by restricting full divinity to the Father or by regarding the three persons simply as three different aspects of one God. Some theologians have found it hard to believe that Jesus is the eternal Son of God, and sometimes he has been regarded as a separate, subordinate being. The tendency in modern times has been to deny that God could truly be united with a human being in one person, and to say that Jesus was a good man who possessed the divine Spirit to an unusual degree, or that true humanity is the same thing as divinity. Another tendency has been to regard the Spirit as less than a full person.

The Christian understanding of the work of Jesus has also been the cause of difficulty. Some Christians have denied that any sort of action is necessary to enable God to forgive sins and have seen in the death of Jesus nothing more than a demonstration of supreme love. Others have carried the idea of sacrifice over into Christian worship and seen the Lord's Supper as some kind of repetition of Christ's sacrifice on the cross.

At times there have been tendencies to legalism; the need for doing good works in order to merit salvation has been taught. The church has on occasions claimed an authority almost equal to that of God, and developed a hierarchy or set of graded authorities surrounded by pomp and prestige. At other times the doctrine of God as judge has been watered down and replaced by a belief that God will ultimately save everyone, no matter how they have behaved in this life.

Over against such views, mainline Christianity affirms that Christian teaching must be firmly based on the Bible, and any developments in understanding must be consistent with its supremely authoritative position as the written form of God's revelation of himself and his will for his people. It therefore insists that people must recognize that the nature of God is a complex unity in which there are three persons, Father, Son and Spirit, and that the Son became a human being in the person of Jesus.

In the life and death of Jesus is seen the activity of the one God entering

The Nicene Creed

'We believe in one God, the Father, the Almighty, maker of heaven and earth, of all that is, seen and unseen.
We believe in one Lord, Jesus Christ, the only Son of God, eternally begotten of the Father, God from God, Light from Light, true God from true God, begotten, not made, of one Being with the Father; through him all things were made.
For us and for our salvation he came down from heaven, was incarnate from the Holy Spirit and the Virgin Mary, and was made man.
For our sake he was crucified under Pontius Pilate; he suffered death and was buried.
On the third day he rose again in accordance with the Scriptures; he ascended into heaven and is seated at the right hand of the Father. He will come again in glory to judge the living and the dead, and his kingdom will have no end.
We believe in the Holy Spirit, the Lord, the giver of life, who proceeds from the Father and the Son, who with the Father and the Son is worshipped and glorified, who has spoken through the prophets.
We believe in one holy catholic and apostolic Church.
We acknowledge one baptism for the forgiveness of sins.
We look for the resurrection of the dead, and the life of the world to come. Amen.'

Common Worship

into the sinful plight of the world and bearing its painful consequences so that believers might be delivered from its guilt and its power and share in the life of God himself.

Within this basic framework of belief, as summed up in the historic creeds and confessions of the church, there is room for confession of people's inability to understand God fully, and there can be variety of understanding over matters that are of lesser significance, as the existence of the various denominations of the church shows. At all times Christians need to go back to the Bible and to test their beliefs and their practice by its teaching. Jesus himself – the Christ of the Bible and of experience – is believed to be far greater than any human formulation of dogma or teaching about him.

BELIEFS

Worship and Festivals

COLIN BUCHANAN

All institutions live by their rituals, and religious institutions are no exception. The New Testament is, from one standpoint, the history of the religious life – including the 'cultic', or worshipping life – of the people of God. Its pages record the beginnings of Christian worship.

It is recorded in the book of Acts that the infant church began a rhythm of church life which in outline is what would be called 'worship' today. (Indeed, a modern pattern for a communion service might well have the same elements.) The believers gathered for the apostles' teaching, for prayer, fellowship and 'the breaking of bread'.

The Lord's Supper, Communion or

Christ inaugurated the Eucharist at the Last Supper. Bread and wine signify his body and blood.

Eucharist was the distinctive event of Christian worship. Jesus himself commanded it and there is reason to think that the church observed it as a weekly (sometimes a daily) event from the outset. Originally, the commemoration of Jesus, especially his death and resurrection which the 'sacramental' bread and wine signified, was held within the context of a larger meal, called an *agape* or love-feast. But

for various reasons this context fell away in the first 150 years after the resurrection, and a ritual meal of solely bread and wine remained.

The New Testament also describes what has been called the Christian 'initiation rite', baptism. This was certainly a means for the new convert to enter the life of the church. But in sharp distinction to contemporary mystery religions, it was open and simple. Baptism was a public 'washing', identifying the believer and his household with the death and rising again of Jesus.

Today the churches which are 'Baptist' in conviction hold that this should only take place on confession of personal faith at an age appropriate for the confession to be credible as the candidate's own. Others baptize not only adults and others able to confess the faith personally, but also young children and newborn infants in believing households. The intention is that such infants and children should be brought up as Christians, but they are usually expected to make a personal profession of faith at 'confirmation' (or a similar rite) at a mature age.

There is other evidence in the New Testament of early church practice. Psalms and hymns were sung. To express corporate solidarity with missionaries, elders or deacons serving the church, there was 'laying on of hands' at their commissioning. The sick were anointed and prayer made for their recovery. Money was collected for other, poorer churches. The 'ministry' of the church was divided amongst those who had the 'gifts of God's Spirit' for both practical and spiritual leadership.

There seems to have been no such concept as 'having a service'. The 'business' part of church life, such as organizing for the care of widows or the relief of famine, was all bound up with the 'worship' part of praying and singing and teaching.

Established patterns

In the post-apostolic years, patterns gradually settled down, and a clear structure of leadership emerged, in which the bishop would normally preside over the worship of the local church. Bishops wrote down for themselves the great thanksgiving prayer they uttered over the bread and wine of communion, and these 'eucharistic prayers' began to be used regularly and over wide areas, as others copied them.

As congregations grew, they sometimes overflowed from the homes in which they originally met. Groups started (even in times of persecution) to put up special buildings for worship. They produced an ever more detailed pattern of the church's year – not only keeping the 'week' of creation (though making the first day of the week holy in place of the seventh), but also keeping annual commemorations: first of all the Passover (when Jesus had died and risen), then Pentecost (when the Spirit had come), and finally Christmas (celebrating Christ's birth) and the 'death day' of the various martyrs.

The Peace of Constantine in CE 313 gave a new boost to church building, and the assimilation of church and state which followed not only encouraged the use of pagan festivals for Christian commemorations (as happened with Christmas), but also started to shape church organization on the lines of the official civic structures. Whole communities were baptized, and the Western concept of 'Christendom' was born. Later, the natural conservatism of the followers of any institution which has rituals ensured that Latin remained in use rather than the language of everyday speech, that fourth-century garments remained in use by those who led the worship (even though fashions changed for other uses) and that church building attracted the energies of architects and builders whilst other civic buildings were neglected.

Worshippers approach the iconostasis (a screen bearing icons separating the sanctuary from the nave) in the church at Yam in Russia.

The importance of the exposition of scripture is shown by the central position of the pulpit at this Protestant church in Shanghai, China.

In many ways the Eastern Orthodox Churches have remained closer than any other to the spirit of the fourth and fifth centuries. Generations of a minority position have built in a great regard for the tradition and its conservation. The East has never had a Reformation or any equivalent of the Roman Catholic Second Vatican Council.

In the Middle Ages in the Western church the role of the clergy became much more dominant. Celibacy added to the mystique of the clergy. They alone took an active part in worship. The concept of their special – indeed miraculous – power to transform the bread and wine into the body and blood of Christ gave them the functions of priesthood. The part of ordinary believers was to attend Mass and to adore the presence of Christ. The people could not understand the Latin used for the Bible readings and prayers. Nor did they receive communion, except at Easter, and then (from the late thirteenth century onwards) only the bread.

Reform

The Reformation, which took a stand against these perceived abuses, was essentially a movement of 'the Word'. It involved the return to God's Word written in the Bible, and also a swing in ritual away from drama, colour and movement to a word-centredness, emphasizing intelligibility and an understanding of doctrine. The reformers themselves often tried hard to bring the celebration of communion into the centre of church life, but the long-standing habits of their congregations defeated them. Weekly worship in most Protestant churches focused on the sermon. In the Lutheran churches there was a growth of hymn-singing to accompany services of the Word and of prayers. The Church of England adopted a sober Prayer Book routine, in which the daily round of Bible readings, psalms and prayers took on more importance than preaching.

The Reformation also gave birth to more distinctive traditions. The Anabaptists, for example, included those who not only rejected infant baptism but also gave voice to their emotions in worship, expressing personal piety in prayer in gatherings 'led by the Spirit'. And in the seventeenth century the Quakers, originally quite literally, 'quaked' before God in worship.

A big change started to affect the whole of English-speaking Protestantism in the eighteenth century. The Evangelical Revival which gave birth to Methodism was characterized by enthusiastic hymn-singing. The hymns were objective in their rich doctrinal content but also expressed emotions towards God. In this revival old metrical psalters were swept aside, and the hymns of Watts and the Wesleys, Cowper and Toplady started to take their place. Also the Lord's Supper was more frequently celebrated.

Hymns apart, Protestantism has tended to be like Roman Catholicism in that its worship is usually dominated by the minister or leader, and in its solemnity: for the congregation religion is not only passive, but also serious. But in the second half of the twentieth century, a 'liturgical movement' among both Catholics and Protestants began to strive for just those ends which seem so often to have been missed – active participation by the whole congregation, understandable services, and a genuine building up of the fellowship of the body of Christ.

Festivals of Christianity

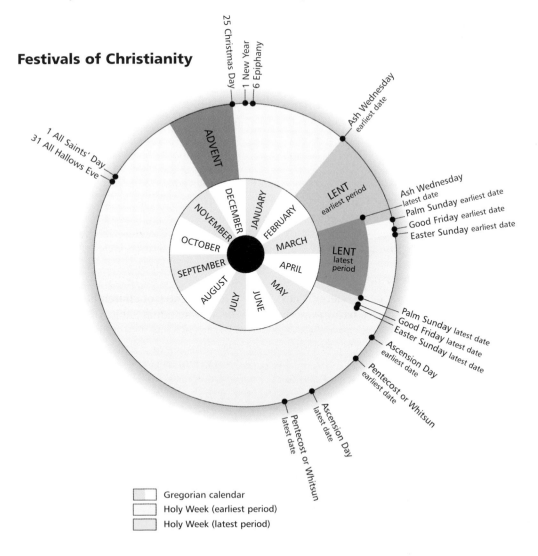

In the Church of Rome this led in time to the Second Vatican Council's reforms of the liturgy, including the admission of local languages into worship, after 1,600 years of Latin. The spill-over from this movement into Protestantism along with other shifts of conviction led to a new emphasis on the corporateness of the sacrament, and on lay participation. Many denominations gained a new sense that worship might be more than a sermon with some formal preliminaries.

As a direct result of this new openness in the Church of Rome there have been many doctrinal conversations designed to clear away misunderstandings. In the area of worship, the Anglican/Roman Catholic International Commission led in 1971 to an agreed statement on the Eucharist, or holy communion. The great multilateral convergence about worship has been precipitated through the World Council of Churches' Faith and Order report, *Baptism, Eucharist and Ministry* (1982), to which churches all over the world responded in the decade following.

> 'A new commandment I give to you, that you love one another. As I have loved you, so you must love one another.'
>
> John 13:34–35

Recent movements

There have always been more radical movements. The twentieth century, for instance, saw the rise of the Pentecostal denominations. These are 'Spirit-directed' rather than 'Word-directed', and the characteristic expression in worship involves a full release of feelings, a free use of body movements and an openness to contributions (not always, but quite often, 'tongues', 'interpretation of tongues' and 'prophecies') from all the worshippers. 'Ministries of healing' are also widely practised within public worship. In South America, for instance, Pentecostalism is the main alternative to Roman Catholicism.

A parallel, indeed related, movement has been the 'charismatic' movement (often initially called 'Neo-Pentecostalist'); here Pentecostalism, instead of separating from the historic churches, has found a strong home *within* the 'mainline' Protestant denominations and even in the Church of Rome.

Into the twenty-first century

Today the religious face of the earth is changing. Eastern Orthodoxy has resurfaced in Russia and other Eastern European nations since the collapse of Communism – whilst Islam and Eastern religions have come (largely by migration) into Western nations.

Christianity is once again in a missionary situation in the West, as Christendom fades into secularism. But the various Western forms of Christianity are not now confined to the West. Young churches flourish in Asia, Africa and elsewhere (see 'Contemporary Christianity in the Non-Western World'). They vary in their worship from being as traditional as the Western churches from which they sprang, to the use of their genuine freedom to be culturally relevant to their contexts. They frequently show a freshness and liveliness hard to find in Western historic churches.

The worship of a truly missionary church loses its respectability, takes on a new edge of realism and, above all, strengthens, unites, and equips believers for their daily life and witness in an alien world. Where worship does not build up the body of Christ, the church perishes. It may be that the churches of the Western world are slowly awaking to this challenge.

I am a Christian

JASON HOOD

I am twenty-seven years old and live in Memphis, Tennessee, USA. My wife Emily and I have a six-month-old boy named Noah. We are members of an Evangelical Presbyterian congregation.

I was raised as a Christian in a family that took the faith seriously. I went to a Christian private school until I was fourteen. At home I was taught to read the Bible daily. I enjoyed reading it (especially the Old Testament books of Proverbs and Psalms) and read it in its entirety before the age of thirteen. My sister and I were raised on Bible stories, right behaviour and respect for our parents and others. More than that, we were encouraged to seek God on our own. My parents held, as I do now, that beliefs must be heartfelt. A relationship with God is personal and must be freely entered into. Although instruction and example guided me in my formative years, my own public profession of faith and a personal prayer of surrender, forgiveness and acceptance seemed to demarcate the beginning of my individual life of faith. It was then, and remains today, a life I base on the fact that God is perfect, I'm not, and Jesus makes up that infinite difference.

I feel confident in my personal relationship with Jesus, who I believe to be Lord and God, and I am continually trying to bring every element of my life under God's authority. This means, with the help of God's Spirit, continually working to understand the Bible and live by its principles, bringing my desires in line with God's guidelines, which I believe are revealed in the Bible. My aim is to live a life of gratitude for the gracious love God has shown me, living in the peace and joy that comes from knowing I am loved and accepted by my maker. I've sometimes tried to live by ideas that run contrary to what I believe the Bible teaches and, frankly, have wound up hurting myself and others.

My practice of faith is not very ceremonial or ritualistic. For me faith is more about believing and practising what the Bible teaches. I believe Christianity is about a relationship with Jesus as a personal saviour, lord and friend. One of my guiding principles is Jesus' commandment to love others in the same way that he has loved us. For example, after college I spent four years teaching and mentoring inner city youths. My wife and I currently live with her parents so that she can help care for her mother, who is paralysed. These experiences have taught how difficult such love and commitment can be. Following Jesus has also helped me to respect others, learn from them and seek ways to increase their health and well-being.

Jesus' example of love has led my wife and me to tithe our earnings (sharing 10 per cent of our income every month with our church and others). That said, we understand 10 per cent to be a bench mark and seek to give more. For example, having won some money on a game show, we felt strongly that at least half of it should be donated to a relief fund. Loving others means making sure that whatever I do in life – including my occupation and all other activities – I do for God's glory and the benefit of others, not primarily for my own gain, reputation or personal satisfaction.

Because God loves the whole world and because a person's greatest good is found in a relationship with Jesus, I feel obliged and privileged to share Jesus with believers and unbelievers (always being sensitive to the needs and rights of others).

The fact that my wife and I were both Christians was of paramount importance to us in our decision to marry and also very important to our families. Having said that, the marriage was not arranged. Our parents were not involved in the decision-making process. However, I did formally ask my wife's father for her hand in marriage. Following this we received the blessing and encouragement of both our families. My wife and I take our relationship of love to each other and to God seriously. We pray together frequently, discuss the Bible and talk honestly as partners on a shared journey, never making big decisions without first seeking God's will.

One of the most important parts of being a follower of Jesus is living in community with other Christians. I feel enormously privileged and grateful to be part of the large, global Christian family – imperfect, to be sure, but a real family nonetheless. The main gathering of our local branch is the church service on Sunday morning, which always includes thanksgiving for what God has done, prayers of petition and confession, hymns of worship, statements of belief about God and salvation and a talk/sermon on a passage from the Bible.

Sunday is a special day to us, when we celebrate a day of rest and worship. It is the Lord's Day, a day of the week that reminds us of Jesus' resurrection. Other important celebrations are Christmas, when we celebrate the event of God becoming human in the person of Jesus, and Easter, when we remember Jesus' death on a cross for sinners and his subsequent victory over death and evil in his resurrection from the dead.

Since our church is quite large, we break down into groups for social and educational purposes, meeting on Sundays and during the week. Our group consists of newly married couples and within this group there are smaller 'mentor groups' which meet for intimate conversation, prayer and Bible study. Whereas the larger groups are led by pastors, the smaller group is led by an older couple with more wisdom and experience in life than we possess. These groups and leaders are important to us. I always pray before making important decisions and seek counsel from my group leaders, pastors and peers.

Finally, the heart of my religion and religious experience can be summed up in the word 'love'. I celebrate the love God has for me and others and I love God in return. My deep desire is that my love for Jesus and his love for me and others will be evident in my life in all places and at all times.

Family and Society

LINDA WOODHEAD

> 'As a way of seeking salvation [monasteries] are all the devil's doctrine and creed... But the holy orders and true religious institutions established by God are these three: the office of a priest, the estate of marriage, the civil government... All fathers and mothers who regulate their household wisely and bring up their children in the service of God are engaged in pure holiness, in a holy work and a holy order'
>
> Martin Luther

Jesus' teaching can be characterized as 'individualist' and 'universalist', insofar as it was directed to the smallest and the largest units of society – to the individual and to a universal 'kingdom'. In the subsequent history of Christianity, however, concern often shifted towards institutions that were intermediate between the individual and the universal, most notably the church and the family.

Pre-Reformation Christianity: the dignity of church and monastery

In earliest Christianity the embryonic institution of the church appears to be of greater concern to Christian writers and leaders than the family. For Paul, for example, it is the church rather than the family that constitutes the 'body of Christ', and which has the stronger claim on loyalty. Not that existing family ties should be disrupted, but Paul counsels those who are not married to remain single in order to devote themselves fully to Christ and his church. The growth of an ascetic emphasis in early Christianity served to confirm his approach. Many early Christian writers counsel against marriage, sexual intercourse, children and family as distractions from the higher purpose of dedicating one's life to the service of God. After all, had not Jesus himself turned his back on family?

But not all early Christians were ascetics, and the growth of Christianity seems to have owed much to its ability to win over married householders. Already in the Pastoral Epistles we see the embrace of 'household codes' that counsel orderly obedience of slaves to

masters, children to parents, and wives to husbands. As more and more respectable Roman families joined the church after the conversion of the emperor Constantine (c. 274–337), the view that family life constituted an inferior and even an ungodly way of life became harder to sustain. Although he shared much of the ascetic sensibility, Augustine of Hippo (354–430) devoted considerable energy to a pioneering theological defence of marriage and the family as an entirely acceptable way of life for Christians. So long as sex and marriage were used instrumentally for the begetting of children, he argued, they were acceptable in God's eyes.

Post-Reformation Christianity: the dignity of the family

Yet the family continued to be considered inferior and subordinate to church and monastery in Christian teaching right through the Middle Ages. It was the Protestant Reformation of the sixteenth century that did most to challenge this view, degrading monasticism and upgrading the family. Instead of viewing asceticism as the highest calling for a Christian, the reformers considered it dangerous and unnatural. They identified 'vocation' not with monastic calling but with the duty to marry and have children. Their vision of the Christian family was patriarchal. The male was to be head of his household and to take responsibility for its moral and economic welfare. Whereas men had 'vocations' to particular public roles and economic callings as well as to family life, the vocation of women was to be limited to domestic duty. Protestantism considerably narrowed the options open to its women, not only by

A view of Monte Oliveto Maggiore monastery in Tuscany, Italy.

abolishing monasticism, but by closing down the possibilities of employment in new trades. On the other hand, it lent new dignity to women's domestic 'calling' and showered praise on women who discharged it with modesty and obedience.

For Protestant Christianity then, church and family were regarded as equally important institutions. Godly Christians must be formed and moulded in both. Not only was the church the ideal family, the family was the ideal church. Although it maintained its support for monasticism and its exalted view of the church, post-Reformation Roman Catholicism soon followed Protestantism in giving a new dignity to the family. Marriage, which had once been viewed as a civil matter, was now brought inside the church – both literally and figuratively. As the early modern world gave way to the modern world, this Christian sanctification of the family gathered pace until today Christianity, both

Protestant and Catholic, is regarded by many as standing first and foremost for 'family values'.

One reason why Christian support for marriage and the family intensified in the modern period may be that, as the churches' control over other aspects of society ebbed away, the domestic sphere remained the one area in which they could still witness effectively. As their control over educational institutions waned too, the task of creating the next generation of Christians fell more and more to parents and families. But these modern factors combine with a historic legacy that has always been hostile to any form of sexual relation outside marriage (although prostitution was considered a necessary evil by the Catholic Church) and which, at least since Augustine, has regarded the (patriarchal) household as a legitimate or even an essential social institution. The reason this position stands out in higher relief in modern society is not

For much Christianity the church is the ideal family and the family the ideal church.

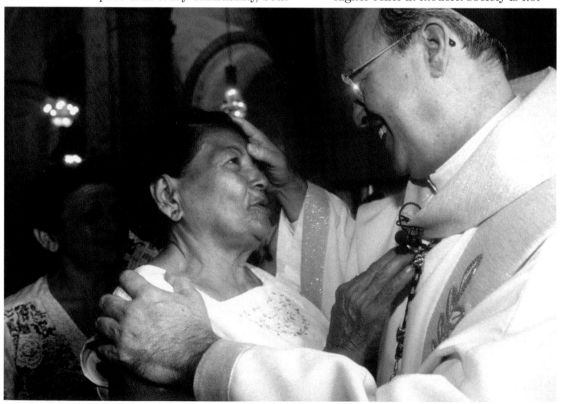

just that the church has changed, but that society has changed. For the 'sexual liberation' which characterized post-1960s society, and which was caused by a coincidence of new technology (the pill) and new values (the internalization of authority and the emancipation of women), has had far more effect on culture outside the churches than within it. In the 1920s or even the 1950s most people would have been suspicious of contraception, sex outside marriage, one-parent families, homosexuality. It could be argued that the churches have remained faithful to these positions, whilst the wider culture has moved on.

Yet not all modern Christians agree with 'traditional' teachings on the family. As the new millennium began, it was clear many denominations and churches were becoming internally divided between those who wished to defend 'traditional family values' and those who took a more liberal stance. In some denominations, such as Anglicanism and Presbyterianism, the division threatened to turn into schism. Nor is the division merely internal to Christianity: it reflects deeper disagreements within modern society as a whole – disagreements not only about gender roles and sexuality, but about the proper shape of society and the institutions which make it up.

Contemporary Christianity in the Non-Western World

DAVID SMITH

The history of the Christian movement across the centuries is full of surprises. From the very beginning this faith has displayed a remarkable ability to take root and flourish in new areas and different cultural settings, often at the very time when it faced difficulties in those lands in which it had previously been strong.

One way of explaining this is to say that Christianity is a faith capable of being *translated* into new languages and cultural forms. This fact is reflected within the New Testament itself when we are told that the early believers who had been scattered by persecutions in Jerusalem went to Antioch and '*began to speak to Greeks*' concerning the story of Jesus of Nazareth. This spontaneous act of witness across linguistic and cultural barriers was to have tremendous consequences. On the one hand, it resulted in the recognition that the faith could be expressed in different cultural forms, so making possible the emergence and growth of Christianity throughout the Roman empire. At the same time, the missionary expansion around the Mediterranean actually kept the faith alive when its original base in Jerusalem was removed with the destruction of the city in CE 70.

What makes the situation at the beginning of the twenty-first century so interesting is that we appear to be witnessing a rerun of this pattern in which Christianity thrives by means of missionary translation even as it

'Give glory to your Son, so that the Son may give glory to you. For you gave him authority over all mankind, so that he might give eternal life to all those you gave him. And eternal life means knowing you, the only true God, and knowing Jesus Christ, whom you sent. I have shown your glory on earth; I have finished the work you gave me to do. Father, give me glory in your presence now, the same glory I had with you before the world was made.'

Jesus' prayer, John 17:1–5

CONTEMPORARY CHRISTIANITY IN THE NON-WESTERN WORLD

experiences decline in its previous heartlands. In this case, the churches of Europe and North America face the well-documented challenges of secularization (the process by which a society becomes increasingly secular or non-religious), while the faith grows at an extraordinary rate in very diverse cultural settings in the non-Western world. Until recently the remarkable growth of Christianity in Africa, Latin America and in some parts of Asia was a well-kept secret, overshadowed by both the reality of the decline of the churches in the Western world and by the much publicized resurgence of Islam. Remarkably, at the very point in the mid-twentieth century at which the colonial empires were receding, indigenous forms of Christianity displayed considerable growth, demonstrating the extent to which the faith had put down deep roots in the soils of local cultures and languages. The outcome of this has been the emergence of what is called 'World Christianity' – which is increasingly recognized as a central feature of our globalized world and one which is likely to prove of enormous historical and social importance.

Christians celebrate the festival of *Timkat* (Epiphany) at one of the twelfth-century rock-hewn churches at Lalibela, Ethiopia.

Christianity in the non-Western world in earlier centuries

Non-Western forms of Christianity existed long before the modern era although they have generally been neglected in studies of church history written from a European perspective. For example, the year CE 635 witnessed not only the arrival of Aidan on the island of Lindisfarne to commence the task of evangelizing the ancient kingdom of Northumbria, but also the entrance of a missionary bishop from Persia into the imperial capital of ancient China, where he began translating the Bible with the support of the emperor. This movement of Christianity eastwards has been a largely untold story but its significance may increase in the coming decades as China moves toward centre stage in the unfolding drama of world history.

Likewise, there has been an unbroken Christian presence on the African continent stretching back across many centuries and the symbolic importance of such traditions in modern times is reflected in the fact that large numbers of independent African congregations scattered across the south and west of the continent have affirmed their African identity by describing themselves as 'Ethiopian' churches. In this way, modern African Christians have signalled their awareness of a Christian tradition on this vast continent which long pre-dates colonization and stretches back to the earliest Christian centuries.

Important as these earlier examples of non-Western Christianity undoubtedly are, the phenomenal growth of the religion across the southern continents in modern times is unprecedented. It is now possible to understand the Western shaping of the Christian faith throughout the many centuries during which it was closely linked to political power in Europe (a phase described by the term 'Christendom') as an important period in the history of the movement, but one that has now given way to a new development, as a faith embraced by millions of non-Western believers is being reshaped through its encounter with the cultures of Latin America, Africa and Asia.

While Western missions played a crucial role in the initial act of communicating the gospel across cultural and linguistic barriers, the key players in the spread of the faith have invariably been local Christians who were able to express their new religion in surprising and dynamic ways in contexts frequently marked by severe social and cultural crisis. This is the case whether we consider the role played in the evangelization of West Africa by repatriated slaves or the contributions of thousands of ordinary Christians who, faced with the new challenge of urban living in the burgeoning cities of the south, have proved amazingly adept at sharing their faith and planting new churches. In addition, an important contribution has come from the ministries of prophetic preachers and evangelists who spontaneously applied the faith to local situations, presenting Christ in ways that resonated with the felt needs of their own people and reaping huge harvests in the form of mass movements of converts on a scale that equals, and probably surpasses, previous revival movements in Christian history.

Christianity in Latin-America, Africa and Asia

This growth of Christianity across the southern continents has resulted in a situation in which it is possible to talk of a shift in the centre of gravity of the religion which now has its roots firmly planted in the soils of non-Western cultures. For example, in South America the extraordinary growth of indigenous forms of Pentecostal Christianity, involving the conversion of upwards of 40 million people, has taken both theologians and social scientists by surprise. Many Western scholars had argued that the decline of Christianity in Europe was merely the start of the global demise of religion in the face of the seemingly relentless advance of secular modernity. However, inescapable evidence of the vitality and growth of churches in Latin America has exposed the shortcomings of such theoretical models and has led to the conclusion that the secular experience of Europe, far from being the vanguard of a global trend, might actually be unusual and exceptional.

The continent of Africa has provided even more remarkable evidence of Christian growth in the course of the twentieth century. Despite the existence of those ancient Christian traditions on this continent to which reference has already been made, the faith arrived in most sub-Saharan countries in the course of the nineteenth century. Yet so extraordinary has been the growth witnessed across this continent that Africa is rapidly displacing Europe and North America as the chief Christian heartland. Both the Roman Catholic Church and major Protestant groupings are being transformed by these changes as the number of their adherents in Africa dwarfs the parent churches in Europe and North America. For example, the Archbishop of Canterbury presides over a worldwide communion of around 80 million Anglicans, of whom the vast majority are to be found in the southern continents, including 20 million in Nigeria alone. One estimate suggests that the total Christian population of that country may reach 121 million by the middle of this century and figures like this can be replicated elsewhere in Africa.

When we consider Asia the picture appears to be rather different. In many countries across this vast region, Christians remain small minorities in contexts shaped by ancient non-

Christian religious traditions. There are exceptions, notably in South Korea, where growing churches display a remarkable missionary passion, and in Singapore and the Philippines. However, a narrow focus on percentages of Christians in the context of the vast populations of Asia may easily conceal the reality of extremely significant Christian movements in the context of Asian religious pluralism. A case in point would be the relatively small Christian community in Japan, which has given birth to some remarkably gifted theologians and writers. Similarly, the church in India has been able to incarnate the gospel in the context of the Hindu-shaped culture of the subcontinent, and there are indications

Worshippers from the Pentecostal Church of Jesus Christ of the Family of God pray during a Sunday service in Guatemala City.

that it is experiencing significant growth. The challenges which these churches present to their Christian friends in the West are many, but perhaps the most important concerns the extent to which Western Christianity has allowed a secular, science-based culture to set the terms of its belief and practice, thereby neglecting both the reality of the spiritual world and the social implications of the gospel.

Above all, the story of Christianity in modern China is of great significance, both in the Asian and the global context. Half a century ago Western scholars were inclined to dismiss the church in China. Its apparently ineradicable foreignness limited its influence and seemed to condemn it to become an ephemeral feature of colonial history. However, following the removal of Western missions after the Communist revolution, the unexpected occurred – so that scholars now speak of a 'flood' of manifestations of the revival of religion and acknowledge that Christianity has shed its image as a foreign import and is now clearly identified as a Chinese religion. Estimates as to the number of Christian believers vary widely between 30 and 100 million; and, while claims at the top end of this range should be treated with considerable scepticism, there is solid evidence of a tenfold increase in the Chinese churches since 1949. Such growth in this region of the world is a phenomenon of enormous importance.

The significance of the emergence of World Christianity

What are the implications of the changes we have described? For Christians in the West the emergence of World Christianity demands a series of fairly radical changes in perspective and attitude. Until recently it was possible to assume that the churches of Europe and North America could simply be transplanted to other continents together with their inherited patterns of theology and practice. This assumption rested on the conviction that Western Christianity was a culture-free expression of the faith revealed through Christ and his apostles and that, therefore, it possessed absolute status and importance. In the new context created by the emergence of the non-Western churches, such assumptions must be abandoned: the church looks very different in societies which stress the importance of the community above the rights of the individual, while theology takes surprising directions in cultures relatively unaffected by Western modernity. As to Christian mission, the older approaches in which this was a one-way affair – *from* the West, *to* the rest – are now replaced by a far more complex pattern, in which mission is 'from everywhere to everywhere'. Indeed, the advent of massive migrations from the southern continents into Europe and North America is resulting in the appearance of 'Southern' forms of Christianity within the great urban centres of the Western world where they often become by far the largest and most dynamic of Christian communities. If they are wise, Western believers will respond to this situation, not with regret and anger, but with thankfulness that the baton has been successfully passed on and the biblical prize of a multinational church is more clearly in sight than ever before.

So far as non-Western Christianity itself is concerned, there is a series of daunting challenges, including the classic issue of precisely how to relate one's faith in Christ to pre-Christian cultures shaped by ancient religious traditions. What are the things from the past that can be sanctified and brought into the kingdom, and what must be left at the doorway? For the vast majority of Christians in the southern hemisphere, religious pluralism is not a new experience resulting from the collapse of the walls which previously

> *'After this I looked and there before me was a great multitude that no one could count, from every nation, tribe, people and language, standing before the throne and in front of the Lamb.'*
>
> Revelation 7:9

Christians in the Southern hemisphere take the spiritual world seriously and know the importance of prayer.

Christianity in the Modern World

PETER BRIERLEY

protected one from contact with people of other faiths, it is simply part of the reality one has always known and experiences every day. Faith in Christ is confessed and the life of discipleship is lived out in continual interaction with one's Muslim, Hindu, Buddhist or Confucian neighbours. This means that the growth of non-Western churches in contexts inevitably characterized by ongoing dialogue with people of other faiths holds the promise that fresh insights into the meaning of Christ and his salvation will emerge from these new heartlands in the course of the twenty-first century.

Finally, we must not overlook the fact that the non-Western churches are overwhelmingly churches of the poor, existing in social and economic conditions largely dictated by forces beyond their control in a world shaped by the phenomenon of economic globalization. Indeed, any celebrations at the indications of growth and spiritual vitality evident in non-Western Christianity need to be tempered by an awareness of the dangers of division within the Body of Christ at a point at which we are being warned of a 'clash of civilizations'. If the dismal prospect of the fracturing of the churches along the lines of division opening up between the so-called developed world and the poorer nations is to be avoided, then Christians in the North and the South need to really listen to each other and, in fellowship together, hear what the Spirit is saying to them. This way there is the prospect that the global church might be able to offer a model of a new humankind and point the way toward a radically different kind of world.

'We are what we have been becoming,' someone once said. That is as true for organizations and churches as it is for individuals, though the timescale may be different. The implication of the statement is that we will be in the future what we have now become – unless by looking ahead we react today to ensure that some of the endemic trends are changed by prayerful attention, persuasive arguments, and positive action.

The twentieth century did not see the decline and fall of religion as the Communists predicted. Instead there was a worldwide increase in Christianity and other major religions, even though in the West, Christian fortunes have been rather different.

Apart from revivals, Western Christianity is much like a modern cargo ship – well-filled, slow-moving and hard to change its direction speedily. Asian and African Christianity is more akin to a pleasure liner – full of enthusiasm, following a definite sense of purpose, and able to take advantage of happenings *en route*. Can the one ship learn from the other?

What does a general inspection of the present situation reveal?

Worldwide Christian growth
In 2001 the second edition of David Barrett's enormous *World Christian Encyclopedia* was published. This he updates with an annual Table in the *International Bulletin of Missionary Research*. His figures show that in 1990 there were 1,750,000,000 Christians in the world, 33.2 per cent

of the world's 5,300,000,000 people. By 2000, the number had grown to 2,000,000,000 or 33.0 per cent. However, he projects an increase in the proportion in the early part of the twenty-first century, so that by 2010 there would be 2,250,000,000 Christians or 33.3 per cent of the world's population.

In the last decade of the twentieth century, some 69,000 people were added *per day* to the church; in the first decade of the twenty-first century this dropped slightly to 67,000 people per day. This drop however simply reflects the decreasing rate of increase in the general world population: the proportion of new births who are Christian was estimated by David Barrett at two-thirds, 66 per cent, in 2000.

These numbers vary by continent as shown in Table 1. David Barrett defines church members as all who call themselves Christian, so many nominal Christians are included in his figures. Not every Christian is an affiliated church member, but for the purposes of Table 1 it is assumed they are.

Table 1 reflects the new definitions of continent introduced by the United Nations in 1992 after the fall of Communism in the former Soviet Union. Estimates for 2010 assume current trends continue, although they rarely do in practice! The top three lines show the Third World continents, two of which are expected to grow a little less quickly in the 2000s than in the 1990s. Africa, however, is expected to continue to grow, if anything, slightly faster in the 2000s.

The bottom three continents in Table 1 show the Western World where the rates of change are slightly less in Oceania in the 2000s than they were in the 1990s, are much less in North America, and are negative in Europe. European Christianity is declining because so many Christians find church irrelevant, boring and not really very welcoming (according to research published initially by Michael Fanstone in 1993 but confirmed by several studies since).

Much of European Christianity (97 per cent in 2000) is also *institutional*, that is, it is Roman Catholic, Orthodox, Lutheran, Anglican or Presbyterian. Institutional Christianity has large numbers of nominal Christians, an inability to change fast, inflexible structures and perhaps a greater inhibition to experiment with new forms of outreach.

Third World Growth

It is important for the Western world to learn from the explosive growth of Third World Christianity. The growth in Asia and Africa comes primarily from their enthusiastic evangelism. In Asia the growth reflects the continuing impact of the Home Church Movement in China, where the number of

Table 1

Continent (millions)	Christian community			Actual change (%)	Estimated change (%)
	1990	2000	2010E	1990–2000	2000–2010
Latin America	409	481	543	+18	+13
Africa	277	360	475	+30	+32
Asia	249	313	373	+26	+19
Europe	550	560	556	+2	-1
North America	240	261	271	+9	+4
Oceania	22	25	28	+14	+12
Total	**1,747**	**2,000**	**2,246**	**+15**	**+12**
World population	5,266	6,055	6,746	+15	+11

congregations increased from some 50,000 in 1970 to 400,000 twenty-five years later.

Africa has seen a plethora of Independent churches, especially in the Zionist tradition, blossom in the 1980s and 1990s especially, as well as many other charismatic and Pentecostal churches. In 1987 in South Africa, for example, there were over 4,200 distinct Zionist denominations. Pentecostal groups start new churches ('church planting' it is called in the UK) anywhere they can. The Synod of the Church of England debated 'Mission-shaped churches' in February 2004 which were warmly endorsed by Archbishop Rowan Williams. Thus might the Western world learn from its Third World brethren.

In Latin America, Pentecostalism has also been hugely important. In his book, *The Next Christendom*, Professor Philip Jenkins quotes a Brazilian, 'The Pentecostal groups have the kind of God that will solve many problems today.' The growth has taken place particularly among the poor, who often come to church for physical healing (not being able to afford doctors and hospitals), and find, in addition, spiritual renewal.

Non-Western Christianity takes the lead

There is another important implication in Table 1. In 1990 the proportion of world Christianity in the Third World was 53 per cent. It was 58 per cent in 2000, and it is set to become 62 per cent by 2010.

It is also the non-Western countries who are most active in spreading the Christian faith outside their own lands. People from these countries living in Britain are very active, and they are supported by UK personnel also. The fourth edition of *Religious Trends* showed that of the 7,200 British mission workers active in 2003 almost 2,200 were working in the UK.

This is seen in the high degree of commitment of Afro-Caribbean church members. Their worship is culturally relevant to those who attend. Their age-structure gives them a degree of homogeneity (in Britain only 6 per cent are over 65), and the similarity of their residential areas and lifestyles facilitates 'people-group' evangelism.

It is not just in the proportion of adherents that the Third World is growing. In 1990 there were 28,600 different denominations across the world, and by 2010 there could be over

A young follower of the Nazareth Church of South Africa puts on her scarf while making her way up the Nhlangakazi Mountain for a pilgrimage. Thousands of followers take to the mountain for a 12-day pilgrimage to pay respects to their ancestors, church founder Prophet Isaiah Shembe, and to pray for peace in the new millennium.

41,000. Two-thirds, 67 per cent, of these are in the non-Western world. Likewise, in 1990 there were 2.7 million churches worldwide, a number likely to increase to 4.1 million by 2010, with again about two-thirds in the Third World. The emergence of new church groups is evident; however, these figures reflect that more church planting takes place from within existing denominations.

Growth in Christian organizations

David Barrett suggests there were 25,000 Christian service organizations in the world in 2003, up from 21,000 in 1990, and, on his trends, there could be 29,000 globally by 2010. These figures seem low since the *UK Christian Handbook* listed over 5,000 in the UK alone in 2004, a figure, however, which is slowly declining.

Parachurch growth in Britain has occurred especially in the services sector, particularly with organizations serving either the church or other parachurch organizations. The proportion of organizations devoted solely to evangelism has diminished. Media, training and accommodation

A female priest celebrates the Eucharist.

agencies have all increased, but the number of Christian bookshops has slightly decreased. So has the number of missionary societies.

The increasing numbers of such organizations are making considerable demands on the church's income. Of all the money given to churches and parachurch organizations worldwide

in 1990, 46 per cent went to the parachurch groups. By 1993, this was 50 per cent and by 2003 it had become 61 per cent, and the percentage will almost certainly increase further. The newer organizations tend to attract money away from the older ones, which are sometimes forced to merge. Yet the newer organizations themselves are not immune from financial pressure (in Britain, a number fail within five to ten years).

Women in leadership

After the Evangelical Lutheran Church in Germany introduced women's ordination in 1976, relatively large numbers of female ordinands came into the church, offset by a decrease in the number of male ordinands. The decision by the General Synod of the Church of England in November 1992 to allow the ordination of women has had considerable impact both in Britain and across the world.

There is some research evidence to suggest that women in church leadership do not attract men into the church. If this is the case, the percentage of women churchgoers in Britain may be set to increase from the 2000 figure of 61 per cent.

Whilst the Salvation Army, many Afro-Caribbean churches and others have always integrated men and women at all levels of leadership, in 2000 in Britain only 10 per cent of all ministers were women, a percentage which an analysis in *Religions Trends* put at 12 per cent for 2005. After these two groups, the United Reformed Church had the highest percentage, 22 per cent, of women ministers, followed by the Methodists with 19 per cent, the Church of Scotland with 15 per cent, and Anglicans with 12 per cent. Of the residential places at British theological colleges and Bible schools in 2003, 41 per cent were for women, yet 60 per cent of mission workers abroad were women.

Worldwide figures for the percentage of church members who are women, or for female church leaders, are not currently available.

Reduced resources

Reference has already been made to the depletion of financial resources available to churches because of the growth of parachurch organizations. The loss of church members in many Western nations is also causing financial pressure. Many Lutheran church members in Germany, and elsewhere in Europe, are opting out of the extra percentage or two they voluntarily pay in income tax to fund the state church. This, together with the declining German population, could lead to a major drop in income for the Lutheran church in coming years. Globally, however, David Barrett predicts that the proportion of a church member's income given to Christian causes is likely to increase significantly from 1.7 per cent in 1990 to 2.3 per cent by 2010. In the Western church finance is likely to become scarcer, but it is not the only resource to do so.

In the United States the numbers being trained for the ministry were too great in the 1990s for the financial resources available to churches, especially in the Baptist and Anglican traditions, with the possibility of clergy unemployment. The same could well happen in Britain. This tends to mean a static or declining number of ministers. In ten European countries where there is a State church, the number of ministers is set to decline 6 per cent in the 1990s, and the decline is likely to continue.

The fall in the number of Roman Catholic priests worldwide has been catastrophic. For example, in France there were over 1,000 ordinations to the priesthood in 1950; by 1990 the number had dropped to fewer than 100. In 1980, there were 42,000 priests in France, but there were only about 20,000 in 1995. This dramatic decline can be attributed partly to the celibacy issue; many are keen to serve as married priests. The Catholic missionary focus continues strongly, however, though fewer Spanish and Portuguese priests now serve in Latin America.

There is a further problem apparently unique to Western countries. The number of church people is falling, primarily because the number of young people joining does not compensate for the mortality rate of older members. Professor Eddie Gibbs identifies a number of key reasons: boredom with adult services; dislike of being one of a small group of young people at church; finding the messages irrelevant to their needs or their family; disagreement with the minister; and, finally, a rejection of the church's moral teaching (at an age when the numbers of those cohabiting are highest). In Asia, particularly, the churches include many young people, and the need to capture youthful hearts may be one reason why some African churches are now sending their missionaries to Europe.

However, this reduction in resources is balanced by increases in other areas. For example, the number of Bibles distributed and the number of Christian radio and television stations have been increasing rapidly and this trend looks set to continue.

The increasing mobility of church attenders

In 1990 the Anglican bishop of Southwark remarked, 'We have moved from where Christianity is culture to where Christianity is choice.' He was right, and his comment holds true not only in Britain, but most notably in Australia and North America as well. Younger and middle-aged people are increasingly moving from one church to another, staying perhaps only a few months or years.

Often it is the Pentecostal and charismatic churches who gain from such 'switching', as do the larger, institutional churches. This means some of the smaller denominations are likely to see fewer attenders.

Sometimes these moves are because of housing or employment changes, but this is not always the case. Some figures suggest that, of those who change, perhaps a quarter stop going to church altogether. This is rarely due to loss of faith, and can apparently be attributed to the reasons of boredom, loneliness and irrelevance already mentioned. This is a challenge to which the Western church needs to respond, as it is not the case in other parts of the world where sometimes a family moving to another town for employment reasons can form the nucleus of a new congregation.

The move towards traditional biblical Christianity

It might have been thought with the prominence of New Age thinking in the 1980s and 1990s that traditional biblical Christianity would decline, but two opposing trends have emerged. On the one hand there is the tendency in the twenty-first century for many to describe themselves as 'spiritual' rather than 'religious'. In a BBC survey in July 2000, 32 per cent of the UK population said they were spiritual, 28 per cent

religious, 22 per cent 'not religious' but only 10 per cent said they were 'agnostic' and 8 per cent 'atheist'. These last two words may not really be the best categorization since 33 per cent in the same poll affirmed 'there is a way to God outside organized religion'. In the 2001 population census in the UK, however, 72 per cent stated they were Christian, 5 per cent belonged to other religions, 16 per cent had no religion and 7 per cent didn't answer the question.

The other trend is the growing proportion within the church of those who would describe themselves as evangelical. This is happening across all parts of the church, and is because the number of mainstream and charismatic evangelicals is growing (up 16 per cent in England in the 1990s), while other ways of believing (or churchmanships) are declining (down 32 per cent). The same occurred in Scotland between 1994 and 2002 according to the Scottish Church census, with mainstream and charismatic evangelicals up 10 per cent and all others down 22 per cent.

The same broad trend is also seen worldwide, according to David Barrett. Evangelicals grew 16 per cent worldwide in the 1990s against 14 per cent non-evangelicals, but are likely to

Table 2

Religion	Adherents (millions)			Actual change (%)	Estimated change (%)
	1990	2000	2010E	1990–2000	2000–2010
Christianity	1,747	2,000	2,246	+15	+12
Islam	963	1,188	1,427	+23	+20
Hinduism	686	811	901	+18	+11
Chinese folk-religion	348	385	409	+11	+6
Buddhism	323	360	381	+11	+6
Animists	200	229	246	+15	+7
Sikhism	19	23	26	+21	+13
Judaism	13	14	15	+9	+4
Other religions	126	141	151	+12	+7
Non-religious/atheists	841	904	944	+7	+4
World population	**5,266**	**6,055**	**6,746**	**+15**	**+11**

grow 15 per cent to 11 per cent in the first decade of the twenty-first century.

The challenge in Britain is reflected in the decline in Sunday School attendance, from 24 per cent of children in 1960, to 9 per cent in 1980, to 6 per cent in 2000, and an estimated 3 per cent by 2010. This, coupled with the general failure of Religious Education classes at school, has the result that many aged under 25 in the early twenty-first century have virtually no Bible memory or knowledge and prove unable to name even the Gospel writers.

Competing religions

If Christianity is increasing worldwide, though not in Europe, other religions are doing the same – and taken together are outpacing Christianity. The figures in Table 2 are David Barrett's, with my estimates from his figures for 2010. Islam is projected to grow fast, as is Sikhism (although this is much smaller in terms of absolute numbers). All the other religions have been growing at a smaller pace than Christianity, and are projected to continue to do so at the beginning of the 2000s.

There are only four groups growing as fast, or faster, than the world's population: Christianity, Islam, Hinduism and Sikhism. Collectively these accounted for 65 per cent of the world's population in 1990, 66 per cent in 2000 and are likely to be 68 per cent by 2010. Given that Christianity remains at 33 per cent of the global population, these other three religions move from 32 per cent to 35 per cent of the total in these 20 years. Islam is the fastest growing religion in the world in the first years of the new millennium.

A turbulent future

The 1980s saw sweeping changes to the world political order with radical changes in the Soviet Union and its satellite countries. The same could happen when the aging Chinese leaders pass on. Changes are already being made in South Africa, Cambodia and other parts of the world. Some changes have been violent (Yugoslavia and Algeria, for example), others continue to evolve in the form of persistent conflict, as they have done for many years (Northern Ireland and Peru).

The vast range and scale of changes experienced have not lessened fear or anxiety. The nuclear arsenal of the former Soviet Union, the developing nuclear capacity of Pakistan (outside the Nuke Club), the continuing testing by China, do not suggest peace. The appalling poverty in Africa, the colossal debts of the Third World, the decline of American economic influence, the increase of AIDS in Thailand and Africa for example, the continuing of many floods in India and elsewhere, and seemingly more earthquakes around the world, all suggest time bombs and turbulence for the future. To this, add genetic engineering, the potential for civil war, the materialism of the West, the problem of global warming, and the world becomes an even unsafer place. Who can tell what will happen?

There is nothing escapist about the Christian faith. The New Testament warns of trouble to come – earthquakes, floods, famines and wars. Christians are called to make the good news of forgiveness and new life known to people of every nation. One day Jesus Christ will return. The world as we know it – all the evil and injustice and pain – will give place to 'new heavens and a new earth' centred on God. Meantime Christians must live in daily readiness to account for their lives: demonstrating in practical ways that love of God and love for fellow human beings which lies at the heart of the faith.

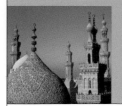

Islam

ISLAM

A Historical Overview

MONTGOMERY WATT

Islam began in Mecca about CE 610. The dominant religion of Arabia at this time was a form of the old Semitic religion, with shrines of various gods and goddesses in many places. There also appears to have been a widespread belief in a high god or supreme god, Allah. The other gods were sometimes regarded as angels, and could be asked to intercede with the supreme god on behalf of the worshippers.

Most of the Arabs were members of nomadic tribes and believed more in human excellence than in any divine power. They believed that what happened to them was determined by Fate or Time, which they thought of not as a being to be worshipped, but simply as 'the course of events'. Some tribes or parts of tribes had become Christian and there were Jewish communities in Medina and elsewhere in western Arabia. Thus, certain Jewish and Christian ideas were familiar to many Arabs.

Messages from God
Islam began not among nomads but

among city-dwellers engaged in far-flung commercial enterprises. Towards the end of the sixth century the merchants of Mecca gained a monopoly of trade between the Indian Ocean and the Mediterranean, which passed up the west coast of Arabia by camel caravan. Mecca had a sanctuary, the Ka'ba, which was an ancient pilgrimage centre, and the surrounding district was sacred. All this facilitated the growth of trade, but the wealth which poured into Mecca led to social tensions, especially among the younger men.

Muhammad was born in Mecca around the year CE 570. It was in about 610 that he came to believe that he was receiving messages from God which he was to convey to his fellow Meccans. These messages or revelations were later collected and form the Qur'an. They asserted that God was *One* (Allah) and that he was both merciful and all-powerful, controlling the course of events. On the Last Day he would judge people according to their acts and assign them to heaven or hell. Part of the conduct which he expected of people was a

Muslims in Malaysia at prayer.

A HISTORICAL OVERVIEW

generous use of wealth. In the revelations, Muhammad himself was spoken of sometimes as merely a warner telling of God's punishment for sinners, sometimes as a prophet or messenger of God. Muhammad sincerely believed that these revelations were not his own composition, but were the actual speech of God conveyed to him by an angel. This is still the belief of Muslims.

Muhammad gained a number of followers, who met frequently with him and joined him in worship of God. But his messages were not all well received. The Meccan merchants were roused to vigorous opposition by the criticisms of their practices implied in the Qur'an. The merchants spoke of the old pagan gods but the Qur'an came to emphasize that there is only one God – that 'there is no deity but God'. As opposition grew, the Quranic messages began to speak of former prophets who had met with opposition, and of the way in which God had preserved them and their followers and brought disaster on their opponents. Among the stories were those of Noah and the Flood, Lot and the destruction of Sodom, and Moses escaping from Pharaoh.

To Medina

Muhammad's followers were now persecuted in various ways by his opponents, who were often their own relatives. Eventually it became impossible for him to carry on his religious activity in Mecca, and in 622, preceded by about seventy men and their families, he emigrated to Medina. This emigration, the *Hijrah*, became the event which marked the beginning of the Islamic era. Medina was a fertile oasis, but the inhabitants were divided into two hostile groups. Most of them accepted Muhammad as prophet and agreed that they and the emigrants from Mecca would form a single

community or federation. Perhaps they were the more ready to accept Muhammad because they had heard from the local Jewish clans that a messiah was expected. They were also hopeful that he would help them to overcome their divisions.

It was at Medina that the religion of Islam took shape. The main ritual forms, modelled on Muhammad's example, were: worship (or prayer), almsgiving, fasting (for the whole month of Ramadan), and the pilgrimage to Mecca (including ceremonies at neighbouring sites). At Medina the messages revealed to Muhammad included legal regulations for matters where Arab custom was unsatisfactory, such as the inheritance of wealth and the avoidance of incest.

The Jewish clans in Medina were associated with Muhammad's federation as allies of Arab member clans but nearly all the Jews refused to accept him as prophet. They mocked parts of the Qur'an and sometimes actively opposed the Muslims. Muhammad expelled two Jewish clans from Medina and had the men of a third executed. Until after the conquest of Mecca he had few contacts with Christians.

At first, Muhammad had no special political powers at Medina beyond being head of the emigrants from Mecca. After a year or two, however, all his followers there (now called Muslims) became involved in hostilities with the pagan Meccans. By 630 Muhammad was strong enough to take Mecca. He treated his enemies generously and won most of them over to become Muslims. Many tribes all over Arabia also joined his federation and became Muslims. Because of his successes his authority as head of state was unquestioned.

The first Caliphs

'He who honours Muhammad must know that he is dead. But he who

> 'He is Allah, besides whom there is no other god. He is the Sovereign Lord, the Holy One, the Giver of Peace, the Keeper of Faith; the Guardian, the Mighty One, the All-powerful, the Most High! Exalted be He above their idols! He is Allah, the Creator, the Originator, the Modeller. His are the gracious names. All that is in heaven and earth gives glory to Him. He is the Mighty, the Wise One.'
>
> The Qur'an, surah 59:23–24

honours the God of Muhammad must know that he is living and immortal.' Muhammad died in 632, and with these words his first successor, Abu Bakr, encouraged the Muslim community and pointed them to the task ahead.

On his death, Muhammad left both a religion and a state. At first the state had the form of a federation of tribes or clans, but as it expanded it became more organized. The head of state was known as the 'caliph' (*khalifa*) – the 'successor' or 'deputy' of Muhammad. Raiding their neighbours had been a normal occupation of the nomadic Arab tribes, and Muhammad and the first caliphs realized that they could not keep peace within the federation unless they found some outlet for the energies of the tribesmen. They therefore organized raiding expeditions (*razzias*) in the direction of Syria and Iraq. The aim of these was to obtain booty, including domestic animals. The first raids from Medina were very successful. There was in fact a power vacuum in the region, because the two great powers of the day, the Byzantine and Persian empires, had been almost constantly at war for half a century and were now exhausted. In a few decisive battles the Muslims overcame such opposition as the empires presented. Instead of returning to Medina after each campaign, they established forward base camps so that they could go further afield in the next expedition. Following this strategy, within twelve years of Muhammad's death they had occupied Egypt, Syria and Iraq, and were advancing westwards into Libya and eastwards into what is now Iran.

The Byzantine and Persian governors of the provinces fled, and the Muslims made treaties with the local inhabitants, giving them the status of 'protected minorities'. These groups ordered their own internal affairs but paid tribute or tax to the Muslim governor. The status of protected minority was open only to 'people of the book' – communities who believed in one God and possessed a written scripture, such as Jews and Christians. They were, of course, a kind of second-class citizen.

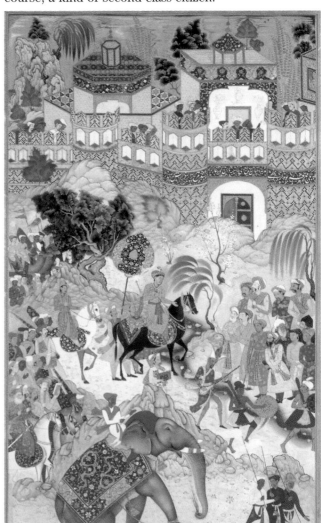

The explosion of Islam

Apart from some periods of civil strife among Muslims, the expansion continued for a century. Westwards the Muslims occupied North Africa to the Atlantic, crossed into Spain, and for a few years held the region round Narbonne in southern France. In the Battle of Tours in 732 a Muslim raiding expedition was defeated by a French army, but this did not loosen the Muslim hold on Spain. Northwards

Islamic art flourished from the Middle Ages onwards. Here is Emperor Akbar's triumphant entry into Surat, from the *Akbarnama* made by Persian artist Abu'l Fazi, 1590–98.

they raided as far as Constantinople (modern Istanbul), but failed to occupy any of Asia Minor (Turkey). Eastwards, after occupying the whole of Persia and Afghanistan, they penetrated into central Asia and crossed the line of the River Indus in modern Pakistan. Until 750 this vast area remained a single state ruled by the caliphs of the Ummayad dynasty.

Most of the inhabitants of these regions were not immediately converted to Islam but became protected minorities. The military expeditions, though dignified with the title of 'holy war' (*jihad*), were raids for booty and not to make converts. The idea that opponents were given the choice of 'Islam or the sword' is false, except in the case of pagan Arab tribes. The protected minorities were on the whole well treated, since Muslim rulers felt it to be a point of honour that their 'protection' should be effective. Members of these minorities, however, saw themselves as second-class citizens, and there was a steady trickle of converts to Islam over the centuries. It is in this way that Islam has become the dominant religion in lands which were the original home of Christianity. In the seventh century though, Zoroastrianism – the official religion of the Persian empire – was in decline, and conversion from it to Islam was quite rapid and extensive.

The prayer of sunset (*maghrib*) performed at the Grand Mosque in Mecca shortly before the annual *Hajj*, when some two million pilgrims gather in the city.

Consolidation

In 750 the Ummayad dynasty of caliphs, based in Damascus, ended. For the next 500 years, the 'Abbasid dynasty ruled from Baghdad. They never took over control of Islamic Spain, however. They also gradually lost control of other outlying provinces. A local governor with a powerful army would insist on being succeeded by a person of *his* choice maintaining only weak links with the caliph. In 945 the 'Abbasid caliph was even forced to delegate supreme political and military authority over Baghdad and the central provinces. But there continued to be 'Abbasid caliphs in Baghdad, though without political power, until the destructive Mongol invasion in 1258.

Whereas the Ummayad period was one of growth and adaptation for Islam and the Arabs, the first century or two of 'Abbasid rule was marked by consolidation. All the cultural forms needed for the life of a great empire flourished. A central place was given to the development and elaboration of Islamic law, the *Shari'a*, which formed the basis of social structure. The *Shari'a* was derived in part from rules in the Qur'an, but to a greater extent from the example of Muhammad. His example was known from the collections of *Hadith* (sometimes translated 'traditions') – stories about his deeds and sayings. This study of law or jurisprudence became the core of Islamic higher education.

Subordinate scholarly disciplines were concerned with the text of the Qur'an, the interpretation of the Qur'an, grammar, lexicology and theological doctrine. There were also the 'foreign sciences' – Greek philosophy, medicine, mathematics and natural science. Many Greek books were translated into Arabic and considerable advances were made in the sciences, in literature, in the arts and in the skills of government and administration.

To the East

After 750, military expansion slowed down, and almost the only advance was that further into India. Here the climax of Islamic power was under the Mughal emperors from 1556 until 1707, when most of the subcontinent was subject to them. Hindus were treated as 'people of the book' because their philosophers (though not most ordinary Hindus) were monotheists. Though there were group conversions to Islam, most of the population remained Hindu.

Islamic rule also spread by peaceful methods. Muslim traders with camel caravans took it into the West African steppe, and sea traders carried it to the East African coast. From India it spread, mainly through trade, to Malaysia, Indonesia and the Philippines; and from central Asia it moved into eastern China.

Local people were impressed by the confidence and high culture of the Muslim traders, allowed them to marry local women, and often after a time decided themselves to become Muslims. Converts often kept many of their old customs, and did not immediately observe the *Shari'a* fully. But over the centuries they moved

closer to standard Islam, and at the same time the number of Muslims kept increasing.

Prior to 1500 the main area where Islam contracted was Spain. Christian military pressure gradually whittled away the area under Muslim control, and in 1492 the last sultan of Granada had to surrender. Muslims continued in Spain for a time, but were executed or driven out by the Inquisition.

The impact of Europe

A new era in the history of Islam began about 1500. The Portuguese sailor Vasco da Gama, having rounded the Cape of Good Hope and disrupted the Muslim trade on the East African coast, reached India in 1498. This was the beginning of the impact of Europe on the eastern part of the Islamic world. In the west the Ottomans took over the caliphate and conquered much of south-eastern Europe and the southern coast of the Mediterranean during the fifteenth and sixteenth centuries, and were then in military and diplomatic contact with European states, as well as having commercial dealings. The full force of the European impact, however, was not felt until after the Industrial Revolution. Napoleon's invasion of Egypt in 1798 is a significant date.

The impact of Europe on the Islamic world (as on Asia and Africa generally) was many-sided: economic, political, intellectual and religious. It began with ocean-borne trade but went on to political interference and finally colonization. As European technology developed in the nineteenth and twentieth century, the richer Muslims wanted to share in its comforts and conveniences, and independent rulers wanted their countries to have railways and other forms of communication, plumbing, electricity for lighting, telephones, and so forth. Military hardware was high on the list, and then it became necessary to train men to use it. Colonial powers also introduced Western-type education to train men for minor administrative posts. After 1800 the Christian churches sent missionaries to most parts of the world, but in Islamic lands they made relatively few converts and their chief contribution was to the development of education and medical care.

By the early twentieth century, intelligent Muslims were aware of their situation. Movements for political independence grew and were eventually successful. Some industry was developed, based on Western technology. Most Muslim countries adopted an essentially Western educational system, because the religious leaders were not prepared to adapt the traditional Islamic education they controlled. The discovery of vast quantities of oil in the Middle East was at first exploited by Westerners, but later, when taken over by Muslim governments, became a weapon in world politics. Until the end of World War II, Muslim countries were united in their struggle to be free of colonialism. Since then, however, splits between 'progressive' and 'conservative' groups have become increasingly apparent; and the conservative and reactionary groups have been strengthened by the development of Islamic fundamentalism.

The Unity and Variety of Islam

DAVID KERR

Islam has two basic groups – the Sunni and Shi'a. Their origins can be traced back to a question which faced the first generation of Muslims: how was Muhammad, 'the Seal of the Prophets', to be succeeded as leader of the Muslim community? For Muslims this question was always a religious as well as a political one.

Sunnis – the community consensus

The answer of the Sunnis, who constitute the Muslim majority of approximately 85 per cent, can be summarized as follows. No one could succeed Muhammad in his nature and quality as prophet, for the Qur'an finalized and perfected the revelation of divine guidance and declared Muhammad to be 'the Seal of the Prophets'. Muhammad's successor could therefore be no more than the guardian of the prophetic legacy. He would be a caliph (*khalifa*) with subordinate authority as leader of the believers, having responsibility for the administration of community affairs in obedience to the Qur'an and prophetic precedent. By the process of consensus (*ijma'*) the community would select its caliph from amongst the male membership of the Quraish tribe to which Muhammad belonged.

Following Muhammad's death in CE 632, caliphal succession passed from Abu Bakr (632–634) to 'Umar (634–644) to 'Uthman (644–656) and to 'Ali (656–661). These, 'the four rightly guided caliphs' are deemed to have lived so close to the Prophet that their example, together with Muhammad's, is taken to comprise the authoritative *sunnah*, or custom, for all

'Whereas the term imam in Sunni Islam simply signifies the leader of the mosque prayers, habitual or actual, in Shi'a Islam the Imam is the agent of the divine illumination of the age.'
Kenneth Cragg

later generations of Muslims to follow.

The Sunnis gradually developed a comprehensive system of community law, the *Shari'a*. This provided cohesion within the community while allowing for variance between four orthodox law schools, the Malikis, Hanafis, Shafi'is and Hanbalis. The principle of *ijma'* remained central. Notionally *ijma'* is the consensus of the whole community, though in practice it is that of the legal scholars.

After the 'rightly guided caliphs' the caliphate became a dynastic institution, regarded as the guardian of the *Shari'a*. But in 1924 it was abolished. The *ijma'* of contemporary Sunni Islam seems to be that if the *Shari'a* is observed by the national governments of Muslim states, there is no need for the transnational office of caliph to be restored.

Shi'a – authority and leadership

For Shi'a Muslims the principal figure of religious authority is the *imam*. Muhammad completed 'the cycle of prophethood', and with it the possibility of further divine revelation. But Shi'a Muslims believe that he instituted 'the cycle of initiation' for the continuing guidance of the community, by appointing as his successor an *imam*. The *imam* was invested with the qualities of inspired and infallible interpretation of the Qur'an. Accordingly the Shi'a speak of

Muslims at the Imam Khomeini Mosque in Tehran, Iran during the midday prayer time.

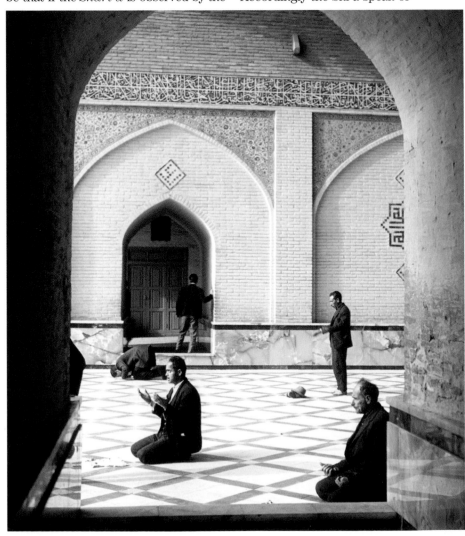

themselves as 'people of appointment and identification'.

The first *imam* was 'Ali. As cousin, adopted son and later son-in-law of Muhammad (by marriage to Fatima), he was not just a member of Muhammad's tribe but also of 'the people of his house'. This intimate family relationship is significant: the Shi'a believe that 'Ali inherited Muhammad's 'spiritual abilities', his *wilayah*. He was infallible in his interpretation of the Qur'an and leadership of the community. And he passed these qualities on to the sons of his marriage with Fatima, Hasan and Husayn, and they to their descendants in the line of *imams*. The Shi'a believe that 'the cycle of *wilayah*' will continue until the end of human history when, on the Last Day, humankind will be resurrected and judged for the afterlife.

The majority of Shi'a, known as Imamis (most of whom live in Iran), believe that the cycle will be completed with the messianic return of the twelfth *imam*, often referred to as the '*imam* of the period'. He is said to have been withdrawn into 'occulation' since the third century of Islam. His guidance is still accessible through 'doctors of the law' (*mujtahidun*) of whom the most senior in Iran are the *ayatollahs*. It is they who have the right to interpret the *Shari'a* and to make religious rulings.

The history of the Imamis has seen two important offshoots. The Zaidis, mostly found in Yemen today, do not limit the number of *imams* to twelve and interpret their function in a manner similar to the Sunni caliph. The Isma'ilis, meanwhile, have developed highly esoteric doctrines surrounding the *imam*. They have two major groups, the Nizaris, who look to the Aga Khan as their *imam*, and the Musta'lis (more commonly known as the Bohra Muslims) who believe in a hidden *imam* who is represented on earth by their leader, the Da'i.

The two dimensions

Sunni and Shi'a Islam reflect the diversity of the Muslim response to divine revelation. Sunni Islam tends to be more concerned to create and preserve structures of society within which the community may fulfil its God-given responsibilities.

Shi'a Islam began in the martyrdoms of 'Ali and his son, Husayn, and has always been conscious of suffering and alienation in the human condition. It searches for answers in a more esoteric interpretation of the Qur'an and *Shari'a*. But there is obviously no hard and fast distinction. Sunni Islam is also concerned with the inner life and Shi'a with the outer. Moreover, the important mystical tradition of Sufism has seen a confluence of Shi'a and Sunni consciousness.

Sufism

Sunnism and Shi'ism represent the major doctrinal varieties of Islam. Sufism denotes the inner spiritual life of both. The Sufis are not a distinct group or sect; they are simply Muslims – Sunnis or Shi'as – who seek intimacy with God through a discipline of spiritual purification.

The heart of Sufism is the love of God. It is built on the Quranic assurance that 'God loves the God-fearing' (*surah* 3:76), and fulfils their devotions in love. 'Nothing is more beloved to Me' – God is heard to say in a *Holy Hadith* – 'than that my servant approaches Me with constant acts of devotion. And when I love him I am the eye by which he sees and the ear by which he hears. When he approaches a span I approach a cubit, and when he comes walking I come running.'

Among the early Muslims remembered for their devotional insight ranks a woman from Baghdad, Rabi'a al-'Adawiyya (eighth century CE), who prayed: 'O Beloved of my heart, I have none like unto Thee, therefore have pity this day on the sinner who comes

'The governments of the world should know that Islam cannot be defeated. Islam will be victorious in all the countries of the world, and Islam and the teachings of the Qur'an will prevail all over the world.'

Ayatollah Khomeini

Sufi dervishes dancing the *Tannura*, a sacred meditative form of dance.

to Thee. O my Hope and my Rest and my Delight, the heart can love none other than Thee.' Later treatises on Sufi devotion defined love as that which 'obliterates from the heart everything except the Beloved'.

It is misleading, therefore, to think of Sufism as an 'ism'. The English word comes from the Arabic *tasawwuf* which could be translated 'self-purification', provided we understand that human endeavour is incomplete unless fulfilled by divine love. *Sufi* (fem. *sufiyya*) denotes a person whose heart is purified from the pollution of this world.

The prophet Muhammad is venerated by Muslims as a Sufi. Religious tradition tells of the miraculous cleansing of his heart as a child, and of his ascension to heaven (*mi raj*) by night when, through prayer, he experienced the mystery of God's all-embracing unity.

Amongst his early followers were the so-called 'people of the bench' (*'ahl al-suffa*) who rarely left the mosque in

Medina due to the constancy of their prayers. They wore a simple tunic made of wool (*suf*), symbolizing their obedience to the example of the many prophets – especially Jesus son of Mary (*Isa ibn Mariam*) – who practised ascetism in rejection of worldly comforts.

Strictly speaking a Sufi should never describe himself, nor a Sufiyya herself, by this term. They use the related word *mutasawwif* (fem. *mutasawwifa*), 'one who tries to be a sufi'. The difference is critical. A classical Persian Sufi authority (al-Hujwiri) explained it as follows:

'The *sufi* is he that is dead to self and lives by the Truth; he has escaped from the grip of human faculties and has truly attained to God. The *mutasawwif* is he that seeks to reach this rank by means of self-mortification and in his search rectifies his conduct in accordance with the Sufis' example.'

The way of purification through self-practice. Acts of self-mortification are called *mujahadat* – a word connected to the Arabic term *jihad* which means 'striving'. The Prophet Muhammad explained that the highest level of *jihad* is the inward striving of the soul for purification.

The Sufi path is like a ladder. Each rung is a 'stage' (*maqam*) of spiritual striving which must be achieved before passing to the next. Sufi orders differ in the ways they identify and arrange the stages, but they typically involve repentance, conversion, renunciation, trust, gratitude, poverty, patience and love. Each stage belongs to the category of acts, and requires ceaseless human striving.

But human effort of itself is insufficient as a means of approaching God. Sufis teach that every stage of spiritual striving needs to be fulfilled by a special grace which God bestows on the heart of the *mutasawwif*. This is called a state (*hal*). They are understood as spiritual qualities of the heart which descend from God, without the recipient being able to attract or repel them by his or her own effort. They also are variously understood in the Sufi orders, but commonly include satisfaction, certainty, intimacy, separation, love, union and knowledge/*gnosis*.

Some say that the states are temporary, others that they are permanent. But all agree that they belong to the category of divine gifts. They complement and transform acts of self-mortification, and bring the *mutasawwif* to the goal of the path.

Through practice of the path, Sufis seek to internalize the worship and law of Islam. In addition to the ordinary mosque service, they developed other forms of worship. These range from the quiet recitation (*dhikr*) of the Names of God, to singing hymns in praise of the Prophet Muhammad, and some orders use music and dance to intensify the emotional side of worship.

mortification involves the spiritual path (*tariqah*). This is modelled on the prophet's heavenly ascent. The prophet Muhammad once said that the paths are equal in number to the true believers, meaning that each person should develop his or her own spiritual practice.

As Islam developed and spread, Sufis saw the dangers of undisciplined spiritual practices. They insisted that a *mutasawwif* must follow the guidance of a spiritual master (*shaykh, pir*); to dispense with a spiritual master is to follow the devil instead. So the path was institutionalized in a variety of spiritual fraternities or orders which followed different masters. They stretched across the medieval Muslim world, and though they varied greatly from one another, each united its followers from different continents in common spiritual disciplines.

All these orders drew a fundamental distinction in the nature of spiritual

'The complete mystic "way" includes both intellectual belief and practical activity; the latter consists in getting rid of the obstacles in the self and in stripping off its base characteristic and vicious morals, so that the heart may attain to freedom from what is not God and to constant recollection of Him.'
Al-Ghazali

'God dwells in the heart, according to the Tradition, "Neither my earth nor my heavens contain me, but I am contained in the heart of my servant who believes."'
Ibn al-'Arabi, Tarjumanu al-Ashwaq

THE UNITY AND VARIETY OF ISLAM

The destination of the path is intimacy with God. The person who reaches it is a *wali* (fem. *waliyya*) or 'saint' (literally, one who is near to God). Only a saint can truly be called a Sufi. A passage from the Qur'an is often quoted to express this highest of spiritual states: 'All upon earth passes away; the face of your Lord, Owner of Glory and Grace, abides' (*surah* 55:27–28). The antithesis of 'passing away' (*fana'*) and 'abiding' (*baqa*) point to the Sufi experience of God. By annihilating all that is impure, only the pure remains.

If God alone is pure, can one who has escaped impurity be separate from God? Answers to this question lead into Sufi metaphysics which explore the mystery of divine unity (*tawhid*). In denying ultimate separation of duality between God and the purified human heart or soul, Sufi mysticism has courted reprimand, even rejection, by other Muslims.

A distinction can therefore be drawn between Sufism as the spiritual internalizing of Quranic teaching and prophetic example, with emphasis on an ascetic life style; and Sufism as mystical doctrine which, with its emphasis on the unitive knowledge of God, has often lived in tension with the mainstream of Sunni and Shi'a thought, verging into the sectarian.

Since the nineteenth century the great Sufi orders of medieval history have shrunk before the pressures of modern renewal movements. These seek to reform medieval practice by re-emphasizing the insight of the Qur'an and the inspiration of the Prophet's practice. On this criterion ascetic Sufism continues to flourish in individual practice, and contemporary Sufis, like people of the spirit in other religions, struggle against the pollution of modern materialistic values.

A little girl in Ibadan, Nigeria reads an excerpt from the Qur'an as her fellow pupils watch.

'When the Qur'an is read, listen to it with attention, and hold your peace: that ye may receive Mercy.'

The Qur'an, surah 7:204.

Sacred Writings

PETER G. RIDDELL

For Muslims the Qur'an represents the supreme revelation of God's word in written form. It is unique among revealed books, universal in its application and eternal in its relevance. It is extracted from a tablet on which God's word is recorded and kept in heaven. Orthodox belief among the Sunni majority considers the Qur'an to be co-eternal with God. According to the great Muslim scholar and jurist Abu Hanifa (d. c. 767), 'its letters, vowel points and writing are all created, for these are the works of man, but God's word is uncreated... he who says that the word of God is created is an infidel'.

Muslims show great reverence for the Qur'an, handling and storing it with great care. Reading the Qur'an is widely considered to bring rewards, increasing with each word read. The reader will be brought closer to God through the act of frequent reading. Memorizing the Quranic text is considered an act of considerable piety. Anyone who memorizes the entire text (a *hafiz*) is highly respected. Furthermore, the pages of the Qur'an are considered by many Muslims to have healing qualities.

There is a supplementary body of sacred writing in Islam: the *Hadith* collections or Prophetic Traditions, much more voluminous than the Qur'an, which serve as a model for Muslims around the world in their daily lives.

Structure of the Qur'an

The Qur'an is divided into 114 chapters. With the exception of chapter one, The Opening, these are arranged in order of decreasing length. Each chapter (*surah*) has a number and a title, which is typically based on a key

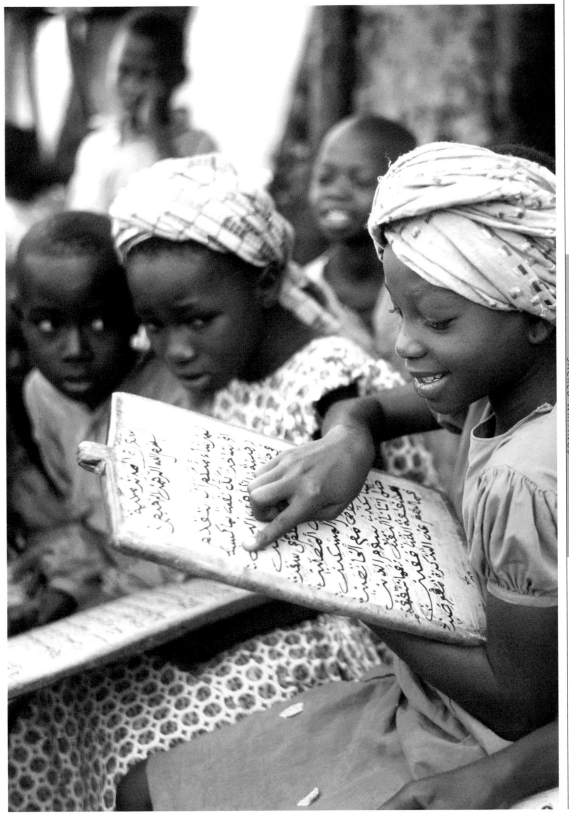

word or theme in the chapter: The Women (4), The Cave (18), The Moon (54). The basic unit of a chapter is the verse (*ayah*). In all, the Qur'an has over 6,200 verses. The Quranic chapters are identified with two periods in time: those revealed to Muhammad at Mecca and those revealed at Medina. The former tend to reflect the voice of Muhammad as protester criticizing the Meccan status quo centred on idolatry, social injustice and other evils. The Medinan chapters reflect Muhammad's role as community leader, addressing legal issues, matters to do with building the structures of state, inter-ethnic and inter-religious relations.

Themes in the Qur'an

The Qur'an presents a holistic theology, claiming authority over all aspects of life, allowing no separation between sacred and secular. It includes diverse themes containing morals indicating right from wrong, as well as injunctions to obey and fear God. There are parables, or allegorical stories teaching a lesson, which Muslim scholars stress are not designed as entertainment but rather for instruction. Passages of sheer ecstasy, relating to Muhammad's revelatory experiences, were later to become models for Islamic mystics. There are legal passages, designed to assist with the organization of the Muslim community; chapters of encouragement, especially those revealed when the embryonic Muslim community was facing dangers and challenges; sections presenting oral traditions relating to Biblical characters and events; sections including sarcasm, argumentation, response, mercy and even ruthlessness; and biographical material from which a life of Muhammad can be constructed.

The ornate Cairo Qur'an, created for the Sultan of Morocco in the 18th century.

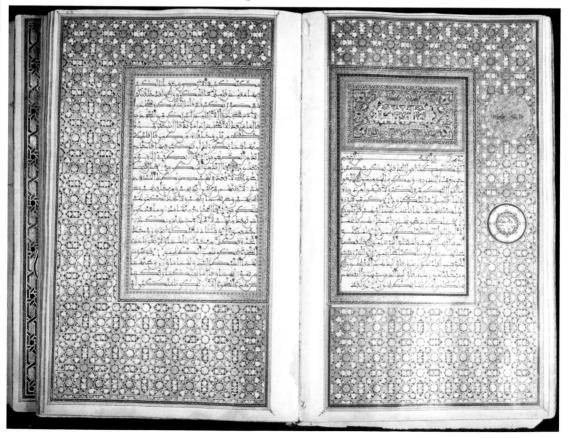

Abrogation

With such diverse themes, revealed over the final twenty-three years of Muhammad's lifetime, inevitably some verses appear to contradict others. This is addressed by the Qur'an itself in *surah* 2:106, which explains that later verses abrogate earlier verses where the content is contradictory. Muslims consider this does not point to error in the earlier verse. Rather, the relevance of the verse being abrogated was specific to a time or context, with the later verse addressing a broader or later context. So prayer in the direction of Jerusalem, referred to in *surah* 2:143, was abrogated by *surah* 2:144, stipulating prayer towards Mecca. This reflected the changing relationship between the emerging Muslim community and the Jewish community of Arabia.

Compilation of the Quranic text

According to the Prophetic Traditions, the first official collection of the Qur'an took place under the first Caliph, Abu Bakr (632–34). However, regional variation occurred in copies of the Qur'an written or memorized, so the third Caliph 'Uthman (644–56) had an official collection made in 649/50. Oral traditions continued to circulate and diversify. This was compounded by the inadequacies of the Arabic language script at the time. Further reform and standardization were considered necessary, and this was undertaken by Abu Bakr bin Mujahid (d. 936). As a result of his efforts, seven readings of the Quranic text were accepted as canonical.

Translation of the Quranic text

The Qur'an in its Arabic original has been prescribed in liturgical contexts by three of the four Sunni law schools since the earliest period of Islamic history. Only the Hanafite school has shown some flexibility, with founder Abu Hanifa allowing worshippers with no Arabic to recite the opening *surah* of the Qur'an in Persian. This right was subsequently extended to speakers of other languages. In the twentieth century there was further liberalization of attitudes towards translation, especially in Turkey and Egypt. Nevertheless, translated texts are still considered as commentaries on the Qur'an, not the Qur'an itself.

The *Hadith*

Hadith accounts are divided into two groups. The sacred *Hadith qudsi* are considered to include God's direct words (mediated through Muhammad) as in the case of the Qur'an. The prophetic *Hadith sharif* record Muhammad's own wise words and deeds. The influential scholar al-Ghazali (1058–1111) shows the importance of the *Hadith* collections when he says, 'God has but one word which differs only in the mode of its expression. On occasions God indicates His word by the Qur'an; on others, by words in another style, not publicly recited, and called the Prophetic tradition. Both are mediated by the Prophet.'

The Torah, the Psalms and the gospel

The Qur'an recognizes earlier sacred writings: the Torah given to Moses, the Psalms to David and the gospel to Jesus. However, it charges both Jews and Christians with corrupting these earlier revelations by changing the text or wilfully misinterpreting it. Hence, the Qur'an sees itself as the final, perfect revelation supplanting those which went before. Some Islamic thinkers recognize a continuing measure of divine authority in the earlier scriptures, but challenge their interpretation by Jews and Christians.

'Whatever communications We abrogate or cause to be forgotten, We bring one better than it or like it. Do you not know that Allah has power over all things?'

The Qur'an, surah 2:106

'The warrior who truly fights for God's cause is he who looks after a widow or a poor person.'

Sahih Bukhari, Volume 7, Book 64, Number 265

SACRED WRITINGS

Beliefs

PETER G. RIDDELL

The Arabic term *iman* is used to designate the system of belief in Islam. It draws on Quranic verses such as 4:136: 'O you who believe! Believe in Allah and His Apostle and the Book which He has revealed to His Apostle and the Book which He revealed before; and whoever disbelieves in Allah and His angels and His apostles and the Last Day, he indeed strays off into a remote error.' This verse presents a concise listing of core articles of faith within Islam.

Oneness of God

The Islamic belief system is centred on an uncompromising monotheism, called *tawhid*, the oneness of God. Many Quranic verses provide an insight into the attributes and characteristic features of God: 'Allah is He besides Whom there is no god, the Everliving, the Self-subsisting by Whom all subsist; slumber does not overtake Him nor sleep; whatever is in the heavens and whatever is in the earth is His; who is he that can intercede with Him but by His permission? He knows what is before them and what is behind them, and they cannot comprehend anything out of His knowledge except what He pleases. His knowledge extends over the heavens and the earth, and the preservation of them both tires Him not, and He is the Most High, the Great' (*surah* 2:255).

God is supreme, eternal and omnipotent. He sees all things and is present everywhere. He is the sole creator and sustainer of the universe, and He controls life and death for all creatures. God has ninety-nine names, according to Muslim belief, representing his numerous attributes

and aspects. The *Hadith* accounts provide the most important source for these names. Some relate to compassion and love, yet the depiction of God within Muslim theology is more of a God whom one reveres, of whom one is in awe and to whom one is obedient.

The nature of God can be gleaned in part by a series of negative statements made within the Islamic sacred writings. 'In the name of Allah, the Beneficent, the Merciful. Say: He is Allah, the One! Allah, the eternally Besought of all! Whom all creatures need. He neither eats nor drinks. He begotteth not nor was begotten. And there is none comparable unto Him' (The Qur'an, *surah* 112). God is not a Trinity, but is one. God has not been created, nor is he in a relationship of father, brother, son with any other. He depends on no one, and has no needs. Nothing resembles Him. He is without imperfections.

Angelic servants

Belief in angels is another important article of faith. The Qur'an records that angels are created from light, and are so numerous that only God knows their exact number. Angels have no offspring, being neither male nor female. Angels serve God in various ways. The classical commentator Tabari defines angels as 'God's messengers between Him and His prophets, and those of His servants to whom they are sent'.

The greatest of the angels is Jibril, or Gabriel, who was, according to Muslim belief, the angel who transmitted the Qur'an to Muhammad. Jibril also functions as the Holy Spirit within Islamic belief. An angel was also the means used by God to tell Mary of the impending birth of her son Jesus: 'When the angels said: O Mariam, surely Allah gives you good news with a Word from Him (of one) whose name is the Messiah, Isa son of

Mohammed's Paradise, a miniature from *The History of Mohammed*, 1030.

Mariam, worthy of regard in this world and the hereafter and of those who are made near (to Allah)' (The Qur'an, *surah* 3:45).

Angels are assigned other tasks by God, according to Islamic belief. They utter continuous praise of God, they bear His throne and they accompany believers in prayer. According to the *Hadith* accounts, angels record the deeds of every person.

The angel Izra'il is responsible for drawing out the souls of the dying, while Israfil will sound the trumpet on the Last Day, the Day of Judgment. Other angels guard hell and direct its affairs. The Qur'an warns that opposing the angels is tantamount to opposing God, as they are His envoys: 'Whoever is an enemy to Allah and His angels and apostles, to Gabriel and Michael – Lo! Allah is an enemy to those who reject Faith' (*surah* 2:98).

Revealed books

Sacred Scriptures revealed to humankind throughout history are of two types. The more substantial ones are called *Kutub* (Books), while the smaller ones are known as *Suhuf* (Scrolls). Over 100 works are believed to have been revealed throughout history. These include scrolls revealed to Adam, Seth, Enoch and Abraham, now lost.

Only four revealed scriptures have survived, according to Islamic belief. They are mentioned by name in the Qur'an. The first is the *Tawrat*, the Jewish Torah, given by divine inspiration to Moses, according to the Quranic record: 'And before [the Qur'an] was the Book of Moses as a guide and a mercy...' (*surah* 46:12). This was followed by the *Zabur* (Psalms), revealed to David; the *Injil* (gospel), revealed to Jesus; and the Qur'an, revealed to Muhammad. The various revealed books represented God's blueprint for people to live according to God's law.

For Muslims the Qur'an is the last and the definitive revelation, the repository of perfect truth. It supplants all earlier revelations sent by God to humankind through the prophets. This is stated clearly in *Hadith* accounts anticipating events in the End Times: 'Narrated Abu Huraira: Allah's Apostle said "How will you be when the son of Mary [i.e. Jesus] descends amongst you and he will judge people by the Law of the Qur'an and not by the law of Gospel?"' (*Sahih Bukhari*, Volume 4, Book 55, No. 658).

Messengers and prophets

God thus sends his angels with revealed books to the created world. A key link in this chain is provided by messengers and prophets, as it is they who must transmit the content of the revealed books to all people.

Islamic belief considers a messenger (*Rasul*) to be a prophet (*Nabi*) of a specific type. The former is given a new set of divine laws and a new revealed book. Prophets who are not messengers are sent to transmit and implement previously revealed dispensations. The Qur'an mentions some twenty-five messengers by name. The *Hadith* collections refer to a total of 124,000 prophets, of whom 313 were messengers. All prophets, whether messengers or not, are considered to perform miracles.

The words of the prophets are not their own, but are of God. The medieval scholar Ibn Khaldun portrays this prophetic role as mediator in the following terms: 'Allah has chosen individuals from among humankind whom He has honoured by Himself speaking to them to mould them according to His understanding, and to make them the mediators between Himself and His servants.' It is in this context that Islamic prophets are believed to be free from sin.

Many of the prophets named in the

Qur'an have counterparts in the Bible: 'And We bestowed upon [Abraham] Isaac and Jacob; each of them We guided; and Noah did We guide aforetime; and of his seed (We guided) David and Solomon and Job and Joseph and Moses and Aaron. Thus do We reward the good' (*surah* 6:84). However, this is not the case with all: for example, Hud, Salih and Luqman are all considered as Arabian prophets.

Muhammad represents the last messenger and prophet of God. Furthermore, according to the Islamic sacred writings, he is the greatest of all the prophets, having been given special functions: 'Narrated Jabir bin 'Abdullah: Allah's Apostle said, "I have been given five things which were not given to any amongst the Prophets before me"' (*Sahih Bukhari*, Volume 1, Book 8, No. 429). These comprise divine assistance in achieving victory over his enemies, the right of prayer for his followers anywhere in the world, the right to take booty after battle, a mission to all humankind, and the right of intercession on the Day of Judgment.

Resurrection and judgment
The message transmitted by the prophets, contained in revealed books, borne by angels and originating from God warns Muslims of an impending Day of Resurrection and Judgment. The exact time of the Day of Judgment is unknown to all except Allah. All that is known is that it will be on a Friday, the tenth day of the month of Muharram.

The *Hadith* collections point to signs of the approaching Day of Judgment. These include an increase in sin in the world, widespread disobedience of parental authority and disrespect for elders, an increase in debauchery, an increase in the numbers of women vis-à-vis men in the world and incompetent people of lowly station assuming positions of leadership.

On the Day of Judgment all people will be judged according to their sincere repentance and good deeds, measured by the degree to which they have followed God's law (the *Shari'a*). Believers will hold a book recording their life's deeds in their right hand, while unbelievers will hold their book of deeds in their left. Everyone's deeds will be weighed on scales. No last minute repentance will be accepted: 'And repentance is not for those who go on doing evil deeds, until when death comes to one of them, he says: Surely now I repent; nor (for) those who die while they are unbelievers. These are they for whom We have prepared a painful chastisement' (The Qur'an, *surah* 4:18).

The Islamic sacred writings describe an afterlife, with the descriptions being especially graphic in the *Hadith* collections. If one earns favour from God on the Day of Judgment, according to good deeds, right belief and sincere repentance of sins, heaven is the reward. This is a place of eternal bliss, resembling a garden with rivers, carpets, cushions, fruit and pure maidens.

In contrast, an eternal hell awaits those who have not followed God's law and held right belief. Hell is a place of great torment with fire and boiling water, where skin is scalded, renewed and scalded again. The Tree of Zaqqum provides bad fruit, and the damned are forced to eat from it: '… the tree of Zaqqum? Surely We have made it to be a trial to the unjust. Surely it is a tree that grows in the bottom of the hell; Its produce is as it were the heads of the serpents. Then most surely they shall eat of it and fill (their) bellies with it. Then most surely they shall have after it to drink of a mixture prepared in boiling water. Then most surely their return shall be to hell' (*surah* 37:62–68).

BELIEFS

All is decreed by God

Belief in God's decrees is the final article of faith. The Qur'an stresses that all is decreed by God: 'And the sun runs on to a term appointed for it; that is the ordinance of the Mighty, the Knowing. And (as for) the moon, We have ordained for it stages till it becomes again as an old dry palm branch' (*surah* 36:38–39).

God controls the past, present and future of each individual Muslim. Among the Muslim masses, this translates to a firm belief in God's preordination of all things, often verging on fatalism. This receives sustenance from Quranic verses such as the following: 'Wherever you are, death will overtake you, though you are in lofty towers, and if a benefit comes to them, they say: This is from Allah; and if a misfortune befalls them, they say: This is from you. Say: All is from Allah, but what is the matter with these people that they do not make approach to understanding what is told (them)?' (*surah* 4:78).

At the level of Islamic scholarship, this article of faith has given rise throughout history to a dynamic debate about the degree of human ability to determine events, within an overall framework of God's predestination.

Worship and Festivals

DAVID KERR

The Qur'an sees men and women as religious beings. 'I created… humankind only that they might worship me,' the Muslim hears God say in the Qur'an. Each individual is an *'abd* of God, a term which conveys the twin meanings of 'worshipper' and 'servant' in a single word. And this description applies to all aspects of human life, all of which is lived under the command of God. There is no distinction between worship and the wholeness of human life.

Submission to God

Islam understands itself fundamentally as being 'natural religion', in that *every* created thing exists in dependence upon God, in obedience to his creative and sustaining power and with the purpose of expressing adoration to God. For the human, this should lead to a conscious commitment to a life of thankful and praise-giving obedience to God. The word *muslim* means one who lives his life according to God's will. *Islam* means 'submission to God'.

Worship (*'ibada*) and the activities of the workaday world (*mu'amallat*) are joint expressions of the character of *'abd*. The mosque cannot be separated from the marketplace, nor politics from praise.

As far as worship is concerned, the Qur'an sees body and spirit as inseparably combined in the wholeness of human worship. Islam has no term for 'spirituality'; for its religious devotion seeks to preserve an equilibrium between the 'outward' and the 'inward' in worship. Believers' external acts of worship depend on their internal intention, and the Qur'an is concerned that both should be 'for the pleasure of God'. So while the holy law provides a code of practice as a framework for Muslim worship, the worship depends on the inner dynamic of thankful and praise-giving obedience, the discipline of the soul to 'remember God always'.

The confession of faith

The Islamic code of conduct is founded upon the bedrock of the testimony of faith, the *shahadah*. This is the first pillar of Islam. When spoken in Arabic and with sincere intention, it is a commitment to obey God and follow the prophet.

'I bear witness that there is no god but God; I bear witness that Muhammad is the Apostle of God.'

These are the first words breathed into a child's ear at birth and the last which Muslims would utter with their dying breath – the lantern for life and the hope for the mercy of God in the life hereafter. They point to the one God who has spoken finally through the Qur'an; and they point to Muhammad, 'the Seal of the Prophets', sent to all humankind to transmit and interpret the Qur'an. The words of the *shahadah* summon Muslims to worship throughout the world, and their meaning is the heart of prayer and meditation.

Praying together

The Qur'an identifies a human being as 'worshipper'. It also places the individual worshipper, male or female, in the context of a worshipping community.

'Hold fast, all of you, to the rope of God, and do not separate… and may

> 'O believers, when you stand up to pray wash your faces, and your hands up to the elbows, and wipe your heads, and your feet up to the ankles. If you are defiled, purify yourselves.'
>
> The Qur'an, surah 5:8

Festivals of Islam

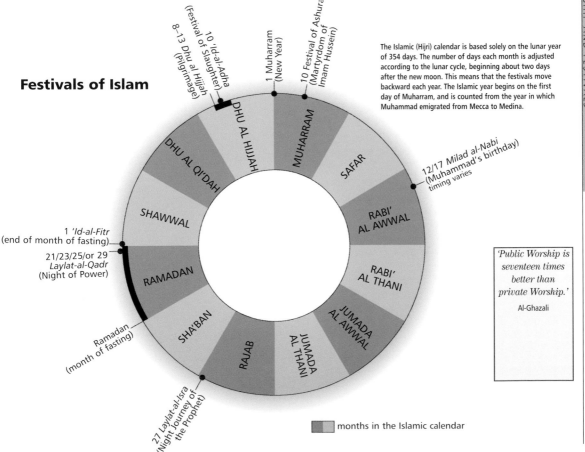

The Islamic (Hijri) calendar is based solely on the lunar year of 354 days. The number of days each month is adjusted according to the lunar cycle, beginning about two days after the new moon. This means that the festivals move backward each year. The Islamic year begins on the first day of Muharram, and is counted from the year in which Muhammad emigrated from Mecca to Medina.

10 'Id-al-Adha (Festival of Slaughter)
8–13 Dhu al Hijah (Pilgrimage)
1 Muharram (New Year)
10 Festival of Ashura (Martyrdom of Imam Hussein)

DHU AL HIJJAH
MUHARRAM
SAFAR
12/17 Milad al-Nabi (Muhammad's birthday) timing varies
DHU AL QI'DAH
RABI' AL AWWAL
SHAWWAL
RABI' AL THANI
1 'Id-al-Fitr (end of month of fasting)
21/23/25/or 29 Laylat-al-Qadr (Night of Power)
RAMADAN
JUMADA AL AWWAL
Ramadan (month of fasting)
SHA'BAN
RAJAB
JUMADA AL THANI
27 Laylat-al-Isra (Night Journey of the Prophet)

months in the Islamic calendar

> 'Public Worship is seventeen times better than private Worship.'
>
> Al-Ghazali

there spring from you a community who invite to goodness, enjoin right conduct and forbid indecency; such are they who are successful.'

The *Shari'a* codifies and coordinates the practice of a worshipping community. Worship is a communal act as well as one of individual commitment. To affirm the unity of God (*tawhid*) is necessarily to affirm the unity of the created order and of humankind in right worship.

This community orientation of Islamic worship is symbolized and demonstrated in the ritual of *salah*, the liturgical form of prayer, which it is the duty of all Muslims to observe at fixed hours. Prayer is the second pillar of Islam. There are five prayer times, each preceded by obligatory ritual washing – dawn, midday, mid-afternoon, sunset

and night – and they serve to remind Muslims in a regular and disciplined manner of their status before God as 'worshipful servants'. From the moment of the *muezzin*'s call and the preliminary washings, Muslims practise *salah*. On Fridays *salah* is a communal act.

An expression of this is the common direction (towards the Ka'ba in Mecca) in which all Muslims turn in prayer. Around the globe all are united in direction and in intention within a human circle of worshippers. At a signal from the prayer leader, the *imam*, men and women assemble separately in rows, at the mosque or in the home or place of work, taking care that each person is close to the next. Carefully following the lead of the

A muslim at prayer in Id Kah Mosque, Kashi, Xinjiang, China.

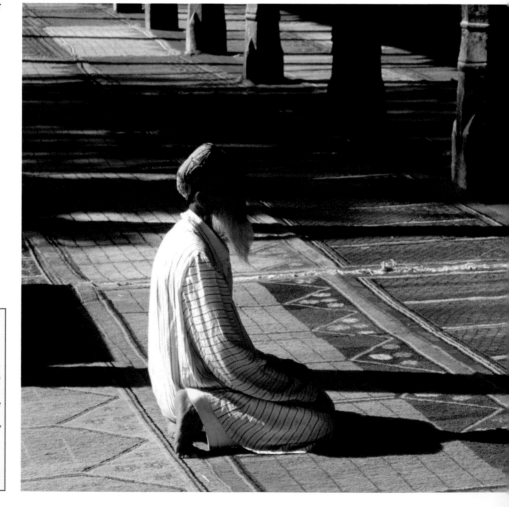

'... proclaim thy Lord's praise before the rising of the sun, and before its setting, and proclaim thy Lord's praise in the watches of the night, and at the ends of the day...'

The Qur'an, *surah* 20:130

imam, they pray as a single body, quietly reciting words of prayer from the Qur'an. At the same time they bow their bodies in a series of ritual movements until, from an initial standing position, all are upon their knees with foreheads touching the floor – the whole congregation enacting as a single body its submission before the majesty of God and asking for his guidance and mercy. Each of the five sets of prayers includes the repetition of *Allahu akbar* ('God is greatest') and of the first *surah* of the Qur'an, itself a prayer. At the end of the prayer each person passes the Arabic words of peace to neighbours on right and left: *as-salamu alaikum*, 'peace be upon you'. Private prayers often follow the public service.

The twofold fruit of giving

'O you who believe, perform the *salah* and give the *zakah*.' Prayer is linked closely with almsgiving, the third pillar of Islam, often described by modern Muslims as the pillar of social action. Externally *zakah* is the duty of sharing one's wealth with the poor, the needy, the debtor, the prisoner, the wayfarer – all who are less fortunate than oneself but equally part of the worshipping community and equally precious to God. The Qur'an is less concerned with the quantity, and more with the quality of giving. When it is offered 'in search of God's pleasure and for the strengthening of their own souls, it is as the likeness of a garden on a hill; the rainstorm smites it and it brings forth its fruit twofold'. The inward attitude is all-important; discretion is preferred to ostentation, and reproach on the part of the giver makes the action worthless.

The *Shari'a* is meticulous in determining the amounts of alms which should be given on different categories of possessions, but contemporary practice simplifies the matter to an annual rate of 2.5 per cent of one's cash balance. But Muslim devotional literature reflects equally the inwardness of *zakah* as 'purification' of the soul. It is a mercy to the giver as much as to the recipient. It is a means to atone for sins which are motivated by human self-centredness or by irresponsible stewardship of possessions.

The most-loved duty of worship

Special alms are given on the two main religious festivals of the Islamic calendar, the first of which, *'Id al-Fitr* or *Bairam*, marks the end of Ramadan, the holy month of fasting. Fasting (*sawm*) is the fourth pillar of Muslim worship, and involves a total abstinence from food and drink through the daylight hours of the entire month, from early dawn to sunset.

In some ways this is the most obviously communal of the duties of

'A mosque that was founded upon godfearing from the first day is worthier for thee to stand in; therein are men who love to cleanse themselves; and God loves those who cleanse themselves.'

The Qur'an, *surah* 9:109

WORSHIP AND FESTIVALS

The minarets of the Golden Mosque of Kazimayn, Baghdad, Iraq, which holds the remains of many revered Shi'a leaders.

Islamic worship. The physical discipline means that social behaviour of the whole community has to change for the duration of the month; the pace of life slows down and there is time for reflection. It is a period when social relationships are reaffirmed, reconciliations encouraged, and the solidarity of the community is expressed. Mosque attendance swells, particularly on the Night of Power (*laylat al-qadr*) towards the end of the month, when Muslims commemorate the descent of the Qur'an from heaven and the beginning of Muhammad's ministry.

The fundamental intention of fasting is thanksgiving. Inwardly the fast is thought of as a disciplining of the soul to wait patiently upon God who guides and provides. This inward aspect is of great importance. Muhammad is reported to have said that of all the duties of worship, *sawm* is the most loved by God since it is seen only by him.

To Mecca

The fifth of the fundamental duties of Islamic worship, to be fulfilled once in a lifetime if at all possible, is the *Hajj*, the pilgrimage to Mecca and its vicinity.

Here are the most holy of holy places for Muslims, full of 'memorials' of God's guidance in times past. There are associations with Muhammad who began his life and ministry in the city, and also with his prophetic precursor Abraham who, according to the Qur'an, built the Ka'ba, helped by his son, Ishmael, as a sign of their submission to God, with the prayer that God would show them 'our ways of worship'.

A visit to Mecca has religious significance for Muslims at any time of the year. But with the twelfth month of the calendar, *Dhu al Hijjah*, the season of the *Hajj* or Great Pilgrimage arrives. (At any other time it is a Little Pilgrimage.) Pilgrims flock to Mecca, each wearing the simple pilgrimage clothing of white cloth denoting the state of ritual purification. They congregate in the Great Mosque and the first rite of pilgrimage is performed – the circumambulation around the Ka'ba. This is followed by running seven times between two small hills, recalling the plight of Hagar and her son, Ishmael, who, in Islamic, Jewish and Christian tradition, were saved from certain death by a spring of water which God caused to break through the desert sands. This well is named in the Islamic tradition as

'... *proclaim among men the Pilgrimage, and they shall come unto thee on foot and upon every lean beast, they shall come from every deep ravine and they may witness things profitable to them and mention God's name on days well-known... Let them finish with their self-neglect and let them fulfil their vows, and go about the Ancient House.'*

The Qur'an, *surah* 22:28–30

zamzam, and from it the pilgrims may draw holy water before journeying a few miles out of Mecca to Mount Arafat where the *Hajj* comes to its climax. Here the pilgrims observe the rite of 'standing' from midday to sunset in meditation before God. Then they begin the return journey to Mecca, stopping overnight at Mazdalifa, where each pilgrim gathers pebbles. The following day these are thrown ritually against three stone pillars in the neighbouring village of Mina, recalling the moments in Abraham's life when he resisted Satan's temptations to disobey God. God had commanded him to prepare his son (Ishmael) for sacrifice as a test of his obedience (*islam*). The Qur'an tells how the child was ransomed 'with a tremendous victim', and in joyful recollection of this act of divine mercy the pilgrims offer the ritual sacrifice of sheep or camels, the meaning of which is clearly stated in the Qur'an: 'their flesh and blood reach not to God, but your devotion reaches him'.

With the intention of magnifying God and remembering him 'with a more lively remembrance', Muslims throughout the world join with the pilgrims in Mina for the Feast of the Slaughter, which brings the *Hajj* to an end. Muslims remember their corporate identity and responsibility as a worshipping community created by Muhammad. Muhammad believed that this festival was the fulfilment of the Muslim community for which Abraham is said to have prayed before the Ka'ba: 'Our Lord make us submissive to thee, and of our seed a community submissive to thee, and show us our ways of worship, and turn towards us. Lo! thou, only thou, art the Relenting, the Merciful' (The Qur'an, *surah* 2:128).

The Law of Islam

NORMAN ANDERSON

Down the centuries the traditional education of Muslims has rested on twin pillars. Theology taught them what they should believe, and the sacred law prescribed how they should behave. And in practice the law has been the senior partner, for Islam has always been far more explicit about the quality of life God has ordained for his creatures than about the nature of the Creator himself. Although the role of Islamic law has changed considerably in recent years, it can still be described as 'the epitome of Islamic thought, the most typical manifestation of the Islamic way of life, the core and kernel of Islam itself'.

The path of God's commandments
The sacred law of Islam is called the *Shari'a* – a word which originally meant 'the way to a watering-place', but came to be used of the path of God's commandments. It is regarded by Muslims as firmly based on divine revelation, derived from four main sources:

● the Qur'an – which, they believe, has existed eternally in Arabic in heaven, and was revealed piecemeal to Muhammad by the angel Jibril (Gabriel) as occasion demanded;

● the *sunnah* – or practice of the Prophet, as enshrined in countless traditions of what he said, did or permitted;

● the *ijma'* – or consensus of the Muslim community or of its leading scholars;

● *qiyas* – analogical deductions from the first three sources.

Orientalists have, however, shown that the raw material of the *Shari'a* was provided by pre-Islamic customary (and even codified) law and the administrative practices of early Islam – systematized and Islamicized by scholar-jurists in the light of those Islamic norms which had come to be

A young muslim couple with their child in Kuching City, Malaysia.

accepted. They also insist that, for a number of decades, the law was wide open to foreign influences current in the conquered territories or ingrained in the minds of converts to Islam.

The *Shari'a* has often been classified under five categories:

● what God has commanded

● what God has recommended but not made strictly obligatory

● what God has left legally indifferent

● what God has deprecated but not actually prohibited

● what God has expressly forbidden

As such its scope is much wider than any Western concept of law, for it covers every aspect of life. Obviously a great deal of it could never be enforced by any human court, and must be left to the Day of Judgment. But, in theory, the *Shari'a* was a divinely revealed blueprint to which every Muslim, from caliph to slave, must attempt to approximate.

In theory, human regulations were only appropriate in those matters which God had left 'legally indifferent'. In practice, though, from a very early date, even the official courts allowed a number of 'devices' which eased the inconvenience of some of the *Shari'a*'s precepts.

Muslim rulers, moreover, found its standards of proof too exacting for the maintenance of public order. Muslim merchants found its prohibitions too restrictive for the life of the markets. And local communities of Muslims found its rigid prescripts too alien to their age-old customs. So less rigid courts soon appeared beside the official *qadis'* courts. But the fact remains that, until little more than a century ago, the *Shari'a* remained the basic (and residual) law – to which lip-service, at least, was almost always paid – through the length and breadth of the Muslim world.

Interpreting the law

But the *Shari'a* was not a system of law which was either codified or uniform. For although it is regarded as firmly based on divine revelation, it has been developed and elaborated by generations of legal scholars.

These scholars interpreted the relevant verses in the Qur'an and those traditions which they accepted as authentic. They also drew from these sources a plethora of analogical deductions. At first, moreover, any adequately qualified jurist had the right of *ijtihad* – going back to the original sources to derive a rule of law to cover any problem that arose.

At a very early date, however, the

Muslim community became divided between the Sunni, or 'orthodox', majority and the Shi'a and Khariji minorities. These two minorities proceeded to split into further exclusive sub-sects, and the Sunni majority divided into a number of different schools or 'rites'. As these schools and sects crystallized, the right of independent deduction was progressively replaced by the duty to accept the authority of the great jurists of the past (*taqlid*). Today even the most learned Sunni jurists are normally considered to be under this authority. The Ithna 'Ashari sub-sect of the Shi'a (which remains the dominant sect in Iran, for example) still recognizes *mujtahidun* who may exercise *ijtihad* in certain circumstances. It is only among the Isma'ili Shi'as that their *imam* – or, in some cases his representative, the Da'i Mutlaq – can give a wholly authoritative ruling.

Civil law

Since about the middle of the nineteenth century, the position of Islamic law has changed radically throughout the greater part of the Muslim world. First in the Ottoman empire, next in what was then 'British India', and subsequently elsewhere, the impact of modern life has loosened the sway of the *Shari'a* in two major ways. The first change is plain for all to see. In many spheres of life the *Shari'a* has been displaced by new codes of law, largely derived from the Western world. In the Ottoman empire in the 1850s and 1860s, for example, the Commercial Code, the Penal Code, the Code of Commercial Procedure and the Code of Maritime Commerce were all based on French models. But when the Ottoman reformers came to the law of obligations (contract, tort, etc.), they debated whether again to turn to European law or to compile a comparable code derived from Islamic sources.

Eventually the latter view prevailed. So the resultant code (commonly known as the Majalla, completed in 1876) was compiled from the rulings of a selection of Sunni jurists – although all these opinions had received some form of recognition from the Hanafi school. The Majalla was thus of immense jurisprudential significance. For the first time in history, a code of law based firmly on principles derived from the *Shari'a* was enacted by the authority of the state. And for the first time, again, a compilation was made of provisions of heterogeneous origin selected on the broad principle of their suitability to modern life, rather than their established precedent in one particular school. Moreover, all these new codes were administered in secular courts by personnel trained in modern law schools. It was only the family law which continued to be applied in the age-old way in the *Shari'a* courts, uncodified and unreformed.

The second change was less obvious but equally important. In 1915 the intolerable lot of Muslim wives under the dominant Hanafi rules virtually compelled the Sultan to intervene even in matters of family law. So he issued two imperial decrees permitting wives to request a judicial dissolution of marriage in certain circumstances sanctified by one or another of the Sunnian schools. Once this dyke had been opened the tide came in very fast indeed. In 1917 the Ottoman Law of Family Rights was promulgated, based on an extended application of these principles.

In one Muslim country after another, much the same happened. In 'British India' the new secular codes were, of course based on the Common Law of England rather than the Civil Law of France. Here both secular law and the uncodified family law of different religious communities were administered by the same courts. In Turkey, by contrast, the *Shari'a* was

'Guide us in the straight path, the path of those on whom thou has bestowed good.'
The Qur'an, surah 1:5–6

'*Ijtihad* means, in its technical sense, enterprise or initiative. It involves diligence and implies great effort, either to understand or to discriminate the right action in any general issue. It is usually held that a *mujtahid*, one judged capable of *Ijtihad*, qualifies only on the grounds of prolonged grammatical, legal, and theological training.'
Kenneth Cragg

THE LAW OF ISLAM

abolished and European codes (only slightly adapted) were adopted in its place.

In Saudi Arabia, on the other hand, the *Shari'a* remains dominant – though even there statutory regulations have begun to proliferate. Most Muslim countries, however, now have largely secular codes in all except family law – which must, they insist, remain distinctively Islamic. And even this has been codified – in whole or in part – in a way which makes it more suitable for modern life. In countries such as Somalia and the People's Democratic Republic of Yemen the presence of Marxist influence in such codes is sometimes plain to see. Thus the present picture is very different from that of the past. Whereas the once-dominant *Shari'a* is now, for the most part, confined to family law, the current tendency is to produce civil codes which incorporate principles derived from Islamic law alongside those of an alien origin. A few countries have, even more recently, begun to introduce some Islamic criminal sanctions and economic practices – a clear evidence of a resurgence of Islamic fundamentalism. In most Muslim countries, moreover, the law – whatever its origin – has been codified by legislative enactments. Thus the authority of the law, once implicit and transcendent, is now, in most countries, constitutional, resting on the will of the people as expressed by their executive or legislature.

The Qur'an revealed to Muhammad during a battle.

Science, Art and Culture

LOTHAR SCHMALFUSS

Islam has produced not only successful army leaders and statesmen but also equally talented poets and musicians, architects and builders. But above all there were the Muslim philosophers and naturalists, whose achievements between the ninth and fourteenth centuries laid the foundations of modern science on which our civilization was built.

For Muslims to start to study the world, they needed a 'supernatural' incentive. Allah was looked on as the Unapproachable, the Impenetrable, so Islam had taught that his creation was similarly unapproachable. It was Ma'mun, caliph of Baghdad from 813 to 833, who supplied that incentive. In a dream, Ma'mun saw the ghost of Aristotle, who convinced him that there is no contradiction between religion and reason. Thus freed from all his scruples, Ma'mun ordered a 'house of wisdom' to be built. In the library all available books in the world were to be collected.

The works of Greek, Persian and Indian writers were brought together and translated into Arabic, and the knowledge obtained was examined, remodelled and developed. So the starting-point and basis of Islamic knowledge was the Greek conviction that behind the visible chaos of the world there is a fundamental order, ruled by general laws and accessible to human reason. Thus scientific effort pursued primarily philosophical goals, the discovery of the 'basic laws' of the world.

Muslim doctors built on the experience and knowledge of ancient Persia. They discovered the principle of the circulation of the blood, evolved treatment methods for smallpox and practised painless operations under anaesthetics. The books of Avicenna (Ibn Sina), a great philosopher and physician, were used as textbooks in the universities of Europe until the seventeenth century.

In mathematics, Islamic academics learnt from India. From there they adopted the decimal system and also the use of the zero. They called this *sifr*, the empty one. Leonardo de Pisa, who had studied with the Arabs, translated this foreign concept as 'cephirum' and it then developed via 'zefiro' to 'zero'. It was the Arabs also who developed the subject of algebra, using symbols to represent unknown quantities.

In the early centuries, the Arabs had used the stars as guides in the desert. When they became familiar with the work of Ptolemy in the eighth century, they also began to investigate the sky scientifically. Star names and astronomical terms such as zenith, nadir and azimuth are an enduring witness to this work. Scholars also collected their geographical knowledge in atlases and travel guides which recorded the main roads of all known countries, as well as the names and positions of the large towns and their distances one from another. They also calculated the circumference and diameter of the earth.

A worldwide influence

At the height of their culture the knowledge of the Muslims extended to all areas. The fascination they inspired in Europe was enormous. Wherever the West met the East, the West started to learn. In Sicily the court of Friedrich II became a centre of Arabian philosophy and science. In the Levant the Crusader knights became familiar with the Eastern way of life. Above all, this contact took place in Islamic Spain. As early as the tenth century towns were thriving. Cordoba had over 500,000

Illustration of a mechanical device for pouring water, from the *Treatise of Mechanical Methods* by Al-Djazari, 1206.

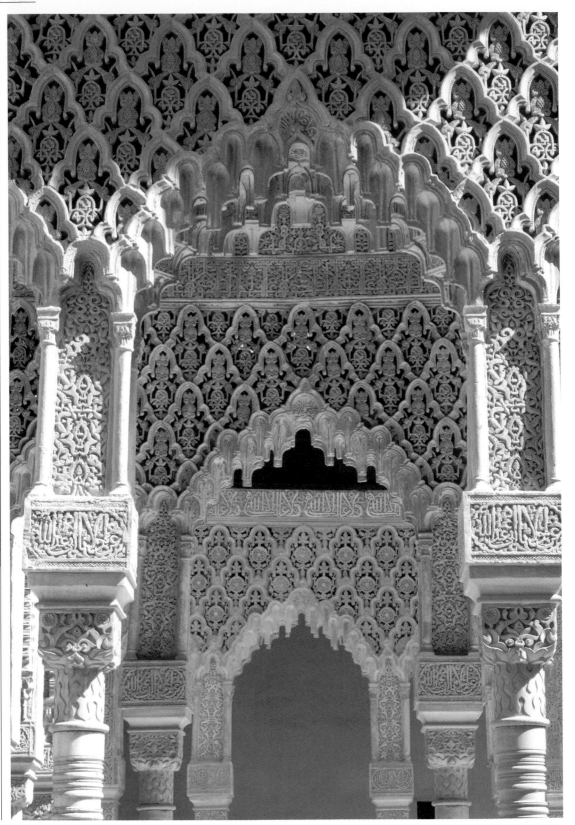

inhabitants with 700 mosques, 300 public baths and 70 libraries. Its streets and squares were paved and brightly lit at night. Everything which made life pleasant was offered for sale: marzipan, soap and perfume, coffee, damsons and sugar, mattresses, caps and jackets, oranges, asparagus. Their influence spread right through Europe. Travelling singers brought their songs and also Arabic instruments – lute and guitar, trumpet, horn and flute. Through Muslim philosophers such as Averroes (Ibn Rushd) and Avicenna (Ibn Sina), Aristotle was rediscovered in the West.

In the fine arts, calligraphy, ceramics and architecture, Islam absorbed influences into itself. It took the cultural inheritance of the peoples it conquered and transformed them, creating an all-embracing culture of a unique type. Islamic architecture can be seen in Cordoba, Granada, Marrakesh and Cairo, in Istanbul and Damascus, Agra and Delhi. All reflect the form and style of the country they are in, as well as the Islamic influence which unites them. The 'Islamic' style has a particular sensitivity for the decorative, and strives to turn the natural appearance of things into the abstract.

The Qur'an teaches that an object and its image are magically united. This was probably why representational art was prohibited.

With the sack of Baghdad by the Mongol invaders in 1258 and the general decline of the Islamic world, the development of art, culture and science in Islam was halted.

Family and Society

THEODORE GABRIEL

The family is a key element of Muslim life and society, one of the cornerstones of social stability and security in the community (*ummah*). The Qur'an and *Hadith* abound in regulations, strictures and caveats regarding the organization and conduct of the Muslim family, and family bonds are the strongest of all social relationships. Loyalty and commitment to the family transcend all other social loyalties.

The Muslim family is established through marriage, Islam frowning on extramarital relationships between men and women. The act of procreation is strictly within the family unit, and fornication and adultery (*zinah*) are sins for which stringent penalties are stipulated in Islamic law. Such infringements are regarded as a source of chaos (*fitnah*). Privacy and modesty are essential for the procreation and proper upbringing of children.

Marriage

Marriage is strongly recommended by the Qur'an and the *Hadith*. Celibacy is not considered a virtue in itself, except in special cases such as the inability to support a wife properly. Whereas marriage (*nikah*) is a social and legal contract, not a sacrament as in some other religions, the Qur'an and *Hadith* provide many guidelines and laws testifying to the fact that it has divine and prophetic sanction. Islam takes human needs and fallibilities into account, and Muslims consider that timely marriage allows one to avoid the sin of fornication. People of marriageable age are advised to marry, rather than run the temptation of extra-marital sexual relationships.

Columns and hanging spandrel work adorn the open courtyard of the Court of the Lions in the Moorish Alhambra Palace, Granada, Spain.

Contrary to Western misapprehension, the consent of both male and female is required for *nikah*. According to Islamic law the prospective bride and bridegroom are not only allowed to meet before marriage, they are advised to. There is no scriptural sanction for forced marriages or so-called 'honour killings'.

Marriage is a public affair, not a purely private or secret act. Technically, at least two witnesses are required to the signing of the marriage contract by

A muslim wedding ceremony in Pakistan.

the bridegroom and the bride's legal guardian. Usually a *qadi* (Islamic judge) is present. The bridegroom gives the wife a dowry (*mahr*), which can be in cash or in kind. This belongs to the woman to use at her discretion (even if the marriage ends in divorce, unless divorce is initiated by the wife).

Polygyny

The Qur'an permits polygyny: a Muslim man may marry up to four wives. (A wife may only marry one husband). This is not a licence for unbridled promiscuity, but a concession to circumstances requiring the care of widows or orphans through marriage, such as the death of large numbers of Muslim males in war (*surah*: 4:3). This message of the Qur'an was revealed in the context of the Battle of Uhud where about 10 per cent of the Muslim males in the community were killed. The Prophet himself – although

> '*O Lord, grant us in our wives and in our offspring the joy of our eyes.*'
>
> The Qur'an, surah 25:74

monogamous from age 25 to 52 (until his wife Kadijah died) – married war widows and orphans to set an example to his disciples. The concession for polygyny came with many stipulations which make it clear that the ideal in Islam is monogamy. The injunction to treat all wives equally comes with the caveat that it is humanly impossible to do so (*surah* 4:129).

Divorce

Divorce (*talaq* – untying of a knot) is permitted in Islam, but was said by the Prophet to be most hateful to God. Men have greater authority to effect divorce, but the Quranic verses permitting this power are combined with exhortations to charity, compassion and justice to women. A waiting period of three months (*idda*) is stipulated to ensure that the wife is not carrying a child, and the divorce can be revoked during this waiting period. Three pronouncements of *talaq* are required to make the divorce final. Though they can all be spoken at the same time and such divorce is binding, this is considered to be irregular or innovative divorce (*talaq bida*) and looked upon as offensive. Remarriage of divorcees is permitted, but when divorce has become final and irrevocable the man cannot marry the divorcee again until she has married some other person and divorced him. This is evidently to ensure that divorcing a woman is not undertaken lightly.

Children

The many stipulations regarding children in the Qur'an, the *Hadith* and *Shari'a* (Islamic Law) testify to the importance placed on the care of children. The Qur'an shows particular concern for the welfare of orphans. Children are treated with great care, affection and responsibility. In return children are expected to love, respect and obey their parents (*surah* 6:152–54).

A parent's first responsibility is to

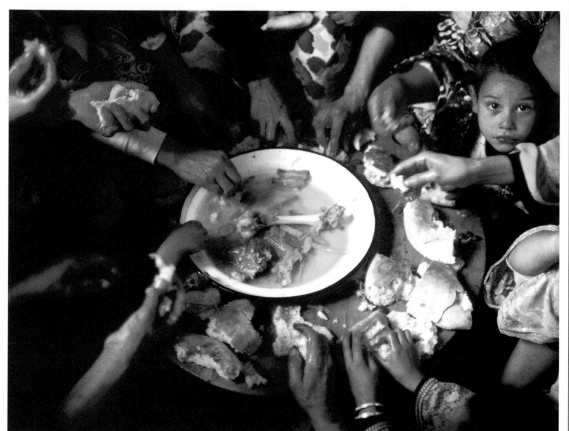

the proper care and upbringing of children, and there are *hadith* which confirm the adage 'charity begins at home'. The care of the family takes priority even over charity for religious purposes. Contrary to Western perception both boys and girls are equally prized by Muslim parents. Children are looked upon as a gift from God, and there are specific injunctions in the Qur'an not to harm children, especially with reference to the pre-Islamic practice of burying female children alive in the sand. The father has primary responsibility for providing for the children, but in cases of divorce or separation the mother has custody.

Conclusion

The Quranic injunctions regarding married life make it clear that the underlying principle is equality and mutuality (*surah* 2:187 and 228), reiterated by Muhammad in his farewell address at Mount Arafat. However, the husband's and wife's duties are not the same. The husband is provider to his wife and children, giving them proper food and clothing, and the wife's role is in maintaining the home in good order and the direct nurturing of children. This equality reflects the theological equality of men and women that many verses in the Qur'an emphasize (such as *surah* 4:1).

A bowl of stew is shared at a name-giving ceremony at Fez, Morocco.

> *'The Qur'an regards the home as a micricosm of the ummah and the world community. It emphasises the importance of making it "the abode of peace" through just living.'*
>
> Riffat Hassan

I am a Muslim

MOHAMMED A. KHAN

I had my first lessons in religion, Islam, on my mother's lap, and learnt to utter a few verses from the Qur'an by heart. Her recitations of the Qur'an in the early hours of the morning left a lasting impression on me, which resounds in my ears to this day whenever I remember her. I lost my father when I was barely one year old, and my young mother had a hard time bringing up a family of six children, hence she sought refuge in religion and prayers, and took special care in our religious education. The verses she memorized carry us through in our daily prayers all our life.

During my youth and working life I was not a particularly devout Muslim. My religion has become much more important following my retirement. Part of this rekindled interest is undoubtedly influenced by my association with fellow Muslims. Even so, I wouldn't call myself a strict follower of the faith. I shun some of the practices and puritanical teachings of the so-called 'fundamentalists'. I pray daily, but wouldn't like to be coerced into religious rituals. Rather, I find comfort and solace in praying to Allah in solitude. Although praying in congregations can be inspiring, I sometimes find it too repetitive and ritualistic.

I have a family with two grown-up children, both born in the West. Being raised in a Western society made a significant difference in their upbringing. In particular, compared to my upbringing in India, they had minimal religious teaching. This concerns me, as I feel responsible for alienating them from their faith. I now believe that religious education is an essential part in moulding the character of a person, irrespective of the religion they decide to follow. The moral and religious aspects of life have become all the more important in the present-day world, where families struggle to stay together and societies seem to be going through a period of upheaval. My wife and I are, therefore, taking extra care with our grandchildren, making sure that they receive basic lessons in religious and moral education.

A few years ago I performed the *Hajj* pilgrimage with my family, which has left another lasting impression on me. The annual *Hajj* is a once in a lifetime occasion for Muslims to meet fellow pilgrims from all over the world. Although things have improved nowadays, it is an experience that tests one's patience, tolerance and physical endurance. It also inspired a sense of fellow feeling for others.

A mosque is supposed to be a place for prayers and social contact. Unfortunately, I find there is little scope to talk with and enquire about others. The only other way to socialize with fellow Muslims is at private parties or weddings. There seem to be few clubs or community centres within the communities of the ethnic minorities, especially amongst the Muslim communities in the United Kingdom.

Muslims have very few religious festivals, the main two being after Ramadan and *Bakrid* ('*Id-al-Adha*). Therefore, young and old, rich and poor alike meet to celebrate these with great fervour. My recollection of '*Id* (*Eid*) celebrations in childhood is one of rejoicing and excitement, as well as days of preparations. We all dressed in our new clothes and visited friends and relations. I remember there being plenty of delicious food, which was prepared and exchanged. The best part for the children was collecting money from the elders and then all visiting the cinema house. Everybody knew everybody else in the town, and it was important to visit them to make up any differences. It was a time of renewing ties and friendships. Unfortunately, I find that there is little community life in this country. It is probably this feeling of isolation that impels us to our religion.

Although my religion is not so important to me, at times of trouble my thoughts go automatically towards religion. A feeling of helplessness makes me submit to God Almighty.

I feel that my religion is my personal affair and I don't like the intervention of a third person, but I do regard the prophet Muhammad as a good role model who has left marvellous examples of compassion, piety, simplicity and honesty. There is no walk of life for which he has not left guidance. Although I pray daily, I only read the scriptures occasionally. Because the Qur'an is written in Arabic, which I hardly understand, I read translations, as well as various interpretations and commentaries.

I get comfort in submission to Allah and thank Him for His bounty, my good health, the air we breathe, the water we drink, the sunshine and the seasons we enjoy without our asking or paying for it. If living in a secular society means not recognizing these gifts of God, then I don't want to live in such a society. I would much rather be a religious person.

As a religious person, I observe certain food regulations. Islam has strict guidelines about what to eat and what not to eat. For example, it forbids the consumption of any intoxicating drinks. I wear Western clothes for the convenience and climatic reasons and I think it is everyone's right to wear (and eat) what they want. That said, I think it is good for people to dress in a way that reflects their distinctive culture. Otherwise this world becomes a monotonous and boring place to live in.

I'm not a strict follower of Islam, yet our family life is very much influenced by our faith. We follow our religion in matters relating to marriage, birth and death. My wife performs prayers five times a day and recites the Qur'an daily. My son also attends the mosque once a week, work permitting. However, living in a Western society it is not always possible to meet the requirement that a Muslim should pray five times a day. Again, there is no fixed day for our festivals (unlike, say, 25 December, a fixed day for Christians to celebrate Christmas) and sometimes they fall on a workday. This can present difficulties. For example, during the month of Ramadan a Muslim is supposed to fast from daybreak to sunset. Because this may mean sixteen or seventeen hours of fasting, depending on the season, it becomes very strenuous for a working person. Hence, there are limitations to following our religion in the strictest terms.

Islam in the Modern World

DAVID WAINES

The story of the Islamic world from 1700 has often been described in terms of the 'decline of Islam' confronted by the 'rise of the West' or the struggle between a vanishing 'tradition' and a triumphant 'modernity.' This is now rejected as an over-simplified picture.

Eighteenth century: rival camps

The increasing political corruption and military weakness of the once powerful imperial structures of the Ottomans of Turkey, the Safavids of Iran and the Mughals of India was paralleled throughout the eighteenth century by the economic expansion of the British, French and Dutch empires. Economic penetration alone, however, had little immediate impact upon Muslim religious developments which were directed at the social and moral reconstruction of Islamic societies and a reorientation of the Sufi tradition. Sunni revival movements arose out of local conditions, while ideas of reform were disseminated by traditional means such as the annual pilgrimage to Mecca. Indeed the holy cities of Mecca and Medina were centres of study visited by scholars from as far afield as India and Morocco.

Two outstanding but contrasting figures were the Indian Sufi, Shah Wali Allah (1702–62) of Delhi and the puritan Arab Muhammad bin Abd al-Wahhab (1703–92). Although each stressed the Qur'an and the Prophet's *sunnah* (model example) as binding sources for faith and law, and each rejected the blind imitation of generations of medieval legal scholarship, Wali Allah accepted the possible vision of an immanent God, while Abd al-Wahhab emphasized the transcendence of the One Unique, and unknowable, God. Their influence has come down to the present. In Shi'ite Iran, a bitter controversy between rival camps of religious scholars may be seen as a forerunner of Ayatollah Khomeini's revolution two centuries later.

Nineteenth century: modernizers

By the end of World War I the three Muslim empires lay dismembered. European colonial power occupied or directly influenced the entire Muslim world. 'Modernity', understood as a cluster of social, political, economic and cultural institutions and values, was a transformation historically originating in European and North American societies. In the European overseas dominions, Muslims experienced modernity within a power relationship between themselves and their colonial masters, which ensured that their responses to it would differ significantly. Specifically, Muslims experienced Europe's power not as secular, but as Christian power. While Muslims welcomed the material benefits of science and technology, they remained ambivalent to certain modern values such as democracy and hostile to missionary propaganda against the core of their faith. In places such as India, Algeria and Palestine the retreat from colonial rule down to the 1960s left much suffering and bitterness in its wake. Not surprisingly, modern Muslim reformers of the late nineteenth and twentieth centuries found it difficult to embrace either social change as secularization or the marginalization of religion away from concerns for political, economic or social problems.

Two early major Sunni modernist reformers were the Indian Sayyid Ahmad Khan (d. 1898) and the Egyptian Muhammad 'Abduh (d. 1905). Both received a more or less traditional education, had an early relationship with Sufi spirituality and later gained

> *'In your despairing, you are a free man; but in your coveting, you are a slave.'*
>
> Sufi saying

> *'Hope goes hand in hand with deeds; otherwise, it is just wishful thinking.'*
>
> Sufi saying

first-hand experience of Europe. These influences informed their efforts at social reform focused upon education and the need to modernize Islam. They held that, rather than interpreting the Qur'an in terms of the Prophetic Traditions (*Hadith*), revelation could be understood solely in its own terms. Implicitly, modernists proposed that every Muslim could search scripture's meaning for him/herself. The banner of all modernist thought was *surah* 13:12: 'God does not alter what is in a people until they alter what is in themselves.' Rather than adhere literally to the past, Muslims must shape their future in the public interest in order to deal with the dramatic new circumstances of the modern era. Religious debate and controversy has continued through the twentieth century to the present day.

Twentieth century: radicals

The aim of more radical reformers was to Islamize modernity rather than modernize Islam. Two key radicals who helped to shape movements sometimes called 'fundamentalist' or 'Islamist' were the Indian/Pakistani Abu al-Ala Mawdudi (d. 1979) and the Egyptian Sayyid Qutb (d. 1966). Both deeply believed that Muslims should conduct their entire lives according to God's law. Their work also provided a strident, if not trenchant, critique of secular Western societies. A similar impulse moved Ayatollah Khomeini's revolution in Iran in 1979. Radicals became the chief target of secularists who formed the backbone of the new political elites of the new Muslim nation states following independence from colonial powers. Underlying these controversies is a contest over rival claims of authority to interpret the foundational religious sources. Some secularists even attempted to justify the separation of religion from politics by

Ayatollah Khomeini waves to a crowd of enthusiastic supporters on his return to Tehran in 1979.

appealing to the Prophet's model community in Medina.

Beyond 9/11

Over the past quarter of a century, Western observers and governments have noted the phenomenon of a 'resurgent Islam'. The tragic events of 11 September 2001 seemed to some to confirm fears of a 'clash of civilizations'. In this perception, two important factors have been overlooked. First, discussions among Muslim leaders worldwide, conservatives included, expressed long-held concern over the dangers of mounting religious extremism within the community, well aware that their own agendas were in danger of being hijacked by a minority. Second, extremists have articulated in religious terms current social-political problems that plague their own and other Muslim societies. Such problems include the corruption of, and repression by, regimes closely supported by Western governments, some of whose policies are widely regarded as perpetrating injustices upon Muslim peoples in areas such as Palestine, Chechnya, Afghanistan, Algeria, Iraq and Bosnia. Effective resolution of such conflicts would help to undermine solutions proposed by extremist religious groups and give moderate Muslim voices a forum for debate with often equally immoderate and unrepentant secularist power holders.

In this multifaceted debate a growing contribution is to be expected from Muslim women. The individual's sense of the broader Muslim community is strong; men and women pray as equals in the eyes of God, and the contribution of each to community life is accepted equally by God: 'I will deny no man or woman among you the reward of their labours' (The Qur'an, *surah* 3:195). Whereas the spiritual equality of men and women has been traditionally agreed upon, questions of patriarchal

Traditional female burqa, Afghanistan. Headscarfs are worn today by vastly greater numbers of women.

power and social equality have been hotly contested for over a century. Modernist thinkers, male and female, (challenged by radicals, both male and female) have sought to reduce male privilege in the family, for example, by arguing that the Qur'an's true intent supported monogamous marriage, not polygny; by raising the marriage age and thereby abolishing union with or between children; by restricting the male right of divorce and increasing the grounds upon which women may seek divorce. Yet the overall goal of change is still to preserve a harmonious and stable family life contributing to the greater good of the community, with the relationship of its parts – men, women and children – based upon equity. It is part of the contest over who may 'speak for God' in interpreting the divine message. Female scholars and laywomen, albeit slowly and quietly today, are insisting their voices be heard too. As the future unfolds, observers should be more attentive to what Muslims, men and women, say as well as do.

'Worship God as though you see Him, for even if you don't, He sees you.'

From the Gabriel *hadith*

The Religions of East Asia

Sages and Immortals: Chinese Religions

JOHN BERTHRONG

Chinese religion is unique. This is partly due to the fact that, alone among the great religions of humankind, Chinese religion first developed in isolation, without the influence of the other great world religions. Confucianism and Taoism (or Daoism), two of the three faiths of China, developed their distinctive forms before there was any significant contact with the rest of the world. For this reason, Chinese religion has taken a form which often seems quite unlike any other. For example, neither Confucianism nor Taoism is like Judaism, Christianity or Islam – monotheistic religions with God at the centre. Confucianism, especially, became a religion without any great speculation on the nature and function of God. For this reason it was often not even considered to be a religion. However, it is clear that Confucianism *is* a religion, and that it was the dominant tradition of pre-modern China.

THE SHANG

The earliest forms of Chinese religion are not clear. We know hardly anything definite about the religion of the great Shang dynasty (1766–1122 BCE), the first historical dynasty. But although we know little of the detail, we are certain that religion played a very important part in the life of the Shang. In fact, the Shang lived in a world of spirits and powers who directly influenced the lives of the living – their success or failure – and who required sacrifice and appeasement.

The Shang sought to fathom the wishes of these spirits through a complicated system of divination. We still have the records of these divinations, the famous 'oracle bones'. The diviner, at the request of the king, would put the question to the spirit, and record the question and its answer on the carapace of a turtle or the shoulder-blade of an ox. The Shang were concerned to know the will of the spirits for just about everything they did.

Although the nature of Shang religion is clouded in mystery, a certain continuity remains between the Shang and later Chinese religion. There is a persistent belief in the balance of nature, an idea which was later explicitly defined as the famous concepts of *Yin* and *Yang*: the forces of dark and light, of soft and hard, of female and male. Another important idea which continues throughout the history of Chinese religion is a constant concern for the well-being of the people. This idea of the well-being of the people later became the concept of *t'ien-ming* or the Will of Heaven.

SENSE OF CONCERN

Prior to the rise of Confucianism, certain elements of the Shang and Chou dynasties took more definite shape. This is not surprising, since all great civilizations make certain choices about religion which give them their historical distinctiveness.

If there is one idea, one characteristic which informs the entire history of the development of Chinese religion, it is a 'consciousness of concern'. Even in the western Chou and eastern Chou one finds the persistent claim that high Heaven itself has concern for the well-being of the people. In fact, Heaven is said to hear and see, as the people hear and see, and hence to have a most active concern for them.

This sense that concern is the basis of the cosmos makes Chinese religion different from such religions as Judaism, Christianity or Islam, where a sense of awe or dread of a supreme power informs religious consciousness. This is why Chinese religion has always had such a close connection with the ethical thought of the people. A sense of concern and participation pervades the Chinese understanding of humanity's relationship to the transcendent and with other people.

PHILOSOPHY OR RELIGION?

In Chinese terms, what then are Confucianism and Taoism? Are they philosophies or religions? Do they have any kind of mystical traditions which seek to aid the faithful to achieve the perfected aims of a religious life?

There is a common Chinese distinction which is helpful in answering this question – the distinction between the terms *chia* (schools of thought, philosophy) and *chiao* (teaching, religion). The former refers more to the great thinkers and their teachings, and the 'great traditions'. The latter refers to the religious and, by extension, to the unique ways in which the great traditions have been appropriated by the people at grass-roots level. A distinction between the great intellectual traditions and the cultic and

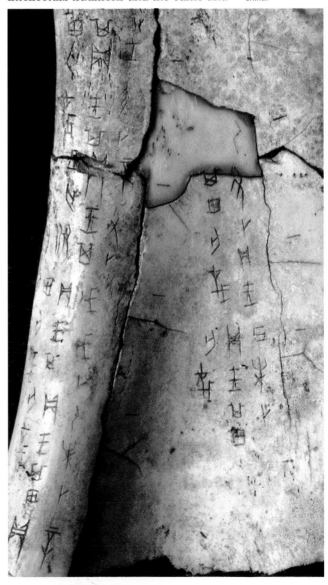

Chinese oracle bones with inscribed questions on display at the Anyang Archaeological Station, Henan, China.

devotional side of religious life has been made in all the Chinese traditions, Confucianism, Taoism and also Buddhism, after its introduction into China in the second century CE.

The Chinese traditions have never felt the need to contrast *chia* and *chiao* in a hostile fashion. In a very characteristic way, they are said to represent two different parts of one continuum. They are different yet related. In traditional China, each of the great religions operated on both levels: there were great Confucian, Taoist and Buddhist philosophers, as well as masters of the various religious arts of meditation, liturgy and ritual.

Confucianism

The Latinized name, Confucianism, is a Western invention which has come down from the seventeenth-century Jesuit missionaries. Interestingly, these early Western missionaries clearly saw the religious nature of Confucianism, even if they did not agree with its traditions and rituals.

The Chinese term for Confucianism, *Ju* (scholars, literati – with the special meaning of Confucian from the T'ang dynasty), points to its broader character as intellectual culture. It is usually regarded as philosophy (*chia*), although such terms as *Ju-chiao*, *K'ung-chiao* (K'ung being Confucius's family name), or *Li-chiao* (*Li* referring to Confucian rituals) are also used. All of these terms refer to those elements of worship, ritual and sacrifice which are religious teachings, which is, of course, what *chiao* itself refers to.

MORAL PHILOSOPHY
Confucianism is best known for its moral philosophy, represented by Confucius (551–479 BCE), Mencius (371–c. 289 BCE) and Hsün-tzu (fl. 298–238 BCE).

It is clearly grounded in religion – the inherited religion of the Lord-on-high, or Heaven. Even the great

An eighteenth-century print of the moral philosopher Confucius.

'His life was glorious, his death bewailed. How can such a one ever be equalled?'

Confucius

rationalist Hsün-tzu sees society founded on the penetrating insight of the sagely mind. And though Confucianism is less known for its mysticism, the *Book of Mencius* as well as other works cannot be fully understood except in the light of mysticism.

The *Chung-yung*, one of the 'Four Books' which became the basis for Confucian self-cultivation in the southern Sung (1126–1279 CE), explicitly states that the sage, having realized true integrity (*ch'eng*),

becomes one with Heaven and Earth. Confucian moral metaphysics reaches over into the religious quest for unity with the ground of being.

None the less, Confucianism gives primary emphasis to the ethical meaning of human relationships, finding and grounding the moral in the divine transcendence. The perfect example of this is Confucius himself. He is best remembered as a great teacher. The basis of his teaching was the concept of humanity (*jen*). Just as compassion is the greatest Buddhist virtue, and love the Christian, *jen* is the ultimate goal of conduct and self-transformation for the Confucian. And whereas most of Confucius's teachings stress the ethical dimension of humanity, he made it clear that it was Heaven itself which protected him and gave him his message: 'Heaven is the author of the virtue that is in me.'

THE WAY OF HEAVEN

Confucius stands as a prophet, giving an ethical teaching grounded in religious consciousness. Mencius projects the image of a teacher of mysticism. He proclaims an inner doctrine, alluding to the presence within the heart of something greater than itself.

'All things are present in me. When I reflect upon myself in all sincerity, my joy is boundless.' What was an implicitly religious message in Confucius, becomes explicit in Mencius. For example, Confucius is said not to have discussed the relationship between human nature and the Way of Heaven. Yet Mencius made his whole system of thought revolve around these two concepts. He attempted to show how the very essence of the Way of Heaven, the divine power of the cosmos, became human nature. He felt that if this human nature could be correctly cultivated and nurtured, even the common person could become a sage.

The Confucian classics (there are thirteen of them) prefer to discuss the work of spiritual cultivation in terms of emotional harmony and psychic equilibrium – a harmony of due proportions, rather than the absence of passions. The 'Doctrine of the Mean' (*Chung-yung*), one of the 'Four Books', distinguishes between the two states of fundamental mind, the 'pre-stirred' state (before the rise of emotions), and the 'post-stirred' state (after contact with

the things and events of the world). The meaning best expressed by the concept of true integrity (*ch'eng*), lies in the harmony of emotions which have arisen, but resembles the equilibrium of the 'pre-stirred' state.

The *Chung-yung*, as we have seen before, claims that this harmony puts a person in touch with the cosmic processes of life and creativity. 'If they can assist in the transformation and nourishing process of Heaven and Earth, they can thus form a trinity with Heaven and Earth.'

PRACTICAL CONDUCT

The third of the founding fathers of Confucianism, Hsün-tzu, is best remembered for his doctrine of ritual action (*li*). If Confucius begins Confucianism with the dramatic, almost prophetic, demand that we live a life of *jen* or perfect humanity, and Mencius expands upon the concept of *jen* to show that this is a life of heightened inter-subjectivity and intuition into the boundless joy of the enlightened sage, Hsün-tzu provides the practical side of Confucian religion.

It is his genius to demonstrate the power of correct ritual action needed to transform the human heart, which is prone to err, into the mind of a sage. In doing so, Hsün-tzu provides a model for daily life which supports the religious and ethical intuitions of Confucius and Mencius. Without a life of ritual – a liturgy of daily life ennobled by humility and graced by beautiful conduct – the supreme insights of religious geniuses such as Confucius and Mencius would be impossible to maintain.

In the course of time, the meaning of the word 'Heaven' becomes ambiguous, shifting from the early reference to a supreme deity (the *Analects* of Confucius), to a vacillation between that and moral force (Mencius), to the universe itself (Hsün-tzu).

'The master said, I have transmitted what was taught to me, without making up anything of my own. I have been faithful to and loved the Ancients.'
Confucius

'Everything has its own destiny, and it is for us to accept our destiny in its true form.'
Mencius

'Which is the greatest service? The service of parents is the greatest. Which is the greatest of charges? The charge of oneself is the greatest. I have heard of keeping oneself, and thus being able to serve one's parents. But I have not heard of failing to keep oneself, and yet being able to serve one's parents.'
Mencius

> 'Human nature is disposed to goodness, just as water flows downwards. There is no water but flows down, and no men but show this tendency to good.'
>
> Mencius

> 'The nature of man is evil, his goodness is acquired. His nature being what it is, man is born, first, with a desire for gain. If this desire is followed, strife will result and courtesy will disappear... Hence it is only under the influence of teachers and laws and the guidance of the rules of decorum and righteousness that courtesy will be observed, etiquette respected, and order restored.'
>
> Hsün-tzu

NEO-CONFUCIANISM

Confucian mysticism, especially in its second great phase, Neo-Confucianism, leans more and more in the direction of pantheism. This is borne out by the later philosopher, Chang Tsai (1020–77). It is here that Confucian religion and mysticism show the imprint of Taoist – and Buddhist – influences. Yet Chang Tsai still shows a profoundly Confucian bent to his mystical vision of the unity of the world, by expressing this as one of a perfected family. In this vision all the world becomes related to him as his own family. The note of inter-subjective concern sounded by Confucius and Mencius is reaffirmed.

TWO WAYS

The first great flowering of Confucianism produced such diverse thinkers as Mencius and Hsün-tzu. Neo-Confucianism gives us Chu Hsi (1130–1200) and Wang Yang-ming (1472–1529). Both started from a desire to reform the Confucianism of their day, and then sought to give practical guidance for the perfection of the mind. Their schools, respectively, were called 'the teaching of principle' (li-hsüeh) and 'the teaching of mind' (hsin-hsüeh). In actual fact, both were primarily concerned with the task of achieving sagehood. The great debate between them centred on how to achieve this.

Chu Hsi believed we must go through a long and arduous process of self-cultivation and ethical activity in order to reach jen. He stressed the method of 'the examination of things' (ko-wu), as the best means to achieve this end. But this was more than a scientific interest in the material matters of the cosmos. It was to be an examination of all the various ethical and spiritual states of the mind, an attempt to know the self, in order to perfect the original nature, which he held to be good.

Chu Hsi expressed his spiritual goal in this way:

'The mind of Heaven and Earth, which gives birth to all things, is humanity (jen). Man, in being endowed with matter-energy, receives this mind of Heaven and Earth, and thereby his life. Hence tender-heartedness and humanity are part of the very essence of his life.'

Wang Yang-ming agreed on the goal of sagehood, but rejected Chu Hsi's gradualist method. For Wang, only the 'enlightenment experience' of the absolute unity of our minds with the mind of the Tao (or Dao) would suffice to achieve sagehood. All other methods, including Chu Hsi's attempt at gradual self-cultivation, were a waste of time if they did not provoke this realization of the enlightenment experience. After Wang himself had had such an experience he wrote:

'My own nature is, of course sufficient for me to attain sagehood. And I have been mistaken in searching for principle in external things and affairs.'

LIFE MODELS

The great Neo-Confucians gave Confucianism a new lease of life. They provided a whole new explanation of the Confucian vision which could compete philosophically with Taoism and Buddhism. But, even more, they provided a practical set of life-models for the earnest seeker of sagehood. Although Chu Hsi consulted gradualism and Wang Yang-ming immediate experience, both sought that moment when the human mind, precarious in its tendencies to good and evil, would be transformed into the Mind of Heaven, the state of perfected excellence.

Taoism

The great Taoist religion is, in many ways, the opposite of Confucianism. Confucianism seeks to perfect men and women within the world, a goal of the secular as sacred. Taoism prefers to turn away from society to the contemplation of nature, seeking fulfilment in the spontaneous and 'trans-ethical'. The Tao, a metaphysical absolute, appears to have been a philosophical transformation of the earlier personal God. The way it teaches leads to a union with itself – a way of passive acceptance and mystical contemplation. Such is the teaching of the great Taoist thinkers, of Lao-tzu and Chuang-tzu. Little is known about their lives, if indeed they ever existed. This is perhaps fitting for men who had allegedly chosen a life of obscurity and taught a way of silence.

Taoism is not just passive contemplation. The texts of Lao-tzu and Chuang-tzu (also the name of the book, *Chuang-tzu*) served a later generation of religious-minded thinkers anxious to transcend the limited conditions of human existence. Their ambition was to 'steal the secret of Heaven and Earth', to wrench from it the mystery of life itself, in order to fulfil their desire for immortality.

The goal of the Confucian was to become a sage, a servant of society. The goal of the Taoist was to become an immortal (a *hsien*). They revived the belief in personal deities, practising a ritual of prayer and appeasement. They fostered the art of alchemy – the external alchemy, which 'internalized' the golden pill of immortality – and sought it through yoga and meditation. They also saw sexual hygiene as another means of prolonging human life.

This new Taoism has been called 'Taoist religion' to distinguish it from the classical philosophy of Lao-tzu and Chuang-tzu and its acceptance of both life and death. This Taoist religion developed its own mystical tradition, embellished with stories of marvellous drugs and wonder-working immortals, of levitations and bodily ascensions to heaven. Basing itself on the early texts – the *Lao-tzu, Chuang-tzu, Huai-nan-tzu,* and *Lieh-tzu* – the Taoist religionists created long-lasting religious institutions.

Some of these groups still exist today, and can trace their roots back to the Taoist movements at the end of the second century CE. With their esoteric and exoteric teachings, their lines of orthodox teachers, their social organizations, they more closely resemble the other great religious traditions of humankind. But their persistent Chinese style comes through: they seek unity with the Tao which cannot be named.

QUEST FOR FREEDOM

How can Taoism be distinguished from its great sister religion, Confucianism? One major goal of all the various schools and sects of Taoism was the quest for freedom. For some it was a freedom from the political and social constraints of the emerging Confucian state. For others it was the even more profound search for immortality. And for others it was the search for oneness with the Tao itself. This Tao was the sum total of all things which are and which change, for change itself was a very important part of the Taoist view of reality. As the *Chuang-tzu* tells us, the Tao is 'complete, all-embracing, the whole: these are different names for the same reality denoting the One'.

This One, this totality of the Tao, worked as a liberating concept for the Taoists. Within the ceaseless flux of the Tao they found the power to live life in a spontaneous fashion. Probably the most famous statement of the freedom of the Taoist immortal is that of Lao-tzu where he says, 'The ways of men are conditioned by those of Heaven, the

'The highest good is like that of water. The goodness of water is that it benefits the ten thousand creatures; yet itself does not scramble, but is content with the places that all men disdain. It is this that makes water so near to the Way.'

Tao Te Ching

ways of Heaven by those of the Tao, and the Tao came into being by itself.' The Tao is therefore the principle of the universe and is also a pattern for human behaviour, often called 'uncontrived action' (*wu-wei*).

'All things alter and change,
Never a moment ceasing,
Revolving, whirling, and rolling
away,
Driven far off and returning onward,
Like the mutations of cicada,
Profound, subtle, and illimitable
Who can finish describing it?'
'THE OWL', CHIA YI (200–168 BCE)

A suspended Taoist temple on the sacred mountain of Heng Shan, North China.

The Taoist imagination was totally unfettered by the confines of Confucian etiquette or sensibility. They provided the magic garden of the Chinese people. Some took this magic very seriously. Some found that this too was just another illusion of the changing Tao. For example, at the end of a report of a magical spirit journey attributed to King My of the Chou dynasty, the magician who has been his guide for the trip explains:

'Your majesty feels at home with the permanent, is suspicious of the sudden and temporary. But can one always measure how far and how fast a scene may later turn into something else?'

Or, as the next story in the *Lieh-tzu* puts it:

'The breath of all that lives, the appearance of all that has shape, is illusion.'

But unlike many of the great religions of India and the East, the Taoists never felt that the Tao could be called a conscious god.

'How can the Creator have a conscious mind? It spontaneously

'Tai gave them birth; the power of the Tao reared them, shaped them according to their kinds, perfected them, giving to each its strength. Therefore of the ten thousand things there is not one that does not worship Tao and do homage to its power.'

Tao Te Ching

takes place but seems mysterious. The breath and matter collect together, coagulate and become shape: constant with transformation it continues on without ever ceasing.'

LIFE ROLLS ON
Throughout its whole history, the diverse masters of Taoism have sought, in various ways, to become part of this 'self-so-ness' of reality. Life rolls on by itself in an unbroken wave of creative spontaneity. Neither the Confucian Heaven, nor the rule of earthly kings and emperors, nor the folly of demons or goblins can defy it.

'Being of themselves as they are
Silently brings them about,
Gives them serenity, gives them peace,
Escorts them as they go and
welcomes them as they come.'

The true immortal lives to learn a life in tune with the Tao.

In all Taoist religion there is a poetic touch, a realization that life is a beautiful, and frightening, panorama of transformations. No religion has been more successful at invoking the sense of wonder which these transformations cause to human beings. Set within their mountain retreats and their lake pavilions, the Taoists have truly been the poets of nature. The great T'ao Ch'ien (365–427 CE) expresses this sense of wonder tinged with serene resignation and hope.

'Just surrender to the cycle of things,
Give yourself to the waves of the
Great Change,
Neither happy nor yet afraid,
And when it is time to go, then
simply go,
Without any unnecessary fuss.'

Today this sense of poetic beauty and desire to achieve oneness with the Tao still informs the Taoist religion. Because of the great revolutionary

Two young monks standing before the distinctive structure of a wooden pagoda in Yunnan Province, China.

changes in China, and the determined animosity of Maoism against traditional 'superstition' it was hard to tell if and how Taoism could survive on the Chinese mainland. In recent years, however, a distinct detente concerning religious affairs has been noticeable. And it turns out to be true that Taoism has always been at odds with the government. Yet it survives as long as Chinese culture itself exists.

Cross-fertilization

The great Chinese religions have always influenced each other's development. In early China great

debates and arguments went on between the Taoists and Confucians. But the arguments helped both sides develop their own distinctive attitudes.

The picture becomes even more complicated with the introduction of Buddhism into China. Both Taoism and Confucianism borrowed a great deal from the new Indian religion. The Taoists reformed their religious structures, founded monasteries and wrote a huge canon of sacred texts in imitation of Buddhist models.

The great Neo-Confucian revival in the twelfth and eleventh centuries CE would also be unthinkable without the stimulus and challenge of Buddhist philosophy. Although the Confucians did not borrow nearly as much as the Taoists from the Buddhists they were certainly stimulated to work out their own mature philosophic response to Buddhist thought. And on the practical level, they learned a great deal about meditation, which they called 'quiet-sitting', from the Buddhists.

'THE THREE ARE ONE'
The great heyday of cross-fertilization of religions in China came in the Ming dynasty (1369–1644). At this period many great religious thinkers such as Lin Chao-en (1517–98), sought to effect a harmonization of the three great religions of China. Their cry was that the three religions are one.

Lin sought to combine the best features of Taoist and Buddhist meditation with a Confucian sense of shared concern for fellow creatures in a uniquely Chinese synthesis. This kind of syncretistic religious life is still present in China today. And, in fact, it would not be far wrong to say that most religious Chinese are in fact a mixture of all three great religions. The syncretists had such a great effect that no one thinks it odd to be a Buddhist, Taoist and Confucian at the same time.

Finally there is the element of Western culture in modern China's intellectual development (see 'Christianity in Contemporary China'). Religious and secular Western influence will no doubt have just as great an impact on China – witness the tremendous transformative power of Maoist thought, based in part on Marxist concepts – as did Buddhism. It is impossible to say what will survive. But we can be absolutely certain that what will emerge will be distinctively Chinese at all levels.

Christianity in Contemporary China

EDWARD A. IRONS

A century ago the Chinese still regarded Christianity as an imported, 'foreign' religion. Today throughout large swathes of the countryside China resembles a Christian culture. The country is dominated by a single political party with near-absolute powers, yet in many ways the multitude of local communities can largely control their own fates. Towns allow traditional beliefs and practices of all religions to flourish, even if such expressions are not allowed in the cities.

Out of a total population of 1.262 billion in 2000, approximately 16 million are Protestants, according to the China Christian Council, the official Protestant church, and another 8 million are Catholic. A recent estimate by other observers is 70 million Protestants and 12 million Catholics. If these larger estimates are accurate, China with over 80 million Christian believers would contain the fourth largest Christian population in the world, after the USA, Brazil and Mexico.

A unique blend
Chinese Christianity, like Chinese Buddhism, has undergone a process of 'sinicization' or indigenization, becoming an embedded part of the Chinese cultural landscape. While worship, ritual, preaching and other elements of religious culture retain their recognizable Christian character, they are now also stubbornly Chinese. Many of the categories familiar in other parts of the world do not apply here.

The first thirty years of Communist rule, from 1949 to the end of the Cultural Revolution in 1978, showed how firmly Christianity had become rooted, especially in the Chinese countryside. Local preachers and networks of worshippers sprang up, many completely cut off from outside contact. They often had limited knowledge of the Bible or traditional doctrine, but they taught the message. Since liberalization in the post-Mao era, the Chineseness of China's Christianity has only strengthened. It is not immune to the forces of globalization. International Christian organizations maintain relations with Chinese groups; some organizations have been known to enter and spread their teachings without official approval; and many English teachers in China are young people sent to spread the Christian message. Yet Chinese Christianity is unique:

● About 80 per cent of believers live in rural areas, often poor, with no resources to build churches or purchase Bibles or hymnals. The educational level is low and many clergy prefer to work in urban environments, leaving congregations dependent on oral teaching and with a weak grasp of doctrine or the church's broader role in society. Sermons often focus on filial piety, a recurring topic throughout Chinese history. Other topics include forbearance, forgiveness and obedience, mixing easily with local folk traditions.

● As with many Chinese religions, Christianity is primarily a *female* activity. Approximately 70 per cent of believers are female (although women do not make up the same percentage of church leaders).

● A *cultural Christian* is an indigenous term from the 1980s for certain academics who, unlike practising church Christians, were relatively free to write and publish on Christian topics. It came to mean an academic who might secretly be a Christian but for workplace reasons did not want to publicize this. Ironically, cultural Christians, though rarely church members, are seen by many Chinese as legitimate spokespeople for Christianity.

● Religion was equated by the post-1949 Chinese state with superstition, feudalism and imperialism and simply not allowed. Yet people clung to their beliefs and this approach was soon softened. Since 1978 state control has been increasingly liberalized. The official church structure, the *Three Self Church*, has reopened churches throughout the countryside and in cities, and worship is allowed. There are significant numbers of believers not under the *Three Self* umbrella: they may belong to banned groups and their offshoots or their leadership may choose not to cooperate with the official church structure. However, the term *underground church* – used widely in the 1980s – is not a very accurate description today. Often rural believers meet in the open or in homes simply because there are no buildings available. Such groups are not officially counted as 'churches', yet hardly constitute any form of organized opposition.

Earlier history
Christianity was present in China as early as 635, when a Nestorian Christian community was established in the capital Chang An (now Xian). A stone monument found there in 1625 narrates the story of Nestorian Christianity and its first monk, Aluoben. By the mid-800s there were several monasteries and communities throughout China. Their activity evidently ceased in 845 with the wider prohibition against Buddhism and other

'I believed in Christ in 1997 when my son was ill and I was seeking his healing. Later this eight-month-old did not get well and was taken by the Lord... He caused me to understand that following Christ is not just so we can get bodily healing but something far more important – healing of our spiritual sicknesses.'

Zhou, farmer

religions, but Nestorian activity began again in the Mongol period (1277–1368) and by the time of Marco Polo there were other types of Christians in China, including Armenians, Byzantine, Jacobin, and Roman Catholics. Most Christians were not of ethnic Chinese extraction, however.

In 1556 the Portuguese established an outpost which later became their colony of Macao. In 1583 Jesuits were granted permission to live in mainland China and then allowed to propagate. They used European advances in astronomy to entice the court and scholars into discussions, but were tolerant of such Chinese values as ancestor veneration. A papal announcement in 1704 denounced the Jesuits' accommodative policy. There were three concerns: the names of God used in China (Shangdi, Tian, Taiji were forbidden), ceremonies to honour Confucius, and the practice of contributing to community festivals in which non-Christian divinities were honoured. The Qing dynasty (1644–1911) had initially adopted a

Prayer at the Damazhan house church, one of the largest unregistered Christian communities in China.

'No state organ, public organization or individual may compel citizens to believe in, or not to believe in, any religion. The state protects normal religious activities. No one may make use of religion to engage in activities that disrupt public order, impair the health of citizens or interfere with the educational system of the states.'

From the Chinese Constitution

positive attitude to Christianity. However, in 1724 it was outlawed. Missionary activity became illegal and Christianity went underground.

Still, Christian missionaries flocked to China in the 1800s, often supported by the imperialist designs of their home countries in Europe and North America. Host populations in turn perceived missionary activity as one of the three legs of imperialism, along with trade and military power. There were no Protestant missions to China until the Treaty of Nanking in 1842. By 1949, the eve of the Chinese Communist victory, there were 936,000 Protestant members and 2,963 clergy. In the twentieth century missionary orientation changed. Many missionaries saw their primary roles as educators. They established universities and private schools, offered foreign language training and also offered medical care in distant places.

What is the Outlook for Christianity in China?

During the Cultural Revolution many Protestants attended clandestine 'house meetings' which later grew into more-or-less open networks of worshippers. The government no longer or rarely uses force to limit such meetings. Family meetings or prayers are of even less concern. The core of state policy toward Christianity in China today is the *Three Self Policy* (self-support, self-government, self-propagation) which was adopted by all officially-sanctioned religious groups in the 1950s. As one Protestant bishop stated in 1988, 'The government doesn't bother us now. They see that Christians have better moral behaviour than others; they don't cause trouble.'

In the 1980s some offshoots of the 'Shouters' (a network of Protestant congregations in Central China which call out words during worship) were deemed harmful 'cults' and their leaders arrested. Still, this is a far cry

from the blanket suppression of all religious activity which prevailed in theory in the early years of the People's Republic.

The Catholic Church has a particular problem due to the rift in official state-to-state relations between China and the Vatican. The officially-sanctioned Chinese Catholic Patriotic Association controls the 'reopened' churches, but in some parishes certain believers refuse to attend those churches, instead practising in private and showing their disapproval by holding chanting sessions outside a church during Mass. Both Protestant and Catholic congregations suffer from a lack of trained clergy, and much local Protestant activity is beyond the control of the formal church. Christians gather for market days and visit private homes to pray, often for days at a time. Preachers are commonly self-taught and recent converts. Often there are no Bibles at all within a congregation.

Inevitably China's absorption of Christianity will result in new organizational forms. Already there are several well-established indigenous churches such as the *Little Flock* and the *True Jesus Church* which began in China in the early decades of the twentieth century. Today both movements flourish in such locations as Hong Kong, the USA, the UK and South-east Asia. Future growth in the numbers of Christians in China is probably a safe bet, with creative mixes of Chinese sensibilities and the Christian message continuing to influence the Chinese and world scenes.

The Worship of Ancestors

CHUA WEE HIAN

Ancestral worship was first introduced to China at the beginning of the Chou dynasty (1122–325 BCE). It was Confucius (551–479 BCE) who popularized this practice by his teaching on filial piety decreeing that parents and elders are to be honoured and respected while they are alive. This sense of reverence continues after their deaths.

The Chinese believe that at death the soul of the deceased ancestor resides in three places. One part goes to heaven, the second remains in the grave to receive sacrifices and the third is localized in the ancestral tablet or shrine.

The soul has to be assisted as it journeys to heaven. Hence, at Chinese funerals, elaborate rituals are meticulously carried out to ensure that the soul is amply provided for on its course. With the help of a Taoist priest members of the family chant prayers, offer sacrifices of food and burn paper money – and in some cases even paper cars, planes and servants – so that there will be no lack of provisions. Evil spirits who oppose the deceased are propitiated by appropriate sacrifices and by loud wailings.

The siting of the grave is very important. A geomancer, in Chinese *Feng shui sien sheng*, is consulted to determine the ideal location. The tomb must be maintained, and occasional offerings are made to the part of the soul which resides in it. The heirs continue to visit it, especially during the spring festivals (*ts'ing meng*).

Within 100 days of the burial a memorial service is held in the home of the oldest male heir. The ancestral tablet is dedicated by a Buddhist or Taoist priest; this now normally contains a photograph of the deceased with the name, rank and status in life. Incense-sticks are burned and placed on the tablet and on certain feast days food offerings are included. Newly married couples in the family have to bow before this tablet. Its presence strengthens family solidarity, and it also offers protection and blessing to all in the family.

Chinese Christians have sometimes been accused of not honouring their ancestors by not becoming involved in ancestral worship rites. Their firm but gracious reply is that they will always respect and honour their elders while they are alive. Many are prepared to be the first in cleaning family tombs, and some Christians have even set up halls of remembrance for their forebears. Non-Christian relatives and friends may be invited to special memorial services where Christ is proclaimed as victor over the grave.

> 'While they (the parents) are alive, serve them according to the ritual (li): when they die bury them according to the ritual; and sacrifice to them according to the ritual.'
>
> Confucius

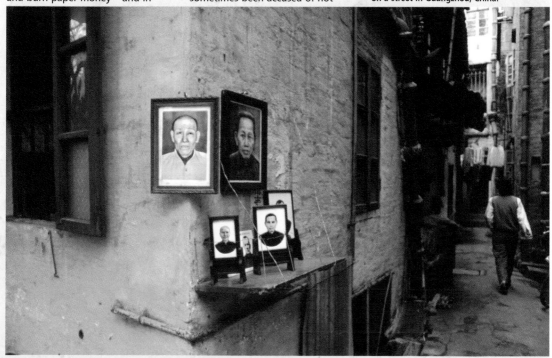

Framed pictures of ancestors form a shrine on a street in Guangzhou, China.

Sinkyo: Korea's Traditional Religion

HARVIE CONN

Korea's traditional religion, Sinkyo, has been called 'the religion without a name'. It is not so much a structured set of uniform beliefs as a religious way of seeing the world and a person's sacred link with it. This used to be called 'animism'. Like other religions it has five 'magnetic points':

● **I and the cosmos:** Humanity is in rhythm with the world. The forces of nature controlling life and death, fertility and sterility, become personified and god like. This world is a religious arena inhabited by spirits of heaven and the soil, water and the trees.

The well-known *Yin* and *Yang* symbol painted onto a door in the folk village of Suweon, South Korea.

● **I and the norm:** The myth of Tangun, legendary founder of Korea, underlines that sense of cosmic norm to which the Korean must conform. Ung, the son of heaven, changed a bear into a woman. The bear-woman could find no one to marry. Ung changed his form, married her and fathered her child, Tangun. The myth is remembered on 'opening of heaven day' (*Kaechonjol*), an annual national holiday. Similar tales surround the archetypal tribal leaders, and mythical ancestors of present-day clan families.

● **I and destiny:** How do we reconcile the fact that we are active beings and also victims of fate or destiny? Borrowing from pre-Confucian roots, Sinkyo finds its answer in a cosmic pattern where heaven, humankind and nature make a harmony of opposites. These opposites complement each other. They are the great forces of the

Yin and the *Yang*, non-being and being. The *Yin* is negative, passive, weak and destructive. The *Yang* is positive, active, strong and constructive. As they act and interact, harmony is achieved and recreated again and again. Our individuality comes from these opposites. The *Yin* is the female, mother, soft, dark, wet. The *Yang* is male, father, strong, hard, bright.

Out of these opposites comes the system called 'geomancy'. 'Where shall we live?', becomes a religious question of choosing a good house-site or grave-site in harmony with these opposites. The house or burial place, for instance, must be arranged in conformity to the cosmic workings of *yin-yang* and the harmony of the five elements: wood, metal, fire, water, earth. The interacting flow of these forces must not be disturbed.

● **I and salvation:** Since this harmony is often broken, Sinkyo must also meet people's craving for salvation. When the rice paddies are ploughed in the spring, a farmers' band pacifies the spirits of the earth with music and ritual. When the ridge pole of a new house is raised, wine and food are thrown at it, while a member of the household chants, 'Please, Grandfather and Grandmother of the ridge pole, bless us with good luck and long life, and many sons!'

Life is under a curse, a shadow darkening the cosmic harmony. The way back to 'paradise lost' is by ritual sacrifice. Throwing a stone on a simple altar keeps you from getting sore feet on a journey. Spitting on the altar is a sign of purification, and wards off evil spirits. Earth spirits must be satisfied before a corpse can be laid to rest. The 'sin' is not that of a personal violating of the will of a personal 'god' but the corporate breaking of cosmic unity.

The chief role in restoring unity is often played by the Mudang. Always a woman, her most important task is curing mental and physical disease. Like the shamans of Siberia, she also conducts communal sacrifice, assures the farmers of good crops, fishermen of safe journeys and a good catch. She will produce sons for a barren woman, recall the spirits of the dead after a funeral, or lead them to the kingdom of the blessed. She will pacify the spirits of those who die violent or tragic deaths. Her role is regarded as beneficial.

Sinkyo feels deep horror at the threat of death which destroys cosmic harmony. Some 2,000 years ago, it was common for Koreans to bury the dead with their personal belongings, including gold and silver.

With the growing influence of Confucianism on Korea from the third century CE, Sinkyo saw the spirit world in a new way. The Confucian concept of filial piety as the summit of all virtues strengthened, if it did not create, Korea's early ancestor-cult. Food was offered to kinsmen at death and at memorial times in the following years. They hoped the ancestor would favour the descendants.

● **I and the Supreme Being:**
Koreans read about the gods in the great picture-book we call the cosmos. Among the spirits of nature, the spirit of heaven (Hananim or Hanunim) has a special place. Not a 'high god' remote and supreme, he is said to bring sunlight and rain. Lightning, drought and other disasters are his judgment on the wicked. By his favour we live and breathe. When national disaster came, the king used to appeal to Hananim by confessing his own sins and those of his people. In some sense a 'heavenly father', Hananim was the grandfather of Tangun, the aboriginal hero of Korea.

Sinkyo and the new religious movements

As Korea was invaded by Confucianism, Buddhism and Christianity, Sinkyo did not shrink but was altered and strengthened. From Confucianism came the ethical codes surrounding the ancestor-cult. Taoism and Neo-Confucianism strengthened the magical side of Sinkyo and its geomancy. From Buddhism came a stress on suffering and pain, now linked with healing and divining.

Sinkyo has also provided the background for Korea's new religions. Chondogyo was founded in the mid-eighteenth century in reaction to the coming of Christianity. It reinforced humanity's sacred links with the universe. Sun Myung Moon (b. 1920), the Korean founder of the Unification Church, can be seen as the great link-man between the people and the spirit world.

SINKYO: KOREA'S TRADITIONAL RELIGION

When the rice paddies are ploughed, the spirits of the earth are pacified with music and ritual.

A Tapestry of Traditions: Japanese Religions

MICHAEL PYE

Religion in Japan is a rich tapestry of diverse traditions with a history of nearly 2,000 years. Many Japanese people display some kind of allegiance to more than one religion; a person will usually be expected to have a Shinto wedding and a Buddhist funeral, though Buddhist and secular weddings are also possible. With this may go a personal or family interest in a particular Buddhist denomination or practice, or membership of one of the various new religions which attract almost a third of the population.

These different forms of religion have separate organizations, buildings, festivals, sacred writings, ministers or priests and so on. However, it should always be remembered that the paths of these religions have touched at many points in Japanese history, and that they still meet in the lives of many Japanese people. For this reason it is possible to speak both of 'Japanese religions' and of 'Japanese religion' – especially as the Japanese language itself does not usually distinguish between the singular and the plural.

Land and religion

The general pattern of Japanese religion is in some ways a reflection of the country's geographical position and character. Japan has received a great deal from the Asian continent, but almost entirely from or via Korea and China. The major imported religions are therefore Buddhism, mainly in its Mahayana form, and Confucianism. The influence of Taoism has been largely indirect, bearing partly on divination practices and partly on the style of Zen Buddhism. It was in reaction to the powerful Buddhist and Confucian systems, with their scholarly prestige and political influence, that Japan's native Shinto faith first became clearly organized and defined. Indeed, the impact of Chinese and then of Western culture, and Japan's responses to these, provide the overall cultural perspective in which Japanese religion can be understood.

The fact that the country consists mainly of four great islands, spread over a vast distance from north to south, has also had its effect.

The most famous historic Shinto shrines and Buddhist temples are found in the southern part of the main island, Honshu. Extremely ancient Shinto shrines which are still of national importance are located at Ise, where the sun-goddess Amaterasu is revered and where a new prime minister usually 'reports' on the formation of the cabinet, and at Izumo, where all the gods, or *kami*, of Japan are said to return once a year.

Between these two sites are the former capitals, Nara and Kyoto, which themselves boast not only some well-known Shinto shrines such as the Kasuga Shrine at Nara, but also many fine Buddhist temples and images. The thirteenth-century sectarian development of Buddhism is reflected in the temple buildings and images at Kamakura, also on the main island of Honshu, but further east near modern Tokyo.

The smaller island of Shikoku which together with Honshu cradles the scenic Inland Sea, has never been of the slightest political importance and so lacks major religious monuments. But it does have a famous pilgrimage route which takes in no fewer than eighty-eight Buddhist temples. Today these are frequently visited by coachparties of tourists, an example of the intimate link between holiday travel and religion in Japan today. Other pilgrimage routes are found in other parts of the country, the most famous being the thirty-three places in western Honshu where the Bodhisattva Kannon-sama is revered.

The island of Hokkaido in the north was largely undeveloped until the nineteenth century, when young Tokyoites were sent out in a pioneering spirit to cope with its less favourable climate. The main city, Sapporo, was a centre of Protestant missionary effort at that time, although its people today practise the more usual forms of Japanese religion.

Kyushu, the southernmost major island, claims some of the oldest known historical sites in Japan, because of its proximity to Korea. Its importance as a maritime trading approach from the west meant that it became the main base for Roman Catholic missions in the sixteenth century, and also the scene of martyrdoms, especially at Nagasaki; Roman Catholic Christianity was suppressed partly because it was espoused by feudal lords in Kyushu who showed separatist tendencies. In a similar way, Kyushu was also the geographical base for the Shinto-inspired reassertion of imperial power in the mid-nineteenth century, when the central military government in Edo (now Tokyo) came to the end of its two and a half centuries of undisturbed rule.

MOUNTAIN-TOP SHRINES

The mountainous terrain of the country has also had a major effect on the forms of Japanese religious life. Many mountains have shrines at their summit, and not a few attract pilgrim groups who seek purification and heightened spiritual powers. The most famous is, of course, Mount Fuji itself, which is a quasi-religious symbol for the whole nation.

Buddhists had already used mountains in China as isolated retreats from the world, and this practice was carried over to Japan. The most famous example was Mount Koya, one of the leading headquarters of Shingon Buddhism (see below).

The mountain cult encouraged one of the most fascinating syncretistic movements in the history of religion, the Shugendo movement, which linked Buddhism and Shinto. This movement used ascetic exercises aiming at enlightenment in a quest for shamanic magical powers, performing spiritualist healing and fire-walking rites. Though it flourished in historical times, it has by no means died out today, and indeed has had considerable influence on the formation of new religions.

Shinto

Shinto is the name given to a wide conglomeration of religious practices with roots in prehistoric Japan. Little is known about Japanese religion before the emergence of a unified state in the Yamato period (fourth to seventh centuries CE), but in its simplest forms it was broadly animist, believing that a supernatural living force resided in natural objects such as mountains, trees and animals.

The oldest literary works in Japan were composed on a basis of the combined myths and legends of the various clans which had been forged into political unity. The oldest of these official works is the *Kojiki* (CE 712), but this was soon replaced by the *Nihongi* (CE 720) also known as the *Nihonshoki*. These two works retain to this day an honoured position in the minds of most Japanese people and are considered especially important by the advocates of Shinto. On the other hand, they are not recited or even studied by ordinary believers.

From the Yamato period onwards the imperial household took a central position within Shinto. Its ancestry was traced back through legendary

'Now when chaos had begun to condense, but force and form were not yet manifest, and there was nought named, nought done, who could know its shape? Nevertheless Heaven and Earth first parted, and the Three Deities performed the commencement of creation: the Passive and the Active essences then developed, and the Two Spirits became the ancestors of all things.'

Kojiki

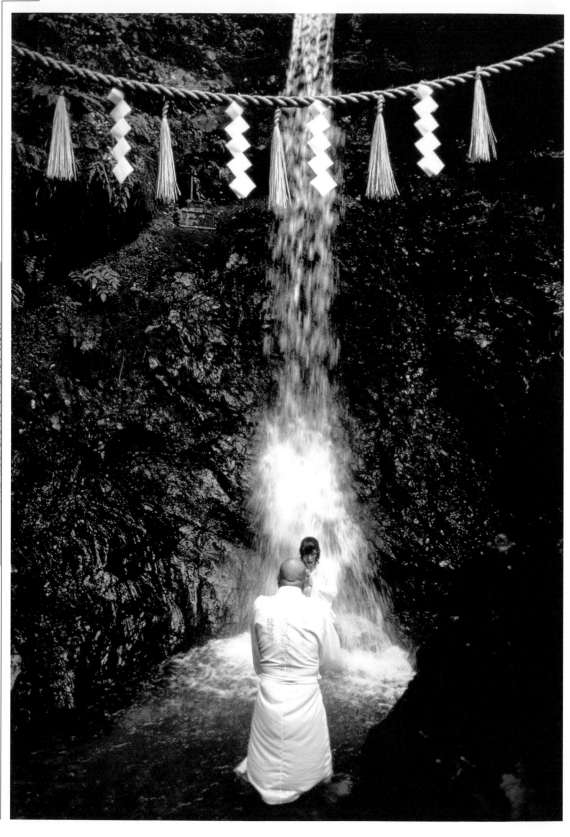

emperors and empresses as far as Ninigi, believed to have been the grandson of the sun-goddess Amaterasu. For this reason, Ise Shrine has always had a close connection with the imperial household. From 1868 onwards, when the monarchy was restored to a central position in Japanese politics under Emperor Meiji, up until the end of the Pacific War in 1945, the Shinto religion was focused sharply on Ise Shrine and the emperor cult. After the war the emperor's semi-divine status was officially denied and Shinto was disestablished. Since then, religious teaching has no longer been given in state-run schools and the observance of Shinto practices has become a voluntary matter. Nevertheless, the imperial family still enjoys very high esteem among the people, and leading Shinto shrines remain important symbols of Japanese nationhood.

SHINTO SHRINES
Shinto today is based fundamentally on each individual shrine. Although most shrines large enough to have an organizing staff are affiliated to the Association of Shinto Shrines, most of the people who visit a shrine or take part in a festival are hardly aware of this. Each shrine has some individual reason for its existence, whether it be a natural phenomenon such as a mountain, a historical event of importance to the local community, or an act of personal devotion or political patronage. There is an endless variety.

For example, the ancient shrine at Kashima, near the Pacific coast of Honshu, is patronized particularly by those devoted to the martial arts such as swordsmanship and *kendo*. At the same time it has various sub-shrines within its grounds.

One of these celebrates a spring of fresh water tumbling out of the side of a hill and has its symbolic gate planted in the pool at the foot. Another is a

fenced enclosure surrounding a mighty stone, of which only the rounded top is visible sticking up through the sand. This stone is supposed to hold down beneath the earth the giant catfish which is believed to be responsible for earthquakes.

The god or *kami* of a shrine may be the natural object itself, it may be one of the divinities mentioned in the *Kojiki* or the *Nihongi*, or it may be a legendary or historical person. In shrines where a specific object is kept in the inner sanctuary it is usually not known what the object is, for nobody ever sees it.

Shinto shrines have certain common features which are almost always to be seen. The first of these which the visitor will notice is the large symbolic gate consisting of two uprights and two crossbars, marking the entrance to the shrine. These gates (*torii*) sometimes stand quite far off at the bottom of a busy street with shops and stalls catering for visitors; there may be two or more, or even a long line of them, leading to the shrine itself. Inside the precinct there is a large trough of clean water, usually sheltered with a roof and provided with clean wooden ladles. Here the worshipper rinses face and hands in a simple act of purification. The main shrine buildings, of which there are several traditional architectural types, consist of a worship hall (*haiden*) and a main hall (*honden*) standing behind. The main hall is usually smaller and is not entered, being the physical location of the *kami* itself.

The worship hall is entered from time to time by small groups for petitionary prayer. Individual visitors to the shrine simply stand outside before the worship hall, toss a coin into the offerings box, pull on a dangling rope with a bell or clanger at the top, clap their hands twice, bow briefly in prayer, clap their hands again and leave. The sound of the clanger and of the handclap are intended to alert the

A religious ascetic performs water austerities, or *suigyo*, symbolizing his regeneration in the ice-cold water. The thick rope, stretched across the falls, is a common Shinto symbol defining sacred and pure space. The lengths of folded paper recall the paper strands attached to the purifying wands used in Shinto rites.

A TAPESTRY OF TRADITIONS: JAPANESE RELIGION

'At festivals we serve the deities by purifying ourselves, with sincerity revere the dignity of the deities, return thanks for their benefits, and offer earnest prayers.'

Kokutai no Hongi

kami to the believer's presence.

The front of the worship hall is often decorated with a thick rope (*shimenawa*) and folded white paper strips, which are regularly used to designate a sacred area or sacred object. Sometimes these are simply strung around a rock or a tree, indicating that these too are considered as shrines for the *kami* of the rock or the tree.

There are three main types of shrine:

● shrines of purely local significance, housing the *kami* of the locality (*ujigami*);

● shrines of a particular recurrent type, such as the Inari Shrines, which are visited with a view to winning business success. These may be found in any part of the country;

● shrines of great national and semi-political importance, such as the Ise and Izumo Shrines mentioned earlier, the Meiji Shrine in Tokyo, honouring the former emperor Meiji, and the Yasukuni Shrine, also in Tokyo, commemorating the souls of Japan's war dead.

Since the end of the Pacific War, the status of Ise Shrine and of Yasukuni Shrine has been a matter of some controversy, because critics fear a revival of Shinto-led nationalism if relations with political leaders or with the imperial household become too close or too formal.

Other types of shrine that recur throughout the country include the Hachimangu Shrines, dedicated to the *kami* of war and martial prowess; the Toshogu Shrines, sacred to the memory of the dictator-general Ieyasu (d. 1616) and reflecting the colourful pomp of his mausoleum at Nikko; and the Tenmangu Shrines where a loyal but wrongfully banished aristocrat is revered and believers pray for success in literature and study.

'The term Kami *is applied in the first place to the various deities of Heaven and Earth who are mentioned in the ancient records as well as to their spirits (*mi-tama*) which reside in the shrines where they are worshipped. Moreover, not only human beings, but birds, beasts, plants and trees, seas and mountains, and all other things whatsoever which deserve to be dreaded and revered for the extraordinary and preeminent powers which they possess, are called* Kami.*'*

Motoori Wonnaga

SHINTO PRACTICES

Much of Shinto practice is an individual matter, as when a person simply visits a shrine to make his or her own request – before a journey, before an examination, before some new enterprise, or perhaps because they just happen to be passing that way. In such cases the form of worship is as described earlier. Family occasions also involve visits to the shrine. It is common, though not universal, to take a newborn baby there so that prayers may be said for its health. Shinto priests officiate at the majority of Japanese weddings, though these usually take place in a purpose-built hall run on business lines with reception rooms and other facilities.

Shrines are visited by particularly large numbers at New Year, especially on 1 January but also on 2 and 3 January. Some people go just after midnight on 31 December, while others go at dawn. Some visitors to mountain shrines make a point of observing the rising sun and bathing their faces in its first rays.

At the New Year visit there is a brisk sale of feathered wooden arrows (to drive off evil), protective charms and stiff paper strips bearing the name and seal of the shrine (*fuda*). These are taken home and kept on the *kami* shelf if there is one, or just in a high place, for the coming year. Last year's accessories are taken back to the shrine at the New Year visit and burned on a bonfire or handed in to be burned later by shrine staff.

Another personal charm sold in great numbers at this time of year is the papier mâché *daruma* doll, originally a representation of the Zen Buddhist master Daruma (or Bodhidharma). Though Buddhist in origin, these dolls are on sale at the entrances to many shrines and are also brought back to shrines for burning.

Some Buddhist temples share in the New Year practices by encouraging a

Shinto priests
in traditional
vestments take part
in the *Takayama*
Festival in Japan,
while shielding
themselves from the
rain with umbrellas.

first visit on a specified day in January, selling various kinds of talisman and offering prayers for safety in the home, traffic safety, prosperity in business and avoidance of bad luck.

FESTIVALS

Perhaps the most important feature of Shinto practice is the festival (*matsuri*), since this forms the main occasion on which a particular shrine takes on meaning for all its worshippers at once.

A Shinto festival usually includes a procession or a fair with stalls and side-shows, and so it easily draws large numbers of people, many returning to visit relatives at the same time. The more spectacular festivals bring in visitors and sightseers as well, thus being good for trade; for festivals which achieve national fame, special trains may be laid on and accommodation booked for months in advance.

One shrine may hold several festivals in a year, but among these just one or two may be of special importance, particularly in spring or autumn.

Festivals famous throughout Japan for their huge floats hauled along in procession are the *Gion* Festival in Kyoto, the *Takayama* Festival in the Hida region and the *Chichibu* Festival in the mountains north-west of Tokyo. In the last of these the vehicles, representing various parts of the town of Chichibu, are illuminated by lanterns and drawn through the town at night as the *kami* from the town shrine is brought to meet the *kami* of the nearest large mountain.

In many cases, the floats or the standards and banners are taken through the town by groups of young men wearing clothes representative of their part of the town. Sometimes they wear only a loincloth because of the strenuousness of the work, especially if they have to wade through water. Almost always they are fortified by plenty of rice wine (*sake*), which is particularly associated with Shinto and often offered at shrines in neatly wrapped bottles or large casks. Sometimes the processions recall a historical event such as a battle, in which case period costumes are worn.

Very often, the focal point of a procession is a portable shrine (*mikoshi*) which is taken from the main shrine to various points in the locality, symbolizing a journey made by the *kami*. Not all of those taking part in a procession enter the worship hall of the main shrine on arrival. Usually it

'The magokoro or "true heart" is pure and sincere. This links with the belief that the divine light which illuminates the kami is also found in the human heart. It is like a mirror which needs polishing and cleaning, to clear away the dust and dirt which obscure it.'

Ninian Smart

is representatives only who go inside with the priests to present offerings such as evergreen branches of the *sakaki* tree, and to offer prayers for the safety and prosperity of the neighbourhood.

Japanese Buddhism

The history of Japanese Buddhism can be traced back to the early sixth century CE when images and *sutras* (Buddhist scriptures) were sent from Korea. The first major act of patronage took place when Prince Shotoku, regent from CE 593–622, established Buddhism as a national religion, linking it to Confucian ideals of morality and statecraft.

A stream of eminent monks brought more knowledge of the new religion from Korea and China, and the early traditions at the capital of Nara were superseded in CE 805 by a much bigger Buddhist establishment on Mount Hiei, overlooking the new capital of Kyoto, This new Buddhist centre drew its inspiration from the Chinese T'ien T'ai school, which came to be known in Japan as Tendai Buddhism.

This in turn was rapidly affected by the doctrines and practices of an esoteric form of Buddhism, not unlike that of Tibet. Almost immediately a rival headquarters for this type of Buddhism was set up on the then almost inaccessible Mount Koya, some distance to the south of Kyoto, This school, Shingon Buddhism, was established by the famous monk Kukai (744–835), posthumously known as Kobo Daishi and revered as a great saint.

The Tendai and Shingon sects were rapidly supplemented by others, partly drawing on special trends in Chinese Buddhism and partly resulting from Japanese innovation. The *Lotus Sutra* had already been of great importance in Tendai Buddhism, but Nichiren (1222–82) gave it a new centrality, and his interpretative writings provided the basis for a number of sects. Among these are counted some of the most influential lay Buddhist movements of modern times. Nichirenite sects share in common the recitation of the simple formula '*Nam(u) Myoho Renge Kyo*' ('Hail Wonderful *Dharma Lotus Sutra*').

In their various ways these sects all express significant themes in the tradition of Mahayana Buddhism which spread from India across East Asia. While some people have a clear allegiance to one or other sect, especially in the case of the *nembutsu* sects or the Nichirenite sects, there are many features of popular devotion which cut across sectarian distinctions.

Two of the most widely revered saviour figures are the Bodhisattvas Jizo-sama and Kannon-sama. Jizo-sama is believed to care especially for children or for infants who have died during childbirth or pregnancy. Kannon-sama (*Avalokiresvara* in Sanskrit) offers many kinds of protection and solace and is found in many places, not least in the precincts of Soto Zen temples.

BUDDHISM IN THE HOME
In the home many families are reminded of Buddhism by the presence of a domestic Buddhist altar (*butsu-dan*). This usually contains a central Buddhist image or other symbol, tablets commemorating ancestors, a booklet with portions of Buddhist scriptures, a place for lighting incense, and various other accessories. As a morning devotion a small offering of food may be placed on the altar, a passage recited from a *sutra* and a stick of incense lit. Individual sects introduce many variations.

Buddhism is also particularly influential as the religion of funerals and cemeteries. Again the different sects make slightly different provisions, though cremation and a stone memorial are universal. Thin wooden posts

---

'Namu Myohorengekyo: "Homage to the Lotus of the Perfect Law."'

Nichiren

'At that time the World-honoured One addressed the eighty thousand great leaders through the Bodhisattva Medicine-King: Medicine-King! Do you see in this assembly innumerable gods, dragon kings... human and non-human beings, as well as... male and female lay devotees... seekers after pratyeke-buddhahood, seekers after bodhisattvaship, or seekers after buddhahood? All such beings as these, in the presence of the Buddha, if they hear a single verse or a single word of the Wonderful Law-Flower Sutra and even by a single thought delight in it, I predict that they will all attain to Perfect Enlightenment.'

Lotus Sutra

placed by visitors at a tombstone bear
texts written in heavy black ink which
reflect the distinctive faith of the
temple in question.

Cemeteries are visited particularly at
higan, which occurs twice a year at the
spring and autumn equinoxes. The

other main commemoration of the dead
is in midsummer at *o-bon*, which is
marked by outdoor fires and dancing.

BUDDHIST FESTIVALS
To some extent Japanese Buddhism
borrows the characteristic Shinto

An ornate float in
procession through
Kyoto, Japan,
during the *Gion
Matsuri* Festival.

concept of festival (*matsuri*). In early April, for example, some Buddhist temples celebrate a flower festival which centres on the commemoration of the Buddha's birthday on 8 April. At this time a small standing statue of the infant Buddha is placed in a framework decorated with flowers, and worshippers anoint it with liquid from a bowl beneath.

Another well-known festival climaxing at a Buddhist temple in Tokyo, is that of the forty-seven masterless Samurai (*ronin*). These feat inspired by loyalty.

The theme is worked out in the well-known traditional drama *Chushingura*, regularly shown at the time of the festival in December. The festival itself consists of a procession re-enacting the arrival of the forty-seven Samurai at the temple to report the completion of their deed of vengeance. Following this, crowds of people light incense at their tombs.

Buddhism is linked to Japanese culture at many points: through the traditional way of the Samurai,

A monk sweeps gravel from a path in a Zen rock garden at the Daitoku Temple at Kyoto, Japan.

forty-seven have been applauded for centuries because they avenged the unjustly forced suicide of their master and then committed suicide themselves. This is one of the classic cases of premeditated ritual suicide (*hara-kiri*), carried out in connection with a generally known as *bushido*; through the austere *no* drama with its many Buddhist themes; through the tea ceremony which is intended to communicate simplicity and naturalness; through calligraphy and painting, and so on. The most lively aspect of Japanese Buddhism however remains the popular faith directed towards the various Buddhas, Bodhisattvas and saints of the Mahayana Buddhist tradition.

The flowering of new religions

Innovation is an accepted feature of Japanese religious life. Many Shinto shrines are the result of some fresh religious experience or message from a medium, long since incorporated into the general pattern of Shinto. In some more recent cases such initiatives have led to the growth of separate religious bodies.

One of the best known of these is the Religion of the Heavenly Wisdom (Tenrikyo), founded in the early nineteenth century by Nakayama Miki (1798–1887). This religion began with her revelations and healings, but instead of merging into the wider pattern of Shinto it formulated its own independent sacred writings, constructed its own sacred city named Tenri, and shaped its own forms of worship including a special dance.

Another well-known example is the popularly-named Dancing Religion (Odoru Shukyo) which also has the longer formal name of Tensho Kotai Jingu Kyo, incorporating alternative names for the goddess Amaterasu and Ise Shrine. The foundress, named Kitamura Sayo (1900–67), believed that a *kami* was speaking through her abdomen, and these revelations are the basis of the religion's teaching. She also initiated a form of ecstatic dance which encourages believers to experience a state of not-self (*muga*).

It may be noted that this is one of the 'three marks' of Buddhist teaching. The religion known as the Teaching of the Great Source (Omotokyo) is also a major independent religious group having a Shinto background combined with belief in a new revelation of its own.

Other new religions have moved further afield from the traditional faiths of Japan.

The Syncretic House of Growth (Seicho no Ie) claims to overcome disease and suffering through its new teachings propounded by Taniguchi Masaharu (1893–1985), a former Omotokyo member.

The Church of World Messianity (Sekai Kyuseikyo) is also loosely derived from Omotokyo. The leader, Okada Mokichi (1882–1955), preached freedom from disease and from poverty, and his following grew rapidly after the Pacific War. The movement now boasts a fine art gallery.

PL Kyodan, which claims a membership of about 2 million, sees the whole of life as art, and religion as a means of realizing this vision in the member's experience. The 'PL' in the name of this group stands for the English words 'Perfect Liberty'.

There are many different explanations for the appearance of new religions, but at least it is clear that they provide a kind of barometer of the needs and aspirations of much of Japan's population.

NEW BUDDHIST MOVEMENTS

Japanese Buddhism also gives plenty of scope for innovation since the proliferation of sects and independent temple organizations is accepted as a normal feature of religious life. It is hardly surprising that several of Japan's new religions are in fact recently developed forms of Buddhism.

The most influential are those based in some way or other on the *Lotus Sutra*, for together they claim about a fifth of the population as adherents. Of these, the Reiyukai began as a movement caring for untended tombs and stressing the virtues of gratitude and loyalty towards ancestors. Today it boasts a huge central hall in Tokyo.

Several groups split off from the Reiyukai, however, in a series of organizational and doctrinal disputes.

'Looking all over the world and through all ages, I find no one who has understood My heart. No wonder that you know nothing, for so far I have taught nothing to you. This time I, God, revealing Myself to the fore, teach you all the truth in detail.'

From the *Ofudesaki* (the revelation received by Nakayama Miki, the founder of Tenrikyo)

A TAPESTRY OF TRADITIONS: JAPANESE RELIGIONS

Of these the largest is the Rissho Kosei-kai, claiming over 6 million members. This movement was strongly influenced in its beginnings by the religious messages of Mrs Naganuma Myoko (1899–1957). The dominant figure, however, was the founding president, Niwano Nikkyo (1906–99), who emphasized the exposition of the *Lotus Sutra* as the doctrinal basis of the movement. After taking the leadership, his son Nichiko (b.1938) has also emphasized political activities such as anti-nuclear campaigns and the promotion of world peace.

It is notable that this is a lay movement which is entirely independent of any previously existing monastic sect. As far as practices are concerned, the main emphasis is on a form of group counselling in which the individual's problems are analysed in Buddhist terms, though, of course, the *Lotus Sutra* is recited and studied as well.

Also based on the *Lotus Sutra*, but with different doctrinal tendencies, is the lay movement commonly known as the Soka Gakkai. This is linked with a monastic sect named Nichiren Shoshu, claiming a direct tradition back to Nichiren himself, and the full name is therefore Nichiren Shoshu Soka Gakkai. The members support one of Japan's larger political parties, the Komeito (Clean Government Party) which was founded under the stimulation of Soka Gakkai leaders, although remaining legally distinct.

The future of Japanese faiths
The new religions draw in many ways on the wider religious culture of Japan. This is formed mainly by traditional Shinto and Buddhism, but is also influenced by Confucian ideas and values, and to a lesser extent by a rather Western-looking Christianity. Historically, Confucianism has provided the main moral backing for Shinto, emphasizing family duty and loyalty and extending these concepts to school, industry and state. Though Confucianism has no organization of any note, many religious bodies in Japan stress such values as loyalty or sincerity (*makoto*), gratitude, correctness of behaviour and brightness of attitude.

Modern Christian missions have had little impact numerically or even ideologically, but they have had some unintentional influence on other Japanese religious bodies. A number of Buddhist sects now run Sunday schools, for example, and some of the new religions use books looking remarkably like Christian Bibles and prayer-books, but with different contents. Christianity itself has a total membership of less than 1 per cent of the population, probably because it is strongly identified as belonging to the Western world. The Christian churches in Japan have only the most tenuous links with the general religious culture of the country.

SECULAR JAPAN?
In spite of the startling success of several of the newer religious movements, it would be quite wrong to think that Buddhism and Shinto have lost support in recent times. In some ways, particularly in politics and education, Japan has become remarkably secularized, and there is much ignorance about the deeper teachings of the religions. At the same time, most Japanese people are involved in various kinds of religious behaviour at certain times of the year and at the appropriate points in their lives.

The Bahá'í Faith

A Historical Overview

MOOJAN MOMEN

Sayyid 'Ali Muhammad was born in Shiraz in Persia (modern-day Iran) in 1819. He put forward a claim to be a Messenger of God, and called himself the Báb, meaning 'the gate' as part of his mission was to the prepare the way for the coming of a greater Messenger. His new religious movement caused a great stir culminating in a fierce persecution of its adherents as Islamic heretics and in 1850 he was executed. Mirza Husayn 'Ali Nuri (1817–92) from Tehran, who had become a follower of the Báb in 1844, took the name Bahá'u'lláh, meaning 'The Glory of God', and went on to found the Bahá'í Faith.

Founded in exile
Exiled by the Iranian government in 1853, Bahá'u'lláh went to Baghdad (then part of the Ottoman empire). Here in 1863 he claimed to be the bearer of a new message from God, a message built on the previous religions of the world and destined to take humanity on to the next stage of its social development: the stage of world unity. Bahá'u'lláh was summoned to Istanbul by the Ottoman authorities and exiled to Edirne from 1863 to 1868 and finally to 'Akka (in what was then the Ottoman province of Syria and is now the state of Israel), a city to which the Ottomans frequently sent religious and political prisoners. Bahá'u'lláh remained in or around 'Akka until he passed away in 1892. His shrine just outside 'Akka is the holiest site in the world for Bahá'ís, and the world spiritual and administrative centres of the Bahá'í Faith are in the Haifa-'Akka area.

The legacy
Bahá'u'lláh appointed his son 'Abdu'l-Bahá ('Abbas Effendi, 1844–1921) to be his successor as head of the Bahá'í Faith and also the authorized interpreter of his writings. In 1911 and 1912–13, 'Abdu'l-Bahá travelled to Europe and North America, consolidating the newly founded Bahá'í communities there. He was invited to speak at churches, mosques and synagogues, to meet prominent people and to address many organizations. Upon his death in 1921 his grandson Shoghi Effendi (Rabbani, 1897–1957) succeeded as head of the Bahá'í Faith and authorized interpreter of the Bahá'í scriptures.

> 'Religious fanaticism and hatred are a world-devouring fire, whose violence none can quench. The Hand of Divine power can, alone, deliver mankind from this desolating affliction... The utterance of God is a lamp, whose light are these words: Ye are the fruits of one tree, and the leaves of one branch. Deal ye one with another with the utmost love and harmony, with friendliness and fellowship.'
>
> Bahá'u'lláh

'Abdu'l-Bahá, successor of Bahá'u'lláh as head of the Bahá'í Faith.

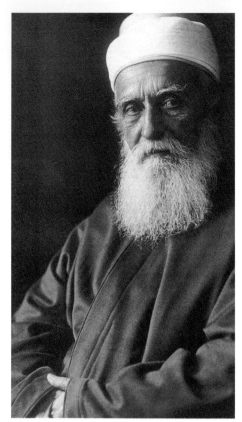

'In the corner where the divan met the wall sat a wondrous and venerable figure, crowned with a felt head-dress of the kind called taj *by dervishes (but of unusual height and make), round the base of which was wound a small white turban. The face of him on whom I gazed I can never forget, though I cannot describe it. Those piercing eyes seemed to read one's very soul; power and authority sat on that ample brow; while the deep lines on the forehead and face implied an age which the jet-black hair and beard flowing down in indistinguishable luxuriance almost to the waist seemed to belie. No need to ask in whose presence I stood, as I bowed myself before one who is the object of a devotion and love which kings might envy and emperors sigh for in vain!'*

A pen-portrait of Bahá'u'lláh from Professor E.G. Browne, Cambridge University, 1890

Shoghi Effendi spent the early years of his ministry building up the Bahá'í administrative system, then began to use this administrative framework to spread the Bahá'í Faith to all those parts of the world where there were not already Bahá'ís. The Bahá'í Faith is not spread by paid missionaries but rather by ordinary Bahá'ís who choose to relocate to another place and work there in whatever occupation they can find. Shoghi Effendi also extensively developed the Bahá'í World Centre and drew up plans for this which have shaped its development to the present.

After Shoghi Effendi passed away, there was an interregnum until 1963, when in accordance with the writings of Bahá'u'lláh the Universal House of Justice was elected. This supreme administrative body of the Bahá'í Faith has continued the task of taking the Bahá'í Faith to all parts of the world and of developing Bahá'í community life.

Worldwide growth

At various times during the twentieth century the Bahá'í community faced persecution in some Muslim and Communist countries. The fiercest persecution erupted in Iran in 1979 after the Islamic Revolution. Many Bahá'ís were executed and others were abducted and are presumed to have been executed. Although international pressure averted a genocide, the government of Iran has put in place a systematic campaign to demoralize and forcibly convert the Bahá'í community there. Nonetheless, the Bahá'í Faith has continued to gain adherents in all parts of the world, from every type of religious, ethnic and social background. A series of plans starting from 1937 and continuing to the present have resulted in the spread of the Bahá'í Faith to every country of the world (except the Vatican) and to the establishment of Bahá'í administrative institutions in all countries where these are not banned by law. By the early twenty-first century there were more than 5 million Bahá'ís living in over 230 countries and dependent territories, with the largest community in India and other large communities in Latin America, Africa and South-East Asia.

Sacred Writings

MOOJAN MOMEN

A decorative depiction of the name of God by the famous Bahá'í calligrapher, Mishkin Qalam.

During his lifetime Bahá'u'lláh wrote a number of key works as well as many letters (known as *Tablets*) in response to questions from his followers and others. These are all regarded as part of Bahá'í scripture and are loosely described as comprising 100 volumes. The most important works of Bahá'u'lláh are the *Kitab-i-Aqdas* (the Most Holy Book), which contains laws and social ordinances, and the *Kitab-i-Iqan* (the Book of Certitude), which addresses theological questions and also explains how the prophecies of the Bible and Qur'an have been fulfilled spiritually and metaphorically, rather than literally. Other highly regarded works include his *Hidden Words*, a condensation of his spiritual and ethical teachings, and the *Seven Valleys*, his foremost mystical work.

'Abdu'l-Bahá wrote on many themes, especially the social teachings of the Bahá'í Faith, the Bahá'í interpretation of the Bible and other scriptures, and philosophical questions. The writings of Bahá'u'lláh's forerunner, the Báb, and of 'Abdu'l-Bahá are regarded as scripture, although some of the laws and social ordinances of the Báb were repealed by Bahá'u'lláh. Scripture is considered to be much more than just the repository of the words of the founder. It is seen itself as a creative transforming impulse.

Authoritative Texts

Shoghi Effendi's interpretations of the writings of Bahá'u'lláh and 'Abdu'l- Bahá are regarded as authoritative, but not scripture. A large part of Shoghi Effendi's writings consists of answers to questions regarding the development of the Bahá'í administrative system. He also wrote an interpretative history of the Bahá'í Faith and translated many of Bahá'u'lláh's writings into English. Only the writings of these central figures are considered part of the Bahá'í canon; reports of their spoken words are not authoritative.

The Universal House of Justice is authorized to act as the head of the Bahá'í Faith and legislate in those areas not already covered by the scripture. Its words are authoritative, although any ruling it makes can be altered or repealed by a subsequent House of Justice if circumstances change. Thus far, the House of Justice has preferred to exhort the Bahá'ís to make their own decisions based on spiritual and moral principles rather than to depend on detailed legislation.

'O ye that dwell on earth! The distinguishing feature that marketh the preeminent character of this Supreme Revelation consisteth in that We have, on the one hand, blotted out from the pages of God's holy Book whatsoever hath been the cause of strife, of malice and mischief amongst the children of men, and have, on the other, laid down the essential prerequisties of concord, of understanding, of complete and enduring unity.'

Bahá'u'lláh

Beliefs

MOOJAN MOMEN

The Bahá'í teachings maintain that the purpose of life in this physical world is to show to the greatest extent possible such spiritual qualities as love, justice, patience, compassion, wisdom, purity and trustworthiness. All human beings are capable of exhibiting all of these virtues, although each individual will exhibit them to varying degrees. The physical world is seen as the arena for the development and perfection of the human being, a classroom for the spiritual education and maturation of the soul, where progress can best be achieved by following the teachings of one of the founders of the world's religions, who are the spiritual educators of humankind. Since these spiritual qualities are also the attributes of the divinity, acquiring them is tantamount to drawing nearer to God. The divine potential is already present in everyone, so the Bahá'í scriptures speak of education as the process of mining the gems that exist within each human being.

The whole of one's life is sometimes described as a journey towards God. On the way one may come across tests and difficulties, but these should be seen as opportunities to make progress, illuminating one's shortcomings and offering a chance to transcend them. For Bahá'ís salvation is not a state that one either has attained or not. It is a process that begins at birth and continues after death. Only God can know where each human being started on this process, what status has been attained and the rate of progress being made. Human beings, therefore, should not judge each other with respect to these matters.

Seeking truth

To play the piano well, one must discipline oneself to practise every day. Similarly, in order to assist individuals with their spiritual progress, Bahá'u'lláh has given some laws such as a daily requirement to pray, to read the scriptures and to meditate, and an annual period of fasting. From these, as well as from group consultation, can be obtained the spiritual guidance that in other religions is given by religious leaders since Bahá'u'lláh has forbidden any type of priesthood or religious leadership among the Bahá'ís. All Bahá'í have the duty to investigate truth for themselves, through prayer,

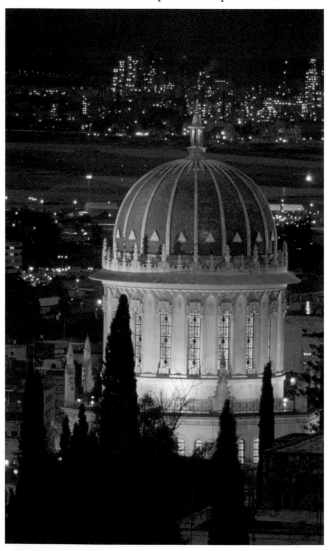

The shrine of the Báb on Mount Carmel, overlooking the city of Haifa, Israel.

study of the scriptures, meditation and reflection upon their experiences. Wisdom should be used in teaching others, in order to prevent confrontation and contention, but denying one's faith is not permitted. Although the many martyrs that the Bábi and Bahá'í Faiths have had are praised, martyrdom is not to be sought deliberately and suicide is condemned.

Manifestations of God

Bahá'u'lláh asserts that there is a supreme reality, which in Western religions is called God. Since God is infinite and our minds can only conceptualize the finite, humanity has no access to knowledge of the supreme reality. Neither the formulations of God made by Western religions, nor the descriptions of various types of ultimate reality in Eastern religions (for example, Brahman, Dharmakaya, Nirvana or the Tao [or Dao]) are adequate or accurate. The only certain knowledge that human beings can gain of that supreme reality is that brought by certain intermediaries who arise from time to time and found the great religions of the world. These intermediaries – among whom Bahá'ís recognize Abraham, Krishna, Moses, Zarathushtra (Zoroaster), Buddha, Christ, and Muhammad – reveal the attributes of the ultimate reality to human beings both in the scriptures they produce and in their own person. In the Bahá'í scriptures they are called 'Manifestations of God'. Bahá'u'lláh claims to be the latest in this chain of manifestations of God. The Báb is also considered to have been a manifestation of God.

These manifestations of God bring teachings to the world which are necessary for humanity's spiritual and social progress. Since each of them has come at a different time in various parts of the world, each message has been adapted to the needs of the time and place and has built on what came before. Bahá'u'lláh claims that he has brought the latest in this series of messages from the supreme reality and that his message is the one relevant for today, namely that now is the time for all of humanity to come together in a world-embracing unity. Bahá'u'lláh claims to be of equal station and indeed spiritually the same reality as the preceding founders of the world's religions. Bahá'ís believe that his message, being the latest, is the fullest and most relevant revelation of God's will, and that this makes his revelation of greater importance to the people of this age. Bahá'u'lláh claims that all the scriptures of the world religions contain prophecies of a future world saviour and that he is the fulfilment of all of these prophecies.

Life after death

Bahá'u'lláh states that the human being survives after death as a spiritual entity (a soul) and continues to progress in further spiritual worlds towards its ultimate goal of reunion with God. In this physical world, human beings are preparing themselves for the next world. The analogy is drawn in the Bahá'í writings of the embryo in the womb of its mother, where it does not even know the outside world exists. Just as it is developing arms and legs and eyes, the need for which only becomes apparent to it when it is born, so we are developing spiritual qualities, the importance of which will only be appreciated after death. The scriptures of many religions have written of heaven and hell in relation to life after death. Bahá'ís believe that these are metaphors for the state of being near to or distant from God. In this sense, one can be in heaven or hell while in this world.

Good and evil?

All major religions have asked why there is evil and suffering in this world, especially when, in the case of the

> 'Religion and science are the two wings upon which man's intelligence can soar into the heights, with which the human soul can progress … Should a man try to fly with the wing of religion alone, he would quickly fall into the quagmire of superstition… with the wing of science alone he would also make no progress, but fall into the despairing slough of materialism.'
>
> 'Abdu'l-Bahá

BELIEFS

Western religions, God is said to be merciful and good. One answer is that, unless human beings had the potential to do evil and cause suffering, they could not be said to possess free will, which is one of the attributes of God – and human beings have the potential to acquire all of the attributes of God. Some suffering is of course the direct result of one's own actions: something that one has done wrong or unwisely. The Bahá'í teachings assert that the universe is governed by physical, moral and spiritual laws. If one breaks or goes against these laws, one must expect to suffer the consequences. Another answer is that suffering can help human beings to advance spiritually. Indeed it often causes human beings to realize the emptiness of this world and turns their attention to the importance of the spiritual life. In fact the Bahá'í scriptures assert that there is no force of evil (such as Satan) in the world. Such concepts refer in reality to the animal side of human beings which, if allowed to dominate the spiritual aspect, turns a human being into an entity that is lower than the animal.

Bahá'u'lláh writes that humanity is reaching maturity and much that was previously part of religion – concepts such as Satan, heaven and hell as literal physical entities and practices such as confession and priestly forgiveness of sins – can now be dispensed with. Such things can now be discarded, or re-conceptualized in a more sophisticated manner. The fractiousness and belligerency of human society is similarly something that humanity will leave behind as it grows into maturity.

> *'The best beloved of all things in My sight is Justice; turn not away therefrom if thou desirest Me, and neglect it not that I may confide in thee. By its aid thou shalt see with thine own eyes and not through the eyes of others, and shalt know of thine own knowledge and not through the knowledge of thy neighbour.'*
>
> Hidden Words, Arabic, no. 2

Worship and Festivals

MOOJAN MOMEN

There are few rituals or acts of public worship in the Bahá'í Faith and there are specific instructions not to allow these to develop. At Bahá'í meetings and commemorations, appropriate prayers and passages of scripture are usually recited.

Prayers
Bahá'u'lláh and 'Abdu'l-Bahá wrote many prayers which Bahá'ís use for their personal devotions and at meetings. Three of Bahá'u'lláh's prayers have a ritual status and Bahá'ís are obliged to say one of these daily. There is also an obligatory funerary prayer. Other prayers by Bahá'u'lláh and 'Abdu'l-Bahá, while not obligatory, are suitable for marriages, funerals or times of difficulty or illness.

Special days
The nine Bahá'í holy days commemorate events in the life of the Báb and Bahá'u'lláh and include the Bahá'í New Year, which falls on 21 March (the first day of spring in the northern hemisphere). Bahá'ís do not work on these days if possible.

The Bahá'í calendar has nineteen months of nineteen days and there is an annual fast of nineteen days, during which Bahá'ís fast from dawn to sunset, a period of spiritual regeneration and a symbol of detachment from the things of this world.

Bahá'ís who are able go on a nine-day pilgrimage to the Bahá'í holy places in the Haifa-Akka area, including the shrines of Bahá'u'lláh, the Báb and 'Abdu'l-Bahá and places where Bahá'u'lláh and 'Abdu'l-Bahá lived.

Regular meetings

The Bahá'í community as a whole meets once every nineteen days for the Nineteen Day Feast, which has three portions: devotional, consultative and social. The lack of set rituals means that artistic and local cultural elements can be incorporated. Most Bahá'í communities have meetings for introducing the Bahá'í Faith to enquirers, devotional meetings, study circles and children's classes. Unless there are a lot of Bahá'ís in an area, meetings will often be held in homes. Eventually each Bahá'í community will be centred on a House of Worship, a building dedicated to worship, especially dawn prayers. At present there are seven of these: in New Delhi, Sydney, Apia (Western Samoa), Kampala, Panama, Frankfurt am Main and Wilmette (near Chicago).

Family and Society

MOOJAN MOMEN

The Bahá'í teachings view the family as both the bedrock of the individual's spiritual development and the foundation for society's stability and progress. The best and strongest marriages are those that are based on both the spirit and the body. One of the most important functions of marriage is raising children. The family unit is the best way of providing a balanced, stable background in which children can grow up and learn to become moral and social beings. Divorce is strongly discouraged. However, if there are irreconcilable differences and antipathy between the partners, divorce is permitted after a year of waiting, during which efforts should be made to bring about a reconciliation.

The Bahá'í wedding vows are simple, the bride and groom each saying, *'We will all, verily, abide by the will of God.'*

See *Kitab-i-Aqdas, Questions and Answers,* no. 3

The terraces that form part of the Bahá'í gardens on Mount Carmel, Haifa, Israel.

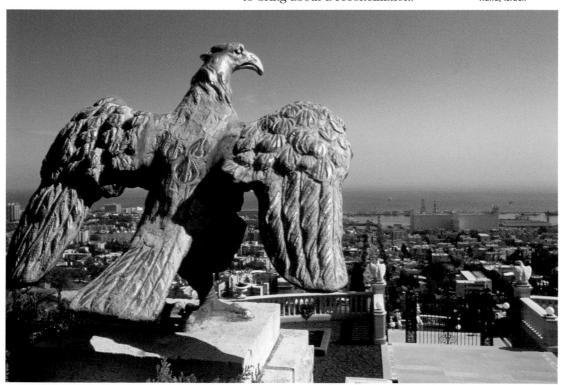

An organic unity

The Bahá'í teachings aim for a spiritualization of the individual, the individual's immediate society and the whole human race. Individuals are responsible for their own transformation, but as social beings they also have a responsibility to transform their society. Bahá'ís see the social teachings in the various religions of the world as the cause of humanity's social development. The next stage of this process is to occur though the teachings of Bahá'u'lláh by uniting humankind and establishing world peace.

The Bahá'í scriptures give the principles that must guide all social policies and laws if they are to create a new social reality. One aspect is that people's consciousness will be raised to a global level, so they no longer think of themselves in terms of narrow racial, religious, ethnic or class identities but as citizens of the world, experiencing such a sense of unity and solidarity that the suffering of human beings in any part of the world becomes like the suffering of one's own brother or sister. The vision underlying this is the organic unity of the human world, likened in the writings of Bahá'u'lláh to the human body, which consists of masses of cells, each contributing to the whole and receiving from the whole its nourishment while retaining its individuality.

Equality of men and women

A prerequisite for world unity is the elimination of the prejudices and hatreds that divide human beings and the injustices that set up anger or resentment, leading to alienation, vandalism and terrorism. One of the most deeply rooted prejudices is gender prejudice. For most of recorded history, human society has been mainly under the rule of men. The values of patriarchal societies, such as power, victory and domination, are the very values that promote aggressiveness and war. Therefore the Bahá'í scriptures refer to the need to achieve a balance between the masculine and feminine elements in society. This in itself will be a powerful means for promoting peace. Since women are usually the first educators of their children, the importance of educating the girl child, so that she can in turn be a good educator of her children, is much stressed. (Indeed, in one of his tablets, Bahá'u'lláh prescribes identical education for women and men but stipulates that when resources are limited first priority should be given to the education of women and girls.)

Governments and individuals

One of the major questions facing humanity is the balance between individual rights and the needs of society for order and a sense of responsibility in its citizens. In the twentieth century the cult of individualism was strongly promoted by politicians and others, primarily in the West. But Bahá'u'lláh warned that if liberty is carried to excess, it can become a great source of evil, leading to licentiousness and depravity. He advocated moderation. The individuals in society, he said, need to be spiritually transformed in order to utilize their freedoms in a responsible and aware manner.

The Bahá'í scriptures recommend democratic forms of government and consultation as the key way of making decisions. Humanity must move away from the situation (which can happen in democracies as well as in authoritarian regimes) where a single person or group makes all the important decisions. Those in positions of authority and the elected representatives of the people are to maintain the highest moral standards and be just and selfless in the carrying

'All men have been created to carry forward an ever-advancing civilization. The Almighty beareth Me witness: To act like the beasts of the field is unworthy of man. Those virtues that befit his dignity are forbearance, mercy, compassion and loving-kindness towards all the peoples and kindreds of the earth.'

From a tablet of Bahá'u'lláh

'The world of humanity is possessed of two wings: the male and the female. So long as these two wings are not equivalent in strength, the bird will not fly.'

'Abdu'l-Bahá

I am a Bahá'í

FIDELMA MEEHAN

I have been a Bahá'í for ten years and am currently a Bahá'í Projects manager. This involves working with other Bahá'ís, all volunteers, to plan and implement the various projects and activities of the Spiritual Assembly of the Bahá'ís in the area. We aim to assist people to develop a spiritual dimension in their lives. Unfortunately, 'spirituality' and 'religion' are often confusing terms for people. So, in some ways, my work is to help remove the barriers that stop people from exploring the transforming role of spirituality and religion in our lives.

All of this is very different to my upbringing and I am often asked how a Catholic girl ended up becoming a Bahá'í. I was always known as a questioning Catholic, even to the point of being called 'a doubting Thomas' by some members of my church. Many simply assumed that, not only is a faith something you're born into, but the faith you're born into should stay with you throughout your life. The problem was that this way of life wasn't for me. The burning question for me in my teenage years was why there are there so many different religions in the world. Millions of people belong to this faith; millions belong to that religion; and many in one faith oppose those in another faith. I wondered whether God was playing games with us. It didn't make sense. Unfortunately, no one I knew could give me, the questioning teenager, a satisfactory answer. I nearly stopped believing altogether. Then I met a Bahá'í.

I first heard about the Bahá'í Faith at university. It was here that I was befriended by the quick-witted comic Omid Djalili, a brilliant and versatile performer – and a Bahá'í. His humour and his deep love for Bahá'u'lláh (the founder of the Bahá'í Faith) were a potent mix that attracted the interest of many students. Omid would join us as we socialized a few miles from the university. As Bahá'ís don't drink alcohol, Omid would sip his orange juice and make us laugh until we cried, while we took advantage of the cheap beer and free entertainment. At the end of the night we would all crowd into Omid's little student flat and discuss religion until the early hours.

Hearing for the first time about Bahá'u'lláh's teachings on unity – the oneness of religion, the oneness of humanity and the oneness of God – was like someone switching on the light. I had always known this to be true and I had finally discovered a religion that had this belief as one of its key principles. I had to know more. During our late-night discussions, Omid would quote from the Bahá'í sacred writings and explain that it wasn't an accident that there are different religions in the world, but that these religions are all the necessary progressive stages of one faith, the eternal Faith of God. These teachings made perfect sense to me in the late-1980s. However, I still didn't consider myself a Bahá'í. Although I agreed with everything at an intellectual level, I felt no connection with the founder of the Bahá'í Faith, Bahá'u'lláh, or his forerunner, the Báb.

According to 'Abdu'l-Bahá, son of Bahá'u'lláh, the longest journey is from the head to the heart, and it was only when I heard the moving story of the martyrdom of the Báb that this journey truly started. When I heard this story, the long journey from my head to my heart had ended, and another spiritual journey as a Bahá'í was about to begin.

While being a Bahá'í is a deeply personal spiritual journey, it is not intended to be a self-centred existence. Spiritual growth requires that faith is translated into action for the good of everyone, not just Bahá'ís. Individual Bahá'ís, as well as Bahá'í institutions, are all encouraged to have an outward-looking orientation, rather than focusing exclusively on the Bahá'í community.

I'm involved in exploring ways through which Bahá'ís can serve the spiritual needs of the local population. The Tranquillity Zone (an inspirational place for people to relax and reflect) and the Youth Empowerment Project are examples of projects that we have developed over the past five years to respond to the spiritual needs of people of all ages. Managing these and other projects can sometimes be hectic – but I put it down to the sense of urgency that being a Bahá'í has instilled in me.

With a busy lifestyle, it's important to have some time to unwind with friends. As a Bahá'í I don't drink, which was not easy at first. Transformation is a slow process. A friend of mine told me that faith is not something you're born into – you acquire it. So, as I acquired my faith in Bahá'u'lláh, a Bahá'í lifestyle followed naturally. For me, the best opportunity to unwind and socialize is at the Bahá'í Nineteen Day Feast. Bahá'u'lláh has stated that the main purpose of this feast is to create love and unity in the hearts of people. Every nineteen days I get together with the Bahá'ís in my town to enjoy the spiritual uplift of a time of devotion, consult on local and national Bahá'í activities and socialize. More regularly, I meet with Bahá'í friends once a week for prayers and attend study groups. Children's classes are also a very important part of community life and I love to participate by telling stories and getting involved in drama.

My lifestyle as a Bahá'í is surprisingly free of rituals. I don't have to eat any special kind of food, nor do I wear special clothes, but daily prayer and reflection on the sacred writings is obligatory, as is a period of fasting every year. All in all, I have found in the Bahá'í Faith a new meaning of the word 'religion'. For me it's not about rituals or traditions, but is a source of inspiration and a way of life suited for this day and age.

out of their duties.

According to the Bahá'í teachings, most of the economic policies of governments today are doomed to failure because they are based on incorrect assumptions. One is that happiness and contentment can be achieved merely by increasing wealth. According to Bahá'í teachings and those of other religions, true happiness comes from being detached from wealth and being of service to others. Economic problems are, at their deepest level, spiritual in nature, they are a symptom of a spiritual malaise, and so they can only be solved by correcting the underlying spiritual problems – such as injustice, corruption and selfishness. The wealthy should realize that their spiritual health is dependent on sharing their wealth.

All should learn useful arts and sciences and engage in work, which if carried out in a spirit of service is regarded as worship. Education should be concerned primarily with the establishment of morals and values in the child and only secondarily with the transfer of knowledge. In this way it also becomes a major factor in the improvement of society and the reduction in crime.

Towards a united world

Bahá'u'lláh stated that the problems of the world cannot be solved unless and until the world becomes united. He called on the kings and rulers of all the nations of the world to convene an international conference to resolve all remaining border disputes and outstanding contentious issues, either by agreement or by arbitration, and then sign a binding agreement to maintain these recognized borders and rise up jointly against any aggressor transgressing the agreed borders. This mutually guaranteed security will, the Bahá'í scriptures assert, enable the nations of the world, particularly the poorer nations, to reduce their arms expenditure and channel the savings into areas such as health and education that will bring benefit to their peoples.

Environmental pollution, the gap between the rich nations and the poor, global warming and drug trafficking, are global problems that can only be effectively tackled at a global level. Similarly, multinational companies and world trade and finance are now beyond the ability of any individual nation to regulate effectively. Eventually therefore, the Bahá'í writings assert, it will become necessary to establish global institutions, including a world legislature, a world executive, and a world tribunal.

Other social teachings to be found in the Bahá'í writings are similarly based either on the underlying spiritual principle of justice or they promote a global vision and a truly integrated world order. Among these is the injunction for the governments of the world to adopt a universal language that will be taught in all schools besides the mother tongue of each nation; the adoption of a universal system of weights and measures; the adoption of a universal standard of human rights; and the universal compulsory education of children. The primacy of agriculture is also emphasized. Among those things to be found in other religions but which are specifically abolished by Bahá'u'lláh are: the waging of holy war; asceticism and monasticism; the confession of sins; the burning of books; the use of pulpits; and regarding certain people or things as impure.

Unity and diversity

The Bahá'í writings specifically warn against any tendency towards uniformity. The Bahá'í idea is not to have everyone submerged under one dominant culture. Excessive centralization is to be avoided and decisions made, as far as possible, at

'O my God! O my God! Unite the hearts of Thy servants, and reveal to them Thy great purpose. May they follow Thy commandments and abide in Thy law. Help them, O God, in their endeavour, and grant them strength to serve Thee. O God! Leave them not to themselves, but guide their steps by the light of Thy knowledge, and cheer their hearts by Thy love. Verily, Thou art their Helper and their Lord.'

A prayer of Bahá'u'lláh

the local and national levels. Nations will continue to exist (and people will continue to have a moderate degree of patriotism) but they must cede certain rights to global institutions, including the right to make war. It is important for unity to be established in the presence of a diversity of cultures. The Bahá'í aim is to preserve the rich diversity of human language, culture, tradition, and thought on this planet, while at the same time removing the causes of conflict and contention that exist.

To some, the Bahá'í vision may summon up George Orwell's nightmare vision of authoritarian social control in *1984*. While agreeing that Orwell's novel has a powerful emotive appeal, Bahá'ís would deny that it reflects their aims. Greater degrees of unity, provided they are within a democratic structure, give individuals more rights, not fewer. Citizens of the UK, for example, their country having joined the Council of Europe, can take their own government before the European Court of Human Rights.

Other people may claim that Bahá'ís are dreamers wishing for the impossible. To them Bahá'ís would answer that, far from being dreamers, it is they who have woken up to the reality of the interconnected, interdependent world in which we now live. It is those who imagine we can continue to run the world along present lines without running into disaster who are the dreamers.

The Bahá'í Faith in the Modern World

MOOJAN MOMEN

Bahá'ís believe Bahá'u'lláh not only provided the teachings needed to bring about unity in the world, but created the instrument for bringing this about through his instructions for the creation and functioning of the Bahá'í community. The Bahá'í community is thus considered to be both a model for and an embryonic form of the future united world envisaged in Bahá'u'lláh's writings. The Bahá'í Faith has no clergy or other forms of individual leadership. All Bahá'ís are to regard each other as equal and are encouraged to participate as actively in Bahá'í community life as their circumstances allow. What Bahá'ís are trying to do is to build up communities that are not patriarchal, communities in which there are not hierarchies of individuals, where people of every race, minority group, class and gender can participate, can voice their opinions and feel that their contribution is valued. This task has not been accomplished but is a 'work in progress'. In contrast to many religions that look back to a primordial golden age, Bahá'ís are very conscious that they are building towards their ideal.

Deciding together

The affairs of the Bahá'í community are run by 'Spiritual Assemblies', councils that are elected annually at the local and national level and every five years at the international level (for the Universal House of Justice). Elections are held in a prayerful

> *'Bahá'ís believe that the "Administrative Order" created by Bahá'u'lláh and built up by His successors 'Abdu'l-Baha and Shoghi Effendi, defines a pattern of cooperative decision-making and social interaction that cultivates the moral and creative capacities latent in human nature. It provides a model of the institutional structures necessary for global community life – a pattern of living that embraces diversity and fosters mutuality of purpose, compassion, and rectitude of conduct. A singular feature of this administrative system is the balance it strikes between preserving individual freedom and promoting the collective good.'*
>
> Statement on the Bahá'í International Community website

atmosphere and without any electioneering. Those elected have no rank or authority in themselves. Only the institution has authority and this is as decentralized as possible, with local decisions being made at the local level.

Decision-making is through consultation and the spiritual qualities said to be necessary for participation include purity of motive, radiance of spirit, detachment from all else save God, humility and patience. The aim is to foster a pooling of ideas and creativity, out of which will emerge the best decision or the best understanding based on the collective wisdom of the group. This process of consultation is used at the Nineteen Day Feast when the affairs of the community are discussed. It can also be used for obtaining spiritual guidance from the scriptures and for making personal decisions.

Unity and obedience

> 'Take ye counsel together in all matters, inasmuch as consultation is the lamp of guidance which leadeth the way, and is the bestower of understanding.'
>
> From a tablet of Bahá'u'lláh

The ethos of the Bahá'í community is very focussed on unity, which could be said to be the highest value in the Bahá'í Faith. A religion whose mission is to bring unity to the world can hardly itself be disunited and measures are in place to prevent sectarian groups forming around charismatic leaders or particular ideologies. While all Bahá'ís are encouraged to read and interpret the Bahá'í scriptures for themselves, no one is allowed to claim that his or her interpretation is correct or authoritative. The cornerstone of the unity of the Bahá'í community is the concept of the Covenant. This refers to the designated authority of the successive heads of the Bahá'í Faith and requires each Bahá'í to be loyal to and obey the head of the Faith (the Centre of the Covenant) in his or her own time (which currently means the Universal House of Justice). Whereas belief in a particular creed or

adherence to a particular school of law may be the identifying factors in some other religions, the identifying factor of a Bahá'í is obedience and loyalty to the Centre of the Covenant.

Development

The rapid growth of the Bahá'í Faith in the 1960s–80s brought into the community a large number of poor, illiterate, rural and indigenous peoples in India, Africa and South America, setting the Bahá'í

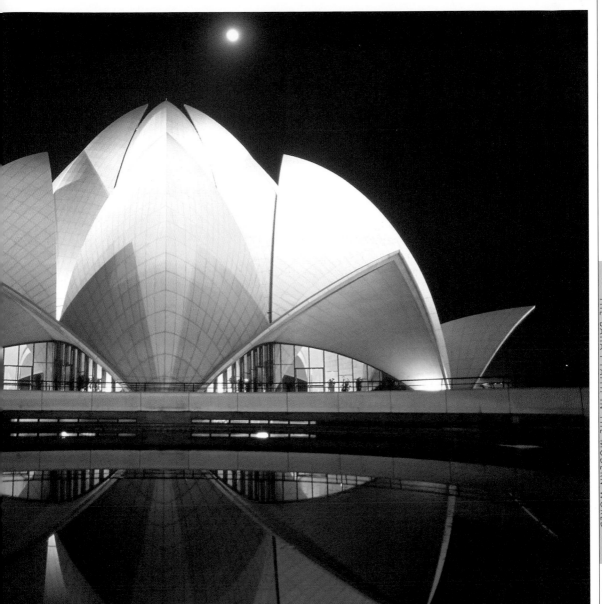

community an enormous challenge. The Bahá'í teachings place great emphasis on education and the elimination of extremes of poverty and wealth. Also the Bahá'í administrative system does not function well unless there is a certain level of literacy present. The Bahá'í community has thus had to grapple with the problem of the social and economic development of communities. The Bahá'í teachings reject the concept that such

development should be just about increasing the wealth of a community. Rather development should be about improving the human resources of each community, increasing their self-reliance, improving their communal solidarity, giving them access to knowledge, and removing sources of injustice wherever possible. Of course some of these goals cannot be achieved without the input of material resources, but these should be adjuncts not the primary goal. The

The Bahá'í Temple at New Delhi, India.

aim is to link together spiritual, moral and material development.

Bahá'ís have initiated many thousands of projects around the world. Some of these are short-term such as health camps, training seminars, tree-planting and environmental clean-up projects. Others are long-term and include literacy, health care, agricultural and environmental projects. The largest number of such Bahá'í projects are in schools, ranging from simple village tutorial schools to large secondary schools, and even some universities. Not all Bahá'í educational projects involve children, however. The Barli Development Institute for Rural Women in Indore, India, for example, trains tribal and village women in literacy, vocational and organizational skills as well as making them a source of knowledge on hygiene, health and environmental issues in their communities. It was placed on the Global 500 Roll of Honour by UNEP in 1992, on UNESCO's INNOV database as one of eighty-one successful basic education projects in developing countries in 1994, and was recognized by UNICEF as representing best practice in educating the girl child in 2000. Similarly, FUNDAEC (*Fundación para la Aplicación y Enseñanza de las Ciencias*) is a Colombian foundation created by a group of university professors, aiming to develop secondary and university-level education among the rural population. In some thirteen departments of the country it has been adopted by state institutions or private, non-governmental institutions reaching more than 15,000 students and its methods have now been adopted by another Bahá'í-inspired programme in Honduras.

In South America, because of the difficulties of travel and communication, radio stations have been found to be particularly effective as tools of social development. The Bahá'í station in Otvalo, Ecuador, is used not only to broadcast programmes on literacy, education, agriculture and health, but it is also committed to raising and reviving the culture of the Quichua people, which is often relegated to a second-rate status below the dominating Hispanic culture. Bahá'í communities run six radio stations in the Americas.

One feature of all of these Bahá'í projects is that their benefits are not restricted to the Bahá'ís in the places where they operate but are open to the whole community. Another feature is that these projects are developed in consultation with those whom it is intended that they should benefit. They are not imposed from outside the community.

United Nations

Because of its concern for world unity, the Bahá'í community has fully participated in the activities of the United Nations (while at the same time having reservations about the present structure and constitution of that organization). The Bahá'í community is represented at the UN by a non-governmental organization called the Bahá'í International Community which has been affiliated to the UN since its start in 1947. For several decades it has been one of the most active of the non-governmental organizations at the UN and has achieved consultative status with many of its subsidiary organizations (such as ECOSOC, UNICEF, UNIFEM) as well as having a significant presence at all of the major UN conferences. Among the goals pursued by the Bahá'í International Community in the UN and its agencies are human rights, the advancement of women and moral education.

> '*O people of God! Do not busy yourselves in your own concerns; let your thoughts be fixed upon that which will rehabilitate the fortunes of mankind and sanctify the hearts and souls of men. This can best be achieved through pure and holy deeds, through a virtuous life and a goodly behaviour.*'
>
> Bahá'u'lláh

Religion in Today's World

Introduction

Throughout the modern period there has been speculation about the collapse of religious belief and rumours of the death of God. Modernity, it has been said, inevitably entails secularization. The progress of the sciences in particular leaves little room for traditional religious belief. However, while it is true that there has been, and continues to be, a haemorrhaging of people from mainstream churches, religion is still alive and well in today's world. Indeed, it is experiencing robust health in the non-Western world where faiths such as Islam and Christianity flourish. In the Western world, while many are disillusioned with traditional religious institutions, authorities and hierarchies, and have even abandoned religious belief altogether, growing numbers are finding spiritual fulfilment elsewhere. Some believe without feeling the need to belong to an institution. Others turn to the increasing number of new religions and alternative spiritualities on offer. Yet others, particularly since the 1960s, have been attracted to Eastern traditions, such as Hinduism and Buddhism. More typical of believers in today's world are those who, influenced by postmodern, consumer-oriented, religiously plural cultures, 'pick and mix' from a range of traditions, beliefs and philosophies.

From Existentialism to Postmodernism

ANTHONY C. THISELTON

Much of the mood of secular thought today can be traced to a general suspicion of reason, argument and objective truth. In historical terms Immanuel Kant (1724–1804) was the first philosopher who went further than simply using reason. He raised difficult questions about the scope and limits of reason itself. The upshot of his work was to emphasize the role of human will, rather than human reason, for issues concerning ultimate truth and value.

The limits of reason
In the nineteenth century, following Kant's work, thinkers assessed the role of reason in different ways. The word 'existentialism' stresses finite 'existence' as the concrete here-and-now. In this context 'existence' stands in contrast not to 'non-existence', but to 'essence'. 'Essence' seems to denote the inner nature of things at some profound level. But essences elude the power of human reason. On

the other hand, flesh-and-blood 'existence' concerns the human will, and indeed the whole human condition. It is not (in contrast to essence) a product of some flight of reason alone.

Georg W.F. Hegel (1770–1831) attempted to reinstate the place of reason by stressing that, although all reasoning is admittedly embedded in finite historical situations in life, it is still possible to talk about 'the Absolute' which lies behind these finite acts of reasoning.

The first existentialist thinker, Søren Kierkegaard (1813–55), rejected Hegel's philosophy as too sweeping, too optimistic and not sufficiently concerned with human existence in all its finite limits. Existentialism takes a variety of forms, but all share a deep suspicion, and often a pessimism, about the capacities of human reason. We cannot reach issues of ultimate truth by mere theory or argument, because we cannot jump outside the limits of our own point of view. I see what I see because I already stand where I stand.

In spite of their differences from one another, all whom we may call existentialists share the following perspective:

● the priority of the human will over against human reason;

● the priority of practical interest over theoretical speculation;

● the priority of the personal over the abstract;

● the priority of individual existence over general essence;

● the priority of first-hand involvement over detached objectivity.

Christian or secular?

The most interesting feature of these

characteristics is that they can lend themselves equally to a Christian emphasis (with Kierkegaard) or to secularism and atheism (with Friedrich Nietzsche, 1844–1900). Across the spectrum, Kierkegaard was a Protestant individualist; Nietzsche was a militant atheist; Karl Jaspers (1883–1969) saw value in religion but rejected the exclusivism of traditional Christianity; Martin Heidegger (1889–1976) left no room for God. Gabriel Marcel (1889–1973) wrote as a Roman Catholic. But Jean-Paul Sartre (1905–80) and Albert Camus (1913–60) attack religious and Christian belief.

Their different use of the same perspective is easy to explain. Into the vacuum left by the absence of reason and of theory Kierkegaard put *faith, decision, venture* and *obedience*. Into the same vacuum or 'abyss' Nietzsche placed *self-interest, wishes* and *the disguise of power-play* as illusory truth-claims. Kierkegaard saw reason as a false alibi which distracted people from authentic faith and obedience to God. Nietzsche saw reason as a false alibi which allowed people to put forward claims which served their interests *as if* these were objective truths.

Christian existentialism as Kierkegaard expressed it stresses that:

● God's existence cannot be proved by argument, it must be accepted in faith.

● Christian faith is not assenting to doctrinal truths, it is commitment and obedience.

● God is far beyond human reason: truth about God entails paradox.

Atheistic existentialism as Nietzsche expressed it stresses that:

● Humans project a notion of God to

> 'There is an infinitely qualitative difference between God and man. This means, or the expression for this is, that man is capable of nothing, it is God who gives everything, who gives man faith, and so on.'
>
> Søren Kierkegaard

make their own wishes and interests appear legitimate and capable of fulfilment.

● 'God' is therefore an instrumental construct or functional cipher to support a manipulative rhetoric: a product of decision.

● All claims to objective or ultimate truth are illusory; religion is a system of value and interests disguised as a system of truth.

EXISTENTIALIST THEMES AND THINKERS

Nietzsche has been described as the first 'postmodernist' (see below), as his views lie behind many assumptions in late twentieth-century secular ideologies. However, to complete our sketch of existentialism we must comment first on Jaspers, Heidegger, Marcel, Sartre and Camus.

Karl Jaspers worked in psychiatry as well as philosophy. He stressed that what often passes for 'objective truth' reflects only the conventional beliefs of the day. How can one know what is genuine? He noted that in situations of crisis in which patients came to the end of their own resources, all artificial or contrived second-hand values often fell away, leaving only that which was genuine or authentic *for the patient*. On one side, this approach can be therapeutic in restoring reality to a person. On the other side, what is deemed to be authentic truth still varies from person to person.

Martin Heidegger argued that even the seemingly 'general' questions of philosophy can be asked only concretely, from the standpoint of where the thinker already is. He or she can philosophize only from within their own pre-existing horizons. A thinker can never completely escape the boundaries and problems imposed by this radical finitude.

Heidegger believed that traditional philosophy had failed to take adequate account of this finitude and of the boundaries imposed by the horizons of the individual. He followed Nietzsche and anticipated postmodernists in diagnosing the 'end' of philosophy (including theology) in any traditional sense, looking in his later writings for a kind of rebirth of 'listening' thinking through some kind of visionary renewal for which one might endlessly wait.

Gabriel Marcel attempted to recapture existentialist perspectives for more positive purposes within a Christian or humanist framework. Rationality and the sciences too often viewed human persons as 'cases' or 'statistics' within some scientific theory. But a more participatory and less rationalistic approach might restore the dignity of personhood to humans who, after all, were not mere 'data' for scientists (including medical or social scientists) but active agents or subjects.

Sartre and Camus follow Nietzsche in attacking every notion of universal or objective truth as illusory. Whereas Nietzsche saw *religion and philosophy* as the worst culprits in disguising self-interest or group interest as truth for all, Sartre and Camus *also* attacked the entrapping constraints of what seemed to pass for truth in the mere *conventions of society*. The individual must not be deceived into imagining that society's notion of 'God', 'truth' or 'the right thing' holds any necessary validity or constraint for free-thinking individuals. All convention must be viewed with suspicion.

A DEATH AND REBIRTH: POSTMODERNISM

This approach reached its climax in the post-war years, especially in Paris. But by the late 1950s a reaction had set in against the confusion between subjectivity (the human person is an agent, not an object) and subjectivism (everything is relative to the wishes and views of the individual).

If existentialism had died in the 1950s, many of its claims were renewed in a transposed form in the movement led initially by Roland Barthes (1915–80) and Jacques Derrida (1930–2004) around 1967. 'Modernity' is often associated with universal, rational truth-claims, especially those put forward by mathematics and science. By contrast, 'postmodernism' expresses a loss of confidence in any *universal* truth. *All* claims to truth are viewed as *constructs* which only *serve the interests of particular groups*. Its chief difference from existentialism lay in its recognition not simply of the radical finitude and fallibility of the *individual. Society as a whole* cannot reach outside the values and supposed truths which it has constructed. Every power-group defines what is 'normal' for society in ways which promote its own interests.

SITUATEDNESS AND FRAGMENTATION

Following Heidegger's emphasis on what he called 'radical historical finitude', exponents of the postmodern perspective stress the 'situatedness' of every person within the pre-given historical and cultural horizons into which they were born. Our place in history and society not only conditions how we think, but also in effect constructs our view of what *counts as* true or useful. *No single overall viewpoint* is possible for everyone. We are faced with a radical *fragmentation* of human understanding, truth and values.

Thus the French postmodern philosopher, Jean-François Lyotard (1924–98), defined postmodernity as a suspicion of all 'grand narratives', that is, of all holistic or universal accounts of human life and history.

David Lyon tried to distinguish between postmodern*ism* and postmodern*ity*. Postmodern*ism*, he argued, reflects first of all a *philosophical and intellectual* rejection of rationalism and of the scientific world view of modernity. Postmodern*ity*, by contrast, reflects a *social* phenomenon, in which the 'truth' becomes largely absorbed into a series of *virtual reality* worlds, constructed by consumer profiles, information technology and what different classes or groups in society construct in accordance with their own norms. Many call this *social constructionalism*. Such a distinction might serve a useful purpose, but it now seems too late to try to put the clock back, since so many use both terms indiscriminately.

FURTHER CONTRASTS IN POSTMODERNISM

A significant difference emerges between more optimistic, postmodern philosophical perspectives in America, and more pessimistic, suspicious, critical postmodern philosophy in continental Europe. The first rests on pragmatism, i.e. we decide what is true by what succeeds; the second is often associated with 'deconstruction'. The most notorious American postmodern pragmatic philosopher is Richard Rorty (b. 1931). Well known European postmodern philosophers include Michel Foucault (1926–84) and Jacques Derrida.

Rorty rejects traditional accounts of the truth. There is no such task as 'getting reality right'. All claims to truth remain entirely relative to the values and perceptions of given 'local' communities. They are relative to the practices of these sub-groups or peer groups, and to what they count as 'success' on their own terms. Although he concedes that this is relativistic, Rorty prefers to use the term 'ethnocentric' to denote what 'local' or specific social or political communities construe as useful and thereby, in effect, also truthful.

We may trace the origins of the continental European version to Friedrich Nietzsche (1844–1900). The phenomenon of *disguise* provides a key. Nietzsche argued that many claims on behalf of Christian truth or belief are in fact disguised bids for power over others. In the 1960s Roland Barthes pointed out that even the choice of clothes or furniture may tell us more about someone's social aspirations or self-image than their concerns about comfort. Foucault stressed that 'knowledge' often reflects 'power'. Bureaucracies and 'regimes' claim expertise about what is right, but too readily constitute and hide an oppressive power on behalf of those in control under this guise. In hospitals and prisons we find 'the smiling face in the white coat' that controls our lives.

Derrida applies this no less radically to question the very status of philosophy, metaphysics and traditional notions of truth and language. Following Nietzsche, Freud and Heidegger, he diagnoses their claims to truth as 'mythologies'. They pretend to a universal status, but simply promote the power of the ruling intelligentsia who use them as instruments to promote their own values, well-being or power. These myths are candidates for 'deconstruction'. This exposes their disguise.

DECONSTRUCTIVE OR
CONSTRUCTIVE EFFECTS
Some perceive the postmodernism of European writers as more destructive than postmodern perspectives in America. However, we may question this. Nietzsche's attack on illusion and disguise in religion, for all its cynical skepticism, may also serve to alert us to the difference between inauthentic religion, driven by selfish power interests and genuine religious faith as a response to revelation from beyond the self. Foucault's strictures about power interests in institutions may alert us to self-serving authoritarianism, not least within churches. American postmodernity may free us from the tyranny of a supposed scientific objectivism, but it may also leave truth hostage to the mere market forces of consumerism and to the changing criteria of 'progress'. It may merely affirm what communities choose to do, and betrays a lack of moral seriousness. Dollars and tanks may, at worst, become the sole substitutes for a lost 'ultimate'. '*Truth*' quits the stage for '*winners*'.

It is impossible, therefore, to pin down a neat package of postmodern beliefs. Postmodernity is more strictly a way of approach, a perspective or a mood. David Harvey, a respected commentator on this subject, endorses a rule-of-thumb contrast between the modern and the postmodern. Where modernity reflects purpose, design, hierarchy, determinacy, form and mastery, postmodernity reflects play, chance, anarchy, indeterminacy, chaos and exhaustion or silence. This is not a bad summary of the 'feel' of the respective moods.

In religions, the contrast becomes further sharpened as one between authority and egalitarianism; reason and rhetoric; truth and power; individual and sub-group or peer group. However, religions often challenge both secular modernity and secular postmodernity in certain respects. For example, religions tend to value traditions more highly than is the case either in modernity or in postmodernity, seeing them often, but not always, as sources of cumulative wisdom gathered through history over the generations. But postmodernity stresses disruption and differences

'God is dead; but considering the state the species Man is in, there will perhaps be caves, for ages yet, in which his shadow will be shown.'

Friedrich Nietzsche

rather than continuities (especially in Foucault) and places a heavy emphasis on social constructionism. By contrast many religions, especially Judaism, Christianity and Islam, often stress the 'givenness' of many beliefs, values and practices, sometimes ascribing to them the status of divine decrees.

EFFECTS ON SOCIETY AT LARGE

Postmodernity may in theory appear to promote a new found tolerance, since no one sub-group is deemed to have the right to impose its values upon another. However, this may be illusory. Different ethnic groups, different genders and different class and professional interests all seem to operate with different criteria of truth. But this leads to the collapse of any dialogue that crosses community boundaries. Rational argument becomes reduced to manipulative rhetoric. People look in vain for some global vision or global overview.

If claims to truth are thought to represent only the manipulative power play of interest groups, this generates (understandably) suspicion, conflict and violence. Everything that goes wrong is blamed on the power interests of some group. Here is *secular ideology* in the fullest sense of the term. Postmodernism is finally unmasked as offering not the freedom which it claims, but conflict and uncertainty, and an invitation to blame the power interests of competing groups for all ills.

New Religious Movements

GEORGE D. CHRYSSIDES

The term 'New Religious Movements' (NRMs) covers a variety of religious organizations that have emerged in recent times, commonly referred to as 'cults'. The term 'cult' is inappropriate, being pejorative and lacking a clear definition. Some scholars have defined a new religion as an organization that has arrived in the West since World War II, while others regard 'new' as spanning the last 150 years. NRMs are a global, not merely a Western, phenomenon: there are some 10,000 NRMs in Africa alone, around 3,000 in the USA and 500–600 in Britain. There are an estimated 31 million followers in Japan.

NRMs tend to fall outside mainstream religion, sometimes because of doctrinal disputes, at times because of controversial practices. The mass deaths of followers of the Peoples Temple in Jonestown, Guyana (1978) and of David Koresh and the Branch Davidians in Waco, Texas (1993), and the deaths of members of the Solar Temple in Switzerland and Canada (1994), the UFO religion Heaven's Gate in California (1997) and the Movement for the Restoration of the Ten Commandments of God in Uganda (2000), and Aum Shinrikyo's sarin gas attack on the passengers of the Tokyo underground, killing twelve and injuring many others (1995), reinforced the perception that NRMs are violent, although such incidents are rare.

Christian-related

Nineteenth century NRMs in the West were predominantly Christian. William Miller (1782–1849), an early proponent of Adventism, proclaimed that Christ's second coming was imminent. He named 1843 and subsequently 1844 as the year of Christ's return and his followers' disillusionment in 1844 became known as the 'Great Disappointment'. His ideas were nonetheless influential. Ellen G. White (1827–1915), who founded the Seventh-day Adventists in 1861, taught that Jesus had returned, but that his presence was invisible. Charles Taze Russell (1852–1916) who founded Zion's Watch Tower Society in 1874 also taught the doctrine of Christ's 'invisible presence', although the Jehovah's Witnesses, as Russell's successor, Joseph Franklin Rutherford (1869–1941), named them in 1931, now regard 1914 as the date of this event.

Not all movements accepted the inerrancy of scripture. The Church of Jesus Christ of Latter-day Saints (the 'Mormons') claims a new revelation,

Thousands of couples gather for the blessing ceremony that lies at the heart of the Unification Church.

afforded to Joseph Smith, its founder-leader. The angel Moroni reportedly lent him a set of gold plates from which he translated *The Book of Mormon* (1830), which tells of Jesus Christ preaching in the USA after his resurrection. Smith was murdered in 1844, after which Brigham Young took over the leadership and led the 'saints' to the Great Salt Lake in Utah.

Another important strand was New Thought, which emphasized health improvement through mental 'affirmations'. This idea influenced Mary Baker Eddy's (1821–1910) Christian Science and the Hopkins Metaphysical Association, set up by Emma Curtis Hopkins (1853–1925) in 1887. Some of Hopkins' students set up their own organizations, the best known of which is the Unity School of Christianity.

Contact with spirits was a further strand. Modern spiritualism can be traced back to the 'rappings' heard by the Fox sisters of Hydesville, New York, in 1848, although it should be noted that spiritualist churches emphasize healing as much as contact with the departed. Helena P. Blavatsky (1831–91), one of the founders of the Theosophical Society, claimed contact with a number of 'Ascended Masters', advanced spiritual beings who once lived on earth. Ascended Masters, sometimes called the 'Great White Brotherhood' feature in other organizations such as the Rosicrucians, and the Church Universal and Triumphant, and also in the New Age 'channelling' movement.

NRMs in the 1960s and 1970s

The post-war wave of NRMs occurred in the 1960s. Bible-based and charismatic, the 'Jesus Movement' (or 'Jesus People') gained momentum within the youth counter-culture of that period and involved communal living and sharing of possessions. Converts had often been on drugs: the Church of

Jesus Christ of Armageddon (a.k.a. Love Israel) and Stephen Gaskin's The Farm in its early years encouraged their use. Other groups, such as the Alamo Christian Ministries, offered rehabilitation. Of the communal groups, the best known are The Family (then known as the Children of God or COG) and the Unification Church (UC):

● Founded by David Brandt Berg (a.k.a. Moses David, 1919–94), COG espoused Protestant fundamentalism, but became controversial for its 'flirty fishing' – or 'FFing' – the offer of sex to seekers, mainly by female members. This practice was abandoned in 1987, for fear of AIDS, but The Family still allows the 'sharing' of marriage partners.

● Although offering an interpretation of the Bible, the UC presents a new revelation, claimed by founder-leader Sun Myung Moon (b.1920). Moon teaches Jesus was unable fully to accomplish his messianic mission, which was to marry and to beget sinless children. Sun Myung Moon and his wife Hak Ja Han Moon are jointly regarded as the new messiahs, and members can be engrafted into their restored family through the Blessing ceremony (the 'mass wedding'). In 1996 the organization's name was changed to the Family Federation for World Peace and Unification, since formal membership was judged to be less important than receiving the Blessing, which is now available to non-members.

Indian-derived NRMs

The first Hindu *swami* (world-renouncer) to visit the West was Ramakrishna's pupil Vivekananda, who spoke at the World's Parliament of Religions in 1893 and founded the Vedanta Society in 1896. Several other gurus arrived, most notably Yogananda, founder of the Self-Realization

'Emperors, kings and presidents... have declared to all heaven and earth that Reverend Sun Myung Moon is none other than humanity's saviour, messiah, returning Lord and true parent.'

Sun Myung Moon

Fellowship, Meher Baba, the Maharishi Mahesh Yogi, Sri Chinmoy, Swami A.C. Bhaktivedanta Praphupada (1896–1977), and Maharaji (the 'boy guru' who led the Divine Light Mission, now Elan Vital), also came to the West.

● Prabhupada arrived in New York in 1965, where he founded the International Society for Krishna Consciousness (ISKCON), popularly known as the 'Hare Krishna' movement. The 'Hare Krishna' mantra was introduced by the ecstatic teacher Chaitanya (c. 1485–1533) and the movement focuses on the Hindu deity Krishna.

● Transcendental Meditation (TM), established by the Maharishi Mahesh Yogi (b. 1911 or 1918), is meditative. Students are given a mantra to use twice daily. TM does not regard itself as a religion, offering pragmatic benefits, such as better health and efficiency, rather than spiritual enlightenment.

● Although Satya Sai Baba (b. 1926) has never visited the West, he is well known as a miracle worker and his followers aver that he can materialize objects such as rings and watches. Followers make pilgrimages to his two large ashrams in India, to receive *darshan*. (*Darshan* traditionally means the appearance of a deity: Sai Baba is held to be God incarnate.)

● Less well known, but equally important, is Brahma Kumaris, founded by Dada Lekhraj (1876–1969). Lekhraj aimed to improve the status of women, and, following his death, the movement has been led by his female disciples. Celibacy is encouraged and Raja Yoga, a mental practice aimed at uniting the soul with the divine, is taught.

● Bhagavan Shri Rajneesh (1931–90), later known as Osho, was born into a Jain family in India, but taught an idiosyncratic form of Zen Buddhism. In the 1970s members dressed in orange or red clothes and became popularly known as 'the orange people'. His teachings rejected authority and extolled sexual freedom and materialism. In 1981 Rajneesh moved to Oregon, USA, and set up his own 'enlightened city' (known as Rajneeshpuram). Following controversies with local residents, Osho was arrested in 1985 and the community disbanded, although the Osho organization survives.

Buddhist NRMs
After arriving in the USA in 1897, D.T. Suzuki (1870–1966) wrote prolifically on Zen. The 1960s US youth counter-culture took the Zen notion of the 'Buddha within' to mean personal licentiousness, and this anarchical counter-cultural version of Zen is sometimes known as 'Beat Zen' – after the 'Beatniks' of the late 1950s. Buddhist NRMs come from various traditions. For example:

● The Vipassana movement promotes a Theravada meditative practice aimed at seeing reality's true nature. Vipassana is an ancient practice, revived in Myanmar (Burma) and Thailand during the twentieth century, but its modern expression is innovative in being taught to Western laypeople and to women.

● Innovative forms of Tibetan Buddhism include the New Kadampa Tradition (NKT), which became controversial in 1996 because of a ritual practice known as Dorje Shugden, which the Dalai Lama had forbidden.

● The Soka Gakkai International (SGI), founded in 1930, derives its teachings from the Japanese teacher Nichiren (1222–82) and his favoured scripture, the *Lotus Sutra*. SGI members regularly chant the mantra *nam myoho renge kyo* (literally 'Homage to the ineffable law of the lotus teaching'), which is believed to have immense power, yielding material pragmatic benefits as well as spiritual ones.

● The Friends of the Western Buddhist Order (FWBO) seek to develop a new form of Buddhism for Westerners. Founded by the Venerable Sangharakshita (Dennis Lingwood, b. 1925), it emphasizes 'right livelihood' (the fifth point of the Buddha's Eightfold Path) rather than the monastic practice of seeking alms from lay supporters.

● Engaged Buddhism is based on the teachings of Thich Nhat Hanh (b. 1926), a Zen monk from Vietnam, and emphasizes active involvement in social and political issues.

Black Power movements and white Islam.

Some NRMs have originated from black communities. Originating in Jamaica, the Rastafarians were initially a Black Power movement supported by the

Raël, formerly known as Claude Vorilhon, with a model of the spaceship he claims to have encountered in 1973.

descendants of slaves. They interpreted the Bible's teachings as pointing to Ethiopia, where they believed Emperor Haile Selassie (1891–1975) was their messiah, who would herald a return to Africa. Following Haile Selassie's death, such ideas have been reappraised, and a variety of expectations now exists.

Other Black Power movements drew on Islam. The Nation of Islam (NOI) was originally a black supremacist organization, established in the 1930s and later led by Elijah Muhammad (Elijah Poole, 1897–1975). Malcolm X (1925–65) joined but left in 1964, having reconsidered NOI's racism.

The white population's interest in Islam tends to focus more on Sufism, originally introduced in the USA in 1910 by Pir Hazrat Inayat Khan and made popular by the writings of Idries Shah (1924–96).

UFO religions, Human Potential and the New Age

UFOs have gained significance for a number of spiritual seekers, and the resulting organizations have come to be collectively known as the UFO religions. Typically, they hold that the gods are extra-terrestrials, who communicate with key individuals.

● The earliest UFO religion in the West was the Aetherius Society, established by George King (1919–97) in 1955.

● Better known is the Raëlian Movement, whose enthusiasm for modern technology includes promoting human cloning, which they believe is the key to personal immortality. Western UFO religions are often Bible-based: Raël (Claude Vorilhon, b. 1946) contends that spaceships are frequently alluded to in Judaeo-Christian scripture, for example the chariots of Elijah and Ezekiel.

Although sometimes classified as a UFO religion, the Church of Scientology is unusual in having no obvious spiritual ancestry. Science fiction writer L. Ron Hubbard (1911–86) gained prominence in 1950 with his best-selling self-improvement classic *Dianetics: The Modern Science of Mental Health*. Dianetics claims to rid the 'thetan' (the self) of harmful 'engrams' (records of unpleasant past experiences) which impede the mind. Once these are removed, the practitioner is regarded as 'clear' and can proceed to the various levels of 'Operating Thetan', which are disclosed only to authorized students.

Scientology is thus one of several groups that form part of the Human Potential Movement (HPM) – an umbrella term for organizations that offer enhanced quality of life. Werner Erhard, founder of Erhard Seminar Training (*est* – now Landmark Forum) previously studied Scientology, but other groups have no such influence: for example Silva Method, PSI Mind Development and the School of Economic Science (SES), the last of which is influenced by TM.

The Human Potential Movement is a loosely defined cluster of groups and ideas, which merges into the equally nebulous New Age Movement (NAM). The NAM is characterized by eclecticism, an optimism about human nature and a disenchantment with organized religion.

From the 1980s the NRM climate changed. Few new religions emerged. Falun Gong is the only significant one: founded in 1992 in China by Master Li Hongzhi (b. 1951), it offers a set of physical exercises similar to *tai ch'i*, with a path to becoming a Buddha.

Other changes in NRMs include less community living, less proselytizing, less media attention and greater institutionalization. Many NRMs have learned from past indiscretions and changed some controversial practices.

Secularization and Sacralization

LINDA WOODHEAD

'Secularization' names the process whereby religion *declines* in significance in personal life and/or society. By contrast, 'sacralization' (or 'de-secularization') names the process whereby religion *grows* in significance in personal life and/or society. There is normally, though not inevitably, a link between the level of significance which religion holds in personal life and in society.

Secularization and sacralization in the West

Levels of secularization or sacralization are normally measured in terms of the numbers of active participants in religious institutions such as churches. By this measure most Western societies have experienced secularization since the late nineteenth century, and the process has accelerated dramatically since the mid-1960s.

Church attendance in England

1851	1903	1951	1979	1989	2000
39%	19%	15%	12%	10%	8%

In Sweden, for example, churchgoing is now down to just 4 per cent of the population. Rates of secularization vary by country, however, as well as by institution. Levels of congregational participation are higher in the USA than in most European countries, and in most places 'liberal' or 'mainline' denominations (both Catholic and Protestant) have declined faster than any other forms of Christianity.

Secularization has been more evident at the social than the personal level.

The important social functions once performed by the churches in Western societies have gradually diminished as the modern state and secular agencies have taken over responsibility for politics, education, welfare and so on. At the national level some modern states instigated a formal separation between church and state, and at the local level the status and importance of the church and the clergy also diminished. In cultural terms too, Christianity has ceased to be a dominant force, being forced to compete with alternative sources and systems of meaning. At the personal level, however, religion still retains widespread allegiance. Whilst religious behaviours like church attendance have declined, religious belief and self-identification remain high. In the 2001 British census, for example, 72 per cent of the population identified themselves as 'Christian', whilst 96 per cent in the USA still affirm belief in God.

When personal 'Christian' belief is interrogated, however, it is often found to be 'nominal' – without accompanying commitment to churchgoing or any other form of active Christian involvement. In recent decades there has also been a noticeable shift away from a commitment to 'religion' towards a commitment to 'spirituality' and away from belief in a theistic God 'out there' towards belief in a more immanent 'Spirit'. In other words, as well as witnessing a decline in traditional religion, the late twentieth century appears to have witnessed the rise of new, more immanent and 'holistic' forms of spirituality which have more to do with the cultivation of unique subjective life than conformity to God-given norms. In this sense both secularization (of traditional religion) and sacralization (of new forms of spirituality) seem to be taking place simultaneously.

> 'The fate of our times is characterized by rationalization and intellectualization and, above all, by the "disenchantment of the world". Precisely the ultimate and most sublime values have retreated from public life either into the transcendental realm of mystic life or into the brotherliness of direct and personal human relations.'
>
> Max Weber

Secularization and sacralization outside the West

If we move beyond the West to the rest of the world, we find evidence of sacralization of a rather different sort, namely the resurgence of traditional forms of religion. Nearly all the so-called 'world religions' including Hinduism and Buddhism have experienced some revitalization since the 1970s, but the most dramatic growth has been enjoyed by resurgent Islam (sometimes called Islamism) and Charismatic Christianity (sometimes called Pentecostalism). Journalists often bracket all these developments together in speaking of the rise of 'fundamentalism', but the term is misleading insofar as it obscures important differences between different forms of religious revival.

Outside the West religious resurgence is most evident in post-colonial regions, and sacralization is often bound up with the assertion of new, 'independent' identities. In the case of resurgent Islam, these identities are importantly national and pan-national, with Islam helping 'the Muslim world' establish itself over and against the cultural, economic and cultural encroachments of the West. In the case of Charismatic Christianity, religion is more often mobilized at the personal and local level, where it helps individuals to establish and defend and strengthen their identities by harnessing the power of God as Holy Spirit. In conditions of poverty, hardship and social dislocation, these religions also have important roles to play in providing much-needed support – material, social and spiritual.

Accounting for secularization and sacralization

The reasons for secularization and sacralization in the modern world are still hotly debated. To date sociologists of religion have devoted far more energy to developing theories of

I am a Rastafarian

BENJAMIN ZEPHANIAH

I am a writer called Benjamin Zephaniah. My full name is Benjamin Obadiah Iqbal Zephaniah. For me, this is significant because it reflects the Muslim and Judeo-Christian religious traditions. Like the hair of Lord Shiva, the Hindu god, my hair is matted in 'dreadlocks' (or *jata*). I also practise Tibetan meditation. What religion am I? In a sense I am all of the above. But ask me what I am and I will tell you that I am a Rastafarian.

It is impossible for me to speak about Rastafarianism without talking about politics. After all, Ras Tafari was the original name of Haile Selassie I (1891–1975), the last emperor of Ethiopia. It is also impossible to talk about Rastafarianism without referring to the fact that I am black. That said, you don't have to be political or black to be a Rastafarian.

My full conversion to the faith happened when I was seventeen years old. It was a matter of life, death and freedom. In the mid-1970s I was one of the many forgotten, unemployed, first generation black youths who roamed the streets, unable to see a future and carrying a feeling of hopelessness. Not only did we have a hopeless future, we were also told that we had a past that started with slavery. The education we were receiving seemed to suggest that black people were incapable of controlling their own destiny. Suddenly Rastafari changed all that. Here was a faith and a movement that pointed to the long and often glorious past of black people. It gave me pride in being black and, most importantly, it taught me that there is nothing wrong with seeing God through black spectacles – from the perspective of a black person.

I stopped walking the streets with my head held down. My head was held high and there was a spring in my step. I now knew that my roots went back much further than Jamaica and I started to look towards Africa. Rastafarians recognize Africa as the home of humanity, Ethiopia as its capital, and Haile Selassie as being directly in the line of Solomon. All this symbolism helped me to stand on my own feet. But most importantly, I was made aware that I could find Jah (as Rastafarians refer to God) by looking inwards. I learnt how to read any of the many holy books, or any scientific book, and apply my own intelligence. I learnt that rituals may be of some use, but that there is a way to find a direct line to Jah through meditation and inner peace. I was no longer concerned with understanding the world, I was now able to 'overstand' it. For the Rastafarian, to overstand is to apply your mind to a subject and discern a greater meaning than the obvious one. Again, in seeking to understand a person, one overstands when one truly empathizes with that person. In other words, overstanding goes beyond basic understanding.

Rastafari is a form of black liberation theology. Although we say that we shall be liberated in heaven, Rastafarians insist that we must also be liberated here on earth. Rastafarian liberation theology has no party manifesto. It is not political in that sense. Rather, it is about social responsibility; and, if that means speaking out about the misuse of power in society, then so be it. I see it as my duty to take a stand and to help those who are struggling to help themselves. Rastafari has given purpose to my writing. I am a scribe of Rastafari bearing witness and writing the third testament. I am full of this sense of purpose. In interviews I have no problem answering that often asked question, 'What is the poet's role in society?' The number of books I sell or my popularity is of little importance to me. Making sure that what I write is written is far more important. Having said that, I do not believe that it is our job to preach. Rastafarians are not out to convert people, which is why I and many other Rasta writers don't write Rasta poetry. Rather, it is poetry about the world; poetry for the body and the soul; poetry for every body and every soul. I have found my role in life and I am perfectly content with it. I have no great ambitions. My only ambition would be to do what I do better and do more of it.

Many Rastafarians live in communes. However, while it is certainly good and pleasant for brethren to dwell together in unity, this is not always possible. I do not live in a commune. Indeed, when I come across other Rastafarians they are often members of an audience I am reading poetry to. Although it would be very difficult for me to live a communal life, fortunately Rastafari has taught me to be at ease with my 'self' and not to fear silence, darkness or solitude. Although I work for and celebrate the community, and value my relationship with others, there is also a great sense of liberation in not relying on the congregation to find strength. Nor do I feel the need for a building as a centre of worship. Jah is always with me. To be precise, Jah is part of me. So I have no real need to look outward for Jah. To find and worship Jah, I must look within.

I used to be very critical of Rastafarians who had children that did not wear dreadlocks, and worse still of those who did not raise their children as Rastas. I thought that if mommy and daddy were Rastas, baby should follow. But I have come to realize that it is up to me (the parent) to live a good life and be a good example to my child. My child should freely want to become a Rasta because of what he sees in me. I have found my spiritual path and my personal relationship with Jah means a lot to me. So even if my child does not become a Rastafarian, but is nevertheless influenced positively by me, I still feel that I have done well before Jah – I am still doing the work of Jah.

When it comes to religious practice, I focus on compassion, which I extend to every living thing. This means there are many practices I won't take part in. I am opposed to violence and war (except in self-defence) and the manufacture of arms. I will have nothing to do with a trade which relies on the unfair exploitation of workers or forced labour. I am also a vegan.

Not only will I not eat animals – I will not even wear leather products unless there are no alternatives. To do so, I believe, would spoil my meditation and disturb my communion with Jah. Although I do understand that there is a time to reap and a time to sow, a time to heal and a time to kill and so on, Jah tells me that such a time is not now. When I feel that every animal is my friend, I find that I have a direct connection with the earth, nature and even that most abstract of things called 'the universe'. I have learned that to have a direct relationship with Jah and with creation makes for a contented guy who is at ease with his 'self'.

secularization than sacralization, mainly because the former process has been of longer duration and had greater impact in Western societies.

Five main varieties of 'secularization theory' may be distinguished, depending on which process of modernization each identifies as the salient cause:

● Theories which focus on *differentiation* argue that religion has lost significance as the process of 'functional' or 'structural' differentiation has separated functions in modern society into specialist spheres (politics, education, the law and so on), each of which seeks to become autonomous from religion.

'One Feather', a New Age preacher of love and peace, with his much-decorated van near Pebble Beach, California, USA. In the West many people are moving away from formal religion to new kinds of spirituality.

● Theories which focus on *rationalization* single out the process by which modern society becomes rationalized, bureaucratized and 'scientific' in its modes of operation as responsible for the 'disenchantment' and 'demystification' of the world.

● Theories which focus on *pluralization* argue that beliefs are plausible when everybody one knows holds them, but become less plausible when one becomes aware that other people believe different things. The gradual pluralization of modern society therefore renders traditional belief

implausible – unless it is able to sustain itself within a bounded subculture.

● Theories which focus on *individualization* suggest that the process by which authority is internalized is damaging to religion, since the latter seeks to have authority over people, rather than let them make their own choices.

● Theories which focus on *societalization* maintain that religion flourishes at the level of the local community and therefore argue that the process by which wider, particularly national, society becomes more important than local societies is destructive of religion.

Although these different theories are often regarded as competitive, they may also be treated as mutually compatible, since each one singles out a different aspect of the general process of modernization as responsible for secularization. In practice, therefore, they may work better in combination than in isolation. There is also a good deal more work to be done in testing these theories to determine their power in relation to specific instances of secularization – whether by investigating historically the ways in which particular institutions have secularized or by researching empirically the reasons why individuals drop out of religion.

Whilst there are no established 'theories of sacralization', it is possible to make some general observations about the conditions under which religion seems to do well. Religions do best, it seems, when they are allied with dominant political and economic power (for example, the spread of Christianity from late antiquity to the Middle Ages) or when they allow peoples to resist such power (for example, the success of religion in Northern Ireland or Poland). In both circumstances

Religion and Globalization

DAVID LYON

religions have much to offer by way of social unity, cohesion and strength of purpose. But religions also do well when they offer empowerment not at the social but the personal level. Historically this is evident in the highly varied manifestations of religion that are often classified, or dismissed, as 'magic'. In the latter, individuals attempt to harness sacred power to their own ends, often for healing or prosperity. Established religions and their representatives inevitably object to 'magic', not least because it threatens their monopoly over the sacred.

In late modern capitalist contexts we see another instance of religion growing because of what it has to offer by way of personal empowerment in the growth of 'spirituality'. Current socio-economic as well as cultural conditions encourage a 'turn to the self', in which secure structures and given roles fall away and individuals are required to fend for themselves in the modern economy. Rather than falling back on what is 'given', individuals have to create and recreate themselves in order to survive and flourish. In this situation it is not surprising to find that 'religion' gives way to new forms of 'spirituality' that offer the healing, enhancement and cultivation of unique subjective lives. God is no longer seen as a being to be obeyed, but as a power, energy or Spirit that can be harnessed to the task of 'becoming all that I can be'. Under these conditions, personal growth becomes identified with spiritual growth, and the sacred finds a new role in societies that had often been expected to become wholly secular.

At first blush, one could be forgiven for imagining that globalization might merely be destructive of religion or that religion would resist globalization. Are not religions bound up with ancient tradition, timeless ritual and local experience? And doesn't 'globalization' suggest cutting-edge economies, jet-setting travellers and instant communication by Internet or cell-phone?

Well, yes and no. Religious tradition does not necessarily imply only looking backwards. And the global world of fast food and transnational corporations cannot shake off religion like yesterday's fashions. For instance, the Islamism (radical, politicized Islam) that produced the attacks on the USA in September 2001 is both planted in the past and has hopes for the future. It used planes and email to achieve its goals.

More broadly, we can safely say that religious activity is both a cause and effect of globalization. Among other things, missionary movements and religious territorial expansion fostered early forms of globalization. At the same time, globalization is both corrosive of, and a carrier for, religions. The multiplicity of media messages may unsettle notions of 'truth'. But cyber-religion has caught on in a big way too, offering new modes of religious engagement online. Thus we cannot grasp globalization without considering the religious dimensions. And we cannot reflect intelligently on religion today without considering its globalizing aspects.

These big words – religion and globalization – are notoriously difficult to define. Rather than a neat capsule of meaning, each is more like a menu or an agenda. 'Religion' and 'globalization' give us an idea of what kinds of dishes we're about to eat or what kinds of topics will engage the discussion. We will start by sampling some aspects of globalization and towards the end suggest some ways in which religion may be understood in fresh ways in a globalized world.

Grasping globalization

To many, globalization is primarily an economic process, typified by corporations such as Microsoft that operate everywhere. Indeed, Microsoft is a good example because it not only exists as a global enterprise, it also supplies the means of operating over vast distances. The world, for Microsoft, has become 'one place' for inventing, manufacturing and selling. This is made possible by both rapid transport and, crucially, communications. They are the *means* of globalization, of making the world one place.

Simultaneously, though, Microsoft has to acknowledge localities. The company headquarters are situated in Washington State, and its products often have to be modified for local use. Languages differ, and so do climates and cultures. Not everyone speaks English or has air-conditioning. Such considerations indicate a demand for products suitable for distinct parts of the world. Corporations such as Microsoft have to be 'glocal' – both global and local.

Similarly, religious activities are increasingly globalized. The Internet has become a key means of shrinking distances that previously separated different segments of the same religious groups. Anglican Christians in the global North, for instance, have become acutely aware of their more numerous dioceses in the global South, especially in Africa, as southern membership has mushroomed in contrast with fairly drastic depletion in the North. Perhaps the northern churches can learn from the experiences of the South, using new means of contact? As well, every religion now has a diaspora, group members scattered well beyond their original place of activity, and Muslim, Jewish, Christian, Sikh and Hindu diasporas can keep in touch using new technologies. In this sense, globalization draws people closer.

Paradox and pain

But globalization is paradoxical. The same forces that seem to unite also divide. Those with great promise may also present dire threat. Take Bangalore, South India, where this piece is written. In the 'new economy' world of globalization, Bangalore is the 'Silicon Plateau' of shiny high-tech offices, a booming software industry and affluent consumers in new shopping malls. But the surrounding state of Karnataka, including Bangalore, is 76 per cent rural, with high poverty rates. Landless labourers are forced to seek work in the city, so that the proportion of poor people living in huts with no services is growing faster than in other Indian cities. In fact, fewer services are available precisely because they're overused by the sprawling science and technology parks.

A key paradox of globalization is seen in political theorist Benjamin Barber's neat phrase, 'Jihad v McWorld'. The fact that you can buy Big Macs anywhere reminds us that one fast-food company has managed to bring its products to the most remote regions. Here, globalization seems to mean 'the world as one brand'. But along with the sameness comes difference. The more the world is remade in the image of big corporations, the more people want to stress their distinctive identities and particular styles and tastes. Barber's point is that the two cannot be separated; they feed on each other or are in tension with each other. Indeed, his phrase recalls the basic theme of religion and globalization. If McWorld

I am a Spiritual Seeker

HELEN SERDIVILLE

My name is Helen Serdiville; I have been married for twenty-five years; I have a son of twenty-three who is a trainee commercial lawyer and a daughter of twenty-one who is a retail manager; I have my own business in the field of accounts and business services. I do not fit into any religious category completely.

From an early age I had strong spiritual feelings that were self-discovered, not taught by any religious denomination. Having been brought up in a divided Roman Catholic-Protestant family, I decided that, although I had been baptized a Roman Catholic, I would make my own mind up when I felt the need.

We lived out of town in a rural area when I was young. Always conscious of a powerful inner sense in God, I felt surrounded by him in the earth, trees, rivers and the wind itself. As an only child I was wrapped up in the seasons and the elements and found inner happiness in the beautiful world that God has given us. In my dreams – or, some would say, astral adventures – I would soar above the world and visit places and people at will. It was not until I was about eleven that I realized not everyone could do this. What I believed to be normal set me apart from my friends and made me realize that I saw the world differently from the way they did.

Now, as an adult, my spirituality has two sides to it. At least that is how it might appear to an observer.

When I married my husband, I accepted his Roman Catholic faith and over the years have found it to be a 'comfort blanket' in times of need or sorrow. I draw upon the community of the church, recognize the strength of the family of God and value the communal spirit of worshipping with others. A Sunday homily provides helpful insights into the meaning of the Bible and the ongoing love that God has for us. I also find the act of confession and contrition within Catholicism a cleansing process that provides renewal for my soul. The traditional church is, therefore, my 'public religious face' that I present to the world.

On the other hand, my private faith is one of spiritual searching. On the outside I say traditional prayers to God which are heartfelt and genuine. But in my inner private meditation, I delve back in time, beyond the confines of the church and the words written and formulated by men (and most *were* men). I look back to the creator, to the source of all life; I search for God; I long to draw upon the divine love to help me become what I am destined to be; I want to understand and accept the path chosen for me; I want God to make me a better person; I want continually to live in the presence of the divine. Every day I try to find some quiet time when I can meditate. This can be anywhere at any time. Sometimes even at work I will take a few minutes if I am on my own. I will close my eyes and go 'inwards' to my special place and cut out the distractions of everyday life. I may need calming if the day is stressful or just a moment to 'touch the spirit within' for a feeling of comfort in a mad world. My meditation also has another purpose, namely self-healing, which can be both spiritual and physical. I believe that the human spirit or life force is connected to God and, moreover, that God is able and willing to heal the soul and mend the body.

I look for guidance. Although I do not consciously have a specific 'spirit guide', I feel that there is a guardian angel that watches over me. Indeed, at times of great stress or sadness I have been fortunate to have experienced 'spiritual cleansing' and empowerment in the form of light and colour that enters my body and gives me inner calm and peace. This experience helps me to face the future with a different outlook altogether.

I feel that my faith transcends cultural barriers and draws elements from many religions. I have heard this described as 'spiritual shopping' and, to a large extent, this is how I see my spiritual path. The stock on the shelves of the spiritual supermarket is extensive and varied and I want to make as much use of it as I can.

As part of my spiritual beliefs, the subject of reincarnation figures strongly. As a child I always knew (before I had even heard the term for it) that I had had a previous life. I often thought to myself, 'I already knew that from before.' And it was often said to me that I was 'an old soul'. I believe that the time spent in this life paves our way for a life ultimately in the presence of God. Through many lives we progress spiritually and draw nearer to God.

Ultimately, I believe that although many *religious* people may be *spiritual*, those who have a deep spirituality of their own do not need to embrace traditional religion at all. Seeking spiritual enlightenment allows our souls to soar and to escape the confines of our cerebral prison to search for our own truth in the light of God's love.

offers a homogeneous diet of beef-in-bread, Jihad warns of scattered scuffles of holy war.

Culture clash

The resurgence of *jihad* has led some, such as political scientist Samuel Huntingdon, to caution about a 'clash of civilizations' overtaking the new global world. This helpfully highlights the vital role of religions in globalization. But there is a danger of tarring all with the same brush ('religions produce violence') or, worse, suggesting that some religions are characterized by their worst elements while others may be considered as basically beneficent but with eccentric margins. The truth is that the main world religions have many manifestations and Muslims may be no happier to be lumped with Islamists than Christians with Zealots (or Appalachian snake-handlers for that matter) or Jews with the fundamentalists of Gush Emunim.

If one explores one icon of globalization, the Internet, one soon finds both mainstream and fundamentalist religion in cyberspace. Helpful resources from major religious organizations are available – including, curiously, re-published classics of sacred or devotional literature – as well as signs of serious spirituality and engaged faith. But strident hate-filled fundamentalist sites also abound and these sometimes even wage cyberwar against each other – including sabotaging each other's sites! The new technologies that foster globalization may be shaped for many purposes. Outcomes are not inevitable, and nor can anything be predicted simply by referring to globalization or the Internet.

One can say, however, that today's fundamentalisms are produced by globalization and the cultural forces at work in its wake. Wherever one voice threatens to dominate, others will assert themselves. And wherever a babel of voices is heard, someone will issue a call back to the 'one true faith'. This is especially so in the case of Western media with their soap operas, MTV and 'reliable' CNN news. These invisible invaders sneak in through satellites and cables, rubbing salt in the wounds of decades of neglect and humiliation. So it is no surprise that, for instance, North African and 'Middle-Eastern' countries can only see a future in the past, in a revival of old verities and strict laws. Religious renewal is a response to globalization in this case.

Hopeful outcomes

Seen both ways, then, the religion-and-globalization theme is not one that will fade away fast. In fact, if this analysis is correct, it will continue to be a crucial arena of activity and site of struggle for the foreseeable future. The challenge is one that must be met if the global world is to be one worth living in. As yet there are few signs that powerful corporations or once-sovereign states will take the lead in shaping the global for humane ends, so perhaps religious voices – paradoxically, again – will have to become clearer. A reading of twentieth-century history shows how quickly religious smorgasbords sour, so those voices will have to acknowledge their particularities.

For example, Christianity has all too often allowed itself to become blinkered, belligerent and bigoted but this is not the whole story. In the twenty-first century opportunities are open to show what contribution authentic spirituality might make to a globalizing world. While some Muslims have resisted the world of Disney and Nike as decadent, all too many Christians have embraced consumerism without even noticing. For, while large corporations tend to direct globalization, they cannot do so without persuading the world's citizens to believe in consumerism as the route to contentment. And that, as we have seen, helps to widen the rich-poor gap and fuel fundamentalisms.

Positively, then, Christians could revisit the gospels to find there a story to live by. This story roots humans not in the world of forests, oceans and cities, but as spiritual beings with material experience. It seeks not merely to know 'who I am' but who is the other? And it sees human contentment not as an outcome of gadgets and gizmos, but coming from genuine commitments to justice and to care. This perspective would oppose neither enjoyment of life's good things nor the development of the world as one place. But it would be a globalization from below, in which Gaza Strip refugees and Bangalore's poor have a place, and where hostility gives way to healing.

Religion and Politics

ROBERT POPE

The common perception in the West is that religion and politics should not mix. This is largely the result of the eighteenth-century Enlightenment, since which it has become common to argue that as a society modernizes so it becomes secular and disentangled from dependence on God. Human ability to control and exploit the environment through scientific discoveries and technological advance meant that the former reliance on God to provide protection, shelter and sustenance was no longer necessary. The consequent separation of church (as the custodian of the sacred) and state (as the political community) is a specifically Western and modern idea, stemming more from secular philosophy than from religious understanding. Although it has won widespread acceptance, such a simplistic separation between religion and politics can be seen to be ideologically and historically mistaken.

Always a 'political' edge

It is historically difficult to see 'politics' and 'religion' as belonging to entirely separate realms. In early animist and tribal religions, cultic practice was intended to ensure the welfare of the group; Roman religious practice was, in part, expressed in emperor worship; Greek religion expected citizens to undertake the civic aspects of ceremonial and sacrifice; and in the present day religious practitioners have held a tremendous influence on Western democracies and governments elsewhere through agitating on moralistic and nationalistic issues. Throughout history, then, religion and politics have maintained a complex, if increasingly ambivalent, relationship.

Separate concerns

Religion is concerned with answering the great metaphysical questions and drawing on the commitment of individuals to the divine call. Religions usually posit eternal and binding values for their adherents to use in interpreting the why and wherefore of the universe. They provide principles, laws and rules which are to be followed and obeyed, but tend to offer little pragmatic advice concerning how adherents should respond to the exigencies of modern life. As a result, religion tends to influence politics either through the teachings of certain pedagogues or through individuals as they follow their vocation in political life.

Politics, on the other hand, is basically the way in which society is organized in order to make social life possible. Its concern tends to be immediate, even when short-term action constitutes a policy for the establishment of long-term goals. Despite its pragmatism, politics remains a branch of ethics because it is vulnerable to abuse. Political organizations can be oppressive and brutal. If they are to serve people well, a commitment is required to goodness, justice and virtue. As these values primarily characterize religious rather than political conviction, they suggest the desirability of a close relationship between the two. Historically, this association can be seen in the teachings of the world's three major monotheistic faiths.

JUDAISM
Judaism emerged out of the biblical history of chosen people and promised land. The Hebrew people had a specifically religious identity: they were Yahweh's people whose life, socially and individually, was to reflect Yahweh's Torah. The result was a

> '[Politics] enters into the self-awareness of a people, their self-identity, and it projects in large measure their sense of historic destiny and accomplishment.'
>
> J. Philip Wogaman

unique political identity which was indelibly linked to religious belief and practice. While officially secular, the modern state of Israel contains many who wish to see the theological understanding of land and people enshrined in political institutions. The Gush Emunim (Bloc of the Faithful) have famously seen the expansion of Israel's territory as the fulfilment of biblical promises, while some rabbis have been keen to confirm the Jewish status as a chosen people and thus the beneficiaries of certain privileges and rights. The Shas Party has been involved in forming coalition governments, bringing together an ultra-orthodox religious understanding and mainstream political activity.

CHRISTIANITY

From its inception, Christianity has recognized a differentiation between religious and political authority, arising partly out of its emergence as a weak and vulnerable social group, partly from the ambiguity in the interpretation of Jesus' injunction to 'render to Caesar' (Matthew 22:21 & parr.) and partly from the influence of Constantine and the role of the church following the collapse of the Roman empire. The Augustinian and Reformation traditions have maintained the sense of believers belonging to two states or cities: the sacred city which has its home in heaven and the earthly city which is ruled over by princes and governments. However, this is not strictly the separation of the secular and the sacred, for the state (the earthly city) is ruled by those whose vocation under God is to govern and whose rule must consequently conform to the divine will. In Christian thought, politics is both the legitimate concern of each believer to act and live in a way pleasing to God and the specific task of keeping the peace under God's law.

> 'Religion may be understood, at bottom, as the essence of what we believe to be true and good.'
>
> J. Philip Wogaman

ISLAM

Islam knows of no separation between the sacred and the secular. Instead all aspects of human life are intended to be drawn under the direct influence of the law of Allah, to which the only response is one of obedience. The obedient life, in all its aspects, individual and social, spiritual and civic, internal and external, should express the divine will. As a result, there is no value in the separation of religion and spirituality on the one hand from politics and social practice on the other.

The influence of religion on politics

In practice, religion has historically exercised a potent influence on political expression and identity. The relationship of church and state, primarily through the established Anglican Church and its privileged status in parliament, influences British society to the present day; the Puritan founders of the USA inspired a later generation to exalt freedom, choice and individual conscience as basic rights. Hinduism played an important role in forging an Indian political identity prior to independence in 1947; Pakistan was founded in the same year as an Islamic state and, as time went on, it attempted to modernize while also upholding *Shari'a* law. Buddhism was an important factor in anti-colonialist movements in Myanmar (Burma), while liberation theology assisted many in Latin America in opposing unsatisfactory secular regimes (although poverty in the subcontinent remains a tremendous problem). All these examples hold a common view of religion, in its various guises, as exercising a liberating influence, influencing politics for the better and challenging corruption and injustice.

From the mid-twentieth century a renewed association developed between religion and politics, resulting from disillusionment with secular values and dissatisfaction with policies of modernization. Hinduism became more of a force in Indian politics, particularly manifest in the Bharatiya Janata Party (BJP) and its association of land, religion and national identity. In Thailand and Sri Lanka, the prima facie other-worldly and pacifist convictions of Buddhism seemed to be set aside as it occasionally embraced violent acts in order to preserve a political system congenial to its own survival. Although from the time of the sixth Guru, Hargobind, Sikhism has maintained that the state and religion are natural allies, it has emerged as a political force in India in recent years, particularly following the declaration of the Sikh state, Khalistan, in 1986. In the USA, Christians have exercised a political influence through organizations such as the Moral Majority and the Christian Coalition as they opposed what they saw as the liberalization of US society.

Much of this renewed interaction has been characterized as an upsurge in religious fundamentalism, which received its most celebrated boost when the Iranian revolution of 1979 swept the Shah from power and replaced him with Ayatollah Khomeini. Islamic militancy had been growing throughout the 1970s, but following this take-over it became a far more potent force in the Middle East and in Africa, perhaps reaching its most infamous expression in the Taliban regime in Afghanistan. Nevertheless, its prominence on the world stage is the result of the threat which it poses to the West through possible control of oil reserves and through direct terrorist action. Perhaps more than any other religion, Islam has been criticized for its political associations and the willingness of its most militant followers to engage in extreme measures to achieve their goals. The dangers of this are only too evident following the attack on the World Trade Center on 11 September 2001. As a result of this, the concern of many that religion and politics held too close an association has, to an extent, given way to the fear that religion has too close an association with terrorism.

Conclusion

It can be seen, then, that religion can relate to politics in several ways. There can be a specifically religious political policy, expressed through a religious political party; religion can hold a theological view of political institutions where the state and its organs have a divinely ordained role to make possible the more exalted work of the religious institution; religion can act as the political conscience of a society, with religious institutions criticizing political policy and calling for action where those policies are seen to contradict eternal values; religion can oppose the political status quo for being too compromising; or it can be involved through theocracy, where God governs directly or at least through the medium of a priestly caste.

In all instances, the association of religion and politics holds the potential to do both good and harm, the latter being most prominent when religious practitioners fail to live up to the highest ideals of their own creed.

Rapid Fact-Finder

This fact-finder has been updated by Christopher Partridge. It is based on the fact-finder by Angela Tilby and John-David Yule in earlier editions of this book. The terms include some that do not appear in this book. These are common terms that are included to give additional information to readers.

'Abbasid dynasty (CE 750–1258) The second great Islamic dynasty which ruled from Baghdad. Under the 'Abbasids the empire enjoyed a period of increased prosperity and trade. Libraries and centres of learning were established throughout the Islamic world.

Abhidhamma Pitaka THERAVADA Buddhist scripture on techniques of mind-training. The aim is to eliminate the idea of the self. It is the key work of Buddhist psychology.

Abraham, Isaac and Jacob The three PATRIARCHS who are continually remembered in the Jewish liturgy as the original recipients of God's promise and blessing. According to tradition they are buried in the tomb of the patriarchs in the cave of Machpelah in the modern town of Hebron.

Absolute, The Term for GOD or the divine often preferred by those who conceive of God predominantly in abstract or impersonal terms.

Abu Bakr MUHAMMAD's father-in-law and traditionally his earliest convert. He was elected CALIPH after the Prophet's death and ruled for two years, fighting tribes who were trying to break away from the Islamic community. He began the compilation of the QUR'AN.

Adi Granth Sacred book of Sikhism. It is regarded as the eternal GURU for the SIKH community. It is the central focus of the Sikh home and of the GURDWARA.

Adonai See YHWH.

Advaita ('Non-dualism') The monist (see MONISM) doctrine of SHANKARA, that all reality is fundamentally one and divine.

Aesir Plural of *'as'*, meaning 'god'. The collective noun used in Norse literature for the pantheon of deities. More particularly, it is used of a particular, majority group that share a common origin, which includes principal deities such as Odin, Thor and Tyr. (See also VANIR.)

African Independent Churches African churches which have arisen in the past 100 years and offer a synthesis of CHRISTIANITY with traditional INDIGENOUS RELIGIONS. Many have prophetic or charismatic founders and emphasize spiritual healing and communication with ancestors. Some have been a focus of nationalistic aspirations.

Afterlife Any form of conscious existence after the death of the body.

Agape Greek word for 'love' which has come to express the Christian understanding of God's love which does not depend on any worthiness or attractiveness of the object of his love. Christians are taught to demonstrate this love to each other in the Christian FELLOWSHIP, and to others.

Agni Indian fire god of Vedic times (see VEDAS). As sacrificial fire, Agni mediates between gods and people and is especially concerned with order and ritual.

Ahimsa Indian virtue of non-violence. It usually applies to abstention from harming any living creature and hence to vegetarianism. The doctrine was developed in JAINISM, BUDDHISM and some HINDU sects. In Jain belief violence carries severe penalties of KARMA. MAHATMA GANDHI applied the idea to the political struggles of the oppressed in his practice of non-violent non-cooperation.

Ahmadiyya sect Offshoot of ISLAM founded in India by Mirza Ghulam Ahmad (died 1908) who is believed to be the MESSIAH MAHDI. The sect denies the authority of the 'ULAMA', IJMA' and JIHAD. It is a missionary sect and has gained converts in Asia and Africa.

Ahriman See ANGRA MAINYU.

Ahura Mazda/Ohrmazd ('Wise Lord') ZOROASTER's name for God. He demands ethical and ritual purity and he judges human souls after death. His symbol is sacred fire.

Akhenaten Name adopted by Amenophis IV, king of Egypt 1353–1335 BCE, in honour of ATEN ('the sun disc') whose cult he promoted to the exclusion of all others in a short-lived reform of Egyptian religion. He built a magnificent new capital at el-Amarna.

Akiba, Rabbi (CE 50–135) Jewish teacher who developed the MISHNAH method of repetitive transmission of teachings. He began the work of systematizing the available interpretations of the TORAH, laying the foundations for the work of JUDAH HANASI. He was also famous for his use of MIDRASH, investing every detail of the Hebrew texts with significance.

Albigensians The CATHARS of southern France who flourished in the late twelfth and early thirteenth centuries. Their theology was a DUALISM that has been compared with that of the MANICHAEANS although they were probably unconnected. They saw CHRIST as an ANGEL whose teachings had been corrupted by the Catholic clergy. Their most rigorous adherents, the 'perfects', abstained from marriage and avoided animal products.

Alchemy Mystical science of chemical manipulation which seeks to change base metals into gold, find the universal cure for illness and discover the secret of immortality. Its study passed from Hellenistic Egypt through the Arabs to medieval Europe. It is also important in TAOISM.

Al-Ghazali (CE 1058–1111) Orthodox MUSLIM legal expert who renounced his post and became a Sufi (see SUFISM). He attacked the incursions of Greek thought into ISLAM and defended the teaching of the QUR'AN. He also defended the Sufi experience of God but denied the possibility of human deification.

Al-Hallaj (died CE 922) Sufi MYSTIC who was crucified because of his confession 'I am the real' which was taken as a claim to divinity. He considered JESUS OF NAZARETH as the supreme example of human deification and at his death forgave his enemies in imitation of the passion of Jesus.

'Ali Cousin and son-in-law of MUHAMMAD who was elected fourth CALIPH in CE 656. War broke out between 'Ali and the governor of Syria who claimed that 'Ali had plotted 'UTHMAN's death. In CE 661 'Ali was murdered and his son, Hasan, renounced any claim to the caliphate.

Allah The Muslim name for God. Allah is one; there are no other gods. As pure, undivided spirit, Allah is the creator and sustainer of all that is known to human beings in the revelation of the divine will in the QUR'AN. Throughout the Qur'an, Allah is declared to be 'the merciful' and 'the compassionate'.

Almsgiving The giving of free gifts, usually of money, to the poor. In ISLAM it is obligatory (see ZAKAH). In THERAVADA Buddhism the lay community is linked to the SANGHA by their provision of food for the MONKS which is collected on a daily almsround. Jain ascetics also rely on alms from the laity.

Alternative Spiritualities One of the more significant developments in particularly Western religious adherence has been the emergence of private, non-institutional forms of belief and practice known as 'alternative spiritualities'. There has been a move away from traditional forms of belief which have developed within religious institutions, towards forms of belief that focus on 'the self', on 'nature', or simply on 'life'. Although there may be particular traditional teachings that are valued by the individual seeker, or particular groups to which the individual belongs, generally speaking there is a suspicion of traditional authorities, sacred texts, churches, and hierarchies of power.

Amida see AMITABHA.

Amidah ('Standing') The principal Jewish daily prayer, also known as the Eighteen Benedictions, recited standing. Today it actually comprises nineteen benedictions, including prayers for the restoration of ISRAEL and for peace.

Amitabha ('Infinite light') Celestial BUDDHA worshipped in China and Japan (where his name is Amida). He is believed to live in a 'pure land' in the far west where those faithful to him go after death (see JODO SHINSHU; NEMBUTSU; PURE LAND BUDDHISM).

Amritsar Site of the Golden Temple, the holiest shrine of the Sikh religion, built by Arjan, the fifth Guru.

Analects One of the four books of the so-called Confucian canon. It contains the essence of CONFUCIUS's teaching and was probably compiled about seventy years after his death.

Ananda One of the most prominent members of the BUDDHA's SANGHA. Traditionally he was the Buddha's cousin and many of the sayings are addressed to him, including the words of comfort shortly before the Buddha's death. He helped to fix the canon of Buddhist SCRIPTURE.

Anatta/Anatman Meaning 'not-self', a Buddhist term indicating that there is ultimately no 'soul' (see SOUL (1)). All beings are merely a series of mental and physical states. *Anatta* is one of the three CHARACTERISTICS OF EXISTENCE.

Ancestor veneration The practice in

INDIGENOUS RELIGIONS of making offerings to the spirits of the dead and expecting to communicate with them through DREAMS.

Angels Spiritual beings who in JUDAISM and CHRISTIANITY act as the messengers of GOD. They have two primary functions: to worship God and to support and encourage human beings. In ISLAM the Archangel GABRIEL (Jibril) is associated with the giving of the QUR'AN.

Anglican Churches Worldwide groupings of churches which recognize the primacy among equals of the Archbishop of Canterbury. They include both catholic and reformed elements and retain BISHOPS.

Angra Mainyu/Ahriman The chief spirit who is opposed to AHURA MAZDA in Zoroastrian belief. His nature is violent and destructive. He created the demons, he rules in hell and has opposed God from the beginning.

Anicca/Anitya Buddhist term for the impermanence and changeability which characterizes all existence.

Animism A term formerly used to describe pre-literary religions. It was dropped because its meaning 'spiritism' was felt to be misleading. (See INDIGENOUS RELIGIONS.)

Anthroposophy Spiritual system invented by Rudolf STEINER. It stresses the threefold nature of humanity as physical, etheric and astral body and proposes a programme for spiritual education which includes techniques of MEDITATION.

Anu The sky god of ancient Sumerian religion and high god of the Sumerian pantheon. He had little to do with human affairs and delegated his authority to ENLIL. From about 2000 BCE he was called King of Gods and Father.

Anubis Jackal-headed god of ancient Egypt who conducted souls to judgment and weighed them in the great balance. Known as 'the embalmer', he watched over mummification and was the guardian of tombs and cemeteries.

Aphrodite Greek goddess of love and patroness of beauty and sexual attractiveness. Her cult was imported from the Near East. The Greeks thought of her as vain and cruel but the Romans identified her with VENUS and honoured her as the mother of Aeneas, ancestor of the Romans. In Cyprus she was worshipped as the MOTHER GODDESS.

Apocalyptic Genre of writing in CHRISTIANITY and JUDAISM, concerned with hidden truths, pointing to the ultimate triumph of faith and the judgment of nations. Daniel and Revelation are examples in the BIBLE.

Apocrypha Historical and wisdom writings found in the Greek version of the Hebrew scriptures but excluded from the canon of the HEBREW BIBLE fixed at the Synod of Jamnia around CE 100. The Roman Catholic Church accepts its authority, though Eastern Orthodox and Protestant Churches distinguish it from inspired SCRIPTURE.

Apollo A major god of both Greeks and Romans, though Greek in origin. He is sometimes seen as the sun and is the patron of the arts (especially music), or prophecy, of divination and of medicine. He was the inspiration of the DELPHIC ORACLE.

Apostle (1) 'One who is sent', name for the twelve original followers of JESUS OF NAZARETH, also PAUL. The 'apostolic age' is a time of great authority for the Christian CHURCH. (2) Title of MUHAMMAD.

Aquinas, Thomas (CE 1225–74) Dominican theologian and philosopher whose teachings form the basis of official Roman Catholic theology. He taught a fundamental distinction between faith and reason, asserting that God's existence can be proved, but that the doctrines of the TRINITY and the INCARNATION are revealed and must be accepted on faith.

Archetypes Term invented by C.G. JUNG to describe the concepts held in common by different people at different times and in different places. He believed that the concept of GOD was the archetype of the self and that it was the object of each individual to discover it.

Arianism Fourth-century Christian HERESY of Arius who denied the divinity of CHRIST, claiming that the Son of God was created and not eternal. It was condemned at the Council of Nicea in CE 325 but flourished until the Council of Constantinople in CE 381.

Aristotle (384–322 BCE) Greek philosopher and scientist who taught on every branch of knowledge valued in his time. His work is characterized by acute observation, close reasoning and orderly exposition. His work was rediscovered in the Middle Ages and laid the basis for the theology of THOMAS AQUINAS and for the HUMANISM of the Renaissance.

Ark (1) Israelite religious artefact, probably in the form of a portable miniature temple, which was carried into battle as evidence of the presence of God (see YHWH). In Solomon's TEMPLE the ark lived in the Holy of Holies. (2) A cupboard in the wall of a SYNAGOGUE that faces JERUSALEM, where the handwritten parchment scrolls of the TORAH are kept.

Artemis Greek goddess and patroness of virginity, hunting, archery and wild animals. She was also the protector of the newly born and the bringer of death to women. At Ephesus in Asia Minor, she was worshipped as the MOTHER GODDESS. (See also DIANA.)

Arthur Legendary hero of Celtic Britain who may have originated as a Romano-British chieftain. His legends were gradually worked into a coherent Christian framework in which he became the medieval ideal of a Christian king.

Aryan Word describing the Caucasian people who invaded India around 2000 BCE and who gradually imposed their language and culture upon the earlier inhabitants. Related peoples settled in Iran and Mesopotamia.

Asceticism Austere practices designed to lead to the control of the body and the senses. These may include FASTING and MEDITATION, the renunciation of possessions, and the pursuit of solitude.

Asgard The home of the gods in Norse religion. It is a mountainous region rising out of Midgard and separated from it by a rainbow bridge.

Ashkenazim One of the two main cultural groups in JUDAISM which emerged in the Middle Ages. Their tradition is from Palestinian Jewry and they live in central northern and eastern Europe. They developed Yiddish as their language, which is a mixture of Hebrew, Slav and German.

Ashram In Indian religion, a hermitage or monastery. It has come to denote a communal house for devotees of a GURU. It functions as a centre for building up the commitment of believers and for transmitting the guru's message.

Astral plane The intermediate world, according to THEOSOPHY and SPIRITUALISM, to which the human consciousness passes at death. Some psychics and visionaries are able to project themselves there at will.

Astrology The study of the influence of the stars on the character and destiny of human beings. The locations of the planets in the field of the zodiac at the time of the subject's birth are the key data considered in the astrologer's analysis.

Aten The sun in ancient Egyptian religion. In the reforms of AKHENATEN he was worshipped as the one true God.

Athanasius (CE 296–373) Bishop of Alexandria who strongly resisted the teachings of ARIANISM and developed the Christian doctrines of the INCARNATION and the TRINITY.

Athena One of the great Greek goddesses of Mount OLYMPOS who sprang fully armed from the head of her father, ZEUS. She is the patroness of war, of the city of Athens and of many crafts and skills. She is usually portrayed in full armour, with an owl on her shoulder and the Gorgon's head painted on her shield. Her Roman counterpart is Minerva.

Atman SANSKRIT word meaning soul or self. The UPANISHADS teach that *atman* is identical to BRAHMAN, i.e. the soul is one with the divine.

Atonement (1) Ritual act which restores harmony between the human and the divine, when it has been broken by sin or impurity. (2) In CHRISTIANITY, reconciliation between God and humanity required because of the absolute holiness of God and the sinfulness of men and women. As human beings are incapable of achieving atonement, it is a work of God's GRACE, through the death of Jesus Christ for human sin.

Atonement, Day of See Yom Kippur.

Augustine (CE 354–430) BISHOP of Hippo in North Africa who was converted to CHRISTIANITY from the teaching of the MANICHAEANS. He stressed the absolute GRACE of God in men and women's SALVATION and the depravity of human beings through ORIGINAL SIN.

Augustus Title of the first Roman emperor, formerly known as Octavian, who ruled 31 BCE – CE 14. He pacified and unified the empire, thus facilitating the later spread of CHRISTIANITY. While he was still alive he was declared a god and after his death he was worshipped throughout the empire.

Austerity Ascetic practice in which one exercises self restraint or denial. For example, the restriction of food during a fast.

Avalokiteshvara ('Regarder of the cries of the earth') Celestial BUDDHA worshipped by Tibetans and in Korea, Japan and China. The DALAI LAMA is believed to be an emanation of him. This Buddha is known under male and female forms and is depicted with a thousand arms symbolizing endless labour for the welfare of humankind.

Avalon Celtic island of immortality replete with miraculous apple trees. Here the hero ARTHUR was taken to recover from his mortal wounds.

Avatar ('One who descends') In popular Hinduism, Lord VISHNU appears on earth at intervals to assert ancient values and destroy illusion. The main tradition refers to ten descents, nine of which have already happened. KRISHNA is the most famous *avatar*. Some modern cults claim to worship a living *avatar*.

Averroes See IBN RUSHD.

Avesta The SCRIPTURES of ZOROASTRIANISM. It includes the *Gathas*, a series of poems reminiscent of the hymns of the VEDAS which may go back to ZOROASTER himself. They may have been used as a liturgy to ward off ANGRA MAINYU and his evil spirits.

Ayatollah ('Sign of God') Iranian term for a great MUJTAHID who has authority in the Shi'a Muslim community.

Aztec new fire ceremony Ritual which took place at the end of every Aztec cycle of fifty-two years. It was performed at night on a volcanic hill visible from many parts of the valley of Mexico. When the constellation Pleiades reached the middle of the sky, the priests signalled that the world would continue for another cycle of fifty-two years. A human victim was sacrificed and a new fire was kindled in his chest cavity.

Aztecs An indigenous people whose empire in central Mexico flourished from the late twelfth century CE until the coming of the conquistador Hernando Cortes in 1519. Their religion centred around a sacred calendar and featured human SACRIFICE in which the heart torn from a living victim was offered to the gods. (See also HUITZILOPOCHTLI; QUETZALCOATL; TEZCATLIPOCA; TLALOC; XIPE TOTEC; XIUHTECUHTLI.)

B

Baal Divinity of ancient Canaanite or Phoenician fertility religion. The name means 'lord'.

Baal Shem Tov (CE 1700–60) Jewish MYSTIC who founded the movement of HASIDISM. His name means 'Master of the Good Name' and it is often shortened to BeShT. His original name was Israel ben Eliezer. At the age of thirty-six he developed powers of healing and prophecy. He taught a kind of mystical PANTHEISM. He was greatly loved and became the source of many Yiddish legends and miracle stories.

Babism See BAHÁ'Í FAITH.

Babylonian epic of creation The story of the god MARDUK's fight with the primordial ocean, Tiamat, who is presented as a sea monster. Marduk slit Tiamat in two and made heaven and earth out of the pieces. This MYTH was probably re-enacted every spring at an enthronement festival.

Babylonian flood story A parallel to the story of the flood in the BIBLE going back to a Sumerian original but best known from the

EPIC OF GILGAMESH. It tells the story of a wise king, Ut-napishtim, who survived the flood caused by the god ENLIL by taking refuge in a huge boat with his wife and various animals. He was rewarded by Enlil by being transported to a land of immortality.

Bahá'í faith A religious movement that arose out of the Persian Islamic Babi sect, led by the 'Báb' ('gate' 1819–50). Founded by Bahá'u'lláh (1817–92), it is based on the idea that there has only ever been one divinely revealed religion, which has been progressively revealed by the teachings of the founders of the world's religions, the most recent of whom is Bahá'u'lláh. Bahá'u'lláh appointed his son 'Abdu'l-Bahá (1844–1921) to be his successor and also the interpreter of his writings. he was succeeded by Shoghi Effendi (1897–1957) in 1921. Following the death of Shoghi Effendi in 1957, there was an interregnum until 1963, when the Universal House of Justice, an institution that had been ordained in the writings of Bahá'u'lláh, was elected. This is now the supreme administrative body of the Bahá'í faith.

Balder The son of ODIN and FRIGG, the wisest and most beautiful of the Norse gods. He was killed by the wiles of LOKI but could not be restored to ASGARD because Loki refused to weep for him. His name means 'lord' and he may be connected with the Middle-Eastern dying and rising gods, Adonis and TAMMUZ.

Baptism The SACRAMENT of entry into the Christian CHURCH (1). By washing in water in the name of the TRINITY, it symbolizes the person's identification with CHRIST's death and resurrection, in dying to sin and being raised to new life. In the case of infants, promises are made on behalf of the child for later CONFIRMATION.

Baptist Churches Protestant churches emphasizing the BAPTISM of adult believers by total immersion.

Bar-Mitzvah ('Son of the commandment') Ceremony by which Jewish boys, at the age of thirteen, accept the positive commandments of JUDAISM and are counted as adult members of the community.

Barth, Karl (CE 1886–1968) Swiss Calvinist theologian who reacted against Liberal Protestantism in theology and declared theology's central theme to be the Word of God.

Beautiful names of God Ninety-nine names which characterize the will of ALLAH in ISLAM. The most important are Al-Rahman and Al-Rahim, 'the merciful' and 'the mercy-giver'.

Beltane Celtic spring festival and origin of May Day. The name means 'shining fire' and it is likely that sacred fires were lit for the people to dance around, encouraging the growth of the summer sun.

Benares/Varanasi/Kashi The most holy city of HINDUISM, situated on the banks of the GANGES and attracts 1 million pilgrims every year. The BUDDHA preached his first sermon here, traditionally in the deer park on the outskirts of the city.

Benedict (about CE 480–550) Monk and reformer who wrote a Rule of monastic life which has been followed by MONKS and NUNS of the Western church ever since.

Bhagavad Gita ('Song of the lord') A section of the MAHABHARATA in the form of a battlefield dialogue between the warrior prince Arjuna and KRISHNA, disguised as his charioteer. Arjuna is unwilling to fight his kinsmen but Krishna encourages him, teaching him that wisdom requires him to fulfil his proper role while at the same time renouncing the consequences of his actions.

Bhagavan/Bhagwan Indian title meaning 'lord' or 'worshipful'. It is frequently used of VISHNU. It is also a title of honour used by devotees of holy men.

Bhagavan Shri Rajneesh (CE 1931–90) Indian spiritual teacher and philosopher who founded his own ASHRAM at Pune (Poona) in India. His daily talks and reflections have been transcribed and widely published in the West.

Bhajana An Indian song or HYMN in praise of God usually sung communally at devotional gatherings and accompanied by musical instruments.

Bhakti Love of, or devotion to, God. It is one of the Hindu paths to union with God (see YOGA). It is expressed in popular religion in which the worshipper develops a sense of personal relationship to God, responding to him as though to a father, mother, friend, lover or child, and looking to him for grace.

Bible The book of CHRISTIANITY, comprising the Hebrew OLD TESTAMENT and the NEW TESTAMENT which, Christians believe, together form a unified message of God's SALVATION.

Bishop The most senior order of ministry in the Christian CHURCH (1) with authority to ordain PRIESTS (2). Many REFORMED CHURCHES do not have bishops.

Black stone Sacred object set in the wall of the Muslim KA'BA sanctuary in MECCA. Tradition asserts that it was received by the biblical Ishmael from the archangel GABRIEL (Jibril). During the rites of pilgrimage (see HAJJ) the faithful try to kiss or touch the stone.

Blavatsky, Helena Petrovna (CE 1831–91) Founder in 1875 of the Theosophical Society (see THEOSOPHY), who claimed to have received the 'ancient wisdom' after seven years in Tibet being taught by various MAHATMAS. She wrote books defending SPIRITUALISM and various OCCULT teachings.

Bodhi In various schools of BUDDHISM, 'awakening', or 'perfect wisdom', or 'supreme ENLIGHTENMENT' (1).

Bodhidharma Traditionally the first teacher of Ch'an Buddhism who moved from southern India to China in CE 520. He introduced the methods of sharp questioning and paradox found today in Japanese ZEN.

Bodhisattva In MAHAYANA Buddhism a saint or semi-divine being who has voluntarily renounced NIRVANA in order to help others to salvation. In popular devotion *bodhisattvas* are worshipped as symbols of compassion.

Book of Mormon Sacred SCRIPTURE of MORMONISM which was revealed to Joseph

SMITH. It describes a conflict between two branches of a family which had emigrated under divine guidance from JERUSALEM to America in 600 BCE. The Mormons regard it as the completion of the biblical revelation.

Book of the Dead Name given to various collections of SPELLS, often illustrated, buried with the dead of ancient Egypt to assist their souls through the judgment. Commonly the soul is depicted as weighed in a balance against *ma'at*, a conception of 'right order' (depicted as an ostrich feather), by the god ANUBIS while the scribe THOTH records the result and OSIRIS presides. (See also TIBETAN BOOK OF THE DEAD.)

Book of Shadows A term used in contemporary WICCA of the book in which rituals, invocations and spells are recorded. While some are kept secret, many allow other witches to copy their contents in order to share good practice. It is believed by some witches that, traditionally, the Book of Shadows was burned when the witch died.

Booths/Tabernacles/Sukkot Autumn Jewish festival marking the end of the harvest. Branch- or straw-covered booths remind JEWS of God's protection during their forty-year journey through the wilderness.

Brahma The creator god of Hinduism. With Vishnu and Shiva, Brahma belongs to the *Trimurti* of classical Hindu thought. Brahma is also understood to be the all-inclusive God behind popular Hinduism's multitude of deities.

Brahman In HINDUISM, the divine, absolute reality. The word is the neuter form of BRAHMA, the creator god of early Hinduism, and originally referred to the holy power evoked through sacrifice.

Brahmans See CASTE SYSTEM.

Breviary Liturgical book containing instructions for the recitation of daily services as followed by the Christian clergy, MONKS and NUNS of the Western church, with the proper hymns, psalms and lessons for each service.

Brighid Celtic goddess of poetry, prophecy, learning and healing. The Romans associated her Gaulish equivalent with Minerva. She was absorbed into Irish Christianity as St Brighid, whose feast day coincides with a Celtic spring festival.

Buber, Martin (CE 1878–1965) Austrian Jewish theologian whose religious roots were in HASIDISM. Although a Zionist, he was critical of the politics of ZIONISM and of Talmudic tradition (see TALMUD). He believed that the central task of JEWS was to build up God's kingdom on the basis of the Jewish belief in an essential dialogue between God and humanity. He has influenced Christian spirituality and social teaching.

Buddha ('The one who has awakened/ enlightened one') (1) Siddhartha GAUTAMA, a sage of the SHAKYA tribe who lived in India in the sixth century BCE, the founder of BUDDHISM. There is little doubt that there was a historical figure at the source of Buddhism though some branches of MAHAYANA regard this as unimportant. (2) Any human being or celestial figure who has reached ENLIGHTENMENT (1).

Buddhaghosa Buddhist writer of the fifth century CE who wrote many commentaries on the scriptures and one original work, *The Path of Purity*. The Burmese believe he was a native of Myanmar (Burma) but other traditions hold that he was an Indian who worked in Sri Lanka (Ceylon).

Buddha image Representation of the BUDDHA used in all forms of BUDDHISM. The Buddha is most commonly portrayed in the LOTUS POSTURE, but there are also versions of him standing or lying on one side. The various postures and position of the hands symbolize the defeat of evil, the achieving of ENLIGHTENMENT, the preaching of the DHAMMA and the final NIRVANA. The images are psychological aids rather than objects of worship, though in MAHAYANA Buddhism they act as a focus for devotion.

Buddhism The religion which developed from the teaching of the BUDDHA and which spread from India into south-east Asia, later expanding into northern Asia, China and Japan. The two principal divisions are the THERAVADA (HINAYANA) and the MAHAYANA. Special features are found in TIBETAN BUDDHISM, also known as VAJRAYANA.

Butsu-dan A Japanese domestic altar to the BUDDHA which contains images or objects of worship and memorial tablets to ancestors. There may be lights, flowers and incense and it is the focus of daily prayer chanting and the offering of food and drink.

C

Caliph ('Deputy' or 'representative') Title of the leaders of the MUSLIM community after the death of MUHAMMAD. The first three caliphs ruled from MEDINA; the UMMAYADS from Damascus, and the 'ABBASIDS from Baghdad. Sunni Muslims revere only four Caliphs. From CE 1517 the caliph was based at Istanbul. Kemal Ataturk abolished the caliphate in 1923.

Calvin, John (CE 1509–64) French theologian who organized the REFORMATION from Geneva. He emphasized justification by faith and the sole authority of the BIBLE and in particular that each person's eternal destiny was decided irrevocably by God and only those destined for salvation would come to faith.

Cao Dai Religious and political movement which started in southern Vietnam around 1920. It is sometimes called the 'Third Amnesty'. Firmly nationalistic, its teachings are a mixture of BUDDHISM and TAOISM.

Cardinal Member of a college of ordained high officials in the ROMAN CATHOLIC Church who, since 1179, have elected the POPE. Cardinals are appointed by the pope.

Cargo cults Term used for new religious movements of Melanesia and New Guinea which imitate European ritual in the hope of thereby receiving European-type material wealth – 'cargo'. They look for the arrival of a MESSIAH who will banish illness and distribute the cargo among the people.

Caste system The division of a society into groups reflecting and defining the division of labour. In Hinduism, caste is traditionally seen as the creation of BRAHMA, each caste emerging symbolically from different parts of his body. There are four chief groups: Brahmans, priests, come from Brahma's mouth; Kshatriyas, warriors, come from Brahma's arms; Vaishyas, commoners, come from Brahma's thighs; Sudras, servants, come from Brahma's feet. Groups of no definite caste were regarded as UNTOUCHABLES and were banished from society.

Catechism (1) Instruction on Christian faith; for example, instruction in question and answer form given to those preparing for BAPTISM or CONFIRMATION. (2) A popular manual of Christian doctrine.

Catechumen Candidate in training for Christian BAPTISM.

Cathars Members of a medieval heretical Christian sect which flourished in Germany, France and Italy before their suppression in the thirteenth century. (See also ALBIGENSIANS.)

Catholicism CHRISTIANITY as practised by those who emphasize a continuous historical tradition of faith and practice from the time of the APOSTLES (1) to the present day.

Celts Population group occupying much of central and western Europe during the first millennium BCE. They included the ancient Gauls and Britons. They worshipped the MOTHER GODDESS and various local and tribal deities. Evidence from skulls excavated in Celtic sacred places suggests that they practised human sacrifice. Their priests were the Druids.

Cernunnos ('The horned one') Celtic horned god associated with the earth and fertility, and protector of the animal kingdom. Usually portrayed sitting cross-legged, he is often accompanied by a stag, or a horned serpent or a bull.

Chac Rain god of the MAYA (3). He is portrayed as an old man with a long nose and weeping eyes. He is in quadruple form and faces in all directions. Benevolent and a friend to humanity, his name was invoked at planting ceremonies.

Chakras According to Indian thought and many contemporary alternative spiritualities, there are seven (sometimes six) chakras (meaning 'wheels') or spiritual energy centres located in the human body. They are: at the top of the head; between the eyebrows; at the throat; at the heart; at the navel; at the genitals; and at the base of the spine where KUNDALINI, the serpent-energy, lies coiled. The chakras are sometimes called 'lotus centres'.

Chant Type of singing in which many syllables are sung on a single note or a repeated short musical phrase. Many religions use chanting in worship. Jews and Christians chant the PSALMS; Buddhists and others their own sacred SCRIPTURES. The repetitive nature of chanting can aid MEDITATION.

Characteristics of existence In the BUDDHA's teaching all existence is marked by the three characteristics: DUKKHA; ANICCA; ANATTA.

Charismatic movement Renewal movement in Catholic and Protestant Churches stressing the work and manifestation of the HOLY SPIRIT in the life of the church and of the individual believer.

Chela In Indian religion, a disciple, student or follower of a GURU.

Ch'i In Chinese thought, chi'i is a universal energy, which manifests in the negative and positive polarities of *yin* and *yang*. The manipulation of ch'i is central to a form of Chinese yoga known as Ch'i Gung (Ch'i Gong, Quigong, Ch'i Kung) to some forms of acupuncture and martial arts, such as tai ch'i.

Chinvat bridge The bridge of judgment in the teaching of ZOROASTER. Good souls found it broad and easy to cross but wicked souls slipped off as it narrowed, and fell into a chasm of torment.

Chorten Tibetan Buddhist shrine, found by roadsides, in fields and at gateways. It is shaped as a pointed dome, often with a spire crescent and disc at the top, and built on a square base. The construction represents the five elements and may contain RELICS or images or texts of sacred scripture.

Christ Greek word for MESSIAH. First applied to JESUS OF NAZARETH by his followers who believed him to fulfil the hopes of ISRAEL, it later became more a proper name of Jesus than a title.

Christadelphians Christian sect founded by John Thomas (CE 1805–71) in the USA, which claims to have returned to the beliefs and practices of the original DISCIPLES. They accept the BIBLE as infallible and are particularly interested in the fulfilment of prophecy. They reject the doctrines of the TRINITY and INCARNATION and have no ordained ministry.

Christian Follower of JESUS OF NAZARETH, the CHRIST, a member of the Christian CHURCH (1).

Christianity Religion based on the teachings of JESUS OF NAZARETH, the CHRIST, and the significance of his life, death and RESURRECTION.

Christian Science Christian sect founded in the USA by Mary Baker EDDY in 1866. It began with a small group fathered 'to re-instate primitive Christianity and its lost element of healing'.

Christmas The festival of the birth of CHRIST celebrated in Western Christendom on 25 December (which is not necessarily the date believed to be the actual date of his birth). The date suggests that it was intended to replace the Roman festival of the birth of SOL INVICTUS in the fourth century CE.

Christology Teaching about the nature of the person of Christ.

Chuang-tzu Chinese Taoist teacher who lived in the fourth and third centuries BCE. He commended a way of life according to nature which disregarded the conventions of CONFUCIANISM. His writings stress spiritual discipline which should lead to MEDITATION on the formless TAO.

Chu Hsi (CE 1130–1200) Chinese philosopher who expounded a system rather similar to that of PLATO. He believed that by quiet daily MEDITATION one could see through diversity to the supreme reality behind all phenomena.

Church (1) The community of all CHRISTIANS, seen in the NEW TESTAMENT as the 'body of Christ', of which he is the head. (2) Building used for Christian WORSHIP.

(3) A local group, organized section or 'denomination' of the church (1).

Circumcision The cutting off of the prepuce in males or the internal labia in females as a religious rite. It is widely practised in traditional African religion, either shortly after birth or at puberty. In JUDAISM boys are circumcised at eight days of age in commemoration of ABRAHAM's covenant with God. Male converts to Judaism undergo this rite. Circumcision is also practised in ISLAM.

Civil religion Religion as a system of beliefs, symbols and practices which legitimate the authority of a society's institutions and bind people together in the public sphere.

Conciliar process The decision making of the CHURCH through the resolutions of specially convened councils or synods in which the will of CHRIST is revealed to the gathered body. Since the second VATICAN COUNCIL member churches of the WORLD COUNCIL OF CHURCHES have pledged themselves to work towards a common stand on important issues in the hope that this would lead to the restoration of a universal council which would speak for all Christians.

Confirmation Christian rite involving the laying on of hands on those who have been baptized, with prayer for the gift of, or strengthening by, the HOLY SPIRIT. It is often the sign of becoming a communicant member of the CHURCH (1). In Orthodox Churches it is performed at BAPTISM. Roman Catholics are confirmed at about seven years of age. Other churches that accept confirmation offer it at puberty or later.

Confucianism The system of social ethics taught by CONFUCIUS and given imperial recognition in China in the second century CE. Opinion is divided on whether or not Confucianism should be regarded as a religion. (See FIVE RELATIONSHIPS; LI.)

Confucius/K'ung Fu'tzu (551–479 BCE) Chinese civil servant and administrator who became known as a teacher, opening his classes to everyone regardless of wealth or class. His teachings, especially the idea of LI, became the basis of a system of social ethics which greatly influenced Chinese society after his death.

Congregationalists See INDEPENDENTS.

Conservative Judaism Movement which tries to stand midway between Orthodox and Progressive JUDAISM. It claims to accept the Talmudic tradition (see TALMUD) but to interpret the TORAH in the light of modern needs.

Conversion A moral or spiritual change of direction, or the adoption of religious beliefs not previously held.

Coptic Church The Church of Egypt, a more or less tolerated minority in Egypt since the coming of ISLAM in CE 642. The Church is 'monophysite', i.e. it rejects the teaching about the INCARNATION OF CHRIST agreed at the ECUMENICAL COUNCIL of Chalcedon.

Corroboree Ceremony of the Australian Aboriginals comprising festive and warlike folk dances.

Cosmology (1) The study of the nature of the cosmos. (2) In religion, cosmologies

concern the relationship between the divine and the natural world. This relationship is usually described in myths or stories of how God or the gods had brought the world, humanity, and particular peoples into existence and how they continue to relate to them. Cosmologies form the frameworks within which reality is interpreted.

Councils of the Church See ECUMENICAL COUNCILS.

Counter-Reformation The revival and reform of the Roman Catholic Church as a reaction to the REFORMATION. Its reforms included those of the Council of Trent (CE 1562–63).

Covenant A bargain or agreement. In JUDAISM the chief reference is to that made with MOSES at SINAI: GOD, having liberated his people from Egypt, promises them the land of ISRAEL and his blessing and protection as long as they keep the TORAH. This confirms the earlier covenants with ABRAHAM and with Noah. The term is also used of God's special relationship with the house of DAVID. With the defeat of the Kingdom of Judah in 586 BCE, Jeremiah's prophecy of a new covenant written on the people's hearts came into its own. In the Christian NEW TESTAMENT the sacrificial death of JESUS OF NAZARETH marks the sealing of a new covenant between God and the new Israel, the Christian CHURCH, which completes and fulfils the old covenant.

Cranmer, Thomas (CE 1489–1556) Archbishop of Canterbury under Henry VIII who helped overthrow papal authority in England and created a new order of English worship in his Prayer Books of 1549 and 1552.

Creation The act of GOD by which the universe came into being. Hence also refers to the universe itself. In JUDAISM, CHRISTIANITY and ISLAM creation is usually thought of as being *ex nihilo*, from out of nothing that existed before. In HINDUISM it is believed that the universe has been outpoured from God and will contract into him at the end of the age.

Creation myth A story that explains the divine origins of a particular people, a place or the whole world. In some INDIGENOUS RELIGIONS and ancient religions it is ritually re-enacted at the beginning of each year.

Creation Spirituality Initiated in 1977 by the Dominican theologian Matthew Fox (b. 1940), it is highly critical of traditional Christianity, which is described as the 'Fall-Redemption' tradition, emphasizing original sin and the fundamental badness of humanity and the created order. Such theologies are, it is claimed, anti-emotional, anti-sensual, hierarchical, patriarchal, and destructively dualistic. Creation spirituality, instead of emphasizing original sin, speaks of 'original blessing', and seeks to provide a life-affirming celebration of humanity and creation. Drawing liberally on the mystical traditions (particularly Christian mysticism), New Age thought, indigenous spiritualities and contemporary eco-spiritualities, it speaks to many Westerners who are disillusioned with mainstream Christianity.

Creed Formal statement of religious belief. In CHRISTIANITY, the two creeds used most commonly today are the Apostles' Creed and the Nicene Creed.

Crusades The military expeditions undertaken by Christian armies from Europe from the eleventh to the fourteenth centuries intended to liberate the Holy Land from ISLAM.

Cybele Phrygian MOTHER GODDESS whose ecstatic rites included a bath in the blood of a sacrificial bull. Her consort was the youthful Attis. Her cult spread to Greece in the fifth century BCE and to Rome in 204 BCE, though here it was virtually banned until the late first century CE because of the scandal caused by her oriental eunuch priests.

Cynic Follower of the eccentric Greek philosopher Diogenes (about 400–325 BCE) who taught that people should seek the most natural and easy way of life, ignoring conventions. He was nicknamed *Kyon* ('dog') and the name stuck to the beggar philosophers who followed him. Some historians believe that JESUS OF NAZARETH may have been influenced by the radical lifestyle and pithy wisdom of the cynics.

D

Dalai Lama Former religious and secular leader of Tibet, widely held to be the reincarnation of AVALOKITESHVARA. Since the Chinese takeover of Tibet the Dalai Lama has lived in India. He is still regarded as the spiritual leader of Tibetan Buddhists. (See also LAMA.)

Daruma Japanese name for BODHIDHARMA. It is also the name of a doll used by Japanese children which resembles Daruma.

Dasara A festival usually celebrated in October. Different parts of India celebrate the festival in different ways and focus on different deities. The celebrations vary from a day to nine days to a month. Those who celebrate it as 'Dussehra' worship the goddess Durga or celebrate Rama's victory over Rawana.

Dastur Parsi priest who is responsible for the rituals of the FIRE TEMPLES and wears a white turban. The priesthood is hereditary. (See PARSIS.)

David King of the Israelite tribes around 1000–962 BCE who united them and extended their territory. He stormed the city of the Jebusites and made it his capital, JERUSALEM. He was a musician and poet, to whom a number of psalms in the BIBLE are ascribed. The belief is common to JUDAISM and CHRISTIANITY that the MESSIAH would be a descendant of David.

Deacon Junior minister in the Christian CHURCH. The word means 'servant' and the deacon's functions originally included the distribution of alms to the poor.

Dead Sea Scrolls Sacred writings of a breakaway Jewish sect which were discovered in 1947 at Qumran on the western shore of the Dead Sea. The several scrolls and fragments include much of the HEBREW BIBLE as well as hymns, treatises and rules for the life of the sect. Many scholars identify the sect with the ESSENES.

Death of God theology Radical American movement of the 1960s seeking to reconstruct Christianity on the basis of atheism. Its two tenets were that God had 'died' in human experience but that it was still possible to

be a follower of JESUS OF NAZARETH. Later developments of Death of God theology are NON-REALISM and the attempt to blend Christian teaching with Buddhist rejection of a personal God.

Deists Followers of a movement for natural religion which flourished in seventeenth-century England. They rejected the idea of revelation and held that the Creator did not interfere in the workings of the universe.

Delphic Oracle Most authoritative source of prophecy and political advice in Ancient Greece. Run by the priests of APOLLO, its prophet was a woman, the Pythia ('pythoness'), who uttered her oracles in a state of induced frenzy. The message was then interpreted by the priests and delivered in a cryptic, often ambiguous, form.

Demeter Greek goddess of fertility and growth. Worshipped throughout the Greek world, she was identified with the Egyptian ISIS, the Phrygian CYBELE, and the Roman CERES as the MOTHER GODDESS. Her MYTH concerns the abduction of her daughter Persephone by HADES; yearly, in autumn, the earth becomes barren while she searches for her child. She initiated her own MYSTERY RELIGION – the ELEUSINIAN MYSTERIES – at Eleusis near Athens.

Demiurge Term used in GNOSTICISM to describe the creator god, seen as willful, passionate and ignorant. His creation is a cosmic disaster which traps in material existence the divine sparks that emanate from the true God.

Demonology Teaching about the demonic and all forms of personified evil.

Dervish Islamic MYSTIC belonging to one of the orders which induce ecstasy by movement, dance and the recitation of the names of God.

Devadatta Cousin of the BUDDHA, and one of his earliest disciples. In some texts he is in conflict with the Buddha and leads a schismatic movement. He was condemned to a period in hell for his misdeeds.

Devil Term generally used to describe an evil spirit. In CHRISTIANITY the devil (SATAN) is the personification of evil who is permitted to tempt and accuse human beings within the overall providence of God.

Dhamma The teaching of the BUDDHA – his analysis of existence expressed in the FOUR NOBLE TRUTHS and his cure as outlined in the NOBLE EIGHTFOLD PATH. *Dhamma* is sometimes represented as an eight-spoked wheel. (See also DHARMA.)

Dhammapada One of the best-known texts of the PALI CANON expounding the essence of THERAVADA Buddhist teachings. It encourages Buddhist disciples to achieve their own salvation, relying on no external saviour or authority.

Dharma In HINDUISM, cosmic order, the law of existence, right conduct. Also, in BUDDHISM, the teaching of the BUDDHA (see DHAMMA).

Diana Italian goddess who was associated with wooded places, women, childbirth and the moon. She became identified with the Greek ARTEMIS. The centre of her cult was a grove on the shore of the volcanic Lake Nemi.

Diaspora (1) The geographical spread of a people who share a common culture. (2) The term was originally used to describe the spread of the Jewish nation. The dispersion from the land of ISRAEL. The dispersion of the JEWS came about partly as a result of war and exile, partly as a result of travel and trade.

Dietary laws Rules about food and drink that are characteristic of a particular religion. Thus JUDAISM prohibits the simultaneous preparation or eating of milk and meat products, bans totally the eating of pork and shellfish and regulates the ritual slaughter of other animals for meat. ISLAM proscribes pork and alcohol. JAINISM bans all meat products.

Digambaras ('Sky-clad') Members of a major sect of JAINS who followed MAHAVIRA in believing in the virtue of total nudity. Numerous in the warm south of India, they tend to wear robes in public.

Dionysus Greek god of wine and of liberation, a dying and rising god identified with OSIRIS. His cult probably came from Thrace or Phrygia. He is associated with vegetation and fertility and appears surrounded by satyrs, nature spirits promoting fertility. He is followed by a host of maenads, frenzied women leading orgiastic rites. Dionysus punishes unbelief with terrible vengeance. In the late Hellenistic world (see HELLENISM) the cult of Dionysus became an important MYSTERY RELIGION.

Disciple Follower of a religious leader or teaching. In CHRISTIANITY it refers to the original followers of Jesus in the NEW TESTAMENT and is widened to include all Christian 'followers' throughout history.

Divination The art of the DIVINER.

Divine kingship The belief that kings and queens are descended from the gods and rule with their authority. The ritual purity of the divine king guarantees the community's welfare. Notions of divine kingship are found in some INDIGENOUS RELIGIONS. (See also PHARAOH; INCA.)

Diviner One who tells the future either by reading the signs of nature in the weather, stars or the flight of birds, or by the manipulation of objects such as sticks, stones, bones or playing cards. An important figure in ancient Roman religion, Chinese religion and many INDIGENOUS RELIGIONS (see I CHING; TAROT CARDS). Diviners may also share the powers of a MEDIUM or SHAMAN.

Divinities Name given to minor gods or spirits in INDIGENOUS RELIGIONS who rule over an area of the world or some human activity – e.g. storms, war, farming, marriage. Divinities are usually worshipped formally with special RITUALS and festivals.

Diwali Festival of light celebrated by HINDUS, JAINS and SIKHS. For Hindus it marks the return of RAMA from exile and his reunion with SITA as told in the MAHABHARATA. For Jains it is the beginning of a new ritual and commercial year and celebrates Mahavira's transcendence to MOKSHA and the enlightenment of his disciple Gautama. For Sikhs it is a commemoration of the release from prison of the sixth GURU and his return to the city of Amritsar.

Doctrine A religious teaching or belief

which is taught and upheld within a particular religious community.

Dravidian Word describing the pre-Aryan civilization based in the Indus valley. It was overturned by Aryan invaders around 2000 BCE. Today Dravidian peoples inhabit southern India.

Dreams One of the chief sources of revelation to the individual in INDIGENOUS RELIGIONS. Dreams may contain warnings or commands or promises of blessing.

Dreamtime In Australian INDIGENOUS RELIGION, the mythical period in which, according to Aboriginal tradition, ancestral beings moved across the face of the earth forming its physical features. The Dreamtime is recreated in art, painting, chanting, dancing and cult ceremonies.

Druidry (1) The priestly caste of Celtic society. It is likely that they presided at sacrifices, made and enforced legal decisions and passed on the traditions of learning, magic, healing and ritual. (2) Since the late-18th century, in Wales and Cornwall, self-identified Druids, many of whom were Christian, established national philanthropic and cultural events. Such cultural events, designed to encourage national pride, are still enormously important, particularly in Wales. (3) In the 20th century there was a revival of specifically Pagan Druidry. It is now a growing and important Pagan tradition, including numerous groups and 'orders'. Worship focuses on ancient pre-Christian sites, such as Stonehenge.

Dualism (1) The belief that reality has a fundamentally twofold nature. Opposed to MONISM it describes the belief that there is a radical distinction between God and the created world. (2) The belief that there are two fundamentally opposed principles: one of good, the other of evil. This moral dualism is the basis of ZOROASTRIANISM. (3) The belief that the mind and the body are fundamentally different yet act in parallel.

Dukkha Buddhist term for unsatisfactoriness or suffering. Birth, illness, decay, death and REBIRTH are symptoms of a restless and continuous 'coming-to-be' which marks all existence as *dukkha*.

Durga ('The inaccessible') In HINDU tradition, the consort of SHIVA in one of her terrifying forms.

E

Easter The festival of the RESURRECTION of CHRIST, the greatest and oldest festival of the Christian CHURCH (1). Its date is fixed according to the paschal full moon and varies from year to year.

Eastern Orthodox Churches Family of self-governing churches looking to the Ecumenical PATRIARCH, the Patriarch of Constantinople, as a symbol of leadership. (See also GREAT SCHISM.)

Ecclesiology Teaching about the church.

Eco-feminism A movement which seeks spiritual enlightenment through a synthesis of feminism with concern for the environment.

Ecumenical councils Assemblies of Christian BISHOPS whose decisions were considered binding throughout the Christian church. These ended with the GREAT SCHISM though the Roman Catholic Church has continued to assemble councils into the twentieth century. The most important of the Ecumenical Councils were held at Nicaea (CE 325, condemning ARIANISM), Constantinople (CE 381), Ephesus (CE 431, condemning NESTORIANISM) and Chalcedon (CE 451, concerning the INCARNATION of CHRIST).

Ecumenical movement Movement for the recovery of unity among the Christian Churches. It dates from the Edinburgh 'World Missionary Conference' of 1910 and today focuses in the WORLD COUNCIL OF CHURCHES.

Eddy, Mary Baker (CE 1821–1910) American spiritual teacher and founder of CHRISTIAN SCIENCE. She believed that orthodox CHRISTIANITY had repressed CHRIST's teaching and practice of spiritual healing and that healing was not miraculous but a natural expression of the divine will. She founded the First Church of Christ Scientist in Boston in 1879; it remains the mother church of Christian Science. She wrote the authoritative work of the movement: *Science and Health* (with *Key to the Scriptures*) and founded the newspaper the *Christian Science Monitor*.

El Great god and 'creator of creation' among the Canaanite and Phoenician peoples.

Elder An officer of the church in the PRESBYTERIAN and INDEPENDENT CHURCHES. Teaching elders also deal with pastoral care; ruling elders help in church government and administration.

Election God's choice of ISRAEL to be his people as expressed in the COVENANT at Mount SINAI and manifested in the gift of the land of Israel. In JUDAISM the election of the JEWS carries responsibility. They are to bear witness to the reality of God in the world by keeping the TORAH. In Christian theology, the concept is widened to include GENTILE converts to CHRISTIANITY who spiritually inherit the promises made to the PATRIARCHS and to MOSES.

Eleusinian Mysteries MYSTERY RELIGION of DEMETER, centred at Eleusis near Athens. The Greater Mysteries were held at the time of the autumn sowing and went on for nine days. The myth of Demeter was probably re-enacted and the climax may have been a revelation of a reaped ear of corn. But only initiates were admitted and the exact nature of the mysteries was kept a secret.

Eliezer, Israel ben See BAAL SHEM TOV.

Elohim Plural form of the Canaanite word for a divinity (see DIVINITIES), usually translated 'God' and used as a name of God by the HEBREWS (see also EL). It is sometimes treated as a common-noun plural, 'gods' or 'angels'. (See also ANGELS.)

Elysium Paradise of Greek religion. It was held to be either far away across the sea, or a section of the underworld ruled not by HADES, but by Kronos, one of the ancient Titan race.

Emperor, Japanese Since the reign of the legendary JIMMU TENNO the emperors of Japan claimed divine descent from

Amaterasu O Mikami. SHINTO thus became an expression of imperial power and nationalism. The divinity of the emperor was formally repudiated in 1945.

Enki The water god of ancient Sumerian religion.

Enlightenment (1) Full spiritual awakening. (2) In BUDDHISM, the realization of the truth of all existence which was achieved by the BUDDHA in his meditation at Bodh Gaya. Enlightenment or final enlightenment also refers to the passing into NIRVANA of anyone who follows the Buddha's way and attains release from the cycle of birth and REBIRTH. (See also BODHI.) (3) Eighteenth-century European movement of philosophy and science which stressed the supremacy of reason over revelation and tradition.

Enlil The wind god in ancient Sumerian belief. He persuaded the other gods to plan the destruction of humankind in a great flood. He rewarded the flood's only survivor with the gift of immortality.

En Sof/Ein Sof Name for God used in Jewish MYSTICISM, in particular in the KABBALAH, meaning the endless, the absolute infinite whose essence is unrevealed and unknowable.

Epic of Gilgamesh Babylonian poem dating from the seventh century BCE which includes much earlier material. It tells the story of Gilgamesh's vain quest for the secret of immortality and includes the BABYLONIAN FLOOD STORY.

Epicureanism Philosophical school founded by Epicurus (341–270 BCE) and holding an atomic theory of the universe. It teaches that the gods are irrelevant to human life, the chief end of which is happiness. Fulfilment comes from the prudent and restrained cultivation of pleasure.

Epistle (1) Letter in the NEW TESTAMENT to a Christian community or individual usually from one of the APOSTLES. (2) Letter on doctrine or practice addressed to a Christian community in post-apostolic times.

Eros Greek god of love, Cupid to the Romans, the son of APHRODITE. In Greek literature his cruelty to his victims is emphasized, also his omnipotence. In the Christian era 'cupids' became angelic beings symbolizing divine benevolence and compassion.

Eschatology Teaching about the 'last things'. In Christianity this includes discussion of the end of the present world order, the SECOND COMING/PAROUSIA, the final judgment, PURGATORY, HEAVEN, and HELL.

Esoteric Word meaning 'inner', suggesting something (e.g. a knowledge or a teaching) that is available only for the specially initiated and secret from outsiders and perhaps even from ordinary believers.

Essenes Jewish group which withdrew to live a monastic life in the Dead Sea area during the Roman period. They were celibates and stressed the importance of ASCETICISM. They also performed exorcisms and rites of spiritual healing and adopted OCCULT practices. Many scholars believe that the DEAD SEA SCROLLS were the scriptures of an Essene community.

Eucharist ('Thanksgiving') The central act of Christian worship instituted by CHRIST on the night before his death. It involves sharing bread and wine which are sacramentally associated with the body and blood of Christ. (See SACRAMENT.)

Evangelicals CHRISTIANS of all denominations who emphasize the centrality of the BIBLE, justification by faith and the need for personal conversion. In Germany and Switzerland, the term refers to members of the Lutheran as opposed to the Calvinist churches.

Evangelism The preaching of the Christian GOSPEL to the unconverted.

Exile (1) The period between 597 BCE and around 538 BCE when leading Jews from the former Jewish kingdoms were held in captivity in Babylon. (2) The condition of Jewish life in the DIASPORA, away from the land of ISRAEL.

Exodus The flight of the people of ISRAEL from Egypt under the leadership of MOSES.

Exorcism Removal of sin or evil, particularly an evil spirit in possession of someone, by prayer or ritual action.

Ezra Scribe of the Babylonian EXILE who was sent with a royal warrant from the Persian king to reform religion in JERUSALEM. Traditionally he arrived in 458 BCE and embarked on a programme to purify the Jewish faith and install the TORAH as the central authority in Jewish life.

F

Faith Attitude of belief, in trust and commitment to a divine being or a religious teaching. It can also refer to the beliefs of a religion, 'the faith', which is passed on from teachers to believers.

Fall of Jerusalem The capture of JERUSALEM and the final destruction of the TEMPLE OF JERUSALEM by the Roman general Titus in CE 70 at the end of a revolt which broke out in CE 66.

Family Federation for World Peace and Unification The new name for the Holy Spirit Association for the Unification of World Christianity, commonly known as The Unification Church or, after the name of the founder, the Moonies. It was founded in Seoul, Korea, in 1954 by Sun Myung MOON. Central to Unificationism is an emphasis on the important of the family unit within society.

Fasting Total or partial abstinence from food, undertaken as a religious discipline. In INDIGENOUS RELIGIONS it is often a preparation for a ceremony of INITIATION. In JUDAISM and CHRISTIANITY it is a sign of mourning for SIN. It is also more generally used as a means of gaining clarity of vision and mystical insight.

Fatwa In Islam, an authoritative declaration, or sentence, as of death.

Fellowship The common life of Christians marked by unity and mutual love, a creation of the HOLY SPIRIT.

Feminist theology A movement developed first in the USA which uses the experience of being female in a male-dominated society as a basis for critical reflection on Christian thought, tradition and practice.

Feng Shui Literally translated as 'wind' and 'water', it is the Chinese art of living in harmony with one's environment in order to ensure happiness and prosperity. It emerged during the Han dynasty (206 BCE–220 CE) and, by the twelfth century, had been developing into the quasi-science of geomancy. Based on the notion that there are five basic elements (earth, fire, metal, water, wood) and two fundamental forces (YIN and YANG), it studies the interaction between these in order to discover the most auspicious and powerful places. Hence, for example, feng shui is used to make wise decisions about the location of buildings, furniture, and gardens, all of which are believed to contribute to human well-being.

Fire sermon One of the BUDDHA's most famous sermons traditionally preached at Gaya to 1,000 fire-worshipping ascetics, in which he explained that all that exists is burning with lust, anger and ignorance.

Fire temples Parsi temples where the sacred fire of AHURA MAZDA is kept continually burning. The fire is kept in a censer on a stone slab hanging under the central dome of the temple. There are no images: the fire symbolizes the purity and goodness of AHURA MAZDA. (See DASTUR; PARSIS.)

Five pillars of Islam Five duties enjoined on every MUSLIM as an appropriate response to God. They are: SALAH (ritual prayer); ZAKAH (almsgiving); SAWM (fasting in the month of RAMADAN); HAJJ (pilgrimage to MECCA); and JIHAD (crusade).

Five precepts Ethical restraints for Buddhists, who are to refrain from: taking life; stealing; wrong sexual relations; wrong use of speech; drugs and intoxicants.

Five relationships The codification and application of CONFUCIUS's teaching to the five basic relationships of human life. These are father and son; older brother and younger brother; husband and wife; elder and younger; ruler and subject. The inferior should show proper deference, the superior proper benevolence. The stress is on reciprocity and Confucius believed that such correct behaviour would weld society together in 'the way of heaven'.

Four noble truths The BUDDHA's analysis of the problem of existence – a four-stage summary of his teaching: (1) all that exists is unsatisfactory; (2) the cause of unsatisfactoriness (DUKKHA) is craving (TANHA); (3) unsatisfactoriness ends when craving ends; (4) craving can be ended by practising the NOBLE EIGHTFOLD PATH.

Four rightly guided caliphs Orthodox ISLAM accepts ABU BAKR, 'UMAR, 'UTHMAN and 'ALI as legitimate successors to MUHAMMAD.

Four stages of life HINDU outline of a man's ideal spiritual life. There are four stages: Student, the Hindu boy learns the scriptures in the house of his GURU and lives a life of chastity; Householder, he marries, has children and earns his living; Forest dweller, when his family are grown up he gradually begins to withdraw from everyday life; Sannyasi (SANSKRIT: 'one who renounces'), he cuts all earthly ties and seeks liberation, often as a wandering beggar.

Francis of Assisi (CE 1182–1226) Founder of the Franciscan order who lived by a simple rule of life, rejecting possessions, ministering to the sick and having a special concern for nature.

Freemasonry Originally a religious brotherhood of English masons founded in the twelfth century. In the sixteenth century it spread to the European mainland where in Roman Catholic countries it became associated with Deism (see DEISTS). In the UK and USA today it is a semi-secret society which retains certain mystical symbols and ceremonies. Members are committed to a belief in GOD as 'the great architect of the universe', symbolized by an eye.

Frey Norse god of beauty with power over rain and sunshine and the fertility of the earth. His name means 'lord'.

Freyja Norse goddess and sister of FREY; her name means 'lady'. She is patroness of love and sorcery and drives a chariot pulled by cats. She possesses half the corpses of those who are slain in battle, the other half going to ODIN.

Friends, Society of See QUAKERS.

Frigg Chief of the Norse goddesses and wife of ODIN; the goddess of love and fertility. She knows the fates of men but cannot avert destiny.

Fundamentalism The doctrine that the BIBLE is verbally inspired and therefore inerrant and infallible on all matters of doctrine and history; from *The Fundamentals*, published in 1909.

G

Gabriel (1) An archangel named in both the Old and New Testaments. In the Gospel of Luke he foretells the births of John the Baptist and Jesus. (2) In ISLAM Gabriel (Jibril) is associated with the 'faithful spirit' by whom the QUR'AN was revealed to MUHAMMAD. Gabriel also transported Muhammad from MECCA to JERUSALEM and from there to the throne of God in the NIGHT JOURNEY.

Gaia Greek name for MOTHER GODDESS, now revived by the hypothesis originated by J.E. Lovelock according to which all living beings on earth are part of a single living organism.

Gandhi (CE 1869–1948) Leader of the Indian independence movement and the greatest spiritual and political figure of modern India. Disowning violence, he advocated political change through non-violent resistance. After independence he tried to reconcile the Hindu and Muslim communities. He also campaigned against the social exclusion of UNTOUCHABLES. He was assassinated by a Hindu fanatic.

Ganesha Elephant-headed god much loved in popular HINDUISM, especially in western India. He is the god of good beginnings and is a symbol for luck and wealth in business and daily life.

Ganges The holy river of India whose waters are sacred for all HINDUS. It is thought to flow from the toe of VISHNU. Pilgrims wash away evil in its waters and the ashes of the dead are thrown into it.

Gautama/Gotama Family name of the BUDDHA. Legend depicts him as a great prince born into a royal household. Modern scholars think that his father was probably the head of an aristocratic family living in the town of Kapilavastu.

Gemara Part of the Jewish TALMUD that takes the form of a series of commentaries on the MISHNAH.

Genius (1) In occult religion, a guardian spirit or familiar. (2) In Roman religion, the spirit of a man, giving rise to his maleness. A LIBATION was poured to the genius of the reigning emperor at every banquet.

Gentile Person who is not a JEW.

Ghat ('Holy place') In HINDU use, a word which can refer to a range of hills, a ritual bathing place or a cremation ground.

Ghost dance A dance which sprang out of a religious movement of the 1870s among Native Americans. It was believed that the dance would lead to the resurrection of all dead Native Americans on an earth free of disease and death. The movement was destroyed at the Battle of Wounded Knee in 1890. (See also WOVOKA.)

Glossolalia Expression in unknown tongues by people in a heightened spiritual or emotional state. In the Christian CHURCH (1) it is used to express WORSHIP to GOD and prophetic messages, in other religions to express a state of religious ecstasy.

Gnosticism Movement of ESOTERIC teachings rivalling, borrowing from and contradicting early CHRISTIANITY. Gnostic sects were based on MYTHS which described the creation of the world by a deluded DEMIURGE and taught a way of salvation through *gnosis*, 'knowledge' of one's true divine self. Gnostics contrasted their 'knowledge' with faith, which they considered inferior.

Gobind Singh, Guru (CE 1666–1708) The tenth GURU of the Sikh community. He militarized the Sikhs, requiring them to adopt a distinctive name and dress. He also shifted the focus of authority from the Gurus to the sacred scripture, the ADI GRANTH.

God (1) The creator and sustainer of the universe; the absolute being on whom all that is depends. (2) A being with divine power and attributes; a deity, a major DIVINITY.

Goddess (1) Female form of god. (2) The supreme being conceived as female as in some modern Pagan religious movements. Worshippers of the Goddess claim that they are continuing the ancient religion of the MOTHER GODDESS who was a personification of nature.

Good Friday The Friday before EASTER, in CHRISTIANITY, kept by the CHURCH (1) as a holy day, sometimes including FASTING, penance and witness, in memory of the crucifixion of Jesus CHRIST.

Gospel (1) One of the four accounts of the 'good news' about Jesus in the NEW TESTAMENT. (2) The Christian message, proclamation of 'good news', referring especially to Jesus' teaching about the KINGDOM OF GOD and to the preaching of the CHURCH about Jesus. (3) The ritual reading of a set portion from the Gospels (1) in the context of the EUCHARIST. (4) A partial account of the life and teaching of Jesus,

usually ascribed to a New Testament figure but rejected by the Church as heretical.

Gospel of Thomas Syriac text of a collection of sayings of Jesus discovered at Nag-Hammadi in Egypt in 1947. It has many parallels with the sayings of Jesus in Matthew and Luke, and some scholars consider it to be as authentic as the canonical Gospels. Its teaching, though, is GNOSTIC.

Gotama See GAUTAMA.

Grace (1) Unmerited favour, especially in the divine salvation of the unworthy. An essential concept in CHRISTIANITY, where it is contrasted with merit, Christians believe that nobody receives SALVATION because they deserve it but only by God's grace. (2) A prayer or blessing before a meal.

Great schism The SCHISM declared in CE 1054 between the Eastern and Western churches resulting from disagreements over the POPE's claim to supremacy, and the doctrine of the HOLY SPIRIT.

Gregory of Nyssa (c. CE 330–95) Christian theologian who helped develop the doctrine of the TRINITY and expounded the BIBLE as a spiritual path leading to the perfect contemplation of God.

Ground of Being Phrase used by German-US theologian Paul Tillich (CE 1886–1965) to describe GOD. It stresses the immanence of God as depth or ground rather than his transcendence as creator.

Gurdjieff, George Ivanovich (CE 1873–1949) Spiritual teacher whose book *Meetings with Remarkable Men* relates his search for wisdom. He invented a system of non-identification with the ego which he believed led to the realization of man's true essence. He was influenced by SUFISM. In 1922 he founded an Institute for the Harmonious Development of Man which attracted a number of Western intellectuals.

Gurdwara SIKH temple and meeting place, consisting of a worship area which houses the ADI GRANTH, and a cooking and eating area for the symbolic meal which ends Sikh worship.

Guru ('Teacher') A spiritual teacher or guide who, in Indian religion, awakens a disciple to a realization of his or her own divine nature. In SIKH religion it refers to the ten teachers, from Guru NANAK to Guru GOBINDH SINGH, who ruled the community.

H

Hades (1) Greek god of the dead and ruler of the UNDERWORLD. He was connected with growth and vegetation and the production of wealth. Because it was considered unlucky to speak his name, he is often referred to as Pluto (the 'rich'). (2) Greek name for the underworld, the abode of the dead. In the Septuagint version of the HEBREW BIBLE it translates *sheol*. In Christian usage it is sometimes used for the interim abode of the departed as distinguished from Hell, the abode of the damned.

Hadith Traditions of MUHAMMAD's words and actions, many of which complement or

elucidate the directions of the QUR'AN. There are many spurious Hadith; one of the major tasks of MUSLIM lawyers has been to categorize Hadith into likely degrees of authenticity.

Haggadah A moral or devotional teaching derived from the midrashic exposition of a HEBREW text (see MIDRASH). There are many of them in the TALMUD where they take the form of narrative tales, poems and metaphysical speculations.

Hajj Pilgrimage to MECCA which is one of the FIVE PILLARS OF ISLAM and which MUSLIMS are obliged to make at least once in a lifetime. *Hajj* must be performed in Dhu al-Hijjah (the last month of the Hijrah calendar). Umra (*Hajj* in miniature) can be performed at any time. On arrival at Mecca, pilgrims make a circuit of the KA'BA and kiss the BLACK STONE.

Halakhah (From HEBREW verb 'to walk') A legal teaching based on the midrashic exposition of a Hebrew text (see MIDRASH).

Hamartiology Teaching about sin.

Hammurabi (Eighteenth century BCE) Mesopotamian ruler who produced a law code laying down punishments for various transgressions and enunciating principles for the conduct of business and social life. The breaking of his code incurred the enmity of the Babylonian gods.

Hanukkah ('Dedication') Eight-day Jewish festival marked by the lighting of ritual candles which celebrates the rededication of the TEMPLE OF JERUSALEM by JUDAS MACCABEUS in 164 BCE.

Hanuman Monkey-god of popular HINDUISM. In the RAMAYANA he led a monkey army against a host of demons. He can fly and cover huge distances at great speed.

Hara-Kiri Japanese expression meaning 'belly cutting' which is used for the Japanese traditional practice of ritual suicide among the warrior classes.

Hare Krishna Mantra used by devotees of KRISHNA to induce ecstatic union with the divine. The most familiar version is a two-line chant, invoking both Krishna and RAMA. (See also INTERNATIONAL SOCIETY FOR KRISHNA CONSCIOUSNESS.)

Hasidim ('The pious') (1) The group of Jewish quietist ascetics who were the forerunners of the PHARISEES. (2) A group of medieval MYSTICS who were particularly important for the development of Judaism in Germany. (3) Followers of BAAL SHEM TOV, who taught a new kind of HASIDISM in the eighteenth century CE.

Hasidism Jewish mystical movement with roots in the KABBALAH which arose in the eighteenth century in response to the teachings of BAAL SHEM TOV after a period of persecution by the Cossacks. It stressed the presence of God in everyday life and the value of prayer. Chanting and dancing were used as aids to ecstatic communion with God. The movement was popular and had a wide appeal among ordinary JEWS.

Heathenism Also referred to as 'The Northern Tradition' or 'Asatru' ('faith in the deities'), Heathenism is a form of contemporary Paganism which focuses on Anglo-Saxon, Norse and Germanic traditions. Runes are used as powerful magical and meditative symbols. Popular Heathen teachings include the belief that this world, MIDGARD/ Middle Earth, is one of nine linked by the 'World Tree', YGGDRASIL. There are two groups of deities, the AESIR and the VANIR. A popular form of Heathenism is Odinism, the spirituality of which focuses on the Norse god ODIN.

Heaven (1) The realm of God or of the gods. (2) In CHRISTIANITY the dwelling place of God and the ultimate home of the saved, regarded both as a place and a state.

Hebrew (1) A member of the Semitic tribes which emerged as the people of ISRAEL. (2) The (Semitic) language of the ancient people of Israel, of the HEBREW BIBLE and of the modern state of Israel.

Hebrew Bible The Jewish SCRIPTURES which comprise the Books of the Law (see TORAH), the PROPHETS and the WRITINGS. According to tradition the canon was fixed at the Synod of Jabneh about CE 100.

Heimdall White god and watcher of the gods in Norse religion.

Hecate An earth goddess who probably originated in Asia Minor. Connected with magic and death, she was sometimes known as the ARTEMIS of the cross-roads. She is shown with three faces, carrying torches and followed by baying hounds. A popular deity in contemporary Paganism.

Hell Realm where the wicked go after death. Religious teachings differ over whether its punishment is reformatory or eternal. In CHRISTIANITY, it is total separation from God. Most religions describe a place or a condition for the wicked following death. ZOROASTRIANISM, JUDAISM and ISLAM all describe such a state following divine judgment after death. Even religions which have a doctrine of reincarnation, such as Buddhism and Hinduism include teachings about hells (although the belief in reincarnation makes them quite different from the teachings of Christianity and Islam).

Hellenism The adoption of the Greek language, culture, philosophy and ideas, particularly around the Mediterranean, from the time of Alexander the Great (356–323 BCE). It was the dominant cultural influence during the rise of CHRISTIANITY.

Hera Greek goddess, the wife of ZEUS and Queen of heaven. She was the protectress of women and marriage and is presented as a model of chastity. She was worshipped throughout the Greek world. Her special bird was a peacock, a symbol of pride. Her Roman counterpart was JUNO.

Heresy The denial of a defined doctrine of the Christian faith. The word means 'chosen thing' and refers to the heretic's preference for an individual opinion over the consensus of the CHURCH (1).

Hermes Greek messenger god and son of Zeus, protector of travellers, bringer of luck and god of thieves and merchants. He is usually portrayed as a young man in winged hat and sandals, carrying a staff twined with snakes.

Hermeticism Mystical movement based on a collection of Egyptian scriptures from the first to third centuries CE. The writings drew on Greek and Eastern ideas, and were ascribed to Hermes Trismegistus (thrice-great HERMES), who is identified with the god THOTH.

Herzl, Theodor (CE 1860–1904) Leader of the Zionist movement (see ZIONISM). He argued that a national homeland for the JEWS was a necessity. He travelled widely raising support from Christian governments for the Zionist cause. He convened the first World Zionist Congress in 1897 which formulated a political programme for the return to Palestine.

Hesiod Greek poet, probably of the eighth century BCE, whose THEOGONY sought to draw together the ancestries of the Greek gods, understanding creation in terms of procreation.

High Priest Traditional head of the Jewish priesthood and organizer of TEMPLE worship. His function was to enter the Holy of Holies and offer sacrifice on the DAY OF ATONEMENT. It was a key political appointment under the Seleucids and Romans. Talmudic tradition criticizes the corruption of some who held the office, which ceased at the destruction of the Temple in CE 70.

Hijrah ('Going forth') The migration of MUHAMMAD, preceded by some of his followers, from MECCA to MEDINA in CE 622). This was the decisive event for the development of ISLAM for it was in Medina that Muhammad established himself as a religious and political leader and organized his followers as an Islamic community. The MUSLIM calendar counts years 'after Hijrah'.

Hillel Pharisaic Jewish teacher of the first century CE. He was known for his humane and lenient interpretations of the TORAH, in contrast to his chief opponent, the stern and rigorous Shammai.

Hinayana ('Small vehicle') Buddhist term used to indicate the doctrine of salvation for oneself alone in contrast to MAHAYANA. Most Buddhists of South-East Asia prefer the term THERAVADA to describe this school of BUDDHISM.

Hindu Word used by Arabs to describe people living beyond the Indus Valley. Today it refers generally to people practising Indian religion who are neither Muslim, Sikh, Parsi nor Jain, and also to their religion, Hinduism.

Hinduism A term coined by Europeans for a religious tradition and social system that emerged in India. It has no founder, no set creed, no prophets, and no single institutional structure. It is actually an umbrella term for an enormous range of beliefs and practices, from the worship of local village deities to the thought of a great philosopher such as Shankara. There are, however, some common beliefs which are basic to most strands of Hinduism. There is an emphasis on DHARMA (the right way of living) rather than assent to particular doctrines. Also found throughout Hinduism is the notion of MOKSHA, or release from the eternal cycle of birth, death and rebirth (SAMSARA) to which one is bound by KARMA. Linked to this set of beliefs is the social stratification known as the caste system. Although some Hindus may not believe in God at all, and others articulate an impersonal conception of the Absolute, and others still others worship numerous deities (some of which are confined to particular localities), very common throughout Hinduism are three chief deities, BRAHMA, VISHNU, and SHIVA, who together form a triad known as the *Trimurti*. (See also BHAGAVAD GITA; VEDANTA; VEDAS; UPANISHADS.)

Hoa Hao Offshoot of the Vietnamese CAO DAI movement. It is Buddhist-based and has been strongly nationalistic.

Holi HINDU spring festival which celebrates the love of KRISHNA and RADHA. It is marked by boisterous games which are reminders of Krishna's amorous pranks with the cow-girls as told in the MAHABHARATA.

Holiness The sacred power, strangeness and otherness of the divine. In the BIBLE and the QUR'AN the term has moral implications and refers to God's purity and righteousness as well as to that which invokes awe. In CHRISTIANITY, believers are called to reproduce God's holiness in their own lives with the help of the HOLY SPIRIT.

Holocaust (From the Latin BIBLE's word for 'whole burnt offering') The name given to Hitler's extermination of 6 million Jews in the Nazi death camps in Europe 1941–45. Mass destruction was envisaged as the 'final solution' to the 'problem' of the Jews. The memory of the Holocaust is the key to modern Jewish theology and made the founding of the state of Israel an event of profound significance.

Holy Communion Name widely used by Anglicans and some Protestants for the Christian EUCHARIST.

Holy Spirit The third person of the Christian TRINITY. In the BIBLE the Holy Spirit is the instrument of divine action and is portrayed as fire or wind. In this sense the Spirit is acknowledged in JUDAISM and ISLAM. The divinity of the Holy Spirit was agreed at the Council of Constantinople in CE 381. The Holy Spirit is the source of faith and new life in the believer and the church, giving 'spiritual gifts', guidance and holiness.

Homer Author of the Greek epics the *Iliad* and the *Odyssey*, which date from between the tenth and eighth centuries BCE. According to the historian Herodotus, Homer was the first to detail the characters and functions of the gods of Mount OLYMPOS.

Honen (CE 1133–1212) Japanese teacher of PURE LAND BUDDHISM. He taught that repetition of the word NEMBUTSU is all that is necessary for salvation. He is said to have recited it 60,000 times a day.

Horus Egyptian hawk-headed sky god, associated with the king. The son of ISIS, conceived on the dead OSIRIS, he defeated the evil SETH and assumed the earthly rule Seth had usurped from Osiris.

House churches/New churches Networks of charismatic, non-denominational churches which started in the 1960s. Members claim that they are restoring the conditions of the primitive Church which met for worship in members' houses. See RESTORATION.

Hsün-tzu Chinese Confucian scholar of the third century BCE who blended the philosophies of CONFUCIANISM and TAOISM. He believed in the correct observance of ceremonial which helped to improve evil human nature. He was critical of superstition and reinterpreted popular religious practices in rationalistic terms.

Huaca Any of the multitude of DIVINITIES recognized by the INCAS; also, an Inca holy place, shrine or temple.

Huiracocha See VIRACOCHA.

Huitzilopochtli AZTEC god of war and the sun. His name means 'hummingbird wizard' and he was perpetually at war with darkness and night.

Hui Yuan See PURE LAND BUDDHISM.

Humanism Way of life based on the belief that what is good for human beings is the highest good.

Hus, Jan (CE 1374–1415) Bohemian reformer who, under the influence of WYCLIFFE's writings denounced the worldliness of the clergy. When he was burnt at the stake he was declared a MARTYR and national hero in Prague. His thought influenced the REFORMATION.

Hymn A sacred song sung in the context of communal worship; a PSALM of communal praise. Hymns are particularly important in Christian and Sikh worship and in the gatherings of the Hindu BHAKTI cults (see BHAJANA).

I

Ibn Rushd (CE 1126–98) MUSLIM philosopher, known in the West as Averroes, who was greatly influenced by PLATO and ARISTOTLE. He believed that the Greek heritage was compatible with ISLAM. His synthesis, however, seemed suspicious to the orthodox and he was banished and his books burnt.

I Ching/Book of Changes One of the five classics of Chinese literature which was originally attributed to CONFUCIUS but is now thought to be much earlier. It gives instructions and interpretations for a form of DIVINATION using six sticks which can fall in sixty-four significant configurations.

Icon A likeness of a divine figure or SAINT painted on wood or inlaid in mosaic and used in public or private devotion.

'Id-al-Adha The great festival of the MUSLIM year. It coincides with the offering of the pilgrim sacrifice at Mina near MECCA.

'Id-al-Fitr The MUSLIM feast which ends the fasting month of RAMADAN. Greetings cards are exchanged, presents are given and sugary sweets are eaten.

Ijma' The consensus of opinion of the MUSLIM community. It is an important principle of Islamic law-making.

Ijtihad ('Enterprise') A way for the Islamic community to develop its law to deal with new situations. It is a ruling given by one MUSLIM teacher, rather than by general consensus (see IJMA'). It is controversial whether Ijtihad is always valid or whether the completion of SHARI'A will render it unnecessary.

Imam Meaning 'model' or 'example', the

term refers to three types of leader within Islam. (1) The leader of ritual prayer in the local community. He is also a Quranic scholar and is therefore respected and often fulfils a leadership function within the local community. (2) Used in a more exalted sense, the term refers to leaders of particular Islamic schools of thought. For example, the founders of the schools of Islamic law are referred to as imams. Similarly, it is an honorific title given to great Islamic scholars (e.g. AL-GHAZALI). (3) It has a special significance in the Shi'ite community. The term refers to a unique intercessor with exceptional spiritual authority, knowledge, and charisma. Imams are agents of divine illumination, indispensable for understanding the relevance of divine revelation for the contemporary community.

Immortals Various beings who live in the Realm of Great Purity, according to the teachings of TAOISM. Best known are the 'eight immortals' who are portrayed with a variety of individual characteristics and symbols and feature in Chinese art and drama.

Inanna The MOTHER GODDESS as worshipped in ancient Sumer.

Inca The divine king who ruled over the INCAS.

Incarnation (1) The Christian doctrine that GOD became human in Jesus CHRIST, so possessing both human and divine natures. (2) A term sometimes used for the HINDU doctrine of the AVATAR.

Incas Empire centred on Cuzco in modern Peru from around CE 1100 until the Spanish conquest (1532). From the late fourteenth century the empire expanded to include parts of modern Ecuador, Bolivia, Chile and Argentina. The first INCA, Manco Capac, was created by and given absolute authority by the SUN GOD. (See also HUACA; PACHACAMAC; VIRACOCHA.)

Incense Sweet-smelling smoke used in worship, made by burning certain aromatic substances.

Inclusive language A response to feminism which tries to eradicate the assumption in speech and writing that maleness is more normally human than femaleness. Churches adopting it modify their hymns, liturgy and Bible translations.

Independence, Day of Jewish festival of thanksgiving on the anniversary of the birth of the state of ISRAEL (4). The liturgy includes prayers for the victims of the HOLOCAUST.

Independents/Congregationalists CHRISTIANS who uphold the authority and independence of each local church, claiming this system to be the earliest form of church order.

Index of prohibited books The official list of books which members of the Roman Catholic Church are forbidden to possess or read, first issued in 1557. The *Index* was abolished in 1966.

Indigenous religions The preferred term for religions which are sometimes referred to as 'primal', 'tribal', 'traditional', 'primitive', and 'non-/pre-literate' religions. That said, indigenous religions are often developments

of the traditional religions of tribal and aboriginal cultures. The problem with the earlier terminology was that it suggested simple, undeveloped, non-progressive, and archaic belief systems. Contemporary indigenous religions include NATIVE AMERICAN RELIGION and AUSTRALIAN ABORIGINAL RELIGION.

Indra ARYAN god of war and storm. There are 200 hymns to him in the *Rig Veda* (see VEDAS). He faded from significance in later HINDUISM.

Indulgence The remission by the Church of a period of correction in PURGATORY. The sale of indulgences by unscrupulous 'pardoners' was one of the abuses which led to the REFORMATION.

Initiation Ceremony marking coming of age, or entry into adult membership of a community. It is also used of the secret ceremonies surrounding membership of the MYSTERY RELIGIONS. (See also CONFIRMATION; NAVJOTE; RITES OF PASSAGE; SACRED THREAD CEREMONY.)

Inquisition Papal office for identifying heretics, founded by POPE Gregory IX and staffed by Franciscans and Dominicans. Torture became an approved aid to interrogation in 1252.

Intercession Prayer offered on behalf of others by a believer on earth or by a SAINT in HEAVEN. In CHRISTIANITY, supremely the work of CHRIST, who intercedes for men and women before GOD.

International Society for Krishna Consciousness (ISKCON) Founded in 1965 by A.C. Bhaktivedanta Swami Prabhupada (1896–1977), and popularly known as the Hare Krishna movement, ISKCON is a modern BHAKTI cult which has been successful in Europe and America. Shaven yellow-robed devotees chant the MANTRA '*Hare Krishna*' as a way of reaching ecstatic union with God.

Inti The SUN GOD of the INCAS.

Ishtar Babylonian goddess, mother and wife of TAMMUZ and associated with the fertility rites of death and resurrection. In mythology she is responsible for the great flood which almost destroyed the earth (see BABYLONIAN FLOOD STORY). Worshipped in various forms all over the Ancient Near East, she was known as Astarte to the Phoenicians and as Ashtoreth to the Hebrews.

Isis Great Egyptian goddess of motherhood and fertility. The sister and wife of OSIRIS, she restored him to life after he was murdered by SETH. Sometimes represented as cow-headed, she had a great temple at Philae.

Isis cult MYSTERY RELIGION based on the MYTH of Isis and OSIRIS which became particularly popular in the Roman world from the first century CE. Its sacred drama and liturgy express the experience of salvation from sensuality which is open to initiates through the grace of the goddess.

Islam (Infinitive of the Arabic verb 'to submit') Teachings derived from the QUR'AN, which is the revelation to MUHAMMAD, a religion of submission to the will of God. (See also ALLAH; MECCA; MUSLIM.)

Isma'ilis A group of SHI'A Muslims who accept the legitimacy of Ismail and his son as the sixth and seventh IMAMS (2) (see also MAHDI; TWELVERS).

Israel (1) Name given by GOD to Jacob the patriarch and hence to his descendants, the 'people of Israel'. (2) The land promised by God to Abram (ABRAHAM) in the early traditions of JUDAISM. (3) The Northern Kingdom of Israel which seceded from Solomon's kingdom in 922 BCE and was destroyed by the Assyrians in 722 BCE. (4) The modern state of Israel, founded in Palestine as a Jewish state in CE 1948.

Izanagi The sky god in SHINTO, and the father of Amaterasu. With his consort, Izanami, he created the islands of Japan.

J

Jade Emperor The supreme divinity in TAOISM, who came into prominence about the tenth century CE. He presided over life and death and kept account of human actions.

Jahannam MUSLIM name for HELL which is frequently mentioned in the QUR'AN as a place of scorching fire and black smoke. Sometimes it is personified as a great monster appearing at the Day of Judgment.

Jain ('One who has conquered') A follower of the religion known as JAINISM.

Jainism Religion of India that derives its name from Jina (conqueror). This term (and the related term Tirthankara) is used of a religious teacher who is believed to have attained enlightenment and omniscience. The most recent Jina was MAHAVIRA, who is regarded as the founder of Jainism. Early in its history Jainism separated into two main sects: DIGAMBARA Jainism and SHVETAMBARA Jainism. (See also DIGAMBARAS; JINA, JIVA; MAHAVIRA; PARSVA; SHVETAMBARAS.)

Janus Roman god of beginnings whose name derives from *janua*, 'entrance' or 'gate'. He is portrayed with a two-faced head, facing both ways. In Julius Caesar's reform of the calendar, his month became the first of the year.

Jarovit Slavic war god.

Jehovah See YHWH.

Jehovah's Witnesses Christian sect founded in 1884 by C.T. RUSSELL. It propagates its own version of the BIBLE (The New World Translation), which it regards as infallible, and stresses the imminent return of CHRIST. Members are pacifists and are forbidden to have blood transfusions.

Jerome (about CE 342–420) Translator of the BIBLE into Latin (the 'Vulgate' version). He wrote many commentaries on the text.

Jerusalem Fortified city captured by DAVID in the tenth century BCE which became the capital and principal sanctuary for the people of ISRAEL. It has remained the focus of Jewish religious aspirations and ideals (see TEMPLE OF JERUSALEM). It is a holy city for CHRISTIANS because of its association with the passion, death and RESURRECTION of JESUS OF NAZARETH. For MUSLIMS it is the holiest city after MECCA. The MOSQUE of the Dome of the Rock stands over the site of Muhammad's NIGHT JOURNEY.

Jesus of Nazareth Teacher, prophet and worker of miracles in first-century Palestine and founder of Christianity. He taught the coming of the KINGDOM OF GOD with forgiveness and new life for all who believed. His claims to be the promised MESSIAH (or CHRIST) roused opposition from the religious authorities and he was put to death by crucifixion. But after his death his followers claimed that he was risen from the dead and he was seen alive by many. CHRISTIANS, members of his CHURCH (1), believe him to be fully divine and fully human, and await his promised SECOND COMING which will bring the fulfilment of the Kingdom of God.

Jew (1) A person who is regarded as a member of the Jewish race. According to Jewish religious law Jewishness is inherited through the female line. (2) A person who identifies with JUDAISM, the religion of the Jews.

Jihad ('Striving') A much misunderstood concept. The relentless fight against worldly lust. Muslims are exhorted to wage holy war only in their defence against the infidel.

Jimmu Tenno Traditionally the first Japanese EMPEROR, who began his reign in 660 BCE. He was thought to be a great grandson of the sun goddess Amaterasu, and was credited with the unification of Japan and the establishment of its government under the guidance of the gods (see KAMI).

Jina Also called 'Tirthankaras' ('ford-makers'), Jinas ('conquerors') are Jain religious teachers who have attained enlightenment and omniscience by conquering SAMSARA (the continuous cycle of birth, death, and rebirth to which those with KARMA are bound).

Jinja The SHINTO sanctuary. They vary in size from roadside shrines to beautifully located halls surrounded by trees and entered through traditional arched gateways (see TORII). They include halls for ceremonial dances, offerings and prayer rooms.

Jinn Spiritual creatures in Islamic belief who are made of smokeless flame. They are capable of belief and unbelief: the good ones are regarded as MUSLIMS.

Jiva A soul or 'life monad' according to JAIN belief. Jivas are infinite and omniscient but in this world KARMA weighs them down into a material existence. Jivas are liberated by acquiring omniscience, and this makes them float up to the summit of the universe.

Jochanan ben Zakkai Creator of the academic SANHEDRIN in Jamnia after the FALL OF JERUSALEM in CE 70. He led the work of Jewish reconstruction within the limits of Roman law and ensured, through the Sanhedrin, that the Jewish community were represented before the Roman authorities.

Jodo Japanese name for PURE LAND BUDDHISM.

Jodo Shinshu ('True Pure Land Sect') A refinement of PURE LAND BUDDHISM founded by SHINRAN. It was characterized by the doctrine of salvation through faith alone and the abolition of the SANGHA.

Judah HaNasi ('The Prince', CE 135–217) Leader of the academic Jewish SANHEDRIN in Galilee. He was responsible for compiling the MISHNAH, which helped the Jewish community

in developing a source of ritual authority in religious teaching. At his death 'Glory departed from Israel'.

Judaism The religion that developed from the religion of ancient ISRAEL and has been practised ever since by the JEWS. It is an ethical MONOTHEISM based on the revelation of GOD to MOSES on Mount SINAI and his giving of the Law (see TORAH). (See also ASHKENAZIM; CONSERVATIVE JUDAISM; ORTHODOX JUDAISM; PROGRESSIVE JUDAISM; SEPHARDIM.)

Judas Maccabeus (died 160 BCE) Jewish revolutionary who opposed the Hellenizing Seleucid emperor Antiochus Epiphanes who had set up an image of Olympian ZEUS in the TEMPLE OF JERUSALEM. Under Judas sporadic guerrilla revolt became full-scale war. In 165 BCE Antiochus was defeated and in the following year the temple was rededicated (see HANUKKAH). Though he achieved religious freedom, he failed to establish a free Jewish state.

Judgment The divine assessment of individuals and the settling of their destiny, a notion found in many religions. Christianity teaches that judgment is based on the individual's response to Christ.

Jumis Latvian harvest god.

Jung, C.G. (Carl Gustav) (CE 1875–1961) Swiss psychiatrist who invented the theory of ARCHETYPES. He investigated the significance of MYTHS, symbols and DREAMS, and found in them evidence for a 'collective unconscious' which was at the root of religion.

Juno Roman goddess, counterpart of the Greek HERA and wife of JUPITER. She was the patroness of women, marriage, childbirth and family life.

Jupiter/Jove Principal god of the Romans, identified with the Greek Zeus. He controlled the weather, particularly lightning and rain and was worshipped throughout Italy as almost a national god.

K

Ka The guardian spirit of each individual which, according to Egyptian belief, survived death and lived on in the next world, where it was reunited with ba, breath.

Ka'ba ('Cube') The sanctuary in MECCA to which all MUSLIMS turn in prayer. Set in its eastern corner is the BLACK STONE. A pre-Islamic holy place, all its religious images were removed in CE 630 by MUHAMMAD when he purified it to be the central sanctuary of ISLAM. The QUR'AN associates Abraham and Ishmael with the building of the Ka'ba.

Kabbalah Jewish mystical tradition which flourished in the teaching of two schools: the practical school based in Germany which concentrated in prayer and MEDITATION; the speculative school in Provence and Spain in the thirteenth and fourteenth centuries. The tradition originates in Talmudic speculation on the themes of the work of creation and the divine chariot mentioned in the biblical book of Ezekiel. The most famous Kabbalistic book is *Zohar* ('splendour'), a MIDRASH on the PENTATEUCH. (See MYSTICISM; TALMUD.)

Kabir (probably 1440–1518) Indian poet and

RAPID FACT-FINDER

hymn writer who influenced the development of early Sikhism. He attempted a synthesis of ISLAM and HINDUISM, rejecting the CASTE SYSTEM and CIRCUMCISION, but teaching the love of God, rebirth and liberation.

Kali Consort of the HINDU god SHIVA, a black goddess who is portrayed with a necklace of human skulls and fangs dripping blood. She is both the goddess of destruction and the Great Mother, giver of life.

Kalki In HINDU tradition, the last AVATAR of VISHNU who will descend on a white horse, with a sword, to kill the wicked and bring the world to an end.

Kami Powers of nature which are venerated in SHINTO. They are beneficent spirits who help in the processes of fertility and growth. They were generated by the gods and the Japanese people are descended from them according to Shinto mythology.

Kamma PALI word for KARMA.

Karaites ('Readers of Scripture') Heretical Jewish school of the eighth century CE which denied the validity of the TALMUD and the oral tradition. They held to a literalist view of the TORAH. By the tenth century they had spread throughout the Middle East and Spain. They refused to mix with other JEWS. Under attack by SAADYA BEN JOSEPH, the movement gradually disintegrated.

Karma SANSKRIT word for work or action. In Indian belief every action has inevitable consequences which attach themselves to the doer requiring reward or punishment. Karma is thus the moral law of cause and effect. It explains the inequalities of life as the consequences of actions in previous lives. The notion of karma probably developed among the DRAVIDIAN people of India. In MAHAYANA Buddhism the concept is transformed by the idea of the BODHISATTVA. Merit can be transferred by grace or faith, thus changing the person's karma.

Karo, Joseph (CE 1488–1575) Jewish legal teacher and MYSTIC. He produced the *Shulshan Aruch* (1565), which is one of the most important and cohesive authorities in JUDAISM, and is considered to be in accord with the purest Talmudic tradition (see TALMUD). His work is characterized by a devotional tone unusual in legal works.

Kashrut The code in JUDAISM according to which food is ritually clean or unclean. It refers particularly to meat, which must be slaughtered so as to ensure the minimum of pain and the draining off of blood.

Kashi See BENARES.

Khalsa Originally the militant community of SIKHS organized by Guru GOBIND SINGH in CE 1699. Now it is the society of fully committed adult members of the Sikh community. Traditional marks of membership are uncut hair, a comb worn in the hair, a sword, knee-length breeches and a steel bracelet.

Khandha See SKHANDHA.

Kharijites MUSLIM party of seceders from 'ALI, the fourth CALIPH. They opposed the UMMAYAD DYNASTY, believing that the succession should be based on a democratic vote. They were puritans strongly critical of

the moral laxity that developed as Ummayad power increased. Their stance inspired later reforming movements. They still exist as a separate sect in North Africa.

Khnum Creator god of ancient Egypt.

Kingdom of God The rule of God on earth. In JUDAISM God is king of the universe, the sole creator and ruler. The JEWS are his witnesses and their task is to work and pray for the fulfilment of his rule among all people. The kingdom will be brought by the MESSIAH and will include the restoration of ISRAEL. JESUS OF NAZARETH proclaimed the arrival of the kingdom in himself. Christians share in the kingdom now, and it will be completed and fulfilled at his SECOND COMING.

Kitab-i-Aqdas Meaning 'the most holy book', this is one of the most important works of Bahá'u'lláh. It contains most of the laws and many social ordinances of Bahá'u'lláh.

Kitab-i-Iqan Meaning 'the book of certitude', this is one of the most important works of Bahá'u'lláh. It addresses a range of theological questions and provides interpretations of the BIBLE and the QUR'AN.

Koan Technique used in RINZAI ZEN to bring about SATORI. It is a mind-bending question given by a teacher to a pupil to help him break through the prison of mental concepts and achieve direct awareness of reality.

Kojiki SHINTO scripture which is the oldest book in the Japanese language, though it is written using Chinese characters. It contains MYTHS and legends about the creation, the founding of Japan and the ceremonies and customs of the Japanese people.

Koko Spirits of dead ancestors in the popular cults of the Zuñi people of northern Mexico. The spirits are represented in ceremonial dances in which all participating males wear god-like masks.

Kol Nidrei See YOM KIPPUR.

Kook, Abraham Isaac Rabbi (CE 1868–1935) First Chief Rabbi of the Holy Land. He believed the Zionist movement to be essentially religious and that the restoration of ISRAEL was necessary for the redemption of the world. He influenced orthodox JEWS in favour of ZIONISM though he was also tolerant of secular Jews.

Koran See QUR'AN.

Kotel See WESTERN WALL.

Krishna The eighth incarnation of VISHNU according to HINDU tradition. His name means 'black'. Though of noble birth, he was brought up as a cowherd. Eventually he obtained his inheritance and ruled in justice. He was also a great lover: the MAHABHARATA describes his romances with the cow-girls which are seen as a type of God's love for the SOUL (1). He is also the main character in the BHAGAVAD GITA, where he appears disguised as the charioteer of Prince Arjuna.

Krishnamurti, Jiddhu (1895–1992) Indian spiritual teacher who was brought up by a leading Theosophist, Mrs Annie Besant, who proclaimed him as a World Teacher. He renounced this role in 1929 and became a solitary traveller, teaching liberation from

dogma and organized religion by the rejection of belief in the individual ego. (See also THEOSOPHY.)

Kshatriya See CASTE SYSTEM.

Kuan-yin Chinese name for the great BODHISATTVA AVALOKITESHVARA, especially when thought of in female form.

Kukai (CE 774–835) Japanese Buddhist teacher who tried to reconcile BUDDHISM with SHINTO. He is sometimes regarded as a manifestation of the Buddha VAIROCANA. Some believe he exists in a deep trance from which he is able to perform miracles and that he will return one day as a saviour.

Kundalini Energy that is coiled like a serpent at the base of the spine according to TANTRISM. When awakened by YOGA it leaps up the spine to the brain giving an experience of union and liberation re-enacting the sexual union of SHIVA and SHAKTI.

L

La ilaha illa Allah The first four words of the MUSLIM confession of faith: 'There is no god but God', which continues 'and MUHAMMAD is his prophet'. To accept this creed is to be a Muslim. It is the first of the FIVE PILLARS OF ISLAM. Its words form part of the Call to Prayer which is broadcast from the MOSQUE five times a day in Muslim communities.

Laity (From Greek: *laos*, 'people') The non-ordained members of a religious community (see ORDINATION), or those with no specialist religious function.

Lakshmi Lord VISHNU's consort. She appears in the *Rig Veda* (see VEDAS) as good fortune. In the RAMAYANA she rises out of the sea holding a lotus. She is involved in Vishnu's descents to earth as an AVATAR. Some associate her with SITA and RADHA, the consorts of RAMA and KRISHNA.

Lama Tibetan religious leader, a title formerly applied only to abbots, but later used of any monk. Lamas have been credited with magical powers which are said to be attained through years of arduous training. Their most common feat is telepathy, but they are also reported to be able to leave their bodies at will, cover huge distances at great speed and know the time and place of their own death. (See also SHAMAN.)

Lao-tzu Traditionally the author of the TAO TE CHING and a contemporary of CONFUCIUS. His name means 'old master', which could have applied to any wandering teacher.

Lares Roman agricultural spirits who were worshipped at cross-roads and in the home as household gods.

Latter-day Saints, Church of Jesus Christ of See MORMONISM; SMITH, JOSEPH.

Lectisternium A Roman feast in which food was offered to images of the gods which were placed on couches (*lecti*) like human guests.

Lent In CHRISTIANITY a forty-day period of FASTING and penitence before EASTER, originally a period of training and examination for those who were baptized at Easter.

Ley lines Straight geological lines of spiritual force which some adherents of NEW AGE RELIGIONS believe were discovered and used in the NEOLITHIC PERIOD. Their existence is said to be demonstrated by the many alignments between religious sites, MEGALITHS and unusual topographical features. There is no archaeological or statistical support for this view.

Li CONFUCIUS'S concept of propriety or reverence which he believed should direct all relationships between members of society. Correct application of *li* was a guarantee of social welfare and harmony.

Libation The RITUAL outpouring of drink as an offering to DIVINITIES or Ancestor spirits.

Liberation Theology Originating in Latin America, associates SALVATION with the political liberation of oppressed peoples. Its insights have been used by black Christians and feminists to understand sexism and racism. It is marked by a stress on the challenges to social action contained in the BIBLE, especially the prophetic books and the NEW TESTAMENT, and the reality of the KINGDOM OF GOD as a coming event.

Limbo According to Roman Catholic doctrine, the dwelling place of souls (e.g. of unbaptized children) excluded from HEAVEN but not subjected to HELL or PURGATORY.

Liturgy ('Public service') (1) Any regular prescribed service of the Christian Church. (2) The EUCHARIST, especially in ORTHODOXY.

Logos Greek for word or principle. In STOICISM it identified the principle of reason, immanent in nature. Speculations about the logos were developed by the Jewish philosopher PHILO OF ALEXANDRIA. The Prologue to St John's GOSPEL identifies CHRIST with the pre-existent logos of God.

Loki The opponent of the AESIR in Norse mythology who is bent on their downfall and the overthrow of the world order. His name may mean 'light' and he is associated with destructive fire. For his part in the death of BALDER he is fettered to underground rocks and poisoned by serpents until the day of RAGNARÖK. His agonies cause earthquakes and volcanoes.

Lord's Supper Name for the Christian EUCHARIST favoured by the Protestant reformers who saw the Eucharist primarily as a memorial of CHRIST's death.

Lotus Type of water lily, a Buddhist symbol of ENLIGHTENMENT. The roots of the lotus are buried in the earth while the flower opens out above the water.

Lotus posture Style of sitting upright and cross-legged, used as a position for MEDITATION in Hindu and Buddhist practice.

Lotus Sutra MAHAYANA Buddhist scripture in the form of a sermon preached by the BUDDHA (1) to a vast throng of gods, demons, rulers and cosmic powers. It contains the essence of Mahayana teachings on the eternity of the Buddha, the universal capacity for Buddhahood and the compassion and power of the BODHISATTVAS. It is especially revered in Japan and is the basic scripture of the NICHIREN Buddhist NEW RELIGIONS.

Lucretius (about 100–55 BCE) Roman poet and philosopher who expounded the materialist and rationalist doctrines of EPICUREANISM in his poem '*De rerum natura*' ('On the nature of things'). He accepted the existence of the traditional gods but located them far away from our world and believed that they had no interest in or influence over events on earth.

Lugh (Irish: 'the Shining One'; Welsh: Lleu) Most honoured of the Celtic gods, a war god, the patron of commerce and moneymaking and prototype of human beings. Skilful in all arts and crafts he is often portrayed as a youthful traveller. His Gaulish name is unknown but Julius Caesar compared him to the Roman MERCURY.

Luria, Isaac (CE 1514–72) Jewish teacher from Spain who developed the Kabbalistic teachings of the *Zohar* (see KABBALAH). He believed in reincarnation and taught that the dispersion of the JEWS was providential and would lead to universal salvation. His teachings inspired devotional poetry and hymns.

Luther, Martin (CE 1483–1546) Founder of the German REFORMATION. He held that people could only be justified before God by faith in JESUS CHRIST, not by any 'works' of religion. So the priesthood and the 'mediating' role of the church are unnecessary.

Lutheran churches Important churches in Scandinavia, other parts of Western Europe and the USA. They value theological study and emphasize the weekly sermons.

M

Maccabees The family and supporters of JUDAS MACCABEUS. They were the forerunners of the ZEALOTS in fighting a holy war against alien rulers.

Madhva (CE 1197–1276) Indian philosopher who founded a dualist school (see DUALISM) in opposition to the MONISM of SHANKARA. He was a devotee of VISHNU, and believed that God was eternally distinct from the natural world. He may have been influenced by Christian teachings.

Magi Priestly class of ancient Persia who at first opposed the spread of ZOROASTER's teachings. By the fourth century BCE they had been drawn into the service of the new religion and stressed the ritual and magic elements of it.

Magic The manipulation of natural or supernatural forces by SPELLS and RITUALS for good or harmful ends.

Mahabharata One of the two great epics of the HINDU scriptures compiled in the third or second century BCE. Ascribed to the sage Vyasa, it tells of the war between two families, the Kauravas and the Pandus. The divine hero of the epic is the AVATAR KRISHNA.

Maharishi Mahesh Yogi See TRANSCENDENTAL MEDITATION.

Mahatma SANSKRIT title of great respect or veneration meaning 'great soul'.

Mahatma Gandhi see GANDHI

Mahavira Great JAIN teacher who

traditionally lived 599–527 BCE, though this is disputed. He abolished the distinctions of the CASTE SYSTEM and tried to spread his teaching among the Brahmans. He starved himself to death at the age of seventy-two, having spent his last years totally naked.

Mahayana ('Large vehicle') The form of BUDDHISM practised in Nepal, China, Tibet, Korea and Japan. Mahayana accepts more scriptures than THERAVADA, and has developed various forms of popular devotion based on the doctrine of the BODHISATTVAS.

Mahdi 'The guided one' who according to SHI'A teaching will come at the end of the world. The Mahdi is identified with Muhammad al-Mahdi who disappeared in CE 880 and is believed to be hidden until his reappearance. There have been a number of false Mahdis in the Shi'a community.

Maimonides, Moses (CE 1135–1204) Jewish philosopher who lived in Spain and later Egypt and attempted a synthesis of Aristotelian and biblical teaching. He listed the THIRTEEN PRINCIPLES of belief which have been treated in Judaism as a creed and are found in the *Jewish Daily Prayer Book*.

Maitreya The Buddha-to-be, or the next BUDDHA to appear on earth according to MAHAYANA teachings. He is at present a BODHISATTVA awaiting his last rebirth.

Mana Polynesian word for the invisible spiritual power which permeates all things. It has been adopted as a general term in the study of INDIGENOUS RELIGIONS. It is not necessarily a personal power, though it can be focused in particular individuals, places and objects.

Mandaeans Members of a Gnostic sect teaching redemption through a divine saviour who has lived on earth and defeated the powers of darkness. The sole surviving practitioners of GNOSTICISM, about 15,000, still live in Iraq and Iran.

Mandala A visual aid in the form of a series of coloured concentric circles used in TIBETAN BUDDHISM. Segments of the circles portray different aspects of the BUDDHA's compassion. Concentration on the *mandala* enables the disciple to see himself in relation to the Buddha's compassion and thus to achieve ENLIGHTENMENT.

Manichaeans Followers of Mani (around CE 216–76), a Persian teacher whose strict ascetic system was designed to release the divine spark trapped in every person by the wiles of SATAN. Their teaching influenced AUGUSTINE.

Manitou Name used by the Algonquin Indians of North America to refer to spiritual powers. It can apply to all kinds of NATURE SPIRITS or DIVINITIES, friendly or unfriendly.

Mantra A symbolic sound causing an internal vibration which helps to concentrate the mind and aids self-realization, e.g. the repeated syllable 'om', and in Tibetan Buddhism the phrase OM MANI PADME HUM. In HINDUISM the term originally referred to a few sacred verses from the VEDAS. It came to be thought that they possessed spiritual power, and that repetition of them was a help to liberation. A mantra is sometimes given by a spiritual teacher to a disciple as an INITIATION.

Mara In BUDDHISM, the evil one, temptation.

Marduk Babylonian deity who superseded the Sumerian god ENLIL. He was associated with the sun and with vegetation. He was addressed as Bel, the Supreme Lord.

Marriage, sacred A religious rite involving real or simulated sexual intercourse which represents the marriage of earth and sky in the fertilization of the soil and the growth of the crops.

Mars Roman war god, regarded second only to JUPITER. Soldiers sacrificed to him before and after battle. Originally he was probably a god of agriculture.

Martyr ('Witness') Title originally applied to Christians who died rather than renounce their faith during times of persecution. Now a term applied to anyone who dies for a religious belief.

Mary, the mother of Jesus Because of her role in the divine plan of salvation, Mary is honoured by all Christians and venerated by Roman Catholic and Eastern Orthodox Christians. The GOSPELS describe her as divinely chosen to be the mother of the Saviour. Roman Catholic churches have attributed an intercessory role to Mary, and developed other doctrines concerning her nature.

Masoretes A group of Jewish scholars from the Babylonian and Palestinian schools who in the ninth century CE supplied the text of the HEBREW BIBLE with vowel points and divided it up into sentences and paragraphs. They also tried to exclude copyists' errors and noted all the variant readings they found.

Mass Name for the Christian EUCHARIST derived from the words of dismissal. The standard ROMAN CATHOLIC term, it emphasizes the sacrificial aspect of the rite.

Matsuri Japanese name for a solemn celebration intended to invoke worship of the SHINTO gods and obedience to their moral will. They take place at stated intervals in Shinto sanctuaries.

Maya (1) Illusion or deception in HINDU thought. Maya is concerned with the diverse phenomenal world perceived by the senses. It is the trick of maya to convince people that this is all that exists and thus blind them to the reality of BRAHMAN and the oneness of existence. (2) Legendary mother of the BUDDHA (1). (3) People of an ancient Central American empire which spread from Yucatan to El Salvador. Mayan civilization was at its height around CE 300–900 and was finally broken up by the Spaniards in the sixteenth century. The Maya developed a complex calendar and a form of writing. Their gods were linked with nature symbols, the most important of which was a double-headed snake. (See also CHAC.)

Mecca Holy city of Islam, in Saudi Arabia, the birthplace of MUHAMMAD, and later the base for his MUSLIM state after its conquest in CE 630. Pilgrimage to Mecca, HAJJ, is one of the FIVE PILLARS OF ISLAM and all Muslims are required to face Mecca to perform ritual prayer five times a day.

Medicine man See WITCH DOCTOR.

Medina Formerly Yathrib, city 100 miles/169 km north of MECCA, the political base for MUHAMMAD from CE 622 until his conquest of Mecca. Pilgrims from Medina were among the first to accept and spread Muhammad's message. The city contains the site of Muhammad's tomb.

Meditation Deep and continuous reflection, practised in many religions with a variety of aims, e.g. to attain self-realization or, in theistic religions, to attain union with the divine will. Many religions teach a correct posture, method of breathing and ordering of thoughts for meditation.

Medium One who is possessed by the spirit of a dead person or a DIVINITY and, losing his individual identify, becomes the mouthpiece for the other's utterance.

Megaliths Large stone monuments dating from the late NEOLITHIC PERIOD. Their original function is uncertain but they mark burial mounds and temples and they may have served as a calendar of times and seasons.

Meher Baba (CE 1894–1969) Indian spiritual leader, regarded by his followers as an AVATAR. From 1925 until his death he did not speak once.

Mencius (born 371 BCE) Confucian teacher who expanded and developed CONFUCIUS'S teachings. He believed that the universe followed a moral order and that knowledge of this order could be attained by MEDITATION.

Mendelssohn, Moses (CE 1729–86) German Jewish rationalist philosopher who taught that the three central propositions of JUDAISM are: the existence of God; providence; the immortality of the soul. He believed these to be founded on pure reason and to be the basis of all religion. The revelation to the Jews preserves the JEWS as an ethnic entity. He translated the PENTATEUCH into German and encouraged Jews to become more involved in European culture.

Mercury Roman god, identified with the Greek HERMES. He presided over trade.

Merit In BUDDHISM the fruit of good actions which can be devoted to the welfare of other beings. The idea develops in MAHAYANA, where it is believed that the BODHISATTVAS have acquired almost infinite supplies of merit which they can transfer to believers.

Merlin Bard and magician in the romances of the CELTS, later the mentor of ARTHUR. He has become a popular figure in some forms of contemporary Pagan spirituality.

Messiah ('Anointed one') A HEBREW word referring to the person chosen by God to be king. (1) After the end of the Israelite monarchy it came to refer to a figure who would restore ISRAEL, gathering the tribes together and ushering in the KINGDOM OF GOD. JUDAISM has known several false messiahs (see ZEVI, SHABBETAI). Modern Jews are divided as to whether the messiah is a symbolic or a representative figure and whether the founding of the Jewish state is in any way a prelude to his coming. (2) In the Christian NEW TESTAMENT, JESUS OF NAZARETH is described by messianic titles, e.g. messiah, CHRIST, 'the King', 'the One who Comes'. The account of Jesus' entry into JERUSALEM is deliberately phrased in messianic terms. Jesus himself was cautious about claiming to be messiah, probably because of its political overtones.

Methodist churches Churches deriving from those which joined the Methodist Conference, first established in 1784 by John WESLEY. They are now spread worldwide, promoting EVANGELISM and social concern.

Mezuzah ('Doorpost') Sign placed at the door of a Jewish house, comprising part of the SHEMA.

Middle Way The BUDDHA's description of his teaching as a mean between the extremes of sensuality and asceticism. It is designed to lead to NIRVANA.

Midgard/Middle Earth The home of human beings according to Norse cosmology. Made from the body of the primeval giant, Ymir, it was defended by Thor from attack by giants. Midgard is the middle of the nine worlds. It is now part of contemporary HEATHEN belief. It has also been popularized in J.R.R. Tolkien's *Lord of the Rings*.

Midrash A method of exposition of HEBREW texts designed to reveal the inner meaning of the TORAH. Great attention to detail was paid because the texts were believed to be of divine origin. The method was originally oral; the most important midrashim were recorded and written down.

Mihrab Semi-circular recess in the wall of a MOSQUE which indicates the direction of the holy city MECCA, which is the direction for MUSLIM prayer.

Miki Nakayama (CE 1798–1887) Founder of the Japanese religion TENRIKYO. In 1838 she was possessed by a divine being who announced he was the Creator and true God and gave her a series of revelations. Miki Nakayama gave away all her money and practised spiritual healing. Her teachings attracted a wide following. Adherents believe she is still alive, in non-physical form, in the shrine built on the site of her home at the city of Tenri.

Mimir In Norse mythology, the fount of wisdom who guards the well of knowledge at the root of YGGDRASIL. He is ODIN's mentor. In one version of the myth, Odin comes to drink from the well and has to sacrifice an eye to do so, in another Mimir's head is cut off and brought to Odin, who preserves it as a talking head which gives him advice.

Minaret ('Place of light and fire') A tower attached to a MOSQUE from which the Call to Prayer is broadcast to the MUSLIM community.

Mindfulness Buddhist method of contemplative analysis. It has two uses: in MEDITATION, where it refers to the practice of observing the arising and passing away of different mental states until one arrives at detachment; in daily life, where it refers to a quality of carefulness in thought, speech and action which prevents the accumulation of bad KARMA.

Ming Chinese emperor (first century CE) of the Han dynasty who, according to tradition, introduced Buddhist scriptures from north-west India. According to tradition he had a dream of a golden man, which he took to be a revelation of the BUDDHA.

Minister (1) A lay or ordained Christian who has been authorized to perform spiritual functions (ministries, literally 'service') in the CHURCH. (2) General title for any member of the clergy especially those of Protestant denominations.

Minoan religion Religion of the Bronze Age civilization of Crete. The Minoans probably worshipped the MOTHER GODDESS and reverenced SACRED SNAKES and SACRED BULLS.

Miracle An event which appears to defy rational explanation and is attributed to divine intervention.

Mishnah A compilation of Jewish oral teachings undertaken by Rabbi JUDAH HANASI in around CE 200. It quickly became second in authority only to the HEBREW BIBLE and formed the basis of the TALMUD. The Mishnah helped Jewish teaching to survive in a period of persecution when the future of the SANHEDRIN was in doubt.

Missal Liturgical book containing all that is said or sung throughout the year at the celebration of the MASS. It also includes appropriate directions.

Mission The outreach of a religion to the unconverted. Whereas understandings of mission vary from faith to faith, the various aims of mission usually include spiritual conversion. However, mission is often conceived more holistically and concerns, not just spiritual conversion, but the transformation of all areas of life. It addresses injustice, suffering, poverty, racism, sexism, and all forms of oppression.

Missionaries Those who propagate a religious faith among people of a different faith. BUDDHISM and CHRISTIANITY have been the most notable missionary religions.

Mithra Originally a god of the Indo-Iranians, he was worshipped in the Hindu VEDAS as Mitra and was an important figure in ZOROASTRIANISM, where he was particularly associated with ideas on judgment and the priesthood. To this day, the term for Zoroastrian FIRE TEMPLES is *dar-i Mihr*, 'courts of Mithra'. To the Romans he was the god Mithras of MITHRAISM. (See also SOL INVICTUS.)

Mithraeum In MITHRAISM a cave-like sanctuary housing a statue of MITHRA slaying the bull.

Mithraism Religion of MITHRA which flourished throughout the early Roman empire. It was found in almost all parts of the empire, but concentrated in Rome, the Rhine Valley and what is now Hungary and Rumania. Popular among soldiers, it stressed the ethical values of courage and endurance. It was not open to women. (See also SOL INVICTUS.)

Moderator MINISTER of the PRESBYTERIAN CHURCH appointed to constitute and preside over one of the courts that govern the life of the church.

Mohammed See MUHAMMAD.

Moksha SANSKRIT word meaning liberation from the cycle of birth, death and rebirth. Permanent spiritual perfection experienced by an enlightened soul after the physical body has died. No further incarnations will be endured.

Monism The belief that there is only one basic reality in spite of the appearance and experience of diversity. It applies particularly to the beliefs of the HINDU philosopher SHANKARA. (See also ADVAITA.)

Monk A member of a male religious community living under vows which usually include poverty, chastity and the wearing of a distinctive form of dress. Monastic orders are found in Christianity and Buddhism and Jainism. The Buddhist monk is a member of a SANGHA and, additionally to the FIVE PRECEPTS, vows to eat only at set times, not to handle money, use a high bed, use scent or go to stage performances. (See also BENEDICT.)

Monotheism The belief that there is one supreme GOD who contains all the attributes and characteristics of divinity.

Moon, Sun Myung (born 1920) Korean engineer, businessman and founder of the FAMILY FEDERATION FOR WORLD PEACE AND UNIFICATION. He claims to have authoritative visions of Jesus. Members of the federation accord him a high, if publicly ill-defined, status.

Moravians Protestant Christians continuing the simple ideals of an earlier group 'The Bohemian Brethren'. They distrust CREEDS and oppose political involvement. They have been active MISSIONARIES since they were founded in CE 1722.

Mormonism Unorthodox Christian sect founded in CE 1830 in the USA on the basis of the visionary experiences of Joseph SMITH. Under its second leader, Brigham Young (CE 1807–77), the Mormons journeyed to found Salt Lake City (1847) where they developed into a strong missionary community. Mormons accept the BIBLE and the BOOK OF MORMON and some other revealed writings. The Mormon Church, officially the 'Church of Jesus Christ of Latter-day Saints', has about 11 million members, half of them in the USA and Canada.

Moroni See SMITH, JOSEPH.

Moses The father of JUDAISM who received the TORAH from God on Mount SINAI having led the people of ISRAEL out of captivity in Egypt. The first five books of the BIBLE are traditionally ascribed to him.

Moslem See MUSLIM.

Mosque MUSLIM place of public worship, consisting usually of an outer courtyard for ablutions and a large unfurnished inner area where Muslims kneel, sit or prostrate themselves in worship. On Fridays special prayers are offered in the afternoon and the IMAM delivers the sermon.

Mother goddess/Great Mother The personification of nature and the natural processes of fertility and growth connected with the earth. Worship of a mother goddess was universal in the Ancient Near East, Asia and Europe (see CYBELE, DEMETER, INANNA, ISHTAR, ISIS). Her worship continues in HINDUISM where the consorts of SHIVA (DURGA, KALI, PARVATI) have some of her characteristics. There is some revival of her worship in feminism, ECO-FEMINISM, and among adherents to the GAIA hypothesis and practitioners of WITCHCRAFT.

Muezzin Person who calls the MUSLIM faithful to prayer.

Mufti A canon lawyer in ISLAM who gives formal legal advice on questions brought to him in accordance with the QUR'AN, the SUNNAH and the law schools.

Muhammad (about CE 570–632) Prophet and apostle of ISLAM, the final messenger of God whose message, the QUR'AN, sums up and completes the previous revelations to the Jews and Christians. Muhammad saw the expansion of ISLAM in terms of military conquest and political organization and he was outstandingly successful as a commander and ruler in MEDINA and later MECCA.

Muharram A commemoration by Shi'ite MUSLIMS (see SHI'A) of the murder of al-Huseyn on the tenth day of the month Muharram. A passion play is performed depicting the martyrdom.

Mujtahid MUSLIM teacher who gives a ruling, legal decision or deduction on the basis of his own learning or authority (see IJTIHAD). In Shi'a Islam, the *mujtahidun* have great authority.

Mullah A Persian form of an Arabic word which means a 'teacher' or 'scholar' – an exponent of the sacred law of ISLAM.

Muslim 'One who submits' to the will of God, a follower of ISLAM.

Muslim brotherhood Egyptian puritanical organization founded in CE 1928 by Hasan al-Banna. The brotherhood was influential after World War II and worked against ZIONISM and Westernization. It fell into disrepute because of terrorist activities and was dissolved in 1954.

Muslim League Organization founded in CE 1906 to promote the interests and political aspirations of Indian Muslims.

Mystery religions Cults based on ancient MYTHS which flourished in Greece, in Rome and throughout the Roman empire. Initiates went through a dramatic and secret ceremony in which they identified with the divinity at the centre of the myth and experienced salvation and the assurance of immortality.

Mystic One who seeks direct personal experience of the divine and may use PRAYER, MEDITATION or various ascetic practices to concentrate the attention.

Mysticism The search for direct personal experience of the divine. There is a distinction between seeing mysticism as leading to identification with GOD (as is common in HINDUISM) and as leading to a union with God's love and will (as in ISLAM, JUDAISM and CHRISTIANITY).

Myth A sacred story which originates and circulates within a particular community. Some aetiological myths explain puzzling physical phenomena or customs, institutions and practices whose origin in the community would otherwise be mysterious. (See also CREATION MYTH.)

N

Nagarjuna (around CE 100–165) MAHAYANA Buddhist philosopher who taught that the truth of reality was void or emptiness.

Namu Myoho Renge Kyo Formula coined by NICHIREN as the essential truth of the LOTUS SUTRA. It means 'Reverence to the wonderful truth of the *Lotus Sutra*' and it is used by a variety of sects based on Nichiren's Buddhist teachings.

Nanak, Guru (CE 1469–1539) Indian religious teacher and founder of the SIKH religion. He intended to reconcile HINDUS and MUSLIMS, and travelled widely preaching a monotheistic faith (see MONOTHEISM) which was influenced by BHAKTI and SUFISM. He appointed a successor to continue his teachings.

Native American Church Religious organization of Native Americans founded in 1870. It teaches a synthesis of native religion and Christianity. Its rituals include the ceremonial use of peyote, a spineless cactus containing the hallucinogenic substance mescaline.

Nature spirits Spirits of trees, hills, rivers, plants and animals which are acknowledged with prayers and offerings in most INDIGENOUS RELIGIONS.

Navjote INITIATION ceremony of the PARSIS at which a child is invested with a sacred shirt and thread symbolic of 'new birth' to adulthood.

Near death experience Visionary sequence of events occasionally reported by those resuscitated. Features include a sensation of being OUT OF BODY, a journey down a long tunnel, the appearance of a being of light who is sometimes identified as CHRIST or an ANGEL, and a flashback of one's past life. Feelings of bliss and oneness are common, which remain for years afterwards.

Nembutsu ('Hail to the BUDDHA AMIDA') The formula of faith taught by the Japanese Buddhist teacher HONEN.

Nemesis Greek goddess who personified the retribution due to evil deeds. Her vengeance was regarded to be inevitable and exact.

Nemeton 'Sacred place' in Celtic religion, usually an enclosed woodland grove.

Neolithic period The New Stone Age, from about 10,000 BCE until the Early Bronze Age.

Neo-Platonism Religious and philosophical movement from the third to the sixth centuries CE. It used the teachings of PLATO as a basis for ascetic practices and mystical experience. Its principal architect was PLOTINUS.

Neptune Italian water god who became associated with POSEIDON and acquired his mythology.

Nestorianism CHRISTIAN HERESY that claimed that two separate persons, human and divine, existed in the incarnate CHRIST (as opposed to the orthodox view that God assumed human nature as one person in Christ). Although condemned in CE 431 it continued to flourish in Persia. A few groups of Nestorians survive in the present day.

New Age With roots in particularly Theosophy, the term refers to alternative spiritualities, which emerged in the mid-1960s principally on the west coast of the USA and spread throughout North America and

Europe. The movements are characterized by a concern to realize the spiritual potential of the individual self, which is often believed to be divine. Also common is the belief that, as we move from the astrological age of Pisces into the age of Aquarius, we are witnessing a spiritual renaissance, a New Age of non-hierarchical, non-patriarchal, eco-friendly self-spirituality. Drawing from discoveries in physics and cosmology, their teachings claim to revive ancient mystical traditions of East and West. They emphasize healing, a healthy and balanced life-style and expansion of self-awareness through meditation and personal counselling.

New religions There is scholarly debate over the precise definition of a 'new' religion. Some scholars limit the definition to those religions that have emerged since 1945 (i.e. since the end of World War II) or, indeed, even later (i.e. since 1960). However, this excludes many older new religions such as the JEHOVAH'S WITNESSES. Hence, other scholars prefer the following general working definition: a religion, sect or spirituality that has emerged or that has arisen to prominence during the twentieth century.

New Testament The second division of the Christian Bible, comprising the GOSPELS, the Acts of the Apostles, the Revelation of John and various EPISTLES.

New Year, Jewish See ROSH HASHANAH.

Nibbana PALI word for NIRVANA.

Nichiren (CE 1222–82) Japanese Buddhist reformer who taught that the LOTUS SUTRA contained the ultimate truth and that it could be compressed into a sacred formula: NAMU MYOHO RENGE KYO. He denounced all other forms of Buddhism. When the Mongols threatened Japan he preached a fiery nationalism, urging the nation to convert to true Buddhism. His teachings have provided the inspiration for some modern Buddhist sects (see NEW RELIGIONS).

Night Journey The journey of MUHAMMAD from the temple in MECCA to the TEMPLE OF JERUSALEM, which is described in the QUR'AN. Tradition asserts that he travelled on a winged horse accompanied by GABRIEL (Jibril). By the sacred rock of Abraham, Muhammad met Abraham, Moses and Jesus. Then he ascended up a ladder of light into the presence of ALLAH. He returned bringing instructions for the faithful.

Nihongi SHINTO scripture which contains the Japanese CREATION MYTH and legends of the gods. It was originally written in Chinese.

Ninigi The son of Amaterasu in SHINTO belief. At a time of chaos in heaven Amaterasu sent him down to rule the islands of Japan, making him the first Japanese EMPEROR.

Nirvana ('Going out, becoming cool') In BUDDHISM, the state when DUKKHA ceases because the flames of desire are no longer fuelled. It is a state of unconditioned-ness and uncompounded-ness beyond any form of known or imagined existence.

Nkulukulu ('The old, old one') Zulu name for God.

Noble Eightfold Path In BUDDHISM, the

way to extinguish desire by adopting: right views; right resolves; right speech; right action; right livelihood; right effort; right mindfulness; right concentration/meditation.

Non-realism Movement arising from DEATH OF GOD theology which claims that religious doctrines refer only to human sources of value and do not refer to objective reality.

Norns The Fates of Norse religion. Of giant origin, they are immensely powerful, controlling the destiny of men. They tend and water the trunk of YGGDRASIL. The names of the three norns mean Past, Present and Future. Their association with time makes them more powerful than the immortal gods of ASGARD, since even they are bound to predestined fate.

Numen In Roman religion, the divine power suffusing nature. From this concept Rudolf Otto developed the idea that the root of religion was a sense of holy power. This he termed the 'numinous'.

Nun A member of a female religious community as found in CHRISTIANITY, BUDDHISM and JAINISM. Nuns live under vows usually including poverty and chastity and often the wearing of a distinctive form of dress. (See also BENEDICT.)

Nut The sky goddess of Egyptian mythology whose body is lined with stars. Every evening she swallows the sun and gives birth to it again each morning.

 O

Obeah Religious and magical practices of the West Indies which are usually of West African origin. (See also VOODOO.)

Occult Teachings, arts and practices that are concerned with what is hidden and mysterious, as with WITCHCRAFT, ALCHEMY and DIVINATION.

Odin Chief of the Norse gods. Originally he was a wild wind god who led the spirits of the dead through the air. The Romans associated him with MERCURY. In later mythology, he visits the earth as The Wanderer. There are two myths of his search for wisdom: the first that he sacrificed an eye as the price for his drinking from the well of MIMIR; the second that he hanged himself upon YGGDRASIL. He is associated with the gallows and there is evidence that victims were hanged on trees in sacrifice to him. As Allfather, Odin watched over the nine worlds and was brought daily reports by two ravens. Variants of his name include Woden (Anglo-Saxon) and Wotan (German).

Odinism See HEATHENISM.

Ohrmazd See AHURA MAZDA.

Old Catholic churches A group of national churches which have separated from Rome. Since 1932 they have been in communion with the Church of England.

Old Testament The HEBREW BIBLE as the first division of the Christian BIBLE.

Olympos, Mount The highest mountain in Greece (9,572 feet/2,917m), held to be the home of the twelve greatest Greek gods under the leadership of ZEUS.

Om mani padme hum ('The jewel in the LOTUS') Tibetan mantra whose six syllables are held to correspond to the six worlds of Tibeten Buddhist teaching: om, 'gods'; ma, 'anti-gods'; ni, 'humans'; pad, 'animals'; mi, 'hungry ghosts'; hum, 'hell'. Each world is present as a state of the human mind. The mantra sums up the whole of human existence and is an indispensable aid to self-realization.

Omnipotence All-powerful.

Omniscience All-knowing. Simultaneous knowledge of all things.

Option for the poor Decision of Latin American churches following Medellin Conference of 1968 and Puebla Conference of 1978 to adopt the tenets of LIBERATION THEOLOGY by insisting that God chose the poor and willed social justice.

Ordination Rite in the Christian CHURCH by which chosen individuals are authorized as MINISTERS of the Word of God and the SACRAMENTS. In BUDDHISM the term denotes entry into the SANGHA.

Origen (around CE 184–254) Theologian who tried to present Biblical CHRISTIANITY using the ideas of HELLENISM. He believed that all creatures would eventually be saved, a view condemned as heretical in CE 553.

Original sin The SIN of Adam and Eve, the first human beings, in eating from the forbidden tree in the Garden of Eden, expressing independence from God. In Christian teaching the inevitable consequence is seen as separation from God: human creatures inherit Adam and Eve's 'fallen' state, resulting in the need for SALVATION.

Orphism Religious movement which began in Thrace and flourished in the sixth century BCE. It was based on MYTHS of DIONYSUS and Orpheus, who was the supreme minstrel of Greek mythology. It taught a way of liberation through ASCETICISM and held also a doctrine of REINCARNATION.

Orthodox Judaism Traditional JUDAISM which is Talmudic (see TALMUD) in belief and practice. It is the largest of the modern groupings and it is the form of religion accepted as authentic in Israel.

Orthodoxy CHRISTIANITY as practised by the Eastern Churches after the GREAT SCHISM. Orthodox Christians are found mostly in Eastern Europe, the Balkan States and Russia.

Osiris Egyptian vegetation god, the force behind the cycle of growth and decay. Mythology tells how he had originally lived on earth as a king. He was murdered and later dismembered by his jealous brother, SETH. His wife, ISIS, searched for the pieces of his body and restored him to life. As a symbol of death and resurrection, Osiris became associated with life after death and the judgment of individual souls.

Ottoman empire (CE 1453–1918) The empire of the Ottoman Turks who were converted to ISLAM. It stretched from the Middle East to the Balkans and at its height to the frontiers of Austria. The Ottomans supported SUNNI orthodoxy against heterodox DERVISH movements. The empire went into

slow decline in the eighteenth century and its religious life stagnated. Muslim communities in the Balkans have been vulnerable since the fall of Communism in Eastern Europe.

Out of Body Experience Sensation of separation of the self from the body occasionally reported in mystical or drug-induced trance, or as part of a NEAR DEATH EXPERIENCE.

P

Pachacamac Leader of the gods in the religion of the INCAS. A great shrine was built for him near the modern city of Lima, Peru.

Pachamama MOTHER GODDESS in the INDIGENOUS RELIGION of the Andes.

Pagan/Paganism The word 'pagan' (derived from the Latin term *pagus*, which literally means 'from the countryside' or 'rural') was first used in a general religious sense by the early Christians to describe the non-Christian gentile religions. It is now generally used to refer to a broad range of nature-venerating religious traditions. Whilst the term 'Neo-Paganism' is sometimes used by academics and even by some devotees, particularly in the USA (e.g. the Church of All Worlds), practitioners generally prefer the simpler term 'Paganism'. Because many contemporary Pagans do seek to learn from indigenous cultures, there are some continuities between the two forms of religion. While there are many forms of Paganism, arguably there are three principal traditions: The largest and most influential of these is WICCA. A second contemporary Pagan tradition is DRUIDRY. Finally, within contemporary Paganism there is a tradition often referred to simply as the 'Northern Tradition'. Northern Tradition Pagans often prefer the appellative 'Heathen' rather than 'Pagan'. 'Heathen' means roughly the same as 'Pagan', but is derived from Germanic languages rather than Latin – it is also a term that has been used pejoratively by Christians. The Northern Tradition/ HEATHENISM draws inspiration principally from Anglo-Saxon, Norse and Icelandic pre-Christian mythology, religion and culture.

Pagoda A Buddhist building in south-east Asia built over Buddhist RELICS and often characterized by a series of superimposed spires.

Palaeolithic Period The Old Stone Age, before 10,000 BCE in Europe and the Middle East.

Pali Vernacular language of northern India in the BUDDHA's time, and hence the language of early BUDDHISM and the THERAVADA SCRIPTURES. It is related to SANSKRIT.

Pali Canon The basic Buddhist SCRIPTURES – the only scriptures valid among THERAVADA Buddhists. Traditionally the collection began soon after the BUDDHA's death when his followers met to receive the TIPITAKA/TRIPITAKA or 'three baskets' of his teaching. The precise wording of the canon was fixed at a council in the time of king Asoka.

Pan Arcadian fertility god, patron of shepherds and herdsmen, usually portrayed with goat's horns and legs.

Panchen Lama Title given to one of the

leading abbots of TIBETAN BUDDHISM, whose authority paralleled that of the DALAI LAMA, though its emphasis was more on spiritual matters. The Panchen Lama was believed to be a reincarnation of AMITABHA.

Pantheism The belief that all reality is in essence divine.

Parousia See SECOND COMING.

Parsis Descendants of the ancient Zoroastrian Persians (see ZOROASTRIANISM) living in India, mostly near Mumbai (Bombay). They practise an ethical MONOTHEISM with a RITUAL life that expresses the purity of AHURA MAZDA. The 115,000 Zoroastrians in the world today are divided into groups that differ over the religious calendar.

Parsva Legendary founder of JAINISM. Born a prince around 850 BCE he renounced his throne and became an ascetic, finally gaining omniscience. He is considered to be the twenty-second JINA.

Parvati ('Mountaineer') Consort of SHIVA in HINDU mythology, like Shiva both beautiful and terrifying.

Passover Seven-day Jewish spring festival marking the deliverance from Egypt (see EXODUS). Since Talmudic times (see TALMUD) the festival has begun with a service in the home where unleavened bread, wine and bitter herbs symbolize the joys and sorrows of the exodus. There is a meal and the evening concludes with psalms and hymns which look to God's final redemption of ISRAEL.

Patriarch (1) 'Father-figure'; especially in family and community; in JUDAISM and CHRISTIANITY, refers to the founders of the faith such as ABRAHAM, ISAAC and JACOB. (2) Head of one of the EASTERN ORTHODOX CHURCHES. The Patriarch of Constantinople is a figurehead for Orthodox Christians.

Paul APOSTLE of CHRISTIANITY who established new churches throughout Asia Minor and Macedonia. Originally a PHARISEE, he was converted by a vision of CHRIST on the road to Damascus. He wrote several New Testament EPISTLES. Tradition asserts that he was beheaded at Rome under Nero.

Penates Spirits or gods who protected the Roman household and family and were guardians over the household stores.

Pentateuch See TORAH (1).

Pentecost (1) Jewish harvest festival, fifty-two days after PASSOVER. (2) Christian festival marking the coming of the HOLY SPIRIT upon the APOSTLES fifty days after EASTER. The second most important Christian festival, it commemorates the beginning of the CHURCH (1).

Pentecostal churches Churches which have formed from a renewal movement which started in the USA in CE 1906. They teach the experience of 'baptism in the HOLY SPIRIT' which shows itself in speaking in tongues (see GLOSSALALIA) and other 'spiritual gifts'.

Perkons/Perkunas/Perun Supreme god of ancient Russia, particularly associated with thunder and lightning.

Peter Apostle and close follower of JESUS OF NAZARETH, from whom he received the name Peter: 'Rock'. He held a position of leadership among the early apostles. Tradition asserts that he was martyred in Rome.

Pharaoh In the BIBLE, the title of the king of Egypt. The reigning king was identified with the god HORUS, and was held to be responsible for the fertility of the land. On death the king became OSIRIS, his body being mummified and buried in a tomb which from the Third dynasty to the end of the Middle Period might be a PYRAMID.

Pharisees Jewish anti-nationalistic party that emerged in the time of the MACCABEES. They believed that God was universal and taught the individuality of the soul and the RESURRECTION. They prepared the way for the survival of JUDAISM after the FALL OF JERUSALEM in CE 70.

Philo of Alexandria (about 25 BCE–CE 40) Jewish philosopher who tried to reconcile Greek philosophy with the Hebrew scriptures. His commentaries used allegorical devices to penetrate the meaning of scripture. He developed the Greek doctrine of the LOGOS or Word of God into the status of 'a second God'. His speculations were widely studied by the early Christians.

Philosophy of Religion The branch of philosophy which investigates religious experience considering its origin, context and value.

Phylacteries See TEPHILLIN.

Pilgrimage A journey to a holy place, undertaken as a commemoration of a past event, as a celebration or as an act of penance (see also HAJJ). The goal might be a natural feature such as a sacred river or mountain, or the location of a MIRACLE, revelation or THEOPHANY, or the tomb of a hero or SAINT.

Pilgrim Fathers Puritan Christian group who left England for America in the Mayflower in CE 1620 and founded the colony of Plymouth, Massachusetts.

Plato (around 427–347 BCE) Greek philosopher and pupil of SOCRATES. He taught the theory of Forms or Ideas, which are eternal prototypes of the phenomena encountered in ordinary experience. Above all is the Form of the Good, which gives unity and value to all the forms. Plato also taught the immortality of the soul.

PL Kyodan ('Perfect Liberty Association') One of the NEW RELIGIONS of Japan, founded in 1926. It is based on SHINTO but accepts KARMA from BUDDHISM and teaches that the ancestors have an influence on the lives of believers. Its motto is 'life is art' and it sponsors games centres and golf clubs as well as shrines and temples.

Plotinus (around CE 205–69) Egyptian philosopher and author of NEO-PLATONISM whose speculations influenced early Christianity. He dealt with the relationship between the world and the soul and blended Platonic teaching with oriental mysticism. His teachings influenced Augustine.

Polytheism The belief in and worship of a variety of gods, who rule over various aspects of the world and life.

Pontifex High priest of Roman religion and member of a guild of priests whose president

was the *pontifex maximus*. From the fifth century CE the title was applied to Christian BISHOPS, usually the POPE.

Pontius Pilate Roman procurator of the province of Judea CE 26–36 under whose authority JESUS OF NAZARETH was crucified. Tradition asserts that he killed himself but the COPTIC CHURCH reveres him as a Christian MARTYR.

Pope BISHOP of Rome, Vicar of CHRIST and head of the ROMAN CATHOLIC Church, regarded as the successor of PETER. Since the First VATICAN COUNCIL his pronouncement on matters of faith and doctrine issued *ex cathedra* have been regarded as infallible.

Poseidon Greek god of the seas and waters, usually presented as a tall bearded figure carrying a trident. He is responsible for sea storms and earthquakes and is also 'Lord of Horses'.

Prayer The offering of worship, requests, confessions, or other communication to God or gods publicly or privately, with or without words; often a religious obligation.

Prayer wheels Wheels and cylinders used by Buddhists in Tibet and northern India. They are inscribed with the MANTRA: 'OM MANI PADME HUM', the powerful effect of which is multiplied as the wheels turn.

Preferential Option for the Poor See OPTION FOR THE POOR.

Prehistoric religion RELIGIONS dating from the period before the development of writing. In the Middle East this is the period approximately up to 3000 BCE.

Presbyter ('Elder') Term for a Christian minister used in the NEW TESTAMENT interchangeably with BISHOP. Later it was held that the authority of the presbyter (from which comes 'PRIEST') derived from the bishop.

Presbyterian churches REFORMED CHURCHES whose teachings and order of worship reflect Calvinism. They are governed by a pyramid of elected, representative courts.

Priest (1) One authorized to perform priestly functions including mediation between God or gods and humanity, the offering of SACRIFICE and the performance of RITUAL in many religions. (2) A Christian MINISTER, the term deriving from PRESBYTER.

Progressive Judaism Term covering the Liberal and Reform movements which emerged in JUDAISM in nineteenth-century Europe. Both movements are critical of the Talmudic fundamentalism of ORTHODOX JUDAISM and welcome scientific research on the Bible. They also tend to use the vernacular in worship and interpret the dietary laws more liberally than do the Orthodox.

Propaganda, Sacred Congregation of Roman Catholic body concerned with MISSION in non-Christian countries. It dates from the COUNTER-REFORMATION.

Prophet One who speaks for or as a mouthpiece of God or a god. (1) The Old Testament prophets were social and religious reformers of ISRAEL (3) and Judah and of the people of God in EXILE. They proclaimed

God's prospective judgment of Israel; they recalled the people to obedience to God, some offering a hope of a future vindication. (2) In ISLAM 'the Prophet' is MUHAMMAD, who brings the word and judgment of God to final utterance. The authority of the Prophet is an article of the MUSLIM confession of faith.

Prophets, The The second division of the HEBREW BIBLE, including the histories and the prophetic books.

Protestantism Christian faith and order as based on the principles of the REFORMATION. It emphasizes the sole authority of the BIBLE; justification by faith; the priesthood of all believers. Since the nineteenth century it has embraced liberal trends which have stressed the subjective side of religion.

Psalm A sacred song or poem. The Book of Psalms in the BIBLE provides the basis for much Jewish and Christian worship.

Ptah The chief god of Memphis in ancient Egypt, usually depicted bearded, in mummified shape and carrying three sceptres. He was a creator-god, the patron of craftsmen. Merged with Sokar and OSIRIS, he came to have a role in the rituals ensuring the survival of the dead.

Puja ('Reverence') Refers particularly to temple worship in HINDUISM, and to the keeping of rites and ceremonies prescribed by the Brahmans (see CASTE SYSTEM).

Puranas A vast corpus of sacred writings (c. 350–950 CE), which include mythologies of Hindu deities and AVATARS of VISHNU, the origins of the cosmos and of humanity, pilgrimage, ritual, law codes, caste obligations, and so on. There are 18 principal Puranas, each exalting a member of the *Trimurti* (Brahma, Vishnu, Shiva). They are very important in popular Hinduism, the most popular being the *Bhagavata Purana*, which deals with Krishna's early life and encourages devotion to him (BHAKTI).

Pure Land Buddhism Buddhist sect founded by a Chinese monk, Hui Yuan (CE 334–416). It was characterized by faith in the BODHISATTVA AMITABHA, who was the creator of a 'pure land' in the west. Through faith his devotees hoped to be transported there after death.

Purgatory In Roman Catholic teaching, the temporary state of punishment and purification for the dead before their admission to heaven. Its existence was denied by the Protestant reformers.

Purim ('Lots') Joyful Jewish festival celebrating the story of Esther, wife of the Persian king Xerxes, who defeated the anti-Jewish plot of the king's steward, Haman.

Pyramid Type of Egyptian royal tomb, usually tapering to the top from a square base, constructed between about 2630 and 1640 BCE.

Pythagoras (about 570–500 BCE) Greek philosopher, musician and mathematician who taught that number was the basis of reality and that mathematics offered insight into the invisible world. He was influenced by ORPHISM, and taught REINCARNATION and a strict vegetarianism.

Q

Qiyas ('Analogy') Principle of Islamic lawmaking by which the answer to a problem may be inferred from the answer to an analogous problem in the QUR'AN or the SUNNAH.

Quakers Members of the Religious Society of Friends which derives from a puritan group which formed around George Fox in the 1650s. They have no SACRAMENTS and no ordained ministry. Instead authority derives from the 'inner light of the living Christ' in each believer.

Quetzalcoatl Mythological figure in MAYA and AZTEC religion. He may have been a king of a pre-Aztec civilization. He is associated with the rediscovery of the complex Mayan calendar. His name derives from the sacred Quetzal bird. In mythology he is a god of the air who descended to earth and taught humanity the arts of civilization. He opposed the practice of human SACRIFICE. His activities aroused the wrath of another deity and he fled in a boat made of serpent skin. He is often symbolized by a feathered serpent. The name Quetzalcoatl was given to the high priests of Aztec religion.

Qur'an The most important sacred text in Islam – their holy scripture. Muslims believe it was revealed to the PROPHET MUHAMMAD, piecemeal, by God and written in Arabic. All Muslims believe the Qur'an to be divine in origin. It is literally divine thought and law in words. It forms part of the 'Mother of the Book' (also called 'the well-preserved Tablet') inscribed in heaven. The Qur'an descended to the lowest of the seven heavens to the 'House of Protection' during the 'Night of Power'. From there it was revealed bit by bit to Muhammad.

Quraysh The tribe of MUHAMMAD, who opposed his attack on idolatry because they were the traditional custodians of the KA'BA. They were defeated in Muhammad's attack on MECCA in CE 630.

R

Rabbi ('My master') Jewish religious teacher and interpreter of the TORAH. In modern JUDAISM he or she is a minister to the community, a preacher and a leader of SYNAGOGUE worship.

Rabbinic Judaism The religion of the medieval RABBIS who expanded the interpretation of the TALMUD and produced authoritative codes of laws, responses, views and judgments, mostly in the form of correspondence with particular communities.

Radha Wife of a cowherd in the MAHABHARATA, who left her husband to become KRISHNA's mistress. The love of Krishna and Radha is a frequent theme of BHAKTI devotion where it is seen as a type of the love between God and the soul. The frank eroticism of the stories of Radha is not welcomed by all Hindus.

Radhakrishnan, Sarvepalli (CE 1888–1975) Indian philosopher who became vice-president and then president of India. He taught that there is a basic unity of all religions and that HINDUISM is a useful meeting ground because of its breadth and tolerance.

Radical Theology Term sometimes used for theology committed to left-wing politics or for theology that tends towards NON-REALISM.

Ragnarök The doom of the Norse gods, the end of the world order. ODIN and the gods ride out with the dead heroes of VALHALLA against LOKI and the hosts of Hel. A great wolf swallows Odin and the whole creation is dissolved in fire. Out of the chaos emerges a new heaven and a new earth. There are Christian influences in some accounts of Ragnarök.

Rama The seventh incarnation of VISHNU according to HINDU tradition. His exploits in love and war are described in the RAMAYANA. He is the epitome of righteousness and moral virtue.

Ramadan Islamic lunar month in which MUSLIMS are obliged to fast from food and water between sunrise and sunset. The old and sick, pregnant women and nursing mothers are exempt, though they are expected, if possible, to make it up later.

Ramakrishna (CE 1834–86) Hindu Brahman (see CASTE SYSTEM) who taught that all religions are paths to the same goal. He laid the foundation of Hindu universalism. He was a devotee of KALI, though philosophically he adhered to the teaching of SHANKARA.

Ramakrishna Mission Indian religious order founded in 1897 by VIVEKANANDA. Its aims are to teach VEDANTA and to care for the sick and needy. It has dispensaries, libraries and welfare centres throughout India and has teaching branches in Europe and the USA.

Ramanuja (died CE 1157) Indian philosopher who opposed SHANKARA's stress on the oneness of being and denied that the divine lord belonged to a lower order of reality. He believed God and the world were related like body and soul, inseparable but distinct. He was a devotee of VISHNU, and believed in the validity of personal devotion to God.

Ramayana One of the two great epics of the HINDU scriptures compiled in the second or first century BCE. Ascribe to the sage Valmiki, it tells of the life of the AVATAR RAMA.

Rammohan Roy (CE 1772–1833) HINDU reformer who founded the Brahma Samaj, an ethical organization with monotheistic tendencies, in opposition to the idolatry of popular religion. He believed the VEDAS taught MONOTHEISM, though he also used Christian and Muslim ideas.

Rastafarianism Religious and political movement centred in the Caribbean. It is a cult of Ras Tafari, better known as Haile Selassie (CE 1892–1975), emperor of Ethiopia (1930–74). Many Rastafarians (not all) are distinguished by keeping their hair in 'dreadlocks' and by their use of cannabis in worship. They helped develop the reggae style of music, which they use to express their political and religious aspirations. The singer Bob Marley has become one of the heroes of the movement.

Re Sun god and supreme god of the religion of ancient Egypt.

Rebirth Buddhist modification of REINCARNATION in the light of the ANATTA teaching. As there is no SOUL (2), there is no reincarnation as such but the karmic (see KARMA) residue of one's life and actions are reclothed in the attributes and qualities acquired in the previous life. After a while this karmic 'bundle' is reborn.

Redemption God's saving work of buying back or recovering what is his. In JUDAISM it refers to the restoration of ISRAEL, in CHRISTIANITY to the ransoming of sinners from the power of SIN and death.

Red Hats Unreformed branch of TIBETAN BUDDHISM whose practices owe much to the former Tibetan religion of Bön.

Reformation The movement within Western CHRISTIANITY between the fourteenth and the seventeenth centuries which led to the separation of the Protestant Churches from Rome. The main issue was the authority of the pope but doctrinal issues such as the precise meaning of the EUCHARIST and the authority and accessibility of Scripture were also important.

Reformed churches Churches which inherit the Calvinist tradition, including PRESBYTERIANS, INDEPENDENTS, Calvinistic METHODISTS and CONGREGATIONALISTS.

Reiki The term is often translated as 'Universal Life Force Energy'. It is a method of spiritual healing founded in Japan by Usui Makao (1865–1926) and introduced into the West by Takata Hawayo. It teaches the existence of a universal energy, *ki*, which is similar to the Chinese notion of *chi*. When the flow of this energy is blocked, the result is a range of ailments, both psychological and physical. Reiki practitioners are able to channel and manipulate this energy by laying their hands on (or over) a person's body.

Reincarnation The belief that individual souls survive death and are reborn to live again in a different body, thus passing through a series of lives. Held in pre-ARYAN India, the belief is associated with the doctrine of KARMA. Some traditions believe rebirth is possible only in human bodies, others envisage hellish or heavenly states, while others suggest a transmigration in which human souls are tied to animal or vegetable forms. Some Hindu apologists explain the doctrine as a mythical way of speaking about the continuity of the human race.

Relics Bones or remains of SAINTS, venerated and accredited with miraculous powers in many religions.

Religion (From Latin: *religere*, 'to pay careful attention to some activity' or *religare*, 'to tie something tightly') A system of belief and worship, held by a community who may express their religion through shared MYTHS, DOCTRINES, ethical teachings, RITUALS, or the remembrance of special experiences.

Renunciation Giving up ownership of material possessions. In some religions, such as Buddhism, renunciation extends to psychological detachment from material possessions, including one's own body.

Restoration Movement to restore the CHURCH to a pristine state in which the

KINGDOM OF GOD is established through a charismatically ordained ministry. Restorationists see themselves as EVANGELICALS and Pentecostalists, but with a new edge to their commitment. Many HOUSE CHURCHES promote a Restorationist theology.

Resurrection (1) The Christian belief that JESUS OF NAZARETH was raised from death by God the Father who thus vindicated him as MESSIAH and revealed his defeat of death and SIN. (2) The raising of all the dead for JUDGMENT as taught in JUDAISM, CHRISTIANITY and ISLAM.

Rinzai Zen School of ZEN which employs startling techniques (e.g. KOANS) to induce SATORI.

Rissho Kosei-kai An offshoot of the Reiyukai movement which is spreading the teachings of NICHIREN Buddhism beyond the boundaries of Japan. The sect claims over 5 million members.

Rita The cosmic order as understood in the Hindu VEDAS. It is the principle of ethical and physical organization throughout the universe and is the work of the sky god VARUNA.

Rites of Passage Religious ceremonies which mark the transition from one state of life to another. In many religions these transitional periods are felt to be dangerous and to require spiritual protection. Examples include birth rites, INITIATION rites, marriage rites and funeral rites.

Ritual Religious ceremonial performed according to a set pattern of words, movements and symbolic actions. Rituals may involve the dramatic re-enactment of ancient MYTHS featuring gods and heroes, performed to ensure the welfare of the community.

Roma The personification of the city of Rome, worshipped by the Romans as a goddess.

Roman Catholic Catholic CHRISTIAN who recognizes the authority of the POPE, the Bishop of Rome.

Rosh Hashanah The Jewish New Year, celebrated as the anniversary of creation. The liturgy is penitential in tone and looks forward to the KINGDOM OF GOD and the MESSIAH. The blowing of the ram's horn proclaims God as king of the universe.

Rosicrucianism Mystical system founded in seventeenth-century Germany and based on an account of a secret brotherhood founded 'to improve mankind by the discovery of the true philosophy'. Several societies came into being based on this originally fictitious 'Meritorious Order of the Rosy Cross' with its private language and magical alphabet. They applied themselves to studies such as ALCHEMY.

Rugievit Slavic god with seven faces from the island of Rügen.

Rumi, Jalal al-Din (died CE 1273) Sufi MYSTIC and poet, author of the *Mathnavi* and founder of a DERVISH order. He was a nature mystic and often used love and wine as allegories of the experience of the divine.

Russell, C.T. (Charles Taze) (CE 1852–1916) US Bible scholar who started a periodical called *Zion's Watchtower* after being influenced by speculation about the return of CHRIST. This grew into the JEHOVAH'S WITNESSES movement.

Russian Orthodox Church The principal church of Russia since CE 988.

S

Saadya Ben Joseph (CE 892–940) Head of the Jewish academy at Susa in Babylon. He defended the cause of Talmudic JUDAISM (see TALMUD) against the KARAITES and the doctrine of the oneness of God against the Christian TRINITY. He was the first Jewish systematic theologian and he believed in the unity and divine origin of both revelation and reason.

Sabbath (Shabbat) Jewish day of worship and rest lasting from Friday sunset to Saturday sunset. The Sabbath is holy because it commemorates God's rest on the seventh day of creation and reminds JEWS (2) of the deliverance from Egypt.

Sacrament 'An outward and visible sign of an inward and spiritual grace' (Book of Common Prayer). REFORMED CHURCHES count only BAPTISM and the EUCHARIST as sacraments, both being instituted by CHRIST. Roman Catholic and Orthodox Churches add CONFIRMATION, marriage, ORDINATION, penance and extreme unction (the anointing of the sick).

Sacred bears In PREHISTORIC RELIGION ritual veneration of the slain bear. It remains common, especially in Arctic and sub-Arctic regions. The Japanese Ainu tribe have bear rituals as do the Lapps, Finns, Eskimos and Native Americans. Eskimo SHAMANS receive the Great Spirit disguised as a Polar bear. Bear worship is frequently associated with the recognition of the constellation Ursa Major; MYTHS concerning the constellation are found among the Greeks and other European and Asian peoples.

Sacred birds Often a symbol of transformation. In Greek mythology ZEUS disguises himself as a swan in pursuit of amorous adventures. The CELTS revere the swan as a symbol of divine transformation and also recognize ravens as appearances of war goddesses. Native peoples of South and Central America venerate the plumed quetzal (see also QUETZALCOATL). The mythical phoenix of Arabia symbolized the cycle of death and rebirth, the ancient Egyptians finding in the similar benu a manifestation of the god Re-Atum worshipped at Heliopolis. A bird often symbolizes the departing SOUL (1) freed from the shackles of earthly life. In the BIBLE, the HOLY SPIRIT is described as being like a dove.

Sacred bulls Symbols of power and strength. They were connected with the worship of the MOTHER GODDESS, especially in the MINOAN RELIGION of ancient Crete where they gave rise to the MYTH of the Minotaur, a bull-like monster who had to be placated with human sacrifices. The slaughter of a bull was important in some forms of Roman religion.

Sacred snakes Frequently associated with the MOTHER GODDESS especially in MINOAN RELIGION. Because they shed their skin they are symbols of immortality. They are also associated with wisdom and healing. In Chinese religion dragons replace snakes as sacred animals. In Norse mythology a Great Serpent, son of the evil LOKI, surrounds the earth. In CHRISTIANITY the snake is a symbol of evil and deceit, especially connected with the biblical MYTH of the Garden of Eden.

Sacred Thread ceremony INITIATION ceremony performed on upper-caste HINDU boys. A sacred thread is placed around the neck indicating that the boy is one of the twice-born and has entered the first stage of life. (See also NAVJOTE.)

Sacred trees Objects of religious significance since they connect the earth to the sky. In Celtic religion tree species were sacred to particular tribes: Irish literature speaks of a sacred ash, a yew and an oak, among others. The connection of DRUIDS with the oak is likely but unproved. (See also YGGDRASIL.)

Sacred wells Springs, rivers and natural wells often have religious significance, particularly in Celtic religion. Regarded as passages to the UNDERWORLD, votive offerings such as brooches, bracelets and even severed human heads were deposited there. The custom of throwing coins into water may reflect these ancient practices.

Sacrifice The ritual offering of animal or vegetable life to establish communion between humans and a god or gods.

Sadducees Aristocratic Jewish party which emerged in the times of the MACCABEES. They rejected the oral law and late doctrines like the RESURRECTION. They were nationalists and collaborated with the Romans to ensure the survival of the Jewish state. The party collapsed after CE 70.

Sai Baba (Born CE 1926) Spiritual teacher from Brindavan in South India who is regarded by his followers as an AVATAR. Probably the most popular and influential GURU in present-day India, he specializes in curing illness and materializing gifts for his disciples.

Saint (1) Holy person or dead hero of faith who is venerated by believers on earth and held to be a channel of divine blessing. The Protestant reformers rejected the practice of devotion to saints. (2) In the NEW TESTAMENT and some Protestant Churches, a term for any believer.

Salafiya Puritan Islamic party which emerged in nineteenth-century Egypt. It accepted the authority only of the QUR'AN and the SUNNAH and rejected the 'ULAMA'. In time it grew closer to the WAHHABI MOVEMENT. It published a journal, *Al-Manat*, which circulated in the Middle East.

Salah Islamic ritual prayer which is carried out five times a day, facing MECCA and using ritual movements to accompany the words. Salah is one of the FIVE PILLARS OF ISLAM.

Salvation (1) In the BIBLE, deliverance of God's people from their enemies, and especially from SIN and its consequences, death and HELL, hence also the whole process of forgiveness, new life and final glorification for the believer. (2) In Eastern religions, release from the changing material world to identification with the ABSOLUTE.

Samhain Celtic festival marking the beginning of winter, celebrated on 1 November with feasting and carousals. Regarded as a period outside the normal flow of time when the dead could freely return to communicate with the living, it was the subject of many MYTHS and legends, mainly concerning death. It is celebrated today by contemporary Pagans.

Samsara ('Stream of existence') Sanskrit word which refers to the cycle of birth and death followed by rebirth as applied both to individuals and to the universe itself.

Sanctuary A place consecrated to a god, a holy place, a place of divine refuge and protection. Also, the holiest part of a sacred place or building. Historically, in some cultures, a holy place where pursued criminals or victims were guaranteed safety.

Sangha Community of Buddhist MONKS which started with the BUDDHA's first disciples. The functions of the *sangha* are to promote through its own lifestyle the best conditions for attaining individual salvation and to teach the DHAMMA to all people.

Sanhedrin Jewish supreme council of seventy which organized religious life during the period of independence following the revolt of the MACCABEES. Under Herod the Great the Sanhedrin was divided: the SADDUCEES dealt with political matters; the PHARISEES concentrated on the interpretation of the TORAH. After the FALL OF JERUSALEM (CE 70) an academic Sanhedrin was organized in Jabneh to reorganize Jewish life.

Sannyasi ('One who renounces') The last of the Hindu FOUR STAGES OF LIFE.

Sanskrit The language of the ARYAN peoples and of the Hindu scriptures. It is an Indo-European language related to Latin, Greek and Persian.

Sarasvati In HINDUISM, the goddess of truth and consort of BRAHMA, the Creator.

Satan In the BIBLE, the personification of evil and identified with the DEVIL.

Satanism Sometimes referred to as 'devil-worship', it should be distinguished from Paganism. Most Pagans do not recognize a being called Satan, which they identify with Christian belief. That said, Satanists will claim that their religion too is not simply an inversion of Christian teaching. Indeed, not all Satanists believe in the existence of a being called Satan, but rather focus on him as a powerful, alternative symbol.

Satguru (1) In SIKHISM, GOD, the true and eternal GURU. (2) In popular HINDUISM a term for a revered teacher such as SAI BABA.

Satori ENLIGHTENMENT in ZEN BUDDHISM.

Saturnalia Roman festival of Saturn, a mythical king of Rome and father of the god JUPITER, which began on 17 December. A time of banquets and present-giving, some of its characteristics were transferred to the festival of CHRISTMAS.

Sawm See FIVE PILLARS OF ISLAM.

Schism A deliberate division or split between Christians that disrupts the unity of the CHURCH.

Scribes Officials who organized the religious life of the Jewish community after the EXILE of 586 BCE. They regulated the observance of the SABBATH, communal prayer and fasting and were the interpreters of the Law. One of their tasks was to develop 'fences' around the TORAH to prevent its infringement.

Scripture Writings which are believed to be divinely inspired or especially authoritative within a particular religious community.

Sebek Egyptian god associated with water and death.

Second Coming/Parousia The personal second coming of CHRIST which, Christians believe, will be a time of judgment and the inauguration of the KINGDOM OF GOD in its fullness.

Sect A group, usually religious (but it can be political), which has separated itself from an established tradition, claiming to teach and practice a truer form of the faith from which it has separated itself. It is, as such, often highly critical of the wider tradition which it has left. For example, the JEHOVAH'S WITNESSES and the SEVENTH DAY ADVENTISTS are sectarian Christian organizations.

Sefirot According to the teachings of Jewish Kabbalistic MYSTICISM (see KABBALAH), the potencies and attributes by which God acts and makes himself known.

Sephardim One of the two main cultural groups in JUDAISM which emerged during the Middle Ages. Sephardic JEWS lived in Spain and Portugal and their traditions go back to Babylonian Jewry. They developed Ladino as their language.

Serapis State god of Ptolemaic Egypt whose worship spread throughout the Mediterranean. He took over many characteristics from the ancient Egyptian OSIRIS, but was also associated with the bull god Apis, in turn associated with PTAH. He was both a healing god and a ruler of the UNDERWORLD.

Seth The evil brother of OSIRIS in Egyptian mythology. He murdered his brother and seized his earthly rule until in turn defeated by HORUS. He became the god of war, storms, deserts and disorder.

Seven Precepts of the Sons of Noah The obligations placed on all men and women, regardless of race or faith, according to Jewish teaching. They comprise abstinence from idolatry, blasphemy, incest, murder, theft, the eating of living flesh, and the implementation of justice.

Seventh-Day Adventists Christian sect which emerged from a number of nineteenth-century groups stressing the imminent return of CHRIST. They observe the Jewish SABBATH instead of Sunday. They accept the BIBLE as infallible and require a lifestyle of strict temperance.

Shabbat See SABBATH.

Shaivism Worship of the Hindu god SHIVA. It is particularly strong in southern India and appeals to extreme ascetics. From Shaivite texts have come the strongest affirmations of MONOTHEISM within HINDUISM.

Shakti ('Energy', 'power') A feminine word, particularly associated with SHIVA and his consorts (see KALI; PARVATI; DURGA). In TANTRISM *shakti* is universal creativity and exists in people as a latent energy located at the base of the spine (see KUNDALINI). In tantric YOGA this energy is awakened to travel up the spine and unite with Shiva, who is present as mind.

Shakyamuni ('The wise man of the SHAKYAS') One of the names of the BUDDHA.

Shakyas Tribe to which the BUDDHA's family belonged. They occupied territory in the Himalayan foothills.

Shaman (1) An ecstatic priest-magician among the Tungu people of Siberia. (2) By extension, a similar figure in other INDIGENOUS RELIGIONS and ancient religions. Shamans induce a trance experience in which they are believed to leave the body and visit other worlds. The shaman's role is to convey sacrifices to the gods, to escort the dead to their destination and to return with divine prophecies.

Shamash Babylonian sun god and lord of justice who rewards honesty and loyalty and brings retribution on the wicked. He is depicted as giving a ring and sceptre to the lawgiver HAMMURABI.

Shammai See HILLEL.

Shankara (CE 788–820) The best-known exponent of classical HINDU philosophy. Developing the thought of the UPANISHADS, he declared that only the eternal being is real; the diverse, phenomenal world is an illusion of MAYA (1). Even the notion of a personal God is part of maya. Liberation comes from realizing oneness with the ABSOLUTE, which is defined as Being, Consciousness and Bliss. (See also VEDANTA (2).)

Shari'a ('The path') Body of law for the MUSLIM community which derives from the QUR'AN, the SUNNAH, and other sources, the legitimacy of which is debated in the different schools of law. Shari'a is regarded as divinely authoritative.

Shavuot See WEEKS.

Shaykh/Sheikh/Shaikh (1) An Arab tribal leader. (2) Sufi spiritual teacher (see SUFISM), somewhat analogous to the Hindu GURU.

Shekhinah The presence or manifestation of God as described in the TARGUMS and later Jewish writings. It came to refer to the indwelling of God in creation. In KABALLAH the Shekhinah is exiled from the eternity of God, EN SOF, because of human SIN and will only be restored at the final REDEMPTION.

Shema The Jewish confession of faith, recited in the morning and evening service. '*Shema*' is the opening word in HEBREW of the confession: 'Hear, O Israel, the Lord our God, the Lord is One…' Three passages from the TORAH confirm that there is one God and that Israel is chosen to witness to him.

Shi'a/Shi'ites The minority group in ISLAM, comprising 15 per cent of MUSLIMS. They reject the first three CALIPHS, believing 'ALI to be MUHAMMAD's true successor. They also hold that authority resides in the IMAMS, who are the infallible messengers of God in every age. The Shi'a live mostly in Iraq, Iran, Lebanon, Pakistan and India. The two main Shi'a

RAPID FACT-FINDER

divisions are the ISMA'ILIS and the TWELVERS.

Shingon 'True Word' sect of Japanese Buddhism founded in the ninth century CE and characterized by a complex sacramental and magical ritual which may have been influenced by TANTRISM and by indigenous SHINTO practices.

Shinran (CE 1173–1263) Disciple of HONEN and founder of the Japanese Buddhist sect JODO SHINSHU.

Shinto The indigenous nature religion of Japan which has provided a focus for nationalistic aspirations. (See also EMPEROR, JAPANESE; IZANAGI; JIMMU TENNO; JINJA; KAMI; KOJIKI; MATSURI; NIHONGI; NINIGI.)

Shirk ('Associating') In ISLAM the greatest sin, that of ascribing equals to God. (See also TAWHID.)

Shiva One of the great gods of HINDU devotion. He is a god of contrasts, presiding over creation and destruction, fertility and asceticism, good and evil. He is the original Lord of the Dance who dances out the creation of the universe. As god of ascetics he is portrayed as a great *yogi*, smeared with ashes, holding the world in being through meditation. His symbol is a phallus-shaped pillar denoting procreation.

Shotoku, Prince Japanese ruler who introduced BUDDHISM as the state religion. During his reign (CE 593–621) he built a Buddhist academy and temple near the state capital at Nara.

Shudras See CASTE SYSTEM.

Shulhan Aruch See KARO, JOSEPH.

Shvetambaras ('White-clad') Members of a major JAIN sect who rejected the DIGAMBARAS' stress on the virtues of nudity. They are numerous in the north of India.

Siddhartha Personal name of GAUTAMA the BUDDHA.

Sikh ('Disciple') Follower of the Sikh religion which developed in the fifteenth century CE in North India as a synthesis of ISLAM and HINDUISM. (See also ADI GRANTH; GOBINDH SINGH; GURDWARA; KABIR; KHALSA; NANAK; SINGH.)

Sin (1) An action which breaks a divine law. (2) The state of rebellion against God which, in Christian teaching, has been the human condition since the Fall of Adam and Eve and their expulsion from the Garden of Eden.

Sin Babylonian moon-god and guardian of the city of Ur. He usually appears riding on a winged bull. He is the father of the sun, SHAMASH, and god of vegetation.

Sinai, Mount Mountain in the south of the Sinai peninsula where, according to tradition, God revealed himself to MOSES and gave him the Ten Commandments.

Singh Surname used by SIKHS. It means 'lion' and expresses the militant stance which Guru GOBINDH SINGH impressed upon the Sikh community.

Sinkyo Traditional religion of Korea.

Sita Consort of RAMA in Hindu tradition.

Skandha/Khandha Term referring to the five factors which compound human

personality according to Buddhist teaching. They are form, sense perception, consciousness, intellectual power and discrimination. The relation between them is continuously changing in accordance with the action of KARMA.

Skilful means Buddhist practice of compassion in sharing the DHAMMA with the unenlightened. Tradition describes the BUDDHA explaining the Dhamma at different levels to different people. In the LOTUS SUTRA tricks and deceptions are among the skilful means employed to lead the lost to salvation.

Smith, Joseph (CE 1805–44) Founder of MORMONISM who claimed to be the recipient of a divine revelation to the former inhabitants of America in the form of golden plates inscribed in ancient languages. With the help of the Angel Moroni, he translated these and they became the basis of the BOOK OF MORMON. Ordained priest by the heavenly messenger, he founded the Church of Jesus Christ of Latter-day Saints in 1830. He died at the hands of a mob.

Socrates (469–399 BCE) Greek philosopher and teacher and mentor of PLATO. He taught by a method of question and answer which sought to elicit a consistent and rational response and hence to arrive at a universally agreed truth. He was executed in Athens for corrupting the youth and introducing strange gods.

Soka Gakkai 'Value-creating society' of lay members of the Japanese Buddhist sect NICHIREN. It was founded in 1930 in a wave of new cults. It is evangelistic, exclusive and highly organized. It runs its own political party and has schools and a university.

Sol Invictus ('Unconquered sun') A name for MITHRA. From the time of the emperor Aurelian (CE 270–75) until displaced by CHRISTIANITY, his was the official imperial cult of Rome.

Soma The juice of the Indian *soma* plant, which may have been fermented or had hallucinogenic properties. It was drunk by gods and men in the VEDAS, and was regarded as a mediating god with power over all plants and as a conveyor of immortality.

Sorcerer A practioner of harmful MAGIC. In INDIGENOUS RELIGIONS sorcerers are sometimes believed to be able to kill others through magic.

Soteriology Teaching about SALVATION.

Soto Zen School of ZEN Buddhism which teaches a gradual and gentle way to SATORI.

Soul (1) The immortal element of an individual man or woman which survives the death of the body in most religious teachings. (2) A human being when regarded as a spiritual being.

Spell A formula of words with or without accompanying RITUAL actions which is believed to have the power to manipulate natural or supernatural forces for good or evil ends. The exact form of the spell is often the secret of the practitioner. In contemporary WICCA, spells are recorded in the Witch's Book of Shadows.

Spiritualism Any religious system or practice which has the object of establishing

communication with the dead. Most modern spiritualist churches derive from a movement which grew up in mid-nineteenth-century America. Spiritualists seek to communicate with the dead through such means as table-turning and automatic writing. All mainstream Christian churches denounce the practices of spiritualism.

Steiner, Rudolf (CE 1861–1925) Founder of ANTHROPOSOPHY. He originally followed THEOSOPHY and ROSICRUCIANISM, but he broke with these groups and developed his mystical ideas into an educational, ecological and medical programme for spiritual progress. He founded a number of highly successful schools which cater for some 120,000 pupils.

Stoicism Philosophical school founded by Zeno of Citium (approximately 335–263 BCE) and named after the porch or *stoa* where he taught in Athens. Stoics believed that the world order reflected the divine intelligence – the LOGOS which was present in all creation. Human beings could attain virtue – harmony with the universe – by learning self-sufficiency and behaving with courage and self-control.

Stonehenge Megalithic monument (see MEGALITHS) on Salisbury Plain, England. It may have been a sanctuary for sun worship or regulated an agricultural and astrological calendar.

Stupa A mound built up to mark a Buddhist holy place or collection of relics. Many stupas in India date from the reign of king Asoka.

Subud Spiritual teaching of the Javanese Muslim teacher Pak Subuh (CE 1901–87). It emphasizes submission to the Life Force through a course of spiritual training designed to open up the individual to the reality of God and to mastery over the lower nature. The Subud training is open to members of all faiths.

Sufism Islamic mystical movement originating in the eighth century CE as a reaction to the worldliness of the UMMAYAD DYNASTY. Sufis claimed direct experience of ALLAH through ascetic practices. The orthodox rejected them at first, but today Sufi orders are accepted among SUNNIS and SHI'AS. (See also ISLAM.)

Sukkot See BOOTHS.

Sundance Four-day ceremony which grew up among Native Americans Plains in the 1870s as a reaction against white attempts to break up the traditions and beliefs of the people. It was held in the summer inside an immense circular area. The ceremony was crushed by the US army and regulations were imposed against such rituals.

Sun God In the INCA religion, the creator of Manco Capac, the first Inca, and father to all the Inca rulers. His names include INTI and Punchau.

Sunnah ('Trodden path') The source of authority in Islamic lawmaking which is second only to the QUR'AN. It refers to the words and actions of MUHAMMAD and, in a lesser degree, to the words and actions of the first four CALIPHS.

Sunni The majority group in ISLAM, comprising about 85 per cent of MUSLIMS.

They accept the authority of the FOUR RIGHTLY GUIDED CALIPHS and the developed process of lawmaking guided by the community's legal experts. Sunni Muslims live in the Arab states in North, West and East Africa and in India and Indonesia.

Sutta Pitaka The most important collection of THERAVADA Buddhist SCRIPTURES. It consists of sermons of the BUDDHA, including the DHAMMAPADA.

Suzuki, Daisetz T. (CE 1870–1966) Japanese ZEN scholar who played a major part in introducing Zen Buddhism to the Western world. He was a member of the RINZAI sect and was sympathetic to CHRISTIANITY.

Swami General term for a HINDU holy man or member of a religious order.

Swami Narayan (CE 1781–1830) Gujurati preacher and founder of a popular sect which attracted Sikh and Hindu followers.

Swedenborg, Emmanuel (CE 1688–1772) Swedish scientist who became a MYSTIC and visionary. He taught a kind of pantheistic THEOSOPHY (see PANTHEISM) centred on Jesus Christ, in whom he found a Trinity of Love, Wisdom and Energy. He founded the New Church.

Synagogue Jewish meeting place for worship and study. Synagogues grew out of the TORAH schools of the SCRIBES during the EXILE. After the destruction of the TEMPLE OF JERUSALEM (CE 70), synagogues became the centres of Jewish life. They are built to face JERUSALEM and contain an Ark (2) in which the scrolls of the law are displayed before a perpetual lamp. Worship in synagogues includes readings from the TORAH, psalms, sermons and communal prayers.

Syncretism The growing together of two or more religions making a new development in religion which contains some of the beliefs and practices of both.

T

Tabernacles, Festival of See BOOTHS.

Taboo Polynesian word applied to an object, place or person which is prohibited because of its holy or dangerous character. It may include the sense of being 'marked off' and therefore separate from everyday usage.

Tagore, Rabindranath (CE 1861–1941) Bengali poet, playwright, musician and Nobel prize-winner, whose passionate espousal of Bengali culture influenced the cause of Indian nationalism. His devotional verses were popular in Britain in the Edwardian era.

Tai Ch'i (1) 'The 'Transcendent Absolute' or 'Great Ultimate' which is the underlying cause and unity of all things in early Chinese Taoist and later neo-Confucian thought. It is the nearest equivalent to GOD in Chinese thought. (2) The name of a martial art often practiced as a form of spiritual development. It takes the form of slow, graceful movements, designed to align the practitioner with the natural flow of the universal Ch'i.

Tallit Jewish prayer shawl fringed at the four corners and used during morning prayer and on YOM KIPPUR.

Talmud The written interpretation and development of the HEBREW scriptures. It is based on the MISHNAH of JUDAH HANASI, with the addition of some excluded teachings and commentary recorded from the debates and controversies of the Schools of Babylon on Palestine. There are two versions: the Palestinian, compiled while the Jews were under duress from the Christian Church, and the Babylonian which is more detailed and complete.

Tammuz Babylonian/Syrian fertility deity. A young god who, in mythology, died and was resurrected after the pattern of the Egyptian OSIRIS.

Tanha ('Craving') The main cause of suffering as analysed by the BUDDHA in the FOUR NOBLE TRUTHS.

Tantrism Tibetan Buddhist practices which aim at direct experience of the enlightened self through symbols, visual images, repetition of sounds, prescribed movements, breath control and ritualized sexual intercourse.

Tao ('Way') In TAOISM, the underlying principle of reality.

Taoism Chinese philosophy outlined in the TAO TE CHING. Its aim is to achieve harmony with all that is by pursuing inaction and effortlessness. Taoism gradually evolved an elaborate mythological system and incorporated notions of spirit possession, ALCHEMY and DIVINATION. (See also JADE EMPEROR; LAO-TZU.)

Tao te ching Chinese religious work compiled in the fourth century BCE and ascribed to LAO-TZU, though it is probably the work of several writers. It describes the TAO as the underlying principle of reality which can only be attained by passivity.

Targum An Aramaic translation of a HEBREW scripture reading. The translator was expected to make a free interpretation. Some of these have become famous in their own right and are used by pious JEWS alongside the appointed text.

Tarot cards Deck of seventy-eight cards marked with various symbolic figures which are shuffled and dealt as a form of DIVINATION.

Tat tvam asi ('You are that') Phrase from the UPANISHADS which expresses the claim that BRAHMAN, the divine power sustaining the universe, and ATMAN, the soul, are one.

Tawhid ('Asserting oneness') The essential MUSLIM doctrine of the unity of God. He is oneness in himself without parts or partners.

Tephillin ('Phylacteries') Small boxes containing scriptural texts written on parchment. They are worn by JEWS (2) on the head and arm during daily prayer.

Temple Building designed for WORSHIP of God or gods, usually containing a SANCTUARY or holy place where SACRIFICE may be offered.

Temple of Heaven Great Chinese temple in Peking where the Chinese emperors received the mandate of heaven (see T'IEN) to rule over the Chinese people. It is still used for great state occasions.

Temple of Jerusalem/Holy Temple TEMPLE first built by Solomon on a site

bequeathed by DAVID. It was divided into the Holy Place and the Holy of Holies where dwelt the presence of YHWH. This temple was destroyed in 586 BCE. The second temple was dedicated in 515 BCE. It was desecrated by the Hellenistic Seleucid king Antiochus Epiphanes but rededicated by JUDAS MACCABEUS. Rebuilding was begun under Herod the Great in 20 BCE. The temple was virtually completed in CE 62, but destroyed by Titus in CE 70.

Ten Gurus In SIKHISM GURU NANAK and his nine successors who are seen as sharing the same essential insights into the nature of God.

Tendai Japanese Buddhist sect based on a former Chinese sect T'ien-t'ai, and founded in the ninth century CE. Tendai was an attempt at a synthesis between MAHAYANA teachings which stressed MEDITATION and those that stressed devotion.

Tengri The supreme god of the Mongols. It was also used as a collective name for gods.

Tenrikyo 'Religion of Heavenly Wisdom' founded in Japan by MIKI NAKAYAMA, and based at the city of Tenri, near Nara, at the site of the founder's home. This is believed to be the centre of the world and it is the place of divine homecoming for the sect's 2 million adherents.

Tetragrammaton See YHWH.

Teutates, Esus and Taranis Gaulish gods mentioned by the Roman writer Lucan (CE 39–65). They required to be appeased by bloody sacrifices. Teutates in particular may have been a god of war, healing and fertility and the guardian of his people.

Tezcatlipoca ('That which causes the Black Mirror to shine') AZTEC god of night and the north, a magician, symbolized by a jaguar. He was one of the most important of the Aztec gods.

Theism The belief in one supreme GOD who is both TRANSCENDENT and involved in the workings of the universe.

Theocracy ('Divine government') Term describing a state which is constituted on the basis of divine law. It is an important concept in ISLAM, where it is sometimes believed that the law of the land should be identical with the SHARI'A. The regime of CALVIN in Geneva was also theocratic.

Theodicy The defence of God as both good and omnipotent, which accounts for the existence of suffering and evil. The term was coined in 1710 by Gottfried Leibniz.

Theology (1) A systematic formulation of belief made by or on behalf of a particular individual or CHURCH or other body of believers. (2) The critical study of RELIGION, particularly CHRISTIANITY, with regard to its origins, SCRIPTURES and other texts, DOCTRINES, ethics, history and practices.

Theophany A divine appearance, revelation or manifestation, usually inducing awe and terror in those who witness it. Examples are the appearance of God to MOSES on Mount SINAI amidst thunder, lightning, smoke and trumpet blasts; the appearance of KRISHNA in his divine form, 'like a thousand suns', as described in the BHAGAVAD GITA.

Theosophy ('Divine wisdom') A term applied to various mystical movements but which refers particularly to the principles of the Theosophical Society founded by Madame BLAVATSKY in 1875. These comprise a blend of Hindu, Buddhist and Christian ideas, together with particular stress on REINCARNATION, immortality and the presence of GOD in all things. Theosophists also believe in a series of World Teachers ('Ascended Masters') who are incarnated to express the divine wisdom.

Theravada ('The doctrine of the elders') The form of BUDDHISM practised in Sri Lanka, Myanmar (Burma), Thailand, Cambodia and Laos, which sticks firmly to the teachings of the VINAYA PITAKA and rejects the doctrine of the BODHISATTVAS.

Thirteen Principles Articles of Jewish faith which were formulated by Moses MAIMONIDES in the twelfth century CE. They assert faith in God as creator, as formless unity, First and Last and only hearer of prayer. They also affirm the words of the PROPHETS, MOSES as the chief of the prophets, the unchanging nature of TORAH, the Creator's knowledge of humanity, the judgment, the coming of the MESSIAH and the RESURRECTION of the dead. The Thirteen Principles are found in the Jewish Prayer Book.

Thomas, John See CHRISTADELPHIANS.

Thor Norse god of thunder and lightning. He is portrayed as wild and red-haired, wielding a great hammer. Thor is the son of Mother Earth and his wife, Sif, is a corn goddess. He is associated with agriculture and is the protector of MIDGARD against the giants.

Thoth Ibis-headed Egyptian god, patron of writing and counting, who recorded the weighing of souls in the judgment after death.

Three Body Doctrine MAHAYANA Buddhist teaching that the BUDDHA exists in three aspects. His human existence was his 'transformation body'. In his celestial existence he appears in his 'enjoyment body'. But the ultimate basis of his Buddhahood is his 'truth body' which unites all three bodies. This is identified with ultimate reality.

Three refuges Brief dedication used by Buddhists and traditionally given by the Buddha himself: 'I go to the Buddha for refuge; I go to the *Dhamma* for refuge; I go to the *Sangha* for refuge.'

Thunderbird A totem (see TOTEMISM) found widely among Native Americans of North America. It represents the eagle, the great bird of the eastern doorway of the world. It also represents thunder spirits who bring rain; the clap of its wings sounds the thunder and the flash of its eyes symbolizes lightning. The Thunderbird is frequently found at the top of Native American TOTEM POLES.

Tibetan Book of the Dead Book of instructions and preparations for death and rites to be performed for the dying. In TIBETAN BUDDHISM the dying must train in advance, helped by a spiritual teacher, to face the clear light of the Void, reality itself, in such a way as to avoid REBIRTH, or at least to ensure a human rebirth.

Tibetan Buddhism/Vajrayana A mixture of BUDDHISM, TANTRISM and the ancient Bön religion of Tibet. The two main groups are the RED HATS and the YELLOW HATS. (See also CHAKRAS; CHORTEN; DALAI LAMA; LAMA; MANDALA; PANCHEN LAMA; PRAYER WHEELS; TIBETAN BOOK OF THE DEAD.)

T'ien ('Heaven') Chinese term sometimes used for the supreme GOD. From around 1000 BCE the Chinese emperors were believed to rule by mandate of heaven.

Tipitaka The 'three baskets' of the BUDDHA's teaching, the canon of SCRIPTURE for THERAVADA BUDDHISTS, comprising the VINAYA PITAKA, the SUTTA PITAKA and the ABHIDHAMMA PITAKA.

Tirthankaras see JINA.

Tlaloc AZTEC god of rain and vegetation. His name means 'he who makes things sprout'. He is portrayed with long fangs and rings around his eyes.

Tongues, Speaking in See GLOSSOLALIA.

Torah (1) The five books of the Law (the PENTATEUCH) revealed to MOSES; the first division of the HEBREW BIBLE. (2) 'The teaching', the correct response of ISRAEL to God, outlined in the rules for purity and social justice. It is God's gift to Israel and the way for Israel to fulfil God's call for holiness. (3) The cosmological principle of order which embraces moral and religious instruction as well as the physical ordering of the universe by God.

Torii Gateway to a SHINTO shrine which consists of two vertical posts supporting two horizontal bars, the higher of which is often curved at each end towards the sky.

Totemism (From a Native American word meaning 'relative') The belief in some INDIGENOUS RELIGIONS that particular animals or sometimes plants or other objects have a special relationship with the tribal group and act as its guardians.

Totem poles Tall decorated posts, found especially among Native Americans, which display tribal relationships with ancestors and guardian spirits.

Towers of Silence Parsi mounds used for the disposal of corpses. In the belief of the PARSIS, sacred fire must not be polluted by contact with the dead. Corpses are exposed on the mounds where the flesh is eaten by birds of prey. The bleached bones are finally thrown down a well.

Transcendent That which is above or beyond common human experience or knowledge.

Transcendental Meditation/TM MEDITATION technique taught by Maharishi Mahesh Yogi which has flourished in the West since the 1960s. Practitioners need no religious beliefs. They are taught to meditate for fifteen to twenty minutes twice a day; this reduces stress and aids relaxation. In some states in the USA it has been ruled that Transcendental Meditation is a religion, of Hindu origin.

Transfiguration The occasion of CHRIST's appearance in glory to three of his disciples during his earthly ministry. It is celebrated as a feast in the Eastern Churches and by many in the West.

Transmigration of Souls The belief held by some Hindus that souls are detached from their bodies at death and are attached to other human, animal or vegetable bodies. What the new body will be depends on the individual's KARMA.

Trinity Christian doctrine of GOD as three Persons, equally God: the Father, the Son and the HOLY SPIRIT, constituting the divine unity.

Tripitaka (1) Sanskrit spelling of the (Pali) word TIPITAKA. (2) The SCRIPTURES of CHINESE BUDDHISM which include translations of THERAVADA texts, SANSKRIT MAHAYANA texts and some Chinese additions and commentaries. Also called the San Tsang.

Triple gem The BUDDHA as teacher, the DHAMMA as his teaching and the SANGHA as the community who live by his teaching. The 'triple gem' is the core of the Buddhist faith.

Tuat The other world in Egyptian mythology, a land of gloom and darkness which is divided into twelve areas, one for each hour of the night. The souls of the dead have to cross this region to enter the judgment hall of OSIRIS.

Twelvers The majority group among SHI'A Muslims who hold that the twelfth IMAM, Muhammad al-Mahdi, will reappear as the MAHDI on the last day. (See also ISMA'ILIS.)

Tyr The oldest of the Norse gods. Originally a sky god like ZEUS or VARUNA, his attributes were taken over by ODIN. The Romans compared him with MARS because he became a war god, an inspirer of warriors. He is portrayed as having great strength and courage.

U

UFO ('Unidentified Flying Object') The subject matter for many speculative groups since the 1950s. Members consider the spiritual and practical significances of UFO sightings.

'Ulama' The doctors of the law in ISLAM. They are the interpreters of the SHARI'A and the upholders of Islamic orthodoxy. They exist in SUNNI and SHI'A communities.

'Umar Caliph after the death of ABU BAKR, from CE 634–44. His rule was a period of dramatic expansion for ISLAM, into Mesopotamia, Persia and Lower Egypt. He was murdered by a Christian slave in the MOSQUE of MEDINA.

Ummayad dynasty (CE 661–750) The Islamic dynasty based on the Meccan family Ummaya. The caliphate was based in Damascus. Under the Ummayads ISLAM spread through North Africa to Spain and as far east as the Indus. There were eleven CALIPHS until the Ummayad period ended in military defeat and the succession of Abu'l 'Abbas as first caliph of the 'ABBASID DYNASTY.

Ummah The MUSLIM community, those who have received God's revelation through MUHAMMAD and live in submission to it.

Underworld The abode of spirits after the death of the body. In many religions the underworld is a shadowy half-real place presided over by a god of death. (See also HADES; HELL; TUAT.)

Unification Church See **Family Federation for World Peace and Unification**

Unitarianism Dissenting movement which spread in England, Poland and Hungary from the sixteenth century. Unitarians reject the Christian doctrines of the TRINITY and INCARNATION and defend a reason-based ethical THEISM.

Untouchables Indians who belong to no caste (see CASTE SYSTEM) and are therefore banished from normal social life. MAHATMA GANDHI called them 'children of God' and worked for their acceptance in Indian society.

Upanishads The last books of the Indian VEDAS which were written in SANSKRIT between 800 and 400 BCE. They develop the concept of BRAHMAN as the holy power released in sacrifice to the point where it becomes the underlying reality of the universe. The soul, ATMAN, is identified with the holy power, Brahman. They include speculation on how the soul can realize its oneness with Brahman through contemplative techniques.

'Uthman Son-in-law of MUHAMMAD who succeeded 'UMAR as CALIPH in CE 644. He was regarded as weak and worldly and was murdered in 656 after a period of rebellion. Under his caliphate the final authoritative version of the QUR'AN was produced.

V

Vairocana A title for the sun in ancient HINDU mythology. In MAHAYANA Buddhism it became a title for one of the great Buddhas. He is regarded as supreme BUDDHA in Java and in the Japanese SHINGON sect. He was said to be identical with the SHINTO sun deity Amaterasu.

Vaishnavism Worship of, or devotion to, the Hindu god VISHNU. Devotees regard him as the sole deity, of whom other gods are mere aspects.

Vaishyas See CASTE SYSTEM.

Vajrayana ('Diamond vehicle') An expression sometimes used for Tibetan Buddhism, a form of MAHAYANA Buddhism which has distinctive doctrines and practices.

Valhalla ('Hall of the slain') The part of ASGARD in Norse mythology reserved for dead heroes waiting for the final battle RAGNARÖK. It had 540 doors and 800 men could march, shoulder to shoulder, out of each door. The dead heroes spent their time drinking, playing games and fighting.

Valkyries ('Choosers of the slain') Female servants of ODIN in Norse mythology who choose which side is to have victory in battle and which warriors are to die. They conduct the dead to VALHALLA and wait on them with food and drink. Some MYTHS portray them as witch-like beings, exulting in blood and death.

Vampyr Spirit of a dead person in Slavic folklore who lives by sucking the blood of the living.

Vanir ('Shining ones') Divine beings of Norse mythology who at first fought with the

AESIR and later allied with them and came to live in ASGARD.

Varanasi See BENARES.

Varuna Indian sky god of the Vedic period (see VEDAS). He produced the cosmic order and was seen as a heavenly ruler and lawgiver as well as a moral guardian of the earth.

Vatican Councils The first was convened by POPE PIUS IX in CE 1869–70. It resulted in the dogma of Papal Infallibility and attacks on 'modern' thought. The second (1962–65) was called by John XXIII. It led to a drastic modernization of Roman Catholic worship and improved relations with other churches.

Vedanta (1) 'The end of the VEDAS'. A name for the UPANISHADS, which close the period of HINDU revelation. (2) Indian philosophy based on the teachings of SHANKARA. Its basic tenet is that only BRAHMAN, the Absolute, is fully real. The world of sense experience is contradictory and dreamlike because it is spun from the illusions of MAYA (1). Release from illusion comes from recognizing the sole reality of Brahman.

Vedas Scriptures which express the religion of the ARYAN people of India. They comprise HYMNS, instructions for RITUAL and cosmological speculations. There are four divisions: *Rig Veda*, hymns to the Aryan gods who are personifications of natural forces; *Sama Veda*, verses selected for chanting (see CHANT); *Yajur Veda*, prose instructions on matters of ritual; *Atharva Veda*, rites and SPELLS in verse, especially concerned with curing illness.

Venus Roman goddess of love, identified with APHRODITE and thus honoured as the mother of the Roman people.

Vesta Roman goddess of the hearth and protectress of domestic life. She was regarded as the guardian of the Roman nation. Her cult was under the supervision of six Vestal Virgins who tended the undying flame (traditionally from Troy) which burned in her temple.

Vestments Special garments worn by the Christian clergy during liturgical services (see LITURGY).

Vinaya Pitaka One of the oldest Buddhist scriptures consisting of the rules of discipline for the SANGHA, and related commentaries.

Viracocha/Huiracocha The uncreated creator-god in the religion of the INCAS. He was god of the ancient city of Tiuhuanaco and the giver of civilization. Pachacutec, the ninth Inca, exalted him as supreme deity over even the SUN GOD.

Vishnu In HINDUISM, the divine as preserver and life-giver, the creator of the cosmos. He and SHIVA are the two great gods of Hindu devotion. As lawgiver and moral guardian, Vishnu appears on earth from time to time as an AVATAR to reawaken people to knowledge of truth.

Vivekananda (about 1863–1902) Follower of RAMAKRISHNA, and founder of the RAMAKRISHNA MISSION in 1897. An apologist for VEDANTA, he criticized the dogmatism of CHRISTIANITY. Attending the World's Parliament of Religions in Chicago in 1893, he commended Vedanta as the highest form of religion.

Voodoo Religion of 90 per cent of the people of Haiti (in spite of the official domination of Roman Catholicism) as well as others in the West Indies and parts of South America. The name derives from a West African word for GOD. In practice Voodoo is highly syncretistic: West African DIVINITIES are worshipped, often as Christian SAINTS, and their sanctuaries are closed during the Christian season of LENT.

W

Wahhabi movement Puritanical Islam movement founded by Al-Wahhab of Arabia (CE 1703–92). Wahhabi accept the authority only of the QUR'AN and the SUNNAH. The movement has revived in the twentieth century and is the dominant religious influence in Saudi Arabia.

Wailing Wall See WESTERN WALL.

Wandering On In Buddhist thought the continual cycle by which the KARMA of past actions causes the coming-to-be of new mental and physical states which in turn produce more karma and further phases of existence.

Wandjina Spirit beings of the Australian Aboriginal DREAMTIME who are believed to have left their shadows on rock and cave walls in paintings and engravings. They are regarded as kindly beings who care for the people, ensure fertility and bring rain.

Weeks/Shavuot Jewish feast celebrated seven weeks after PASSOVER. It has become associated with the giving of the Ten Commandments on Mount SINAI. Also known as PENTECOST.

Werewolf Human being who has been transformed into a wolf in Slavic folk tradition.

Wesley, John (CE 1703–91) Founder of the METHODIST movement. He travelled through Britain on horseback preaching the 'new birth'. Although loyal to the Church of England, he was eventually forced to ordain his own ministers.

Western Wall/Wailing Wall/Kotel Site in JERUSALEM used by JEWS to lament the FALL OF JERUSALEM and the continuing suffering of the Jews and to pray for restoration. It is believed to be part of the original Temple of Solomon, the only part of the Temple left standing after the destruction of CE 70. (See TEMPLE OF JERUSALEM.)

Wicca Also called 'the Old Religion', witchcraft, 'wisecraft' or simply 'the Craft', the term is taken from the Anglo-Saxon *wicce*, meaning 'witch' or 'wise woman'. Many contemporary practitioners of witchcraft prefer the term Wicca for their religion. While some claim that it has ancient origins, many would argue that contemporary Wicca was founded by Gerald Brosseau Gardner (1884–1964), who claimed to have been initiated into the 'Old Religion' in 1939. Although there are many Wiccan paths, it is generally agreed that there are five principal ones: Gardnerian Wicca, Alexandrian Wicca, Hereditary Craft, Traditinal Craft, and Feminist Craft.

Witch Doctor/Medicine man A healer in INDIGENOUS RELIGIONS. The terms are rarely used today as they are felt to have misleading connotations.

World Council of Churches Body including many Protestant and Orthodox Churches, first constituted at Amsterdam in 1948 (see CONCILIAR PROCESS, ECUMENICAL MOVEMENT).

World Fellowship of Buddhists Society founded in 1950 in Ceylon (Sri Lanka) by G.P. Malaleskera to bring together Buddhists of all traditions and nations with the common intention of spreading Buddhist teaching throughout the world.

Worship Reverence or homage to God or a god which may involve PRAYER, SACRIFICE, RITUALS, singing, dancing or chanting.

Wovoka (CE 1856–1932) Paiute Native American PROPHET and MYSTIC who, reacting against white domination, urged his followers to live in peace, fighting the whites through the power of the GHOST DANCE. His hope of imminent regeneration spread among the Native American Plains. The movement was destroyed at the Battle of Wounded Knee in 1890.

Wrath The righteous anger of God against SIN.

Writings The third and final division of the HEBREW BIBLE, comprising the Wisdom literature (such as Job and Proverbs), the Psalms, the later histories and other material.

Wycliffe, John (about 1329–84) English religious reformer who condemned the POPE as Antichrist and began the translation of the BIBLE into English.

X

Xipe Totec ('The flayed one') In Mexican mythology, the god of the west and of agriculture, who was skinned alive like the maize. He was represented by the mask of a skinned human face.

Xiuhtecuhtli ('Turquoise lord') The ancient Mexican fire god. His fire burned in every home and temple and he was regarded as a form of the supreme god.

Y

Yahweh See YHWH.

Yama In the VEDAS the primordial man who crosses through death and becomes immortal. He is therefore god of death who judges men and consigns them to heaven or hell. His significance as judge faded as the pre-ARYAN doctrine of SAMSARA became established.

Yasna The form of public worship in ancient ZOROASTRIANISM, elements of which are retained by the PARSIS. Part of the AVESTA, it teaches the presence of the divine in all things and refers to many lesser divine beings alongside AHURA MAZDA.

Yellow Hats Reformed branch of TIBETAN BUDDHISM whose leader is the DALAI LAMA. (See BUDDHISM.)

Yggdrasil The great ash tree which unifies the creation according to Norse mythology. Its three roots reach ASGARD, MIDGARD and Niflheim, the UNDERWORLD. The tree holds together the nine worlds of giants, dwarfs, human beings, light elves, dark elves, AESIR, VANIR, the dead and the home of the world-destroyers. The tree of knowledge, it is simultaneously being nourished and destroyed. It is also a symbol of the generation of life: the first man in Norse myth is named Ash.

Yhwh The 'tetragrammaton', the sacred name of the God of ISRAEL which was revealed to MOSES. The name means 'I am'. It could not be spoken and the Hebrew 'Adonai' ('the Lord') was substituted when the scriptures were read aloud. The MASORETES put the vowel points for Adonai into the name YHWH which gave rise to the malformation 'Jehovah'. Yhwh was possibly pronounced 'Yahweh'.

Yin and Yang The polarity of energies in Chinese philosophy. Yang is masculine, dynamic, bright and good; yin is feminine, passive, dark and bad. Their production and interplay is represented in a circular diagram (see TAI CH'I). *Yin* and *yang* produce the elements and the cycle of the seasons. They also provided the theoretical basis for the Taoist practice of ALCHEMY (see TAOISM).

Yoga A way to union with GOD in HINDU philosophy. It also forms one of the six classical systems of Indian thought. Traditionally there are eight stages of yoga: restraint; discipline; posture; breathing; detachment; concentration; meditation; and trance. In the *Bhagavad Gita* the three paths to spiritual fulfilment are: *jnanayoga* (the path of knowledge/wisdom), *karmayoga* (the path of work/action) and *bhaktiyoga* (the path of devotion).

Yogi Indian holy man who has reached ENLIGHTENMENT through yogic practices (see YOGA). (See also TRANSCENDENTAL MEDITATION.)

Yom Kippur/Day of Atonement Jewish day of FASTING and repentance, the most solemn day of the Jewish year. The LITURGY includes a solemn chant, the Kol Nidrei, which challenges Jews who have strayed from religion to return to faith.

Z

Zaddiq Jewish teacher in the later Hasidic movement. The *zaddiq* was seen as the perfectly righteous man who was in mystical communion with God. The *zaddiq*'s house became the meeting place for the HASIDIM.

Zakah A 'poor tax' charged at the rate of 2.5% of a person's total income for the year, in ISLAM. It is levied on all who can afford it, and distributed among the poor and needy. It cannot be used for any other purpose.

Za-Zen Japanese term for the form of MEDITATION practised in ZEN monasteries. It involves a sitting posture designed to accompany reflection on a KOAN.

Zealots Jewish nationalistic party in Roman times who believed that the Roman presence was a defilement of the land and a flouting of TORAH. In CE 66 they revolted. The war which followed led to the destruction of JERUSALEM and its Temple in CE 70. The last stand of the Zealots was at Masada, where 960 of them died in CE 73.

Zen Japanese Buddhist movement which developed from the Chinese Ch'an school in the thirteenth century CE. It is characterized by the teaching that ENLIGHTENMENT is a spontaneous event, totally independent of concepts, techniques or rituals. Zen aims at harmony in living and uses secular arts such as tea-making and calligraphy to develop effortless skills.

Zeus Supreme ruler of the Greek gods. Described by HOMER as 'Father of gods and men', he may have originated as a storm god and continued to be regarded as controller of the weather. Although there were many MYTHS about him he did not appear in drama, which suggests that he was held in special awe. Sometimes the name Zeus stood simply for God, as supreme deity.

Zevi, Shabbetai (CE 1628–1716) Kabbalistic RABBI from Smyrna who became the centre of a messianic movement which spread throughout the Jewish world (see KABBALAH). In 1665 he proclaimed himself MESSIAH. He was later imprisoned and, to the horror of his followers, converted to ISLAM. There were attempts to argue that the sin of the messiah was a necessary part of redemption, but the movement disintegrated.

Ziggurat Ancient Babylonian TEMPLE in the form of a tower rising from a broad base to a narrow top.

Zionism The movement to establish a national and permanent homeland for JEWS. In 1897 the first Zionist Congress was organized in Basle by Theodor HERZL in the wake of a wave of European anti-Semitism. Gradually the movement became determined that Palestine was the only realistic place to establish the Jewish state and Jews were encouraged to emigrate and acquire property there. The majority of Jews today support Zionism to the extent that it is manifested in the modern state of ISRAEL.

Zohar Most important writing of the Jewish KABBALAH.

Zombie Term used in Haiti and South America for the 'living dead'.

Zoroaster/Zarathushtra Prophet and founder of ZOROASTRIANISM. He lived in Persia, either in the tenth and ninth centuries BCE, or, more likely, in the seventh and sixth. At the age of thirty he had a revelation of AHURA MAZDA which drove him to preach against polytheism. According to tradition he died performing the fire sacrifice which was the central ceremony of the new faith.

Zoroastrianism The religion of ancient Persia, founded by ZOROASTER, possibly related to the Vedic religion of India (see VEDAS). It was strongly ethical: Zoroaster taught that AHURA MAZDA would judge each individual soul after death. Later there developed a complex doctrinal system speculating about the inner nature of the universe. The expansion of ISLAM drove Zoroastrianism out of Persia (see also AVESTA; PARSIS; ZURVANISM).

Zurvanism Zoroastrian heresy according to which an absolute being called Zurvan ('time') was the origin of good and evil and the source of the two spirits AHURA MAZDA and ANGRA MAINYU.

Contributors

Norman Anderson, Emeritus Professor of African Law at the University of London, England.

Veikko Anttonen, Professor of Comparative Religion, University of Turku, Finland.

George Bankes, former Keeper of Ethnology, The Manchester Museum, University of Manchester, England.

Robert Banks, Professor of the Ministry of the Laity and Chair of the Ministry Division, Fuller Theological Seminary, Pasadena, California, USA.

Axel-Ivar Berglund, Associate Professor in Missiology and Cultural Anthropology, University of Uppsala, Sweden.

John Berthrong, Assistant Professor of Comparative Theology, University of Boston, Massachusetts, USA.

Barbara M. Boal, former Lecturer in Primal Religions, Selly Oak Colleges, Birmingham, England.

Fiona Bowie, Senior Lecturer in Anthropology, University of Bristol, England.

Peter Brierley, Executive Director, Christian Research Association, London, England.

Colin Buchanan, former Bishop of Woolwich, England.

Jeremy Carrette, Lecturer in Applied Theology, University of Kent, Canterbury, England.

Colin Chapman, former Lecturer in Islamic Studies, Near East School of Theology, Beirut, Lebanon.

Eric S. Christianson, Senior Lecturer, Biblical Studies, University College Chester, Chester, England.

George Chryssides, Head of Religious Studies, University of Wolverhampton, England.

Chua Wee Hian, Senior Pastor of Emmanuel Evangelical Church, London, England.

Dan Cohn-Sherbok, Professor of Jewish Theology, University of Wales, Lampeter, Wales.

Harvie M. Conn, (deceased) Professor of Missions, Westminster Theological Seminary, Philadelphia, PA, USA.

Geoffrey Cowling, former Senior Lecturer in History, University of Macquarie, New South Wales, Australia.

James Cox, Reader in Religious Studies and Head of the Religious Studies Subject Area, University of Edinburgh, Scotland.

Clyde Curry Smith, Professor Emeritus of Ancient History and Religion, University of Wisconsin, River Falls, USA: Visiting Professor, Department of Religious Studies, Newcastle University, England.

Douglas Davies, Professor of the Study of Religion, Department of Theology, University of Durham, England.

Andrew Dawson, Senior Lecturer in the Academic Study of Religion, University College Chester, England.

R.T. France, former Principal, Wycliffe Hall, Oxford, England.

Theodore Gabriel, Honorary Research Fellow, University of Gloucestershire, England.

Malcolm Hamilton, Senior Lecturer, Department of Sociology, University of Reading, England.

David Harley, General Director of OMF, former Principal, All Nations Christian College, Ware, Herts, England.

Elizabeth Harris, Secretary for Inter Faith Relations, The Methodist Church, England.

Graham Harvey, Lecturer in Religious Studies, The Open University, England.

John R. Hinnells, Research Leader in Zoroastrianism, Liverpool Hope University College, England.

Åke Hultkrantz, retired Professor of Religions, University of Stockholm, Sweden.

Lynne Hume, Associate Professor in the School of History, Philosophy, Religion and Classics, University of Queensland, Australia.

Ronald Hutton, Professor of History, University of Bristol, England.

Edward Irons, Director of the Hong Kong Institute for Culture, Commerce and Religion, Hong Kong.

Sewa Singh Kalsi, Lecturer in Sikh Studies, University of Leeds, England.

David Kerr, Professor of Islamic Studies, Hartford Seminary, Hartford, Connecticut, USA.

Anna S. King, Senior Lecturer in the Centre for Theology and Religious Studies, University College Winchester, England.

Carl Loeliger, Senior Lecturer in Religious Studies, History Department, University of Papua New Guinea.

David Lyon, Professor of Sociology, Queen's University, Kingston, Canada.

Russell T. McCutcheon, Associate Professor and Chair, Department of Religious Studies, University of Alabama, USA.

Alister McGrath, Professor of Historical Theology, University of Oxford, England.

I. Howard Marshall, Emeritus Professor of New Testament Exegesis and Honorary Research Professor, University of Aberdeen, Scotland.

A.R. Millard, Emeritus Professor and Honorary Senior Fellow, School of Archaeology, Classics and Egyptology, University of Liverpool, England.

Khojeste Mistree, widely respected scholar of Zoroastrianism, and co-founder and Managing Trustee of Zoroastrian Studies, Mumbai (Bombay), India.

Dr Moojan Momen, independent scholar, graduate of the University of Cambridge, England.

J.W.E. Newbery, Professor Emeritus (Native Studies), University of Sudbury, Canada.

Christopher Partridge, Professor of Contemporary Religion, University College Chester, Chester, England.

Robert Pope, Senior Lecturer in the Department of Theology and Religious Studies, University of Wales, Bangor, Wales.

Michael Pye, Professor of the Study of Religions (Religionswissenschaft) at the University of Marburg (Philipps-Universität Marburg), Germany.

Elizabeth Ramsey, Lecturer, Liverpool Hope University College, England.

Peter G. Riddell, Professor of Islamic Studies, London School of Theology, England.

John Ruffle, former Keeper, The Oriental Museum, University of Durham, England.

Joan E. Rule, former Senior Lecturer in English, Dauli Teachers' College, Papua New Guinea.

Tinu Ruparell, Graduate Coordinator, Department of Religious Studies, University of Calgary, USA.

Michael Sadgrove, Dean of Durham, England.

Emma Salter, Doctorate from University of Cardiff, Lecturer at 6th Form College, North England.

Lothar Schmalfuss, Director of Studies, the University of Munich, Germany.

Christopher Shackle, Professor of Modern Languages of South Asia, University of London, England.

David Smith, Lecturer in Mission and World Christianity, International Christian College, Glasgow, Scotland.

Anthony C Thiselton, Research Professor in Christian Theology, University College Chester, and Emeritus Professor of Christian Theology in the University of Nottingham, England.

Harold W. Turner, Presbyterian theologian, directing the Deepsight Trust programme, Auckland, New Zealand.

David Waines, Professor of Islamic Studies, University of Lancaster, England.

Morten Warmind, Lecturer in the Department of History of Religions, University of Copenhagen, Denmark.

Maya Warrier, Lecturer on Hinduism, University of Wales, Lampeter, Wales.

Montgomery Watt, former Professor (Emeritus) of Arabic and Islamic Studies, University of Edinburgh, Scotland.

Fraser Watts, Starbridge Lecturer in Theology and Natural Science, University of Cambridge, England.

Paul Williams, Professor of Indian and Tibetan Philosophy, University of Bristol, England.

Marvin R. Wilson, Ockenga Professor of Biblical Studies, Gordon College, Wenham, Massachusetts, USA.

Linda Woodhead, Senior Lecturer in Christian Studies, University of Lancaster, England.

Index

Acknowledgments
Margin Quotes

10, Brian K. Smith, *Reflections and Resemblance, Ritual, and Religion* (New York: OUP, 1989); 19, Maurice Hocart; 22, Clifford Geertz, *The Interpretation of Cultures: Selected Essays* (New York, 1973); 24, Karl Marx, *A Contribution to the Critique of Hegel's Philosophy of Right* (Deutsch-Französische Jahrbucher, 1844); 26, Sigmund Freud, *The Future of an Illusion* (London: Hogarth, 1962); 30, *Religion and Culture by Michel Foucault* ed. Jeremy Carrette (Manchester University Press/Routledge, 1999); 33, Mary Douglas; 38, F. Max Müller, *Contributions to the Science of Mythology* (London, 1897); 40, E.O. James, *The Beginnings of Religion* (1958); 43, Joseph Kitagawa, *The Quest for Human Unity* (1990); 44, Ninian Smart, *The World's Religions* (1989); 54, ibid; 59, *The Epic of Gilgamesh*; 62, Prayer to Marduk; 74, Homer, *Odyssey*; 77, Homer, *Iliad*; 78, Homeric *Hymn to Demeter*; 81, Critias, *Sisyphus*; 83, *Livius*; 85, Cicero, *The Nature of the Gods*; 87, Roman Proconsul to Provincial Assembly of Asia, 9 BCE; 88, Minucius Felix, *Octavius*; 88, Sallustius, *Concerning the Gods and the Universe*; 90, Julius Caesar, *De Bello Gallico*; 97, The inscription on the seal of Genghis Khan; 103, Taitokerau Whakatauki (Maori); 104, Ifa divination text; 105, Mircea Eliade, *Patterns in Comparative Religion* (1958); 107, Gerardus van der Leeuw, *Religion in Essence and Manifestation* (1938); 107, Piers Vitebsky (2000); 112, Caruana, Wally & Nigel Lendon, *The Painters of the Wagilag Sisters Story. 1937–1997* (National Gallery of Australia, Canberra, 1997); 113, R.H. Codrington, *The Melanesians* (1891); 113, Mircea Eliade, *Patterns in Comparative Religion* (1958); 116, Bronislaw Malinowski, *Magic, Science and Religion and Other Essays* (New York: Doubleday Anchor 1954); 121, John Lame Deer (twentieth-century Sioux shaman); 122, Sword, *Wakan* trans. Burt Means. www.sacred-texts.com/nam/pla/sdo/sdo49.htm; 124, Old Inuit woman testifying to Canadian Judge Thomas Berger; 124, Jimmy Stotts, Inuit from Barrow, Alaska; 125, Weston LaBarre, *The Ghost Dance: Origins of Religion* (New York: Doubleday, 1970); 126, Okot p'Bitek, Ugandan poet; 127, J.S. Mbiti, Kenyan theologian; 133, Geoffrey Parrinder; 137, Mahatma Gandhi, *Hindu Dharma* (New Delhi: Orient Paperbacks, 1987); 142, The *Bhagavad Gita*; 148, Mahatma Gandhi, *An Autobiography or the Story of My Experiments with the Truth* (Harmondsworth: Penguin, 1982); 149, The *Bhagavad Gita*; 152, Mahatma Gandhi, An Autobiography or the Story of My Experiments with the Truth (Harmondsworth: Penguin, 1982); 153, The *Bhagavad Gita*; 155, ibid; 157, The *Mahabharata*; 167, *Kalpa Sutra*, trans. K.C. Lalwani (Motilal Banarsidass, 1999);

167, ibid; 172, Umasvati's Tattvartha, *That Which Is*, trans. Nathmal Tatia (Harper Collins, 1994); 173, ibid; 175, ibid; 179, ibid; 182, John E. Cort, *Jains in the World* (OUP, 2001); 184, Umasvati's Tattvartha, *That Which Is*, trans. Nathmal Tatia (Harper Collins, 1994); 187, Acharya Tulsi; 193, *Dhammapada*; 194, *The Discourse on Loving Kindness, Sutta Nipata*; 195, *Sutta Nipata*; 198, *Anguttara Nikaya*; 199, *Dhammapada*; 202, *Anguttara Nikaya*; 205, *Sutta Nipata*; 206, *The Discourse on Loving Kindness, Sutta Nipata*; 207, The *Kutadanta Sutta, Digha Nikaya*; 211, *The Monastic Code of Discipline*; 213, From the *Cakkavatti-Sihanada Sutta, Digha Nikaya*; 218, *Adi Granth*; 221, *Dasam Granth*; 223, *Adi Granth*; 224, ibid; 226, ibid; 227, ibid; 234, ibid; 237, Bhai Kahn Singh Nabha; 240, Rehat Maryada; 244, *Yasna*; 247, ibid; 248, ibid; 254, *Shkand-gumanig Vizar*; 255, *Denkard*; 265, Old Testament; 267, ibid; 271, Moses Maimonides, *Mishnah Torah* (1170–80); 272, Baruch Spinoza, *The Ethics* (1677); 273, Isaac Bashevis Singer, *Love and Exile* (1985); 283, S.R. Hirsch, *The Nineteen Letters on Judaism* [1836], trans. B. Drachman (New York: Feldheim, 1960); 284, Heinrich Graetz, *History of the Jews* (New York, 1927); 287, Old Testament; 289, ibid; 293, ibid; 295, Rabbi Harold Kushner, *To Life: A Celebration of Jewish Being and Thinking* (Little, Brown, & Co., 1994); 296, Rabbi Norman Solomon, *Judaism: A Very Short Introduction* (Oxford University, 2000); 298, *The Jewish Prayer Book*; 307, *Pirkei Avot*; 309, Mordecai Kaplan; 310, www.jrf.org/recon/perhaps.html; 310, www.shj.org/proclam.htm; 320, C.S. Lewis, *Mere Christianity* (Fount, 1997); 322, New Testament; 322, ibid; 323, ibid; 326, ibid; 327, Second Westminster Confession (1677); 327, H.H. Farmer, *The Servant of the Word* (1941); 328, Leo Tolstoy, *What I Believe* (1884); 331, Brother Lawrence, *The Practice of the Presence of God* (1691); 332, Basis of the Apostles' Creed, from Marcellus of Ancyra; 338, New Testament; 340, Martin Luther; 343, New Testament; 348, ibid; 358, The Qur'an; 363, Kenneth Cragg, *The Call of the Minaret* (1985); 365, Ayatollah Khomeini, speech in 1979, quoted in V. S. Naipaul, *Among the Believers* (1981); 367, *Deliverance from Error* (12th century); 367, Ibn al-Arabi, *Tarjumanu al-Ashwaq* (13th century); 368, A.Y. Ali, *The Meaning of the Holy Qur'an* (new edition) (Beltsville, Maryland: Amana Publications, 1989); 371, ibid; 371, *Sahih Bukhari*; 374, ibid; 377, The Qur'an; 377, Al-Ghazali (11th century); 378, The Qur'an; 379, ibid; 380, ibid; 383, ibid; 383, Kenneth Cragg, *The Call of the Minaret* (1985); 388, The Qur'an; 389, Riffat Hassan; 391, Sufi saying; 391, ibid; 393, The Gabriel *hadith*; 396, Confucius, *Analects*; 397, ibid; 397, Mencius (4th century BCE); 397, ibid; 398, ibid; 398, Hsün Tzu (3rd century BCE); 399, Tao Te Ching; 400, ibid; 404, Zhou, from *China Insight Newsletter*, September 2004,

www.us.omf.org; 406, From the Chinese Constitution; 407, Confucius, *Analects*; 411, *Kojiki*; 413, *Kokutai ni Hongi*; 414, Motoori Wonnaga (1730–1801), *Monnaga*; 415, Ninian Smart, *World Philosophies* (1999); 415, Peter Harvey, *An Introduction to Buddhism* (1990); 416, Nichiren (1222–82); 416, *Lotus Sutra*; 419, From the *Ofudesaki*; 421, Bahá'u'lláh; 422, A pen-portrait of Bahá'u'lláh from Professor E.G. Browne, Cambridge University, 1890; 423, Bahá'u'lláh; 425, 'Abdu'l-Baha; 426, *Hidden Words*, Arabic; 427, *Kitab-i-Aqdas, Questions and Answers*; 428, From a tablet of Bahá'u'lláh; 428, 'Abdu'l-Baha; 430, A prayer of Bahá'u'lláh; 431, Statement on the Bahá'í International Community website; 432, From a tablet of Bahá'u'lláh; 434, Bahá'u'lláh; 436, Soren Kierkegaard, *Papirer* (1849); 439, Friedrich Nietzsche, *Joyous Wisdom* (1910); 442, Sun Myung Moon, 23 March 2004, quoted in *The Guardian* June 24, 2004; 446, Max Weber, *Science as a Vocation* (1919); 453, J. Philip Wogaman, *Christian Perspectives on Politics* (London: SCM, 1988); 454, ibid.

Pictures

Picture research by Zooid Pictures Limited.

2/3 Howard Davies/Corbis UK Ltd; 4/5 Chris Lisle/Corbis UK Ltd; 5t Owen Franken/Corbis UK Ltd; 5c Archivo Iconografico, S.A./Corbis UK Ltd; 5b Anders Ryman/Corbis UK Ltd; 6tc Jeremy Horner/Panos Pictures; 6bc Jeremy Horner/Corbis UK Ltd; 6t Michael S. Yamashita/Corbis UK Ltd; 6b Paul Doyle/Alamy; 7t Michael S. Yamashita/Corbis UK Ltd; 7c Nathan Benn/Corbis UK Ltd; 7b Reuters/Corbis UK Ltd; 8tc Mark Henley/Panos Pictures; 8bc Bahai World Centre; 8t Jose Fuste Raga/Corbis UK Ltd; 8b Sipa Press/Rex Features; 10 Owen Franken/Corbis UK Ltd; 10/11 Bettmann/Corbis UK Ltd; 12 Jed Leicester/Rex Features; 16/17 Mark Campbell/Rex Features; 18 Jacques Langevin/Sygma/Corbis UK Ltd; 21 Simon Arnold/Eye Ubiquitous/Corbis UK Ltd; 22 Felicity Nock/Hutchison Picture Library; 24 Bettmann/Corbis UK Ltd; 26 Bettmann/Corbis UK Ltd; 27 Syracuse Newspapers/The Image Works/Topham Picturepoint; 29 Hulton-Deutsch Collection/Corbis UK Ltd; 32 Henning Christoph/Still Pictures; 33 Penny Tweedie/Corbis UK Ltd; 38 Archivo Iconografico, S.A./Corbis UK Ltd; 42 AKG - Images; 43 Ray Roberts/images-of-France/Alamy; 45 Mike Andrews/Ancient Art & Architecture; 46/47 Roger Ressmeyer/Corbis UK Ltd; 48/49 Catherine Karnow/Corbis UK Ltd; 51 Gianni Dagli Orti/Corbis UK Ltd; 52/53 Yann Arthus-Bertrand/Corbis UK Ltd; 55 Michael Freeman/Corbis UK Ltd; 57 Iraq Museum, Baghdad/Giraudon/Bridgeman Art Library; 60 Erich Lessing/AKG - Images; 63 Erich Lessing/AKG - Images; 66/67 Roger Ressmeyer/Corbis UK Ltd; 69 Sandro Vannini/Corbis UK Ltd; 70/71 Sandro Vannini/Corbis UK Ltd; 72/73 Glen

Allison/Stone/Getty Images; 75 Mimmo Jodice/Corbis UK Ltd; 76 John Heseltine/Corbis UK Ltd; 79 Christie's Images/Corbis UK Ltd; 81 Massimo Listri/Corbis UK Ltd; 86 Erich Lessing /AKG - Images; 91 Werner Forman Archive; 94 Werner Forman Archive; 97 Werner Forman Archive; 100 Anders Ryman/Corbis UK Ltd; 101 Rykoff Collection/Corbis UK Ltd; 102 Chris Rainier/Corbis UK Ltd; 105 Corbis UK Ltd; 106 Corbis UK Ltd; 111 Penny Tweedie/Corbis UK Ltd; 114 Jack Fields/Corbis UK Ltd; 117 Corbis UK Ltd; 120 Werner Forman Archive; 123 Bryan & Cherry Alexander Photography/Alamy; 125 Zooid Pictures; 128/129 Earl & Nazima Kowall/Corbis UK Ltd; 132 Ed Kashi/Corbis UK Ltd; 134 Michael S. Yamashita/Corbis UK Ltd; 135 Chris Lisle/Corbis UK Ltd; 136/137 Wolfgang Kaehler/Corbis UK Ltd; 138 Lindsay Hebberd/Corbis UK Ltd; 141 British Library/AKG - Images; 143 Pierre Perrin/Sygma/Corbis UK Ltd; 145 Angelo Hornak/Corbis UK Ltd; 146 Stout/Christine Osborne Pictures; 147 Ted Streshinsky/Corbis UK Ltd; 150 Jason Burke/Eye Ubiquitous/Corbis UK Ltd; 153 Lindsay Hebberd/Corbis UK Ltd; 154/155 Brian A. Vikander/Corbis UK Ltd; 156 Corbis UK Ltd; 158 Bob Krist/Corbis UK Ltd; 160 Hulton-Deutsch Collection/Corbis UK Ltd; 162 Arvind Garg/Corbis UK Ltd; 163 Sipa Press/Rex Features; 165 Jeremy Horner/Panos Pictures; 166 Prem Kapoor/World Religions Photo Library/Alamy; 168/169 Peter Guttman/Corbis UK Ltd; 170 Jean-Louis Nou/AKG - Images; 174/175 Charles & Josette Lenars/Corbis UK Ltd; 176/177 Robert Holmes/Corbis UK Ltd; 180/181 Gian Berto Vanni/Corbis UK Ltd; 183 William Holtby/Circa Photo Library; 184 Lindsay Hebberd/Corbis UK Ltd; 188 Jeremy Horner/Corbis UK Ltd; 189 Craig Aurness/Corbis UK Ltd; 191 Chris Lisle/Corbis UK Ltd; 192 Jeremy Horner/Corbis UK Ltd; 195 Burstein Collection/Corbis UK Ltd; 196 Chris Lisle/Corbis UK Ltd; 200 Axiom; 203 Horace Bristol/Corbis UK Ltd; 204/205 Luca I. Tettoni/Corbis UK Ltd; 206 Bohemian Nomad Picturemakers/Corbis UK Ltd; 209 Chris Lisle/Corbis UK Ltd; 214 Corbis UK Ltd; 215 Chris Lisle/Corbis UK Ltd; 216 Paul Doyle/Alamy; 217 Christine Osborne/World Religions Photo Library/Alamy; 219 Chris Lisle/Corbis UK Ltd; 222 Christine Osborne/Corbis UK Ltd; 225 Lindsay Hebberd/Corbis UK Ltd; 229 Christine Osborne Pictures; 230/231 Blaine Harrington III/Corbis UK Ltd; 232 Helene Rogers/Alamy; 235 Christine Osborne/Corbis UK Ltd; 238 Desai Noship/Sygma/Corbis UK Ltd; 241 Noshir Desai/Corbis UK Ltd; 242 Michael S. Yamashita/Corbis UK Ltd; 243 Roger Wood/Corbis UK Ltd; 245 Gianni Dagli Orti/Corbis UK Ltd; 246 Paul Almasy/Corbis UK Ltd; 250 Brian A. Vikander/Corbis UK Ltd; 254 Lindsay Hebberd/Corbis UK Ltd; 257 Corbis UK Ltd; 260 Tim Page/Corbis UK Ltd; 262/263 Reuters/Damir Sagolj/Corbis UK Ltd; 265 Nathan Benn/Corbis UK Ltd; 266 Araldo de Luca/Corbis UK Ltd; 268/269 Index/Bridgeman Art Library; 272 AKG - Images; 275 Robert Holmes/Corbis UK Ltd; 279 Richard T. Nowitz/Corbis UK Ltd; 280/281 Marc Asnin/SABA/Corbis UK Ltd; 283 David H. Wells/Corbis UK Ltd; 284/285 Corbis UK Ltd; 288 Peter M. Wilson/Alamy; 290/291 Richard T. Nowitz/Corbis UK Ltd; 291 Liba Taylor/Hutchison Picture Library; 293 Annie Griffiths Belt/Corbis UK Ltd; 295 Richard T. Nowitz/Corbis UK Ltd; 297 Ted Spiegel/Corbis UK Ltd; 299 Richard T. Nowitz/Corbis UK Ltd; 302/303 Carl & Ann Purcell/Corbis UK Ltd; 305 Milner Moshe/Sygma/Corbis UK Ltd; 306 AKG - Images; 308/309 Dave Bartruff/Corbis UK Ltd; 311 Reuters/Corbis UK Ltd; 312/313 Mark L Stephenson/Corbis UK Ltd; 314 AKG - Images; 315 Phillips, The International Fine Art Auctioneers/Bridgeman Art Library; 316 Sean Sprague/Panos Pictures; 319 AKG - Images; 321 Gianni Dagli Orti/Corbis UK Ltd; 326 Bridgeman Art Library; 329 Hans Georg Roth/Corbis UK Ltd; 330/331 Robert van der Hilst/Corbis UK Ltd; 334 John Smith/Circa Photo Library; 335 Thierry Prat/Sygma/Corbis UK Ltd; 336 Bojan Brecelj/Corbis UK Ltd; 340/341 Hubert Stadler/Corbis UK Ltd; 342 Franco Origlia/Sygma/Corbis UK Ltd; 344 Earl & Nazima Kowall/Corbis UK Ltd; 346/347 Carlos Lopez/AP Photo; 351 Rajesh Jantilal/AP Photo; 352 Polak Matthew/Sygma/Corbis UK Ltd; 356 Jose Fuste Raga/Corbis UK Ltd; 356/357 Steve Raymer/Corbis UK Ltd; 359 The Stapleton Collection/Bridgeman Art Library; 360/361 K. Nomachi/Rex Features; 364/367 Roger Wood/Corbis UK Ltd; 366 Sandro Vannini/Corbis UK Ltd; 369 Paul Almasy/Corbis UK Ltd; 370 Corbis UK Ltd; 373 Archives Charmet/Bridgeman Art Library; 378/379 Keren Su/Corbis UK Ltd; 380 Charles & Josette Lenars/Corbis UK Ltd; 382 Rod Johnson/Panos Pictures; 384 Archivo Iconografico, S.A./Corbis UK Ltd; 385 Giraudon/Bridgeman Art Library; 386 Adam Woolfitt/Corbis UK Ltd; 388 Camerapix/World Religions Photo Library/Alamy; 389 Craig Aurness/Corbis UK Ltd; 392 Setboun/Corbis UK Ltd; 393 Rex Features; 394 Mark Henley/Panos Pictures; 395 Lowell Georgia/Corbis UK Ltd; 396 Archivo Iconografico, S.A./Corbis UK Ltd; 401 Tjalling Halbersma/Circa Photo Library; 402 Wolfgang Kaehler/Corbis UK Ltd; 405 Sinopix/Rex Features; 407 Julia Waterlow; Eye Ubiquitous/Corbis UK Ltd; 408 Michael S. Yamashita/Corbis UK Ltd; 409 Carl & Ann Purcell/Corbis UK Ltd; 412 Geoff Howard; 415 Peter Guttman/Corbis UK Ltd; 417 Frank Leather/Eye Ubiquitous/Corbis UK Ltd; 418 Catherine Karnow/Corbis UK Ltd; 421 Bahai World Centre; 422 Bahai World Centre; 423 Bahai World Centre; 424 Richard T. Nowitz/Corbis UK Ltd; 427 Richard T. Nowitz/Corbis UK Ltd; 432/433 Lindsay Hebberd/Corbis UK Ltd; 435 Sipa Press/Rex Features; 440/441 Rex Features; 444 Rex Features; 448 Chris Stowers/Panos Pictures

Additional pictures

131 supplied by Fiona Bowie; 348 supplied by Edward Irons

Lion Hudson

Commissioning editor: Morag Reeve

Editorial team: Olwen Turchetta, David Bygott (freelance), Liz Evans (freelance), David Hutchison (freelance)

Designer: Nick Rous

Production manager: Kylie Ord